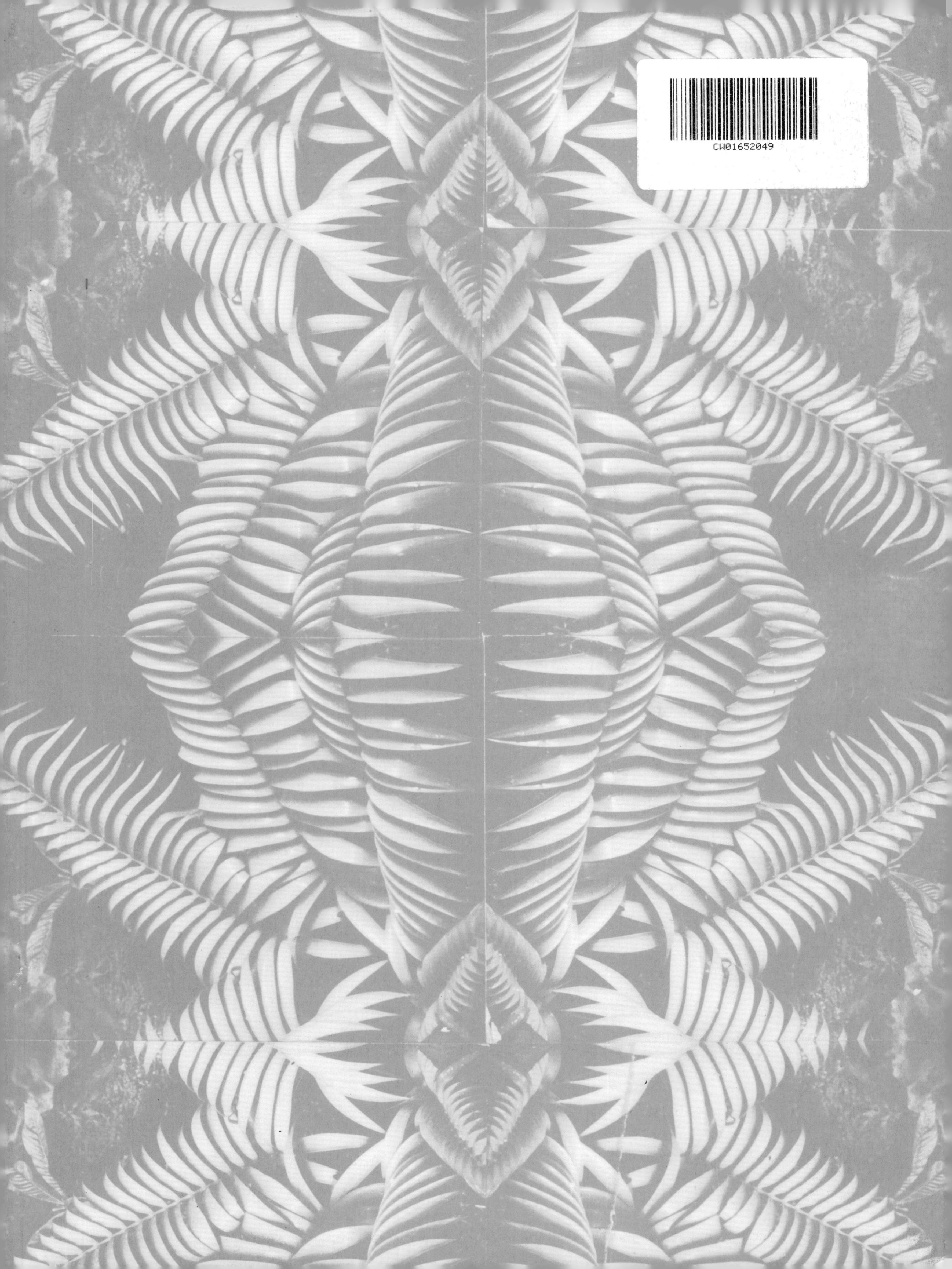

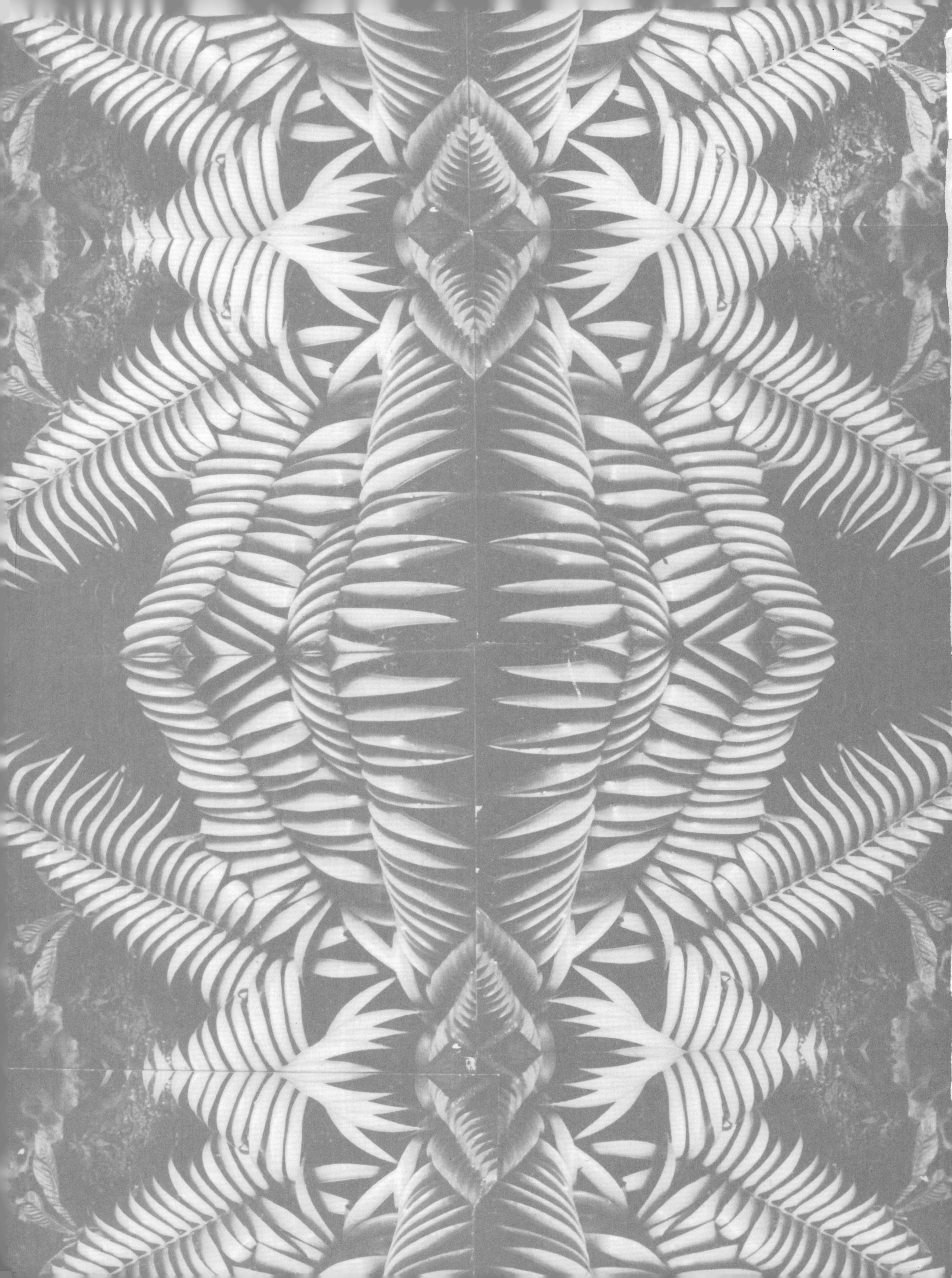

HORST

Photographer *of* Style

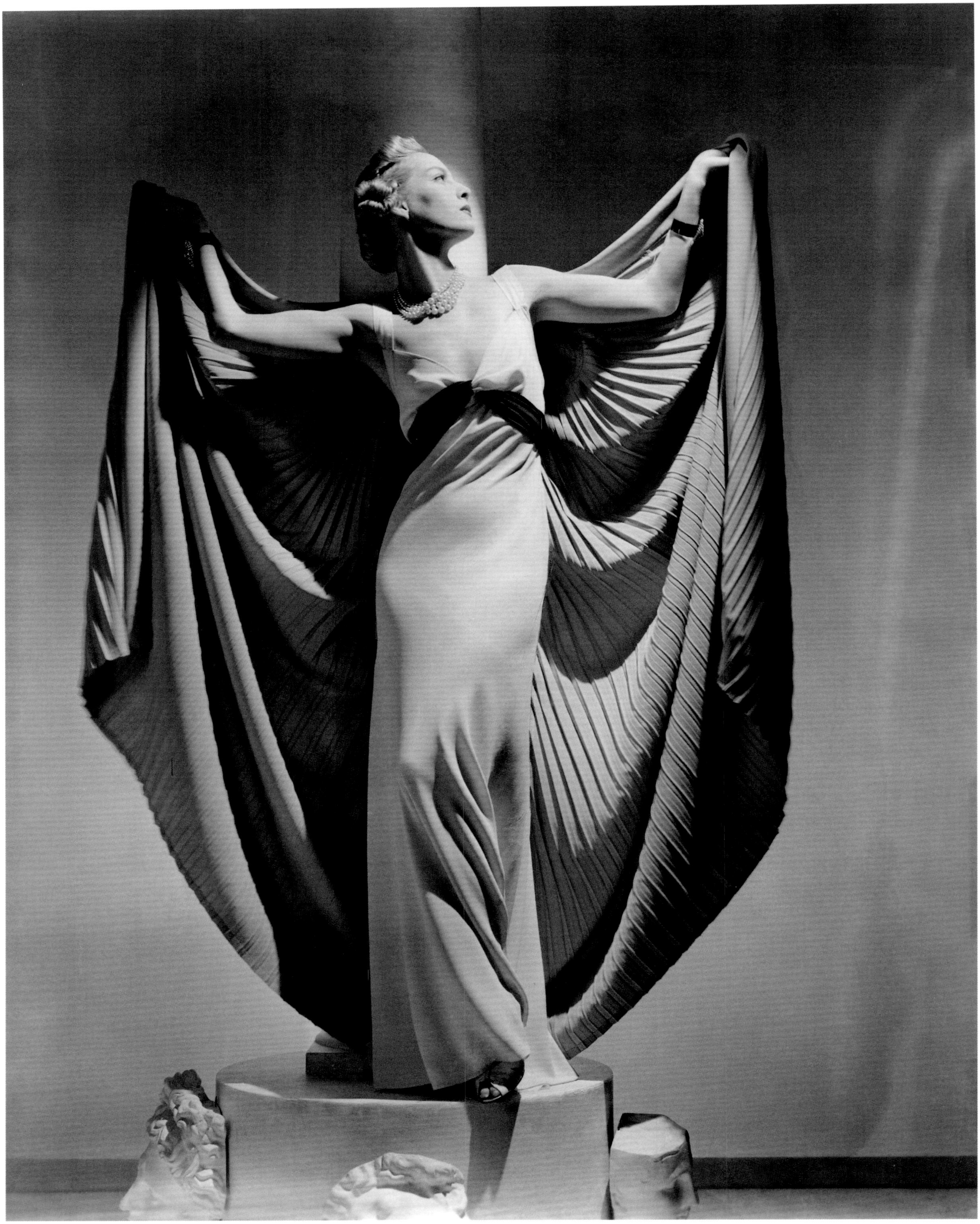

HORST

Photographer *of* Style

Edited by Susanna Brown

V&A Publishing

Travel Partner

American Airlines

With thanks to Bicester Village
and Kildare Village

Supported by the American Friends
of the Victoria and Albert Museum

First published by V&A Publishing, 2014
Victoria and Albert Museum
South Kensington
London SW7 2RL
www.vandapublishing.com

All photographs by Horst P. Horst.
Images reproduced courtesy of the Condé Nast Archive, New York,
Collection Condé Nast, France, and the Horst Estate.

The moral right of the authors has been asserted.

Hardback edition
ISBN 978 1 85177 801 0

Library of Congress Control Number 2014940909

10 9 8 7 6 5 4 3 2 1
2017 2016 2015 2014

A catalogue record for this book is available from the British Library.

Front cover illustration: Sun-bathed, but not Sun-struck, 1941

Frontispiece: Helen Bennett, Paris, 1936

Designers: Daniel Baer with Hannah Montague
Copy-editor: Denny Hemming
Index: Heliotrope Indexing

Printed in Italy

MIX
From responsible
sources
FSC www.fsc.org FSC® C016114

V&A Publishing

Supporting the world's leading
museum of art and design,
the Victoria and Albert
Museum, London

CONTENTS

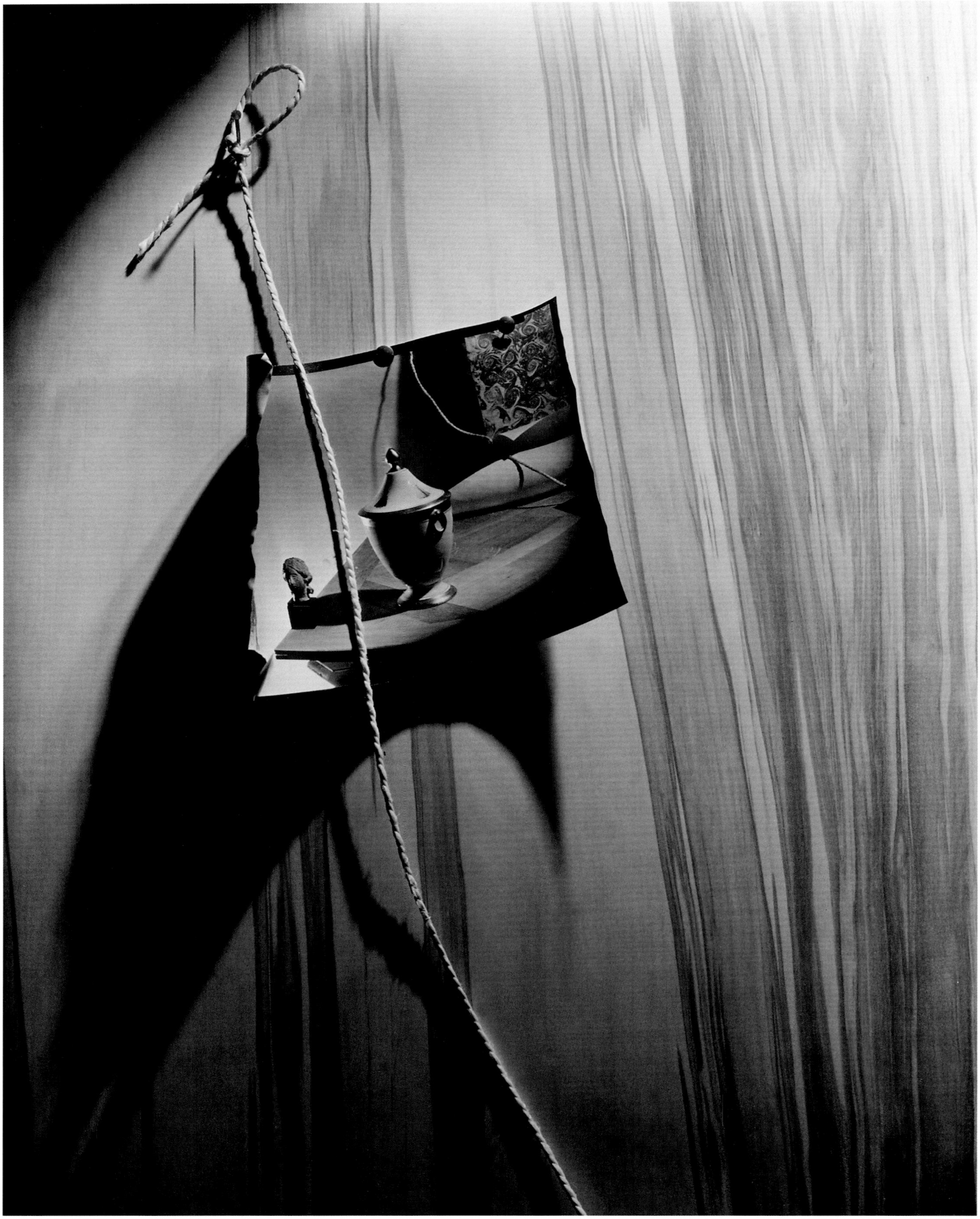

1. Still Life, 1942

DIRECTOR'S FOREWORD

Martin Roth

As the first major exhibition by master photographer Horst P. Horst (1906–99) opens at the V&A, we might consider how Horst himself would feel about the event. He was a man of wit and modesty, who might wonder at all the fuss. Yet, as a frequent visitor to art galleries and a connoisseur of design, Horst would surely feel pleased and proud that his extraordinary photographs should take their rightful place in one of the world's greatest museums of art and design, to be admired by the widest possible audience and bring inspiration to a new generation of image-makers.

One of *Vogue*'s star artists, his one-word photographic byline was synonymous with elegance and supreme style. Horst was an international figure, who chronicled the interwoven worlds of art, fashion, design, theatre and high society. He was born in Germany and shuttled between Paris and New York, becoming an American citizen in 1943. His diverse influences ranged from the designs of the Bauhaus, to surrealist discourse and classical forms. The subjects and style of his photographs resonate across the V&A's collections. They were first exhibited at the Museum in 1975, as part of the group exhibition *Fashion 1900–1939*. This definitive new book, and the exhibition it accompanies, shed new light on Horst's remarkable œuvre.

Through a generous gift from Mr Gert Elfering, collector and photography connoisseur, 32 exquisite Horst photographs will enhance Britain's National Collection of the Art of Photography at the V&A. The Museum began acquiring photographs in 1852 and the collection is unique in covering the history of photography as a fine and applied art. *Horst: Photographer of Style* is the latest in a series of acclaimed major exhibitions drawing on the V&A's world-class collection and curatorial expertise.

The V&A is grateful for the invaluable support given to this exhibition and publication by the Horst Estate, the dedicated staff of Condé Nast in America, Britain and France, and Horst's friends and family members.

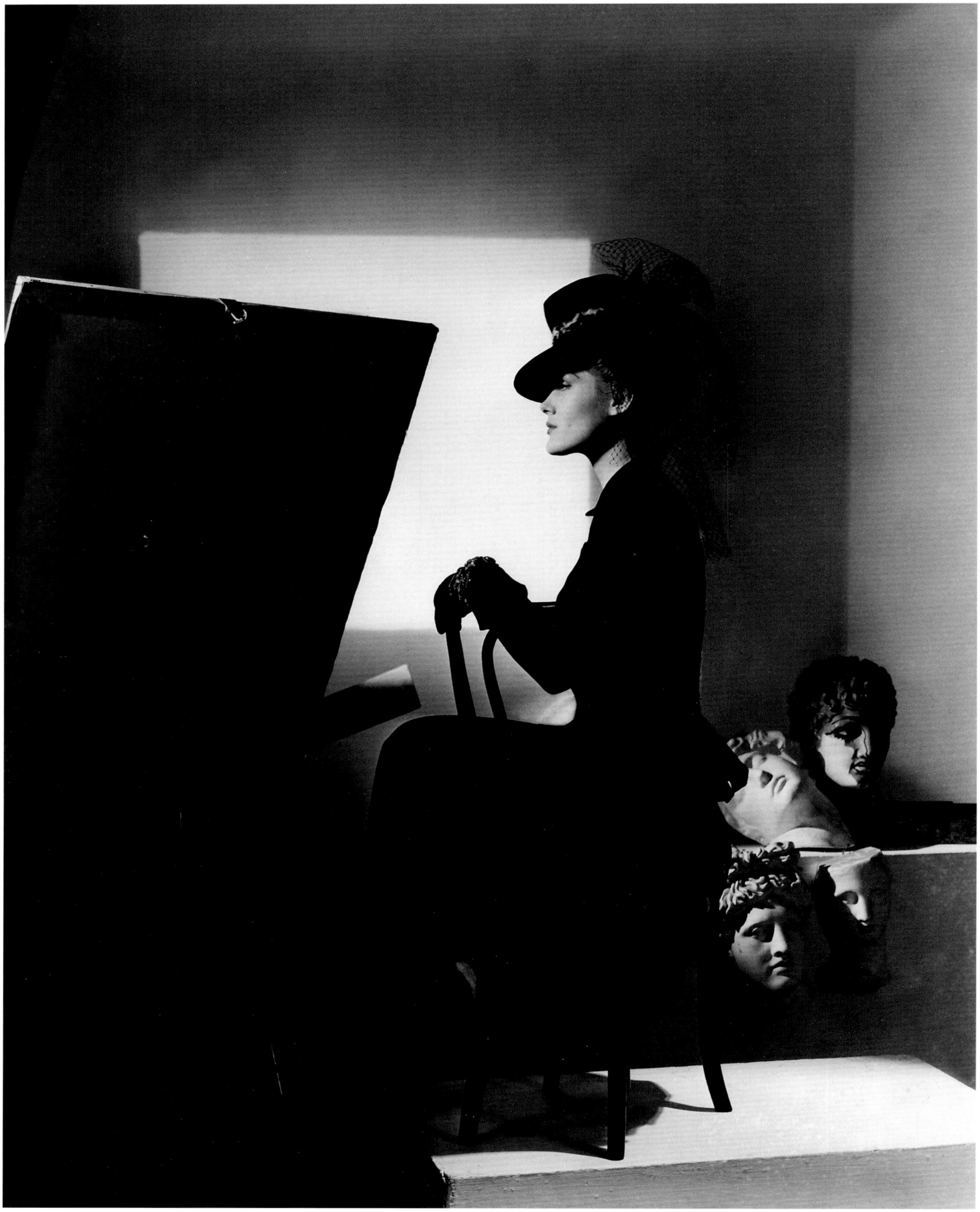

2. Estrella Boissevain, hat and coat-dress
by Bergdorf Goodman, 1938

A LIFETIME OF STYLE

Anna Wintour

When I was creative director at American *Vogue* in the mid-1980s, I frankly didn't have much to do, so every now and again I would have lunch with Horst. We used to go to a rather dowdy Italian restaurant just up from Bloomingdales, and he would talk to me about the old days. He was so much fun. At that time he was feeling rather left out in the cold – Alex Liberman would never hire him as he felt Horst's fashion work was old-fashioned – but Horst never complained. He was a perfect gentleman.

Later, as editor-in-chief of British *Vogue*, I commissioned Horst, together with Grace Coddington, to do a fashion story on Yasmin Le Bon, in spite of the fact that my vision for the magazine was all about being of the moment. Grace was wildly excited to be working with him. I remember her telling me about the shoot afterwards and the extraordinary effect Horst was able to achieve – how he did something to the lights, moved them in a very specific way, and suddenly you had a 'Horst' picture with that signature chiaroscuro, those dramatic shadows. The images were very much of Horst's 'period' but they were also absolutely timely and relevant.

Horst was the Mario Testino of his day. If you were faintly royal, or had social connections, having your photograph taken by Horst really meant something. He made everyone look beautiful, flawless and alluring.

Horst excelled at photographing interiors as well as portraits, capturing rooms so that that they looked not only stylish but also lived-in. He would ask the home owners where they most liked to sit in a room and would take the picture from that vantage point, often shooting through a flower arrangement. The resulting image created the impression that you were a welcome guest, walking into the room for the first time.

After I had returned to the United States as the editor-in-chief of American *Vogue*, Horst was awarded the Geoffrey Beene Lifetime Achievement Award by the Council of Fashion Designers of America. I was extremely flattered when Horst asked me to present him with the award. I wore a glamorous Geoffrey Beene dress once worn by Diana Ross. Of course, Horst loved it!

My great friend Eric Boman, the Swedish photographer, while in Paris shooting the collections for French *Vogue*, found himself at the same *Vogue* studio as Bailey and Horst. He and Horst had dinner together and became firm friends, and so I would hear all the stories. Eric and Peter Schlesinger, David Hockney's muse, were invited to visit Horst and his partner Valentine Lawford to celebrate Labor Day at their house in Oyster Bay, which was a reflection of Horst's sense of style and elegance. Eric and Peter were a little alarmed to discover Horst sitting stark naked by the pool. 'Come on, boys, jump in!' he urged them, but they felt it was too early in their friendship for such intimacy, so they demurred. Instead, he regaled them with stories of how the Sitwells and Greta Garbo had sat exactly where they were sitting, and to illustrate his point, he asked his assistant Hansi to fetch the photographic evidence, a shoe box full of large format negatives. To Eric's horror, Horst proceeded to pull out the one of Garbo 'with his bare mayonnaise fingers'.

To mark the 120th anniversary of American *Vogue*, I was asked to reflect on my favourite *Vogue* images: Horst's *Mainbocher Corset* was one. While Horst himself was old school in the best possible way, a vibrant testament to a lifetime of high style and high culture, lived to the fullest, his genius lay in creating images that are equally of their time, yet timeless.

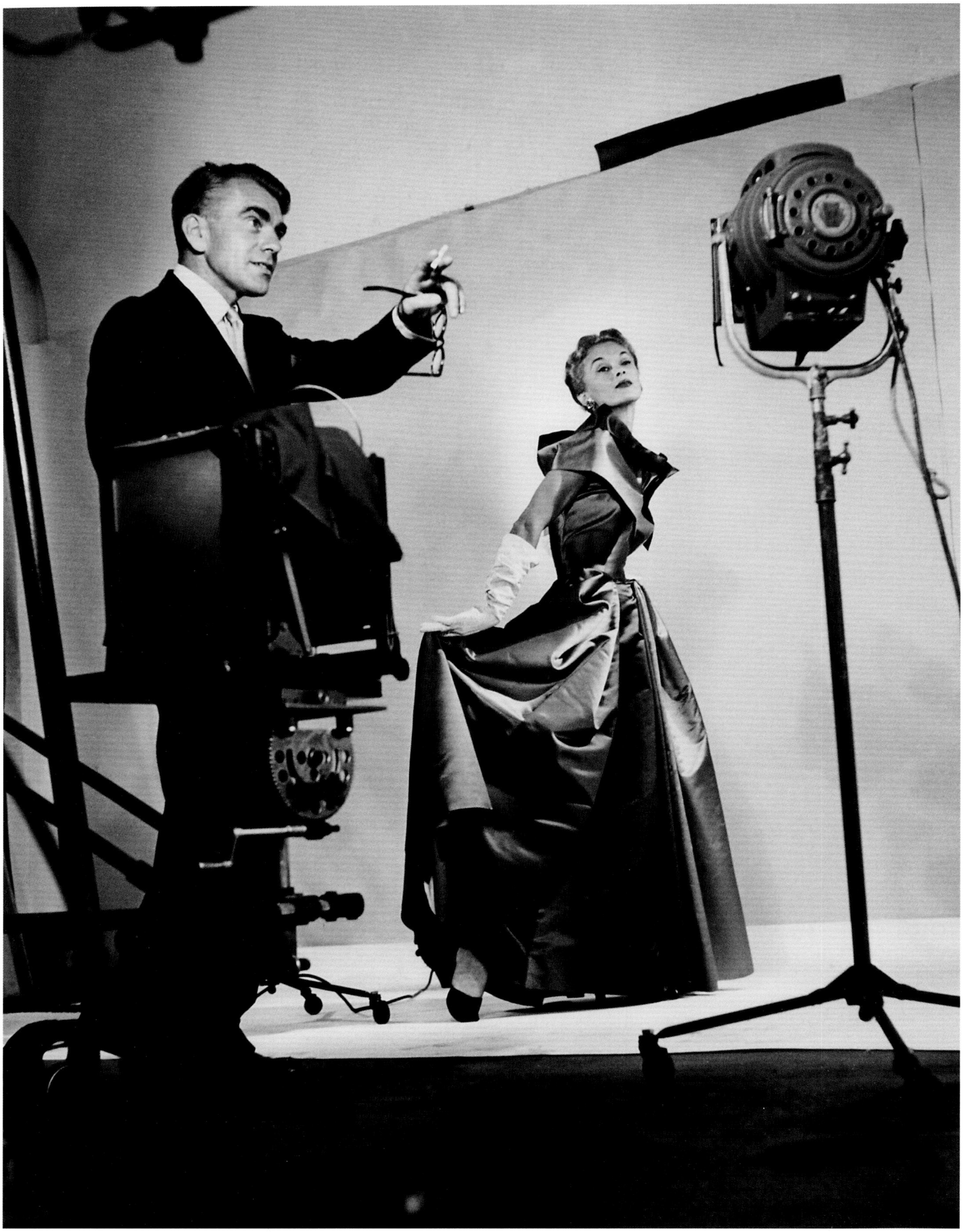

3. Roy Stevens,
Horst and Lisa Fonssagrives
in the studio, New York, 1949

INTRODUCTION: INVENTING ELEGANCE

Susanna Brown

> Fashion is an expression of the times.
> Elegance is something else again.[1]
>
> Horst, 1984

Horst P. Horst created images that transcend fashion and time. More than a century after his birth, his photographs remain as expressive and potent today as they ever were. He was a master of light, composition and atmospheric illusion, who conjured a world of sensual sophistication. In the 1980s, discussing his expansive career and photographic triumphs in pre-war Paris, he reflected:

> For some people the word 'elegance' has acquired objectionable, snobbish connotations. But I myself prefer to regard elegance as an attractive and admirable – if admittedly rare – human attribute: a form of physical and mental grace that has nothing to do with pretension or over-refinement or an excess of money to spend ... Unlike Huene, who had absorbed an infallible sense of elegance from his upbringing, I had to invent it on my own: more exactly, to learn gradually to recognise elegance in others and try to portray it in my photographs.[2]

In the early 1930s, Baron George Hoyningen-Huene was Horst's mentor and partner. The son of a Russian father and American mother, Huene was among *Vogue*'s first star photographers. He was almost as famous for his fiery temper as for his classically inspired fashion images, in which models pose atop columns to resemble caryatids, or lounge in chic beachwear, bathed in light. Horst's relationship with Huene led to lessons with the camera and an opportunity to hone his skills in the photographic studio of French *Vogue*. The attractive, fair-haired Horst even appeared as a model in a number of Huene's photographs.[3]

Horst learnt much from the Baron, but went on to perfect a style all his own, superseding Huene in the mid-1930s as French *Vogue*'s primary photographer and achieving international acclaim for his sublime fashion studies, portraits and nudes. Horst assimilated Huene's neoclassical approach and skilfully combined it with elements of Modernism and baroque, punctuated by surreal and humorous touches: as one writer concluded, 'Horst's eclectic spirit is seen in manifold references to art history ... In a Horst, Neoclassical order lives comfortably with Baroque imagination.'[4] His extraordinary range and his work outside *Vogue* convey Horst's relentless visual curiosity and lifelong desire for new photographic challenges. Personal projects include the detailed exploration of natural forms published as *Patterns from Nature* (pl.178), contemplative still-life arrangements, and powerful documentary pictures from his international travels. An extensive colour series exploring some of the world's most magnificent homes and gardens marked a new phase in Horst's career in the 1960s. When the next generation discovered his early black and white studies in the 1970s, Horst was in demand: his stylish, spotlit fashion pictures appeared in *Vogue* again and in the 1980s he began to produce platinum-palladium prints for collectors and museums.

When Horst joined *Vogue* in 1931, Paris was still the world's undisputed centre of high fashion, and the magazine presented the work of the city's leading couturiers to the minority who could afford such items, as well as those aspiring to a life of luxury, who escaped into a glamorous fantasy world through *Vogue*'s pages. In the 1920s, the medium of photography had begun to eclipse graphic illustration in fashion magazines. The publisher Mr Condé Nast had purchased the American society magazine in 1909. He devoted large sums to improving the quality of image reproduction and hired leading photographic artists such as Baron Adolph de Meyer and Edward Steichen. The Condé Nast empire grew to include titles such as *Vanity Fair*, *House & Garden* and *Glamour*; Horst's photographs would be printed in them all. Mr Nast launched British and French editions of *Vogue* in 1916 and 1920 respectively, and appointed Edna Woolman Chase editor-in-chief of the three. Bettina Ballard, who was an early employee of Condé Nast and *Vogue*'s American representative in Paris, considered the company to be a family 'in which Mr Nast was the father, Mrs Chase the mother.'[5]

The creation of a *Vogue* photograph was a collaborative process, which involved not only the talents of the photographer and model, but also the art director, fashion editor, studio assistant, set builder and hairstylist, among others. Mr Nast's insistence that photographers work with the cumbersome 10 × 8 inch plate camera, prized for its large and detailed negatives, meant that Horst was rarely able to photograph outside the confines of the studio. Each day, he would walk from rue Saint-Romain on the Left Bank to the spacious seventh-floor studio at *Vogue*'s office building on the Champs Elysées, the city's grandest bustling avenue. The studio secretary was Madame Dilé, 'a bright-eyed, gold-toothed little woman' affectionately known as 'La Dilette'. She ran the lives of the photographers and models 'with efficiency mixed with a vicarious pleasure in knowing everything about everybody.'[6] Horst valued Dilé's friendship, as well as the assistance of Maurice, the studio carpenter and painter, who helped transform wooden planks, paper, and simple sheets of fabric into seemingly luxurious photographic sets and backdrops. Having studied design and construction under Walter Gropius at the Hamburg Kunstgewerbeschule, it is not surprising that Horst relished the opportunity to build his own sets and exercise his instinctive 'sculptor's sense of form'.[7]

His favourite props included Baroque gilt scrolls (pls 4, 7), plaster casts of antique statues and vast photographic enlargements of paintings by artists such as Fragonard and Goya. Props that could not be produced in the studio were lent by interior decorators and friends, Jean-Michel Frank among them (pls 8, 9). The designers Emilio Terry (pl.30) and Marcel Vertès (pls 160, 169, 170) were called upon to collaborate on some of Horst's most memorable pictures; the photographer might spend two days preparing for a single elaborate sitting. As well as props, the studio was equipped with about 20 lights, both overhead spotlights and large floodlights of various strengths:

> I preferred to use the spotlights, to emphasize the important points of a dress. Faces presented their own problem. Greek statues, created to be seen in sunlight out-of-doors, could stand overhead lighting. But photographing live faces with a strong overhead light brought out the wrinkles, left the eyes dark, and made shadows under the lips and nose. To show a face at its best and most attractive, I tried lighting it from below or from the side, or sometimes straight on with just the eyes or a cheek lit up.[8]

Chiaroscuro effects and dramatic shadows were key elements of Horst's 1930s photographs. One of his early breakthroughs was to devise a way to photograph black garments without bleaching out the face of the model. The method involved directing all the light onto the dark fabric, leaving the face in shadow, to mysterious and romantic effect. When photographing pale garments, he used much less light on the dress than on the background (pl.13). After a sitting, Horst would look through his prints with the darkroom assistant and Simone Eyrard, the skilful retoucher, who would delicately accentuate eyelashes, slim waistlines and eliminate unwanted details, to craft *Vogue*'s idealised version of beauty. Today, a fashion sitting might be referred to as a 'shoot', but perhaps a more appropriate word in this context is 'séance', better evoking the atmosphere of intense concentration and hushed suspense typical of a sitting; there was certainly none of the speed or violence that the word 'shoot' suggests.

In the early years of Horst's career, there were few professional models, or mannequins, as they were often called. Thus, the women who posed for him were sometimes friends of *Vogue*'s well-connected staff, or the couturiers' house mannequins, such as Sonia Colmer at the House of Vionnet. To be a model required great stamina, as well as beauty. During the thrilling and frenetic weeks of the Paris couture presentations, in spring and autumn each year, garments had to be photographed at night, once the buyers had left the couture houses. Models filled the *Vogue* studio and vied for the best dresses in which to pose, before taking their positions under the heat of the lights. Horst explained the laborious process of making a photograph:

> First you posed the model. Then you put a black cloth on your head, and focused the eight-by-ten camera, which was mounted on wheels. Then you tightened the camera extension.

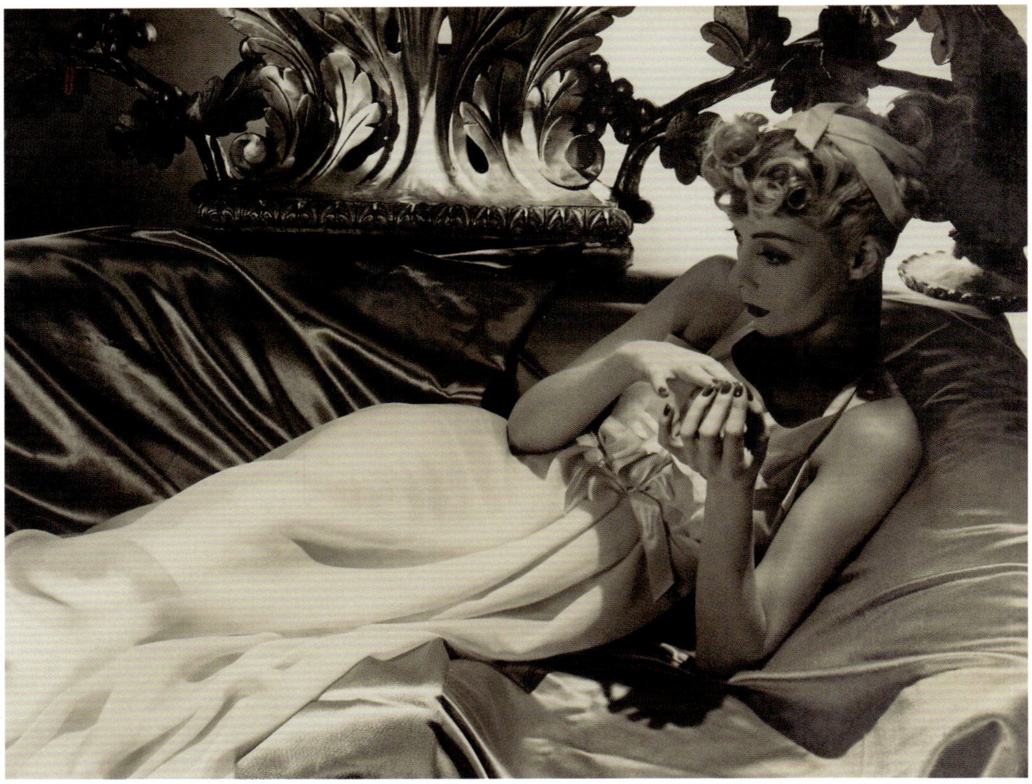

4. Helen Bennett, nightgown by Dubrulle, 1938

> You folded back the black cloth to prevent it covering the lens. Then you took the film holder from its carriage and put it into the camera. You pulled out the slide, and put it away. Then you told the model to 'hold it,' and clicked the camera. Since there were no light meters, you had to guess the correct exposure, generally two to three seconds, and time it with the help of an alarm clock that stood on the box containing the film holders. In other words, you had to watch the clock and watch the model at the same time. Of course throughout this entire cumbrous operation, the model had to hold her pose. In fact, she might as well have been part of a still life.[9]

Horst was instrumental in launching the careers of the most admired models in pre-war Paris, several of whom were Russian émigrés who had fled their native country in the wake of the 1917 revolution and ensuing civil war. Among his favourite Russian models were Lidia Konstantinova Zelenskaya, known in France as Lyla Zelensky, and Ludmila Leonidovna Feodoseyeva, known simply as Lud.[10] Lyla Zelensky was the daughter of the Georgian princess Melita Tazievna Cholokayeva, who had briefly worked as a model for Chanel in the 1920s, and Lyla was capable of carrying off even the most outlandish creations with swan-like grace. Lud was working as a film extra and messenger when Horst caught sight of her delivering some dresses to the *Vogue* studio. He immediately wanted to photograph her, and later recalled: 'She revolutionized the look of the model. She was not at all remote or cold, not at all like a sleepwalker; she was sensual and catlike.'[11] She would look over the garments in the *Vogue* studio before the other models, and would only pose in the ones she liked best. Accounts of Lud paint a picture of a brave, strong-minded woman, almost wild at times: 'She was ruthless with herself, having cut off part of her breasts and thighs for a better figure. We could never put too low a dress on her because the plastic surgery had been badly done ... She rarely smiled, except for Dilé, who could get through to her, or for Horst, with whom I suspected she was in love.'[12]

The Swedish beauty Lisa Fonssagrives was another of Horst's dearest models.[13] Lisa was working as a dance teacher when Horst made some test shots of her at the French *Vogue* studio. Like Horst himself, Lisa spent many hours studying the paintings and sculptures at the Louvre to improve her skills. She attempted to see herself through photographer's eyes:

> I would imagine what kind of woman would wear the gown I was wearing and assume different characters. I would look at myself in the dressing room mirror before going on the set and instinctively try to solve the photographer's problems. I would look at the cut of the dress and try different poses to see how it fell best, how the light would enhance it, and basically try to create a line the way one starts a drawing. I would objectify myself and become more of a director than an actress.[14]

Horst particularly favoured Lisa for her expressive dancer's hands and lithe figure, and it was Lisa who posed for his most accomplished nudes. His charm and rapport with the models meant that many became friends. In 1976, an article was published in American *Vogue* celebrating Horst's 'instinctive and architectural understanding of what makes a dress come beautifully alive', and it was accompanied by

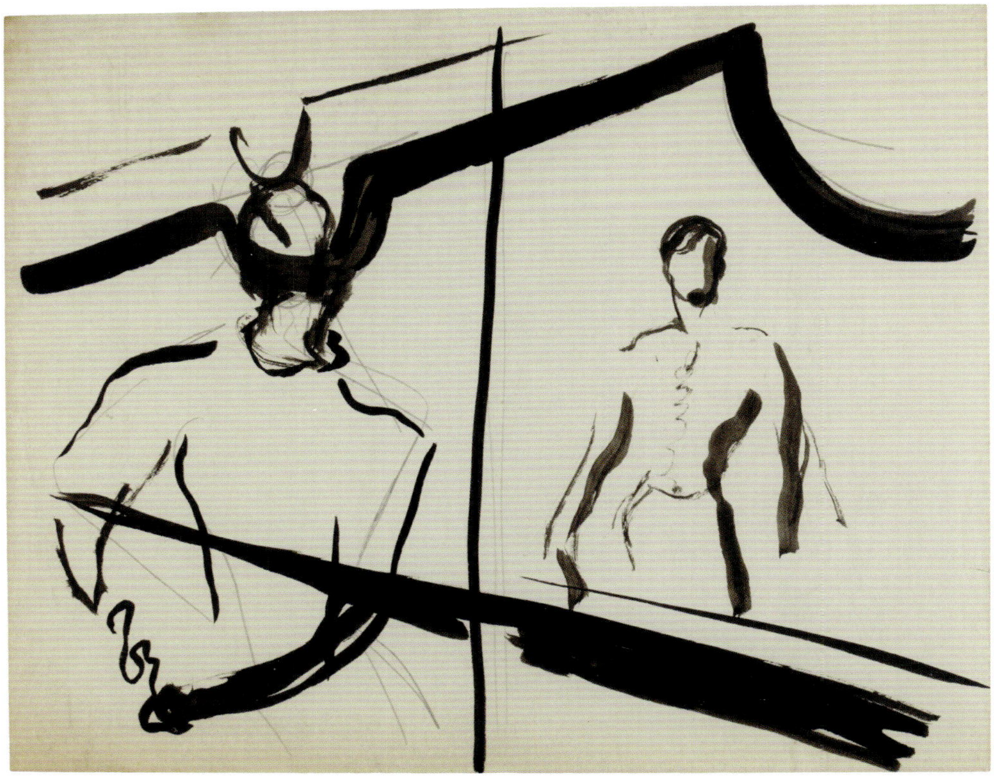

5. Preparatory sketch for a fashion photograph, 1930s

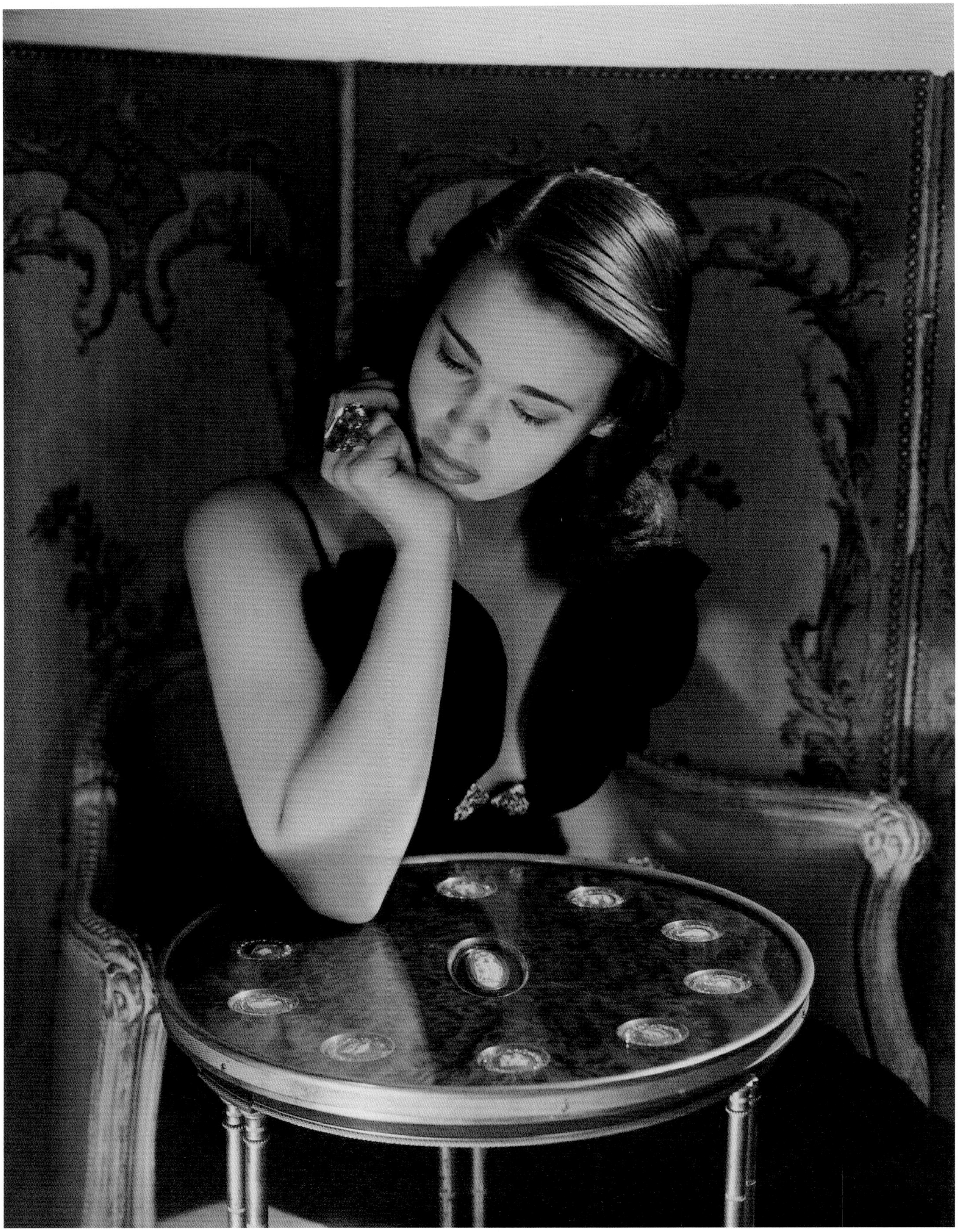

6. Gloria Vanderbilt, New York, 1941

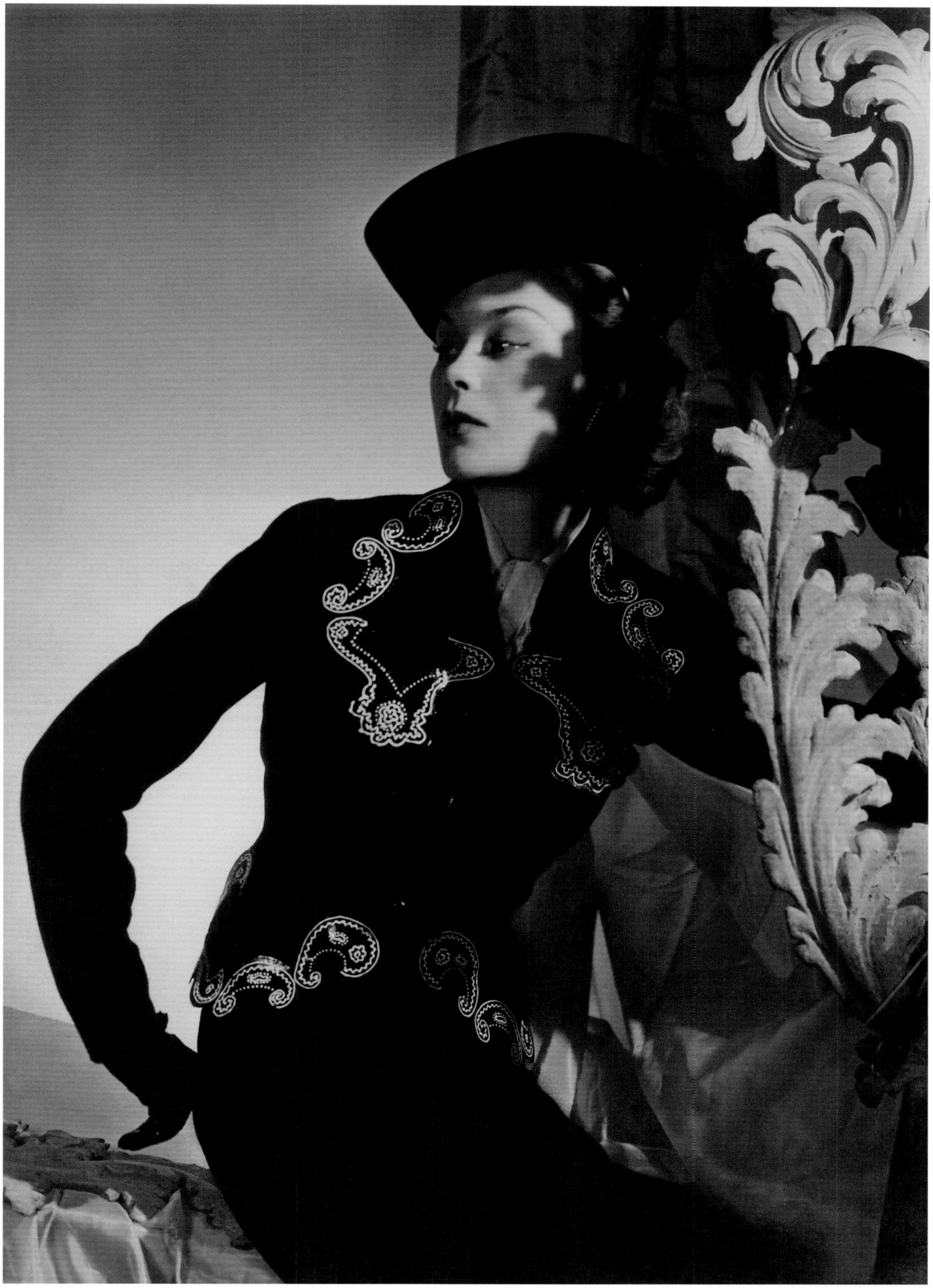

7. Lud, suit and hat by Schiaparelli,
jewellery by Mauboussin, 1937

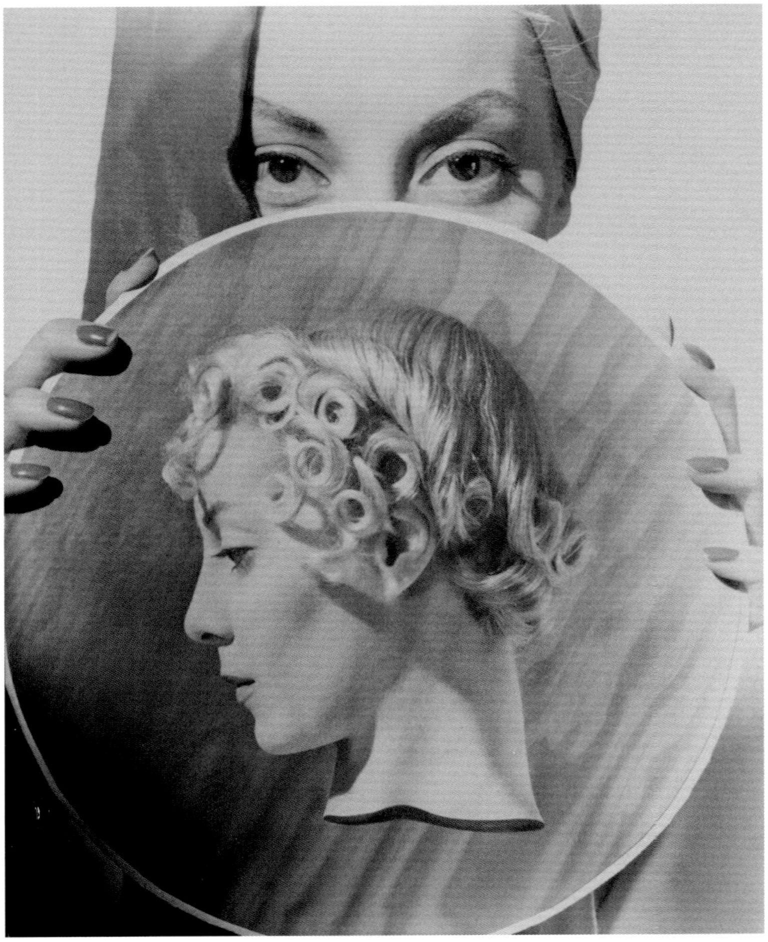

8. Helen Bennett, 1936

a study of Lisa, taken in 1939.[15] On seeing the magazine, she was moved to write to Horst: 'I feel such soothing blessings by your beautiful work – even more so today when we live in a sea of flickering snapshots, bombarded from everywhere.'[16] Speaking years later of her debt to Horst, Lisa said simply, 'I became a model because he made me one.'[17]

Other models with whom Horst worked in the 1930s included Agnetha Fischer, Toto Koopman,[18] Evelyn Grieg, Helen Wedderburn, and Madame Muthe, who was 'like a Bellini Madonna' and would later be killed by the Gestapo.[19] Platinum-haired Helen Bennett[20] and tall brunette Muriel Maxwell were two of the first Americans to be sent by *Vogue* to model the Paris collections. Both featured in vibrant colour on numerous *Vogue* covers by Horst. Bennett went on to make a successful transition into acting and Maxwell became a fashion editor for American *Vogue*.

In the 1930s, *Vogue*'s photographers travelled between London, Paris and New York. Horst visited New York for the first time in 1932 and, later in the decade, he traversed the ocean between France and America more frequently, as a passenger on ocean liners such as the *Ile de France*, the *Normandie* and the *Lafayette* – floating luxury hotels that showcased splendid Art Deco design. In August 1939, with the outbreak of war just weeks away, Horst fled Paris for New York on the *Normandie*; he was unable to visit France again until 1946.

American *Vogue*'s photographic studio was situated on the 19th floor of the Graybar Building on Lexington Avenue. Here, Horst gained confidence photographing in colour with the recently invented Kodachrome film, but the war would bring about a hiatus in his fashion work. On 21 October 1943, Horst officially became an American citizen, changing his surname from 'Bohrmann' to 'Horst'. That year, he spent a gruelling three months training with the American army in Virginia and, as Sergeant Horst, worked as a photographer for the United States Army Signal Corps. After the war, the American fashion industry boomed and Horst was as busy as ever. A new generation of photographers, led by Richard Avedon and Irving Penn, created images that helped to rehabilitate the French couture houses and promote America's blossoming ready-to-wear industry. Horst particularly admired Penn's restrained and technically sophisticated black and white work, and the inventive wit of Erwin Blumenfeld, who – like Horst and many of New York's creative personalities of the era – had left Europe for a new life in America. Condé Nast acquired a larger studio on Lexington Avenue, managed by Claire Malleson. Better equipped, it was filled with lights and a spectacular variety of props. Mr Nast relaxed the rules regarding cameras, allowing the use of smaller and more portable types including the Rolleiflex: 'It took ten years, a world war, and a world-wide shortage of film for us to be permitted to use a Rolleiflex', wrote Horst.[21] The new, lighter cameras enabled the magazine photographers to take up a more journalistic approach and the soaring city took centre stage in the work of photographers such as William Klein and Genevieve Naylor. Yet Horst, the master of studio photography, still produced his best images inside, where composition and lighting could be more carefully controlled (pl.3).

His favourite models in 1940s New York included Bettina Bollegard, Susann Shaw, Betty McLauchlen, Barbara Mortimer and Carmen Dell'Orefice, who paints a vivid picture of their collaborations and enduring friendship at the end of this publication.[22] Horst's kindness and charisma endeared him to every model he worked with. Lillian

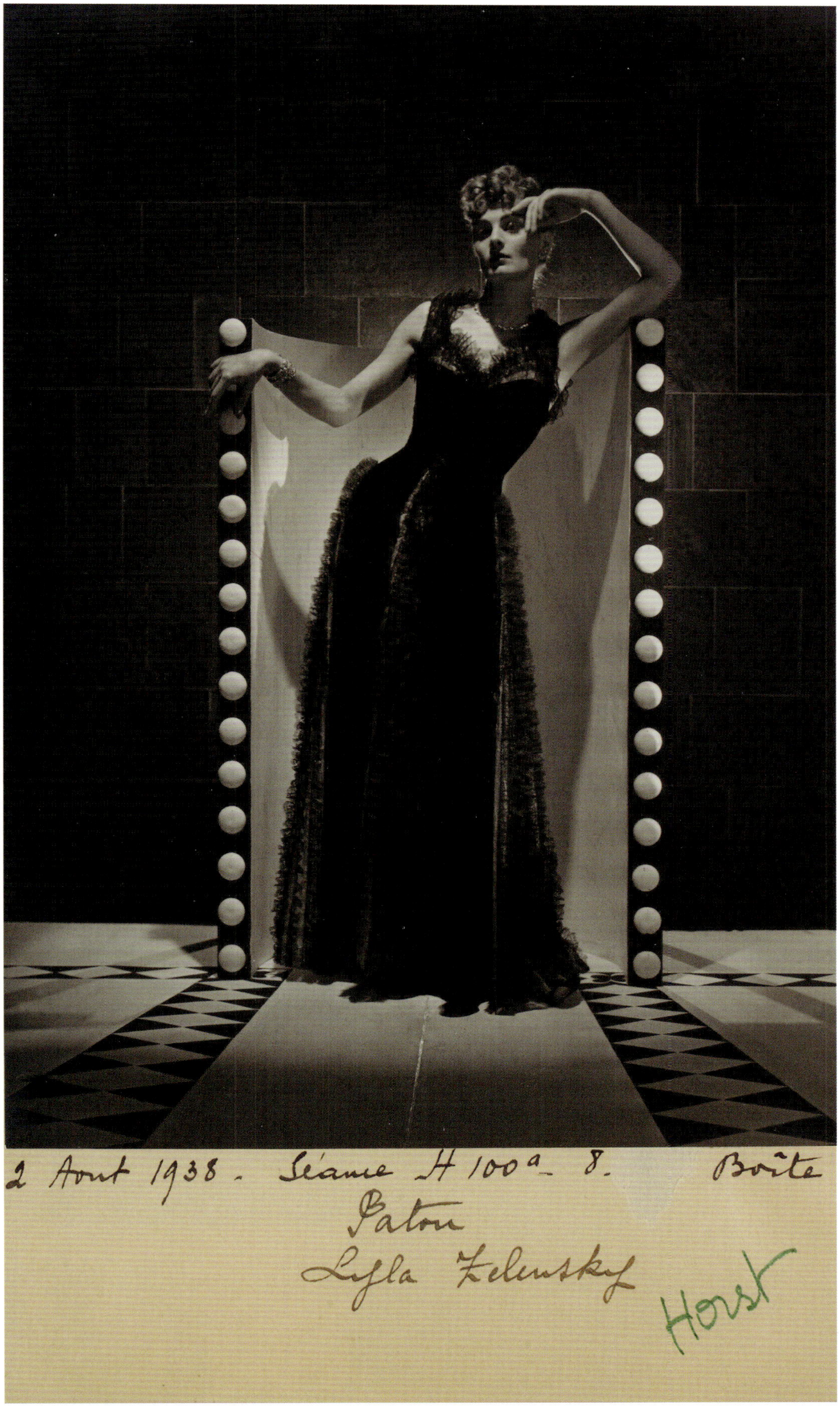

9. Lyla Zelensky, dress by Jean Patou,
jewellery by Boucheron, 1938

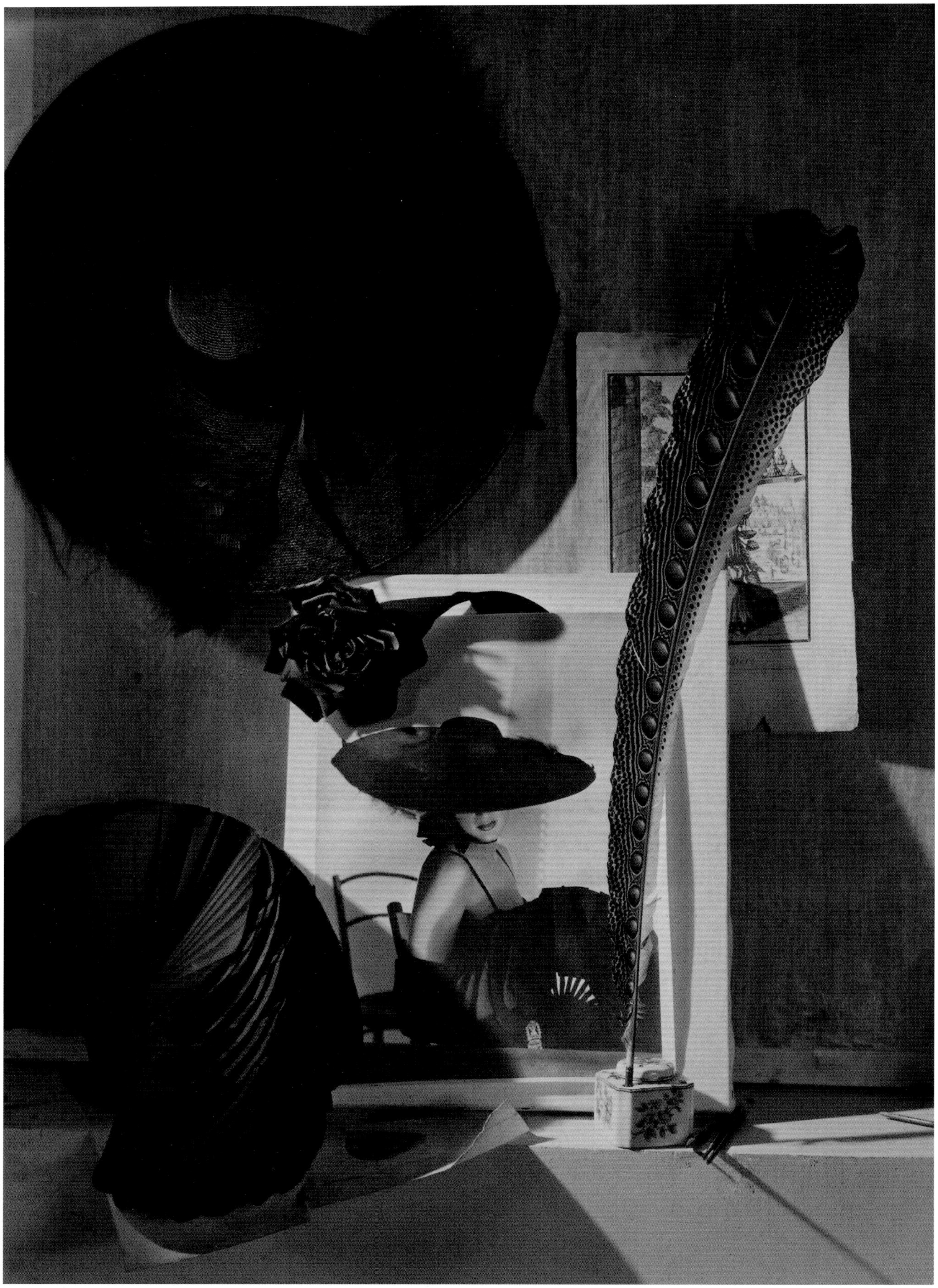

10. Ma-quise de Montesquiou-Fezensac,
accessories by Molyneux, 1938

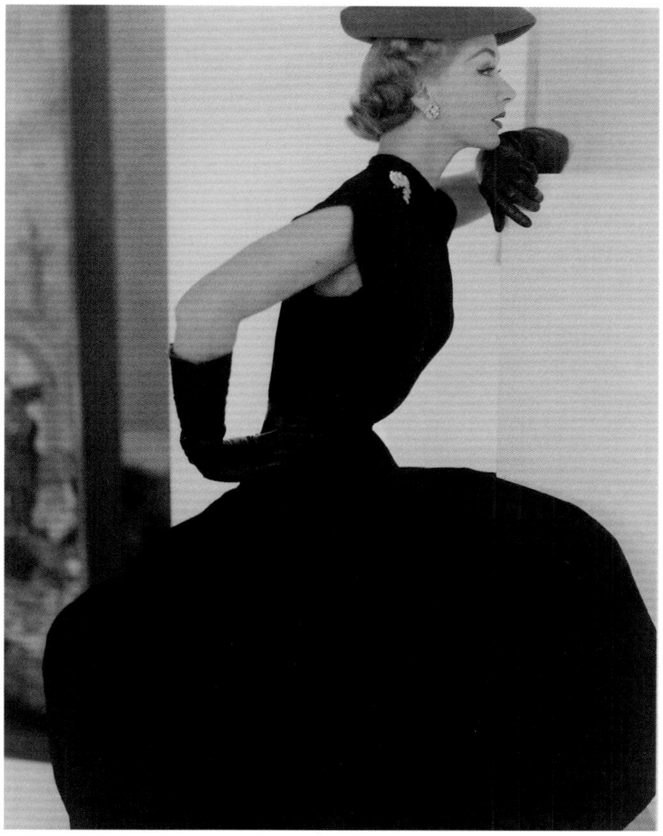

11. Suzy Parker,
dress by Balenciaga, 1951

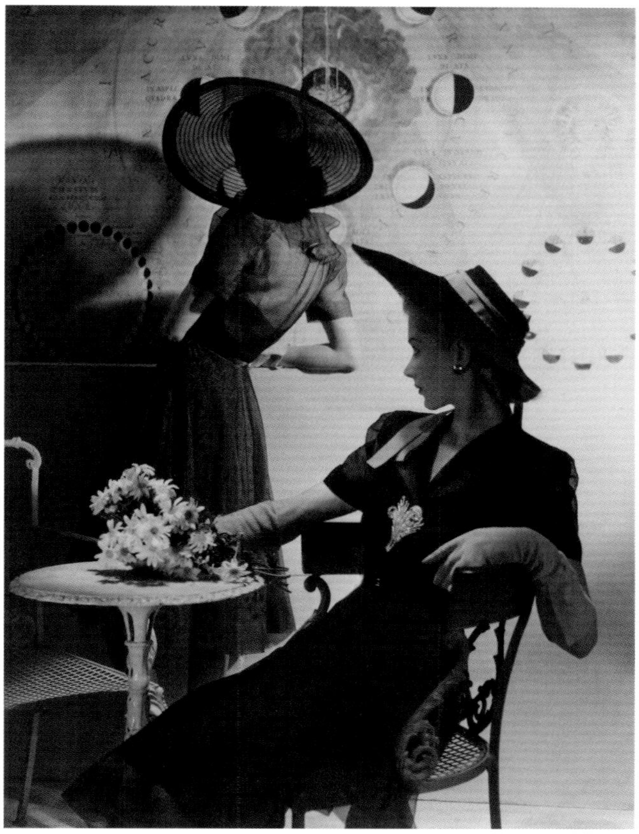

12. Miss Lane and Lisa Fonssagrives,
dresses and hats by Saks-Fifth Avenue, 1940

Marcuson, who spent ten days with him in Paris at the end of the decade, recalled: 'I loved him. He was the sweetest, nicest man, and very handsome as well.'[23] Horst's leading models of the next decade included Dovima, admired by Horst for her 'extraordinary American ease ... an understanding, a feeling, for clothes',[24] Sunny Harnett, Jean Patchett, Dorian Leigh and, later, Leigh's younger sister Suzy Parker (pl.11).[25] The home Horst designed at Oyster Bay, Long Island, became his oasis and a favoured location for shoots. He settled into life at Oyster Bay with his companion Valentine Lawford, a cultured British gentleman and diplomat, whom he first met in the spring of 1947. Horst always remained close to his earlier loves, Huene and film director Luchino Visconti. It is a testament to their lasting friendship that, when Huene died in 1968, he bequeathed his entire collection of photographs to Horst.

In 1951, when Condé Nast closed down the New York studio, Horst found a studio of his own: the former penthouse apartment of artist Pavel Tchelitchew on East 55th Street, with high ceilings and a terrace commanding a spectacular view over the river. Horst developed a new approach to photography in response to the abundance of daylight that flooded into the studio and, for a time, his trademark atmospheric shadows disappeared. He hired as his assistant the young photographer Edwin Pfizenmaier, who would work with Horst for the ensuing 15 years.

Other major changes occurred at *Vogue* in the early 1950s. Edna Woolman Chase, Horst's personal friend and neighbour in Oyster Bay, retired after half a century with the magazine. She was replaced as editor-in-chief by Jessica Daves, but Daves' new rules on photography stifled Horst's creativity and he began to focus more energy on lucrative, but sometimes mundane, advertising assignments. His advertising clients included the department stores I. Magnin and Saks-Fifth Avenue, and the brands Modess and Soft-Weve, Lipton Tea, Cadillac, Ford and RoundtheClock hosiery. One of the more memorable advertising campaigns, for Modess, took Horst to the Austrian Alps with the model Suzy Parker in the winter of 1951–2. During the three-month trip to Europe, Horst also covered the February 1952 Paris collections for *Vogue* and reconnected with his German family, whom he had not seen since 1939. His father, Max Bohrmann, had died, but Horst's mother, Klara, was living in the Soviet-occupied zone of Germany, and was sometimes granted permission to visit West Berlin. His brother, Heinz, had fought in the German army throughout the war and had suffered a serious head wound.

It might be said that Horst created a family of his own choosing in America, with Lawford. A young Austrian, Johann D. Mayr (known as Hans), joined them in Oyster Bay and worked as Horst's assistant after Pfizenmaier. Hans was 18 when he was invited by Horst to embark on a new life, and left his home town of Söll, near Kitzbühel. He explained: 'Horst became like a second father to me, he treated me like family.'[26] Years later, another young man joined the family. Richard, or, as Horst called him, Ricki, met the photographer for the first time at a dinner party in the mid-1970s: 'I found Horst to be a perfect gentleman: handsome, debonair, charming, sophisticated, but very masculine, with his deep voice and dark tan. I believe at that very moment, I became completely infatuated with him.'[27]

The house at Oyster Bay encapsulated Horst and Lawford's shared passion for interior and garden design. They welcomed many friends and visitors, including the dynamic editor Diana Vreeland. She left *Harper's Bazaar* for *Vogue* in 1962 and soon put the couple to work, photographing and writing about opulent homes and the tastes and talents of their owners – everyone from Jackie Onassis to the Duke and Duchess of Windsor, Andy Warhol and Karl Lagerfeld; many were Vreeland's personal friends. Horst's creative chemistry with Vreeland brought him a new lease of life. When planning a visit to Germany, Horst asked her: 'What should I bring back?' 'Splendour!' was her ebullient reply.[28] During the 1970s, he photographed predominantly for *House & Garden*, under the editorship of Mary Jane Pool. Those who opened their homes to Horst and Lawford were invariably thrilled with the results, as their letters convey. The designer Emilio Pucci (see pls 266, 267) wrote from Florence:

> Christina and I have been absolutely delighted with the fantastic pictures published in *Vogue*. Every day I am receiving enthusiastic comments on them from all over the world and I really cannot tell you how impressed I am by your artistry and superb sense of movement and proportion which is so beautifully exemplified by these pictures ... I wish to thank you again for working here so easily and so pleasantly, making it for us a pleasure to have you here rather than a preoccupation as I had originally expected.'[29]

Horst's images inspired other leading photographers, including Richard Avedon, who wrote to Horst upon seeing his pictures of Cy Twombly's home and family:

> Dear Horst:
> I really think your last spread in the November 15th issue is the most charming, rollicking, contemporary, happy and beautiful I have seen all year. I have tacked it up on my bulletin board at home so as not ever to have it out of my sight. Congratulations!
> Dick Avedon [30]

In 1978, Horst's early aesthetic experienced a renaissance, when Francine Crescent, French *Vogue*'s editor-in-chief, invited him to photograph the Paris collections in a style that echoed his atmospheric, spotlit studies of the 1930s. The models he worked with in the 1970s and '80s recall his mastery: 'Walking into Horst's studio, one was walking into history ... He put a little bit of himself into every picture. He was humble, very quiet, very kind. It was as if he didn't understand or couldn't connect to the fact that he held a major place in fashion history and photographic history.'[31] Carol Alt was struck by his generosity after a sitting, when he gave her a set of signed photographs. It was a gesture he repeated with Eva Malmstrom after photographing her for Italian *Vogue*. Malmstrom recounted: 'Mr Horst went out of his way to give me these amazing presents. I found him to be a lovely man to work with, such a gentleman.'[32]

The period also witnessed a flurry of new books, exhibitions, and television documentaries. Staley-Wise Gallery became Horst's New York dealer; Etheleen Staley and Takouhy Wise understood the importance of fashion imagery to the broader history of photography and chose Horst as the subject of their inaugural exhibition in 1981.

Hamiltons Gallery in London presented the first major British exhibition of his work, to coincide with the photographer's 80th birthday in 1986. It comprised 200 photographs selected by Horst and Andy Cowan of Hamiltons, with detailed texts by Valentine Lawford. Horst produced new prints for museums and the collectors' market, selecting emblematic works from every decade of his career to be reprinted in platinum-palladium. These prints are treasured for their nuanced tones, surface quality and permanence. The platinum-palladium process is complex and expensive, employing metals more expensive and more stable than gold.[33]

In 1999, the collector and photography expert Gert Elfering acquired Horst's archive and house at Oyster Bay and has endeavoured since then to bring his work to greater public attention through exhibitions, auctions and publications. In 2006, on the centenary of Horst's birth, Hamiltons Gallery published *Platinum*. In the book's introduction, Cowan recalled a conversation with Irving Penn, who 'described an exceptional talent that Horst displayed with his female models ... Horst had a way of looking at and communicating with the model that somehow elevated her to a slightly higher plane, prising a priceless and intangible extra ounce of magic from the situation.'[34]

The huge collection of prints, negatives, drawings, notebooks, scrapbooks and letters that Horst carefully preserved throughout his life, alongside thousands of prints in the archives of Condé Nast and *Vogue*, bear witness to that glittering talent. His images have become icons of photography; none more so than the Mainbocher Corset of 1939. Decades later, the couturier Mr Main Bocher himself expressed his admiration for Horst's virtuosity: 'Your photographs are sheer genius and delight my soul ... each one is perfect by itself.'[35]

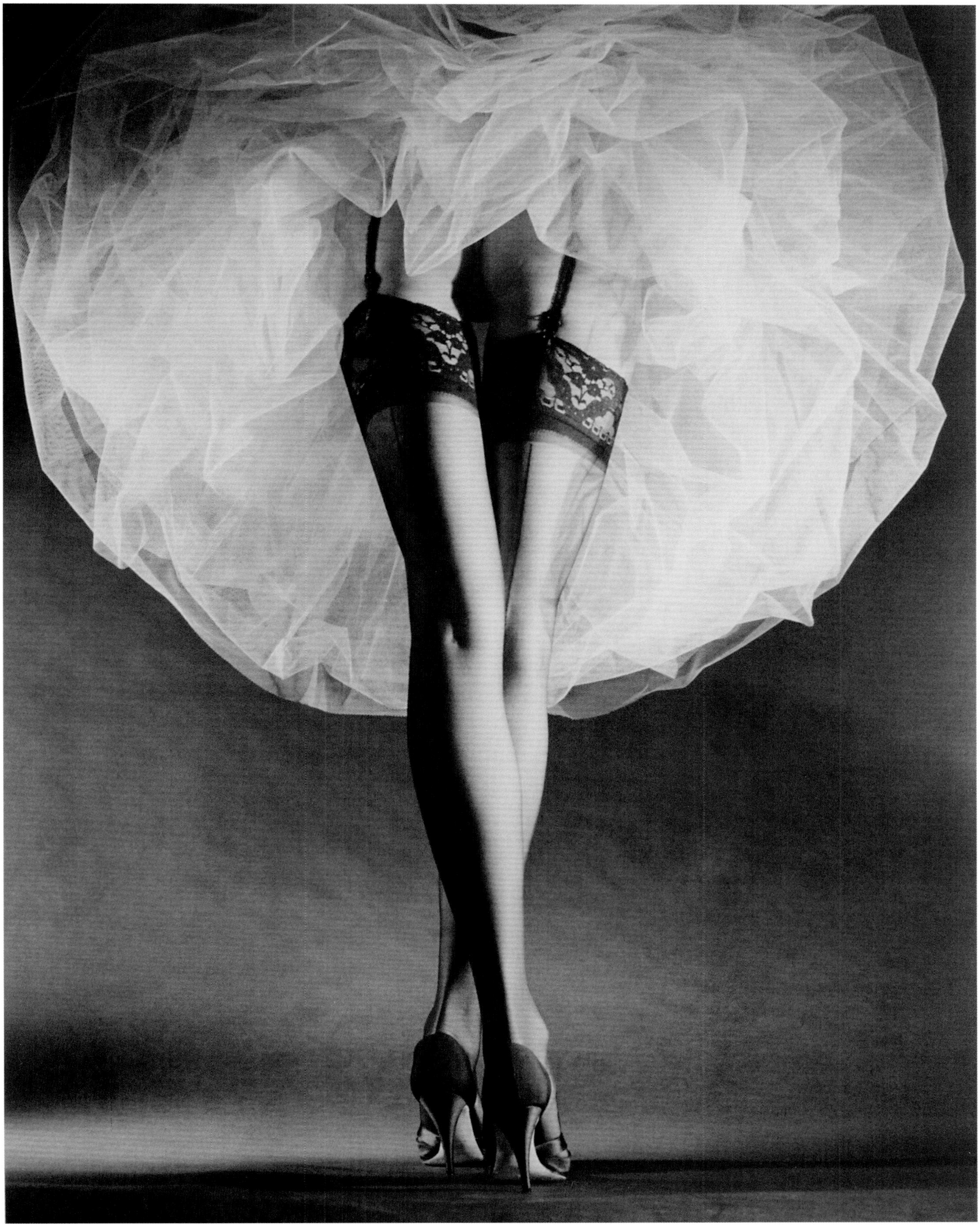

13. Round the Clock, 1987

I
Paris Style

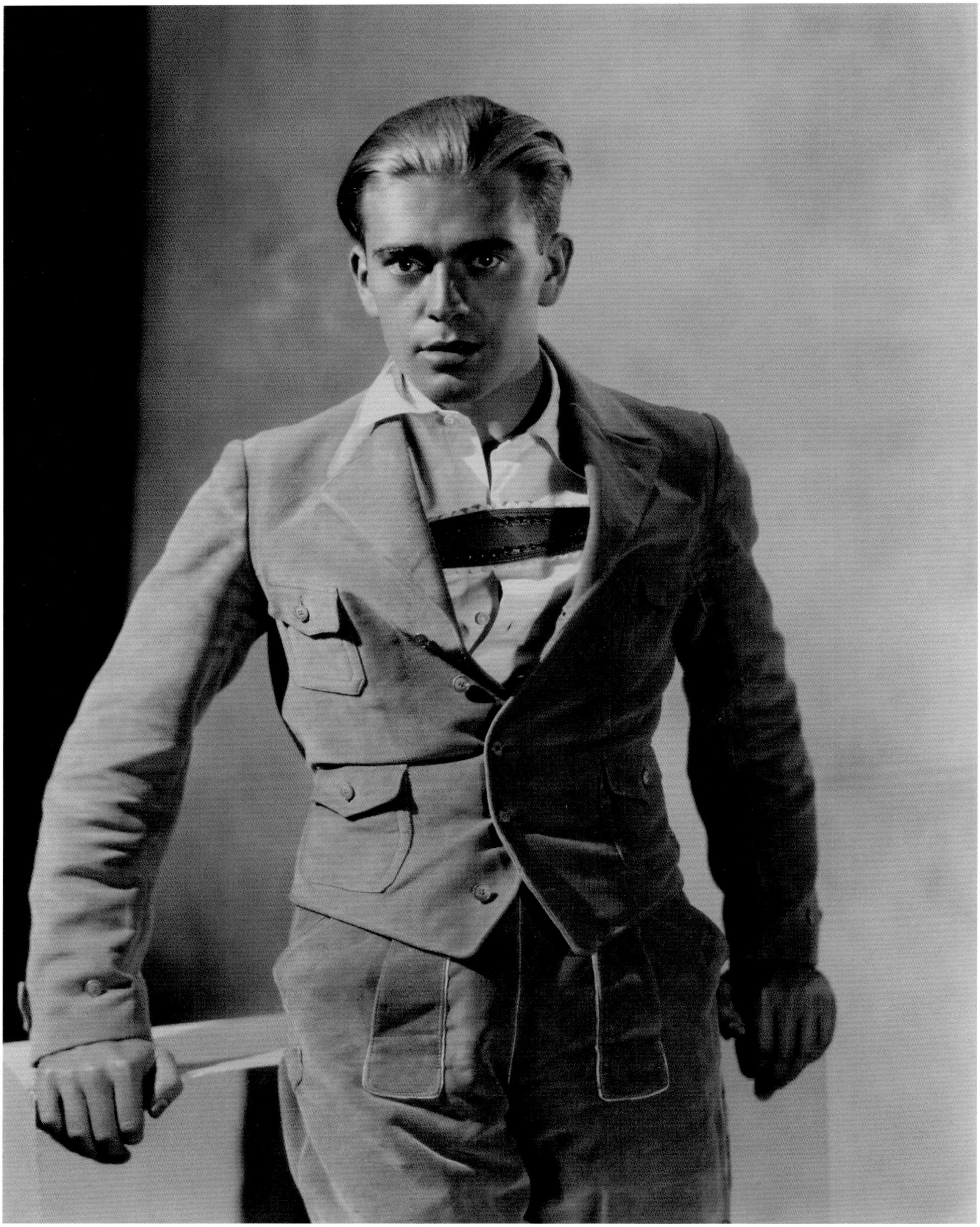

14. George Hoyningen-Huene,
Horst, 1931

1930s PARIS – FASHION, ART, ELEGANCE AND IMAGINATION

Philippe Garner

When 23-year-old Horst P. Horst arrived in Paris early in 1930, he brought with him a complex skein of emotions and of expectations. His adolescent years in Germany had crystallized his desire for a career, indeed a way of life, that would allow him to pursue his intertwined ideals of beauty and creative freedom. While he always preserved key strands of his German heritage – a heritage that significantly shaped his artistic precepts – the single-minded young Horst nonetheless perceived Paris as the most promising stage for the expression of his dreams and of his imagination. The city was internationally recognized as the singular most powerful hub of creativity in the arts. It was the birthplace of the most radical Modernism in painting and sculpture; it was also an unrivalled focal point of elegance and sophistication in the applied arts, interior design, fashion, theatre – a reputation emphatically consolidated in the triumph of French artists and artisans at the Exposition Internationale des Arts Décoratifs et Industriels Modernes of 1925.

'PARIS WAS ALL I EVER DREAMED IT TO BE'

The specific circumstance of Horst's pilgrimage to Paris was an offer of employment in the architectural office of Le Corbusier, arguably the most vocal advocate of the 'esprit moderne' within his profession in France. Already fired with enthusiasm for the new, utopian ideas of modern design promulgated at the Bauhaus in Weimar, and following his own studies and apprenticeship in design at the Hamburg Kunstgewerbeschule, Horst saw Le Corbusier's visionary atelier as precisely the environment in which his chosen destiny might unfold.

Horst left behind the restrictive conservatism of provincial life in Germany in search of the stimulus of kindred spirits. Both in ways hoped for and in ways quite unexpected, the city that he made his base for a decade provided him with exceptional opportunities as he gradually assumed, through his elegant and masterful photographic picture-making, the role of principal chronicler within the interlinked worlds of fashion, the arts, and a brilliant and sophisticated beau monde. Horst flourished in the context of this 'extraordinary working alliance between artists, writers, dressmakers, actors, and dancers'.[1] 'Paris', he reflected at the close of the decade, 'was all I ever dreamed it to be.'[2]

'THE EMBODIMENT OF THE MODERN SPIRIT'

As a teenager in the 1920s, Horst came under the spell of progressive ideas and experiments in the arts. In particular, he was influenced by what he had heard of the teachings of the Bauhaus with its integrated approach and its mission to create a true synthesis of all the arts that would embrace architecture, graphics, photography, product design and expressive dance. At this time, he befriended a young woman, ten years his senior, whom he idolized as 'the embodiment of the modern spirit'.[3] Eva Weidemann was a student of dance at the Bauhaus. A surviving photograph – which Horst cherished – shows a smiling, boyish figure, suggestive of an open, uninhibited spirit. Evoking Isadora Duncan, the founder of expressionistic dance, Eva demonstrated a new, liberating language for the body in movement and filled his head with visions of a world of creative freedom.

The celebration of the body had indeed become central to the post-war German aesthetic, evident not only in an emphasis on modern dance but also in the cult of the athletic figure, the heroic body set in the landscape. A fascination with the culture of ancient Greece had begun in Germany in the late eighteenth century and continued through the nineteenth, infusing the imagery of High Romanticism. As explained by the philosopher Friedrich Nietzsche, the German people aligned their image of themselves with the Hellenic ideal, which found a revitalized authority in the focus upon national identity after the First World War. Horst absorbed this culture that acknowledged 'the intrinsic beauty of the human body. *Nacktkultur*[4] reigned supreme.'[5] It was an influence that would manifest itself in his first nude studies of the model Lisa Fonssagrives.[6] The search for a modern ideal that drew on the perceived purity of classical imagery found emblematic and seductive form in the work of Leni Riefenstahl (1902–2003), first as actress and later as director of the stunning, if ultimately controversial, record of the 1936 Berlin Olympics, with its very specific evocation of classical antiquity.

Health concerns, specifically the symptoms of tuberculosis, forced the teenage Horst to spend a year's convalescence in Switzerland. Valentine Lawford, who was to become Horst's biographer and partner, has emphasized the crucial impact of this period of confinement, spent lying on his balcony, gazing out from the mountain-top sanatorium, 'with nothing to do but read Eva's letters and dream of Mediterranean

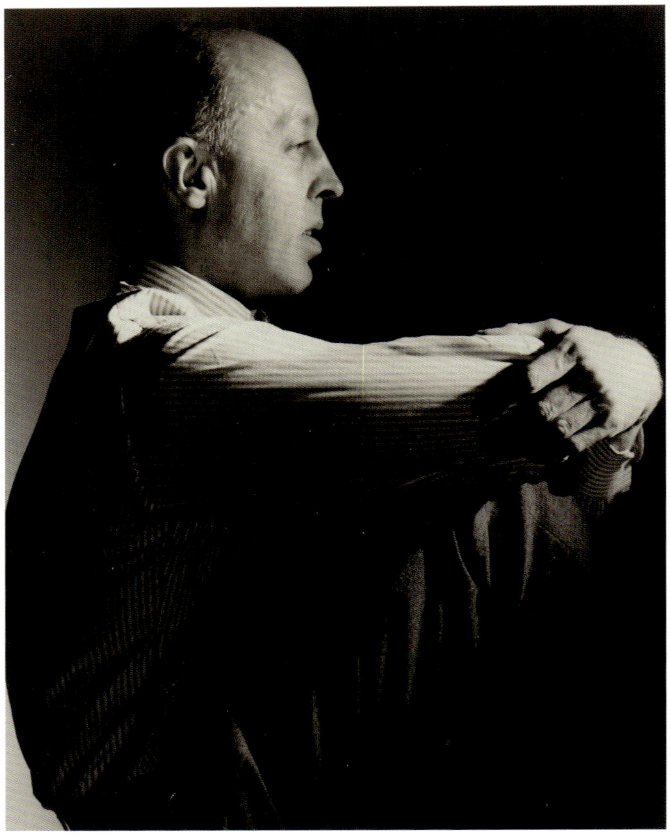

15. George Hoyningen-Huene, 1933

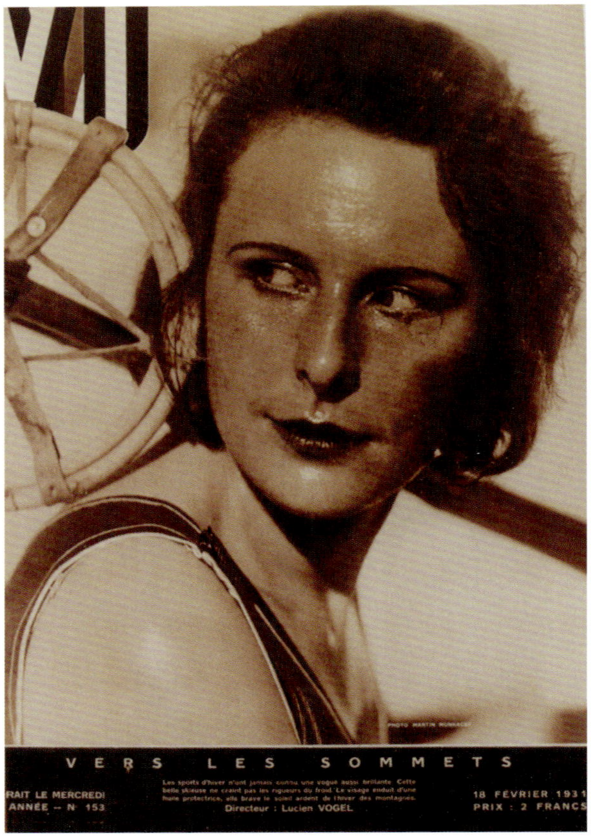

16. Martin Munkácsi,
Leni Riefenstahl, cover of *Vu*,
February 1931

ease and sun and warmth'.[7] Quietly, patiently, Horst found the inner resolve to pursue his ambitions. His journey to Paris was triggered by his choice of architecture as his initial discipline, but serendipitous connections introduced him to a mentor and partner – the Baltic Baron, George Hoyningen-Huene (1900–68, pl.15) – sparking an alternative interest in photography. And his first involvement with the medium was as a model for his mentor, enacting the elegantly stylized Olympian poses that would become central to his aesthetic.

'HORST WAS FANTASTICALLY HANDSOME – A CLASSICAL TEUTONIC BEAUTY'

On arriving in Paris in 1930, Horst took a room at the Hôtel Bréa, near Le Corbusier's studio and the cafés of Montparnasse. His first task was to work on plans for a duplex apartment on the Champs Elysées for Charles de Beistegui, a wealthy connoisseur and socialite, described by Cecil Beaton as one of the 'rich patrons who are themselves dilettante architects, capable of producing results alone or hand in hand with their own architect'.[8] In its first iteration, the architectural scheme, which included a minimalist spiral staircase leading to an upper floor with terrace areas open to the skies, was an exercise in reduction, its modernity reflected in its formal clarity (pl.17).[9] Horst's duties – drafting plans for the bathroom – fell short of his expectations, though he would later cross paths with de Beistegui in a more evidently glamorous context. The apartment itself, however, was to become a metaphor for the sense of adventure, style, glamour and fantasy that characterized Paris in the unfolding decade – qualities so consummately distilled in Horst's photographs. For de Beistegui was to counterpoint the classical simplicity of Le Corbusier's spaces with elements of extravagance and provocation – here 'baroque chichi or surrealist rococo ... reached its fantastic peak ... with its welter of glittering silver, peppermint pink, white ostrich feathers and blackamoors'.[10]

Horst was, in the words of Alexander Liberman (1912–99), art director at American *Vogue* from 1943 to 1962, 'fantastically handsome – a classical teutonic beauty'.[11] These looks and his charm very soon ensured social connections that in turn encouraged Horst to leave Le Corbusier's studio and discover another, richer, more poetic aesthetic, a world of refined and informed historicism, of romantic indulgence, into the very centre of which he was invited by the principal photographer for French *Vogue*, George Hoyningen-Huene. 'It was from him', Horst acknowledged, 'that I learned everything he could then teach me about photography.'[12]

Vogue provided more than a catalogue of the latest trends in dress. It was the journal of a privileged milieu that embraced high society and the arts. Huene's images dominated its pages at the turn of the decade, and positioned him as an arbiter of taste. Around the time he took Horst under his wing, in addition to his fashion pictures he was documenting dance, theatre, film stars and popular revues, as well as the most chic social events. Published images pertaining to the performing arts included studies of dancer Serge Lifar in the 1930 ballet *Les Créatures de Prométhée*, of Jean Cocteau at the time of the first performance of his 1930 play *La Voix humaine*, and of the sensual and exotic artiste Josephine Baker.[13] Huene's portraits of guests at socialite Elsa Maxwell's fancy-dress ball, held the same year, bring together the cast of characters who were to constitute Horst's world. Here was decorator Jean-Michel Frank (1895–1941) dressed as art patron the Vicomtesse de Noailles, set designer Oliver Messel (1904–78) as Serge Lifar, Cecil Beaton (1904–80) as novelist Elinor Glyn.[14]

In the winter of 1931–2, Huene and Horst took the train south to the Riviera. Here, Horst was introduced to the Vicomtesse de Noailles herself, at her spectacular modernist villa overlooking Hyères, designed by Robert Mallet-Stevens (1886–1945) and already the location for avant-garde artistic adventures. It had been the setting for surrealist scenes in the 1929 film *Les Mystères du Château de Dé* by Man Ray (1890–1977). In this respect the villa might be seen as a parallel to the de Beistegui apartment, with its layering of the bizarre, whimsical, and surreal upon the classical purity of modernist lines. Here, in essence, was the stylistic equation that became so central to the era as a whole and came to define Horst's pictorial repertoire in particular.

The crucial introduction effected by Huene was of course into the world, and ultimately the pages, of *Vogue* itself. He first enlisted Horst as a model in such images as those published in the July 1931 issue,[15] in which he models swimwear on a sunny beach, the *plein-air* photographic fulfillment of the heroic sporting figures Horst had visualized in his youthful fantasies. In a similar vein is an image of a bare-chested Horst and a bare-shouldered girl as skiers, published in Huene's first book of photographs in 1933[16] – an echo of the mountain portraits of Leni Riefenstahl shot by Martin Munkácsi (1896–1963), one of which featured on the cover of French magazine *Vu* in February 1931 (pl.16).[17]

Brought to the attention of Dr Mehemed Agha (1896–1978), American *Vogue's* art director from 1929 to 1943, Horst was given the opportunity to observe studio practice, to make his first uncredited pictures for the magazine, and in due course to publish his first credited images. As his skills and confidence grew, so his contribution to the magazine gained momentum. By the time of Huene's departure for New York in 1934 to take the lead on American *Vogue*, and his subsequent defection to *Harper's Bazaar*, Horst was ready to assume the mantle as principal photographer for French *Vogue*. He was by then a central figure in the glamorous, creative world that he was so effectively documenting

'THIS EXTRAORDINARY FEELING ABOUT GREECE'

In 1920, well before he became a portrait and fashion photographer for American *Vogue*, Edward Steichen (1879–1973) had photographed the draped figure of Isadora Duncan against the columns and figures of the Parthenon. In 1929, Greek photographer Nelly (Elli Souyioultzoglou-Seraïdari, 1899–1998) had captured the energy and grace of dancer Nikolska, aloft and near-naked, in full leap on this same symbolic site (pl.18). Her picture became a cover for the French magazine *Voilà* in 1934.[18] Such evocative imagery, aligning classical and modern, was a powerful reference point in those years. Horst's early admiration for the classical ideal was to become a constant throughout his long career as a photographer. Horst was later to explain how he and Huene 'had this extraordinary feeling about Greece. The physical beauty of the men and women, the sun and

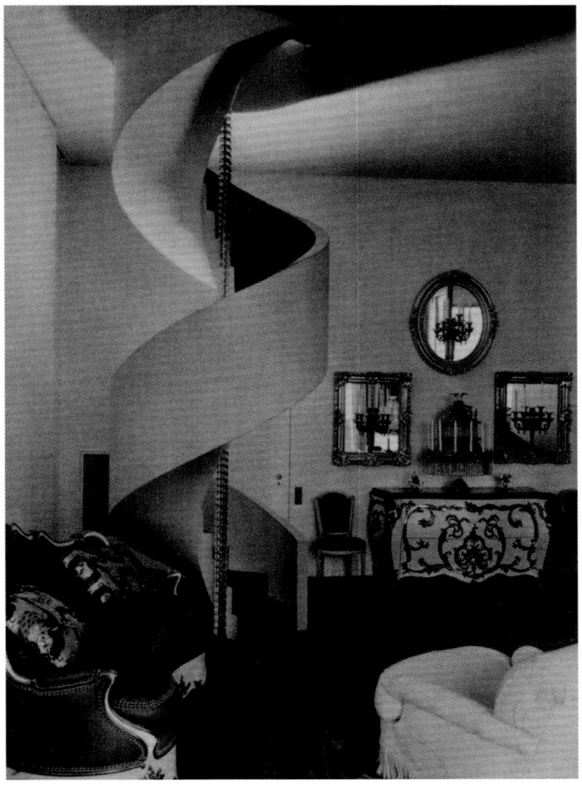

17. Count de Beistegui's apartment, 136 Champs Elysées, Paris, designed by Le Corbusier, 1930s

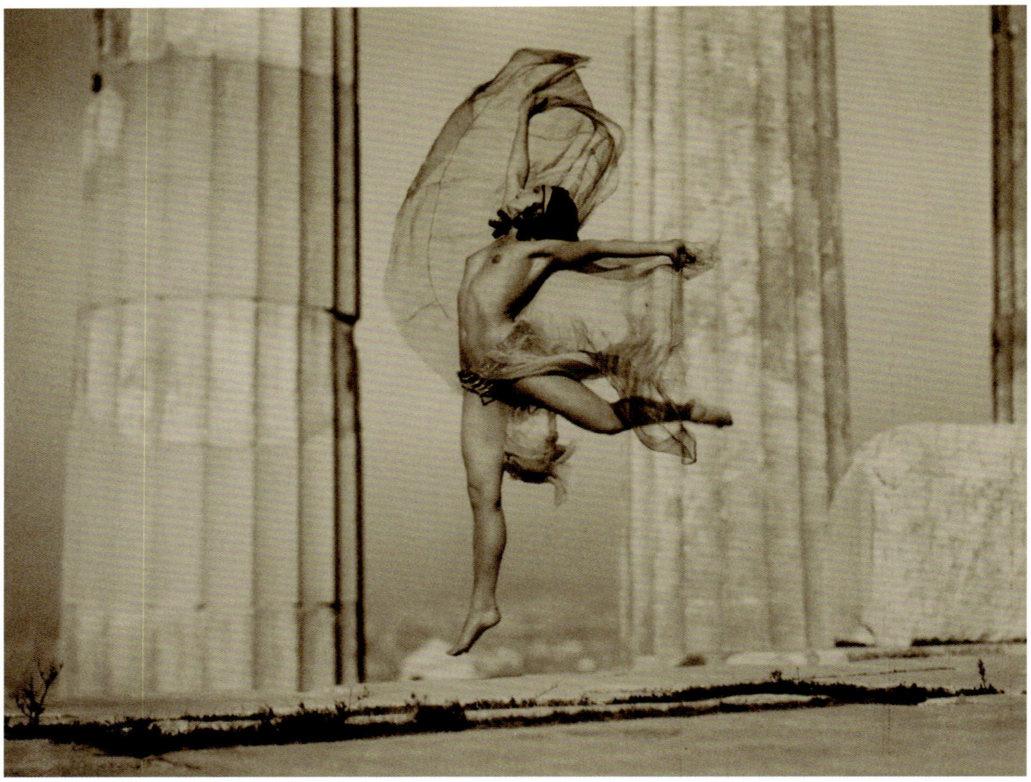

18. Nelly,
Nikolska, Parthenon, Athens, 1929

the fresh air and the sea'.[19] Irrespective of the transient fashions he illustrated or the decorative fantasies he concocted, such sources established the underlying rigour, the discipline in composition and in lighting, that was the hallmark of every image he created.

One of the delights of Paris was the opportunity to see classical sculpture at first hand. Horst visited exhibitions; he spent time in the Louvre, where the Winged Victory of Samothrace, reinstalled in 1934 in prime position, was revered as an icon of antiquity (pl.19). In the winter of 1930, Horst travelled to London with Huene and made a point of visiting the British Museum to see for himself the Elgin Marbles. Huene was to make many photographs of the ruins of ancient Greece, which he published in an anthology, *Hellas: A Tribute to Classical Greece* (1943), a companion volume to *Egypt*. Of his 1930s images of Horst posed as an Olympian, noted earlier, the most arresting were a close-cropped half-figure study in which Horst's arms make a geometric structure with a vertical pole, and a portrayal of Horst seated astride a plaster-cast replica of the celebrated horse's head from the Parthenon frieze (pls 20, 21). This occupied pride of place on the mantelshelf in Huene's apartment.

Dramatically lit with a low, raking light, Horst recalled of these images: 'We had tried to duplicate the lighting of the Acropolis at sunset.'[20] Here were primary elements that would be assimilated in Horst's own work – an instinct for formal clarity, and a profound appreciation of how light can animate its subject. Though for the most part a studio photographer, Horst showed an acute awareness of the ways in which strong directional daylight can render a real sense of volume. In effect, he brought into the studio the powerful Mediterranean light of which he had dreamed in his Swiss sanatorium. Dramatic and theatrical, his most characteristic lighting was a unique hybrid that was at once a meticulously controlled use of artificial studio lights and a wilful evocation of the effects of natural light and shade (pl.20).

A study of a classical torso, executed by Horst in 1932, made evident his finely nuanced skill in using lighting to describe relief. *Vogue's* Dr Agha wrote appreciatively of Horst's distinctive sensitivity: 'His lighting is what the lighting of sculpture in the museums should be and only too often is not: three-dimensional and dramatic, striking without harshness. ... the comparison between interpretative portraiture and sculpture is an apt one', he elaborated, 'and fits particularly well the work of Horst. His photographs are like statues, not in funereal marble but perhaps in the warm terra-cotta of the Greek islands. He takes the inert clay of human flesh and molds [*sic*] it into decorative shapes of his own devising.'[21] 'Horst', Dr Agha went on to observe, 'has the sculptor's feel for form and volume. He works in "*ronde bosse*", not in bas-relief. One has the impression that if it were possible to walk around his models on their pedestals, they would look equally good from the back or from the side – an age-old devise [*sic*] for judging sculpture.'[22] Horst was eventually to own a Roman marble torso, one among a number of sculptures that he acquired and frequently used as props, or in still-life compositions.

Classical imagery significantly informed Paris fashion and design in the 1930s. Couturières Madeleine Vionnet (1876–1975) and Alix (Madame Alix Grès, 1903–93) were foremost among the champions of long vertical pleats or drapes in unadorned alabaster-pale fabrics that followed the contours of the body 'as though they were Ancient Greek statues'.[23] Huene had established the appropriate photographic

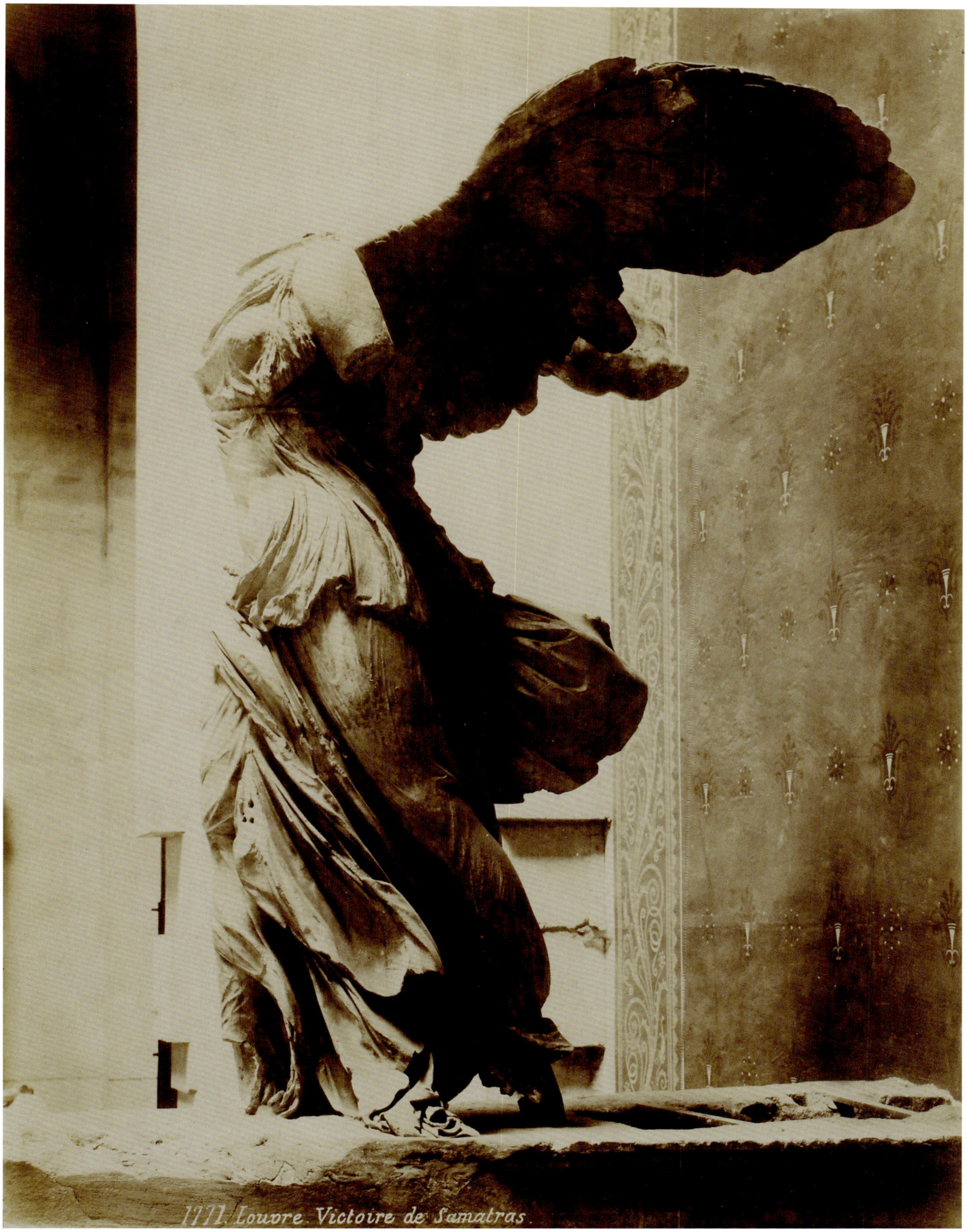

19. Unknown photographer,
Winged Victory of Samothrace c.220–185 BCE,
Musée du Louvre, Paris, 1885

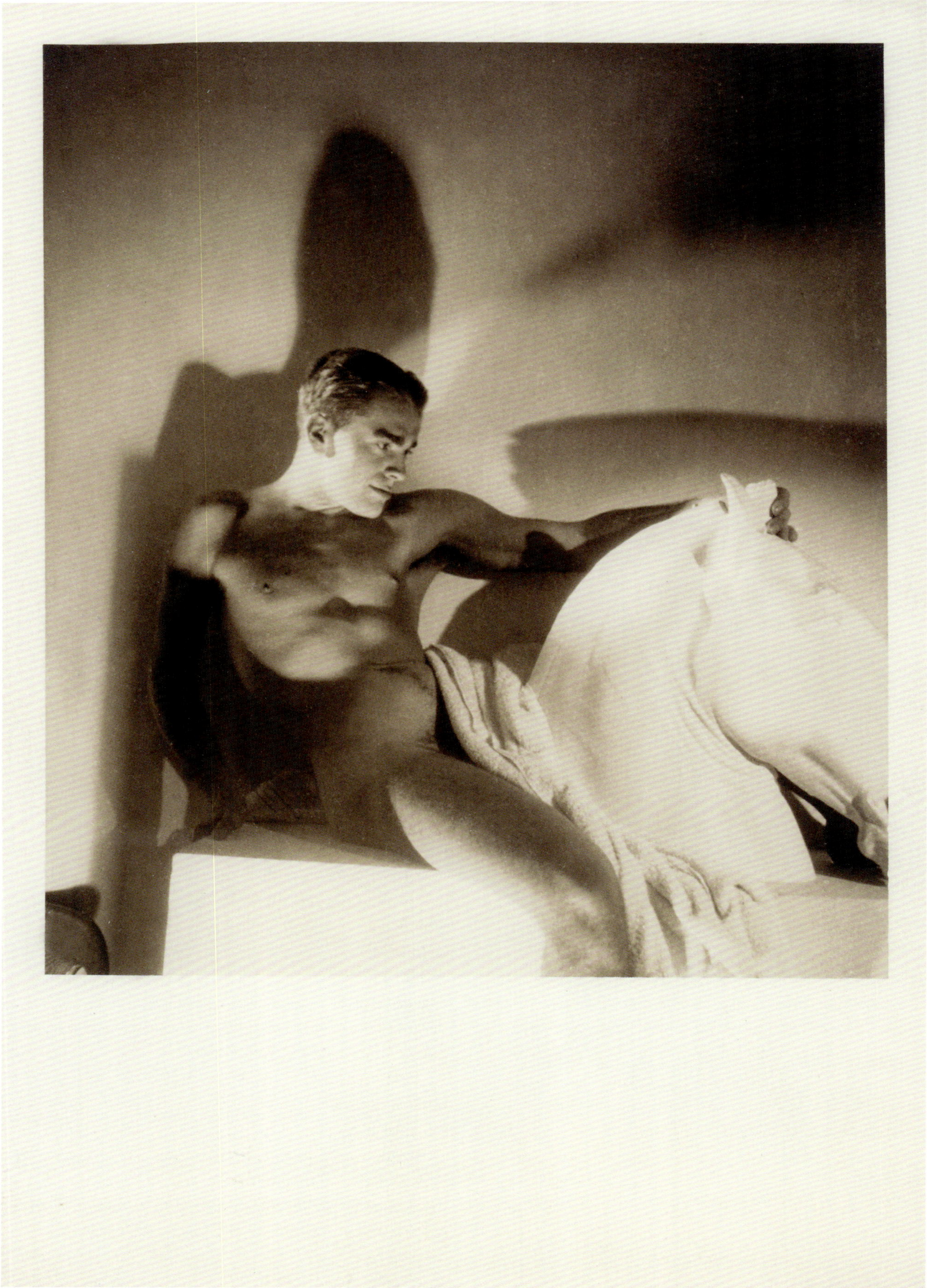

20. George Hoyningen-Huene,
Horst, 1932

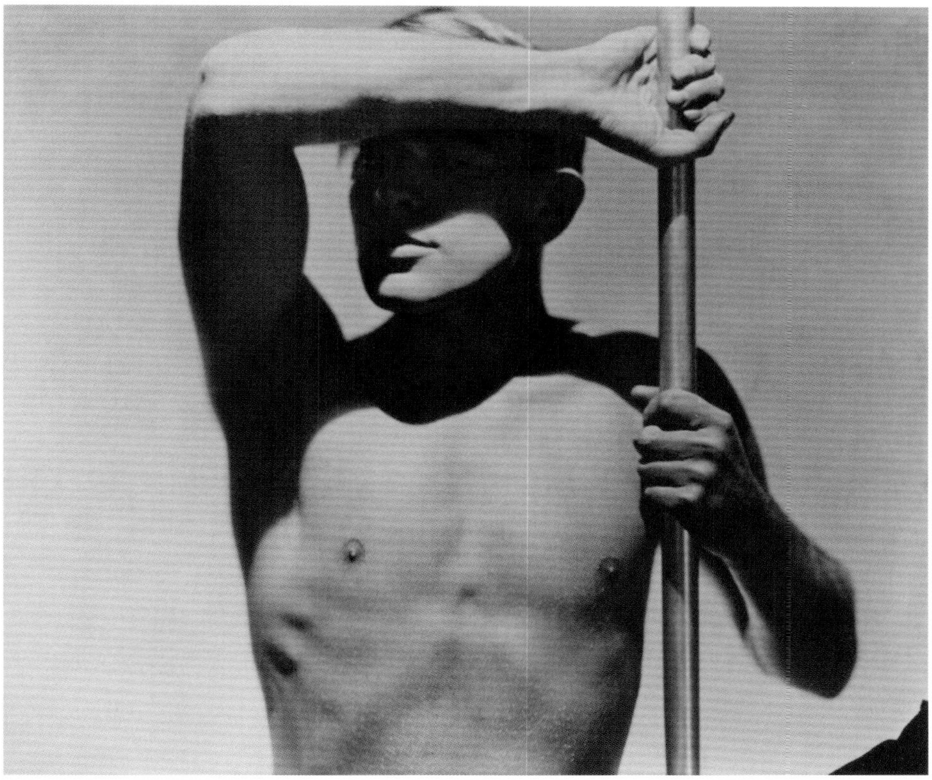

21. George Hoyningen-Huene,
Horst, 1930

styling for such garments, with models standing straight, like the caryatid figures of the Erechtheion on the Acropolis, and columns or clean verticals defining neoclassical spaces. The fashion for classical drapes was translated by couturière Jeanne Lanvin (1867–1946) into the seductive stage costumes for the 1930 production of Jean Giraudoux's *Amphtyrion 38*; leading ladies Valentine Tessier and Lucienne Bogaert were photographed by Huene for French *Vogue*, the epitome of high fashion.[24] A photograph credited to Alinari celebrated the idyll of Greece in a *Vogue* feature in September 1930, 'Dans les montagnes et les îles de la Grèce'.[25] The classical masks and sculptural fragments that Horst loved to incorporate in his photographs meanwhile became a ubiquitous symbol of timeless beauty in numerous advertising images for a burgeoning fashion and cosmetics industry. Surely the ultimate Parisian tribute to the classical was to be seen in the grandiose, theatrical architecture and associated sculptures of the Palais de Chaillot, created in the context of the Exposition Internationale of 1937.

'A SENSE OF FANTASY'

Theatre, in all its forms – modern plays, avant-garde dance and popular spectacle – played a key role in the culture of Paris from the *fin de siècle* through to the 1930s. Ultimately destined to be overshadowed by the ubiquity of film and television, when Horst arrived in Paris, the performing arts were a vibrant, highly creative field of expression, central to artistic life. Sergei Diaghilev's Ballets Russes had re-energized dance in the years before the First World War, providing a showcase for exceptional talent, not only in musical composition and choreography but also in the innovative design of costumes and sets – from the enormously influential exoticism of *Schéhérazade*, lavishly visualized by Léon Bakst (1866–1924) in 1910, to the inventive cubistic costumes by Pablo Picasso (1881–1973) for *Parade*, devised in 1917 by Jean Cocteau (1889–1963).

After the death of Diaghilev in 1929, his legacy was revived by a new generation. The Riviera trip made by Huene and Horst in 1931–2 provided an opportunity for both to catch up with the activities of Colonel de Basil, director of the new Ballet Russe de Monte Carlo, and for Horst to meet Christian 'Bébé' Bérard (1902–49), who was engaged in creating sets and costumes for a new ballet, *Cotillon*, with Bérard's companion Boris Kochno as artistic adviser and George Balanchine as choreographer.

First presented in the Monte Carlo Opera House in January 1932, *Cotillon* captivated its audience, not least through the imaginative, romantic ideas developed by Bérard, the sensitive, poetic, multi-talented artist who was to win the hearts of so many key figures within Parisian high society and high bohemia, and to leave his enchanting mark on the decade. 'It is difficult to overestimate Bérard's influence on taste in Paris and elsewhere, for his advice and approval were sought by dressmakers, interior decorators and leaders of fashion', Horst later observed in *Salute to the Thirties*.[26] Kochno has described, apropos *Cotillon*, how Bérard added 'an indelible air of mystery ... an enchanted world in which the ballet's props ... seemed to become the instruments of magic'.[27] Most memorable was a scene, 'The Hands of Destiny', in which the dancers wore elegant gloves that drew the eye to their gestures.

Horst was captivated by his new acquaintance. 'Bérard taught

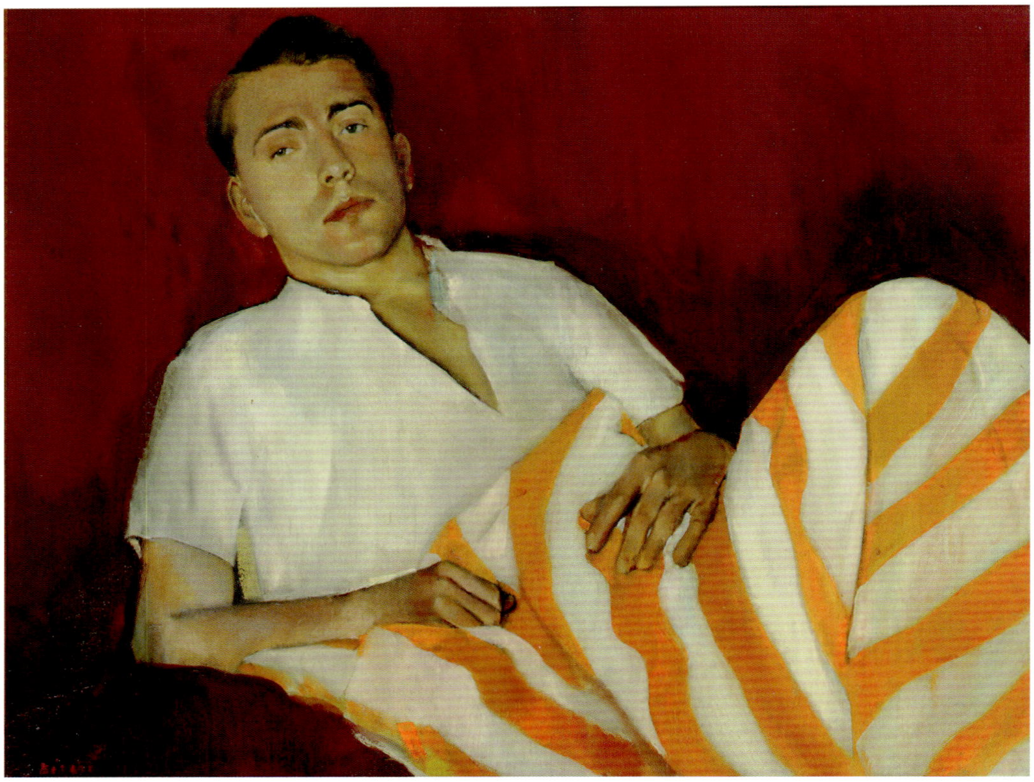

22. Christian Bérard,
Horst, 1933–4

me a sense of fantasy', he later acknowledged.[28] Strong bonds of friendship were soon established, traces of which survived in their various estates, Horst having preserved drawings and his portrait in oils by Bérard (pl.22), the latter commissioned by Huene,[29] Bérard and Kochno having treasured Huene's Olympian portrait of Horst.[30] It was Horst who in turn introduced Bérard to *Vogue* as an illustrator.

If Bérard taught Horst a sense of fantasy, then the stage offered him an imaginary world that encouraged his inventive fashion images. It also focused his attention once more on the language of gesture. The fluid, gracious and expressive lines created by the choreographer provided a kinetic parallel to the grace and elegance that he, as a fashion photographer, had to develop with his models. Sharply observant, Horst came swiftly to appreciate the seductive effect of a sensual contour, the flowing line of an arm, a hand that expressed poise and finesse. The tilt of a shoulder, the curve of a hip, every line and shape was meticulously considered. Horst himself became a veritable choreographer and ensured that the static should never appear rigid.

Among Horst's first signature assignments for French *Vogue*, published in January 1933, was a feature on gloves, a tour de force of subtle modelling, a transposition onto the fashion page of the eloquent gloved scene in *Cotillon* (pl.24). The aura of romance that was so appreciated in the work of Bérard was also a feature of key productions by the short-lived but influential Ballets 1933, the company sponsored by the eccentric British patron Edward James, who used it as a vehicle for his Austrian dancer wife, Tilly Losch. The project presented an opportunity to such uniquely gifted artists as Eugène Berman (1899–1972), André Derain (1880–1954), Pavel Tchelitchew (1898–1957) and Emilio Terry (1890–1969) to develop neo-romantic fantasies that in turn inspired a generation of photographers and decorators. 'Even an esoteric painter such as Tchelitchew had an overt influence,' noted Beaton, 'his decor and costumes for Giraudoux's *Ondine* created a vogue for fish nets, stalactites, coral branches and driftwood ... and photographs were taken by Hoyningen-Huene, George Platt Lynes, Horst, Durst and myself of lost wanderers in a Tchelitchew world of shadows.'[31] For the Ballets 1933 production of *L'Errante*, Tchelitchew confected ethereal silk draperies that proved similarly inspirational (pl.25).

'A CARNIVAL OF LUXURY'

Horst was captivated by the gestural freedom and grace of dance, by the stylization and heightened effects of theatrical *mises en scène*, by the poetry and provocation of avant-garde film. He drew specific ideas and broad inspiration from the multiple facets of the performing arts. He was also, of course, living a life very much abstracted from conventional realities. His good looks and good manners, his profession as a maker of images of elegance, glamour and seduction, had situated him swiftly at the centre of a milieu in which the patrons and supporters of the performing arts were themselves very much committed to spectacle and to their own arts of performance at social occasions, notably fabulous costumed balls. Horst became a player as well as a chronicler in what was later described by Liberman as 'a carnival of luxury' played out by Parisian high society in the 1930s. 'And *Vogue* reported on it. It was incredible splendour', he noted.[32]

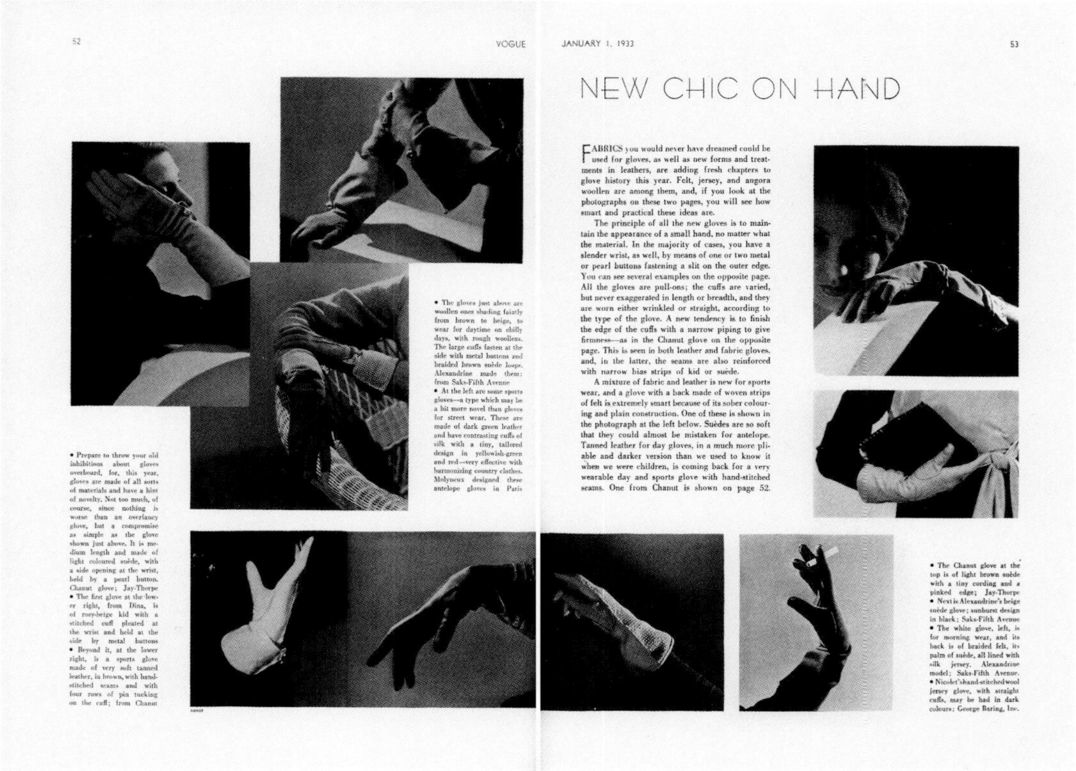

52 VOGUE JANUARY 1, 1933 53

NEW CHIC ON HAND

FABRICS you would never have dreamed could be used for gloves, as well as new forms and treatments in leathers, are adding fresh chapters to glove history this year. Felt, jersey, and angora woollen are among them, and, if you look at the photographs on these two pages, you will see how smart and practical these ideas are.

The principle of all the new gloves is to maintain the appearance of a small hand, no matter what the material. In the majority of cases, you have a slender wrist, as well, by means of one or two metal or pearl buttons fastening a slit on the outer edge. You can see several examples on the opposite page. All the gloves are pull-ons; the cuffs are varied, but never exaggerated in length or breadth, and they are worn either wrinkled or straight, according to the type of the glove. A new tendency is to finish the edge of the cuffs with a narrow piping to give firmness—as in the Chanut glove on the opposite page. This is seen in both leather and fabric gloves, and, in the latter, the seams are also reinforced with narrow bias strips of kid or suède.

A mixture of fabric and leather is new for sports wear, and a glove with a back made of woven strips of felt is extremely smart because of its sober colouring and plain construction. One of these is shown in the photograph at the left below. Suèdes are so soft that they could almost be mistaken for antelope. Tanned leather for day gloves, in a much more pliable and darker version than we used to know it when we were children, is coming back for a very wearable day and sports glove with hand-stitched seams. One from Chanut is shown on page 52.

• Prepare to throw your old inhibitions about gloves overboard, for, this year, gloves are made of all sorts of materials and have a hint of novelty. Not too much, of course, since nothing is worse than an overfancy glove, but a compromise as simple as the glove shown just above. It is medium length and made of light coloured suède, with a side opening at the wrist, held by a pearl button. Chanut glove; Jay-Thorpe
• The first glove at the lower right, from Dina, is of rosy-beige kid with a stitched cuff pleated at the wrist and held at the side by metal buttons
• Beyond it, at the lower right, is a sports glove made of very soft tanned leather, in brown, with hand-stitched seams and with four rows of pin tucking on the cuff; from Chanut

• The gloves just above are woollen ones shading faintly from brown to beige, to wear for daytime on chilly days, with rough woollens. The large cuffs fasten at the side with metal buttons and braided brown suède loops. Alexandrine made them; from Saks-Fifth Avenue
• At the left are some sports gloves—a type which may be a bit more novel than gloves for street wear. These are made of dark green leather and have contrasting cuffs of silk with a tiny, tailored design in yellowish-green and red—very effective with harmonizing country clothes. Molyneux designed these antelope gloves in Paris

• The Chanut glove at the top is of light brown suède with a tiny cording and a pinked edge; Jay-Thorpe
• Next is Alexandrine's beige suède glove; sunburst design in black; Saks-Fifth Avenue
• The white glove, left, is for morning wear, and its back is of braided felt, its palm of suède, all lined with silk jersey. Alexandrine model; Saks-Fifth Avenue.
• Nicolet's hand-stitched wool jersey glove, with straight cuffs, may be had in dark colours; George Baring, Inc.

23. Gloves by Chanut, Alexandrine, Nicolet, Dina and Molyneux, 'New Chic on Hand', American *Vogue*, 1 January 1933

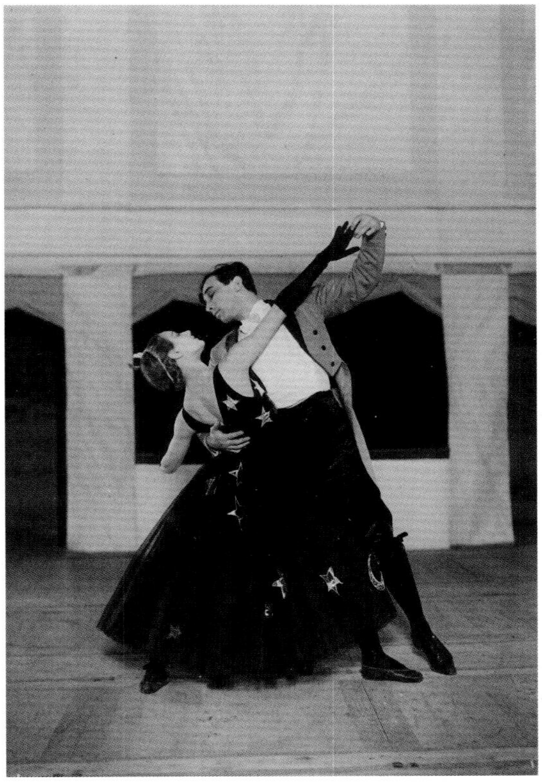

24. Raoul Barbà,
Cotillon, Ballet Russe de Monte Carlo,
sets and costumes by Christian Bérard, 1932

In her introduction to Horst's *Salute to the Thirties*, Janet Flanner, Paris correspondent of the *New Yorker*, tells how 'in Paris a decade of private fêtes and splendid entertainments began in the beau monde ... ten years of elegant, aristocratic hedonism ... modern, luxuriously presented amusements, with the party-givers and the party guests consisting of the most entertaining, intelligent, fashionable Parisian figures of the period.' Foremost among the hosts, she cites the Comte and Comtesse Etienne de Beaumont, whose guests were either 'in the Almanach de Gotha, or very talented or very famous or very beautiful or very handsome', while observing that 'The most intellectual of the Paris mansions' social figures in the 1930s was the eccentric, vigorous Vicomtesse Marie-Laure de Noailles.'[33]

When, in 1930, Jean Cocteau screened his first film, *Le Sang d'un Poète*, a key scene in this perverse, ambiguous drama involved the unfolding of the story beneath the gaze of two groups of spectators – the gentlemen in white tie, the ladies in elegant couture gowns – in two opulently decorated theatre boxes. The 'loge mondaine' comprised André Raval, the Vicomte and Vicomtesse de Noailles, Lady Abdy, Arturo Lopez-Willshaw and Prince and Princess Jean-Louis de Faucigny-Lucinge (pl.27). The production's sponsors and champions thus became an integral part of the spectacle. It was fitting that such a group should be implicated in a work by Cocteau, for it was he who, 15 years earlier, had been instrumental in connecting the avant-garde artists of Montparnasse, and notably Picasso, with the precious community of aristocrats and connoisseur aesthetes. He was a natural catalyst and made social cross-connections that encouraged the mingling of the worlds of creativity and privilege, setting the stage for the intimate rapport that was to flourish in the 1930s. Hosts and hostesses, *mécènes* and collectors, this aristocratic, patrician group were the great enablers of artistic adventure. Their glamorous soirées and extravagant balls defined luxury and filled the pages of French *Vogue* in photographs made by Huene, and then Horst. The names of these events and their guest lists conjure a lost world of mannered, often nostalgic indulgence: the 'Bal Blanc' of 1932, for instance, organized by a consortium of titled gentlemen, for which the guests wore white; or the 'Bal 1900' in the same year, for which the guests – among them Cocteau, Kochno and Bérard, the Vicomte and Vicomtesse de Noailles, and the Prince and Princesse de Polignac – showed 'equal measures of inventiveness and of taste'.[34]

There survives a splendid series of portraits made by Horst of individual guests in their sumptuous historical costumes for the ball hosted in the summer of 1934 by Baron Nicolas 'Niki' de Gunzburg, a pageant of elaborate gowns and court dress, crinoline skirts and braided uniforms (pls 37–40). Among them was Charles de Beistegui, resplendently costumed in an ermine cape. In the August 1935 issue of French *Vogue*, we read of 'Une soirée chez le Gouverneur', an exotic orientalist fantasy hosted by the Hon. Mrs Reginald 'Daisy' Fellowes, which featured a turbaned Bérard and patron Madame José-Maria 'Misia' Sert in fez and mask, photographed by Horst (pl.26).[35]

For 'Une nuit d'art vivant', in 1935, hosted by the Comte and Comtesse de Beaumont, guests staged *tableaux vivants* in the manner of artists and styles from history – from Botticelli to Manet, from ancient Egypt to eighteenth-century Britain and Gainsborough. Horst made their portraits, too.[36] In the last 'Carnets de Bals' before the outbreak of the Second World War, *Vogue* reported the Beaumonts' celebration of the era of Racine – the court of the Sun

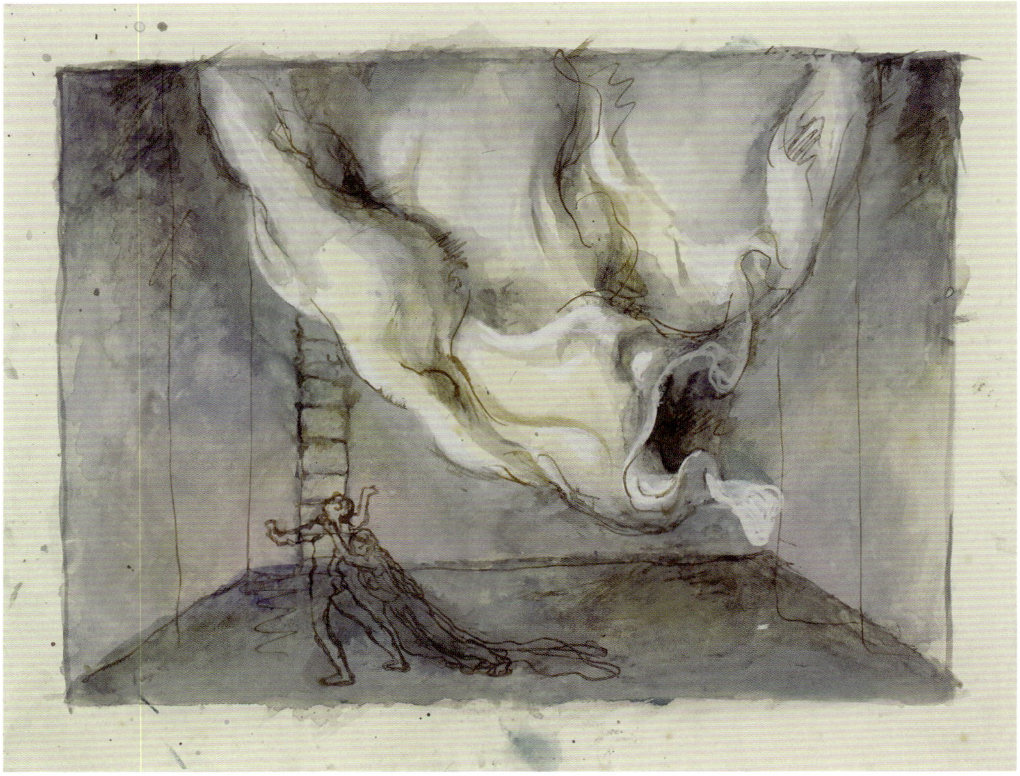

25. Pavel Tchelitchew,
set design for *L'Errante* at the Théâtre des Champs Elysées, Paris, 1933, V&A: S.2092-1986

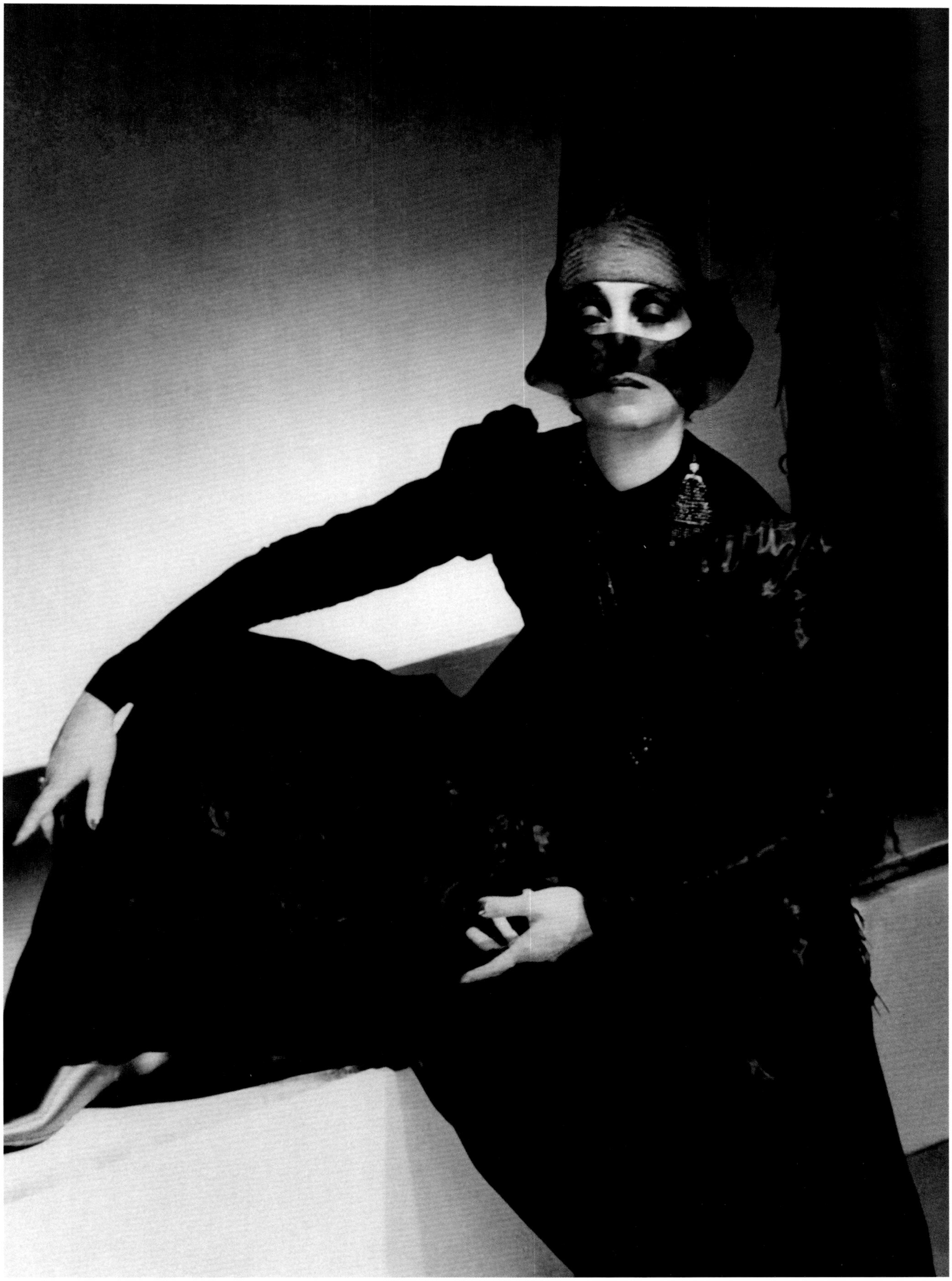

26. Madame José-Maria Sert,
'Bal Oriental', 1935

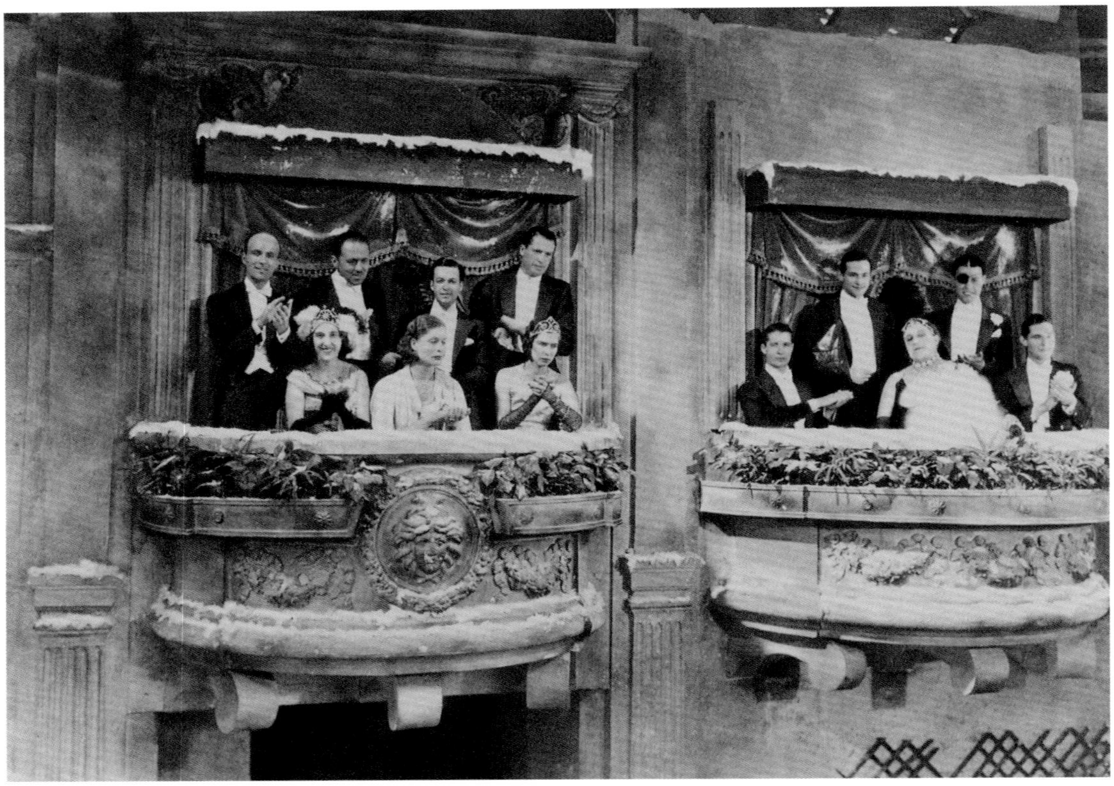

27. Still from the original version of
Le Sang d'un Poète, by Jean Cocteau, 1930

King providing the pretext for fabulous spectacle – and observed that 'Paris has witnessed an epic display of elegance.'[37]

'FANTASY AND INGENUITY BROKE FORTH'

Two strong personalities, with very distinct approaches, dominated Paris couture in the 1930s – Coco Chanel (1883–1971) and Elsa Schiaparelli (1890–1973). Rivals, though sharing many of the same friends and collaborators, each carved an influential position for herself, not just in the area of dress design but also as taste-maker, and through close engagement in myriad facets of style and creativity. Horst admired, befriended, and indeed photographed both, though he asserted that 'Without a doubt, the center [*sic*] of the circle, the star of the circus was Chanel'. Reminding us of the range of her involvements, he wrote: 'Chanel worked closely with Dalí and Cocteau and Balanchine on theatre and ballet costumes.'[38]

In contrast to the understatement of her unstructured clothes, her taste in decoration was rich and eclectic. Horst was to make a flattering series of supremely lavish portraits of her, posed against elaborately decorative volutes. When he refused to charge her, she showed her appreciation by arranging delivery to him of furnishings for his still-sparsely decorated apartment. Horst turned a length of Polynesian fabric into screens that feature in a number of his fashion shoots. From Bérard, he acquired a drawing of Chanel that he copied in petit-point to adorn a Louis XVI giltwood bergère.

Schiaparelli, in her memoirs, acknowledged how 'Working with artists like Bébé Bérard, Jean Cocteau, Salvador Dalí, Vertès, Van Dongen; and with photographers like Hoyninge-Huene, Horst, Cecil Beaton, and Man Ray gave one a sense of exhilaration. One felt supported and understood.'[39] 'Art,' observed Beaton in turn, 'especially under the influence of such painters as Dalí, Picasso and Bérard, was impinging very closely on fashion.'[40]

In a rich tradition of creative cross-currents between the worlds of high fashion, fine art and the decorative arts, Chanel and Schiaparelli followed in the footsteps of Jacques Doucet (1853–1929) and Paul Poiret (1879–1944), who, in the first quarter of the century, had re-cast the role of the couturier as connoisseur, aesthete and patron. In 1935, when Schiaparelli opened her boutique at 21 Place Vendôme, she introduced new retail possibilities for the couture world. She invited Jean-Michel Frank to conceive an appropriate decor. The result was 'a gilded cage for the budding perfume business'.[41]

Frank, who counted the Vicomtesse de Noailles among his significant early patrons, was the defining sensibility in the creation of seductive environments that captured the spirit of 1930s Paris. Schiaparelli stated that it was he 'who revolutionized interior decoration. He invented a new style of furniture combining simplicity with considerable luxury.'[42] Beaton described how 'Jean-Michel Frank invented new surfaces and fabrics, tables made of parchment, banquettes upholstered in sackcloth, and walls covered in great squares of raw leather. He designed low sofas and tables, even encouraging people to sit on leather floor cushions, while sheepskin or raffia were recommended carpets. He prevailed upon Giacometti to design some lamps which are among the most beautiful of modern household objects.'[43] When Frank opened a new showroom in 1935, the event was reported in *Vogue*.[44]

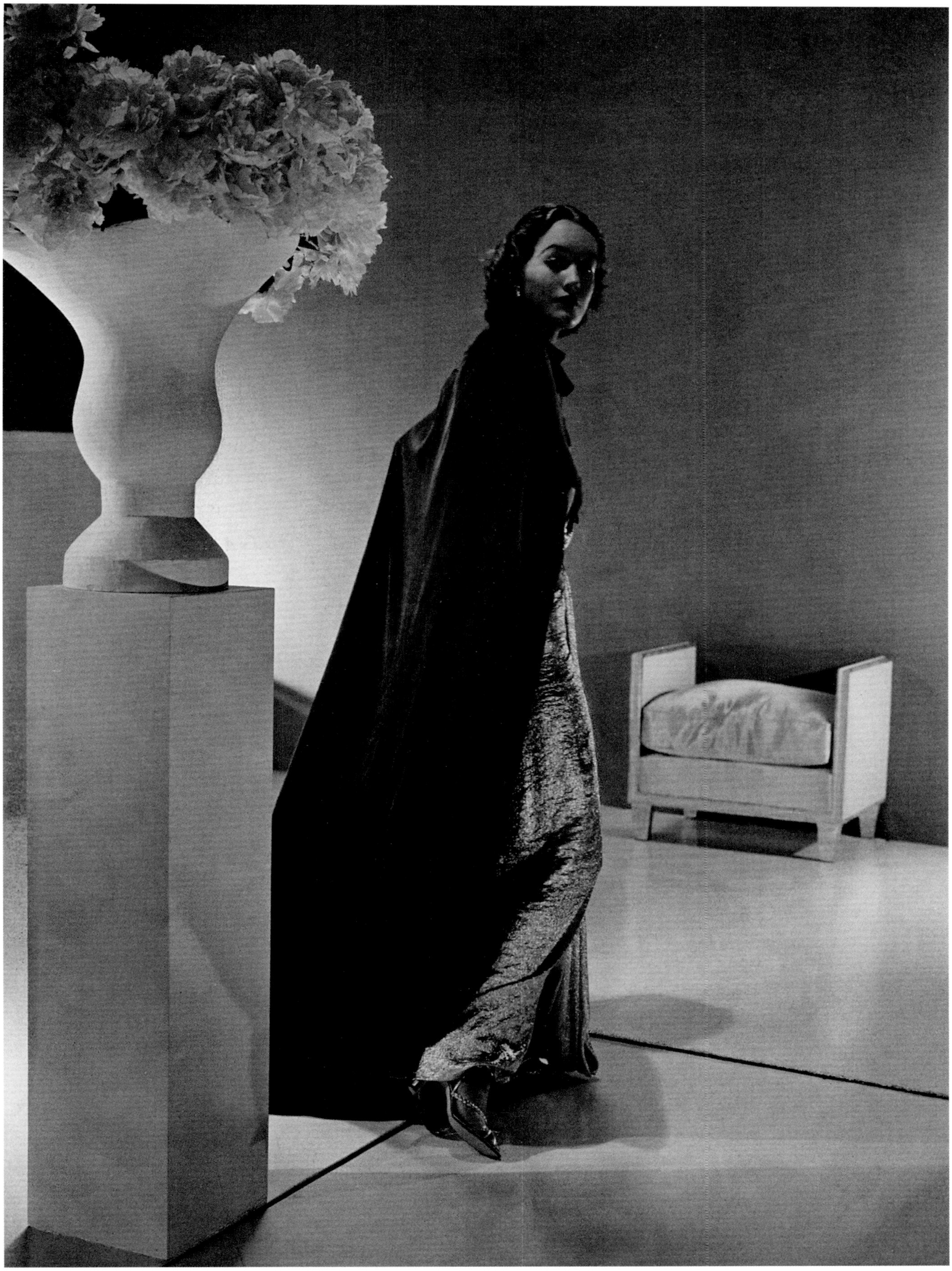

28. Dress and cape by Lanvin, sandals by Bally Bottier, stool by Jean-Michel Frank, vase by Giacometti, 1935

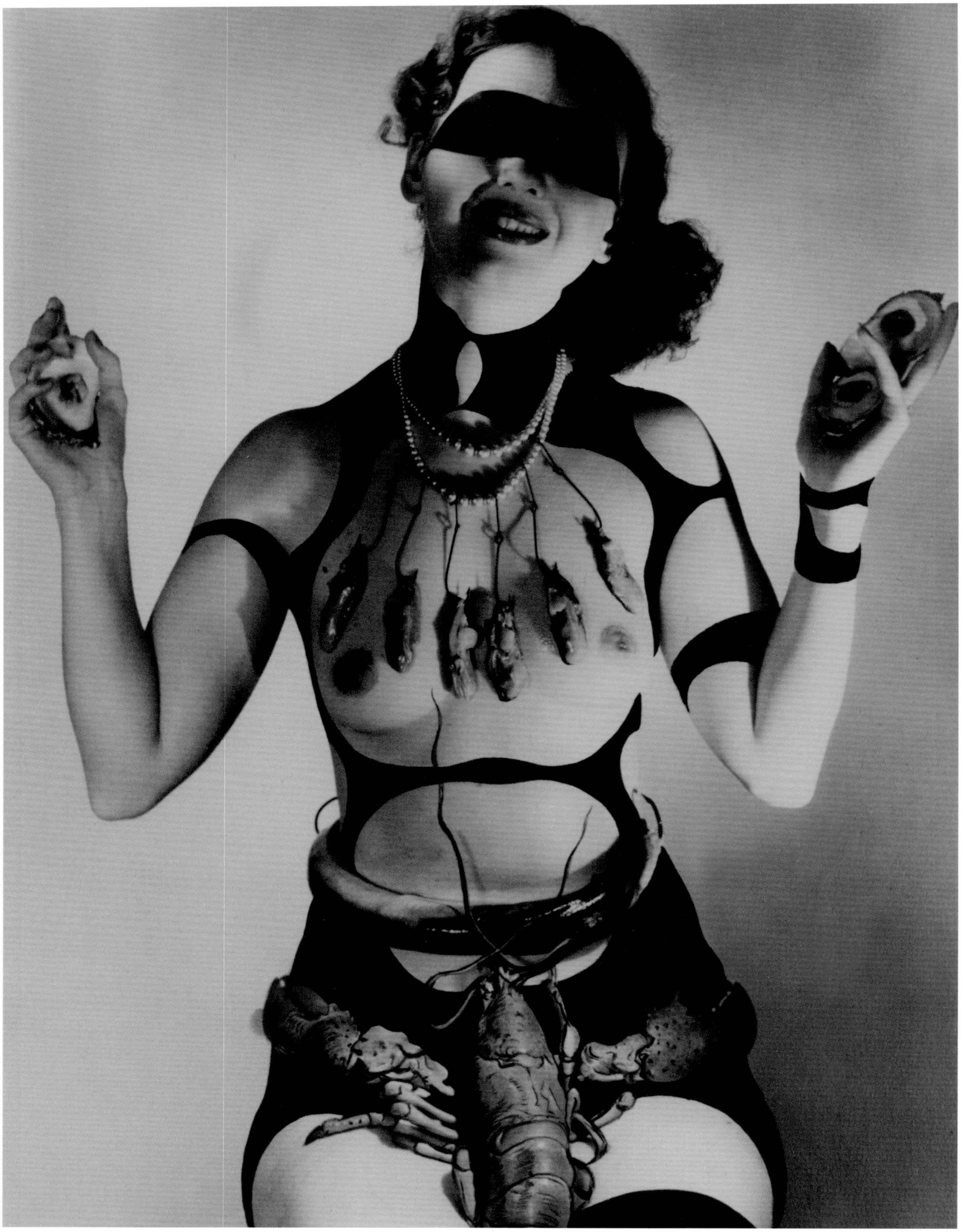

29. Costume for Salvador Dalí's
Dream of Venus, 1939

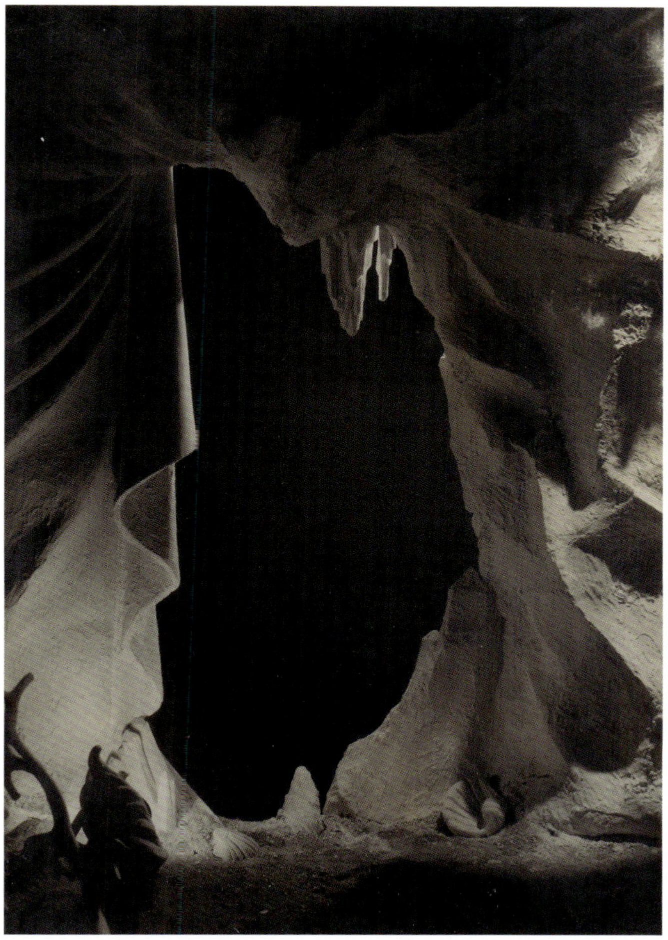

30. Décor for a *Vogue* fashion set, designed by Emilio Terry, 1936

His project was a collaborative one, and, in addition to Alberto Giacometti (1901–66), he enlisted the skills and imagination of Salvador Dalí (1904–89) and Jean Hugo (1894–1984), as well as Bérard and Terry, among others.

The collective ambition was to create an ambience, to devise spaces that would provide tactile and visual delight, sophisticated interiors that would act as a foil to elegant living and social engagement– and that, furthermore, might provide a poetic stimulus to the imagination. 'The artists had a hand in everything', observed Horst.[45] Designs by Frank and his associates were used by Horst, and others, to dress the sets of their fashion images. In one characteristic shot by Horst for French *Vogue* we find a stool by Frank and a plaster vase by Giacometti, filled with peonies (pl.28);[46] in another, a white plaster console raised on swirling columns of long, pointed leaves, credited to Frank and reminiscent of the white stucco palm trees that decorated Mrs Reginald Fellowes's 1935 ball (pl.44).[47] Horst, a great admirer of Frank's taste, bought pieces for his own interiors – stools, chairs, tables, and a dressing table – and white plaster vases and lamps by Giacometti.[48]

The invention of dream interiors was greatly stimulated by the growing influence of surrealist imagery (pls 47, 48). 'Fantasy and ingenuity broke forth', records historian Martin Battersby,[49] as, in the mid-1930s, the movement evolved from its more literary and intellectual beginnings to become a wholesale physical assault on the senses and the imagination. The major surrealist exhibition in Paris in 1938, L'Exposition Internationale du Surréalisme, was conceived as a fully immersive experience. Dalí, more than anyone, became the exponent of the disconcerting space and dislocated object, of such provocative new ideas as his sofa in the shape of Mae West's lips and 'lobster' telephone, both created for Edward James. In this context, we should not overlook the influence of the 'poetic obsession with fantastic architecture ... and disturbing atmosphere of still, magical desolation'[50] of Berman or the strange universe, peopled by sexually ambiguous figures, of Leonor Fini (1908–96). It was Fini who, in 1937, created the bottle for Schiaparelli's perfume 'Shocking' – in the form of a female torso.

For an extended fashion shoot by Horst in the April 1936 issue of French *Vogue*, Emilio Terry created a strange grotto, littered with shells and giant coral, a dream space that anticipated the surrealist exhibition (pls 30, 49, 50). It was also a precursor to the Dream of Venus pavilion conceived by Dalí for the New York World's Fair of 1939, where a bare-breasted siren swam in the grotto's aquarium, and was photographed by Horst adorned with oysters and a lobster (pl.29). Fashion and fantasy, art and artistry, came together in a last extravagant toast to a decade of elegance, invention and imagination, before the outbreak of war.

Electric Beauty
Paris, 1939

In the early decades of the twentieth century, Hollywood films disseminated new ideals of beauty, which the cosmetics industry grew rapidly to fulfil.[1] In 1920 there were 5,000 beauty parlours in America, but by 1930 that figure had risen to 40,000.[2] Women's magazines featured articles on the most impressive innovations in age-defying treatments. Advertisements by companies including Helena Rubinstein, Elizabeth Arden, Klytia and Caron suggested that miraculous therapies could be experienced inside their luxurious professional salons, and that the secret to eternal youth might be found in the creams and lotions they manufactured. Photographs by Willi Eggarter illustrated French *Vogue* articles that extolled the transformative power of the modern beauty machines used in Rubinstein's salons, such as the 'Le Tensiographe', 'Le Beautycult' and 'Le Pulvérisateur', all of which resembled futuristic instruments of torture.[3] Eggarter's photograph of the 'Vopozone' treatment, administered in the Klytia salons, depicts a model's face being blasted with steam. She wears a towel around her hair and a gleaming metal bowl sits beneath her chin; despite the apparent ordeal, her expression remains serene.[4]

Horst's *Electric Beauty* was perhaps intended as a satirical comment on the increasingly extreme beauty treatments of the 1930s, and the futility of such preoccupations at a time when the world was on the brink of war. The spot-lit model is seated next to a table filled with beauty instruments and appears to be undergoing several modern procedures simultaneously. The variant versions reveal how Horst and his model experimented with the pose, and arm gestures in particular. He photographed her with and without the mask over her face, but it was the sinister masked version that Horst chose to reproduce when he made prints in platinum-palladium. The mask renders her blind to her own bizarre appearance and unaware that she is dangerously close to being electrocuted. The same mask appeared in American *Vogue* on 1 June 1939, described as the 'Inspiré Mask', which claimed to utilize electricity and infrared radiation to refresh the skin.[5] Wires from the mask and the electric massage device she holds in her hands encircle her body like serpents, preparing to suffocate or strangle her.[6] The backdrop against which this scene takes place enhances the threatening atmosphere. It shows a greatly enlarged detail of the *Temptation of St Anthony* (*c.*1501), a triptych painted in oil on panel by the Flemish artist Hieronymous Bosch (*c.*1450–1516). Horst and his contemporaries at *Vogue* often used reproductions of historic paintings as backdrops, usually featuring classical architectural details or attractive landscapes. In contrast, this eerie image is filled with the imaginary creatures and visual metaphors that typified Bosch's work. It depicts a bird-like monster on ice skates, approaching three fiends who crouch under a bridge. The monster wears the badge of a messenger and carries a letter. According to the complex symbolic code used by Bosch, the ice skates represent folly, while the funnel on the monster's head indicates wastefulness, and the twig and ball that extend from the funnel represent promiscuity and merrymaking. Given Horst's keen interest in art, it is likely that he understood at least some of the messages encoded in the painting, and composed his photograph to serve as a caution against the vice of vanity.

The fantastical and grotesque elements of Bosch's work led him to be regarded as one of the forefathers of the surrealists, in particular Salvador Dalí, with whom Horst collaborated on several occasions. In the latter half of the 1930s, surrealist art, fashion and commercialism became closely intertwined: Dalí painted covers for *Vogue*, worked with Elsa Schiaparelli on several couture designs, and even created surreal window displays for the New York department store Bonwit Teller. Between 1936 and 1943 Horst, in turn, produced numerous photographs infused with a sense of the surreal, including still lifes, fashion studies and beauty pictures, but none match *Electric Beauty* for its fusion of wit, menace and foreboding.

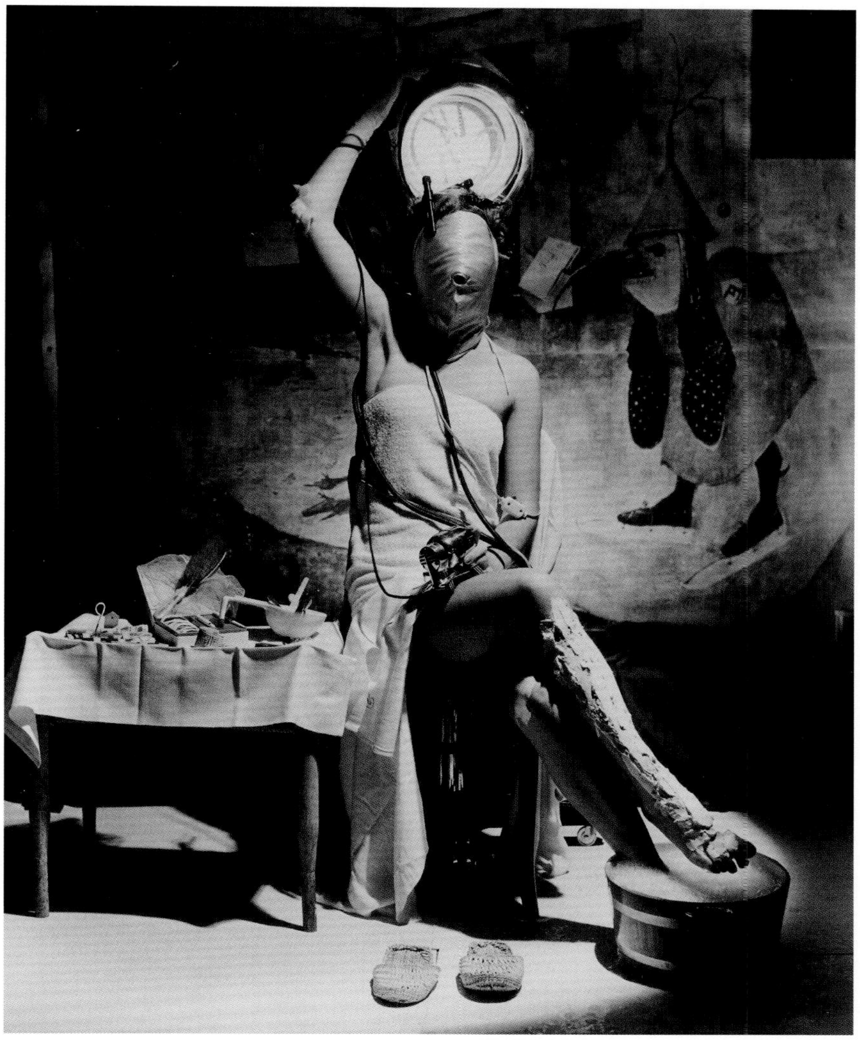

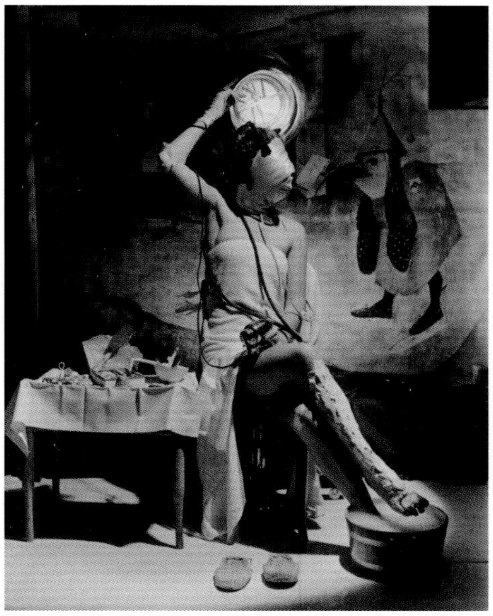

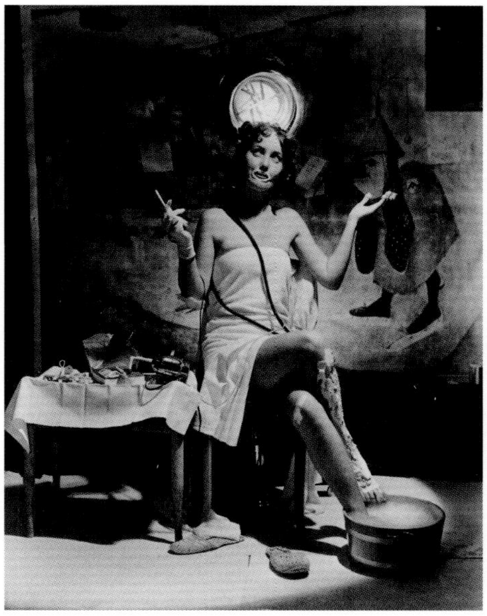

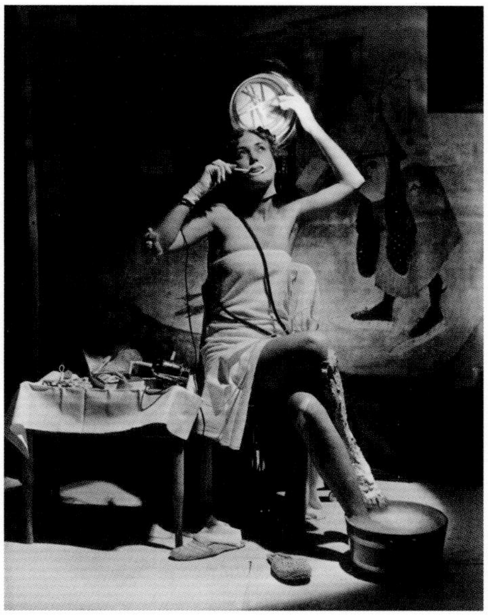

31. *Electric Beauty*, Paris, 1939,
and three variant poses

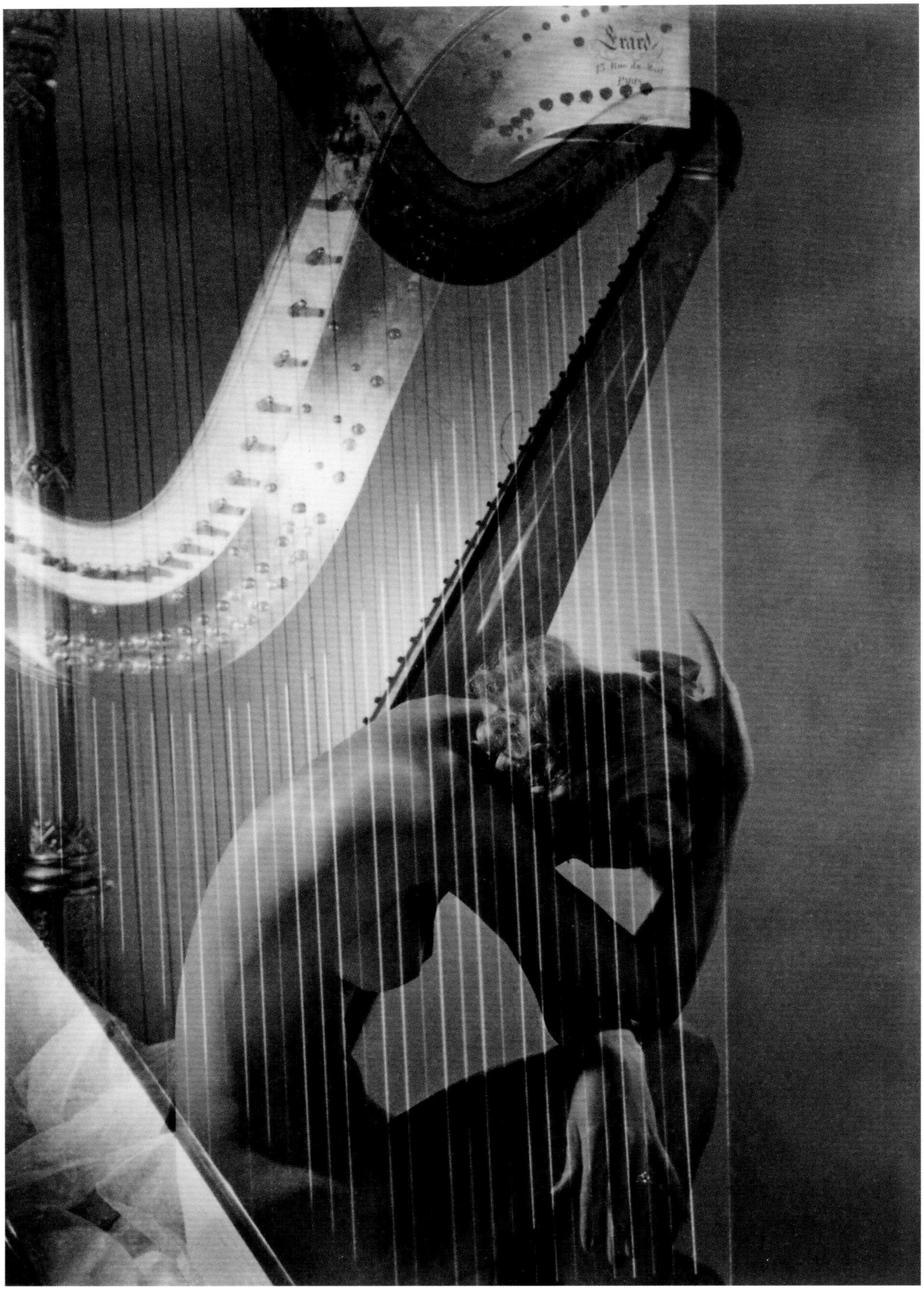

32. Lisa Fonssagrives, *Lisa with Harp*, 1939

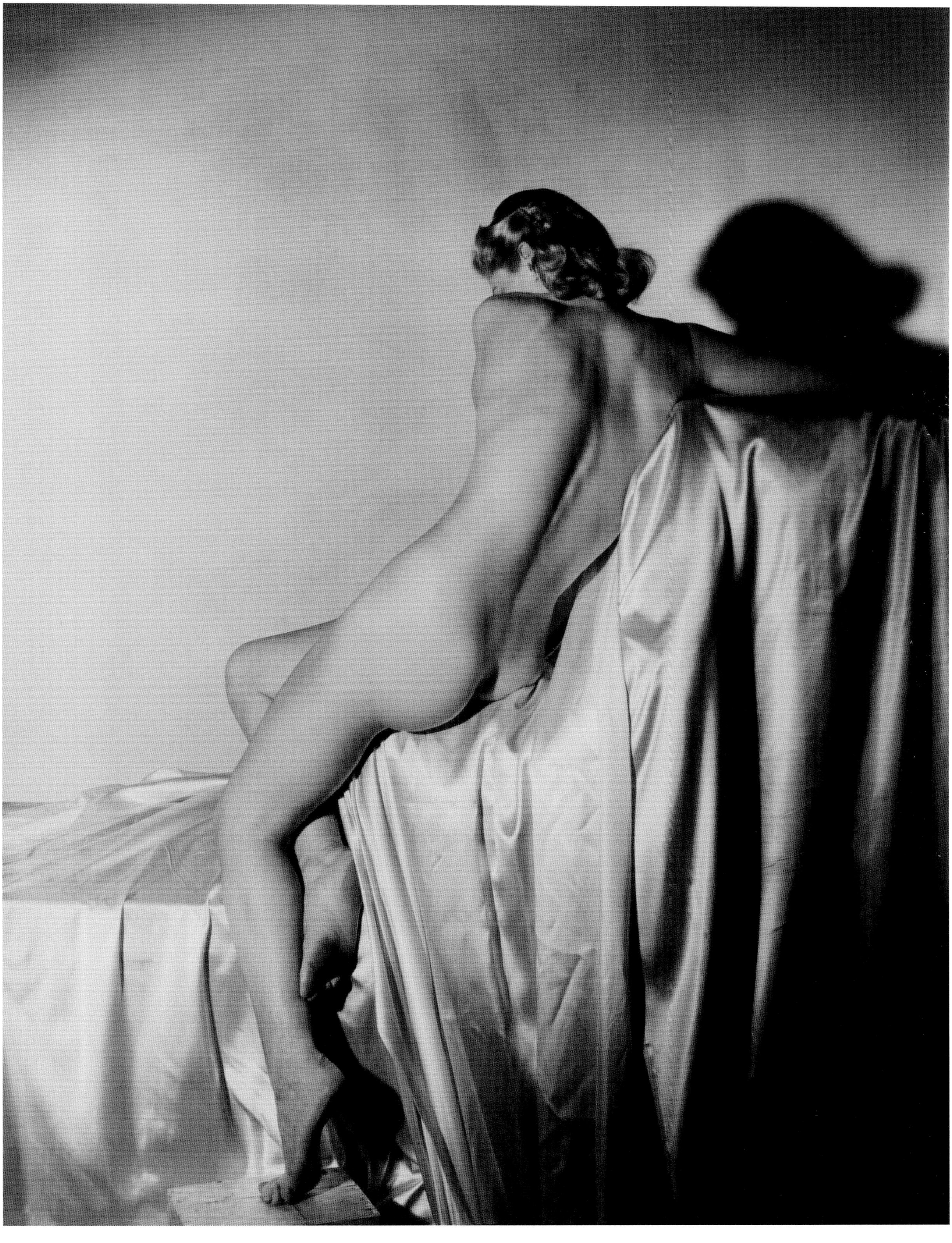

33. Lisa Fonssagrives, *Lisa on Silk*, 1940

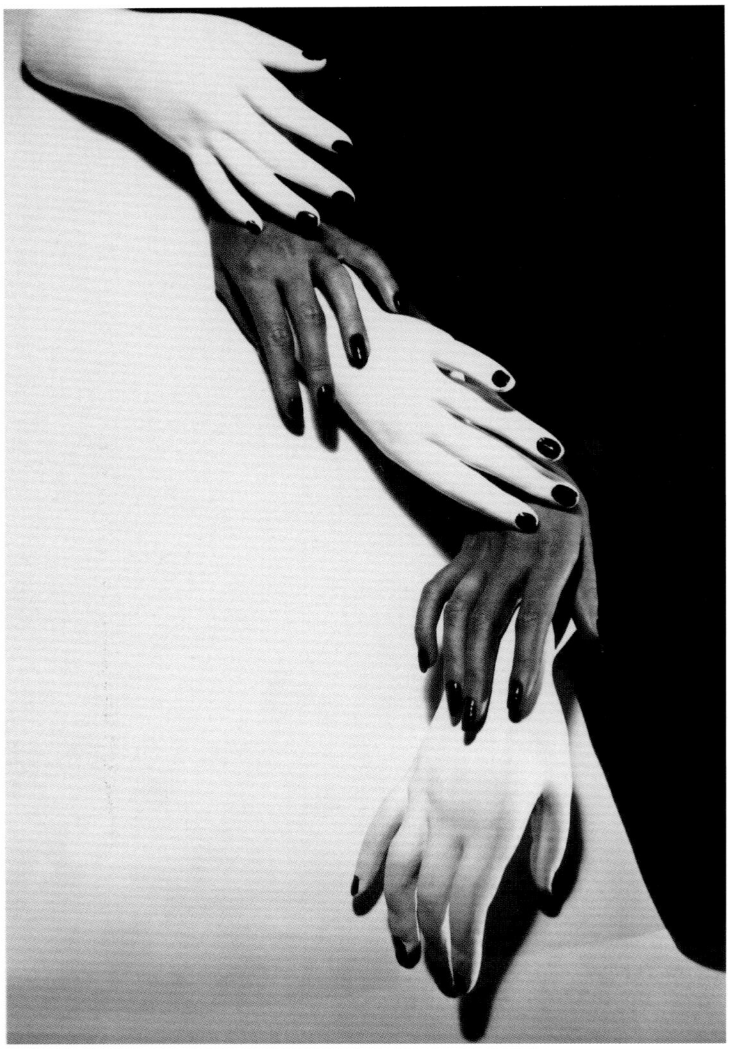

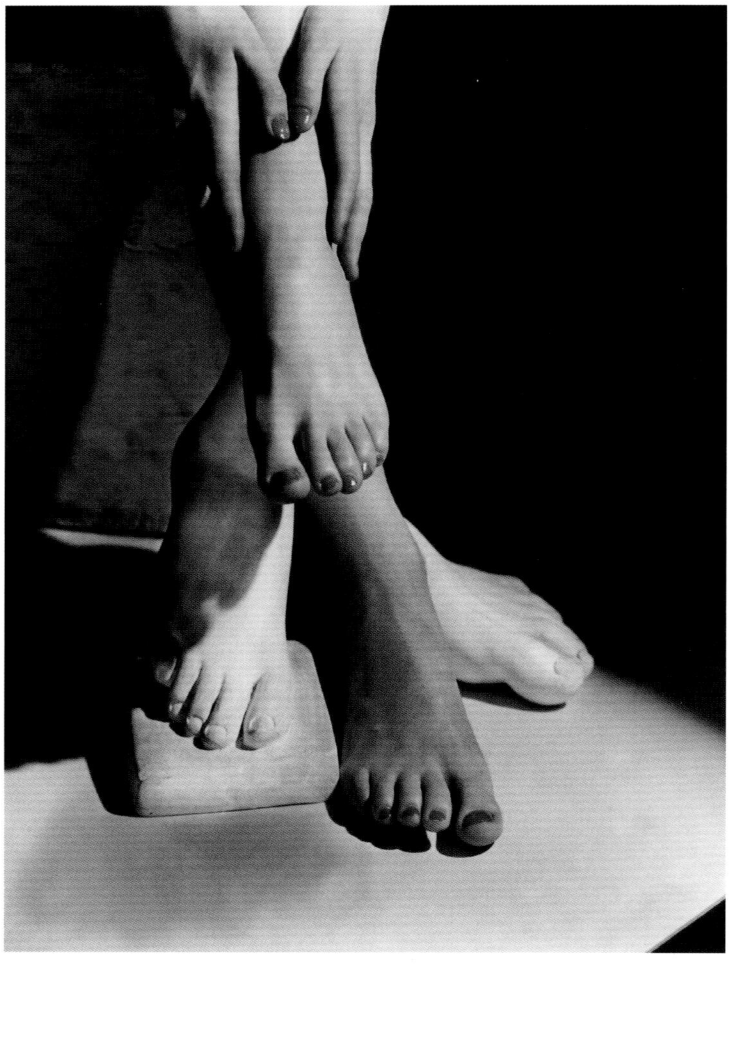

34. *Hands, Hands, Hands*, 1941 35. *Barefoot Beauty*, 1941

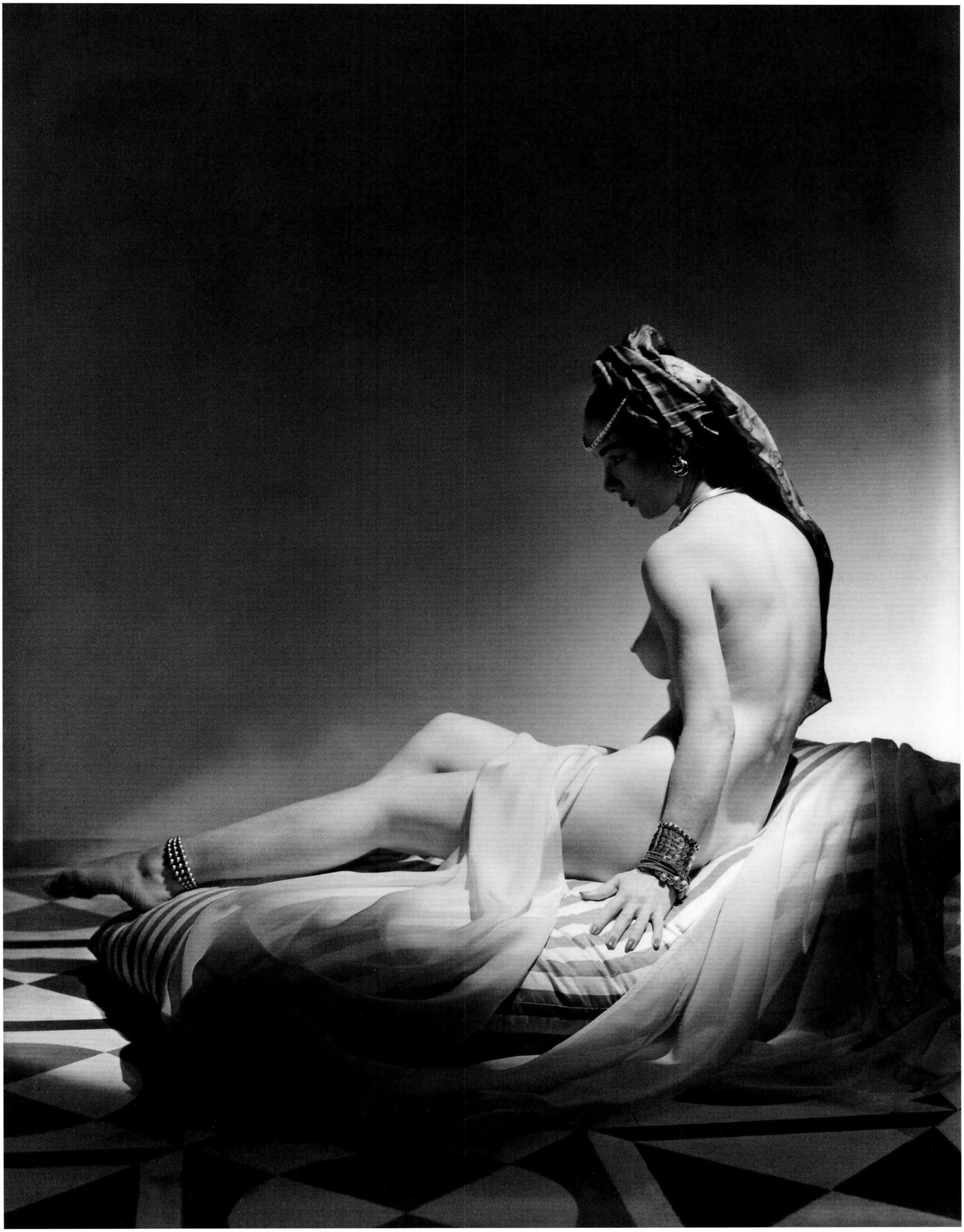

36. *Odalisque II*, 1943

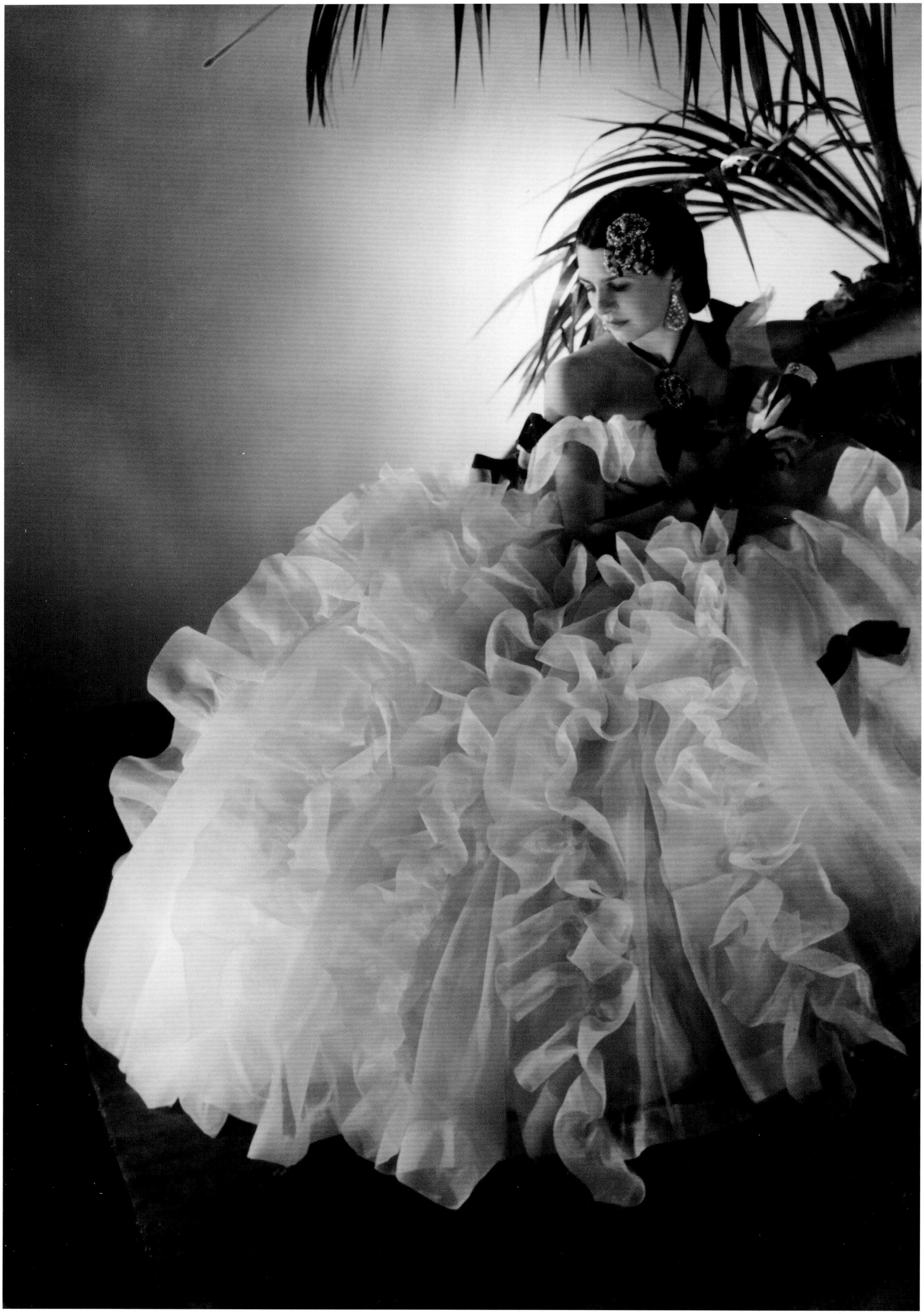

37. Comtesse Gérard de Moustier, 'Bal de Valses', 1934

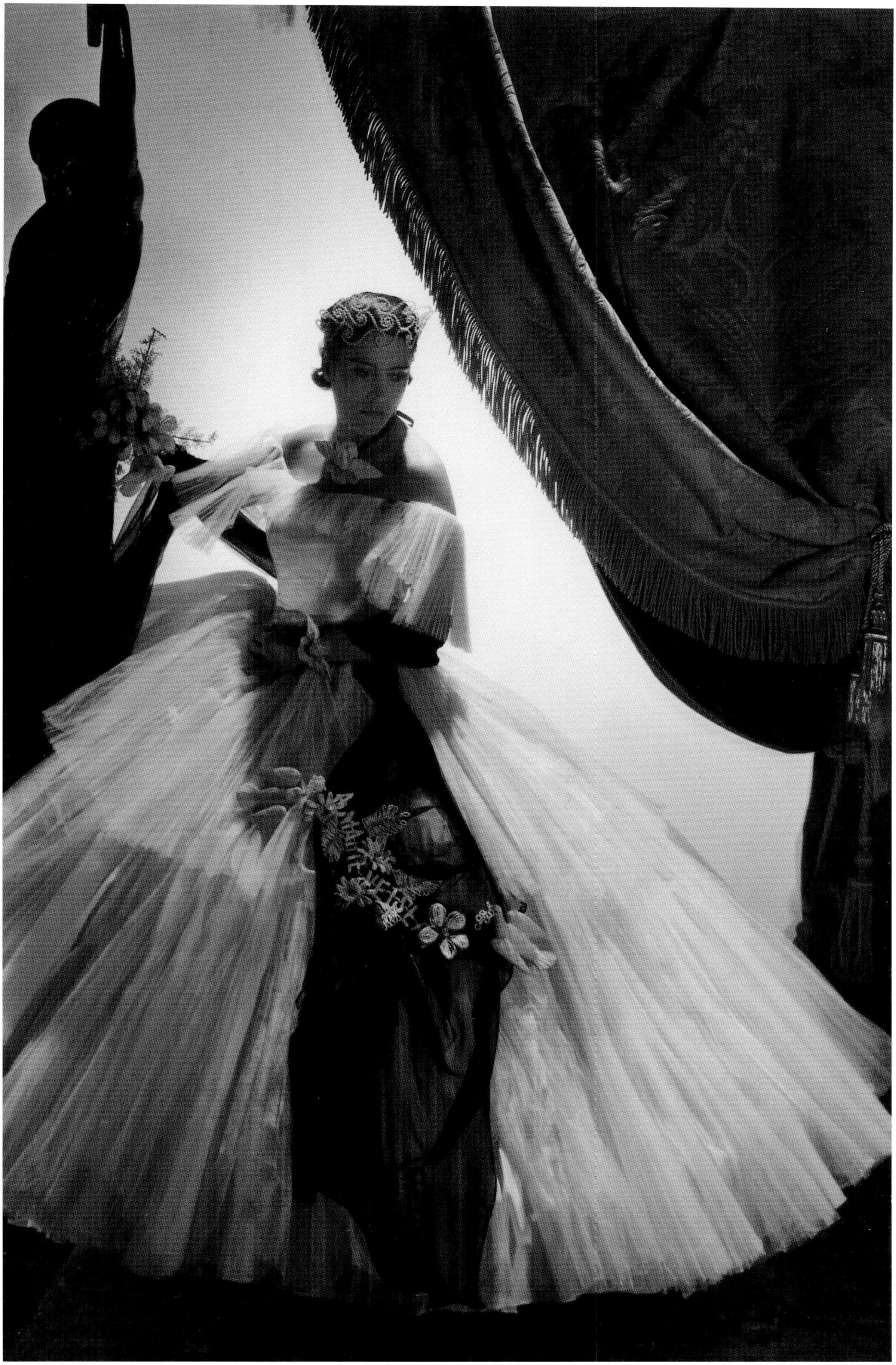

38. Madame Edouard Baurdet, 'Bal de Valses', 1934

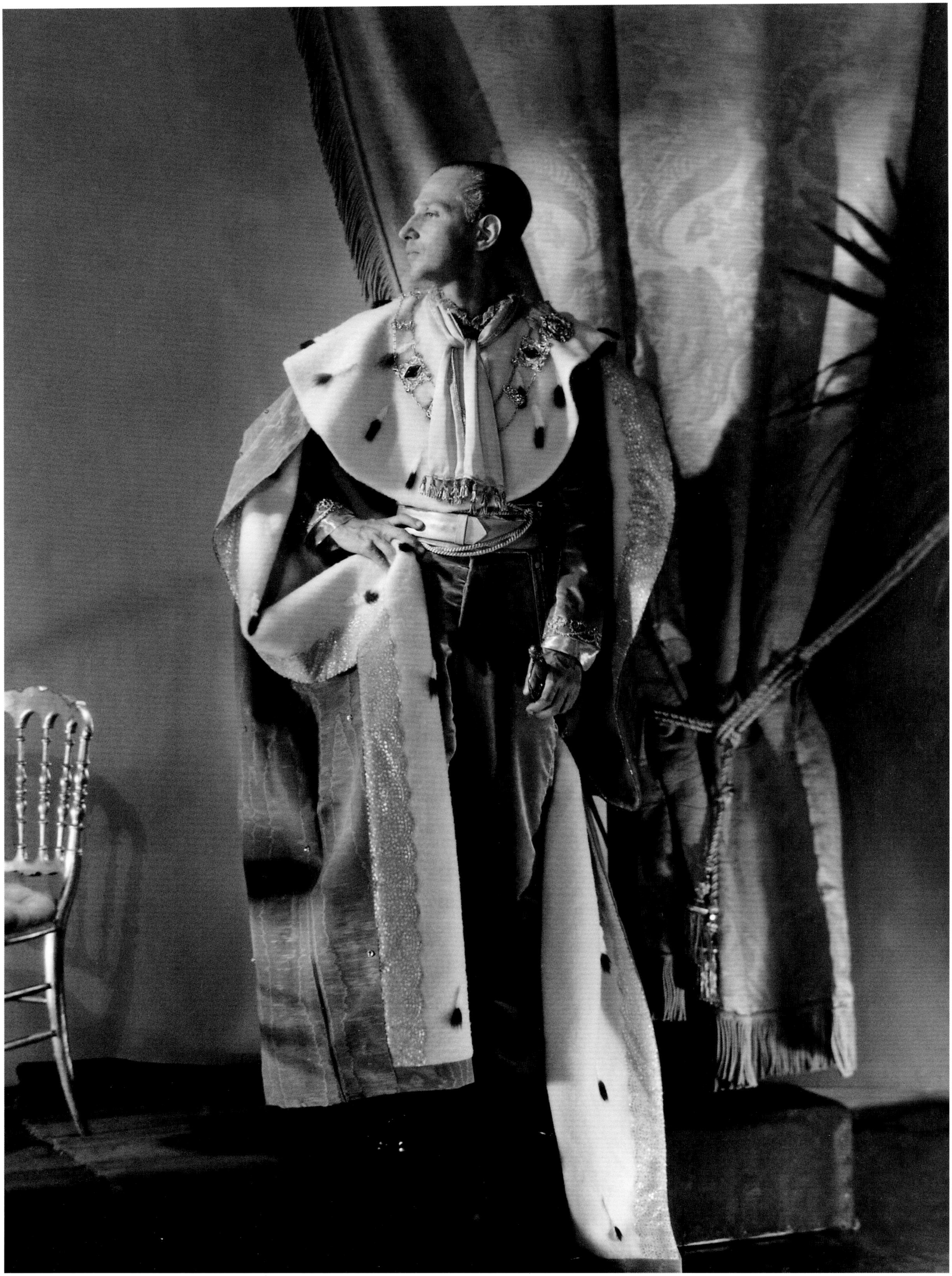

39. Count Charles de Beistegui, 'Bal de Valses', 1934

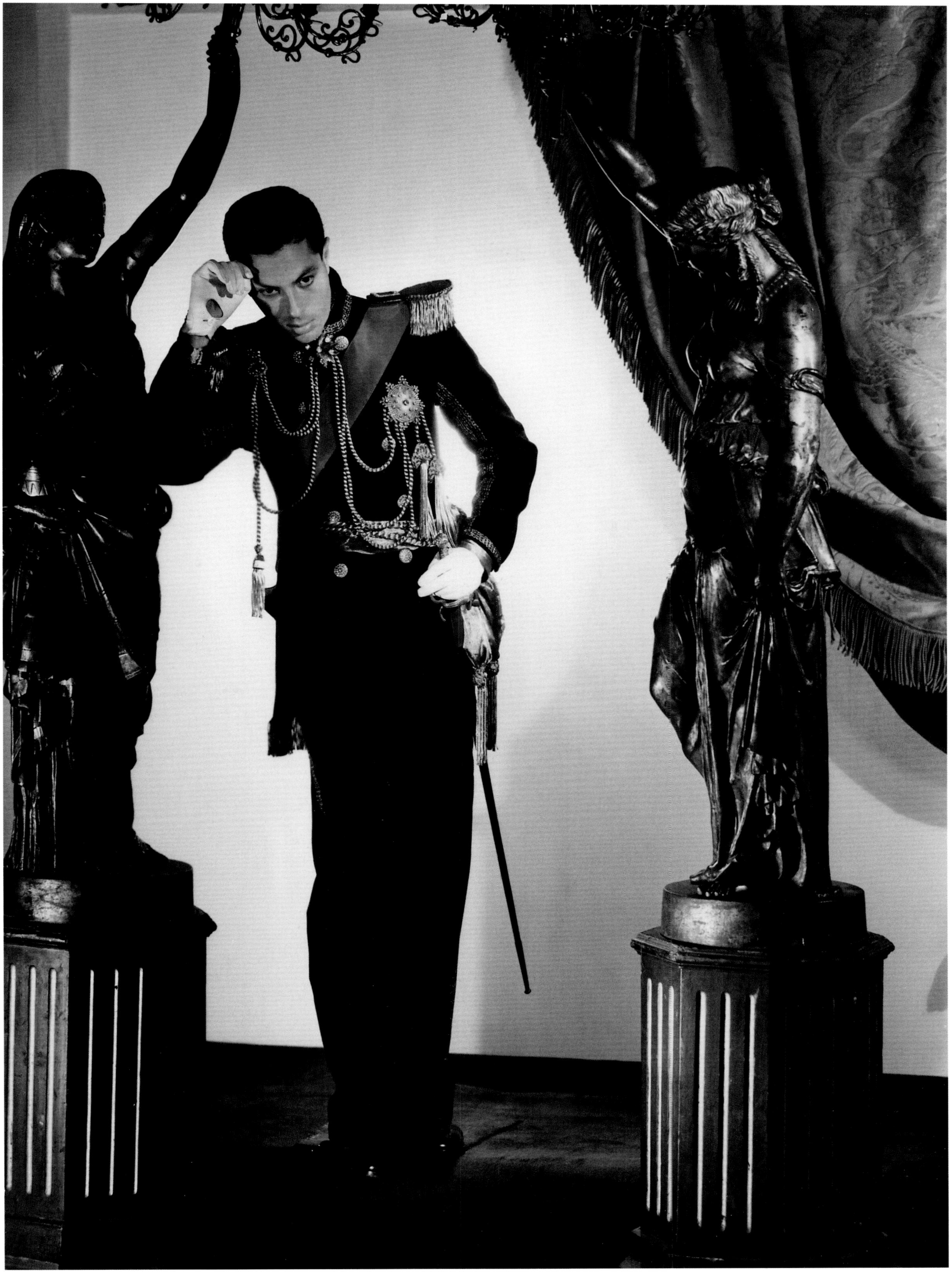

40. Baron Nicolas de Gunzburg, 'Bal de Valses', 1934

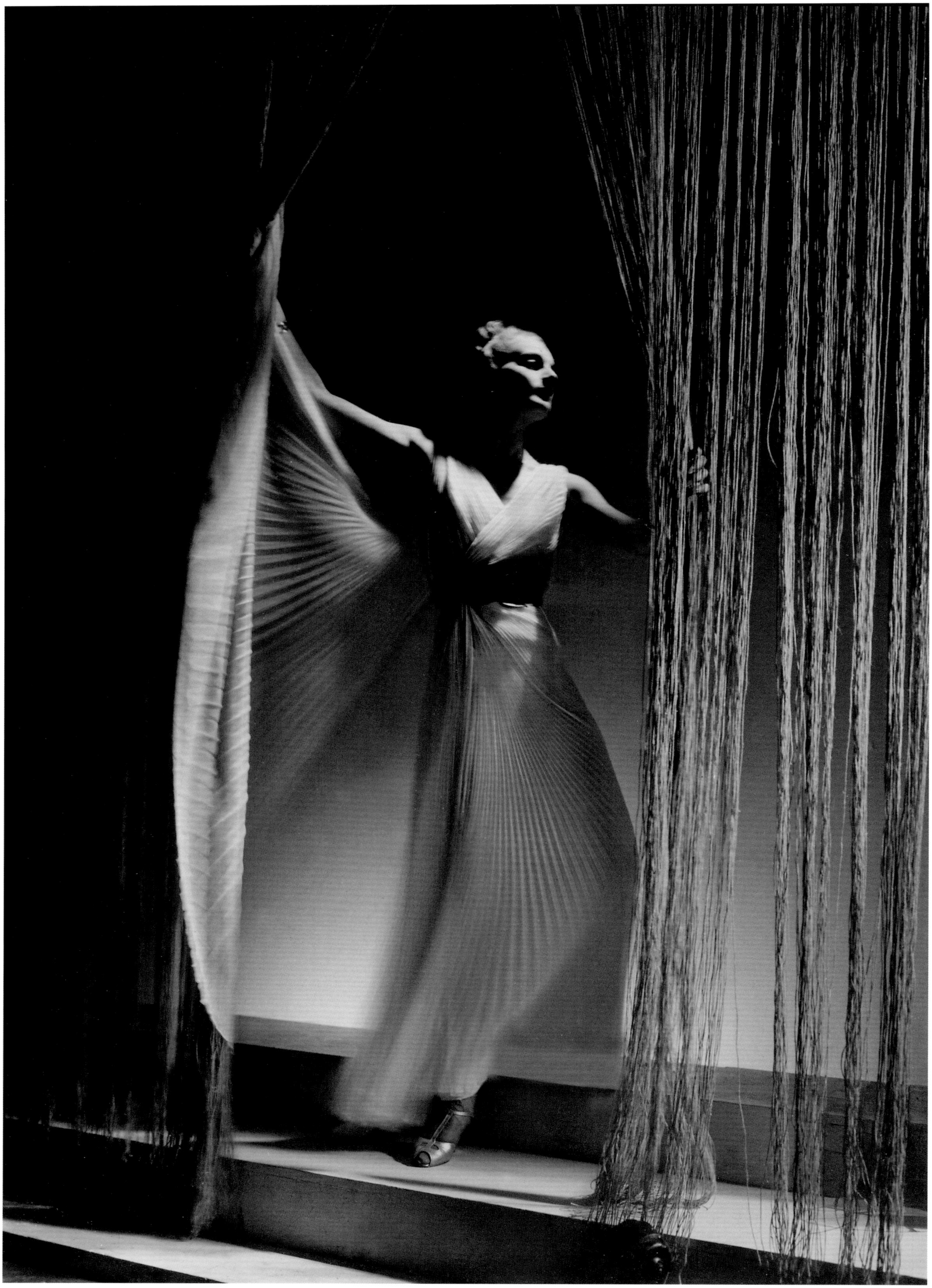

41. Lyla Zelensky, dress by Jean Patou, jewellery by Mauboussin, 1937

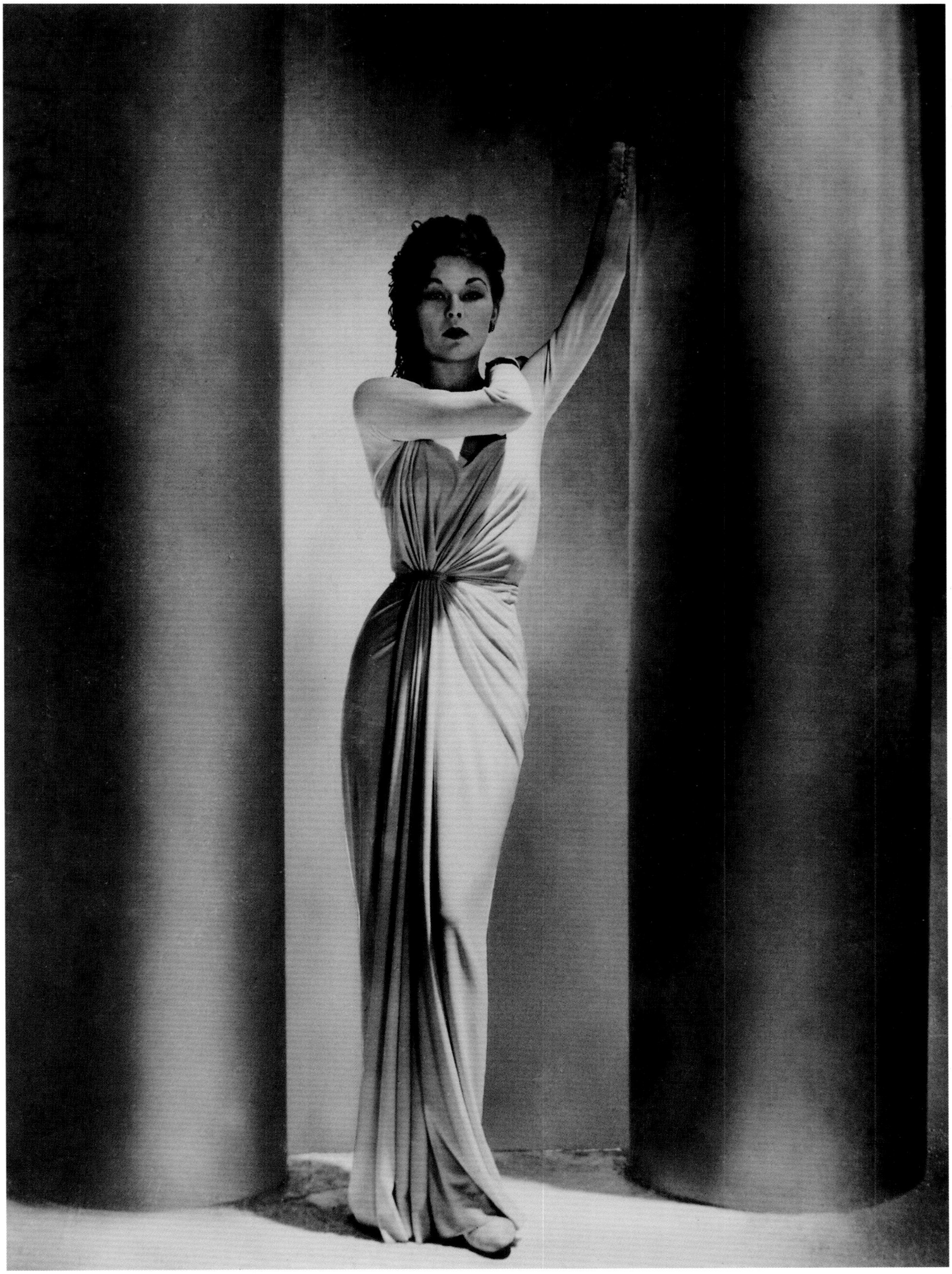

42. Lud, dress by Alix, 1938

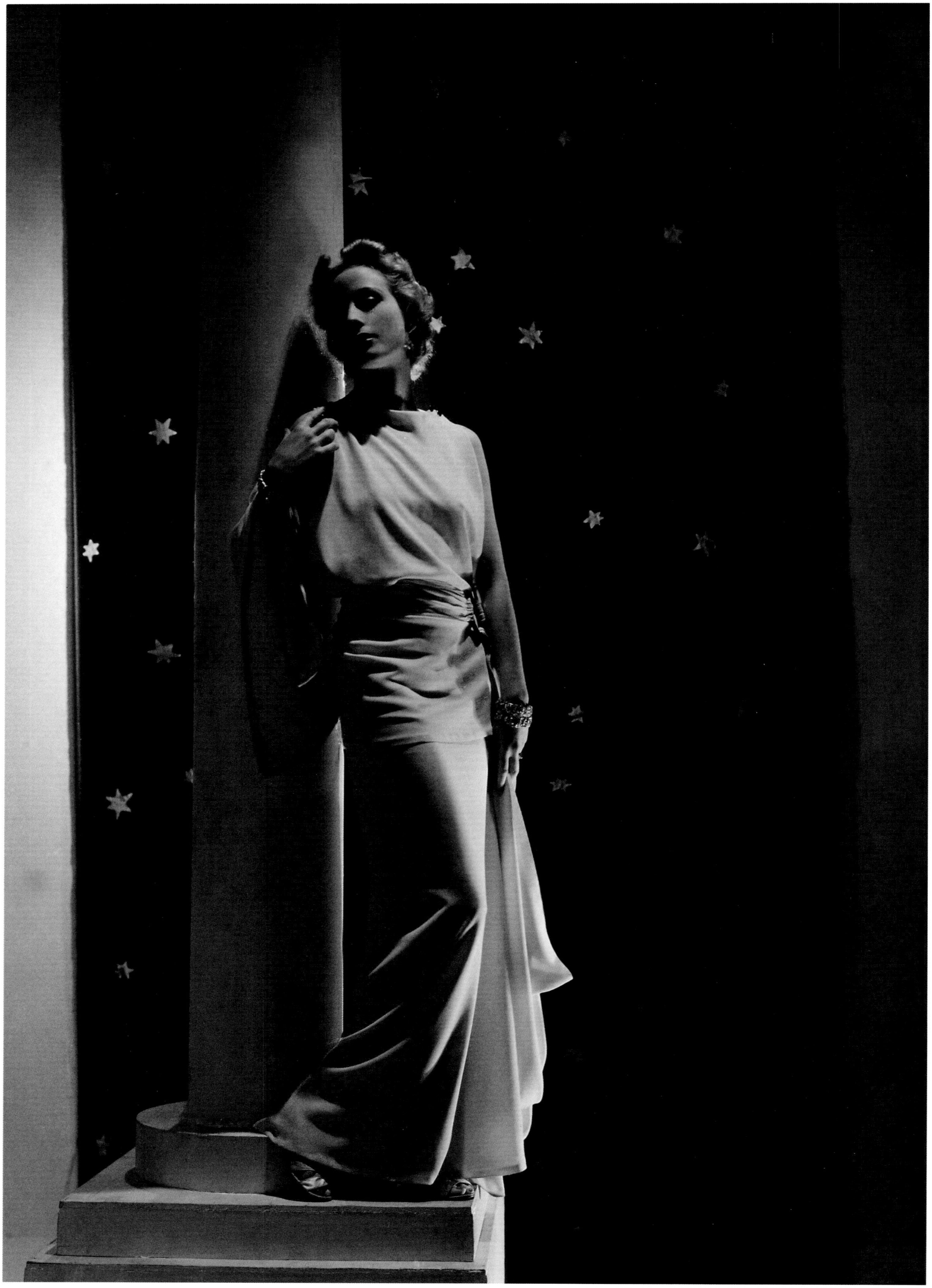

43. Cora Hemmet, dress by Worth, jewellery by Mauboussin, 1935

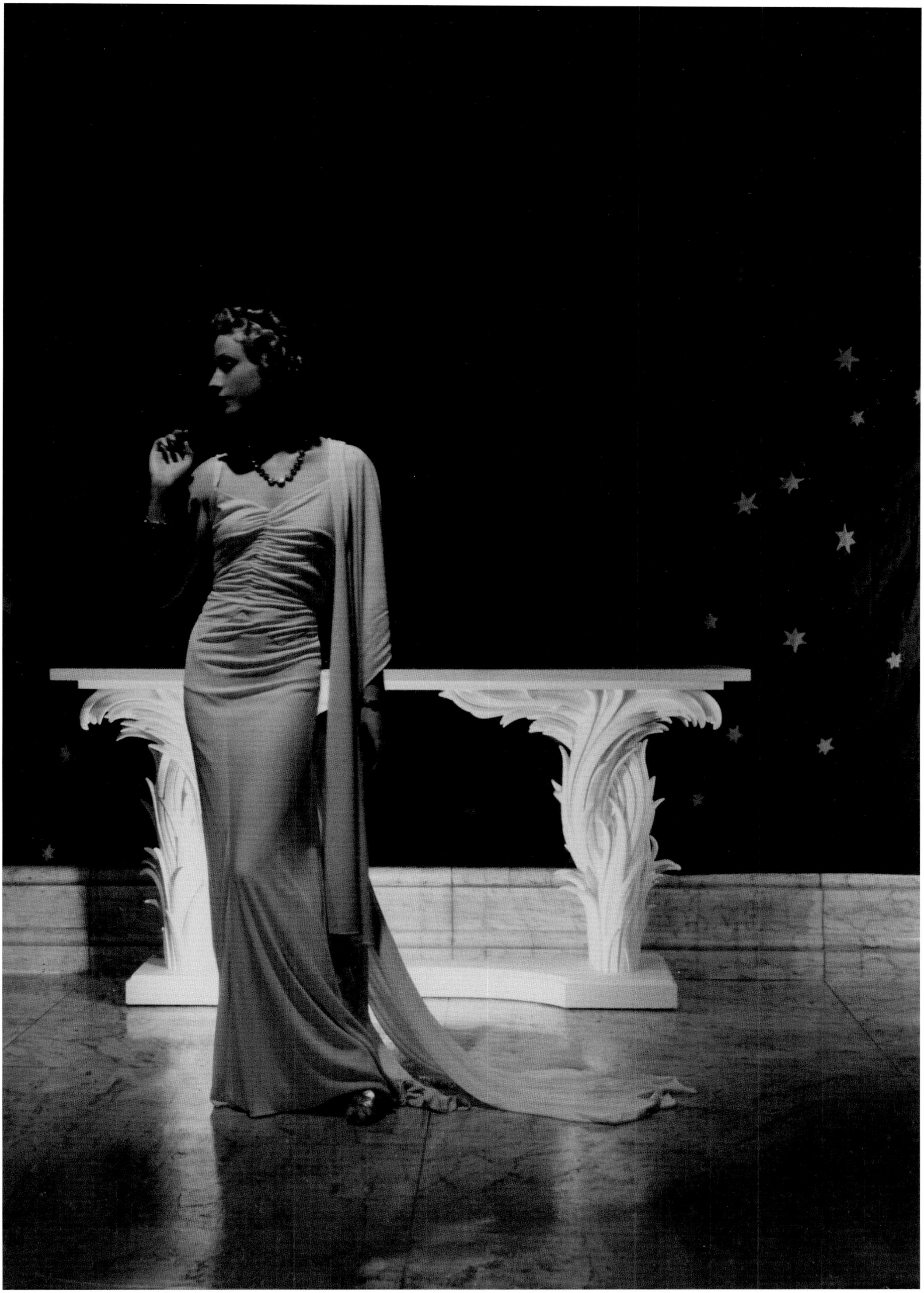

44. Cora Hemmet, dress by Lucien Lelong, jewellery by Cartier, console by Jean-Michel Frank, 1935

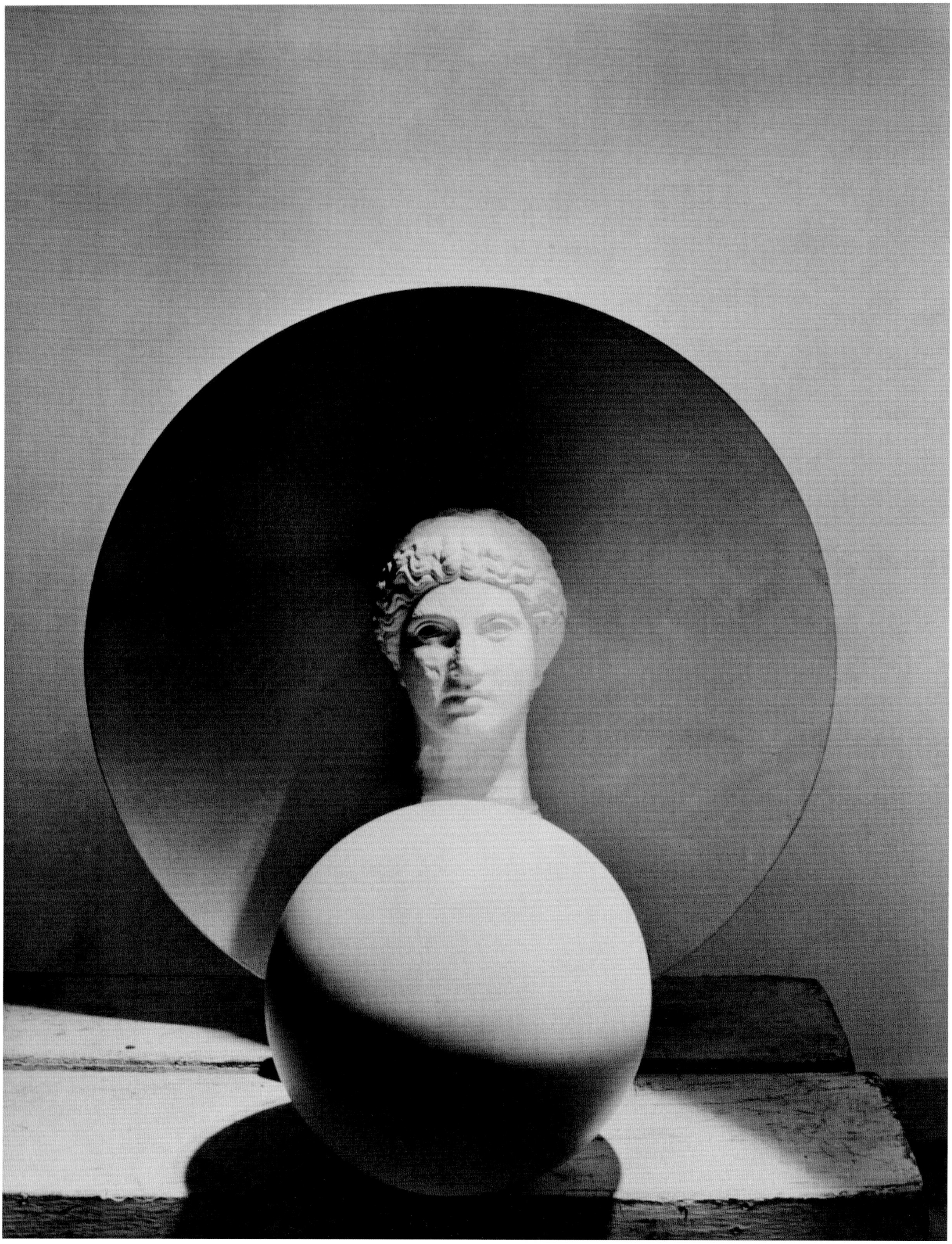

45. *Classical Still Life*, 1937

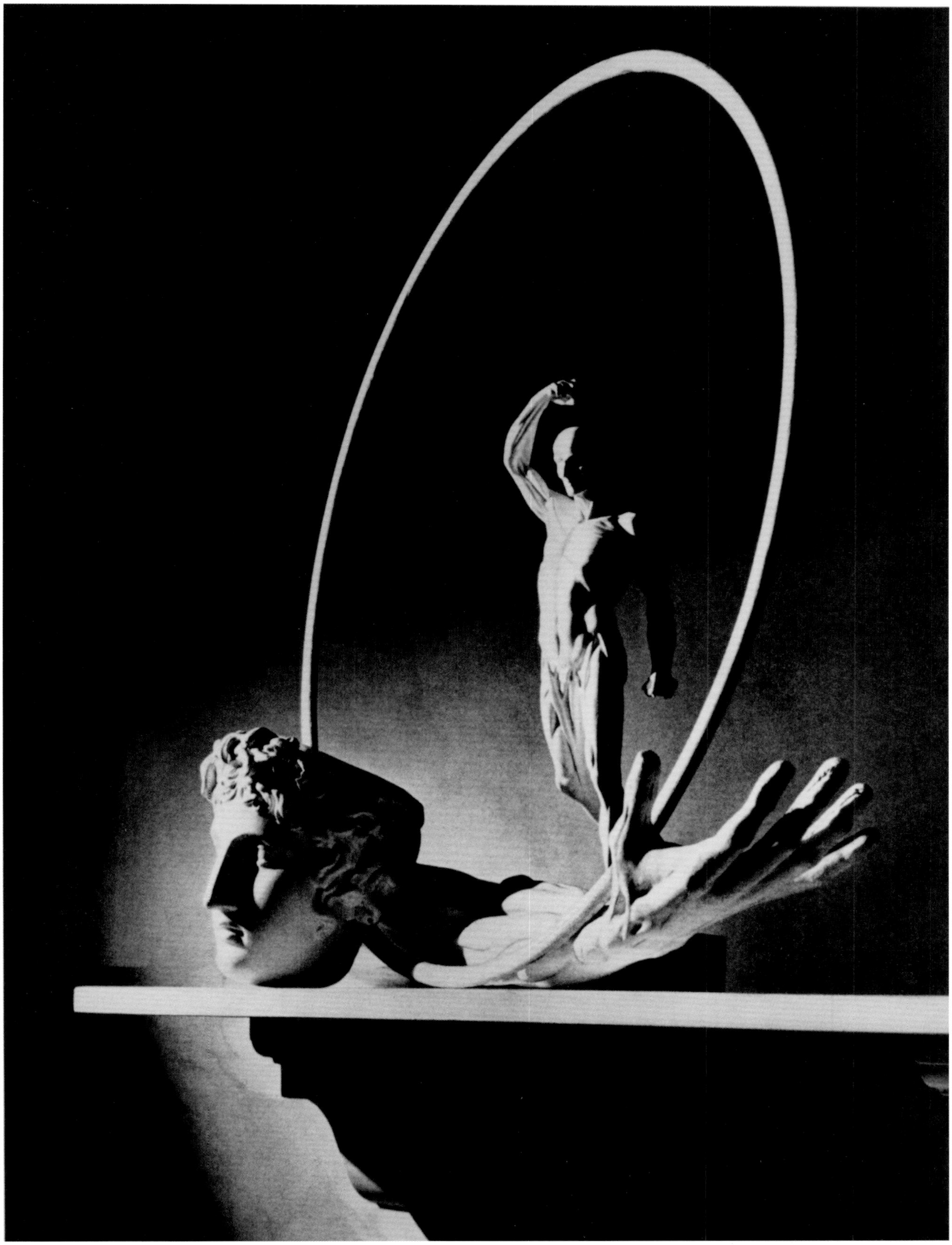

46. *Houdon Still Life*, 1939

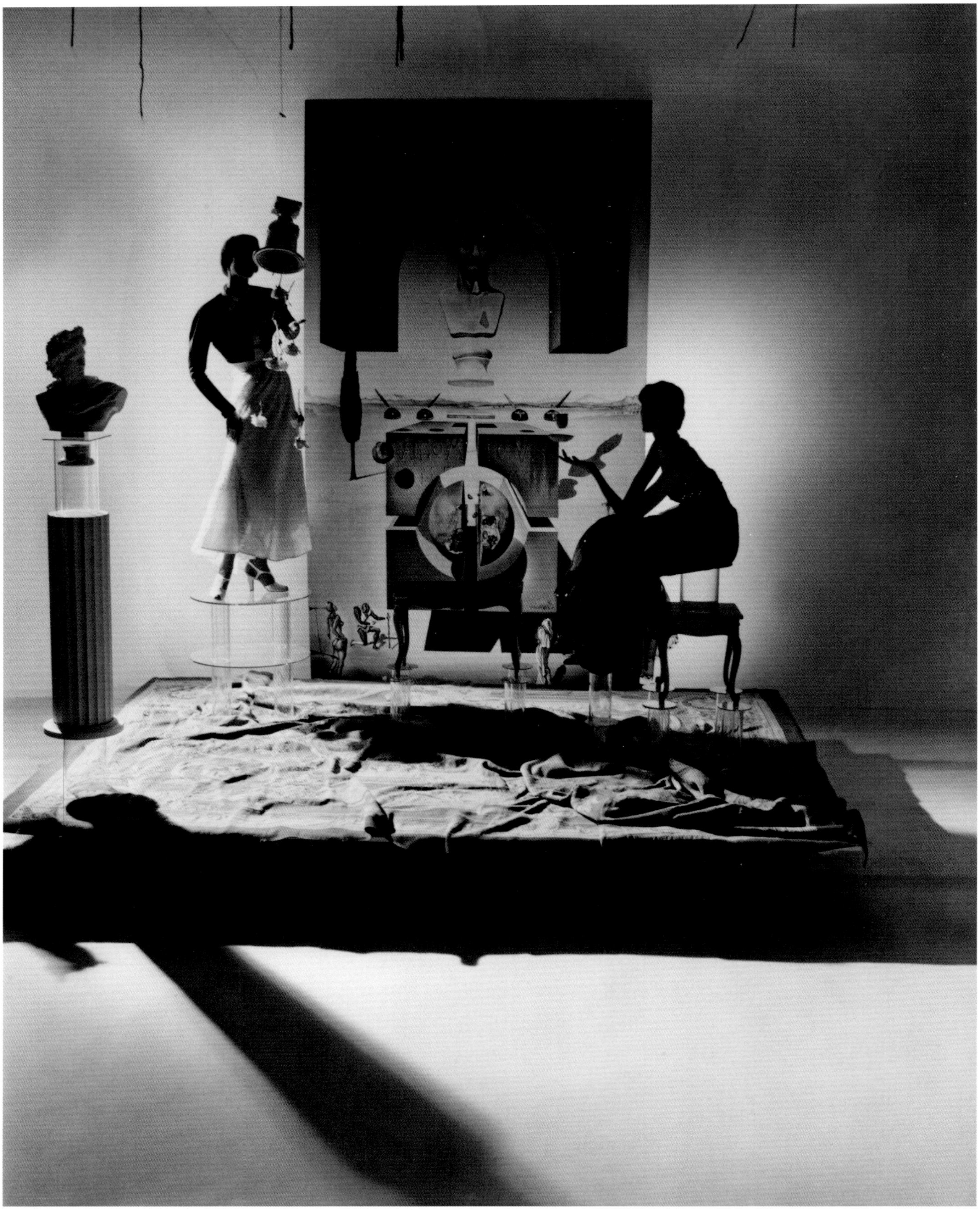

47. Set designed by Salvador Dalí, dresses by Hattie Carnegie, 1947

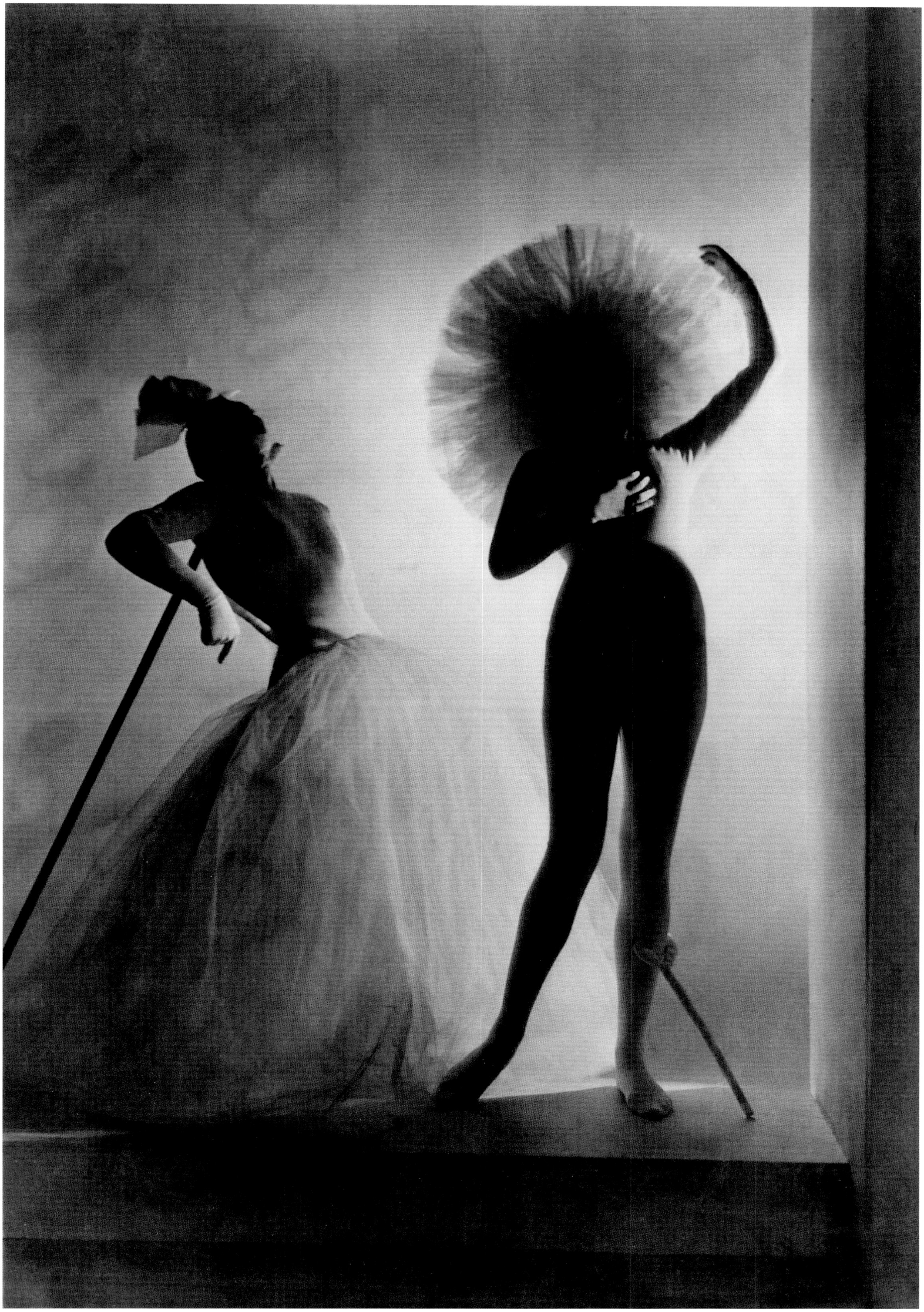

48. Costumes by Salvador Dalí for Leonid Massine's ballet, *Bacchanale*, 1939

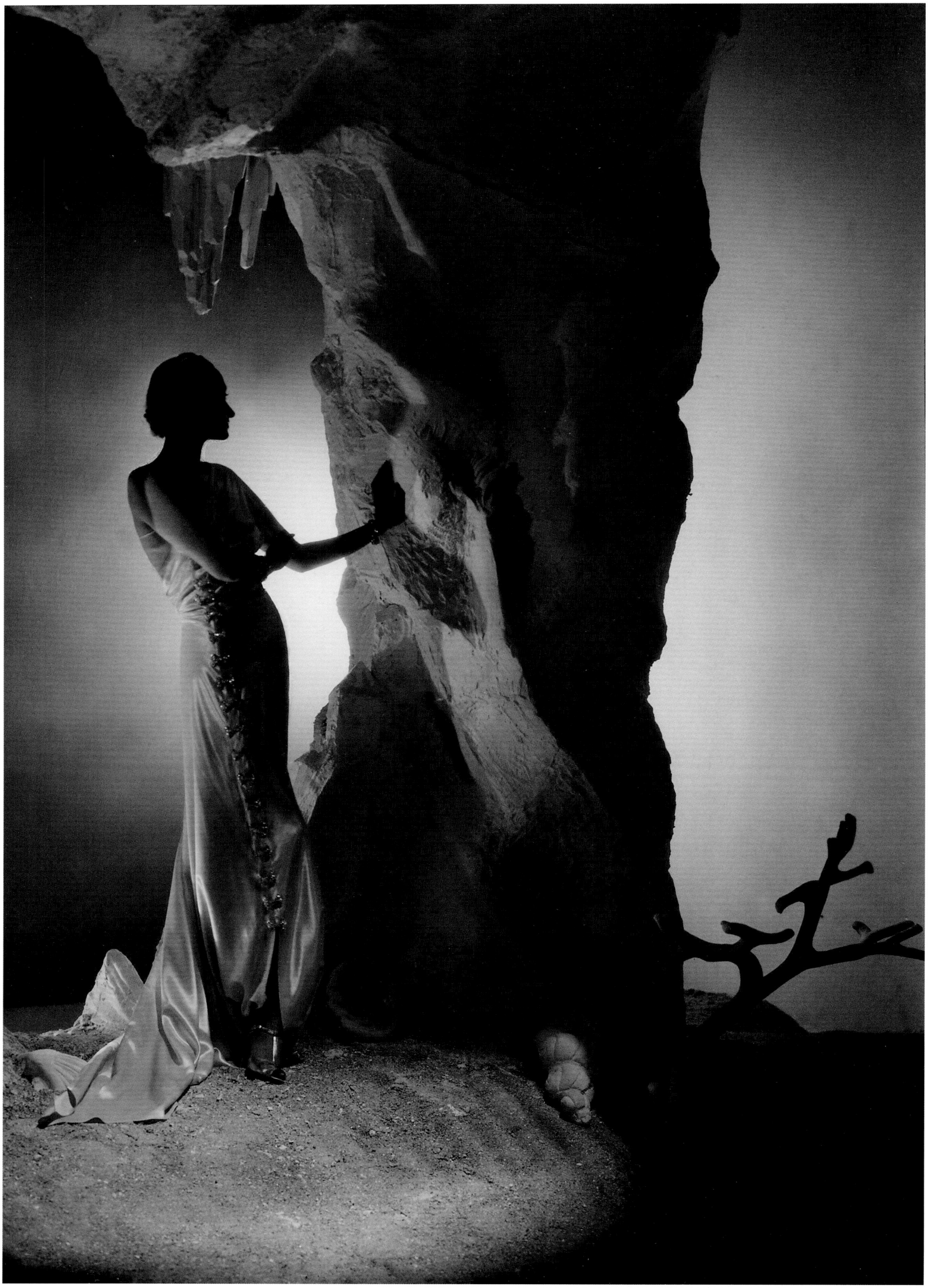

49. Louise Sheldon, dress by Vionnet, jewellery by Mauboussin, 1936

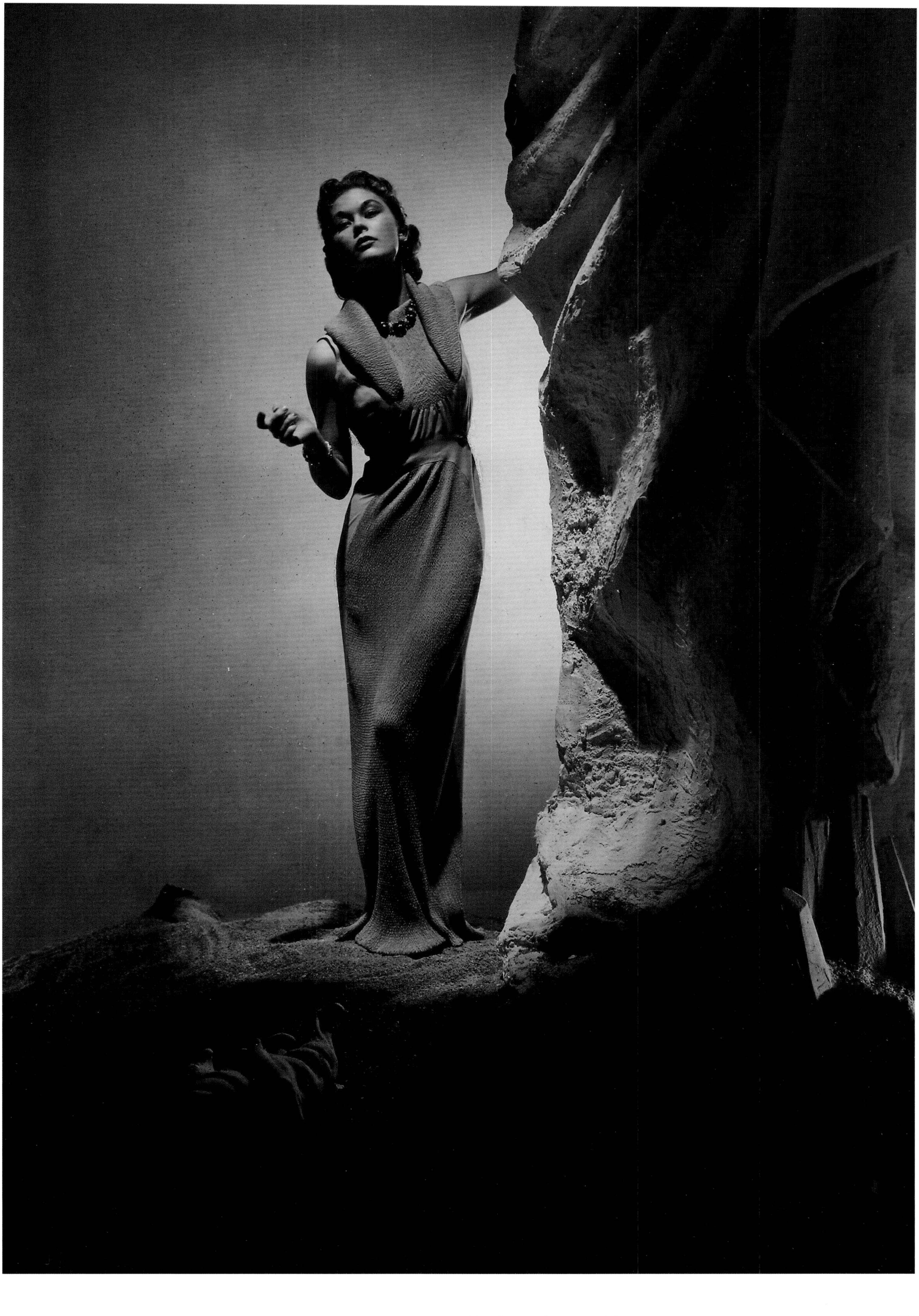

50. Lud, dress by Jean Patou, jewellery by Mauboussin, 1936

II

Couture Fashion in the 1930s

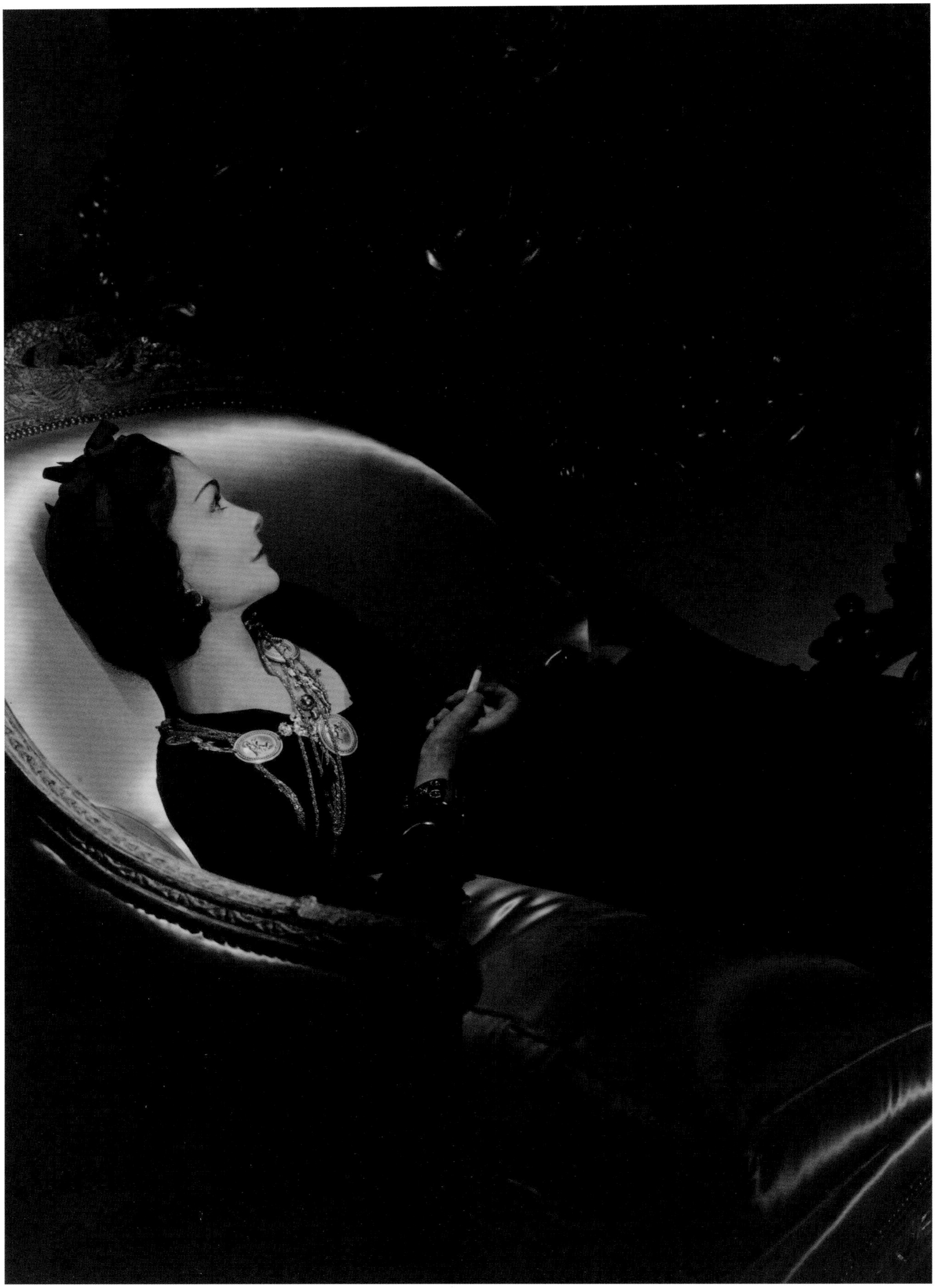

51. Coco Chanel, Paris, 1937

THE AURA OF GLAMOUR: COUTURE FASHION

Claire Wilcox

> Each spring and autumn the Paris dress houses open their doors to the world – and the world walks in. Every spindly gold chair is taken; press and buyers are strung up the staircases; cluttering doorways; peering, scribbling, nudging their neighbours; fastening with professional zeal on every point that may go to the composite picture of the new mode.
>
> British *Vogue*, 16 January 1938[1]

The presentation of the new Paris fashions was the culmination of months of endeavour by an army of highly skilled cutters, tailors, seamstresses and specialist embroiderers. The collections were the creative expression of a couturier's vision and also the measure by which an haute couture fashion house traded ideas for orders, for it was from this series of showings of the latest styles to the international press, buyers and private clients that commissions, overseas sales and editorial in magazines such as *Vogue* would follow.

The Chambre Syndicale de la Couture Parisienne, haute couture's governing body, imposed exacting regulations on couture houses in order to control standards of design, and to protect this unique, luxury industry which was so vital to both the identity and the economy of France. In 1938, *The Times* fashion correspondent explained, 'Others may look at it as mere extravagance but in Paris a dress means more than that. It is ... a vast trade – a trade which enables rich and poor to live, and to which towns and villages throughout France look for their livelihood.'[2] One of the prerequisites for the acceptance of a new fashion business into the elite conglomeration of haute couture houses was the appropriateness of the premises – usually an imposing town house with workshops on the upper levels – and the distinction of its reception rooms, in which fashion shows were staged.[3]

To wealthy French clients, such as the Comtesse Etienne de Beaumont, or Marie-Laure, the Vicomtesse de Noailles (pl.53; an art patron whose parchment-lined salon was created by the fashionable decorator Jean-Michel Frank), the interiors of the great Parisian couture houses echoed the grandeur of their own residences, and were familiar and appropriate settings for the transaction of luxury. Each of the numerous Paris establishments was distinguished by the aesthetic sensibility of its couturier, from the gleaming modernity of Coco Chanel's house with its mirrored staircase on which she sat, hidden, to observe the reaction to her collections (pl.52), to the discreet, pearl-grey elegance of the House of Molyneux on the rue Royale, the premises of Edward Molyneux (1891–1974), the British-born couturier, from the classical setting of Madeleine Vionnet's Grand Salon, with its stained glass windows by Lalique and carved friezes inspired by Grecian temples (pl.54) to Elsa Schiaparelli's surrealist-inspired perfume boutique within her Place Vendôme premises, situated in a giant birdcage designed by Frank. Such atmospheric settings were integral to the theatre of fashion. One American model, employed by couturier Lucien Lelong (1889–1958) to demonstrate to buyers that French couture was suitable for all physiques, recalled: 'As I went through the door to show my first dress, I had the impression of stepping into a perfumed, silk-lined jewel casket, the atmosphere was so strongly charged ... It was hot, so hot, and the air was stifling.'[4]

It is no surprise that the theatricality and grandeur of this uniquely Parisian event should be reflected and emulated in fashion photography. Just as the promenade of in-house models was essential to demonstrate how a design worked in three dimensions, so the studio model's ability to appear to freeze motion was essential to the photographer. As Alexander Liberman observed of 1930s fashion photography: 'The stillness of the pose, the haughtiness of the attitude, and the splendour of the clothes created a distance between the image and the spectator. The woman's expression was hermetic, closed; no emotion was permitted.'[5] It was in this context that Horst began to photograph fashion for French *Vogue*, creating idealized and dream-like environments populated with figures of impossible beauty, wearing clothes far beyond the reach of most. But the necessity for haute couture to appeal to both those who could afford it, and those who could only dream, was part of its paradox. The novelist Célia Bertin once observed that haute couture was 'An art which is extremely difficult to describe, and by its very nature inimitable, [it] has to be interpreted ... the effort to find new markets and outlets for this most individual industry makes it essential to maintain popular interest in a luxury art.'[6] As the vehicle for couture's wider reach, it was also the magazine's role to translate the designer's creative vision for the commercial benefit of the ready-to-wear industry: as Carmel Snow (1887–1961), the editor of *Harper's Bazaar* from 1932, noted, 'The editors must recognize fashions while they are still a thing of the future. The dressmakers create them, but without these magazines, the fashions would never be established or accepted.'[7]

For a newcomer to Paris such as Horst, the camera lens gave a view on, and an entry into, an entirely new world. His apprenticeship under George Hoyningen-Huene ensured the continuation of Huene's

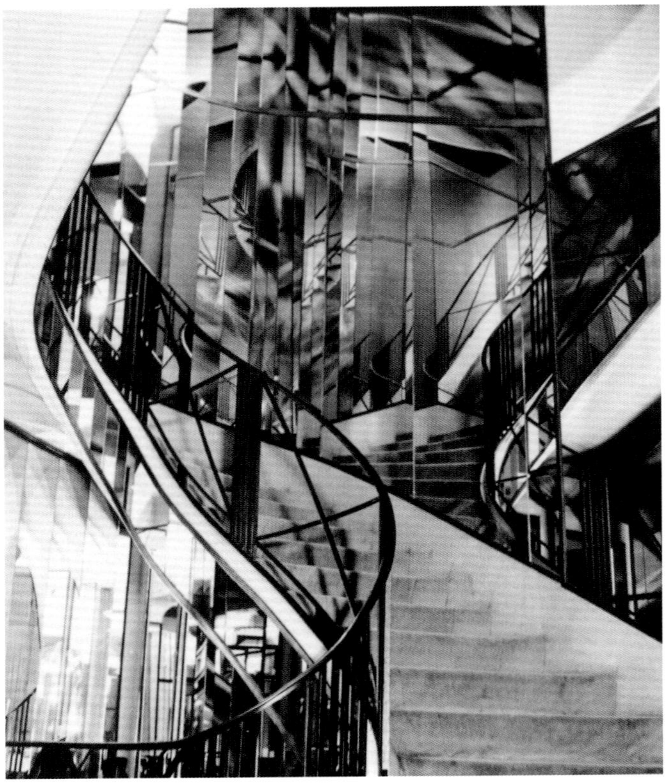

52. Curtis Moffat,
Mirror staircase at the House of Chanel,
31 rue Cambon, Paris, 1925–30,
V&A: E.838-2007

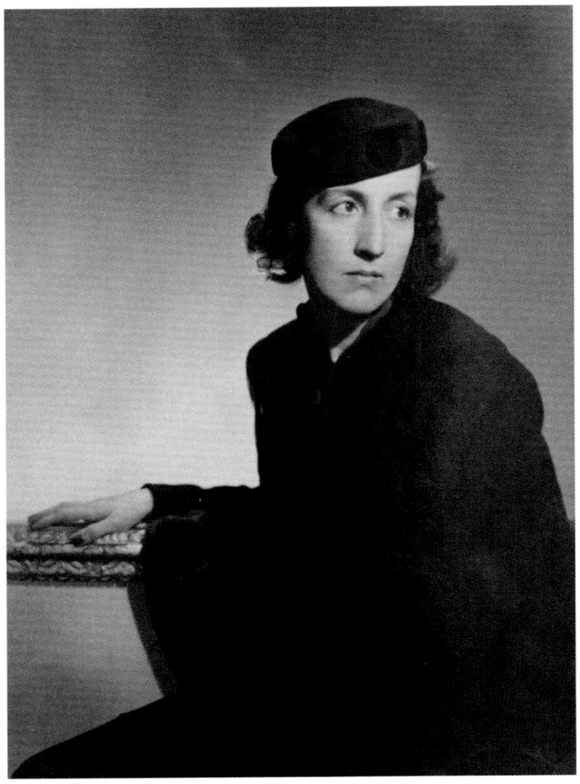

53. Marie-Laure, Vicomtesse de
Noailles, Paris, 1935

melodramatic rendering of fashion perfection. Horst was a witness to the needle and thread, recalling 'One of my most cherished memories is of Chanel at the dress rehearsal of a Cocteau play, ripping apart the costumes she had designed for the production and stitching them together again, sitting cross-legged, tailor-fashion, on the bare boards of the stage.'[8] But his interest, like Huene's, was in the formal, resolved properties of couture. As Babs Simpson (b.1913), then American *Vogue* fashion editor, observed, 'Horst liked things to be polished.'[9] It is no coincidence that both Huene and Horst excelled at the drama of eveningwear, one of the keynotes of 1930s fashion.

The classically inspired mood of Huene's and Horst's fashion photography reflected the wider preoccupations of the time, for the decorative arts in the 1930s were permeated by images and artefacts that paid homage to the ideals of Greek and Roman proportion. Their photographic *mises en scène* began to resemble stage sets for a classical drama, with plinths, columns, drapery and strong overhead lighting inspired by the natural light of Greece, recorded in snapshots taken on Mediterranean trips the pair took together. The rituals of the photographic shoot reflected this dramatic tension. Horst's muse, the Swedish model Lisa Fonssagrives, recalled, 'One was led from the dressing room onto a very dark, dramatic set with a column or stairway or some other Greek-inspired element, and there was silence. It was like some mystic ritual. [Huene] spoke very little and in a very low voice and there was only one assistant, who moved like a cat. No one was allowed on the set in those days, not even an editor.'[10] References to the body as part of a classical landscape also abound in editorial features from this time: 'Close-Up of the Paris Collections' in American *Vogue*, 15 March 1935, featured a Schiaparelli dress of black satin, 'draped to turn you into a human column' with the model standing on a fluted classical pedestal, scattered with laurel leaves (pl.55).[11] Horst often embraced this visual metaphor, most memorably in his 1938 photograph of one of his favourite models, Lud, resembling a caryatid in a white jersey dress by Alix (pl.42). The association with statuary was furthered by the near-nakedness of much eveningwear, with plunging backs and bare arms, while the trend for ivory, white and beige shades of satin gave the appearance of skin, or marble.

Such material qualities were further emphasized by the vogue for cutting fabric on the cross, which allowed it to stretch and cling, a technique developed and perfected by the arch-technician Madeleine Vionnet – 'I was the first to do the bias cut … [it] was fluid, easy, promising.'[12] Like a sculptor, she manipulated fabric in the round: 'You don't take the potentialities of a material into consideration when you're only dealing with drawings. To do this you must work on a lay figure, and that is what I always did.'[13] Vionnet's preference for plain fabrics, without any patterns to distract from the purity … of the garment, was realised in jerseys, chiffons, pliable woollens and matt *crêpe Romaine*, which could be moulded to the body, and draped and fell in folds that appeared to be carved. The complexity of working with such clinging, sensual materials was informed by Vionnet's knowledge of the contours and musculature of the human body, and her belief that 'A woman's muscles are the best corset one could imagine.'[14] Of Vionnet's creations, Bettina Ballard (1905–61), the young Paris-based fashion editor of American *Vogue*, confessed, 'The evening clothes were so statuesquely beautiful with their asymmetric necklines, their bias cut that revealed a hip and the shadow of a bust but never seemed to cling anywhere, that all I could feel was desire.'[15]

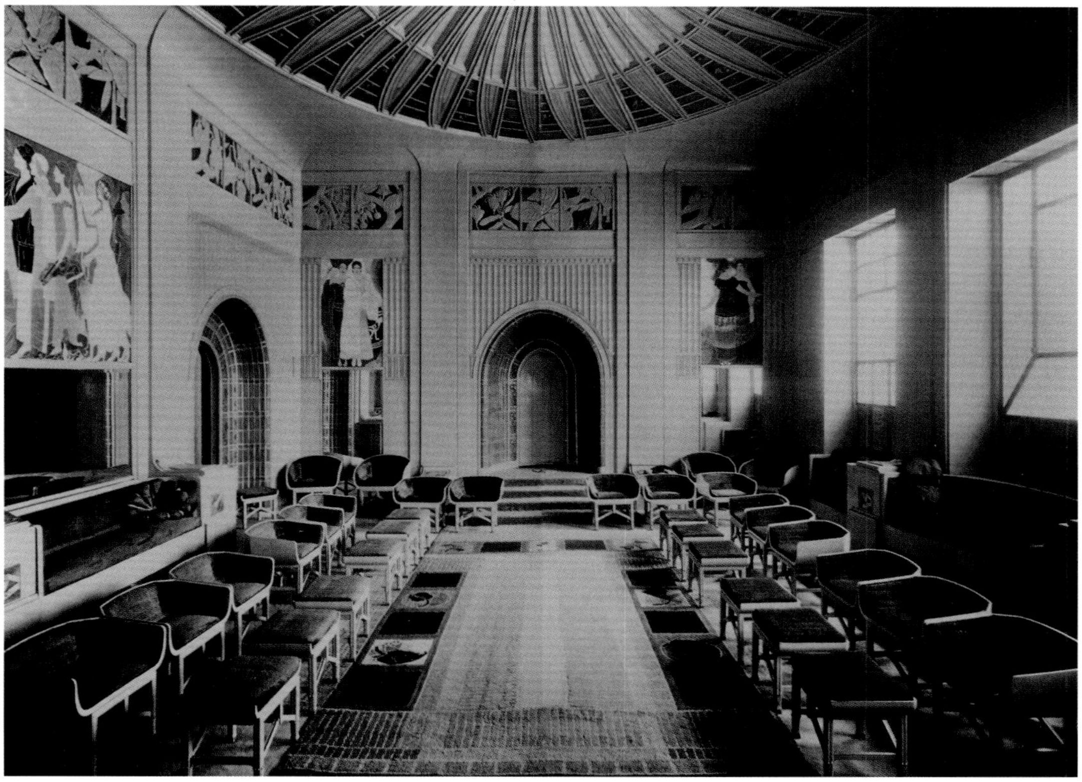

54. Albert Seeburger,
Madeleine Vionnet's Grand Salon,
50 avenue Montaigne, Paris, c.1930

Many designers in the 1930s utilized lustrous fabrics such as silks and satins, characteristically offset by the addition of sparkling diamante buckles and clips (pl.60), or used in combination with reflective materials, from fish-scale sequins to newly developed man-made fabrics including lamé. Technical developments in the 1930s, including the development of aluminium foil thread laminated with plastic film, allowed for such materials to be draped and manipulated, and even cut on the bias, unlike the heavy stiff metallics of the 1920s.[16] New Cellophanes and 'glass' fabric – 'a brittle, fragile, transparent substance – you must handle it with care' – were embraced by innovative designers including Schiaparelli and Alix, and were even used for hats, bags and shoes, as well as gowns (pl.56).[17] Such fabrications were rendered by Horst in a series of photographs that captured the reflective and metallic properties of the garments, as if the figures were apparitions, or as if the images were shimmering stills from a film, in a decade captivated by the illusionistic properties of cinema. Such magic with fabric was familiar to audiences who had marvelled at the alluring outfits of Hollywood film stars such as Merle Oberon and Joan Crawford, numbered amongst the many actresses photographed by Horst at the height of their fame. As Diana Vreeland (1901–89), editor and then editor-in-chief of American *Vogue* from 1962 to 1971, observed of Paris, 'In this brilliantly lighted populace, everyone was a star. There was a strong whiff of celluloid everywhere. Everything was Hollywood. Glamour.'[18]

Despite its beauty, artistic photography created a dilemma for editors who had a requirement to show their readers the details of clothes and were trying to sell copies of their magazine, for their star photographers often disdained the use of lighting as anything other than a dramatic device. Edna Woolman Chase (1877–1957), editor-in-chief of *Vogue* from 1914 to 1952, dispatched a memo in 1937 that declared: 'I have been lecturing Horst about the lack of light in his photography. We have simply got to overcome this desire on the part of our photographers to shroud everything in deepest mystery ... I am sick and tired of having women say to me, "How is this dress made? What is it like?"'[19]

Horst recalled: 'I ... began a series of strong black compositions that made a big inky splash on the magazine page, blotting out everything else. This went so far that one day a *Vogue* editor produced during a sitting a little flashlight – "just for the dress please".'[20]

Vogue did not rely entirely on photography to convey the character and cut of the latest fashions, however. Black outfits in particular tended to be illustrated by means of sketches because their details became lost in the predominantly monochromatic photographs of the time. Illustrators could also capture the line of a new look in hats, or the essence of a collection, 'live' with little equipment other than pen and pad and were often allowed access into the inner sanctum of the couture house. Photography, on the other hand, was a laborious studio-based process, with cumbersome fixed lights, elaborate and theatrical sets and long, controlled exposures that required models to hold their poses.

The conception and production of a fashion photograph, and the investment of time required, demanded that the photographer be both artist and technician, rather like the couturier. Horst's interpretation of the latest fashions found favour with his fellow creatives, for his images had the sheen of luxury and the static elegance of a still life. His tendency to 'edit' and even obscure a

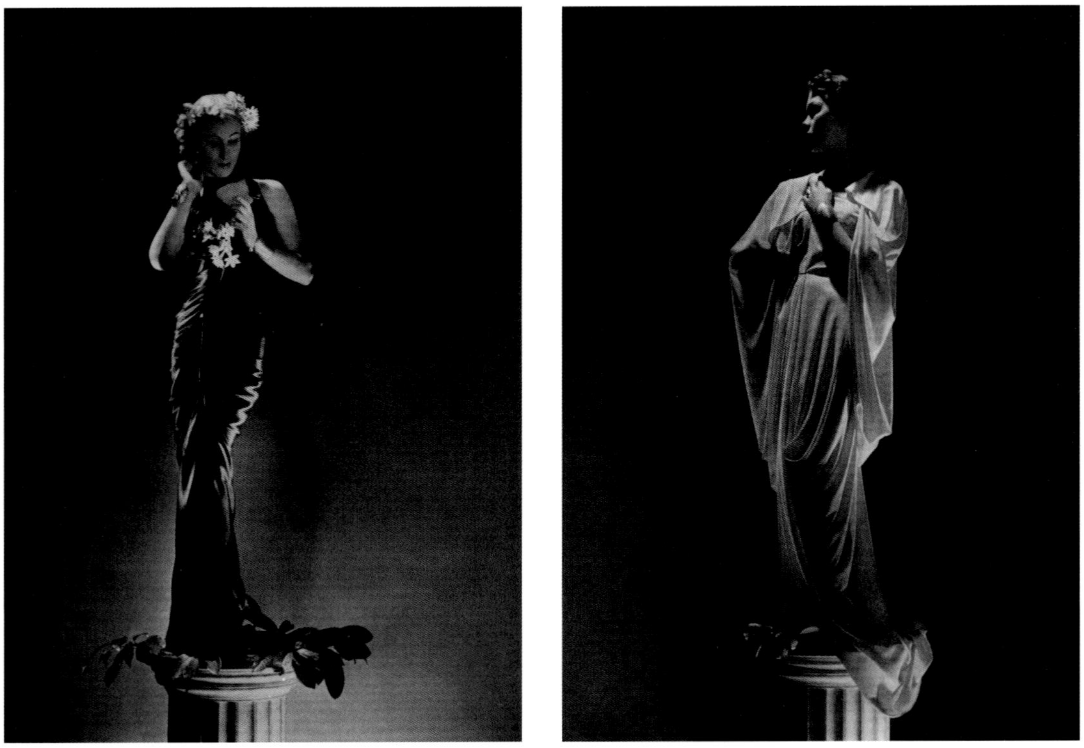

55. Cora Hemmet and Lud, dresses by Schiaparelli and Alix, 'Close-up of the Paris Collections', American *Vogue*, 15 March 1935

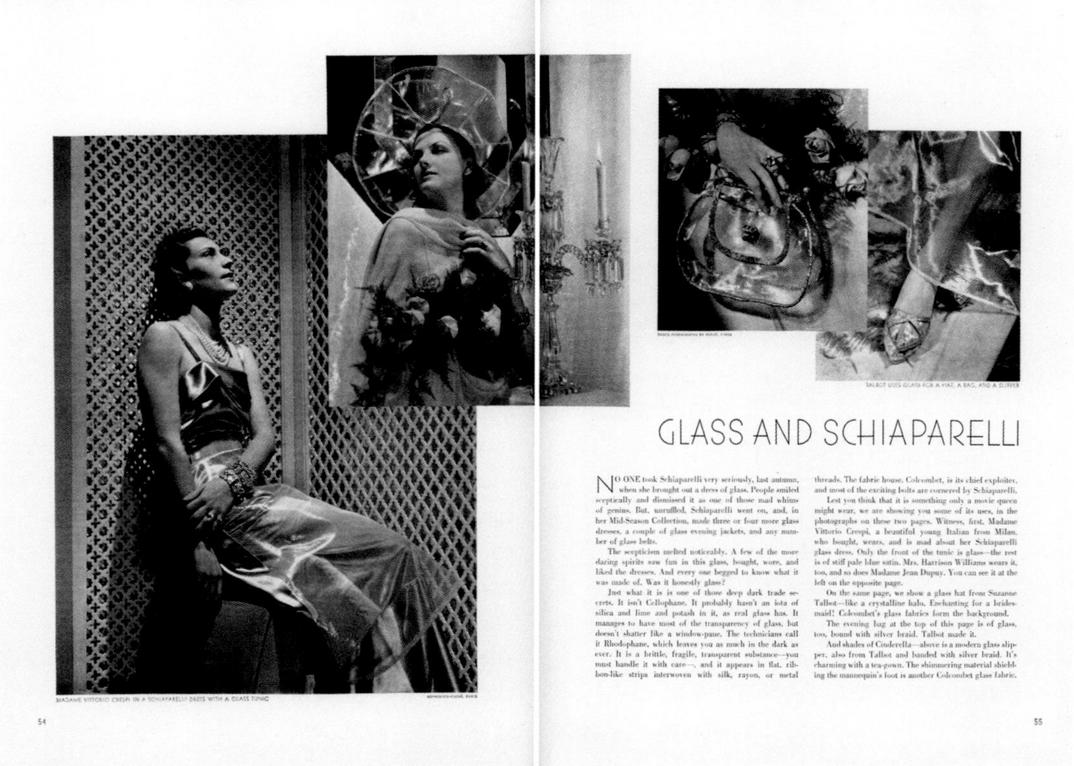

MADAME VITTORIO CRESPI IN A SCHIAPARELLI DRESS WITH A GLASS TUNIC

TALBOT USES GLASS FOR A HAT, A BAG, AND A SLIPPER

GLASS AND SCHIAPARELLI

NO ONE took Schiaparelli very seriously, last autumn, when she brought out a dress of glass. People smiled sceptically and dismissed it as one of those mad whims of genius. But, unruffled, Schiaparelli went on, and, in her Mid-Season Collection, made three or four more glass dresses, a couple of glass evening jackets, and any number of glass belts.

The scepticism melted noticeably. A few of the more daring spirits saw fun in this glass, bought, wore, and liked the dresses. And every one begged to know what it was made of. Was it honestly glass?

Just what it is is one of those deep dark trade secrets. It isn't Cellophane. It probably hasn't an iota of silica and lime and potash in it, as real glass has. It manages to have most of the transparency of glass, but doesn't shatter like a window-pane. The technicians call it Rhodophane, which leaves you as much in the dark as ever. It is a brittle, fragile, transparent substance--you must handle it with care--, and it appears in flat, ribbon-like strips interwoven with silk, rayon, or metal threads. The fabric house, Colcombet, is its chief exploiter, and most of the exciting bolts are cornered by Schiaparelli.

Lest you think that it is something only a movie queen might wear, we are showing you some of its uses, in the photographs on these two pages. Witness, first, Madame Vittorio Crespi, a beautiful young Italian from Milan, who bought, wears, and is mad about her Schiaparelli glass dress. Only the front of the tunic is glass—the rest is of stiff pale blue satin. Mrs. Harrison Williams wears it, too, and so does Madame Jean Dupuy. You can see it at the left on the opposite page.

On the same page, we show a glass hat from Suzanne Talbot—like a crystalline halo. Enchanting for a bridesmaid! Colcombet's glass fabrics form the background.

The evening bag at the top of this page is of glass, too, bound with silver braid. Talbot made it.

And shades of Cinderella—above is a modern glass slipper, also from Talbot and banded with silver braid. It's charming with a tea-gown. The shimmering material shielding the mannequin's foot is another Colcombet glass fabric.

54

55

56. Left: George Hoyningen-Huene, Madame Vittorio Crespi, ensemble by Schiaparelli; centre and right: Horst, hat, bag and slippers by Suzanne Talbot, 'Glass and Schiaparelli', American *Vogue*, 15 January 1935

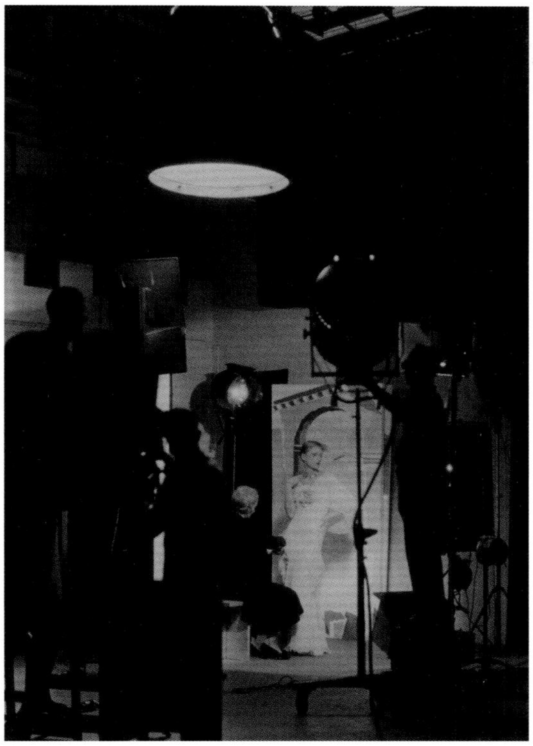

57. George Hoyningen-Huene
self-portrait with Lee Miller
in the *Vogue* studio, Paris, 1931

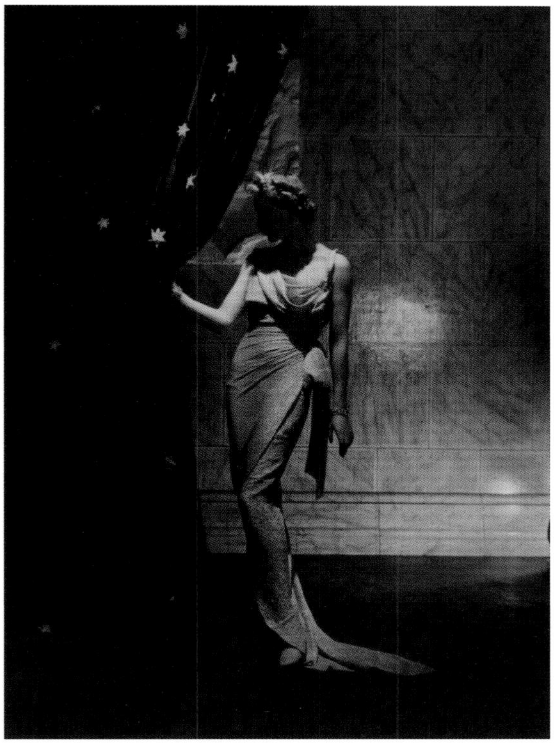

58. Cora Hemmet, dress by Jean Patou,
jewellery by Boucheron, 1935

garment – 'I accentuated the important parts of the dress and chose not to show the whole thing'[21] – may even have appealed to couturiers wary of allowing their work to be easily copied, for, despite the best efforts of the Chambre Syndicale to protect the couturier's original designs, the industry had a morbid fear of counterfeiters. Vionnet was one of the most difficult designers for *Vogue* editors to deal with because of her belief in her work as a unique art. Ballard recalled, 'In 1935 she showed her collection with a pathological fear of being copied and a hatred for the press that made it impossible to give her what she deserved in editorial praise. For every dress that *Vogue* was allowed to photograph, the Duchesse d'Ayen [Solange d'Ayen, 1898–1976, the aristocratic fashion editor of French *Vogue*] would have to go personally, practically on her knees, and beg Vionnet's Machiavellian Egyptian director for it. He might let her have one dress for an hour with one of Vionnet's workers sitting in the studio watching everything we did with it. I remember the magnificent bias gold lamé that Horst photographed on Lud one night in fifteen minutes, the dress so superbly designed that it was impossible not to have a memorable picture.'[22]

Paris between the wars was populated by an artistic milieu of wealthy society figures, intelligentsia, displaced Russian royalty, artists, film-makers and numerous fashion designers. Horst became part of the creative fervour. 'It was quite a big thing to be photographed in the studios by a famous photographer – it was all part of fashion. That is to say, at a certain point if you were a fashionable person a picture could be arranged of you in a fashionable magazine in a fashionable pose taken by a fashionable photographer who, the chances are, you'd later meet at dinner, like Horst.'[23] Temporarily abandoning the studio, Horst was commissioned to photograph fashionable women 'at home' in their chateaux or town houses for society columns, and naturally dressed à la mode.

For French *Vogue*, Horst also took many photographs of the beau monde in fancy dress, for one of the most notable forms of entertainment from the 1930s up to the outbreak of war were the private fêtes and extravagant balls hosted by the wealthy. A gift to Paris couturiers, no expense was spared with regard to dress. In June 1934, Baron Nicolas 'Niki' de Gunzburg staged a 'Bal de Valses' (also known as 'A Night at Schönbrunn'), for which lavish costumes were designed by Bérard, Alix, Mainbocher and Lanvin, and made by Mme Karinska of the Ballets Russes. Such events also provided the opportunity for Horst to widen his circle of fashion luminaries, for it was at the 'Bal de Valses' that Horst first met Coco Chanel. 'Horst found himself being photographed with Chanel. It was the first time he had seen her. He was introduced to her, but she merely said "Bon soir"; and that was that', recalled Valentine Lawford, Horst's biographer and partner.[24]

The relationship between Chanel and the *Vogue* offices was, in the early 1930s, frosty because of, according to Liberman, a falling out with Mr Condé Nast.[25] In 1933, it was recorded that 'She wishes to release no models ... unless they are shown alone on a page, the facing page not containing models from other houses.'[26] Horst's charm prevailed, however: 'For years she had firmly refused to allow her dresses to be photographed, let alone herself, for *Vogue*. But one day in 1937, to the frank astonishment of *Vogue*'s Paris office, she sent word that she would consent to be photographed – on one condition: that I should be the photographer.'[27]

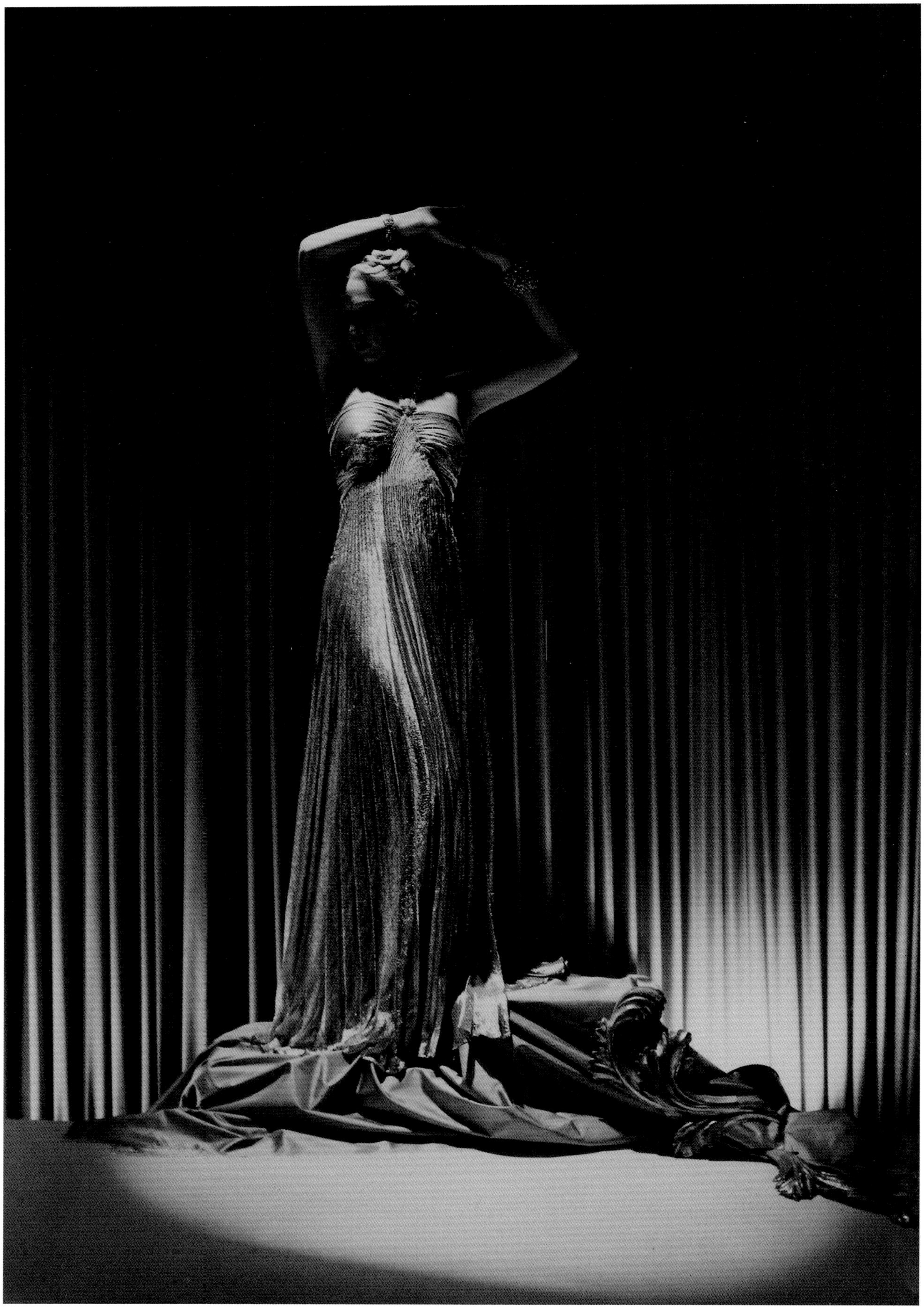

59. Sonia Colmer, dress by Vionnet, jewellery by Mauboussin, 1937

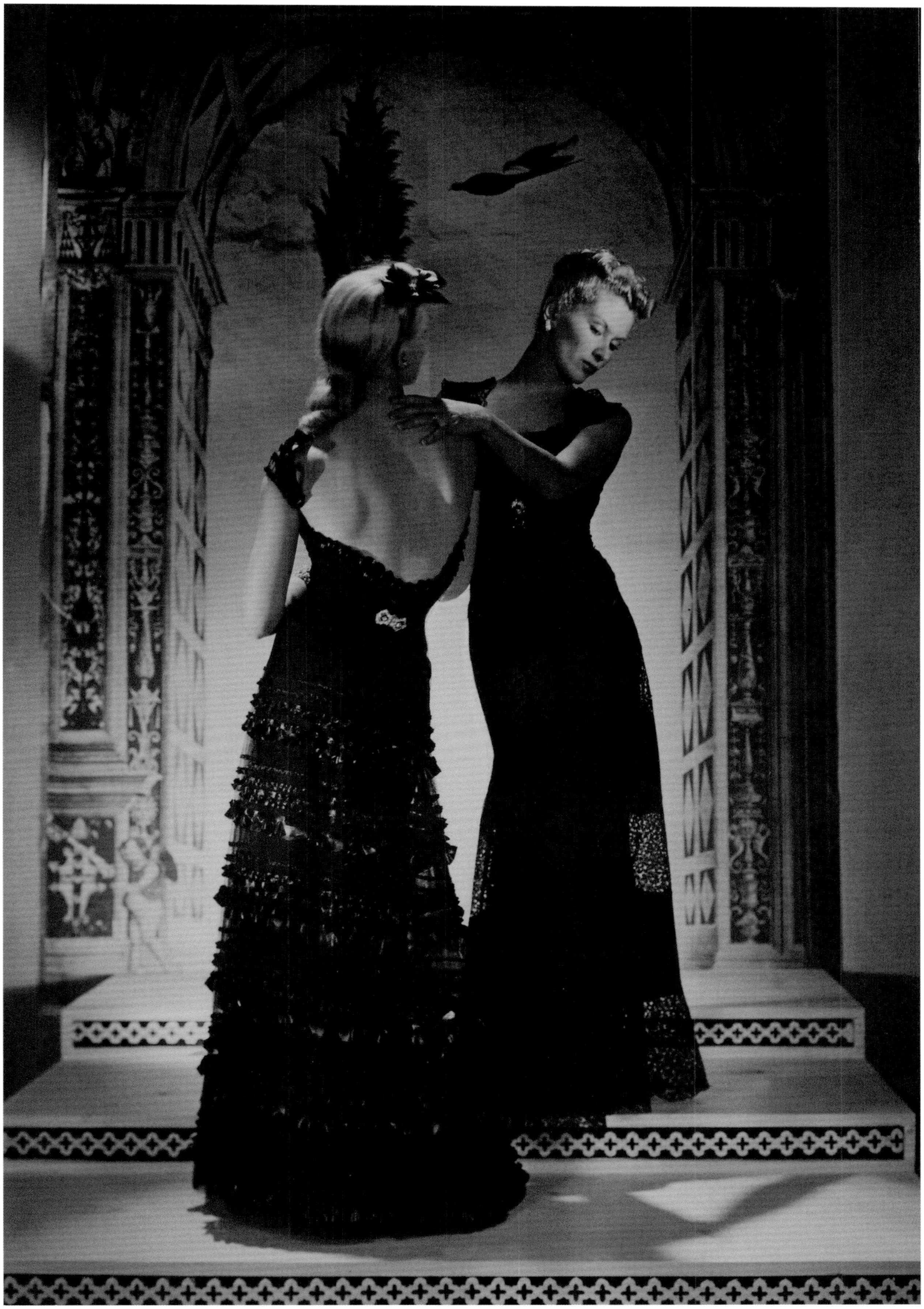

60. Madame Buchardt and
Lisa Fonssagrives, dresses by Chanel, 1938

Although the session was, in Horst's words, 'a flop', a second private sitting resulted in a profile portrait that remained Chanel's favourite throughout her life (pl.51). Diana Vreeland recalled, 'Horst in the 'thirties took tender portraits of Chanel ... There's a gentleness of lighting and a tenderness of expression. There's nothing of the mannequin in her. She's not totally sure of herself. She looks ... away. And this was when Chanel was at the height of her power.'[28] The portrait abounds with rich detail; Chanel reclines in a Louis XVI-style chair that Horst sourced, inspired by a similar item in Chanel's apartment, the delicate outline of her profile set against the satin upholstery. Simply dressed, but with her trademark bold jewellery, and holding her cigarette in a characteristically masculine way, Chanel was the epitome of modernity. Ballard recalled, 'Chanel's own lifestyle fuelled her ideas of how modern women everywhere should look, act, and dress. Her own slim boyish figure and cropped hair became an ideal, as did her tanned skin, active lifestyle, and financial independence.'[29]

A 'Bal Oriental' followed in 1935, hosted by Daisy Fellowes whom Schiaparelli regularly, despite her immense wealth, dressed for free for the publicity. Horst captured the spectacle, not only at the event but also in a series of portraits taken in the *Vogue* studio the previous evening, which recorded the exotic costumes and their wearers. The hostess, her hair elaborately shellacked with black lacquered leaves, is pictured wearing a white Mandarin dress by Schiaparelli. The couturière herself chose to dress as a 'Venetian blackamoor' in gold lamé jacket and turban. In Horst's portrait of her, Schiaparelli is perched on a carved stand holding an African mask, her pose echoed by the looming shadow thrown on to the wall behind.[30]

Lawford wrote of Schiaparelli that she 'swept across the sky of the Paris couture of the thirties like a comet' (pl.63).[31] Her witty, themed collections were extremely chic, and photographs of her designs began to dominate the pages of *Vogue*, 'an infuriating taunt in the faces of all the other couturiers because her models outnumbered the rest in the magazines', wrote Ballard.[32] Although Chanel and Schiaparelli were rivals, Célia Bertin points out how closely connected they were: 'They were at once artists, instigators and patrons; they encouraged fashion and fantasy.'[33] Both introduced new materials and inverted the norms of traditional couture styling – in the case of Chanel, utilizing practical jersey fabric, making it fashionable to wear strings of pearls during the day with tweeds but fantastic costume jewellery at night, and introducing easy, masculine touches such as pockets, into which the designer would characteristically thrust her hands. Schiaparelli's innovations included padded shoulders, often emphasized with folds of fabric or horsehair; fur bracelets; veined gloves with red nails; spectacular costume jewellery; lapel clips and novelty buttons designed by Jean Schlumberger; and zips, even on evening clothes, a development notable enough to be reported in *LIFE* magazine: 'Overnight, the zipper, which since 1913 had been an accepted functional gadget for smooth, secure closings, became important as a style element.'[34]

In her close collaborations with Salvador Dalí and Jean Cocteau, Schiaparelli interpreted Surrealism's shock value and translated it into headline fashions. Horst's photographs of her designs responded to the psychological ploys in her work, and played on the disruption of the body into separated parts, which he depicted as disembodied architectural fragments (pls 64, 65). Dissecting the model with a

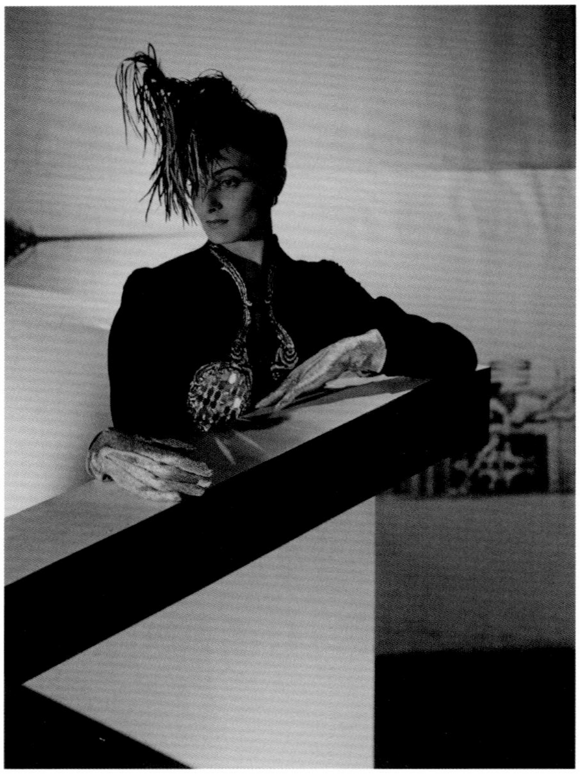

61. Lyla Zelensky, hat and dinner suit by Schiaparelli, 1938

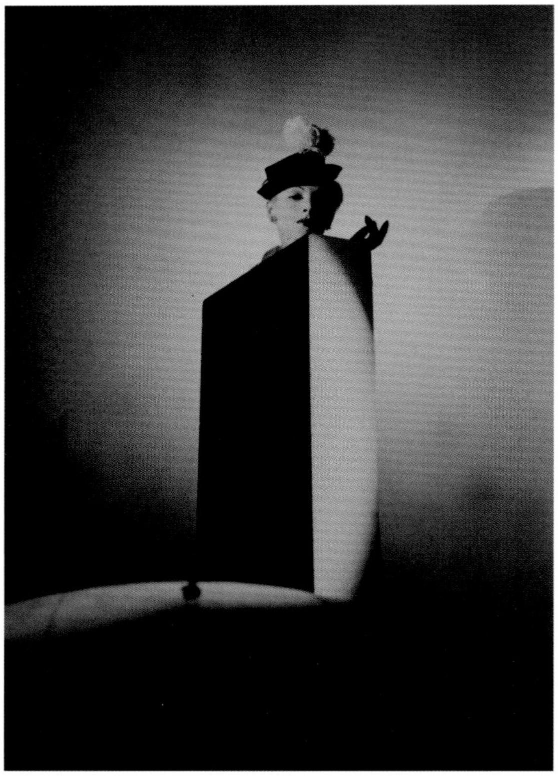

62. Andrée Lorain, hat by Schiaparelli, 1938

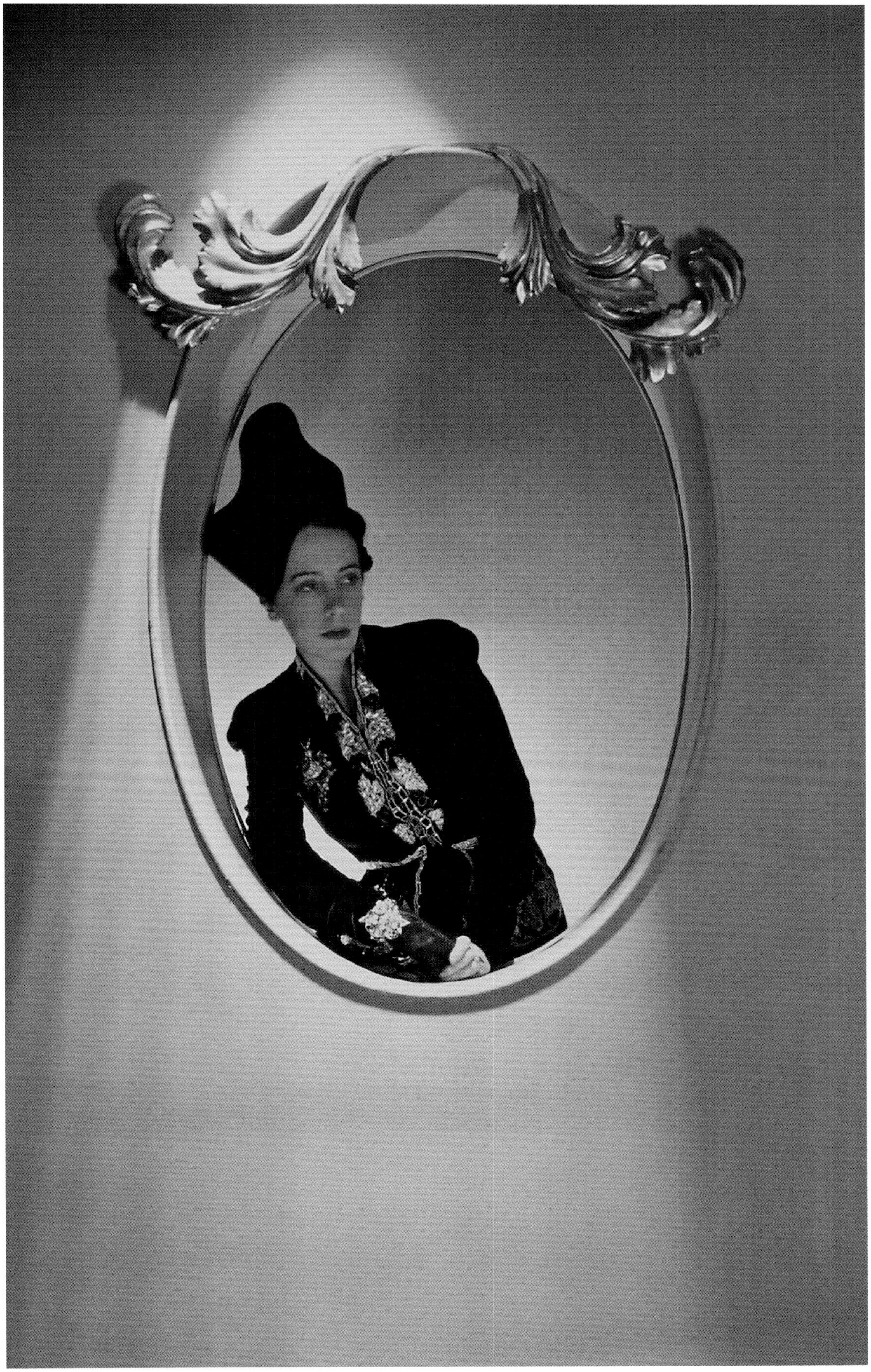

63. Elsa Schiaparelli, Paris, 1937

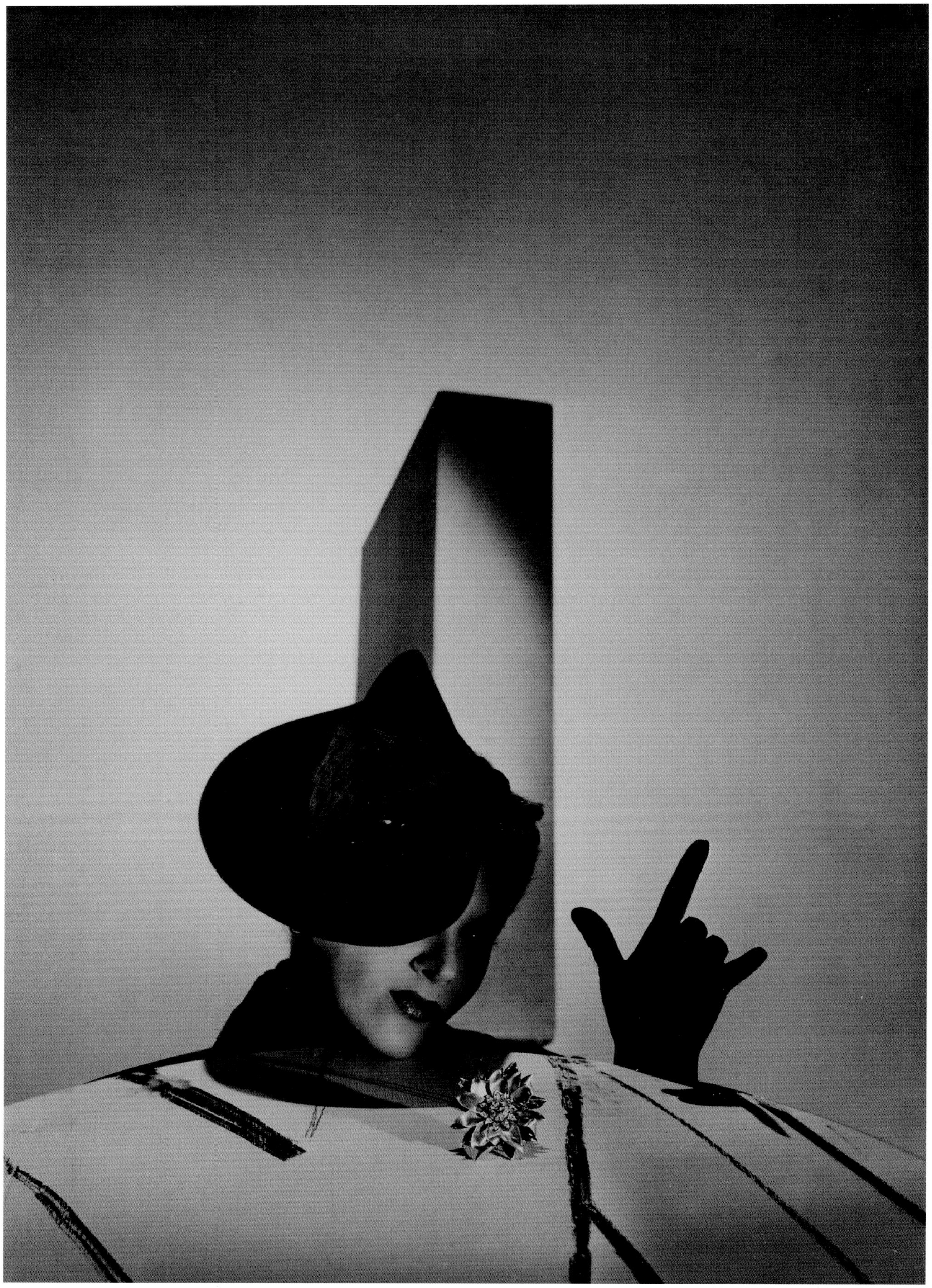

64. Lisa Fonssagrives, hat by Suzy,
jewellery by Boucheron, 1938

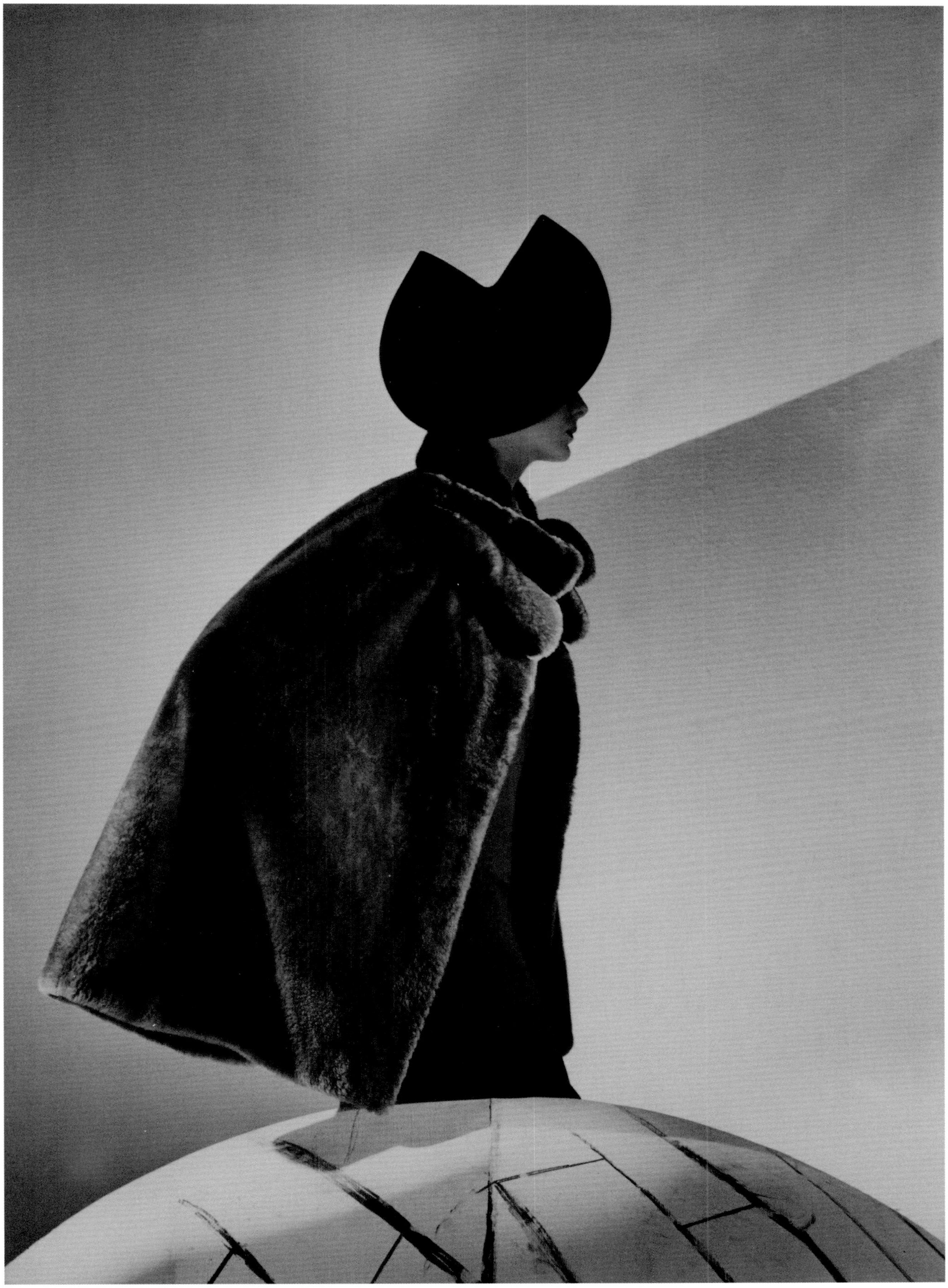

65. Mary Belevsky, beret and cape by Lanvin,
jewellery by Boucheron, 1938

gleaming horizontal surface in order to focus on the torso and hands, he showed an embellished jacket of 1938 with Rococo hand mirrors placed over the breasts and, looming disconcertingly large in the foreground, hands clad in metallic gloves (pl.61).[35] In another series, hats are shown on what appears to be a disembodied head, the body hidden behind a plinth (pl.62), with the caption 'Significant things are beginning to emerge from behind the wall of the future ...', while in another, proportion is distorted, the model wearing a 'doll-size tricorn' hat of black felt, the crown covered in satin bows.[36] Only head and hands are visible amidst the geometric props.

Schiaparelli's themed collections, and what Bettina Ballard called 'her daring nonsense ... plus a true sense of hard chic', made Schiaparelli entirely appropriate for those final frivolous years before the Second World War.[37] In 1937, as Ballard prepared to leave for New York to 'refresh' her American viewpoint, she was determined to demonstrate her transformation from ingénue American fashion editor into fashion sophisticate, a sartorial education bestowed upon her by the capital of haute couture. The contents of her suitcases and trunks were the epitome of Parisian chic of the late 1930s: 'I really worked on my New York wardrobe ... I concentrated on a Handsome black Schiaparelli suit with fancy buttons, a Creed suit, and a Molyneux navy dress and jacket for day with no less than twenty of the most conspicuous hats in Paris from Suzy, Agnes, Reboux, and Rose Descat ... I was hat mad. Chanel lent me, from her own closet, two sublime evening costumes ... Both had soft, long skirts pleated onto bare bodices and their own waist-length bolero jackets – simple and very elegant because of the lavish oriental brocaded lamé fabrics. For a real shocker I took Schiaparelli's gold embroidered black monkey jacket, a long black skirt, and matching high chechia hat.'[38]

As Ballard sailed on her journey from the Old World to the New, on a luxurious ship aptly named the *Paris*, she found herself part of a microcosm of a society in transition. Among the passengers were Marlene Dietrich, bound for Hollywood, who 'wore slacks and a man's jacket and fedora hat all day – the first woman I had ever seen wear pants in public ...'. Another, perhaps inevitably, was that dramatist and 'eye' of fashion, Horst, on one of his last trips to New York before the outbreak of war. His urbane conviviality made Ballard's trip 'wonderful ... a companion to dine with and laugh with'.[39]

Alexander Liberman, who like Horst found refuge within the artistic circles of Paris and then New York, and enjoyed a similarly long career with *Vogue*, viewed the decade as a high point in fashion's chronology: 'A unique collaboration of talent, circumstance and opportunity lifted fashion photography in the 1930s into an instinctive place as a separate visual genre in the arts of the twentieth century.'[40] Looking back on that glittering period, Horst himself reflected, 'We never felt we were just taking a photograph. We were making a record of our time.'[41]

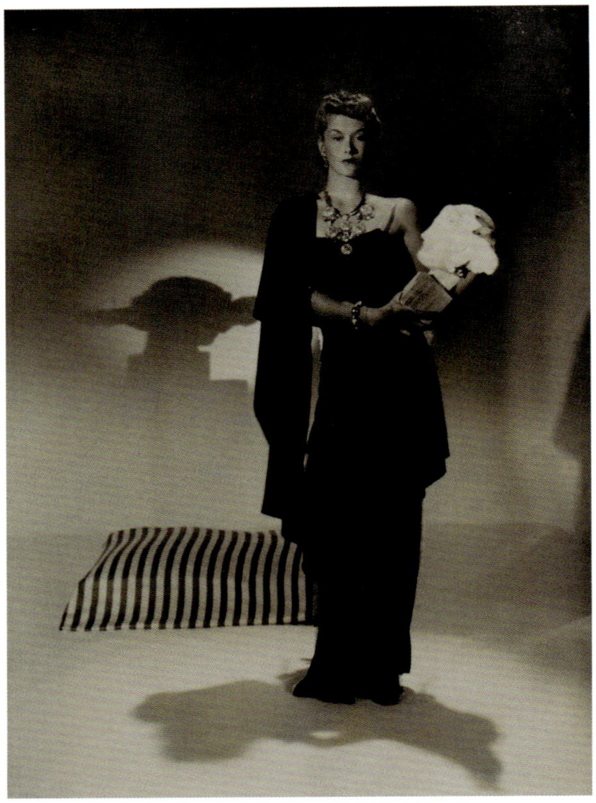

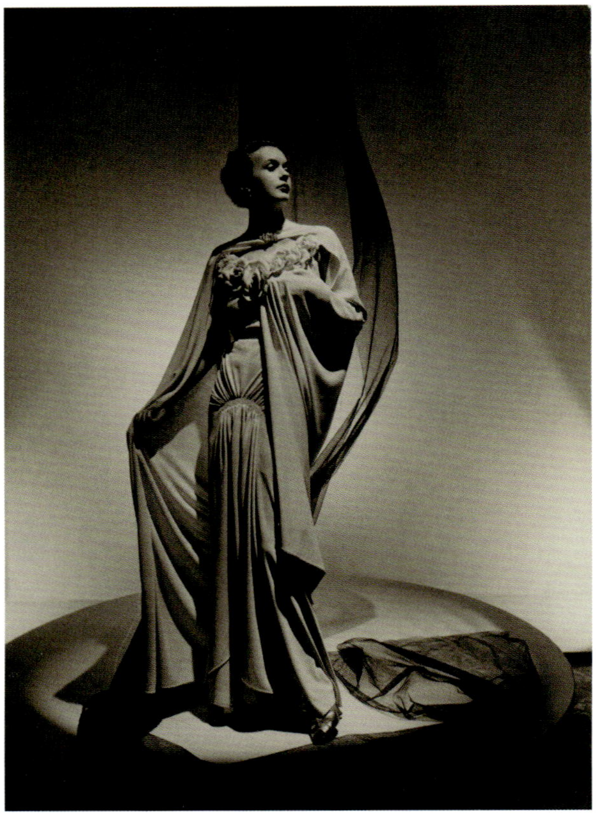

66. Lisa Fonssagrives, dress by Chanel, 1939

67. Dress by Robert Piguet, 1936

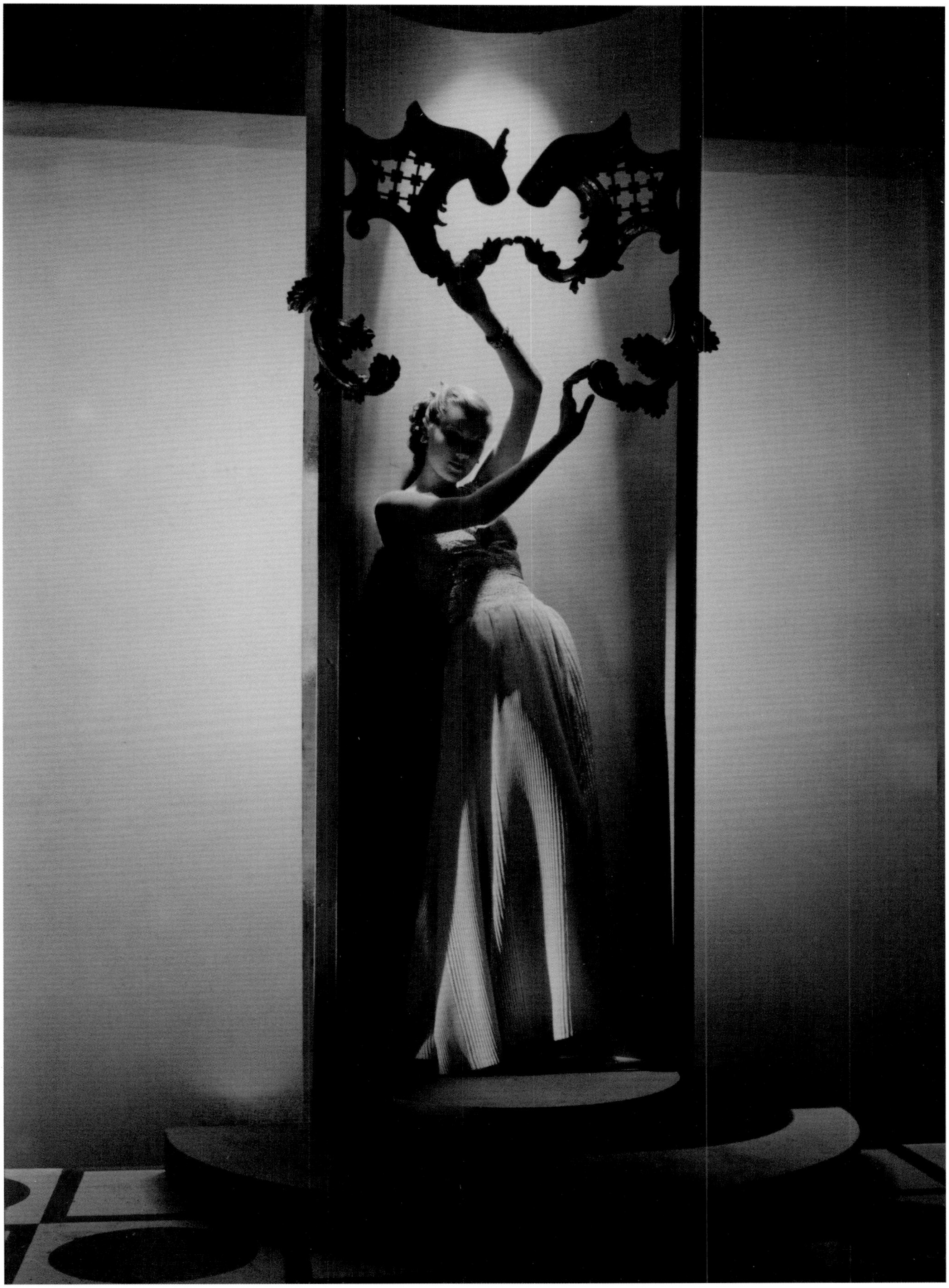

68. Constant, dress by Chanel,
jewellery by Boucheron, 1937

Mainbocher Corset, Paris, 1939

This most alluring of fashion photographs depicts a model wearing a back-lacing corset of pink satin, made by Detolle for Mainbocher's Autumn/Winter 1939 collection. The image is both sensual and melancholy and, for Horst, it came to represent a turning point, the end of a charmed era. He said of it 45 years later:

> It was the last photograph I took in Paris before the war. I left the studio at 4:00a.m., went back to the house, picked up my bags and caught the 7:00a.m. train to Le Havre to board the *Normandie*. We all felt that war was coming. Too much armament, too much talk. And you knew that whatever happened, life would be completely different after. I had found a family in Paris, and a way of life. The clothes, the books, the apartment, everything was left behind. I had left Germany, Huene had left Russia, and now we experienced the same kind of loss all over again. This photograph is peculiar – for me, it is the essence of that moment. While I was taking it, I was thinking of all that I was leaving behind.[1]

The model, known only as Madame Bernon, assumes the role of Aphrodite or Venus, goddess of love, beauty and pleasure, the proportions and contours of her body as perfect as a classical statue. *Vogue* art director Dr Mehemed Agha commented on the photographer's ability to render human flesh: 'Horst has the sculptor's feeling for form and volume ... One has the impression that, if it were possible to walk around his models on their pedestals, they would look equally good from the back or from the side.'[2] The photograph also references painted examples, nude Venuses by Paolo Veronese and Diego Velázquez in particular. Like Velázquez's *Rokeby Venus*, Horst's goddess is without her traditional symbols of roses and myrtle. Horst's sketchbook, however, contains what appear to be two preparatory drawings, in which a plant is included to the right of the figure. Perhaps he originally intended to use such a prop, but removed it for a purer composition. Again echoing the *Rokeby Venus*, the ribbons of the corset that trail in the lower portion of the image evoke Cupid's silken fetters and create just enough 'mess' to balance the model's physical perfection; Horst once commented, 'My best pictures always have a little mess.'[3] The balustrade that bisects the picture plane appears to be made of marble, but was likely painted to look as such and constructed by the studio's craftsmen. Horst used spotlights and reflectors to create the deep shadows and highlights (he was known to spend as long as two days perfecting the arrangement of lights for a single shoot). So complex was the lighting in this photograph, he later commented that he would never be able to recreate it.

The image was carefully retouched before it was printed in *Vogue*: the corset was altered to appear to cling tightly to the body and the model's waist was made even smaller. The original, in which the corset hangs loosely at one side, has a more provocative effect and is the version that Horst himself preferred.[4]

In 1939, the corseted silhouette became front-page news from the couture collections. *Vogue* declared, 'The corset is the key to new Paris silhouettes'[5] and *LIFE* magazine reported, 'Ever since January there has been loud chatter on both sides of the Atlantic about tight waists and back-laced corsets. But Mainbocher's creation was a bombshell, which made the front pages of the U.S. press ... Equally popular were Mainbocher's full-bosomed, hippy evening gowns worn over the same corset. Many other silhouettes were seen in the 4,000-odd models viewed at the 20 important houses. The tight waist was the recurrent theme.'[6] Described as the 'wasp-waist' or 'whittle-waist',[7] the shape harked back to the fashions of the Victorian era. Although magazines promised that these new foundation garments were more comfortable than ever, Mainbocher's boned corset, specifically for evening, did not permit the wearer to bend. Corsets were among the several thousand items purchased by American fashion buyers in Paris and shipped to the United States on the luxury ocean liner SS *Normandie*, which departed Le Havre, France, on 23 August 1939 and arrived in New York five days later. Horst was aboard the ship too, a second-cabin traveller whose name appears on the list of 'Alien passengers' produced for the United States Immigrant Inspector. He could not have known at the time that it would be the *Normandie*'s final Atlantic crossing, or that war would prevent him from seeing Paris again until 1946.

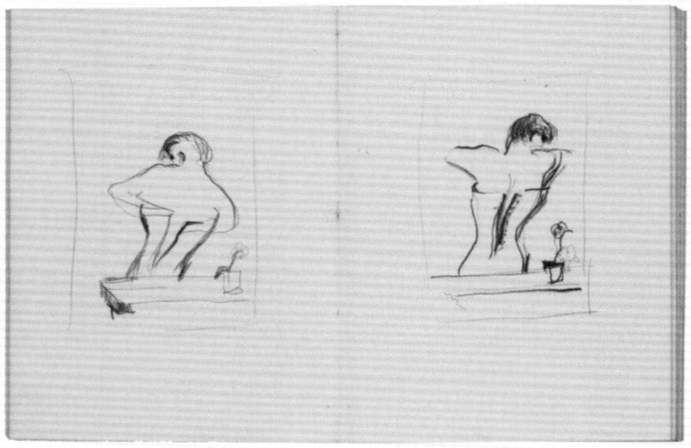

69. Horst's sketchbook, undated

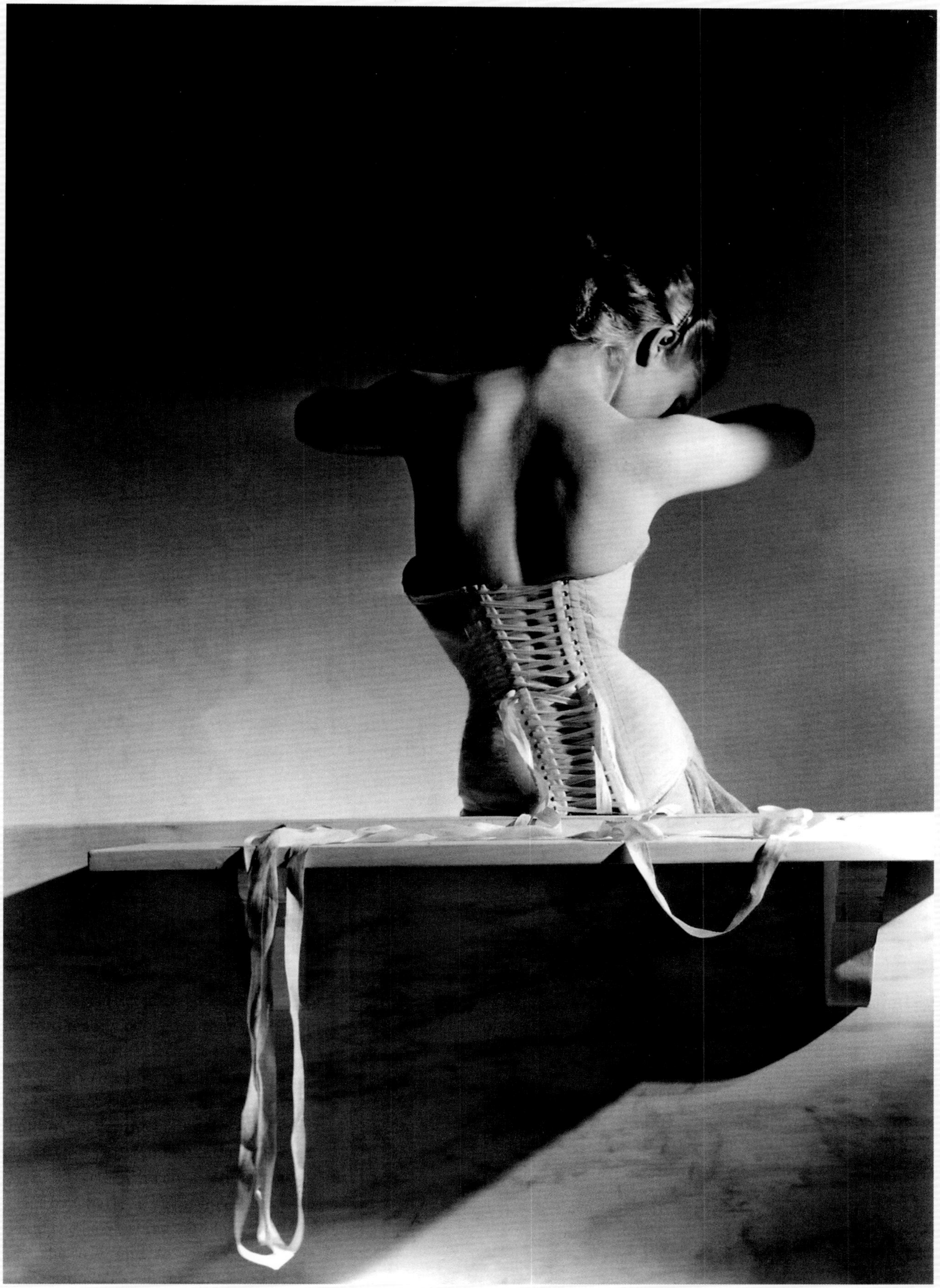

70. Madame Bernon, corset by
Detolle for Mainbocher, 1939

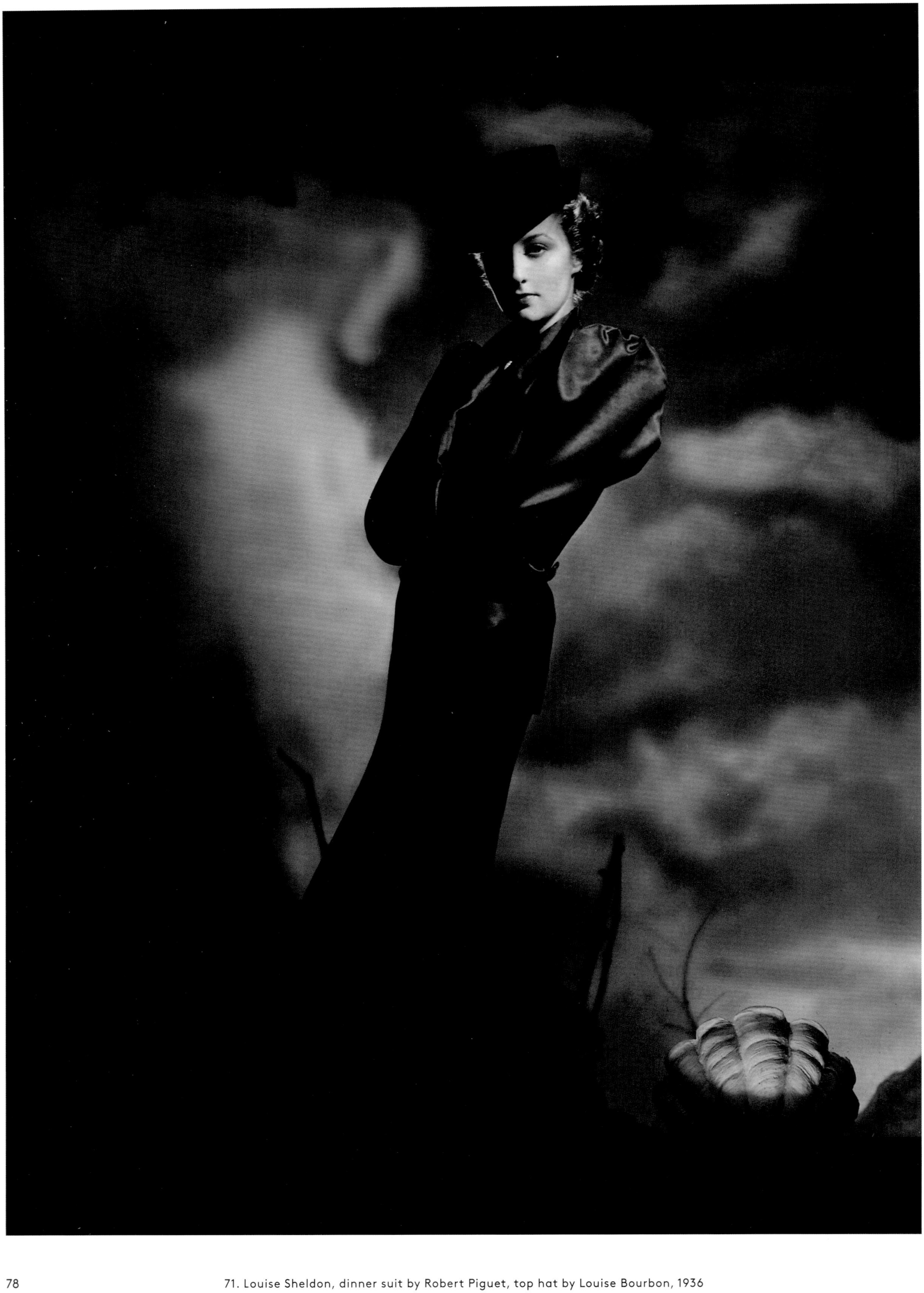

71. Louise Sheldon, dinner suit by Robert Piguet, top hat by Louise Bourbon, 1936

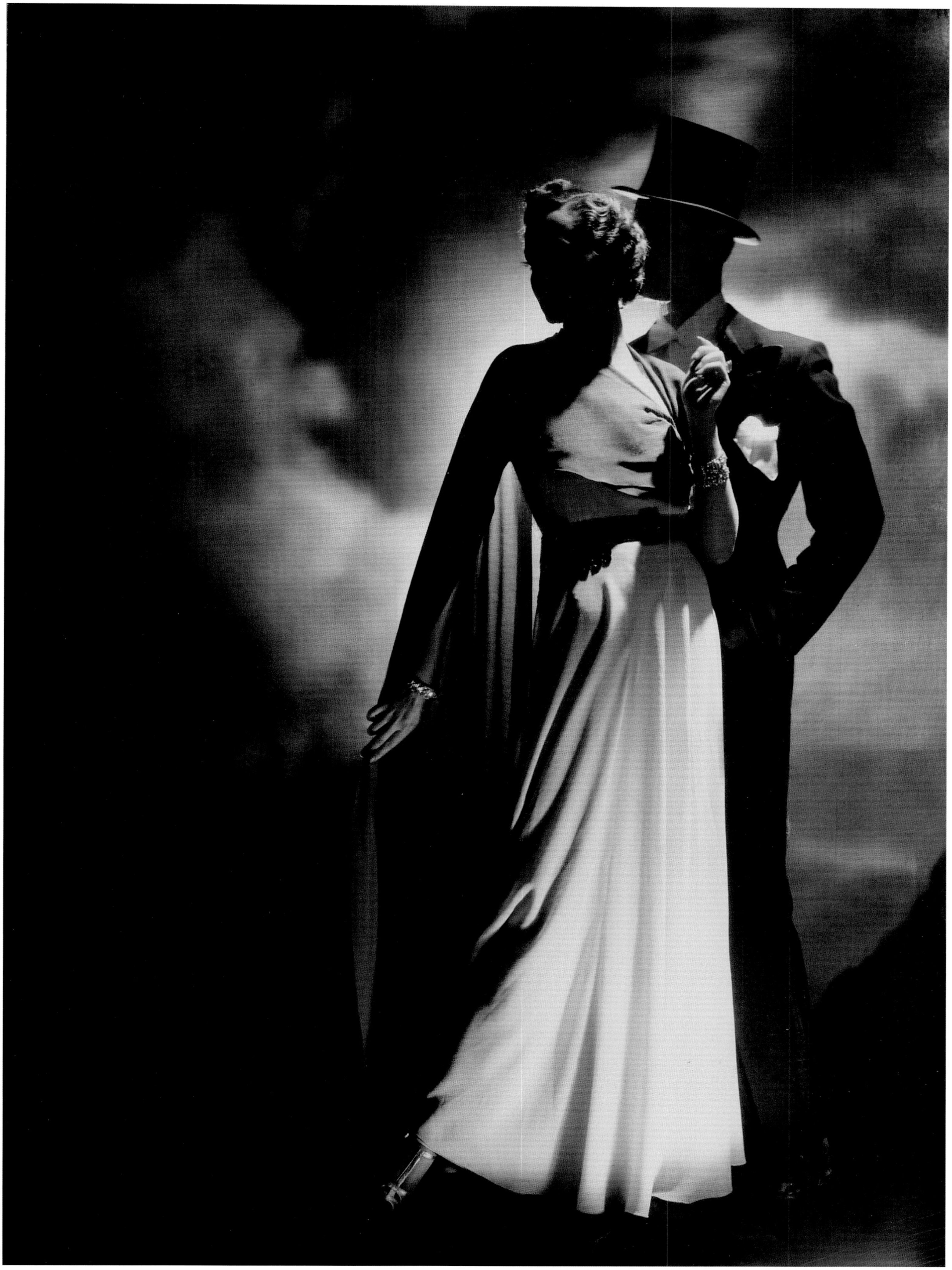

72. Louise Sheldon, dress by Lucien Lelong, 1936

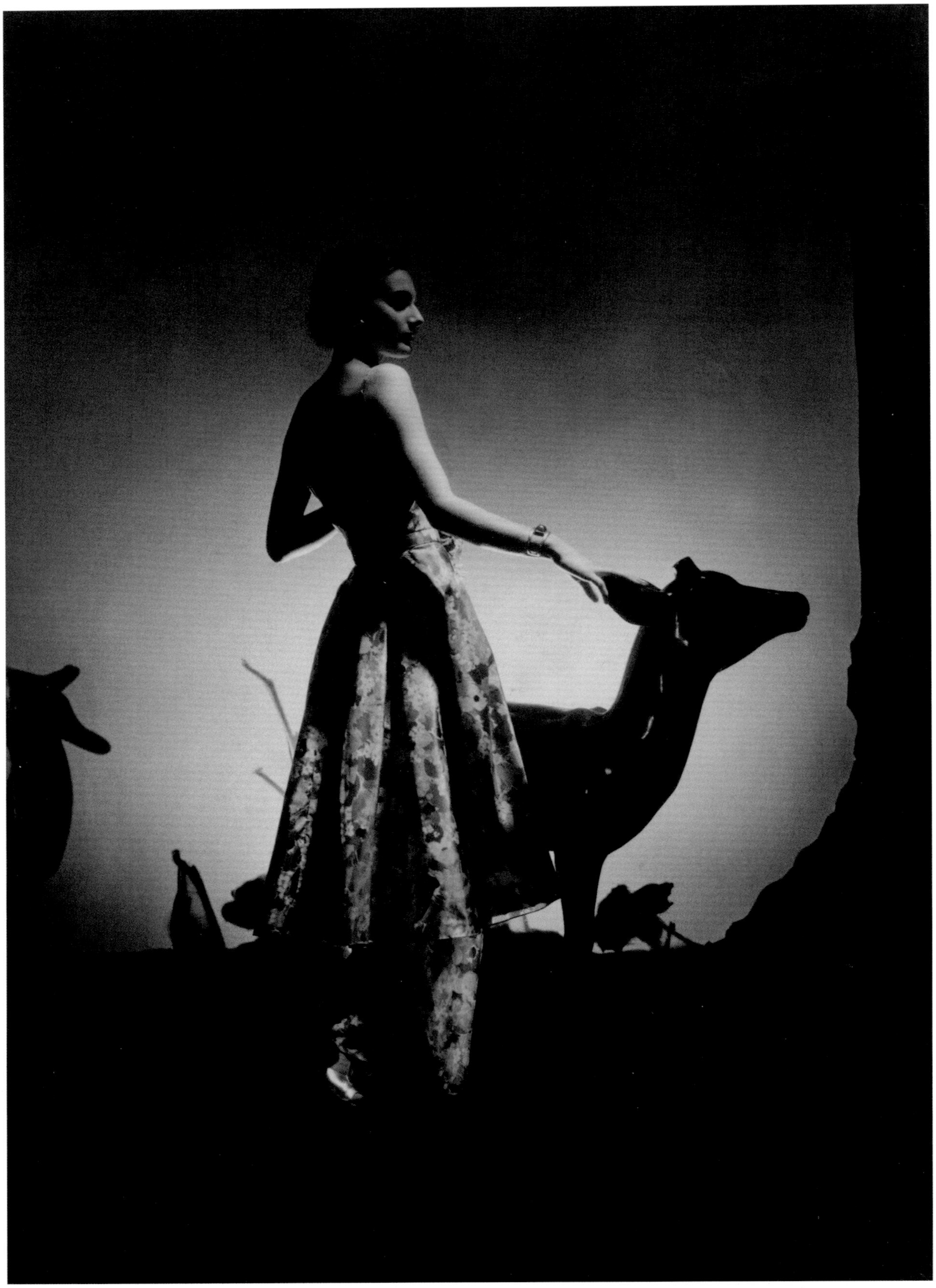

73. Lyla Zelensky, dress by Mainbocher, jewellery by Herz, 1936

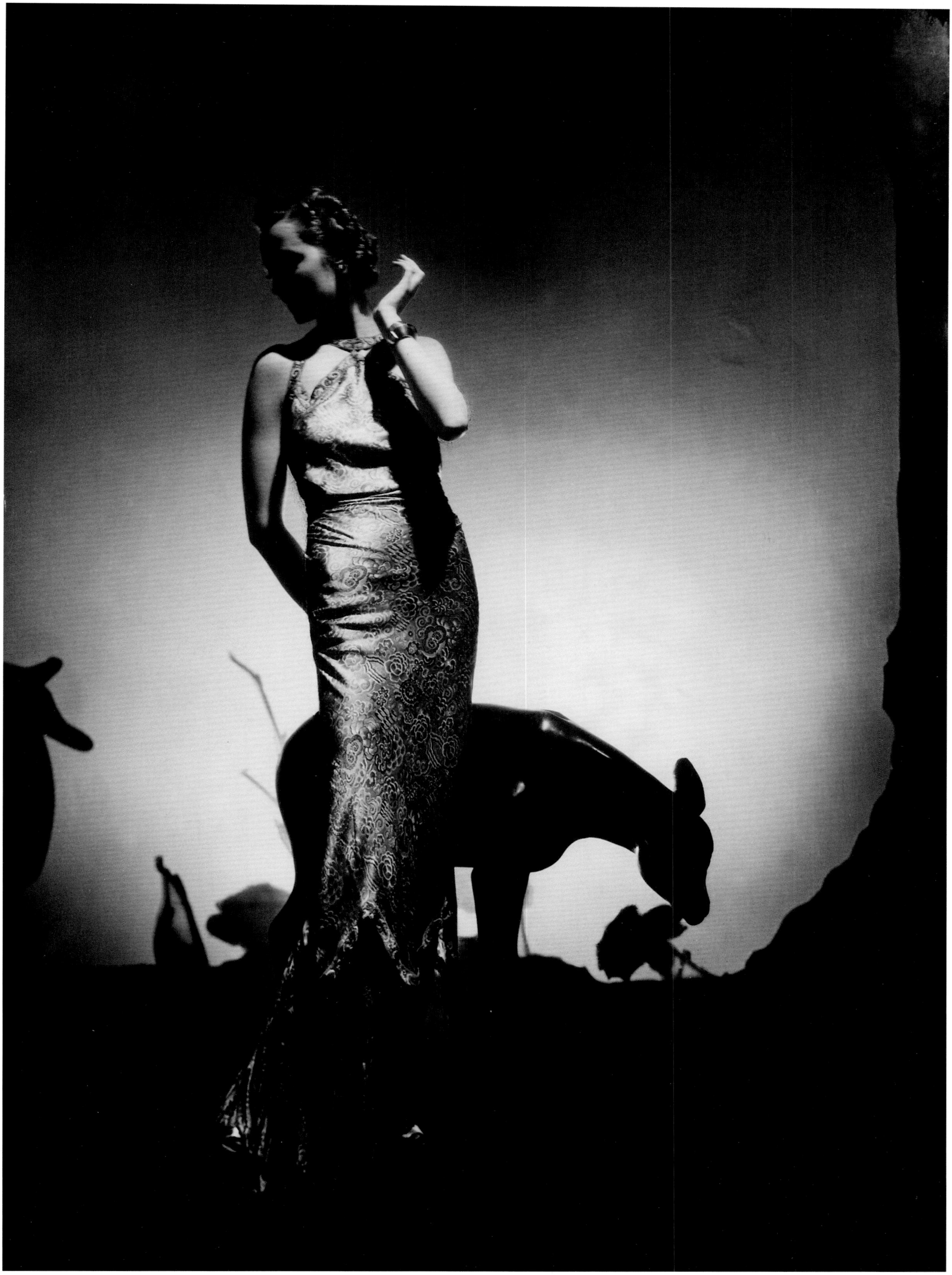

74. Louise Sheldon, dress by Mainbocher, 1936

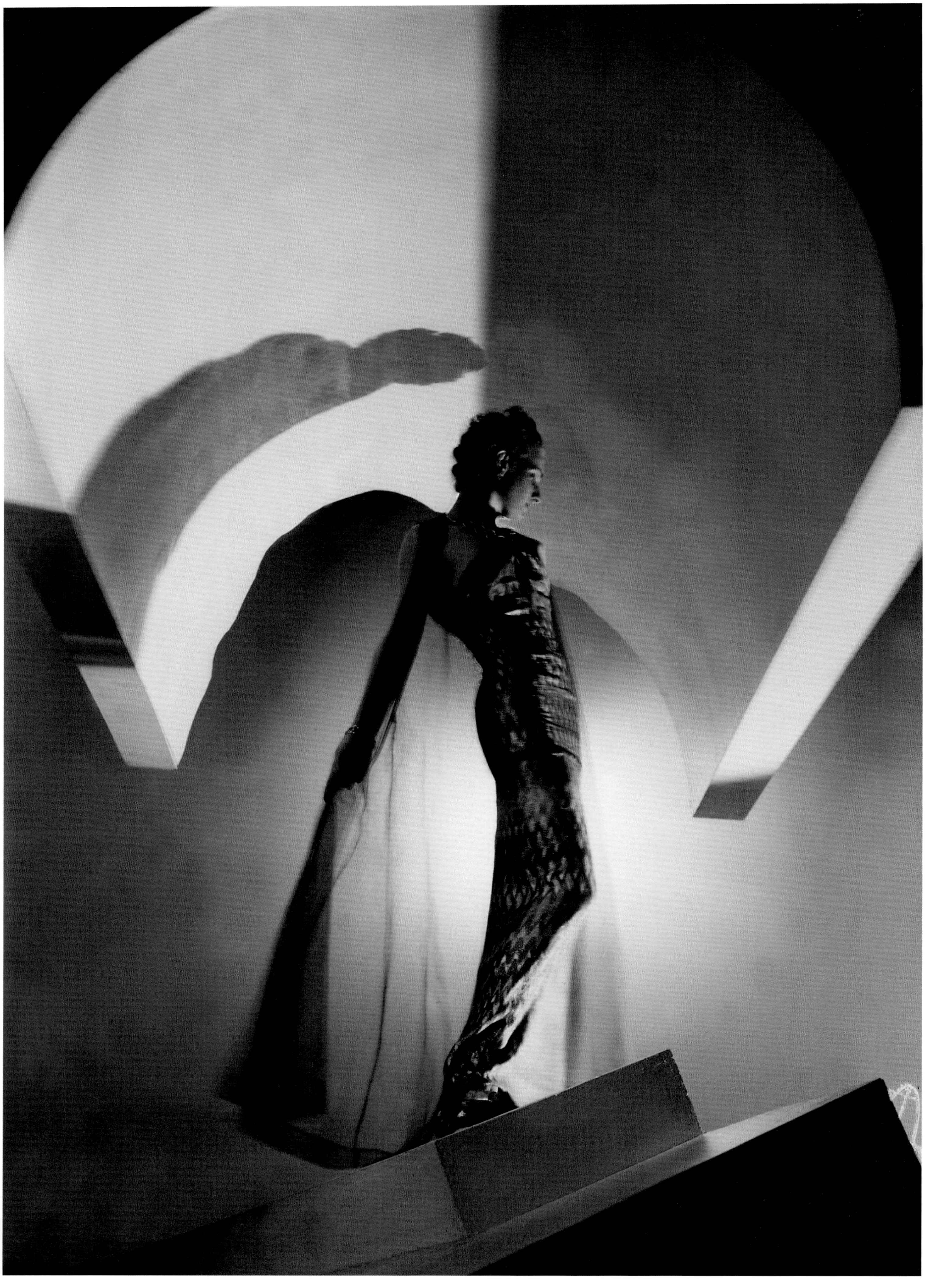

75. Lyla Zelensky, dress by Molyneux, 1937

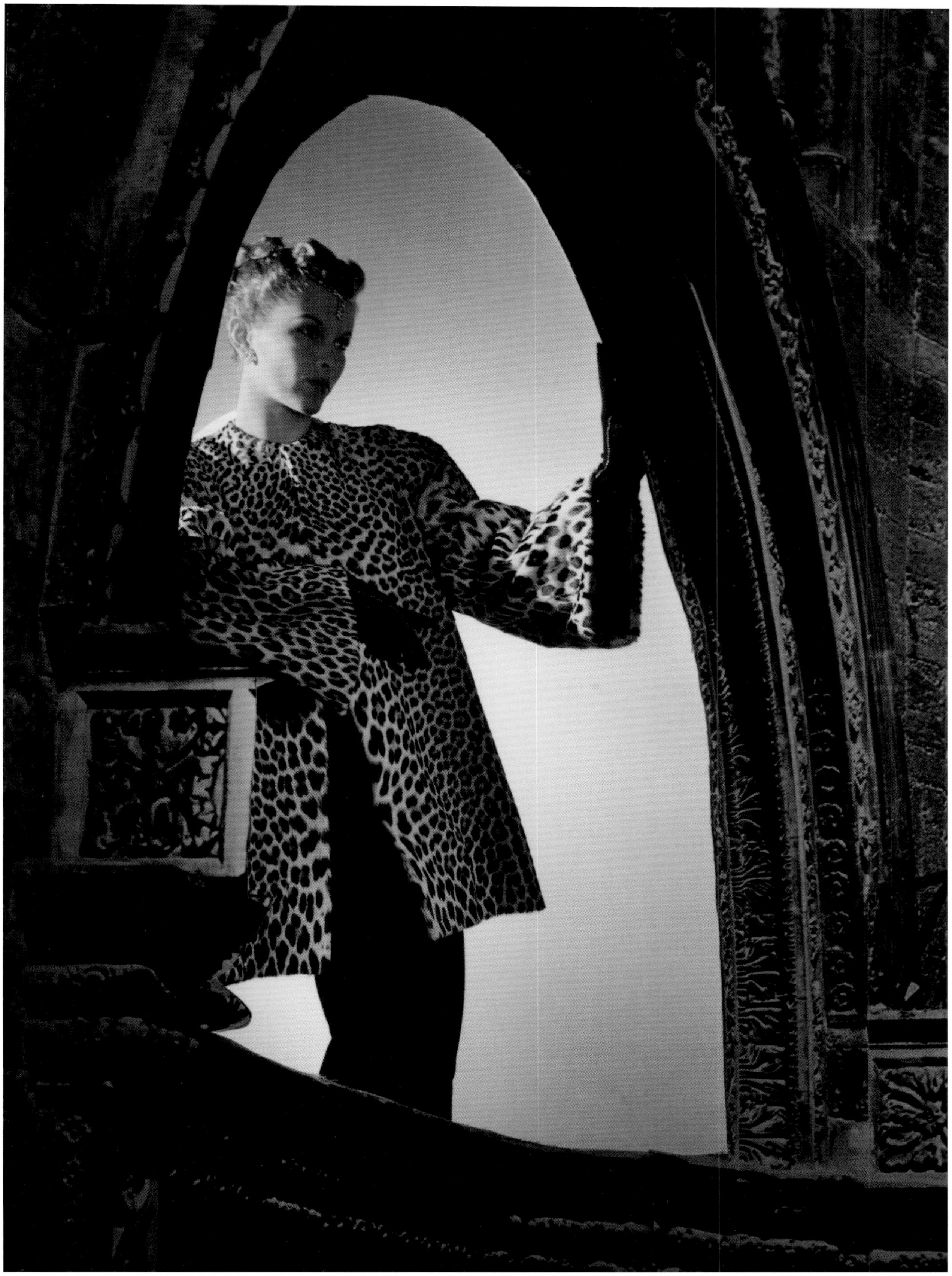

76. Lisa Fonssagrives, coat by Molyneux, 1938

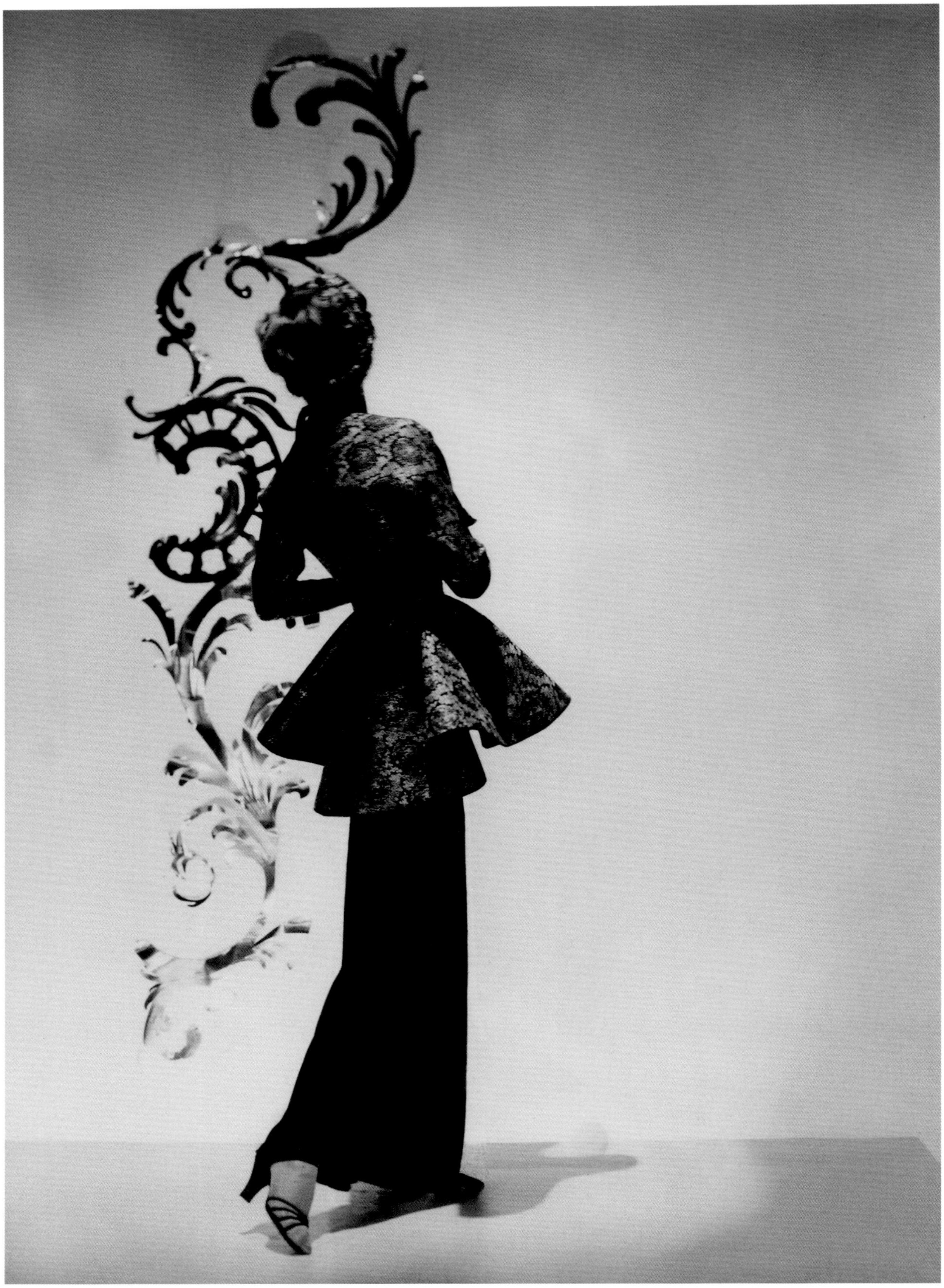

77. Lyla Zelensky, tunic by Alix, sandals by Bally, 1936

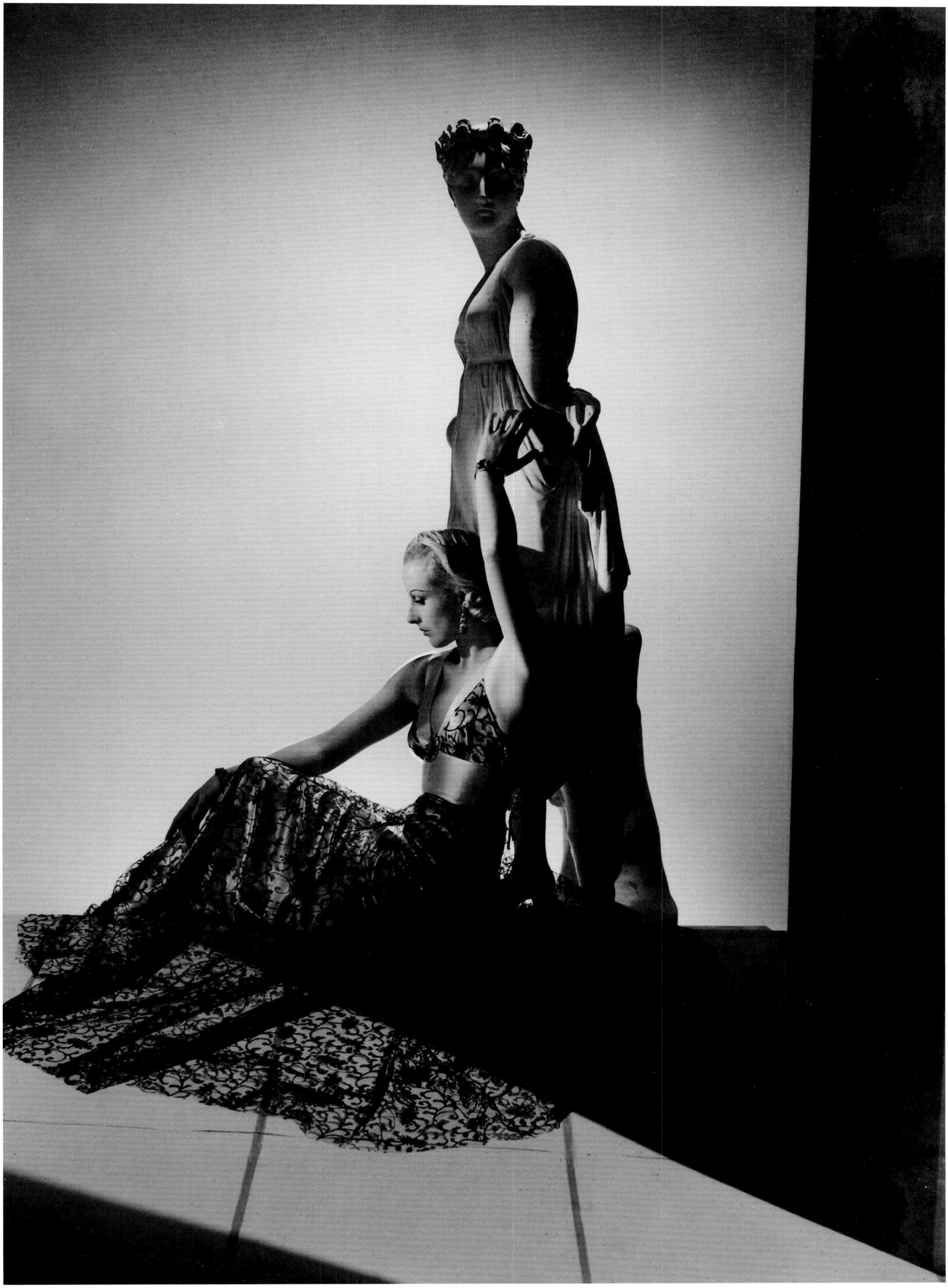

78. Cora Van Millingen, dress by Lucien Lelong, jewellery by Mauboussin, 1937

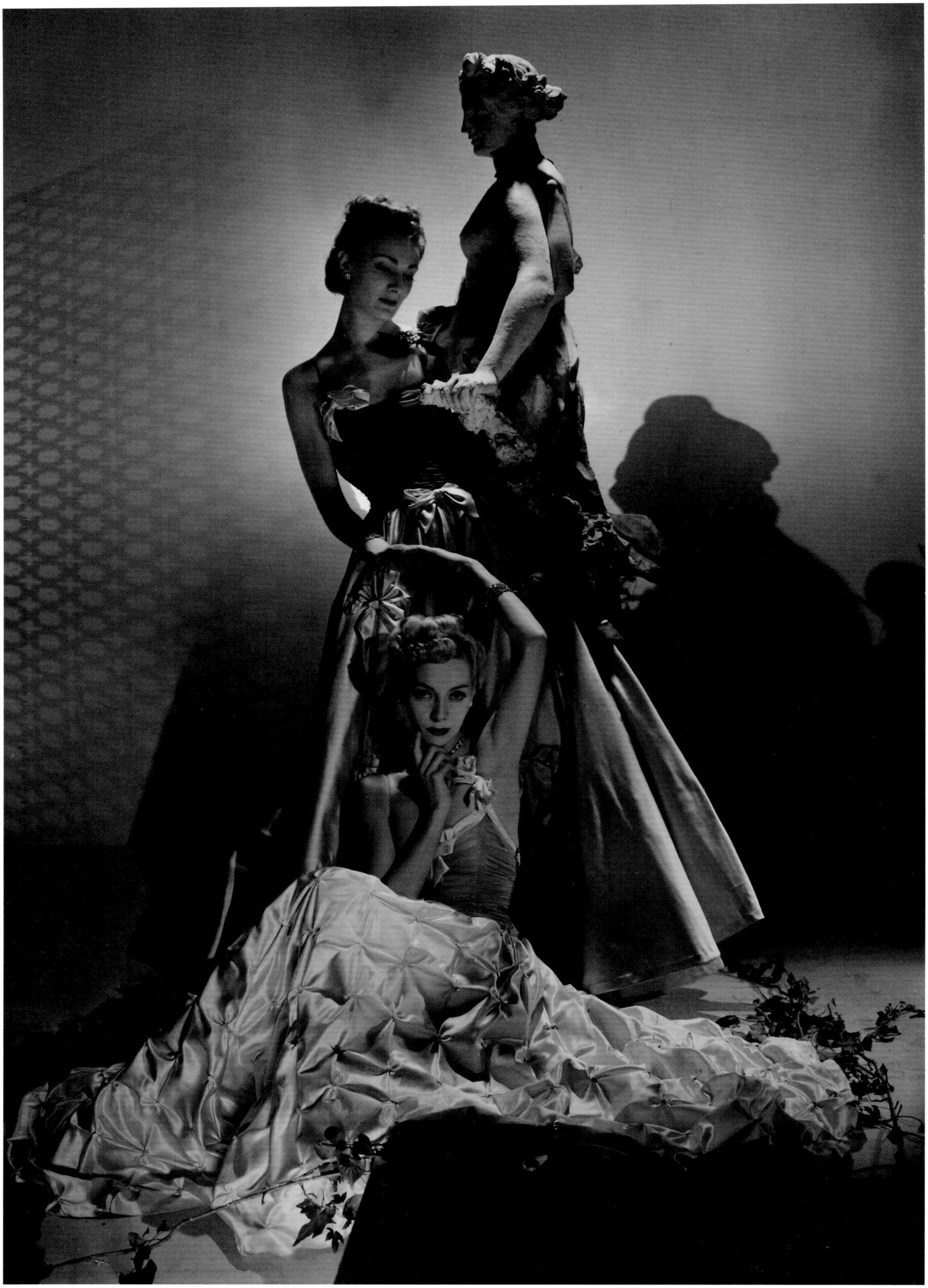

79. Helen Bennett and Lyla Zelensky, dresses by Maggy Rouff, jewellery by Mauboussin, 1938

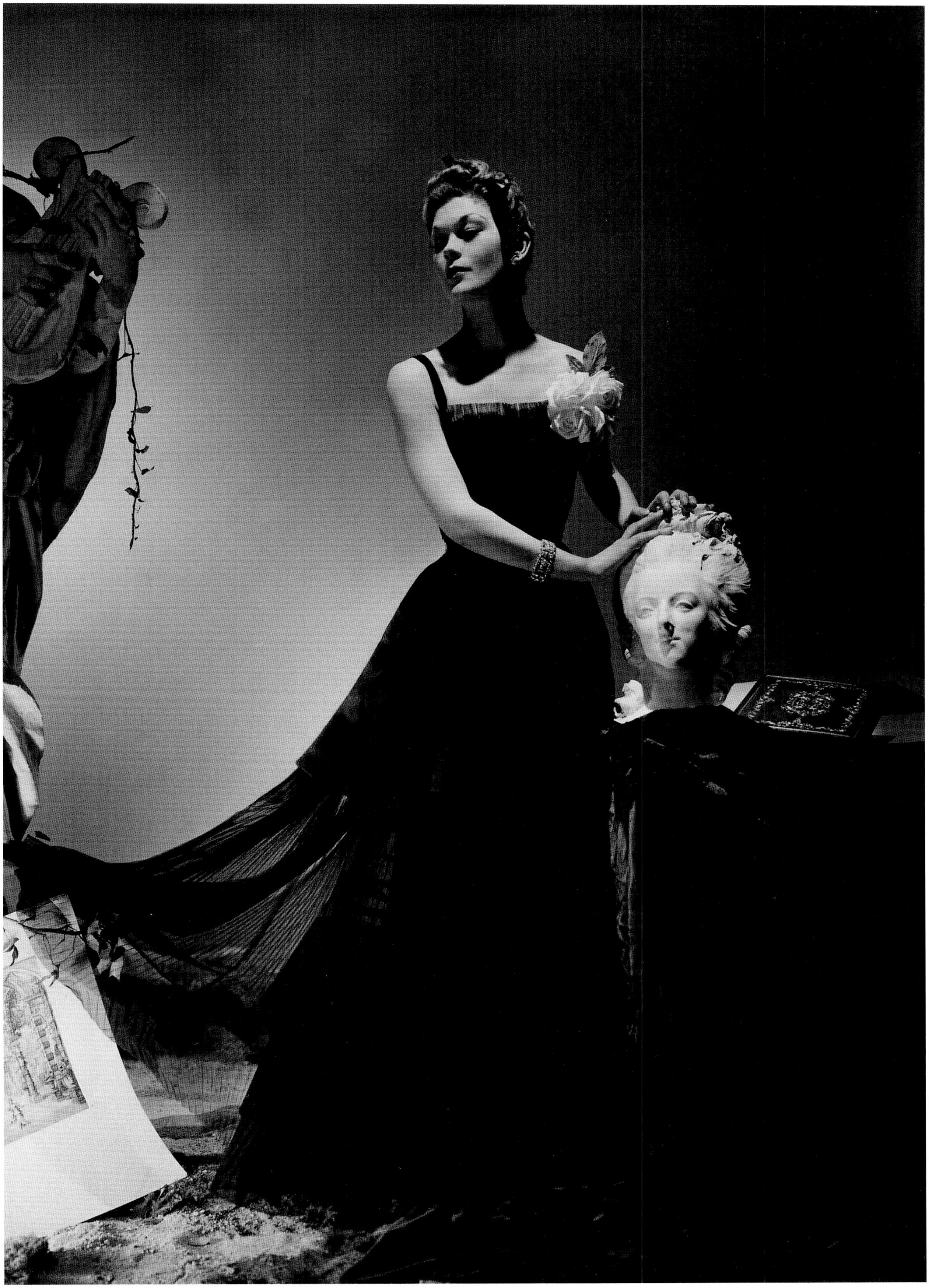

80. Lud, dress by Jean Patou, jewellery by Mauboussin, 1938

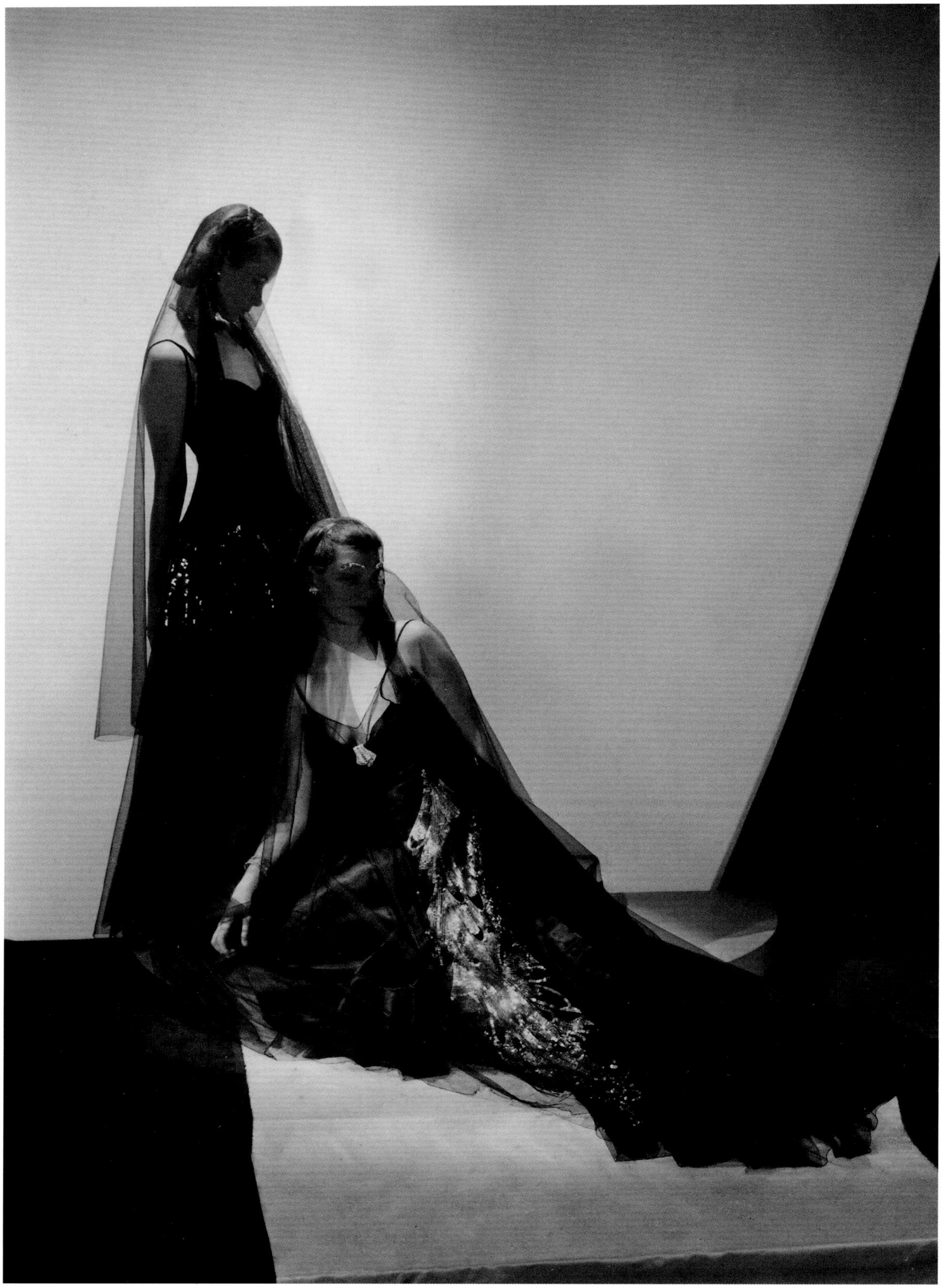

81. Margaret Healey and Margot Taylor, dresses and veils by Mainbocher, jewellery by Boucheron, 1937

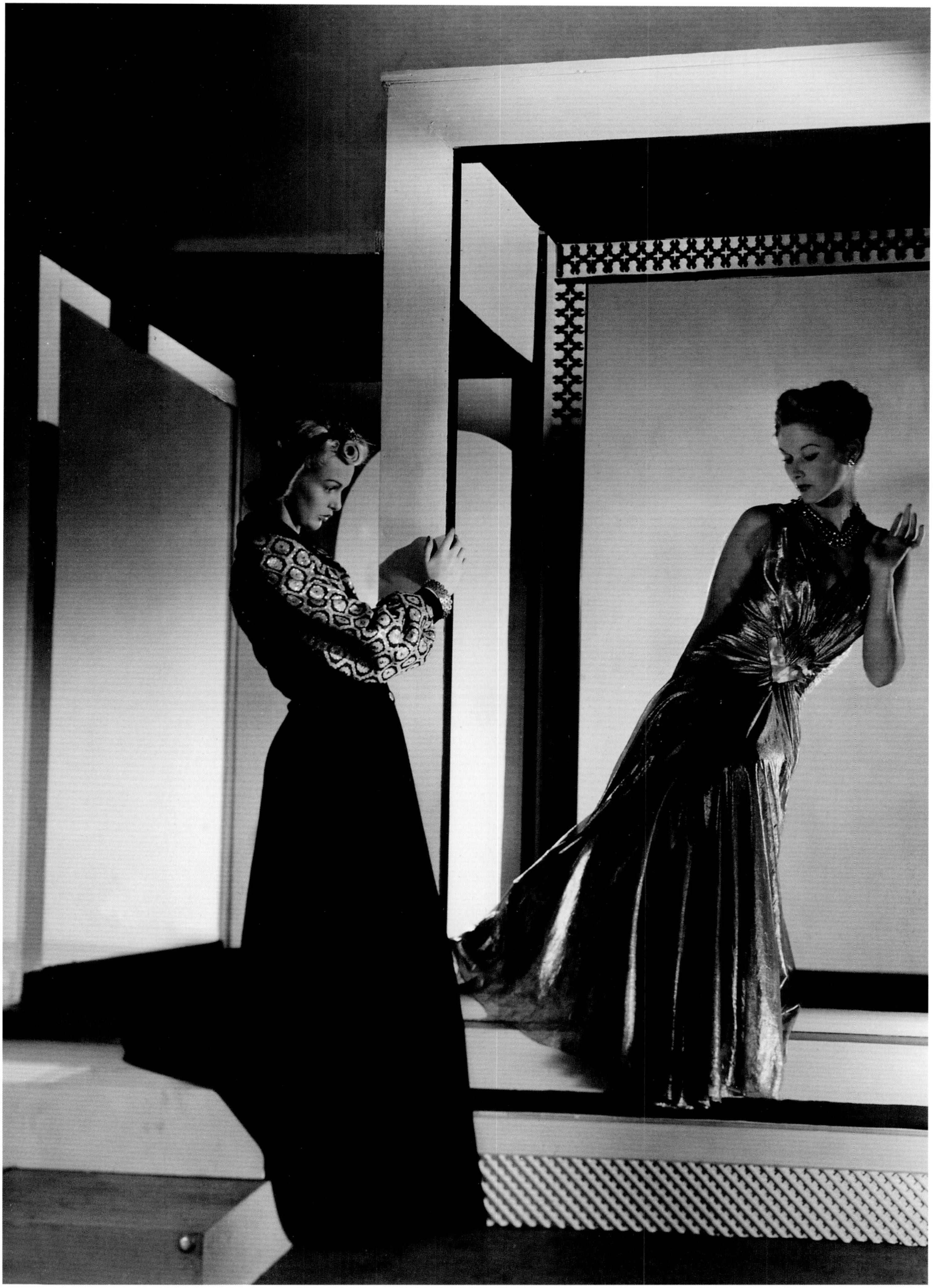

82. Madame Buchardt and Lisa Fonssagrives, dresses by Lucien Lelong, 1938

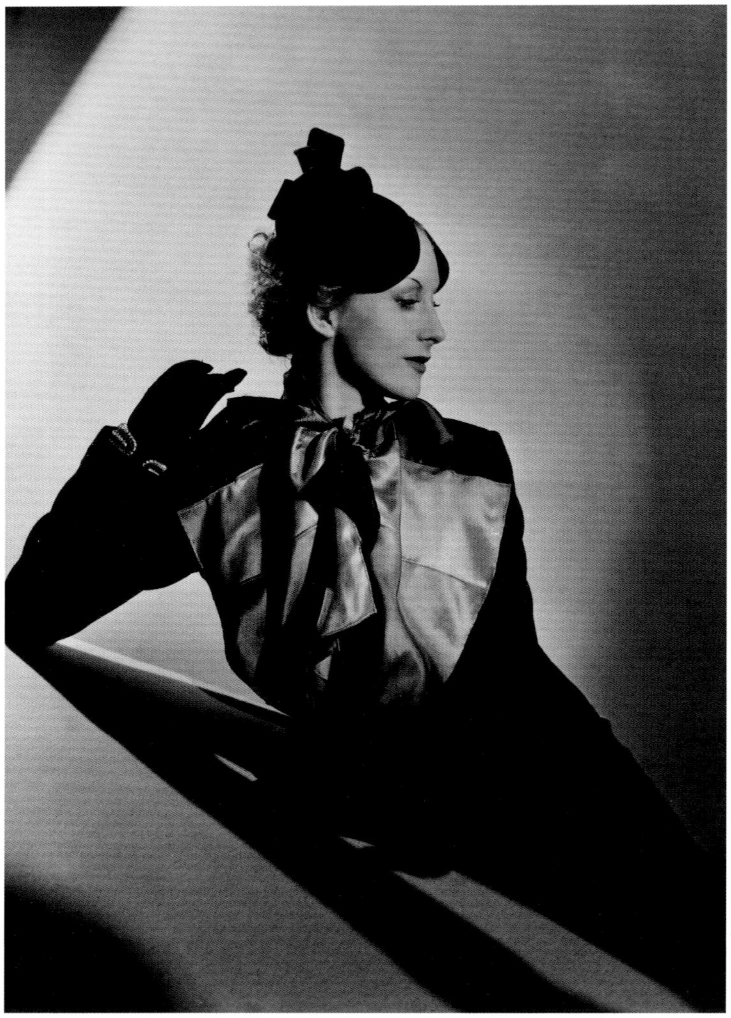

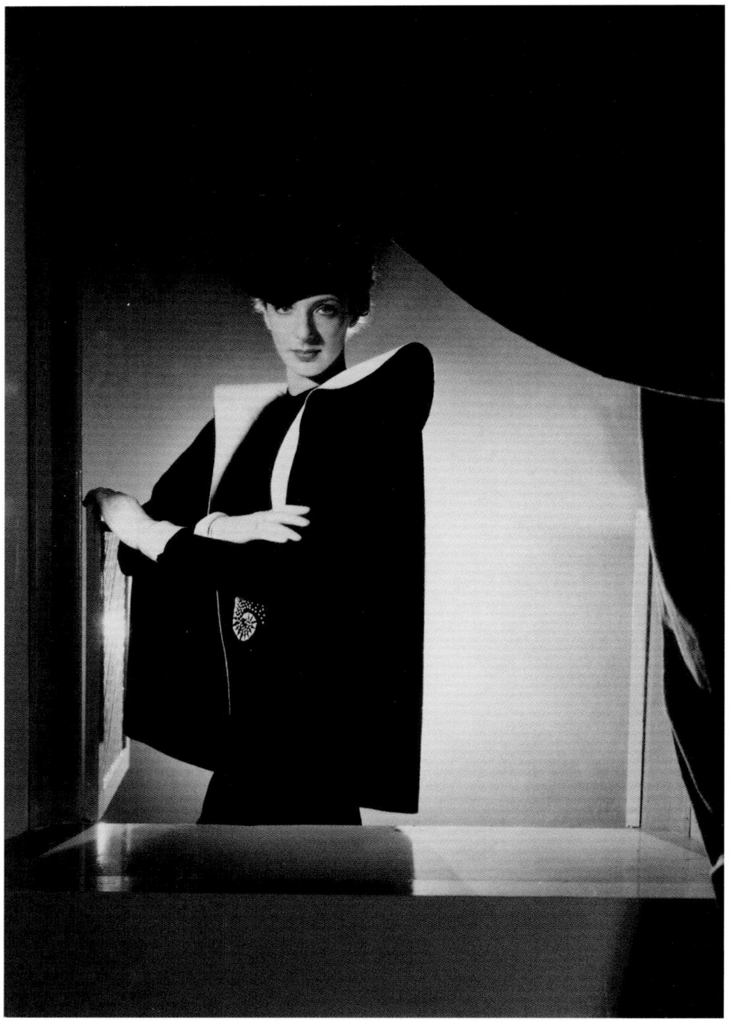

83. Cora Hemmet, hat by Reboux, jewellery by Boucheron, 1935

84. Agnetha Fischer, ensemble by Robert Piguet, hat by Louise Bourbon, 1936

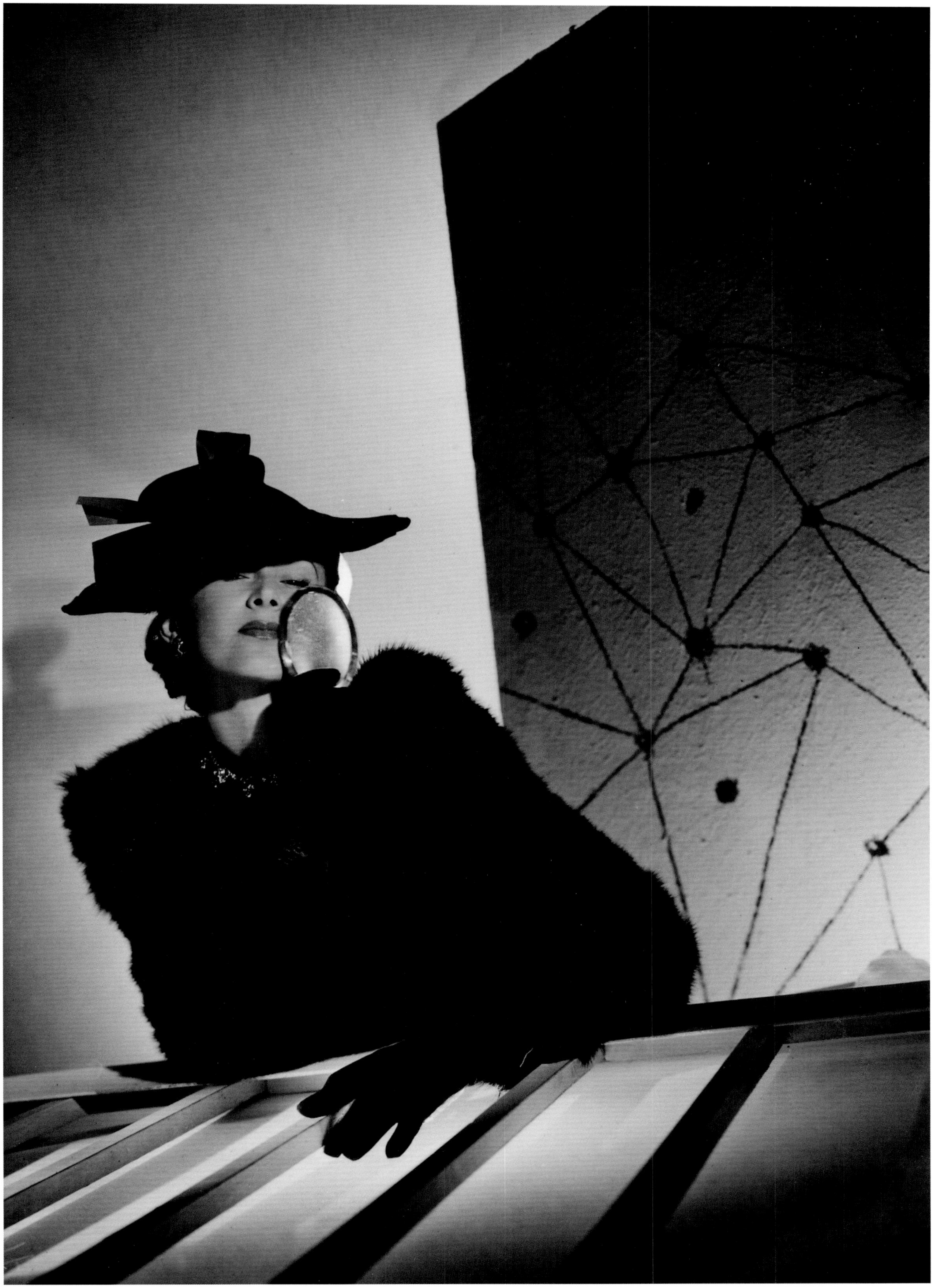

85. Lisa Fonssagrives, jacket by Francevrament, hat by Maria Guy, 1938

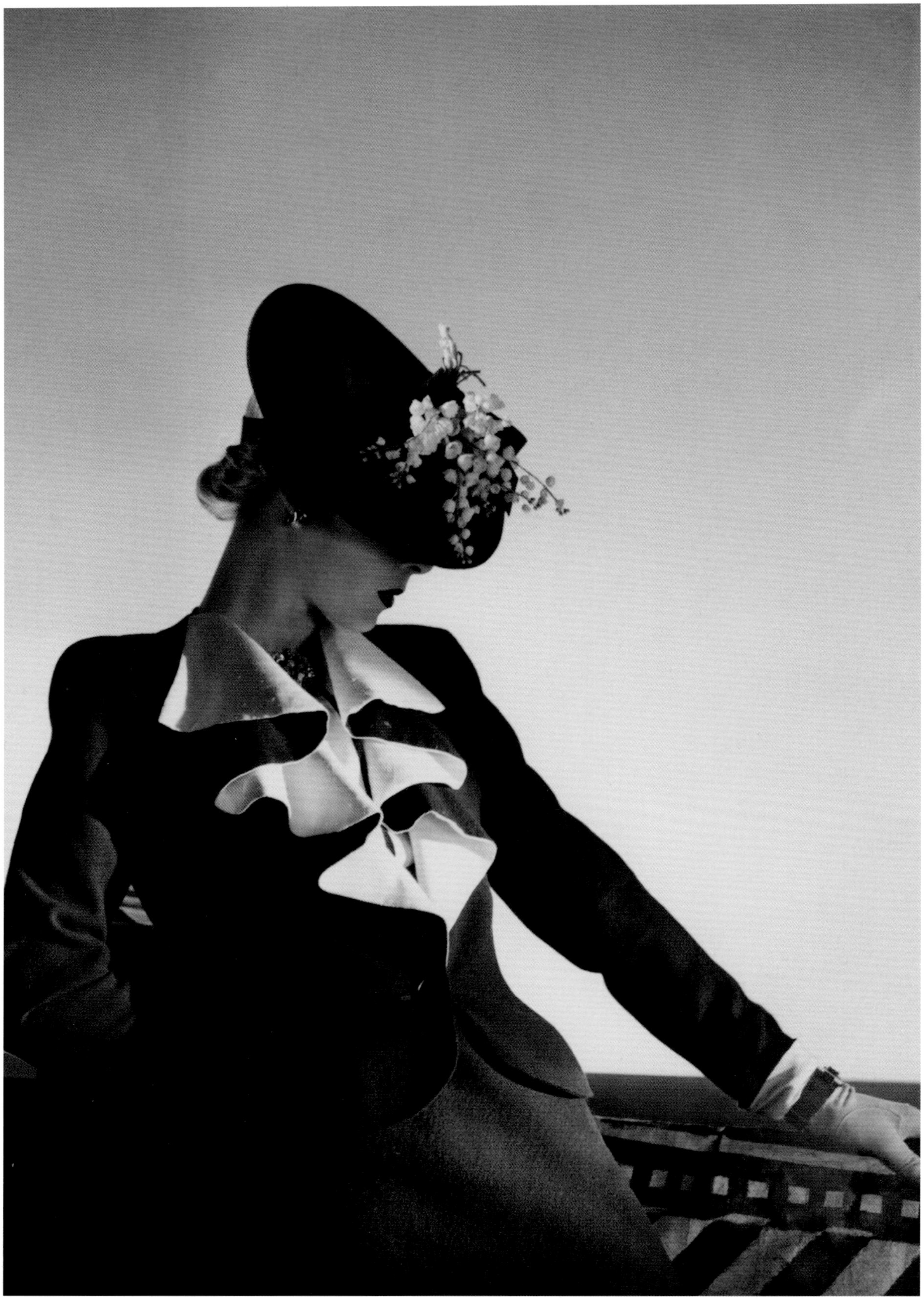

86. Helen Bennett, jacket and blouse by Molyneux, jewellery by Boucheron, 1938

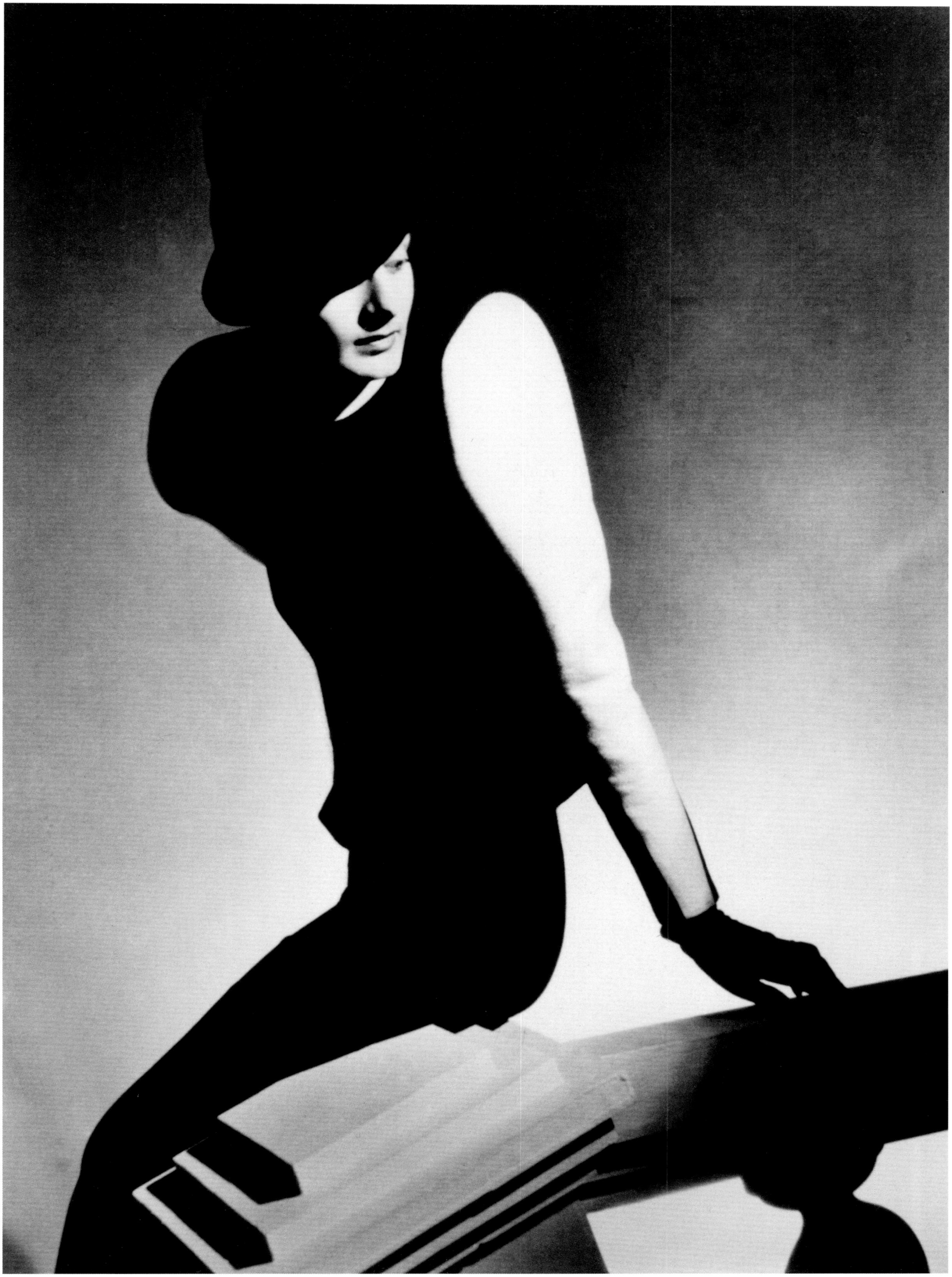

87. Lyla Zelensky, suit by Robert Piguet, hat by Suzanne Talbot, 1936

III

Stage and Screen

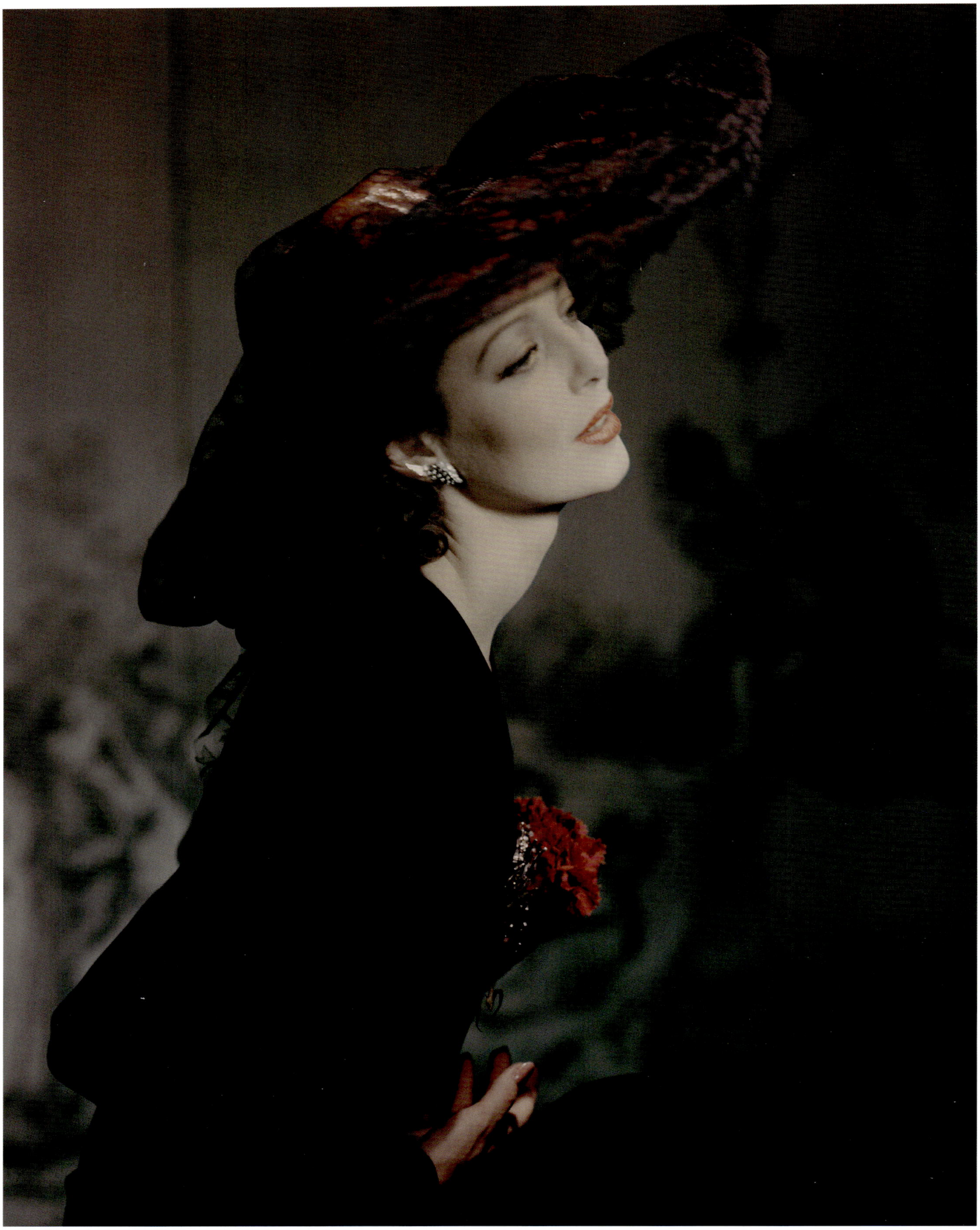

88. Loretta Young, New York, 1941

FROM LIMELIGHT TO STARLIGHT: PORTRAITS OF STAGE AND SCREEN STARS

Terence Pepper

The 1980s saw a resurgence of interest in Horst's work. Valentine Lawford's magisterial book *Horst: His Work and His World* was published in 1984, shortly after a book of new portraits, *Return Engagement*, with text and commentaries by James Watters, entertainments editor for American *Vogue*. These joined *Salute to the Thirties* (1971), a popular compendium of celebrity portraits of the period by Horst and George Hoyningen-Huene.[1] In the late 1980s, Horst's classic works started to become available to institutions and private collectors through the promotion of his art and aesthetics by Etheleen Staley and Takouhy Wise of the Staley-Wise Gallery in New York, and in London by Andy Cowan and Tim Jefferies, the energetic directors of Hamiltons Gallery. A series of carefully curated displays showcased Horst's exquisite prints, including platinum and palladium editions, prized for their beautiful tonal range and permanence. In 1989, I chose to include one of Horst's most stylish portraits, a 1933 study of Noël Coward (pl.98), in *Camera Portraits*, the National Portrait Gallery's exhibition and publication to mark the 150th anniversary of the birth of photography.

Ten years later, the National Portrait Gallery was offered an amazing opportunity to stage the first museum retrospective of Horst's portrait photographs.[2] Amongst the varied works in the exhibition, it was Horst's studies of leading stars of stage and screen that were particularly entrancing. Two star portraits were selected as key images for the lavish exhibition catalogue: Jessica Tandy appeared on the cover, while Rita Hayworth featured as the catalogue frontispiece and also the exhibition poster. These beguiling images were thought likely to seduce visitors not already familiar with Horst's captivating compositions and interpretations. Jessica Tandy was a British-born actress, wife of Jack Hawkins and later, and more lastingly, of Canadian actor Hume Cronyn, with whom she frequently starred. Fifty years before her Oscar-winning performance in *Driving Miss Daisy* (1989), Tandy posed for Horst's camera to create an image that perfectly represents Horst's 1930s style: her half-lit silhouette forms a sculptural composition against an Art Deco-style studio prop (pl.92). Nine years later in 1947, Horst photographed Rita Hayworth in an even more alluring half-light (pl.91), after the success of her role in *Gilda* (1946). Indeed, one of Horst's *Vogue* covers had itself made an appearance in an earlier film (*Cover Girl*, 1944) in which Hayworth starred. The cover depicted American model Susann Shaw (pl.89).[3]

While Horst's interest in architectural interiors was to have a profound effect on his future photography, much of his early inspiration resulted from his association with Huene. Both shared an interest in Greco-Roman art mixed with 1920s and 1930s Modernism. Both photographed a number of the same stage and film personalities, such as Gertrude Lawrence, Tilly Losch, Katharine Hepburn, Gary Cooper and Sybil Thorndike.

Horst's first portrait to appear in *Vogue* was a study of the German model Agnetha Fischer (pl.93), who had previously posed for Huene and went on to become a photographer herself. Published in the November 1931 issue of French *Vogue*, neither Horst nor Fischer is credited but the image is important because it was used to advertise the quality of photography at *Vogue*'s Paris studio. The December issue, however, contained several Horst images that were credited.[4] Like many *Vogue* photographers, Horst's portraits spanned a wide cross-section of subjects, from artists and writers to presidents and royalty, but towards the end of the 1930s Horst became aware of a new sort of subject. Hollywood movie stars were imperceptibly assuming the place left vacant by Europe's vanishing royal families, as he later noted in *Salute to the Thirties*. With the approach of war, the escapism offered by both the theatre and the cinema gained in popularity. Horst now began to photograph these new, classless celebrities and continued to chronicle the stars of stage and screen for the next 60 years.

Although his first portrait was taken for French *Vogue*, it was for the British edition of the magazine, in April 1932, that Horst took his first 'celebrity fashion portrait' of a named and well-known star, Gertrude Lawrence, then appearing in Ronald Jeans' play *Can the Leopard...?* at the Theatre Royal, Haymarket (1931). The magazine caption reads: 'There is only one Gertrude Lawrence and there she is on the opposite page looking her own provocative self, with a blue scarf caught around her lemon-yellow dress. "*Can the Leopard?*" provides her with the sort of part she excels in and talking of leopards, the rug she stands on is from Rowland Ward, Piccadilly.'[5]

A portrait from the same sitting appeared in American *Vogue* three months later, this time – as Lawford relates – with Lawrence standing on a bold zebra skin, chosen by Horst. Interestingly, a studio chair in Howard Coster's studio had a zebra-striped cushion, which was used on a number of sittings including one in 1931 for Noël Coward's set designer Gladys Calthrop. Horst and Huene both used Coster's studio on a number of occasions when visiting London and this may have provided another inspiration that the photographers shared. Lawrence and her close friend and collaborator Coward, who had written *Private Lives* for its British premiere in 1930 (followed by Broadway success in 1931), were to be subjects for many more Horst

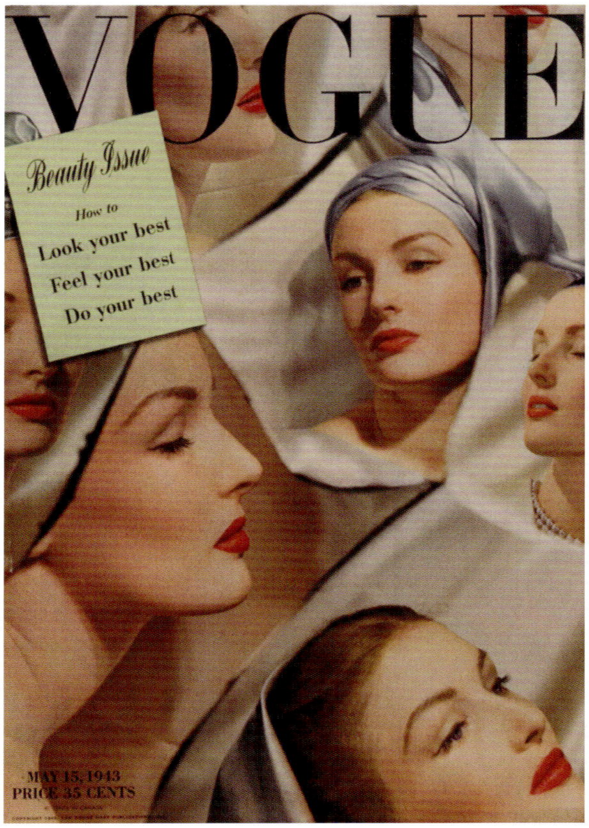

89. Susann Shaw,
American *Vogue* cover, 15 May 1943

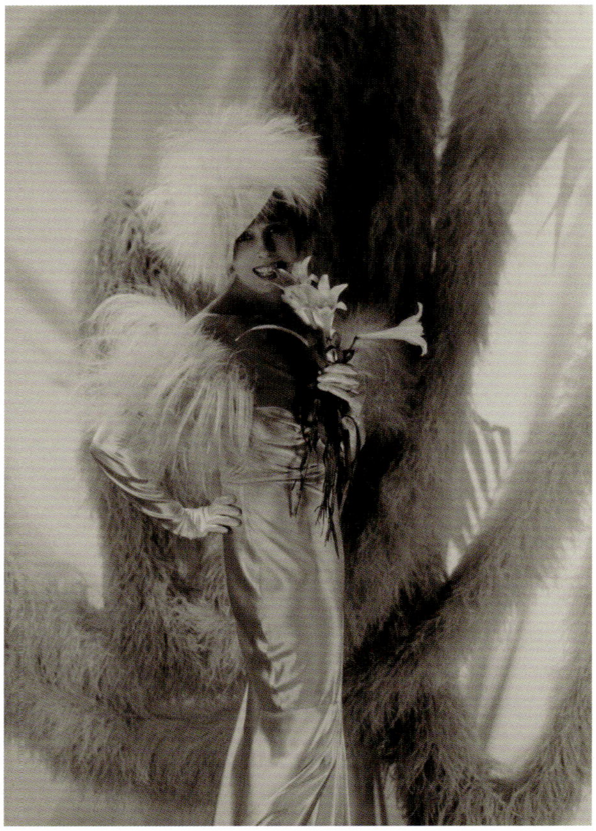

90. Mistinguett, Paris, 1933

studies (pl.106). However, the real importance of that first Lawrence portrait was how well it was received by Condé Nast in New York. Horst subsequently received an invitation to visit the studios of American *Vogue*, which he did in 1932. Although the episode was not an unqualified success, it did lead to Horst's first portrait of a Hollywood actress, Bette Davis, which appeared in *Vogue*'s sister magazine, *Vanity Fair*.[6] Horst, lacking confidence and experience, thought the sitting a failure, but the photograph has been much reproduced since, particularly in anthologies celebrating the history of *Vanity Fair*.

Shortly before his New York trip, for the 25 May 1932 issue of British *Vogue*, Horst had captured the 'vivacious personality' of British dancer and actress Jessie Matthews, wearing one of the magnificent costumes for the musical *Hold My Hand* (1931) by Desmond Carter and Noel Gay, which was performed at London's Gaiety Theatre. It prefigures a similarly feathered study of the French star Mistinguett, taken at the end of 1933 in Paris, to announce her appearance in her new revue *Folies en Folies* at the Folies-Bergère (pl.90).[7] Outrageously theatrical and seductive, the portrait befits the projected persona of 'Miss', whose legs were reputedly insured for a million francs. Her feather-crowned headdress set against spiky shadows cast by grassy fronds, she holds a bunch of lilies suggestively to her mouth. She is shown wearing a silk sheath dress designed by Edward Molyneux, the British couturier whose fashion house in Paris was frequented by actresses, high society and royalty.

Mistinguett was a rare, older subject for Horst – she was 58 when this portrait was made, a legendary performer with a career that had begun in 1895. Back in London, he was to photograph younger, newly emerging stars, such as Elsa Lanchester,[8] Douglas Fairbanks Jr[9] and the exotic and mysterious Merle Oberon,[10] later to become the wife of film producer Sir Alexander Korda. Oberon (born Estelle O'Brien Thompson) was talent-spotted by Korda, who helped her find stardom in well-chosen film roles. She was the daughter of a British railway engineer in India and a Ceylonese mother, but claimed to have been born in Tasmania, fearing that her race would inhibit her future career. Horst's lighting and elaborate plaster set creations emphasized her beautiful and unusual looks (pl.94). Oberon appeared in *The Private Life of Don Juan* (1934), as did Natalie Paley, the fashion model turned actress, who played 'the jealous husband's poor wife' in a costume designed by Oliver Messel. Paley had first met Horst in Paris in 1930 and he was immediately captivated by her beauty (pl.95). A cousin of Tsar Nicholas II and daughter of a grand duke, she was, between 1927 and 1936, married to fashion designer Lucien Lelong.

The following year Horst made his first trip to Hollywood, where he photographed Katharine Hepburn, crop-haired and in male attire for her role in the film *Sylvia Scarlett* (1935), and met up with Paley, who had a small, uncredited part in the film as Lily Levetsky. Horst also photographed Messel, who was working on the set designs for the film *Romeo and Juliet* (1936). Away from the constraints of the *Vogue* studio, Horst was able to experiment with smaller format photography, using a Rolleiflex camera for these *plein-air* studies rather than the 10 × 8 inch plate camera he used in the studio.

An intriguing and recently rediscovered portrait of Vivien Leigh (pl.96), taken for British *Vogue* in March 1936, includes a handwritten note on the reverse claiming that the image shows Leigh as Jenny Mere in the Ivor Novello production of *The Happy Hypocrite* (1936).

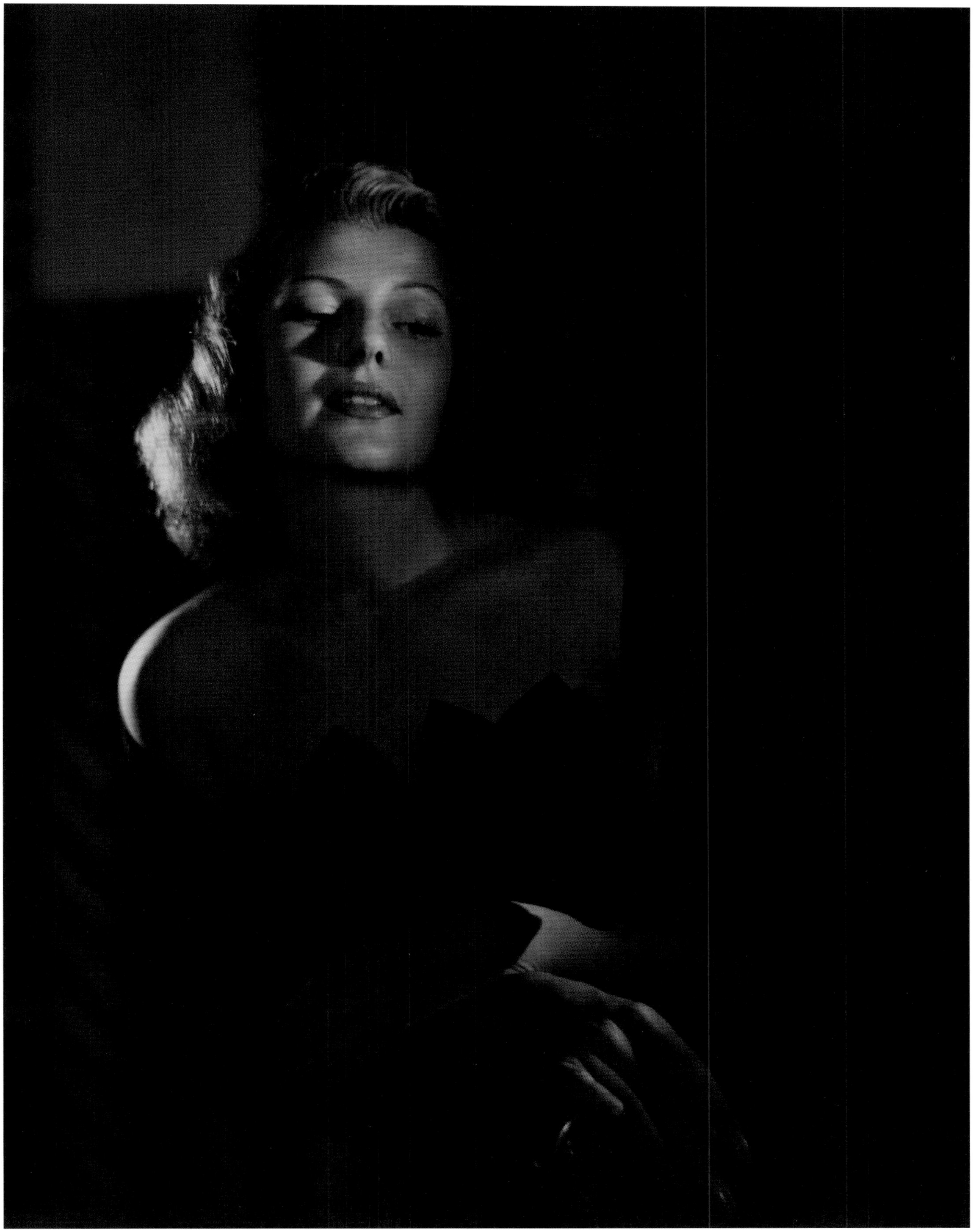

91. Rita Hayworth, New York, 1947

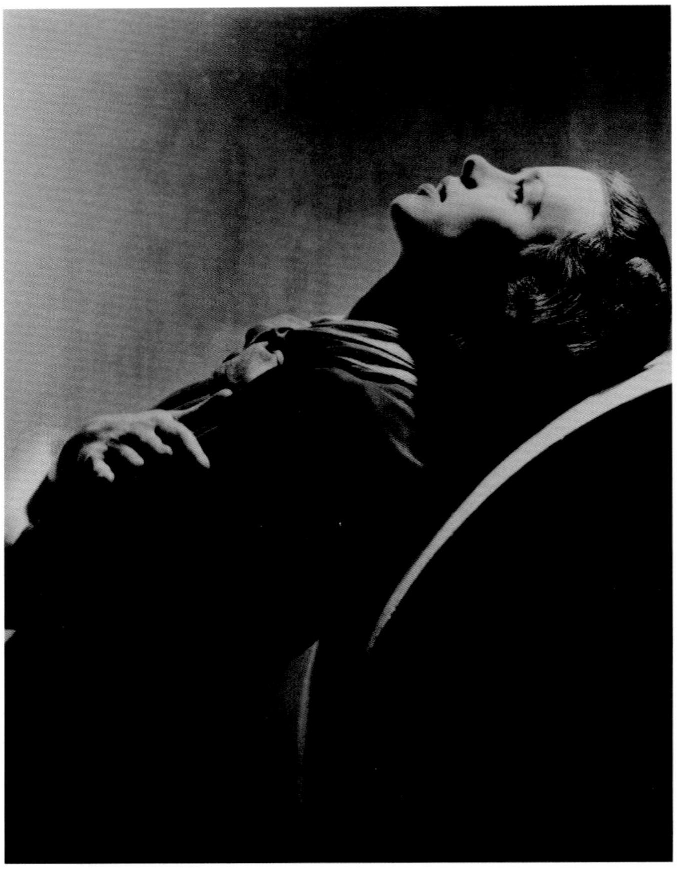

92. Jessica Tandy, New York, 1938

However, a study of the production photographs[11] rules out this possibility. The play opened in London on 8 April 1936 after a successful pre-London regional tour, but despite the good notices it received, it did not please Novello's core audience and closed shortly afterwards. British *Vogue* did indeed run the image in its 15 April issue, but the spread was essentially a fashion feature, entitled 'London Lines', for which Horst had photographed a number of subjects in designer outfits, set off against mysterious *objets d'art* including a suit of armour. The caption describes 'a black braid-edged town suit with hand tucked organdie blouse' from the newly launched fashion designer Dilkusha, followed by a four-word credit, 'Miss Vivien Leigh posed.' Subsequently this fashion image, and another full-page study showing Leigh in a 'cellophantasie' of a Victor Stiebel dress in pleated white Cellophane over white taffeta, would reappear in *Vogue* after Leigh's Oscar-winning performance in the film *Gone with the Wind* (1939), proof of *Vogue*'s prescience in giving Leigh early exposure after her first major theatrical success in Carl Sternheim's *Mask of Virtue* in 1935.

Horst's other significant portraits of 1936 included studies of the dancers Pearl Argyle, Tamara Geva and most significantly Ginger Rogers, wearing a dress by American fashion designer Muriel King (1900–77) and photographed in a series of five poses, which were published as 'Rhythm in Chiffon' in November 1936.[12] Seen from behind in a backless chiffon gown, her right hand arm holding an antique lamp standard, this atmospheric image conjures up the graceful dance moves that secured her enduring reputation as Fred Astaire's dancing partner in *Flying Down to Rio* (1933), *The Gay Divorcee* (1934) and *Top Hat* (1935).

Actress Olivia de Havilland, born in Tokyo of British parents, had been brought to California with her sister Joan Fontaine, also to become a major star. One of her most important moments came when she starred as Melanie with Vivien Leigh in *Gone with the Wind*. Horst's portrait of de Havilland was one of four he took for Allene Talmey's 'Vogue's Spot-Light', published in the American edition of the magazine in January 1937. Taken at the time of her appearance in the film *Call it a Day*, she is shown posing with an Old Master picture frame, a favourite device of Horst, creating a slightly surreal 'portrait within a portrait' (pl.105). It echoes other Horst compositions with pictures frames, such as his portrait that year of the couturière Elsa Schiaparelli (pl.63) and one of Tilly Losch, an altogether more elaborate study inspired by Old Master paintings in which the dancer, posed in a Descat beret and holding her painted self-portrait, is set against an architectural background, Horst's photographic enlargement of an archway (pl.97).

In the same genre are Horst's magnificent studies of Joan Crawford, 'looking more glamorous than ever', according to British *Vogue* in February 1939 (pl.109).[13] Wearing an enormous wide-brimmed hat, with jewelled ornamentation, Crawford was dramatically posed once more against an architectural backdrop, this time Horst's photographic enlargement of an engraving of Giovanni Paolo Panini's imaginary study of Roman Baths, the original of which is in the National Gallery at the Palazzo Corsini, Rome.

Horst's portrait of Ethel Waters, a blues singer who made the transition to the stage, shows Waters in her role as Hagar in the Broadway production of *Mamba's Daughters*, written originally as a novel by DuBose Heyward in 1929 but adapted by him for the theatre (pl.100). Horst's portrait, like those he took of other theatre stars, focuses on the dramatic gesture, as can be seen in his study of British actor Emlyn Williams.

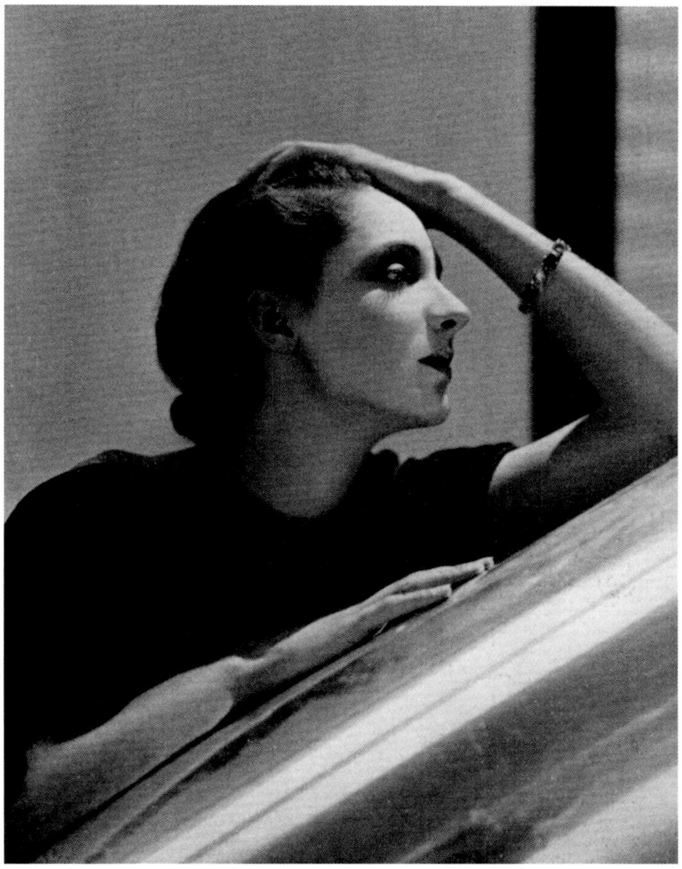

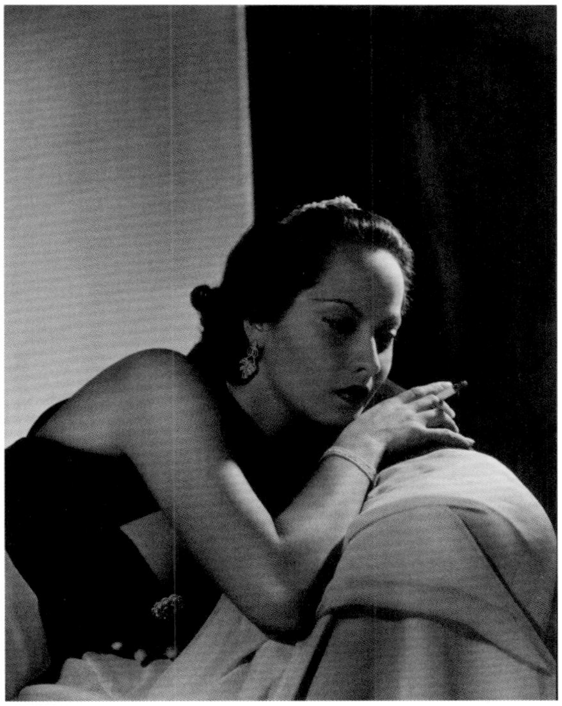

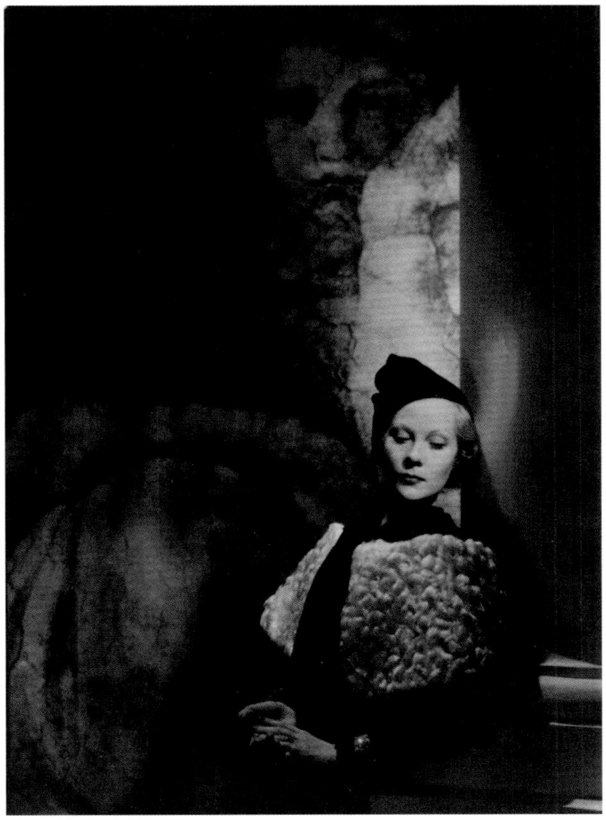

Top left
93. Agnetha Fischer, Paris, 1931

Above
94. Merle Oberon, London, 1934

Left
95. Natalie Paley, Paris, 1934

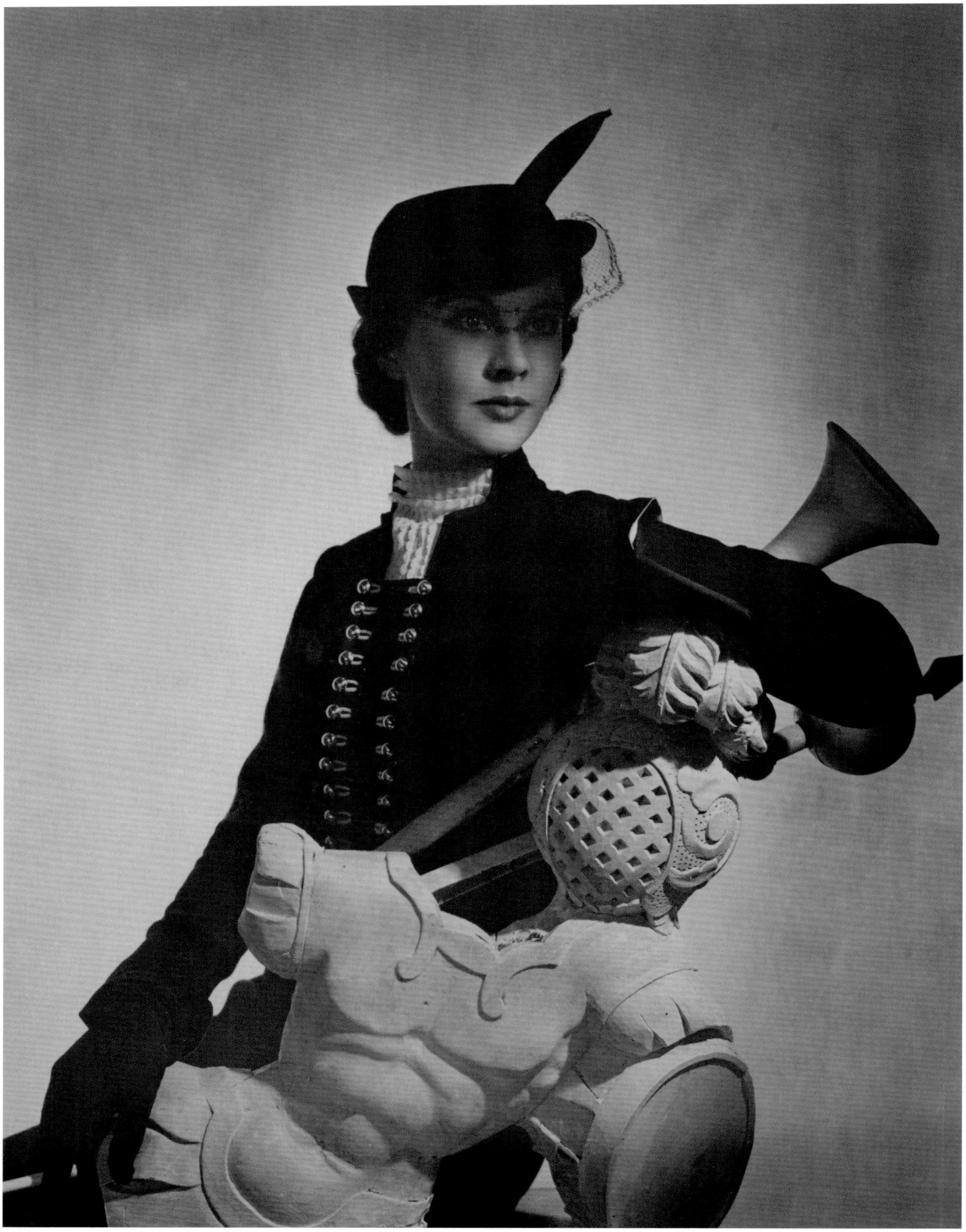

96. Vivien Leigh, London, 1936

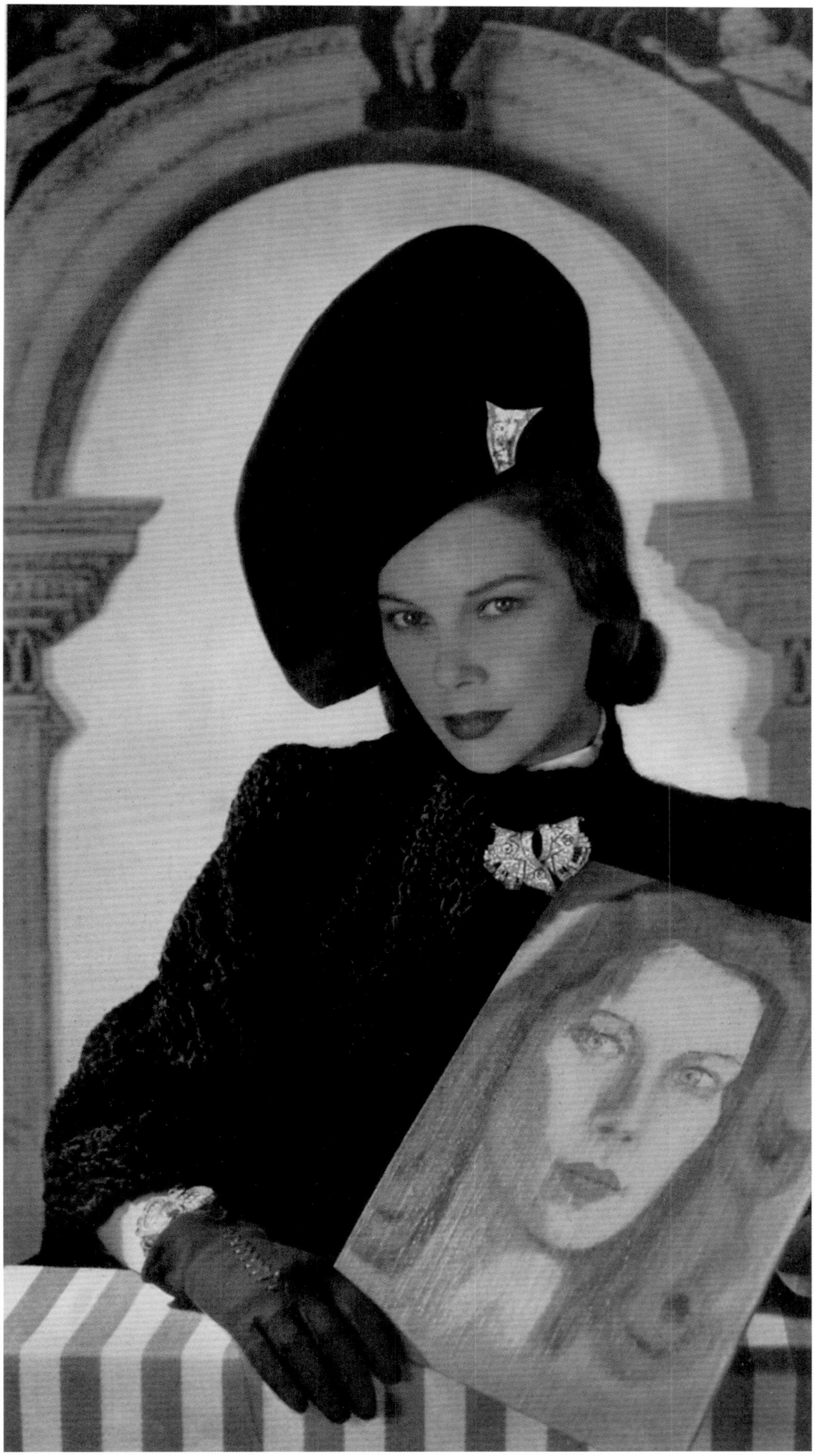

97. Tilly Losch, 1939

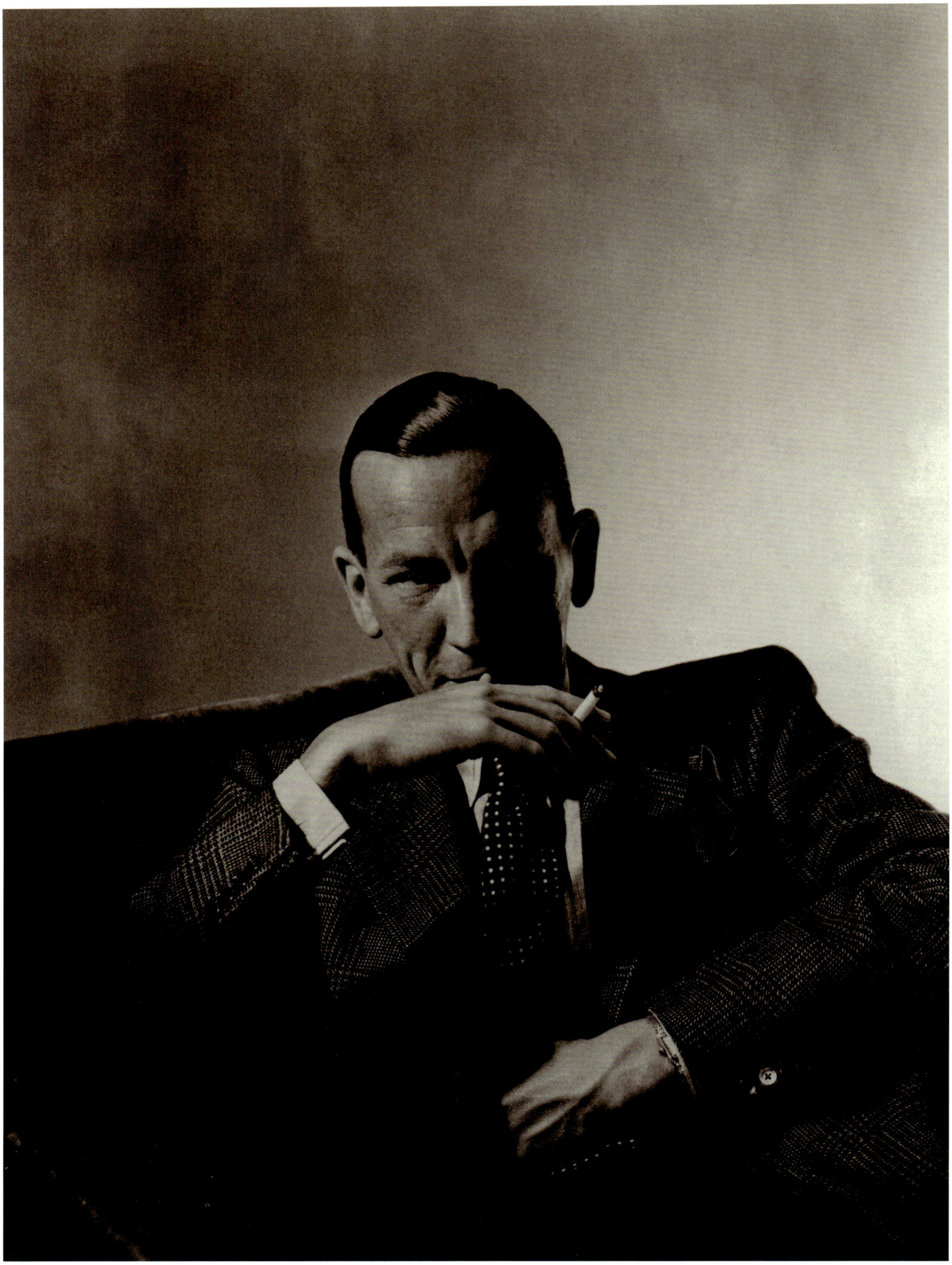

98. Noël Coward, Paris, 1933

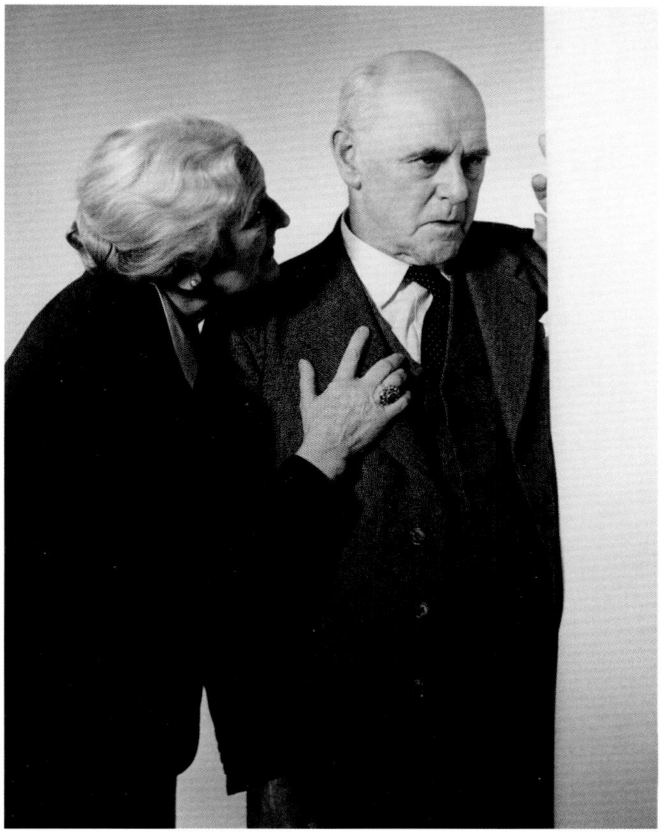

99. Sybil Thorndike and Lewis Casson
in *The Potting Shed*, New York, 1957

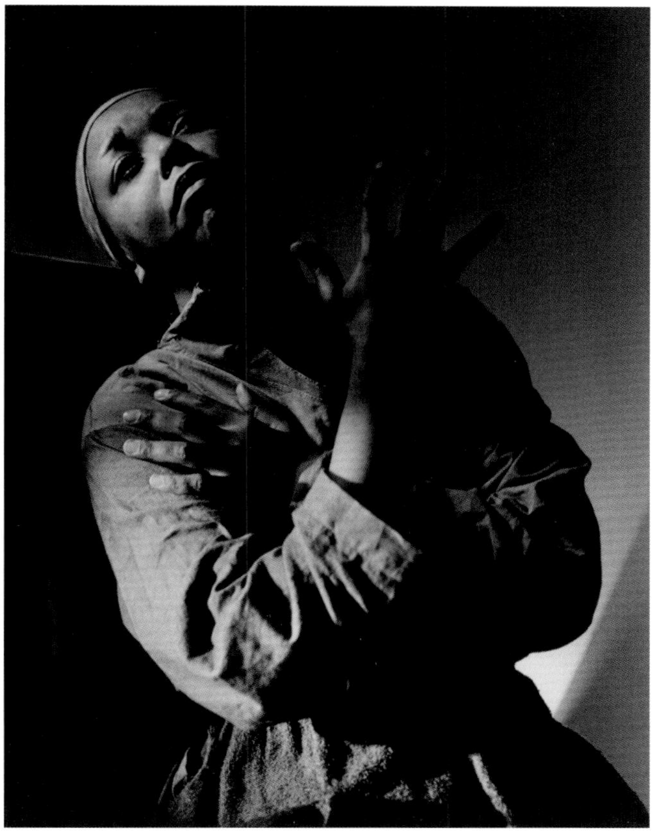

100. Ethel Waters as Hagar
in *Mamba's Daughters*, New York, 1939

Around this time Horst also photographed a number of double portraits of leading stars such as Ingrid Bergman and Burgess Meredith in *Liliom* (1940) and Janet Gaynor and her husband, the Hollywood fashion designer 'Adrian' (1940). The relationship he portrays in his brooding photograph of Gary Cooper and his wife 'Rocky' Veronica Balfe (1938) seems slightly uncomfortable and makes for a thought-provoking comment on a long-lasting, but at times troubled, marriage (pl.101).

Two of Horst's most remarkable cinematic portraits, photographed in colour, are of the actresses Paulette Goddard and Loretta Young. Horst had first photographed Young in 1937, posed 'in a froth of lavender, pink and grey tulle', for the promotion of her film *Cafe Metropole*.[14] On the second occasion Horst was contributing to a special photography issue of American *Vogue* (15 June 1941), which attempted to map the history of photography and included new iconic images, such as Horst's portrait of a 'Photogenic Loretta Young', in a 'huge picture hat of black lace over yellow spun glass [*sic*]'. Technical notes were supplied by all the photographers, revealing that Horst had used 10 × 8 inch Kodachrome film with a 3-second exposure time and 6,000 watts of spot-lighting. Young's photogenic attributes were captioned in full from her 'fine-boned face' and 'long, graceful neck' to her 'fine-textured, flawless skin', subtle elements conveyed by the photographer's skill (pl.88).

The actress Paulette Goddard, at one time the wife of Charlie Chaplin, was another subject Horst photographed on a number of occasions.[15] It was Chaplin's *Modern Times* (1936) that established her reputation, after which she co-starred with him in *The Great Dictator* (1940). In Horst's portrait, taken in New York in 1940, Goddard is shown seated in a beachwear costume of shorts with matching silk crepe jacket, designed by Hattie Carnegie (pl.111). Strange shapes scattered in the foreground, possibly surreal manifestations of seashells, complete this intriguing fashion portrait. Horst's ultimate film star session, however, would be in 1942 with Marlene Dietrich (pl.107), whom he caught 'between films' when on a tour of army camps, singing for the troops to lift morale during the Second World War. His other portraits of 1942, both shot in New York, again included Merle Oberon and also Myrna Loy, these stunning images forming part of the 'Bundles for Britain' wartime campaign and whose captions spoke of the stars' contributions to the war effort.

Horst's great star sittings of the late 1940s and 1950s included portraits of Tallulah Bankhead on stage in the Jean Cocteau play *The Eagle Has Two Heads* (1947), which added to his earlier, equally formidable stage portrait of Bankhead in *The Little Foxes* (1938). In 1957 Horst made a double portrait of the famous husband-and-wife British actors Sybil Thorndike and Lewis Casson, who were appearing on Broadway in the Graham Greene play *The Potting Shed* (pl.99), and in 1958 he photographed for the third time Ingrid Bergman, then nearing completion of her film *The Inn of the Sixth Happiness*.

In the 1960s film actor Steve McQueen was one of the most successful American international box office stars, due to his charismatic appearances in films such as *The Magnificent Seven* (1960) and *The Great Escape* (1963), which established his action-hero reputation. Horst photographed McQueen for the 'Men in Vogue' section of the magazine, which described him as 'cool, hip, easy, very much his own man, the sort that didn't exist before right now'.[16] Horst portrayed him standing nonchalantly in front of a picture

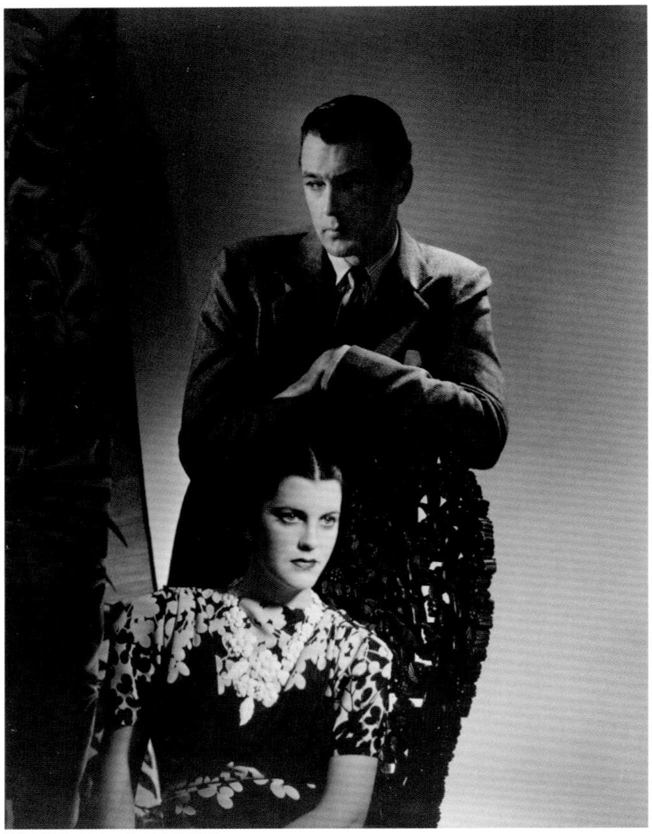

101. Gary Cooper and his wife Rocky, New York, 1938

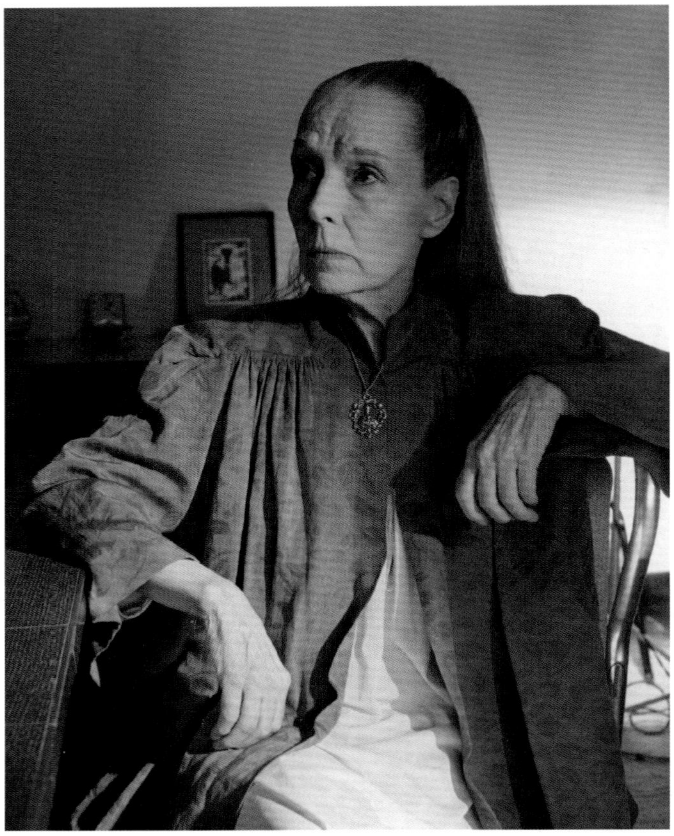

102. Louise Brooks, New York, 1979

window, high above the San Francisco cityscape which would become the backdrop to another defining screen presence, that of Lieutenant Frank Bullitt in the car-chase film of the same name (1968).

Horst continued consistently in his own iconic style, although in the 1970s and 1980s this tended to be more stripped back with fewer props, generally eschewing a plain light background in order to emphasize the sitter's face and body, as seen in such portraits as those of Paloma Picasso (1979), or Arthur Miller (1980).

Although the many editions of *Vogue* and other Condé Nast titles had been Horst's primary outlets for his work in his 60-year photographic career, his images did appear sporadically in other publishers' publications. *LIFE*, one of the world's most popular mass readership magazines from its creation in the later 1930s, featured occasional references including a 15-picture spread publicizing his book *Horst: Portraits of a Decade* (1944).[17] In 1979, however, the magazine decided to run one of those popular features on what had happened to famous film stars of the past, with images from classic vintage film magazine covers shown alongside new portraits and updated details on their lives at the end of the decade. Various photographers were considered for what was to be called 'Whatever Became of Mary Astor and Other Lost Stars'. Then *LIFE*'s assistant picture editor, Mel Scott, suggested that Horst would be the perfect choice of photographer. James Watters was responsible for compiling a list of ideal surviving subjects to be photographed and argued strongly that the pictures should be in black and white rather than colour. On completion, the project became the cover story for the February 1980 issue and featured nine Horst portraits. At over 1.5 million copies, it was the highest selling issue of the year.

Due to this success a follow-on book was commissioned. Horst, working mainly with assistant Richard Stanley, and Watters, who interviewed the subjects, travelled from the East to the West Coast, taking two years to complete 74 sittings, the results of which were published as *Return Engagement: Faces to Remember: Then and Now* (1984). The book went on to sell 25,000 copies. Horst's image of Bette Davis was accompanied by his earlier portrait, a surreal study of the actress shown seated in a giant chair that had been published in American *Vogue* in 1941 (pl.108). Other subjects included Loretta Young, Lillian Gish, Mary Astor, the 1920s vamp Pola Negri, and Claudette Colbert, who was again photographed by Horst for the newly relaunched *Vanity Fair* in 1983.

Two of Horst's most memorable studies of film stars to be included in *Return Engagement* were, first, of Louise Brooks, the extraordinary star of G.W. Pabst's 1920s films *Pandora's Box* and *Diary of a Lost Girl*, photographed in her small apartment in Rochester, New York in 1979 (pl.102) and, second, of Katharine Hepburn, photographed in 1981, the year the film *On Golden Pond* was released. It was Hepburn's portrait that appeared on the book's cover, bringing the concept full circle for she was one of the few stars that Horst had met and photographed in the 1930s and who was still working as a film actress. These two images were both issued in signed, editioned prints and rank with many of Horst's best portraits. Indeed, they form an appropriate coda to his contribution to portraiture, his photographs of celebrities from the worlds of stage and celluloid having become synonymous with style and glamour.

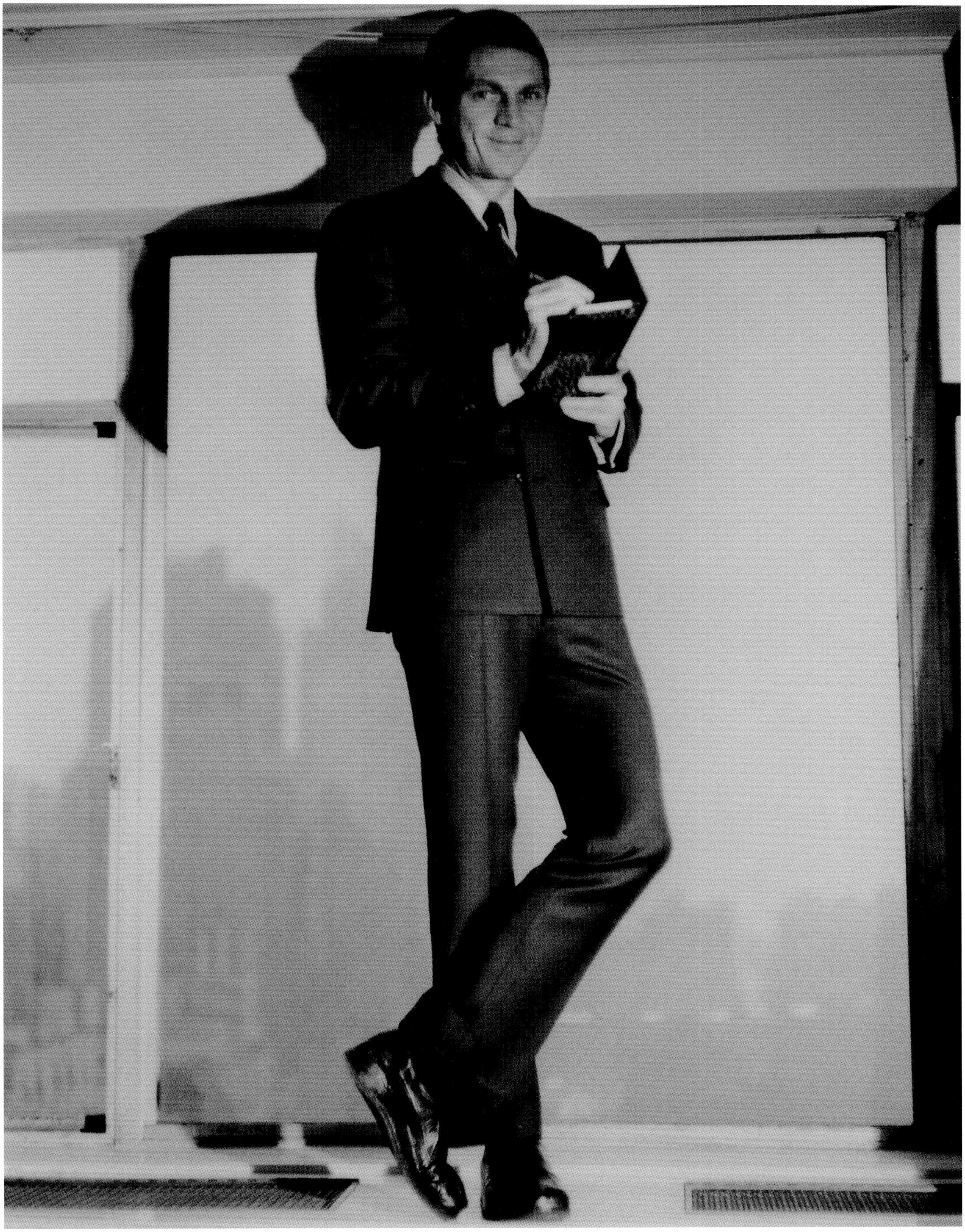

103. Steve McQueen, San Francisco, 1967

Marlene Dietrich, New York, 1942

Marlene Dietrich (1901–92) gained international fame starring in Paramount films such as *Morocco* (1930), *Blonde Venus* (1932) and *The Devil is a Woman* (1935). The director Josef von Sternberg was instrumental in shaping the actress's femme fatale image in those, and several other visually arresting movies. In close-ups, von Sternberg frequently employed a technique known as 'butterfly lighting' to enhance Dietrich's facial features.[1] He used two lights: one key light directly in front of her, fairly high up above the camera, and a rim light to the side. This set-up emphasized the cheekbones and produced a distinct shadow, shaped something like a butterfly, below the nose. Dietrich instructed Horst to use the same dramatic technique when she posed for him in *Vogue*'s New York studio in 1942. He recalled, 'She came in with this terrible hat and said in that voice, "Remember the von Sternberg lighting."'[2] Horst chose not to take her advice. Instead, he placed a mirror next to the camera and moved the light down slightly below her face; the overall mood was softer and 'all the wrinkles disappeared'.[3]

Despite her immense stardom, Horst did not consider his fellow countrywoman a great beauty, commenting that 'without makeup, her face had typical flat German features. She projected sex but she was not sexy.'[4] The screen celebrities of the era were often known for specific attributes: Bette Davis for her eyes, Louise Brooks for her dark bob, and Dietrich for her perfect legs – reputedly insured for a vast sum by Lloyd's of London. Yet, for this portrait, Horst obscured the famous legs altogether, placing a chair directly in front of her. The chair was Horst's own, a Louis XVI giltwood bergère dating from the late eighteenth century. The needlepoint panel on the back is based on an elegant still life photograph he took in Paris before the Second World War.[5] It comprises a hoop and three plaster casts of sculptures: a Roman bust, a hand and an écorché figure[6] by Jean-Antoine Houdon. Objects such as these were most commonly found in art schools of the nineteenth century, used as an aid to the teaching of figurative drawing. It has been suggested that by grouping classical and neoclassical objects with the hoop, a symbol of the cyclical nature of the arts, Horst was inferring that he himself was among the new generation of classical followers (pls 45, 46).[7]

The focus of the image is Dietrich's face, with its slightly open mouth and heavily lidded eyes that gaze into the distance and effect an expression of longing. Though undoubtedly bewitching, she is depicted here as a real woman rather than a celluloid siren. There is no elaborate set, just the single chair and the shadow of a diamond-shaped trellis to enliven an otherwise stark background. *Vogue*'s columnist commented: 'On this page, you see her as she herself likes to look. As she looked when she came to *Vogue*'s studio to be photographed. Her suit of black alpaca shrewdly understates her glamour, but has the force of an exclamation-point.'[8] The front of the hat's brim echoes the line of Dietrich's shoulders, while the back of the brim creates the inverse of the line, emphasizing her sharply-tailored form. Always meticulous in her attire, Dietrich had all her clothes made to order: 'She's a crank about the fit of her shoulders. Her skirts are sinuously narrow. She likes to look like a triangle on tiptoe.' The woman who, in her youth, had worked in a glove factory to pay the bills now carried a spare pair of white gloves, 'she's that fussy about white-whiteness.'[9]

During the Second World War, it is unlikely that Dietrich had much time to dwell on clothes. Staunchly anti-Nazi, she became an American citizen in 1939 and when the country entered the war she became one of the first stars to raise war bonds. When Horst took this photograph, she was on a break from her long tour of the US Army camps. More intensive tours followed in 1944 and 1945, during which she risked her life to perform to the Allied troops close to the front lines in Europe. When Horst and Dietrich met again in New York in the winter of 1944, both were dressed in their American army uniforms as they chatted in German over dinner at Le Pavillon restaurant. Afterwards, in her apartment at the St Regis hotel, she played him the records she had recently made to be broadcast to German troops on the Western Front. She was keen to hear Horst's views on songs designed to persuade the German soldiers to abandon their resistance to the Allied invasion.[10] After the war, Horst would have the opportunity to photograph Dietrich once again. She posed with her daughter, Maria, in a spectacular New Look dress by Dior, ushering in a new phase in fashion.[11]

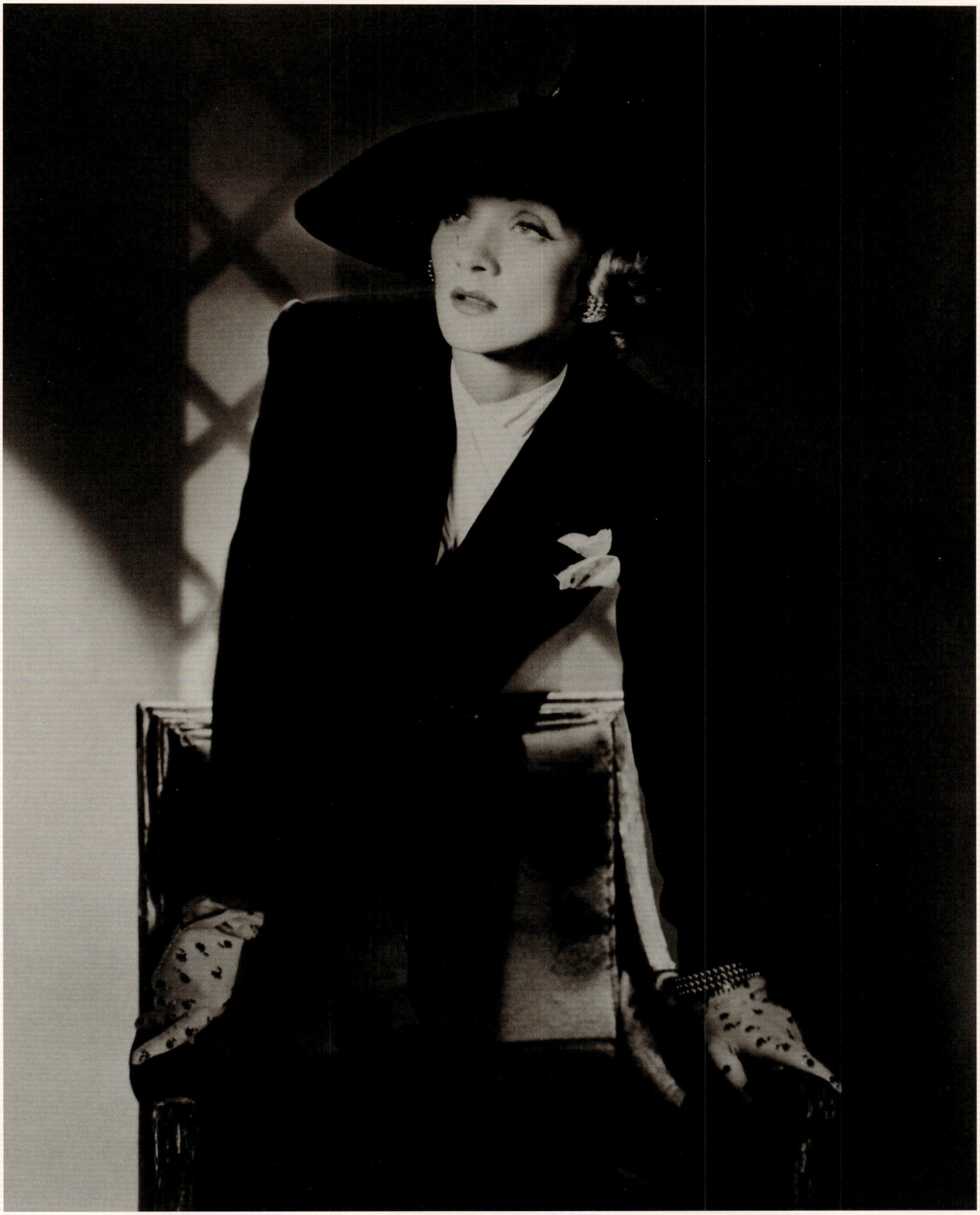

104. Marlene Dietrich, New York, 1942

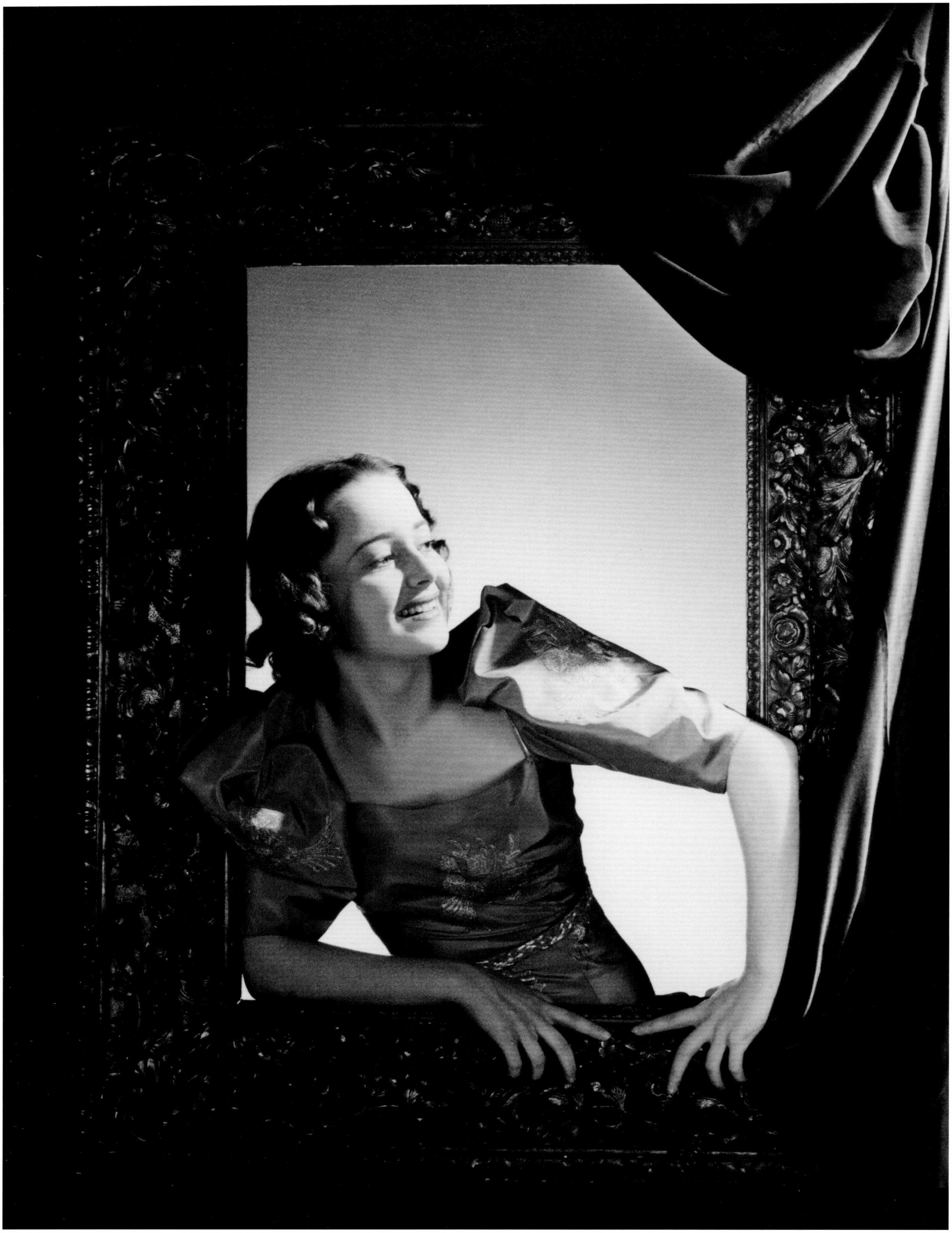

105. Olivia de Havilland as Catherine Hilton in *Call it a Day*, New York, 1936

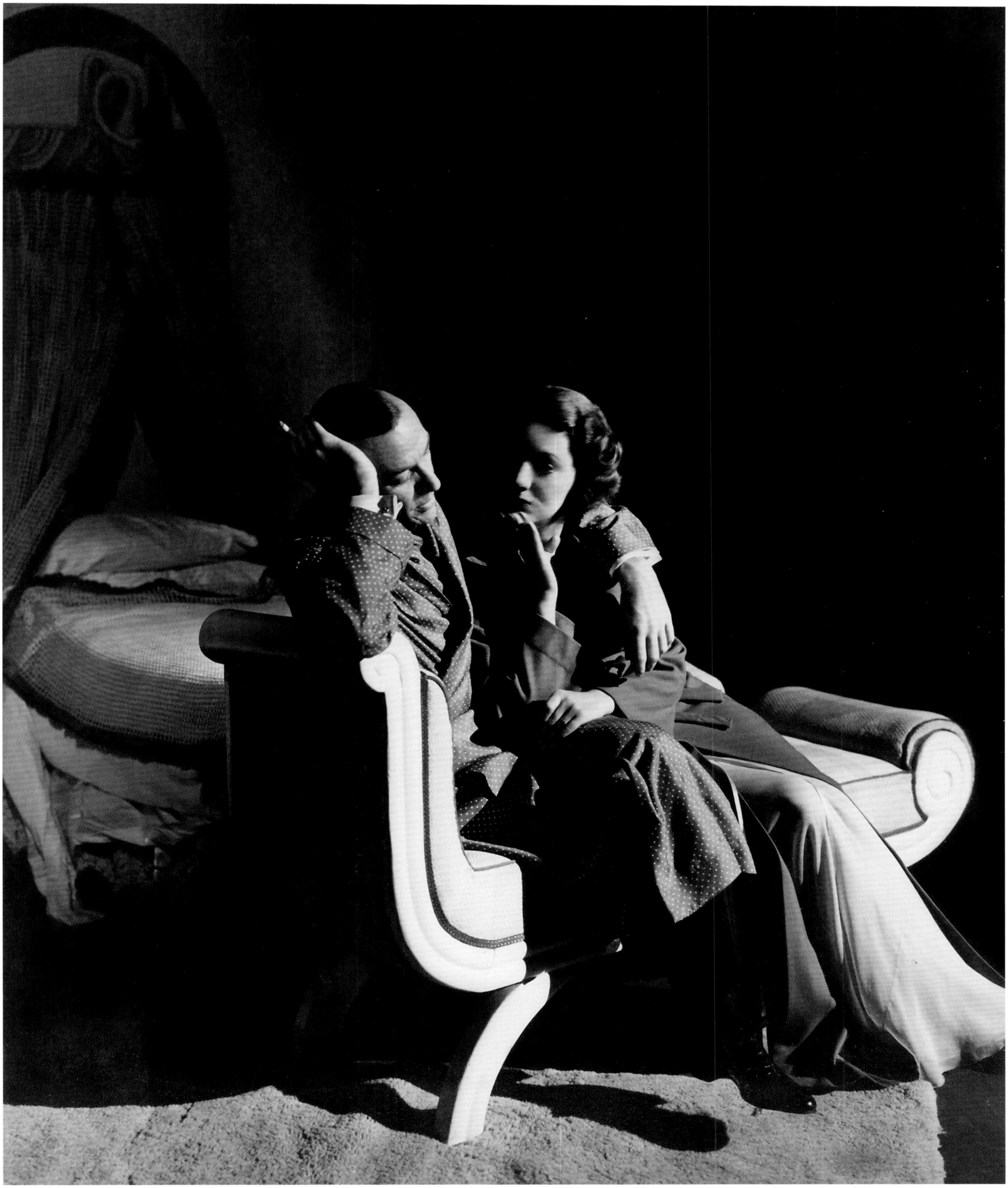

106. Noël Coward and Gertrude Lawrence on the set of *Tonight at 8:30*, 1936

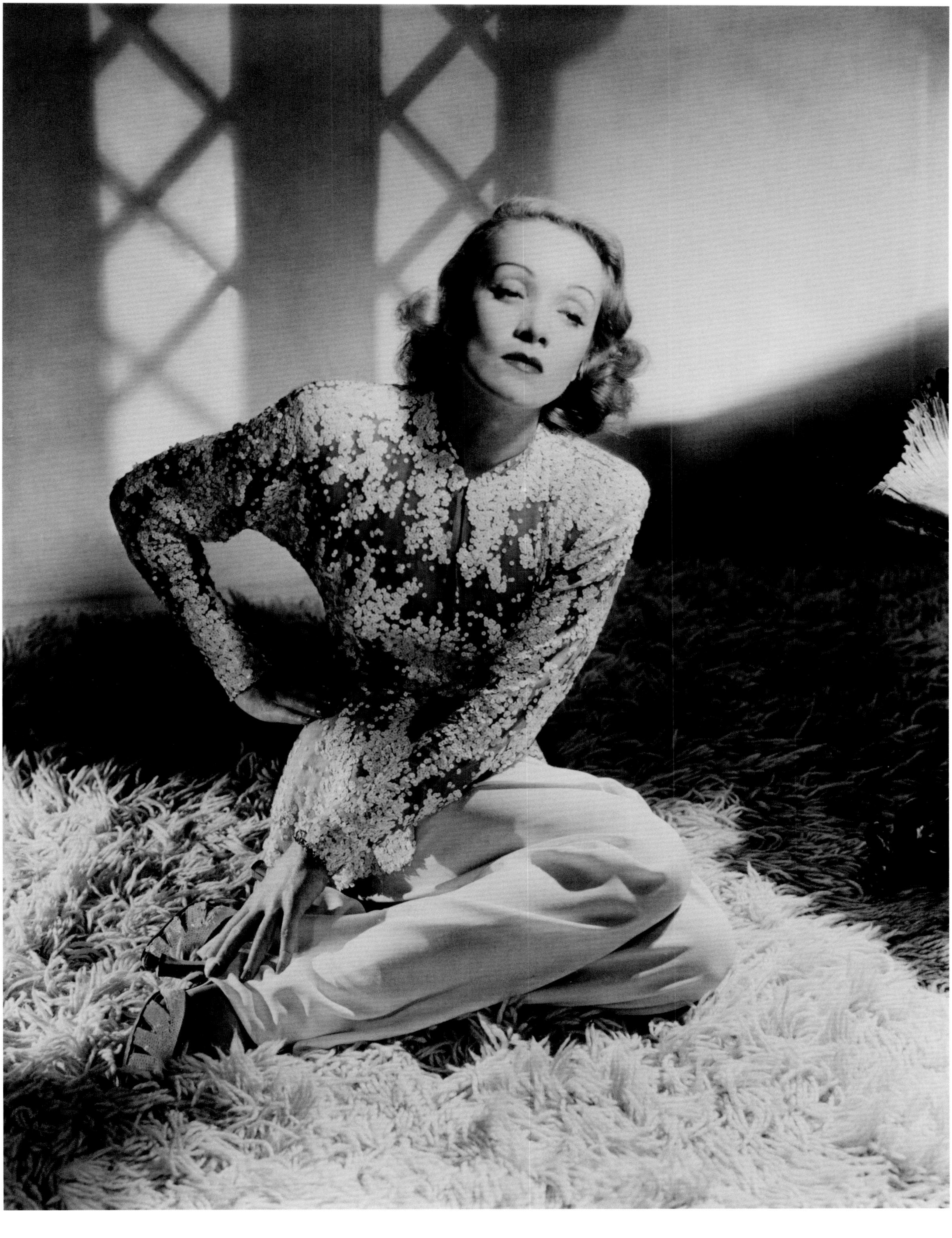

107. Marlene Dietrich, New York, 1942

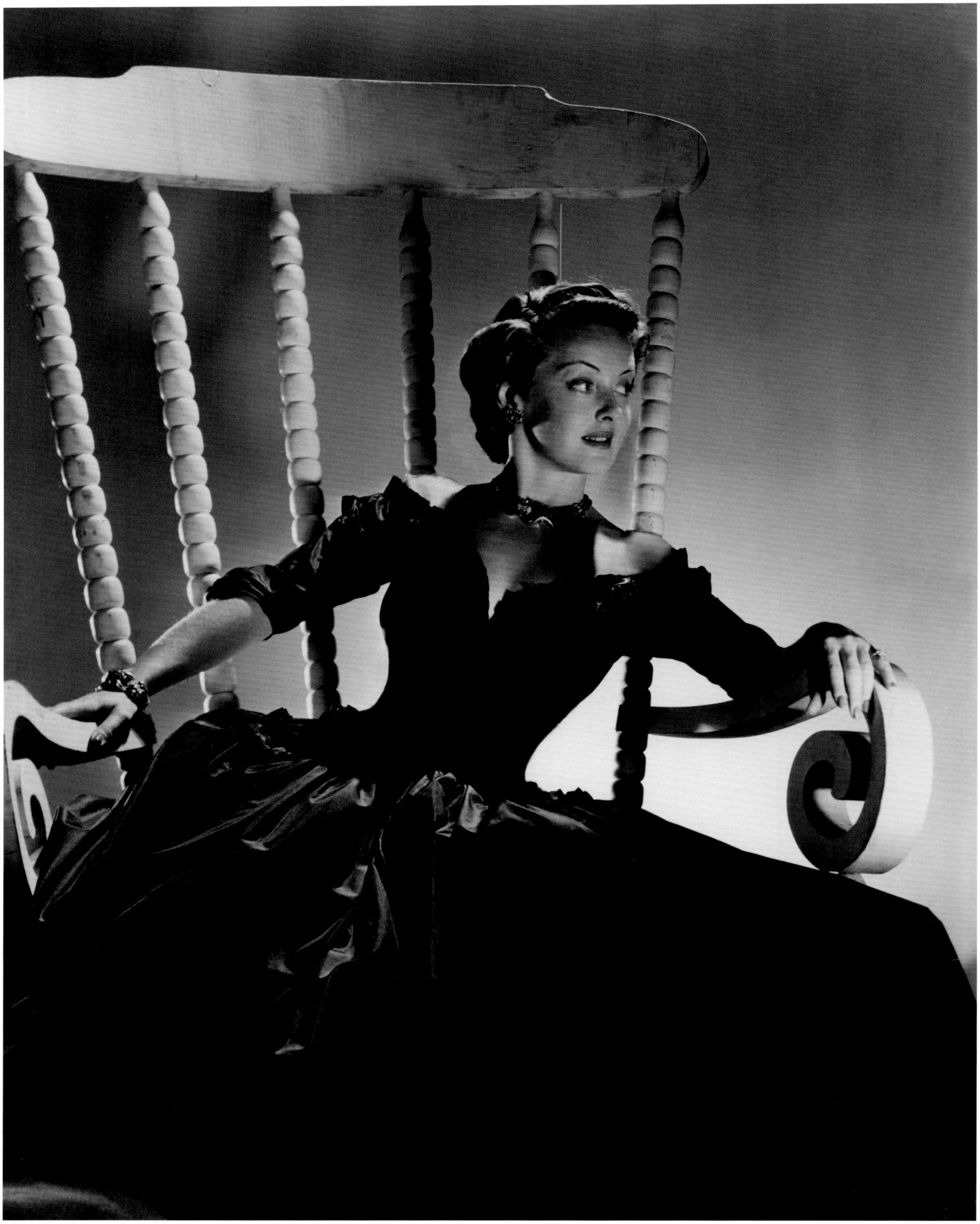

108. Bette Davis, New York, 1939

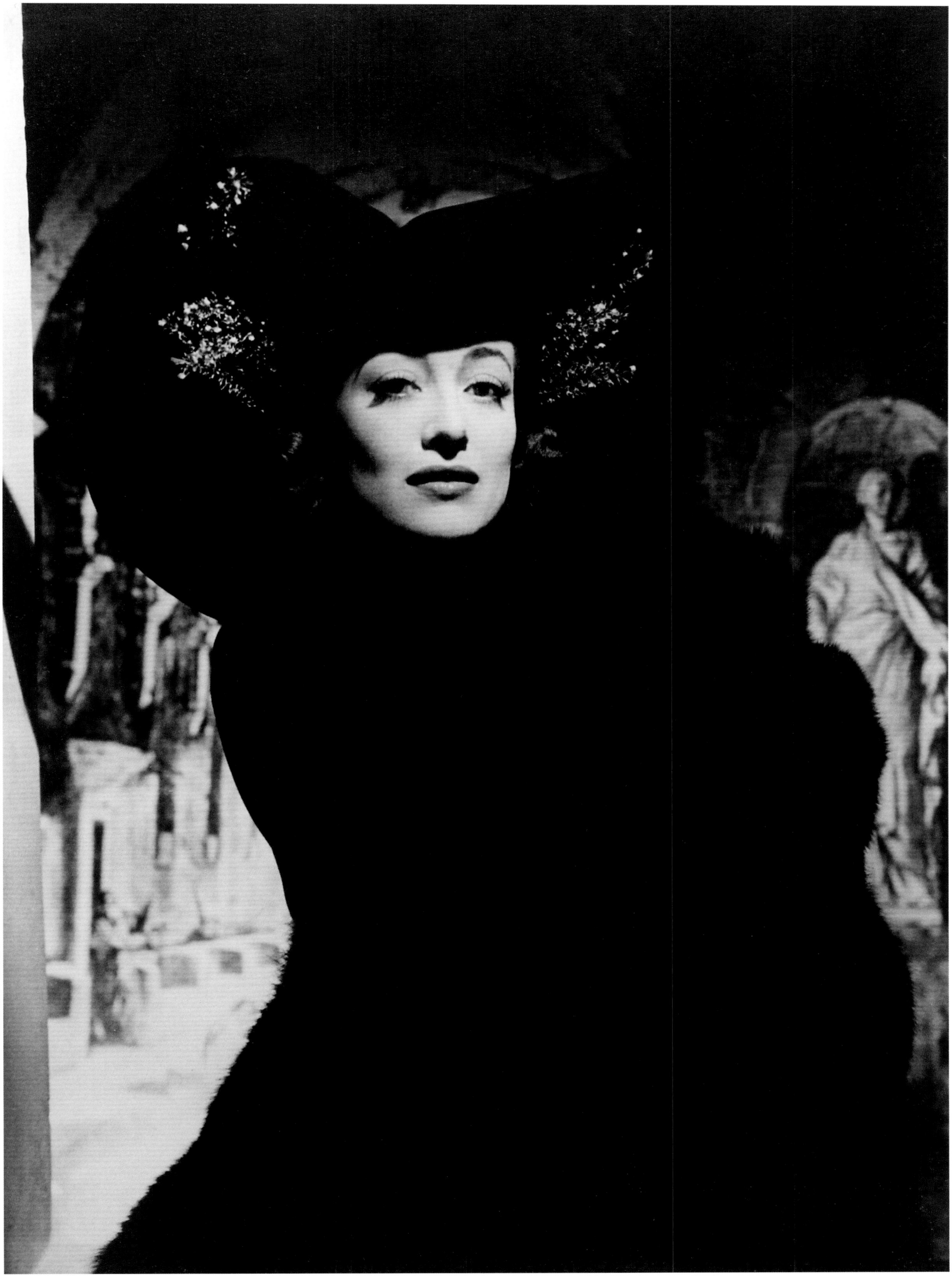

109. Joan Crawford, New York, 1938

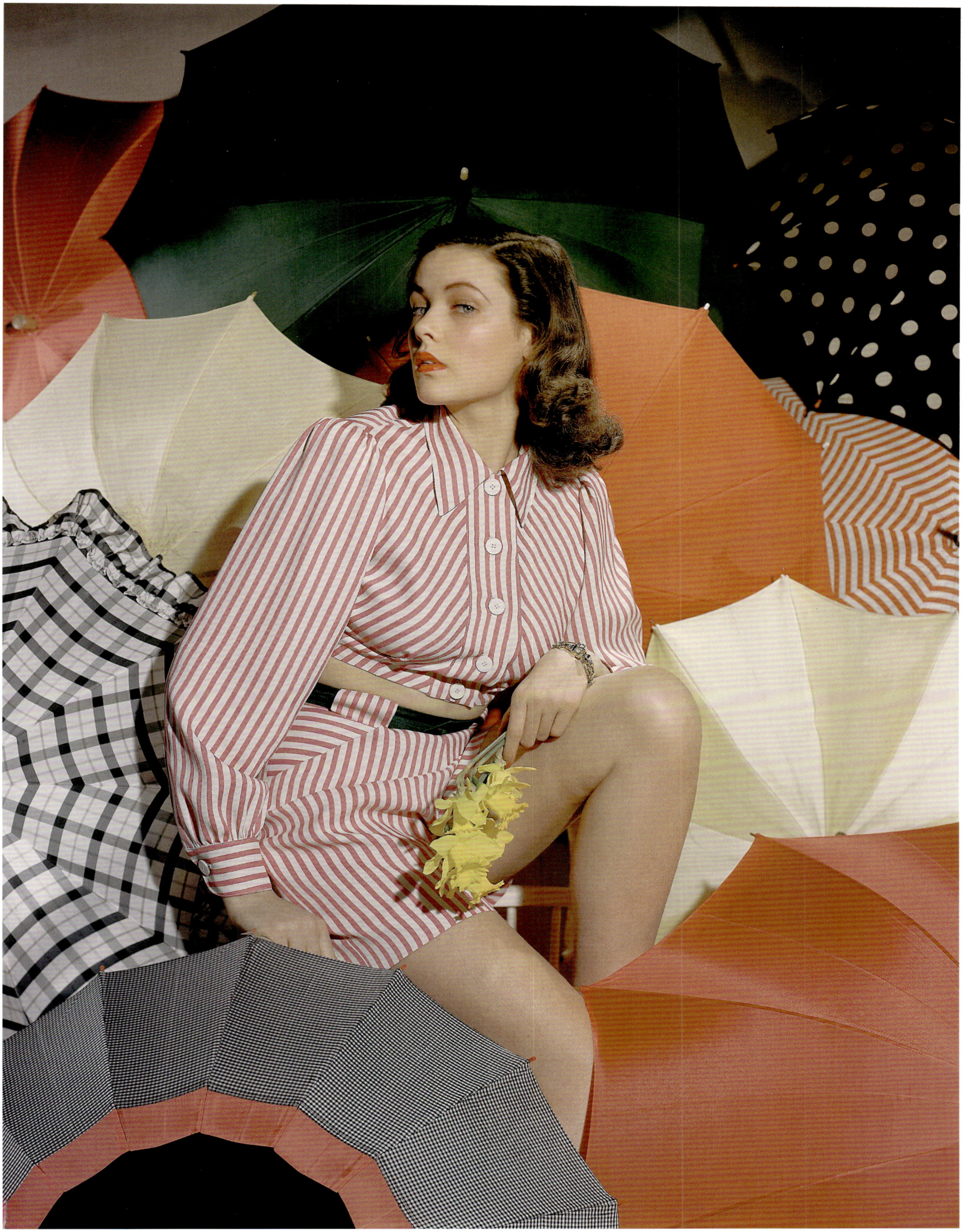

110. Gene Tierney, New York, 1940

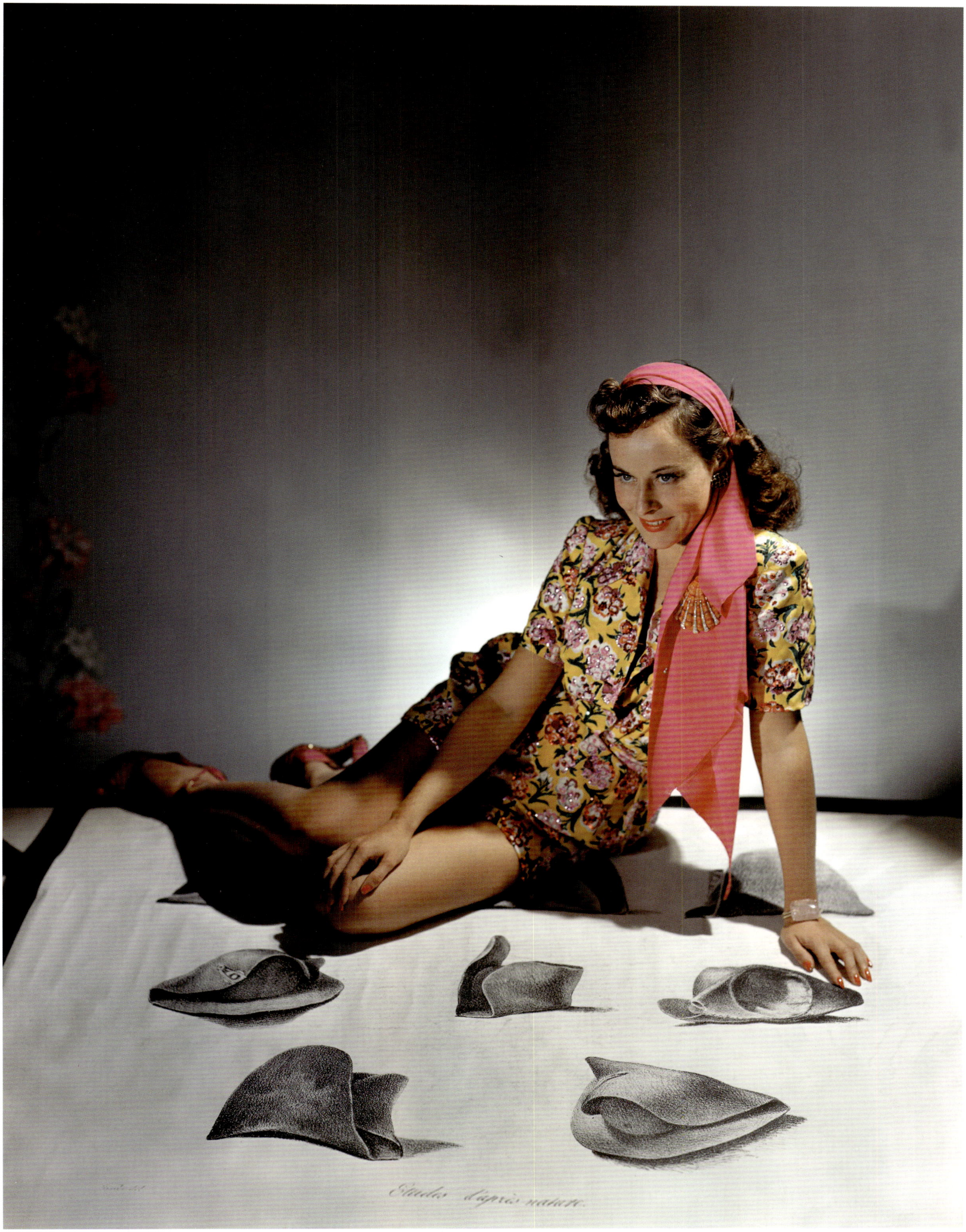

111. Paulette Goddard, New York, 1940

IV

Horst and Britain

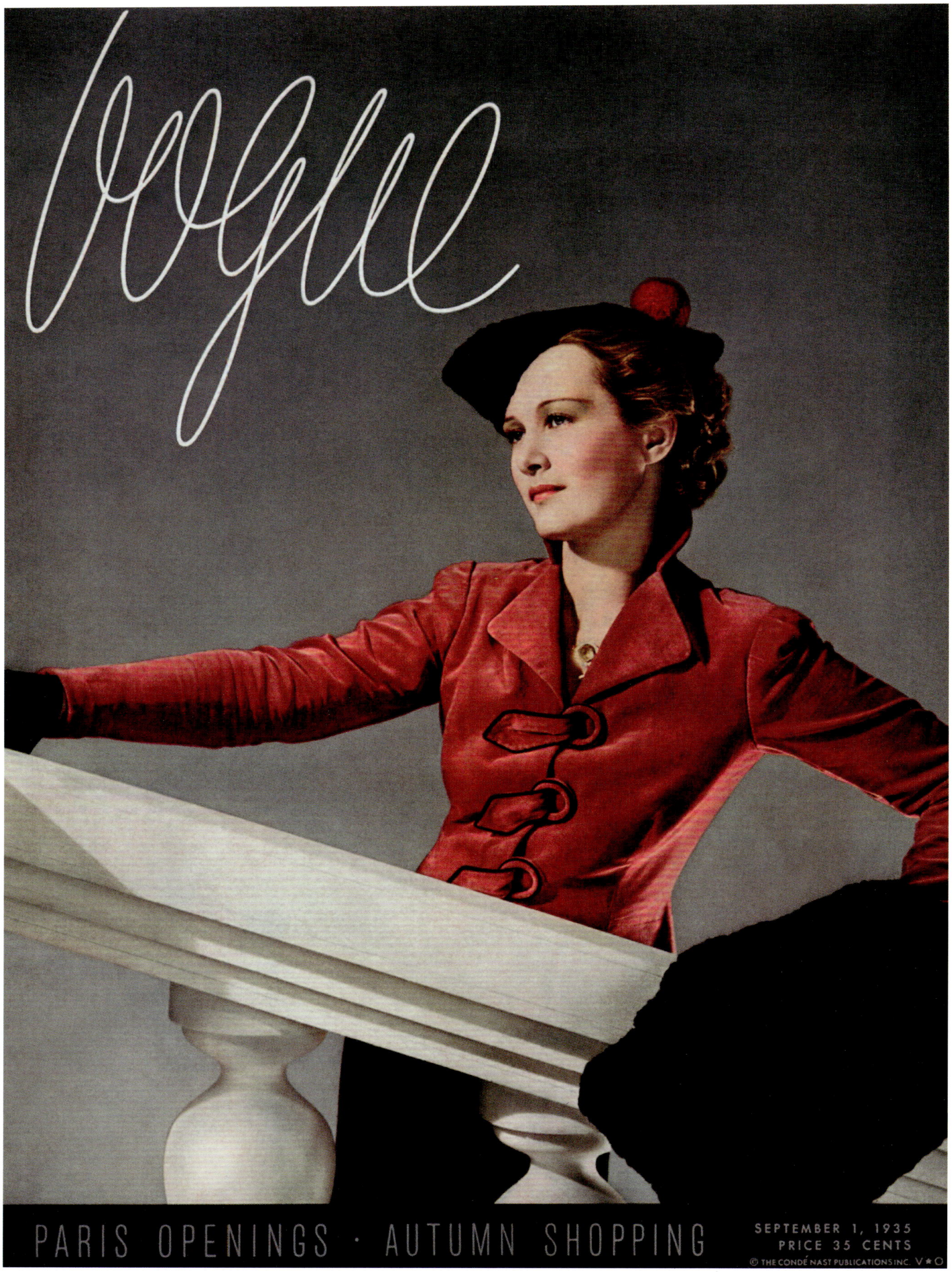

112. *Vogue* cover, September 1935

AN ENGLISH INTERLUDE

Robin Muir

The exhibition *Horst Portraits: 60 Years of Style*, arranged by the National Portrait Gallery, London, in 2001, barely 18 months after Horst's death, celebrated his best-known images, those that cut across the barriers of art, fashion and high society to present a vision of the 1930s, his heyday, as an era of avant-gardism, creativity and stylishness nonpareil. For Horst, this had crystallized in the decade's early years with photographs for the Condé Nast magazines *Vanity Fair* and *Vogue* in New York (starting in 1932) and in Paris for the French edition of *Vogue* where his pictures first appeared – though unattributed (in 1931).

A point of departure was a survey of unseen and unpublished portraits with a commentary and chronology by curator Terence Pepper, disclosing that while many had been made in London they had slipped from view in the intervening years. In the historiography of Horst this is a small body of work, but considered with his still little-known fashion photographs taken for British *Vogue* between 1931 and 1937, it is not an insignificant one. The British edition provided him with his first breakthrough as a published photographer, commissioning over 200 of his earliest pictures and sharing with the American and French editions his first cover image.[1] If exposure to the Parisian beau monde taught him the rudiments of fashionable taste, Horst believed his early sojourns in England were equally formative with regard to the sense of 'style' by which his work would come to be defined. There was – as his friend Jean Cocteau pointed out, not least by his own example – '[a] close association between theatrical gesture and good tailoring'.[2]

Horst's first visit to London was in 1930, a five-day trip accompanying his friend and mentor the established *Vogue* photographer George Hoyningen-Huene. Horst later recalled being impressed by 'the immaculate style of an extraordinarily high proportion of the men I saw on the street'. He continued: 'It was an entirely new world to me. I felt like some eighteenth-century traveller seeing his first mandarins in China. The English gentleman in those days dressed with a phenomenal blend of ease and precision. And they had a way of walking that added to their elegance. In fact, I was so lost in admiration for their appearance – the dark-blue suits, the red carnation in the buttonhole, the bowler hats and neatly-furled umbrellas – that I tried to copy them.'[3]

That Horst's fashion work for British *Vogue* has been neglected is regrettable but unsurprising. The negatives were presumed lost, only to be rediscovered in *Vogue*'s London archives in the mid-1990s and returned to his studio thereafter; too late for *Horst: His Work and His World* (1984) by Valentine Lawford, the starting point for any study of the photographer's work in the context of his life. Pictures taken for British *Vogue* could only be reproduced from tear sheets.

In April 1934, in its account of the spring collections, British *Vogue* reported that 'a modish young man comes over from Paris and looks at the London fashion collections with a fresh and unbiased eye'. This reference was to Johnnie McMullin, a writer for American *Vogue* and keen observer of the rich and fashionable at leisure, but it might equally have described the photographer accompanying him. The observation continued: 'Some of the loveliest models from the English dress houses are photographed here by Horst.'[4] There followed 18 photographs by Horst over 12 pages. Interposed among the fashion pictures were his portraits of actress Yvonne Printemps (pl.134) and actor Louis Hayward in costume for Noël Coward's *Conversation Piece*, which had opened in February with a set design by Gladys Calthrop, also photographed. Coward, who had assumed a lead role, posed in costume.[5]

In identifying Horst, *Vogue* was recognizing a contribution born of necessity, one that had begun in 1932 and over the next five years would give the British beau monde a veneer, in Cecil Beaton's words, of '*boîte-de-nuit* drama' and the London couture a continental 'chic'.[6]

In 1931, even as British *Vogue* celebrated its 15th anniversary, it relied on fashion photographs imported from the American edition. The take-up rate was considerable and frequently the same material appeared in both magazines.[7] This was partly in the spirit of economic expediency but also partly due to the fact that the new discipline of fashion photography (the course of which, in Britain, *Vogue* and its newly-established rival *Harper's Bazaar* would determine) was unfamiliar to the hieratic society portrait photographers upon whom *Vogue* then relied. Few could bring to the magazine freshness or enthusiasm. Under contract from 1927 until 1955, Cecil Beaton was a sure-footed exception.[8]

Harry Yoxall, managing director of British *Vogue* from the 1920s to the 1960s, bewailed the lack of home grown talent: 'Until the arrival of Cecil Beaton and Norman Parkinson our London studio was lamentably short of native aptitude; and even when they arrived they were constantly being whisked off to Paris and New York.'[9] Newly contracted to French *Vogue*, Horst was released from his duties to aid the British edition at the end of 1931. He made his base the well-equipped, if gloomy, studio of Howard Coster, near Fleet Street.[10]

The first results appeared in March 1932, an eight-page, highly-stylized portfolio of London fashions. Taken in the controlled

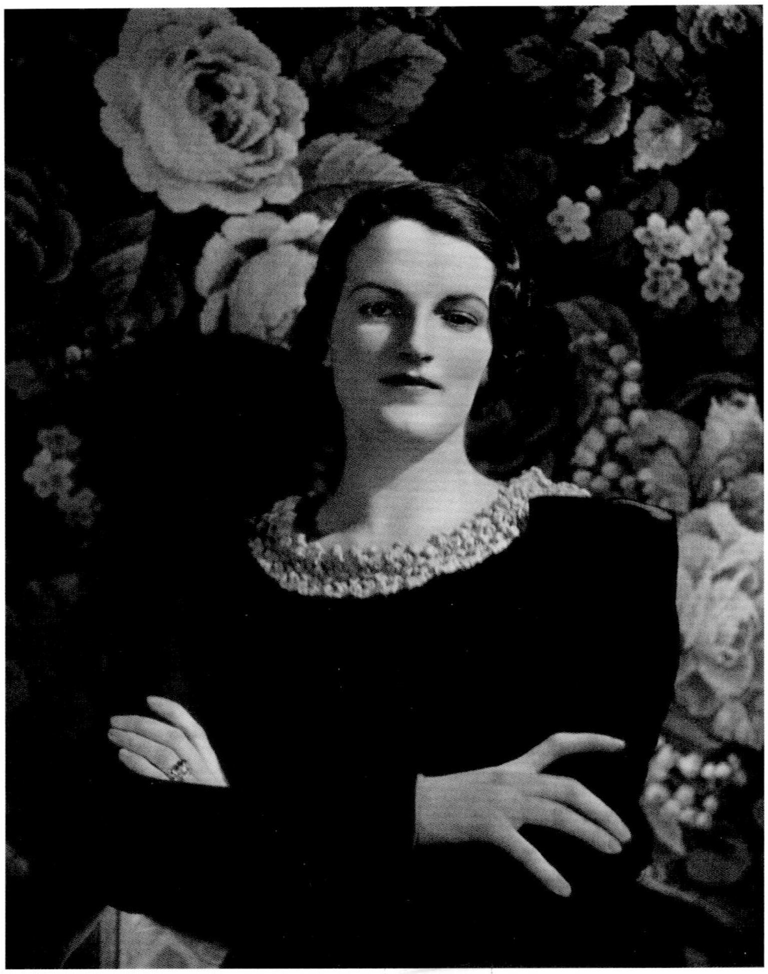

113. Mrs Anthony Eden, 1934

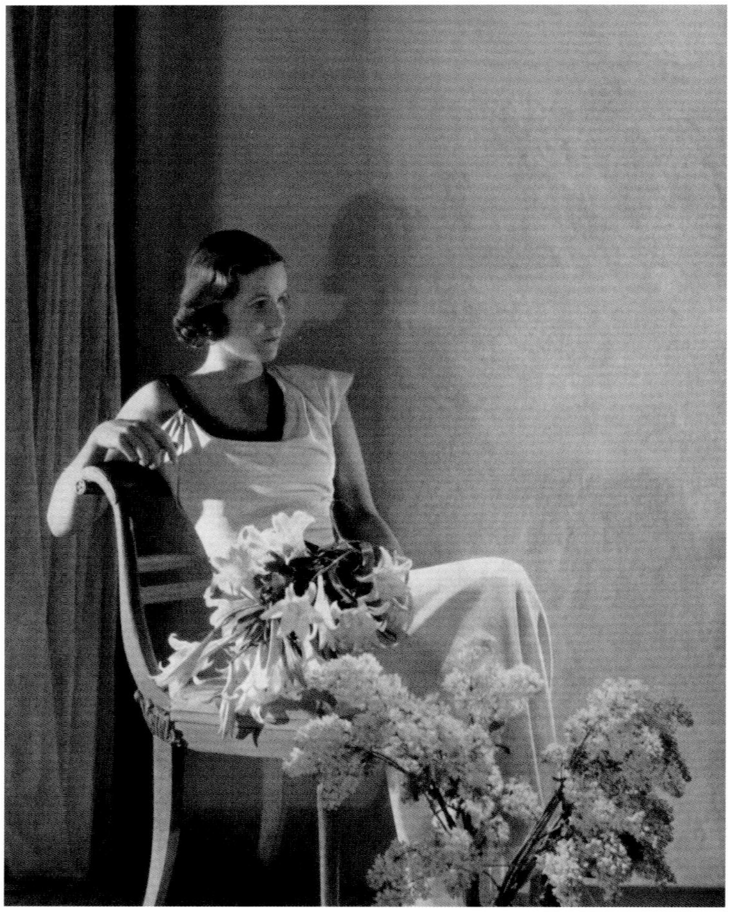

114. Mrs Anthony Jenkinson, 1932

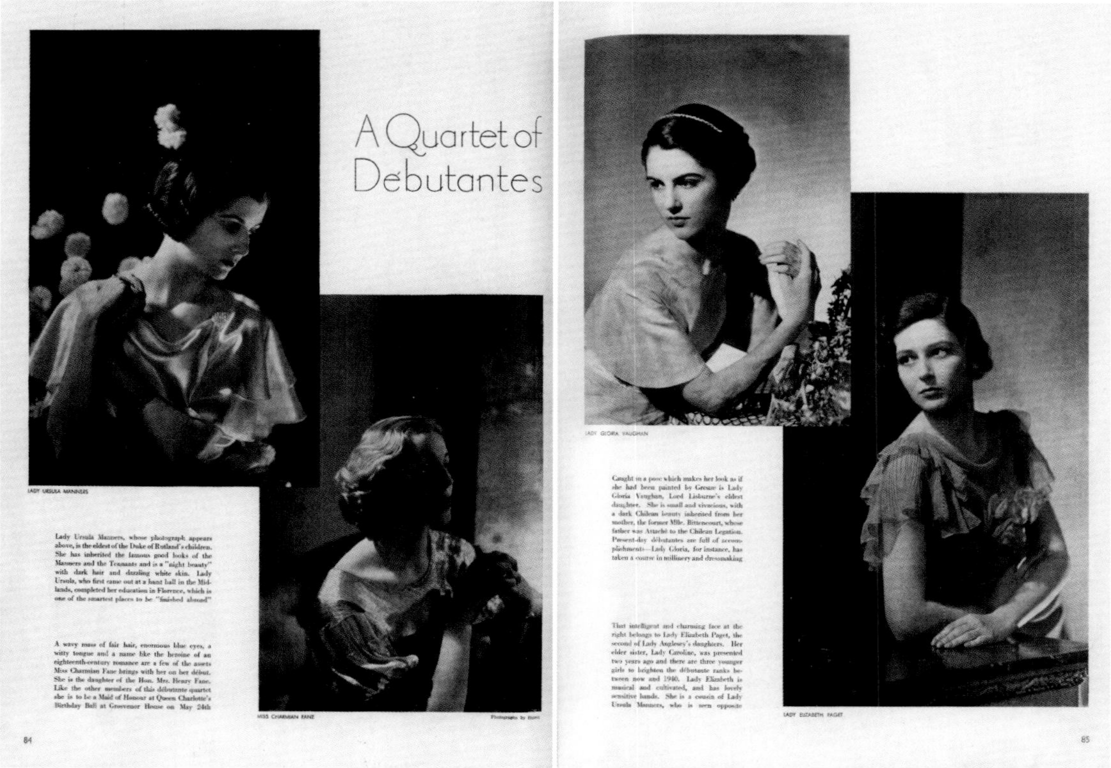

115. Lady Ursula Manners, Miss Charmian Fane, Lady Gloria Vaughan, Lady Elizabeth Paget, 'A Quartet of Débutantes', British *Vogue*, 2 May 1934

environment of the studio and on a large format plate camera, they were indebted to Horst's mentor Huene, the *mise en scène* meticulously arranged and lit to display the construction and fine detailing of the clothes and the human form as sculptural. As was customary for *Vogue*, Horst's models were drawn from the ranks of emerging actresses who could hold a pose with equanimity, and the ornamental daughters of the British establishment who could not (pl.115). Felicity Seddon in a lace and organdie confection by Glenny had appeared in Noël Coward's *This Year of Grace* (1928). In a 'dance frock' by Norman Hartnell (1901–79) was the promising musical comedy actress Norah Henderson, while the issue's frontispiece showed Mrs Anthony Jenkinson, daughter of the Canadian financier Sir James Dunn, her inexperience all but concealed by an arrangement of cut flowers (pl.114). Further pages followed in the April, May and June issues, including portraits of the popular musical comedy star Jessie Matthews, socialite Edwina d'Erlanger and against a floral tapestry Mrs Anthony Eden, wife of the Lord Privy Seal (p.113).

This pattern of debutantes, English beauties, revue artists and stage and film actresses, classically composed, would be repeated over the next few years. In selecting the props and backdrops for these early photographs Horst sought to convey, in the words of his biographer Valentine Lawford, 'his untutored impression of the kind of ideal and beautiful world in which he imagined that the women who bought the dresses must live'.[11] As the settings grew increasingly baroque, the more meticulous and complex was their construction, the human form as architectural as the scenery. The *New Yorker*'s correspondent in Paris, Janet Flanner, had already praised (in 1932) Horst's 'instinct for linear romance' and 'the special constructive values of one who has worked first with skeletons of steel and wood'.[12] By 1944, Horst was more direct: 'My first pictures were loaded with background – perhaps because of my training in architecture, which made me more interested in décor than in the human element. I was continually dismantling palaces, hauling in small forests and entire hothouses meant to enhance but really crushing the little woman posing in their midst ...'.[13]

A portrait of actress Gertrude Lawrence in a daring ensemble by Schiaparelli was also taken in London, a simpler *mise en scène*. Horst's first contribution to American *Vogue*, it was considered innovative because he had posed her on a zebra skin. Lawrence, a Broadway sensation after Noël Coward's *Private Lives* (1931), was the first luminary Horst had photographed and his first significantly successful portrait, not least because, as he explained, 'she knew how to stand and move' (pl.130).[14]

At this time Horst enjoyed London life in the company of the theatre designer Oliver Messel and the art collector and patron Peter Watson, lunching with two of the Mitford sisters, Diana and Unity, and having himself fitted for a suit from Anderson & Sheppard, then of Savile Row.[15] English taste entranced him: 'the only real male elegance was English and any foreign imitation of it, whether American or French made me wince'.[16] To Horst, the perfect example of style was the Duke of Windsor, whom later he came to know. The German illustrated magazines of Horst's youth were in thrall to the Duke (then the Prince of Wales). He was, as Horst recalled, 'unforgettably handsome: blond, blue-eyed, youthful, not tall but well built ... the very picture of health'. Time did not diminish the former king's appeal. In 1963, Horst photographed him at the Moulin

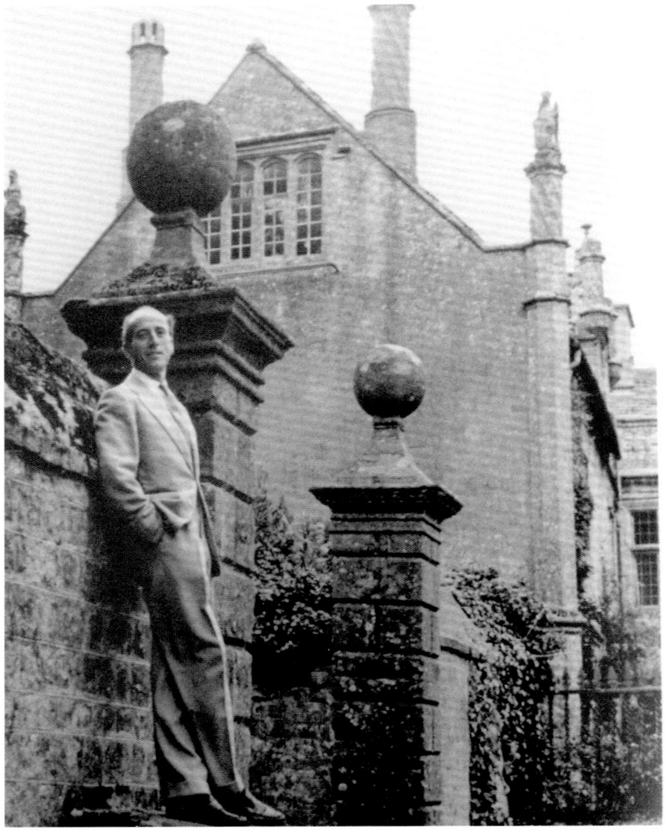

116. Valentine Lawford, Dorset, 1948

de Tuilerie, Paris: 'I took a quick snapshot. It turned out to be one of my favourite portraits. He was wearing a bright, dark-blue tweed suit with a white windowpane pattern … That suit was an astonishing one. It certainly astonished me. It had an outspoken, almost flashy elegance. But he looked wonderfully well in it …'.[17] He found in Noël Coward another epitome of English style, 'urbane, amusing and light of touch, a mixture of show-off and throwaway …', and in addition he admired the easy-going charm of anglophile Douglas Fairbanks, Jr.[18]

By the autumn of 1934 at British *Vogue* Horst was emerging as a star in his own right, photographed by Howard Coster (1885–1959) and given the endorsement: 'without whom the loveliest dress would not make a lovely picture'. The same issue saw Horst's first *en plein-air* photograph for *Vogue*, a fashion picture taken on the steps of the Albert Memorial, Kensington.[19] A year later, his first *Vogue* cover image was published (pl.112).

In 1934 Horst's prestige was confirmed with an invitation to photograph Princess Marina of Greece and Denmark, in Paris, in advance of her marriage to Prince George, Duke of Kent, the younger brother of the Prince of Wales (pl.133). The suite of royal portraits – the result of painstaking set construction involving Savonnerie carpets, drapery and a detail from a photographic enlargement of a Veronese painting – was a tour de force, conspicuously successful and, although intended exclusively for *Vogue*, much reproduced elsewhere.[20]

Early magazine images of the Prince of Wales aside, the effortless elegance of the English was not new to Horst. Many years earlier, while a trainee at a Hamburg-based import-export business, Horst had heard of, if not glimpsed himself, a 'kleiner, englischer Lord', immaculately dressed in a grey flannel suit, who was reputed to have 'stopped the traffic'. This was Valentine George Nicholas Lawford, known to his family as Valentine, though many, including Horst, called him Nicholas (pl.116).

Their paths would cross in 1947. That Horst's taste for English decoration, horticulture, reading matter and much else would be informed by Lawford, a cultured and urbane Englishman, was inescapable. They lived together for over 40 years, setting up home at Oyster Bay, Long Island, their relationship ending only with Lawford's death in 1991. Lawford was a highly polished product of the English upper middle classes and destined for the Foreign Office.[21] In 1936, as an Under-Secretary at the British Embassy, Paris, he glided dextrously between the bureaucrats and public servants of embassy life and, after office hours, the artistic circles around Gertrude Stein and Nancy Cunard. Even Cecil Beaton admired him: 'He is one of the most delightful, refreshing, un-selfconscious companions one could ever meet. He has an incredibly well-trained brain, never forgets a fact, date or name, is quite as flash, witty and kind.'[22]

On the eve of war, Lawford was summoned back to Whitehall and served as Private Secretary to three successive Foreign Secretaries: Lord Halifax, Anthony Eden and Ernest Bevin. Certain mandarins may have regarded him critically, but this may have been connected to a subsequent event: his unexpected decision to leave the diplomatic service at short notice to join Horst in the United States. The politician and diarist Sir Henry 'Chips' Channon dismissed Lawford in his diaries as a 'rather "Second Empire" secretary', but conceded that as a rival diarist, Lawford's observations 'would live but they would be too precious, too distinguished …'.[23]

Despite writing Horst's photo-biography, Lawford would be far

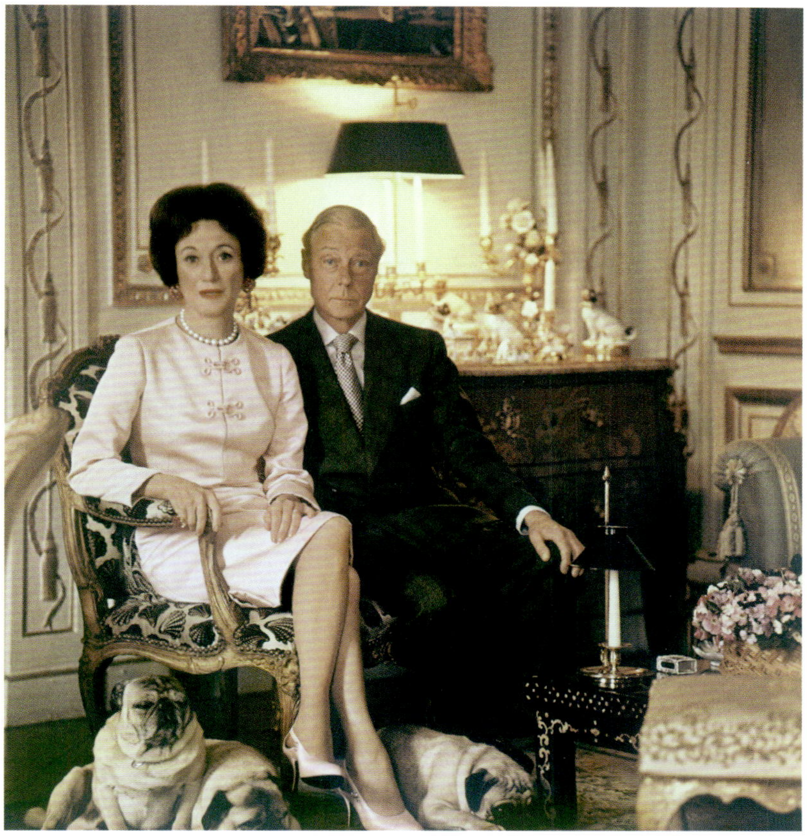

117. Duke and Duchess
of Windsor, 1963

118. Duke of Windsor,
Paris, 1963

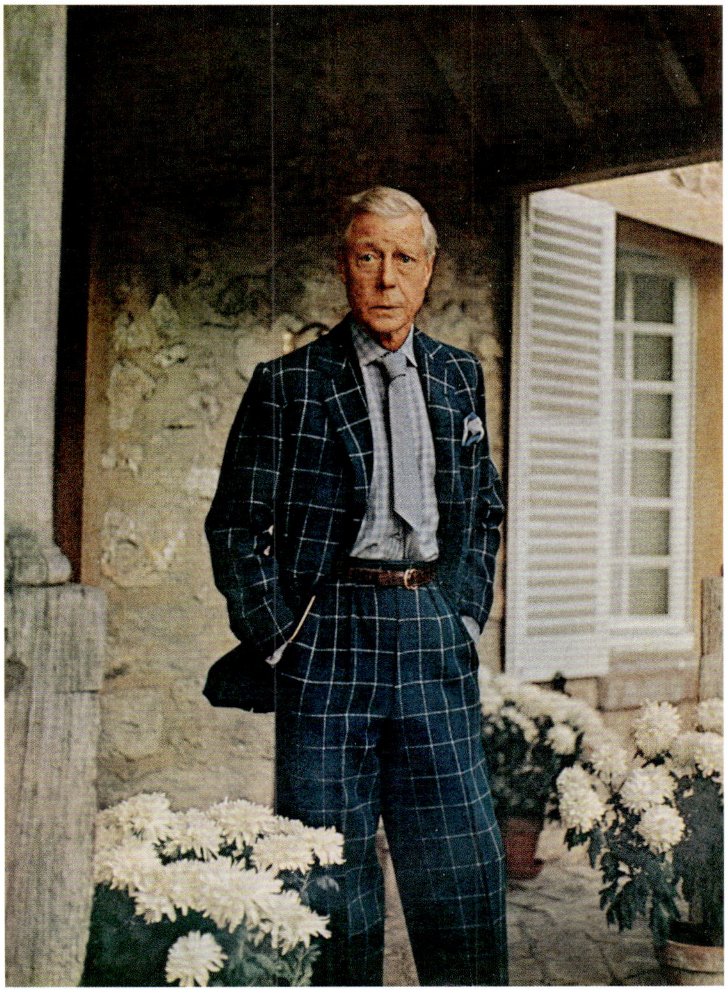

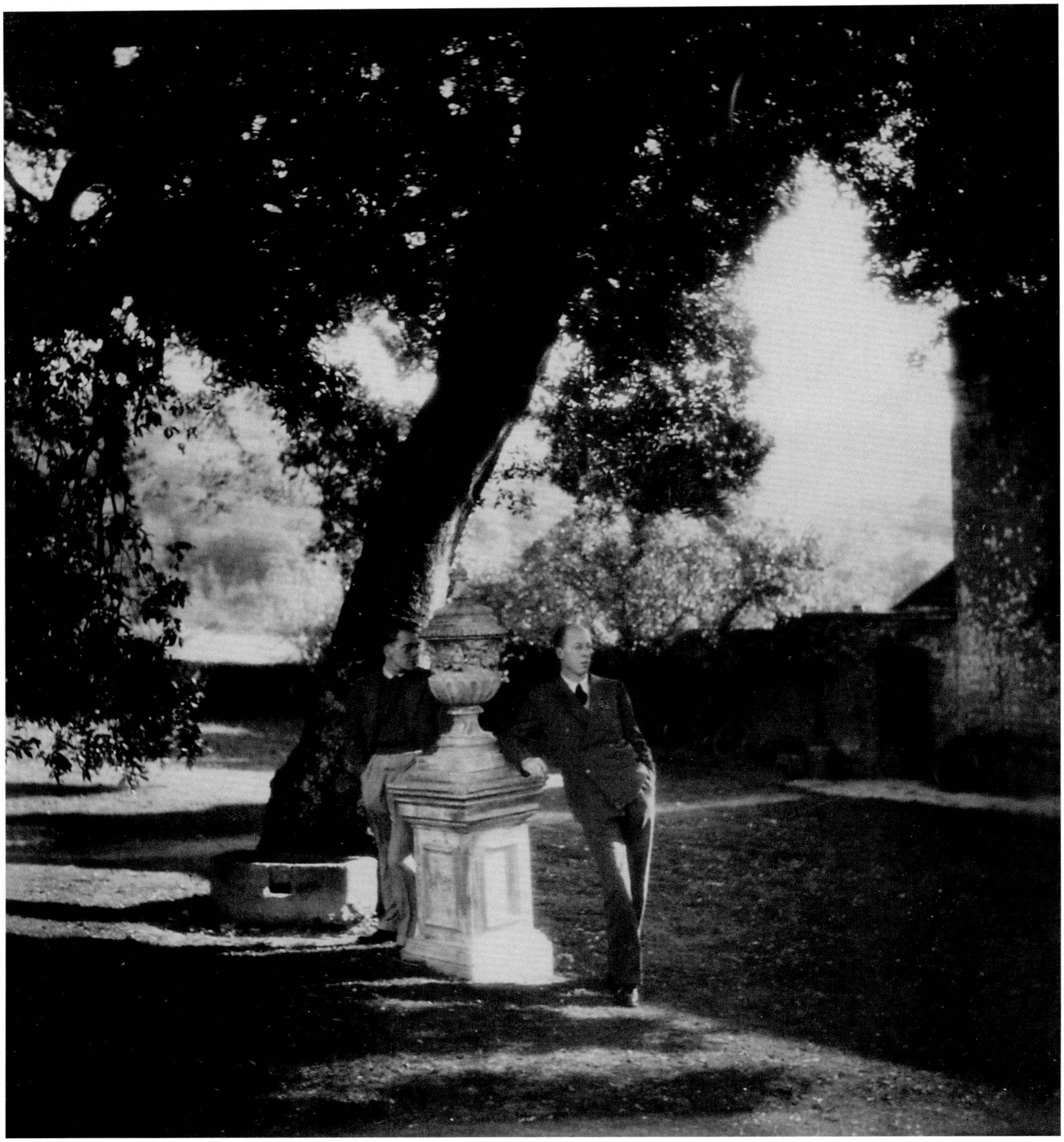

119. Cecil Beaton,
Horst and George Hoyningen-Huene, 1930

more than an amanuensis. When Horst's career entered a second phase in the 1960s at American *Vogue* – he became a photographer of domestic interiors and gardens for editor Diana Vreeland – Lawford's role would be a vital one, and his charm, social connections and descriptive writing skills were crucial to the success of the *Vogue* features.

By 1935 Huene had quit as *Vogue*'s chief Paris photographer and his protégé was appointed in his place. With new demands on his time, Horst's arrangement with the British edition officially ended in 1936, though he would continue to make many trips to London until the autumn of 1937. It would take another half century for Horst to be commissioned again by British *Vogue*.

As Horst's reputation escalated in Paris, so too did Cecil Beaton's in London. Querulous and suspicious, the two photographers enjoyed an uneasy relationship that lasted their long professional lives. It started badly. The culmination of Horst's and Huene's 1930 trip to Britain was an invitation to Ashcombe, Beaton's country home in Wiltshire (pl.119). Ashcombe afforded a vignette of English country life, and one in particular that intrigued Horst was a view glimpsed through a window of a shooting party: guns, keepers, beaters and dogs, all making their way up the valley. Horst photographed Huene posing with garden statuary and Huene photographed Beaton in his 'Circus Bedroom' (pl.123). However, a game of charades during the course of the weekend gave Beaton the opportunity to humiliate Horst, who spoke little English. 'If Cecil had known what was to come, I wonder what even more artful humiliation he might not have cooked up,' recalled Horst.[24]

By the autumn of 1935, *Vogue*'s editor-in-chief, Edna Woolman Chase, was advising Beaton not visit the New York office as his rival would be there. Age did not diminish their mutual enmity. A pointed review by Beaton of Horst's compilation of photographs *Salute to the Thirties* (1971) prompted another row and several conciliatory letters on the part of the reviewer.[25]

As the decade closed and the outbreak of war became a certainty, Horst left Paris for New York in 1939. There he became aware of antipathy towards his nationality. On a wartime goodwill mission to New York, Lady Louis Mountbatten – 'stiffly and properly British' – left the studio on learning Horst was German and could only briefly be cajoled back.[26] Horst assumed American citizenship in 1943. He continued photographing fashion and portraiture for *Vogue* throughout the 1940s and 1950s, but his career took an auspicious turn in 1963 when Diana Vreeland assumed the editorship of American *Vogue*. She commissioned from Horst and Lawford a series of articles on the lifestyles of the 'Beautiful People', the successors to the international beau monde of the 1930s. Their surroundings, whether conservative or innovative, urban or rural, were always creative and glittering, and were illuminated in words by Lawford and pictures by Horst. The project, conceived by Vreeland to capture, in the words of her biographer, 'the complete worlds of imaginative people whose distinctive taste and determination turned fantasy into reality', continued even after her dismissal from the magazine in 1971.[27] In Vreeland's own words, 'My soul craved something that was tangible. I didn't want still lifes, I wanted secrets of the house, of the garden, of the countryside ...'.[28]

Horst had already been contributing, albeit intermittently, to American *House & Garden* since 1941, and had been marked out as 'a photographer of great decorative ingenuity' by Frank Crowninshield

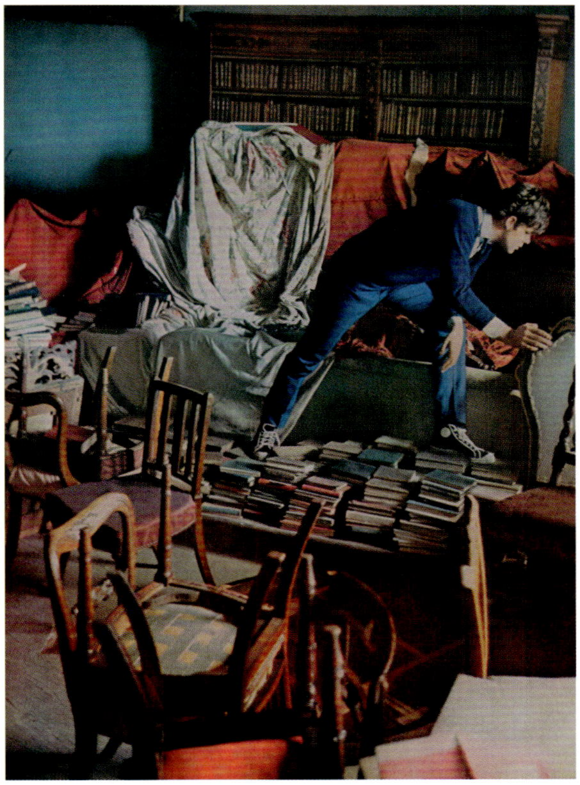

120. Lord Eliot, Port Eliot,
Cornwall, 1966

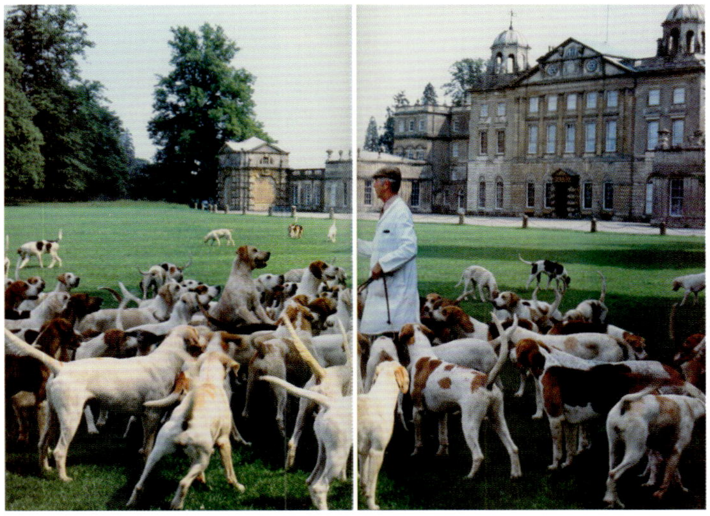

121. Duke of Beaufort's hunt,
Badminton Estate,
Gloucestershire, 1983

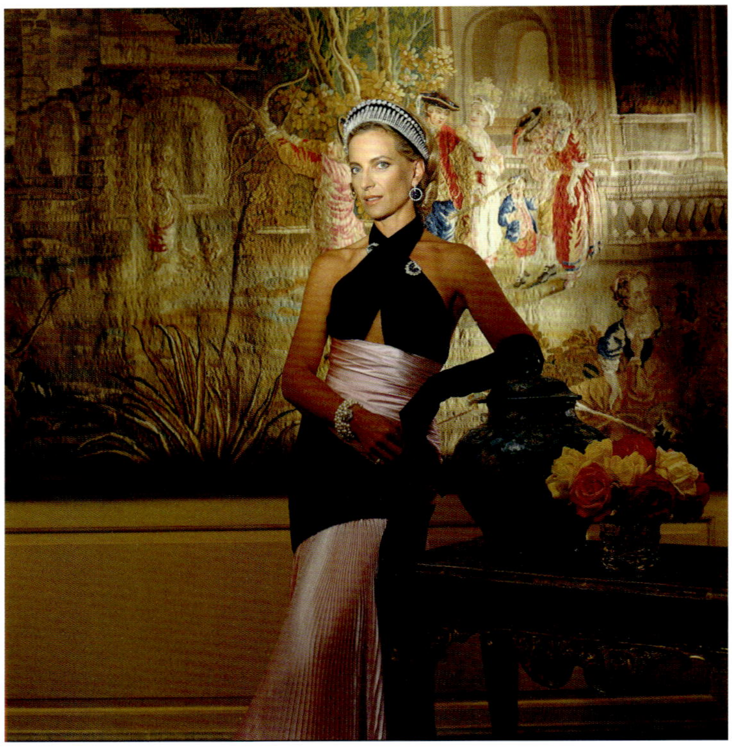

122. Princess Michael of Kent, 1991

(1872-1947), editor of *Vanity Fair* from 1914 to 1936.[29] But for Horst, 'having Diana as my editor was like having a new lease on life. She rejuvenated me and my work when I least expected it'.[30]

With Lawford as Vreeland's 'historian' and with suggestions from the younger but equally well-connected Englishman, Nicholas Haslam, it was inescapable that English taste – and American approximations of it – would shine through. Vreeland sought originality in taste and though this was usually underpinned by wealth, inherited or acquired, and possessions, inherited or acquired, it was not always the case. The young Lord Eliot at his ancestral home Port Eliot, Cornwall, had inherited possessions but limited means with which to care for them, and a perceptible disinclination for order. The haphazard domestic harmony made for eye-catching 'fashions in living' (pl.120). 'It was', considered Horst, 'the first cosy and congenial English country house I had stayed in.' If American interpretation of English taste led to a riot of colour and drama, so much the better. Virginia-born Nancy Lancaster's house and garden at Haseley Court, Oxfordshire, represented for *Vogue* the apogee of English country house style (unsurprisingly, as she was the co-owner of decorating firm Colefax and Fowler). A 'furor [*sic*] of flowers' and 'flooded in history', the article began, running to 15 pages of photographs and text.[31] The Duke and Duchess of Windsor's 'Englishness in exile' at the Moulin de Tuilerie in the Bois de Boulogne ran to 17 pages (pl.117).[32] At Turville Grange, Buckinghamshire, Princess Radziwill – formerly Caroline Lee Bouvier of New York – presented a Queen Anne house alive with colour – 'ravishing pinks and sharp Cantonese Greens, faded Russian-y blues and enamelled yellows'.[33]

But it was his own house – a low-lying, single-storey, whitewashed Bauhaus-inspired pavilion of modest proportions, which Horst built in 1947 on the Tiffany estate at Oyster Bay, Long Island – that would be his own contribution to a fashion of living. Lawford joined him there in 1950, and it duly featured in *Vogue* in 1966.[34] Vreeland may have considered the symbiosis of Horst and Lawford 'like the sun and the sky at the right time of day',[35] but Haslam has observed that 'Nicholas [was the] polar opposite of Horst; he was carefully spoken almost la-di-da compared with Horst's cascading sentences, neatly buttoned-up as opposed to Horst's easy elegance'.[36] Horst's and Lawford's home was accordingly a harmony of dissimilar tastes. Horst's admiration for 1930s European style, particularly the furniture of Jean-Michel Frank, had led him to aquire several of the designer's oak and cloth x-stools, a dressing table, and plaster lamps and vases designed for Frank by the Giacometti brothers (Alberto and Diego), a case of rare artistic prescience as interest in Frank was to increase. These pieces were later regrouped at Oyster Bay to dramatic effect and featured thereafter in many of Horst's photographs.[37]

This modernist style was at odds with Lawford's own tastes, which tended towards the rhetoric of 'English traditional' – book-lined walls, family memorabilia, floral prints – and several visitors remarked upon the clash of aesthetics at each end of the pavilion, not all of them favourably.[38] However, a fondness for English rusticity was not Lawford's alone: Horst had acquired an English refectory table for entertaining and a nineteenth-century British officer's campaign desk, and upholstered his library chairs in a strong flowered chintz while his study was dominated by a nineteenth-century British military portrait.

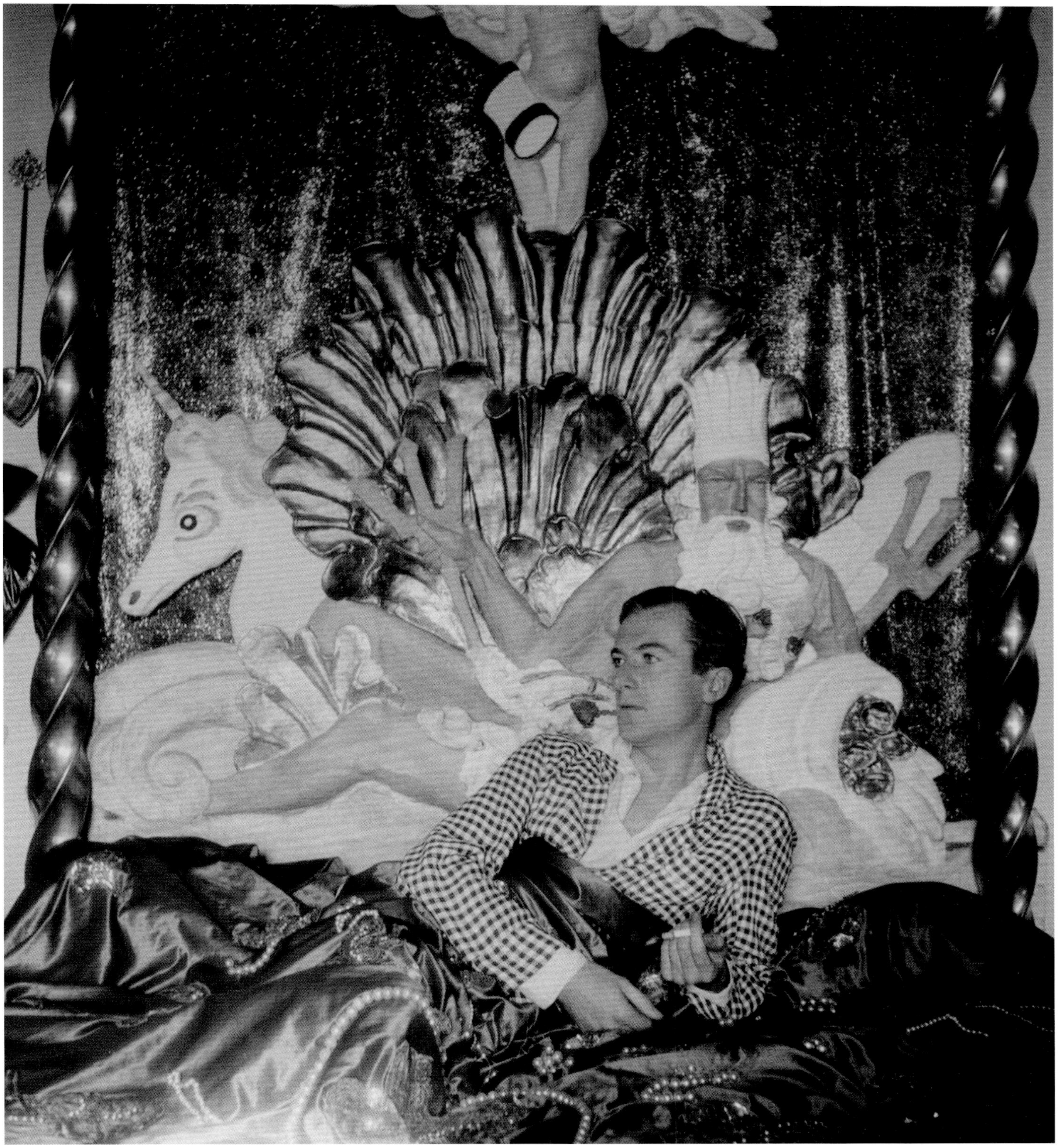

123. George Hoyningen-Huene,
Cecil Beaton in his 'Circus Bedroom', 1930

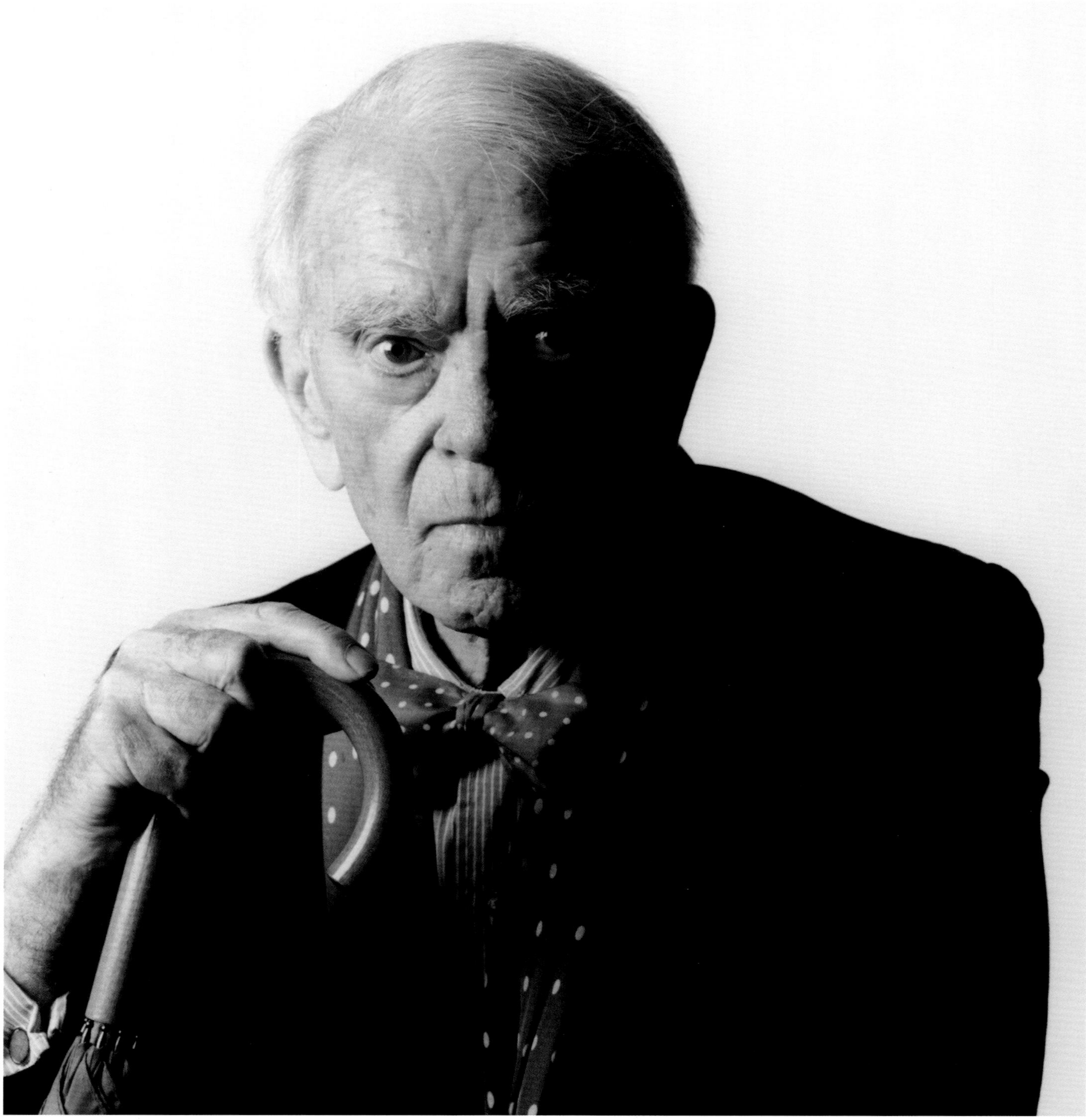

124. David Bailey, Horst, 1989
(image © David Bailey)

In 1969 Leo Lerman, then a contributing editor to Condé Nast's *Mademoiselle* magazine and a friend to both Lawford and Horst, described Oyster Bay's decorative schemes in his diaries, struck by its debt to the vernacular of the English country house – unexpected within its modernist frame. (He mentions specifically Bulbridge, the Georgian home in Wilton, Wiltshire, of their mutual friend Lady Juliet Duff, as a source of inspiration.) 'The house: meticulously arranged; [a] Picasso was sold to help build the house, with its triple transecting allées, an index to Horst's and Nicholas's lives, each detail cluing the stops upon their journeys to this place, this time – Russian silver cups, batiks, photos of Maestro [Toscanini] and so many others ... drawings by Nicholas of his grandparents – these good and very English-German, sometimes a Juliet feeling here – very Bulbridge (especially in Horst's loo with a wall of Turner engravings), much blue and white ...'. Spending the night there, Lerman was reminded of another aspect of English country life: '... [in] the coldest bedroom since my weekends in the Statelies those long-ago six months in England. I love being here, because it is having one foot in my lost world.'[39] What had once caused in the locality, as Lawford wrote in American *Vogue*, a 'minor architectural scandal', by the end of the 1960s had achieved a harmony with its landscape of tall trees and sloping lawns, and appeared almost to be moulded into it, assuming 'the elegance of an eighteenth-century hunting lodge'.[40]

As he approached his 80s, Horst was not yet finished with England. In 1983, he was despatched to Gloucestershire to photograph for American *House & Garden* the Dower House, home to David Somerset, heir to the Duke of Beaufort, on the edge of the grand sporting estate around Badminton House (pl.121). It was England at its most romantic and picturesque with the hounds of the Duke of Beaufort's Hunt on display.[41] Two years later he was back for *House & Garden* at another Dower House, this time at Arundel Park, the estate of the Duke of Norfolk in Sussex. With the landscape dipping towards the coast, Horst captured horses from the Duke's racing stables riding the gallops.[42]

As he celebrated his 80th birthday in 1986, British *Vogue* commissioned Horst to make a series of fashion pictures as dramatic as his chiaroscuro-lit tableaux of 1932.[43] In London again in early 1988, he photographed a cover for *Vogue*'s sister publication *Tatler* and, for the inside pages, a group portrait which included Margaret, Duchess of Argyll, who was a fixture in *Vogue* during the 1930s.[44] A year later, in 1989, Horst returned to England to accept an Honorary Doctorate from the University of Bradford and made more pictures for *Vogue*. The model was Catherine Bailey (pls 136, 137, 139); her husband, the *Vogue* photographer David Bailey (b.1938), in turn made a portrait of Horst to accompany the pictures (pl.124).[45] His last portraits for *Vogue* comprised, in black and white, a photograph of the gracious and elegant shoe designer Manolo Blahnik (b.1942) in 1990 (see pl.141); a re-interpretation of his portrait from 1934 of the equally elegant Baron 'Niki' de Gunzburg; and the following year, in colour, Princess Michael of Kent against a tapestry backdrop (pl.122).[46] The Princess wore a tiara belonging to her mother-in-law, Princess Marina, who nearly 60 years previously had been Horst's most socially prominent sitter.

Horst's last fashion sitting was also for British *Vogue*, two pictures specially commissioned for the magazine's 75th anniversary from its oldest living photographer (Horst was 10 years older than the magazine). In one of these photographs, to the right, stood a familiar motif – a Giacometti plaster vase he had acquired from Jean-Michel Frank in 1936 (pl.140).[47] The following year, in 1992, with his eyesight failing, he finally gave up photography but the magazine's anniversary celebrations provided a fitting opportunity for Horst to comment that *Vogue* had provided him with a '*raison d'être*'.

Royal Still Lifes

Horst's still lifes typically fall into three categories: 'classical', 'surreal' and 'domestic'. The classical studies are visual essays in form and shading and comprise sculptures and plaster casts from the photographer's collection. The surreal pictures, dating predominantly from the late 1930s, include trompe l'oeil flourishes and tropes such as disembodied hands or feet, mirrors and double images. Horst was often inspired to photograph a domestic still life after lunch at his Long Island home in Oyster Bay, arranging objects from the table and flowers picked from his garden in pleasing compositions suffused with natural light.[1]

A series of 17 intriguing still lifes forms a fourth category, which could be titled 'pictures within pictures'.[2] Each one depicts an assemblage of printed images from the 1930s – magazines, scrapbooks and albums – grouped against a wall and shelves resembling Carrara marble. Some incorporate swathes of fabric, ribbons, flowers and fruit, or items from a designer's toolkit: pencils, colour swatches, string and tape measure. These photographs are undated, but the paper on which they were printed, and their nostalgic mood, suggest they were made late in Horst's career. The similarities in composition and lighting from one to another indicate they were created during a fairly short period, possibly around 1970, when he was preparing his book *Salute to the Thirties*. The publication, which features 111 photographs by Horst and 51 by George Hoyningen-Huene, celebrates the creative individuals who shaped that decade. In Horst's words, *Salute to the Thirties* was intended to commemorate 'the astonishing vitality, in literature, art, music, ballet, theatre, opera, films, fashion, and private entertainment' of the era, and pay tribute to the talent of Huene, 'my mentor and friend'.[3]

Every image from the series of 'pictures within pictures' might be considered a salute to the 1930s, although none appear in the publication. Each still life references a different aspect of culture or politics from that auspicious decade in Horst's career. The subjects are wide ranging, from Europe's brightest theatre stars to American workers during the Great Depression. One marks the important contribution artists such as Bérard and Dalí made to *Vogue* (pl.127); another features classic sports cars. Two pictures from the series comprise portraits of the British royal family. Unlike his fellow photographer Cecil Beaton, Horst rarely had the opportunity to photograph royalty. The most significant of Horst's royal sitters were Princess Marina, Duchess of Kent and, later, the Duke and Duchess of Windsor. Yet these still life studies feature more prominent royals: one shows King George V and Queen Mary on the occasion of their 1935 Silver Jubilee (pl.125); the other depicts the new royal family of 1936 (pl.126). After the death of George V, and the swift abdication of Edward VIII, Prince Albert, Duke of York unexpectedly came to the throne at the end of 1936, taking the regnal name George VI.

Horst's still life of the new royal family centres on drawings and photographs of the King, his consort Queen Elizabeth, and their young daughters Elizabeth and Margaret Rose. The composition is split in two by the strong horizontal line of the shelf, reminiscent of the balustrade in Horst's Mainbocher Corset. Two oval picture frames temper the straight edges of the paper leaves and scrapbooks, while a flowing ribbon links the top and bottom sections of the picture plane. The larger frame contains a portrait of the King in full military uniform. His mother, Queen Mary, is pictured in the smaller oval frame below. Both Horst and Huene kept scrapbooks and albums throughout their lives and the inclusion of a glue bottle (LePage's Grip Spreader Mucilage, with its distinctive bell-shaped packaging), in the lower right corner, might suggest that these particular scrapbooks are still being assembled.

Horst's early understanding of English culture was shaped by his travels with Huene in the winter of 1930, and later by his relationship with the diplomat Valentine Lawford. Both royal still lifes convey an interest in British history, which is in keeping with Horst's wider admiration for the country's traditions and the sartorial elegance of the English gentleman.

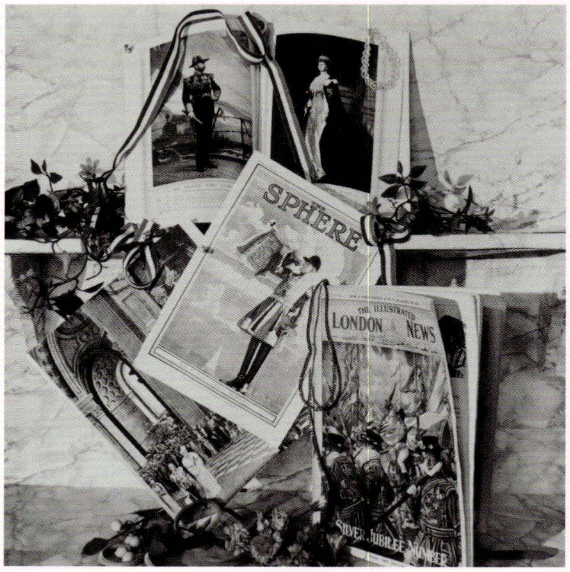

125. Still life, the Silver Jubilee of King George V and Queen Mary, undated

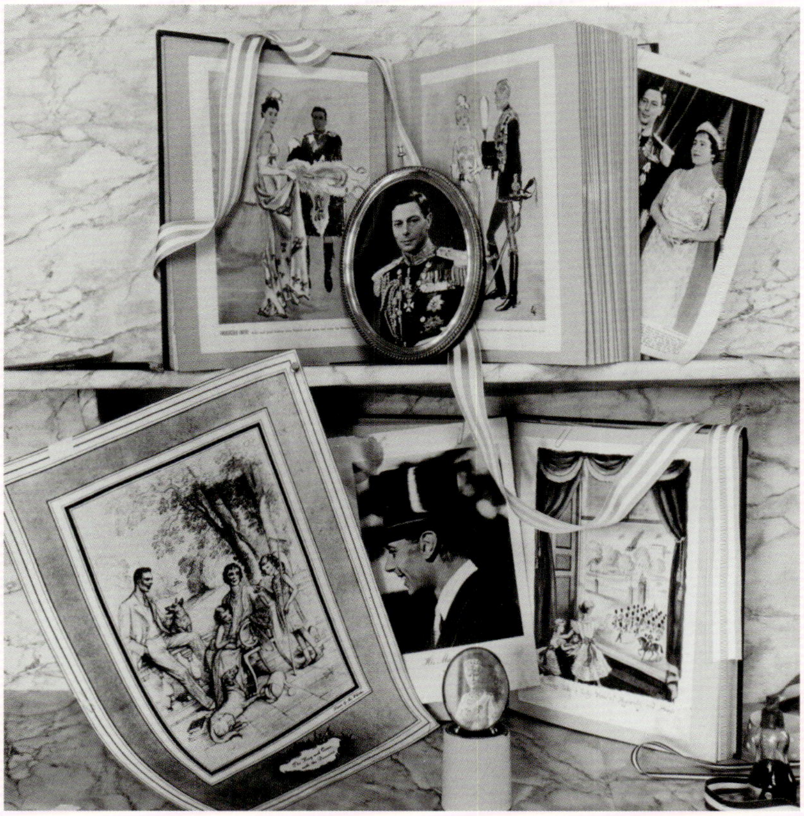

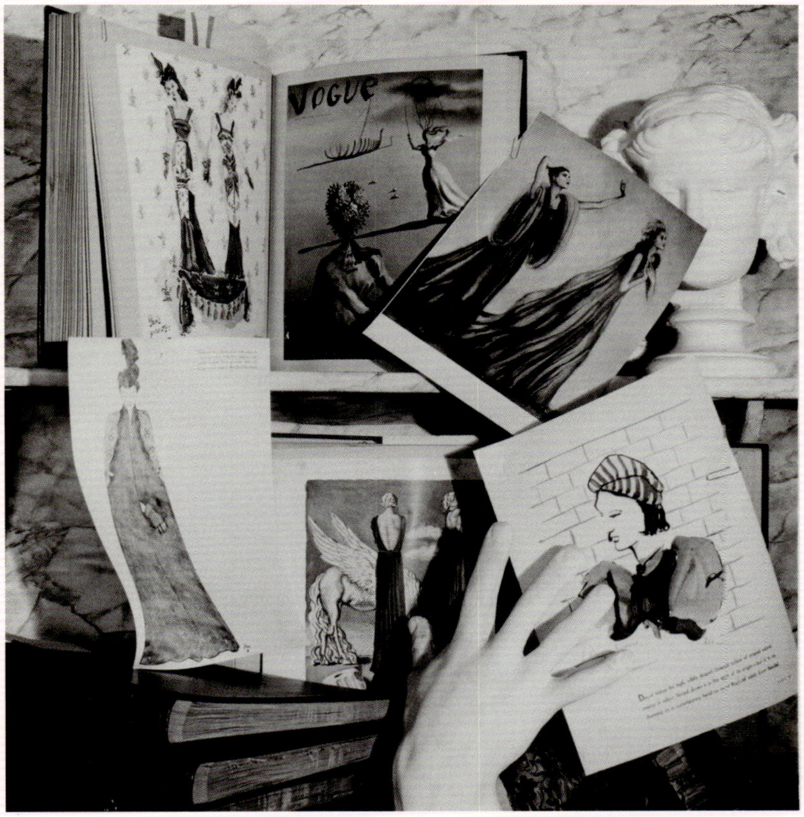

Above
126. Still life, King George VI
and the British royal family, undated

Below
127. Still life with fashion illustrations
by Bérard, Dalí, de Chirico, Cocteau
and Tchelitchew, undated

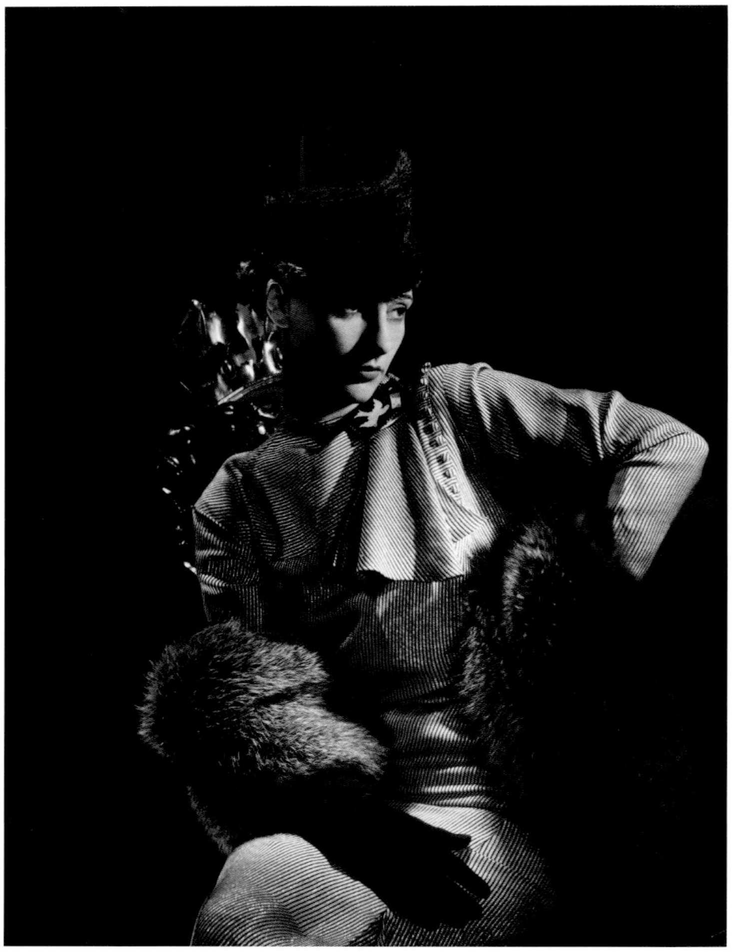

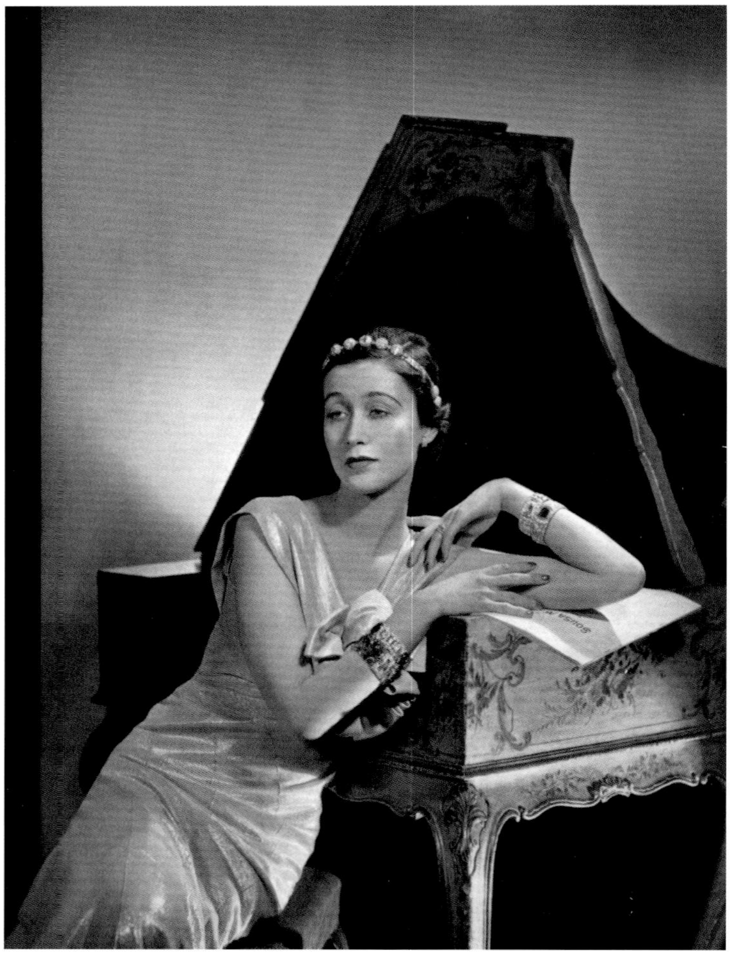

128. Doris Hilditch, dress by Norman Hartnell, 1934

129. Toto Koopman, dress by Victor Stiebel, jewellery by Chaumet, 1934

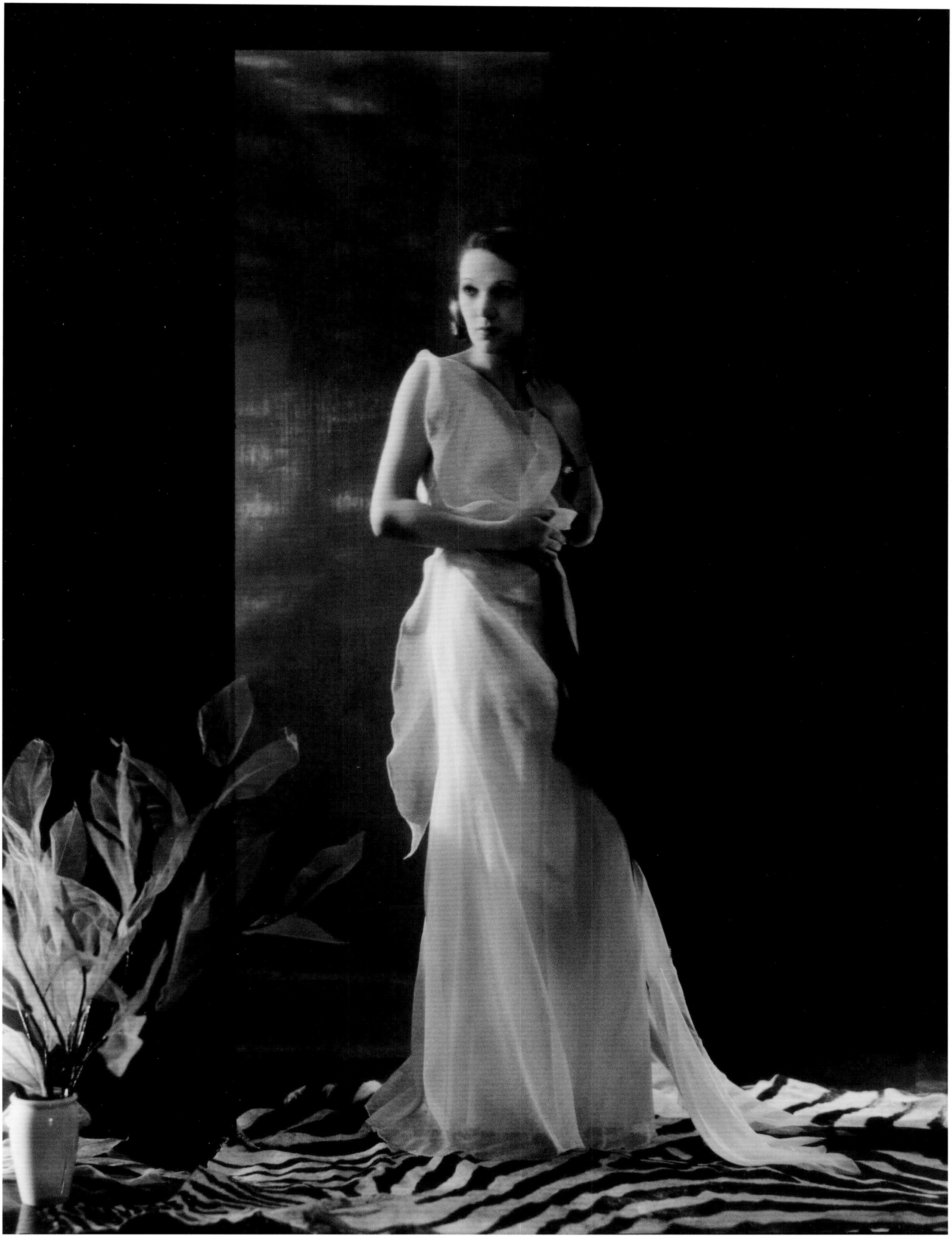

130. Gertrude Lawrence, dress by Schiaparelli, 1931

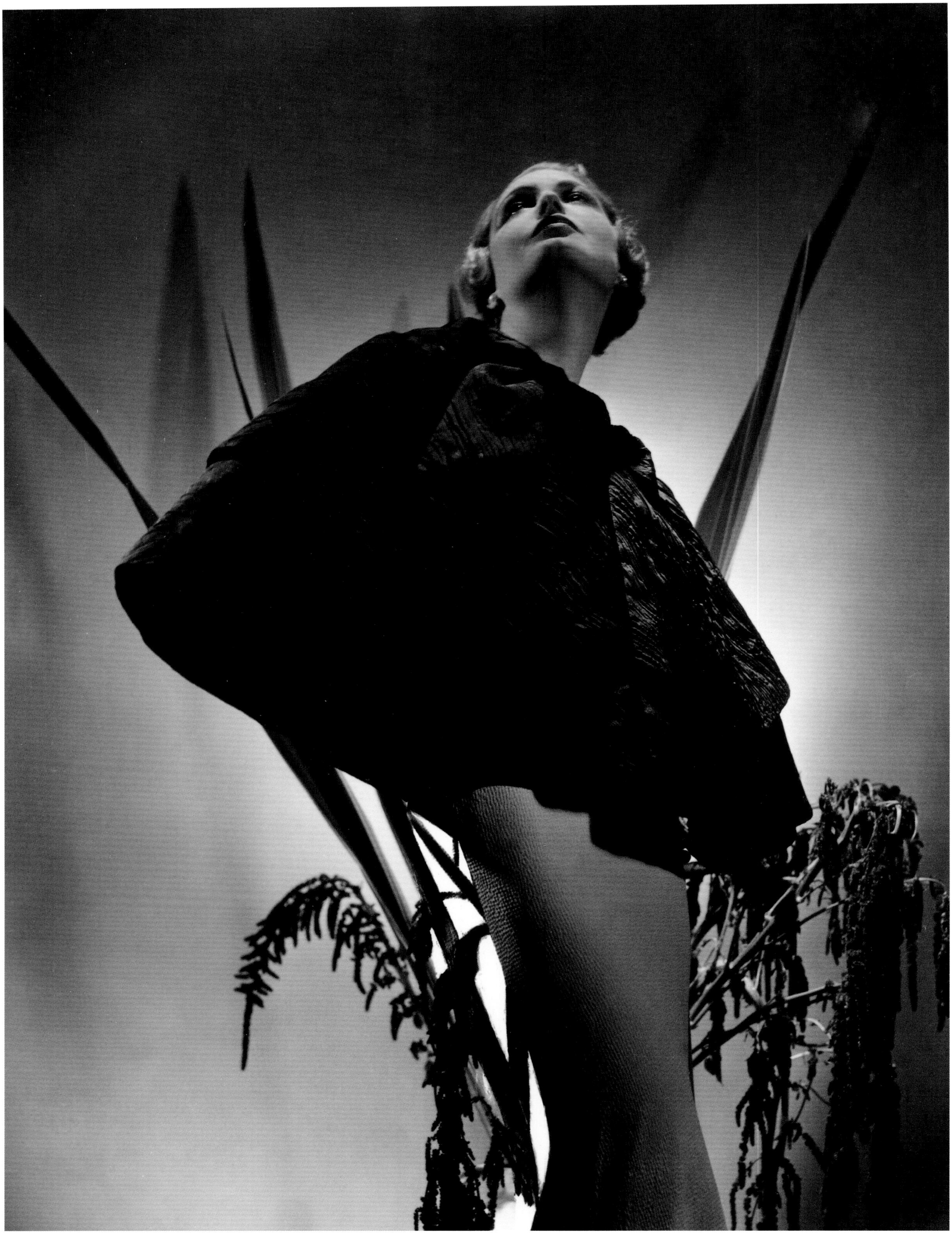

131. Ensemble by Victor Stiebel, 1934

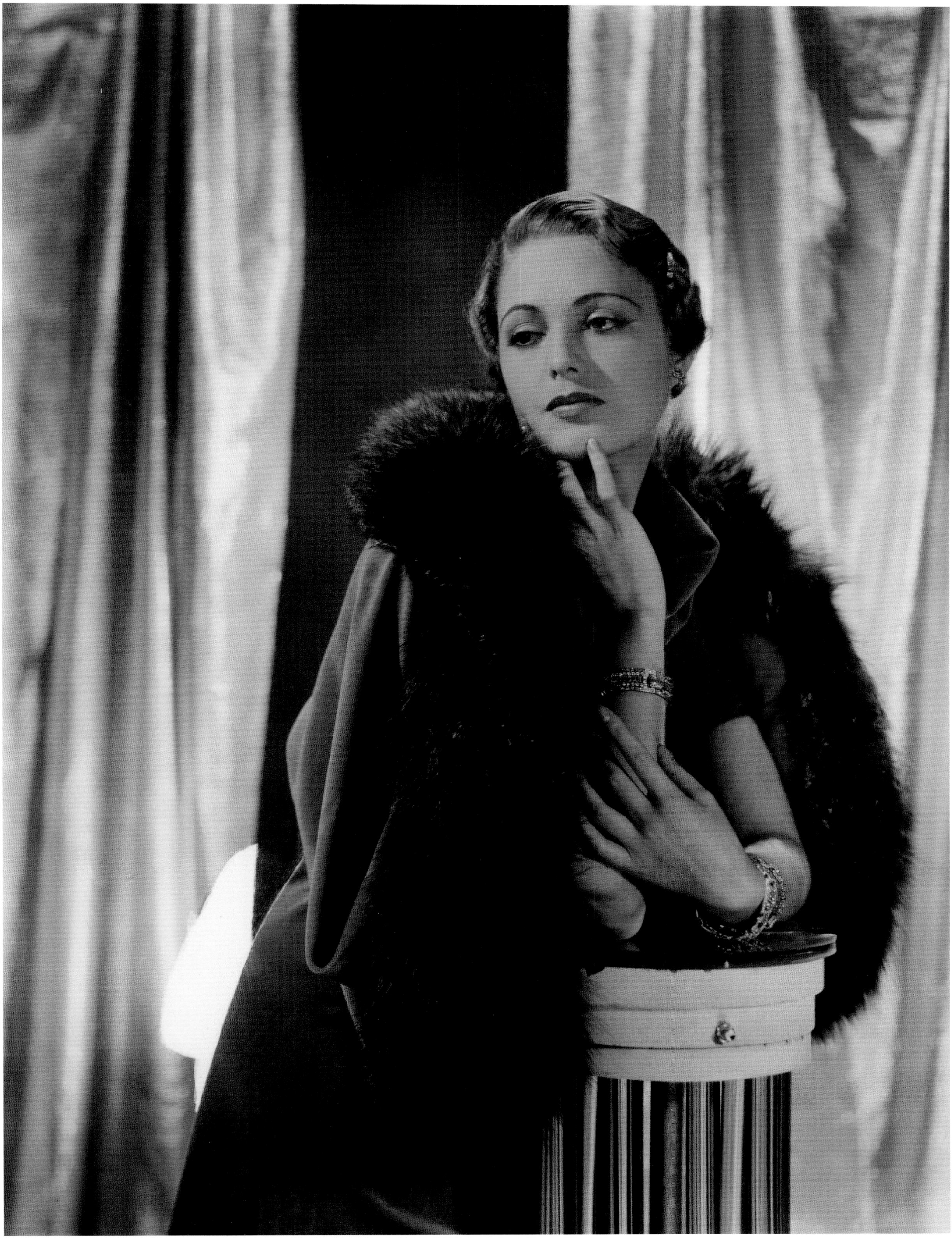

132. Elizabeth Jenns, cape by Enos, jewellery by Lacloche, décor by Syrie Maugham, 1934

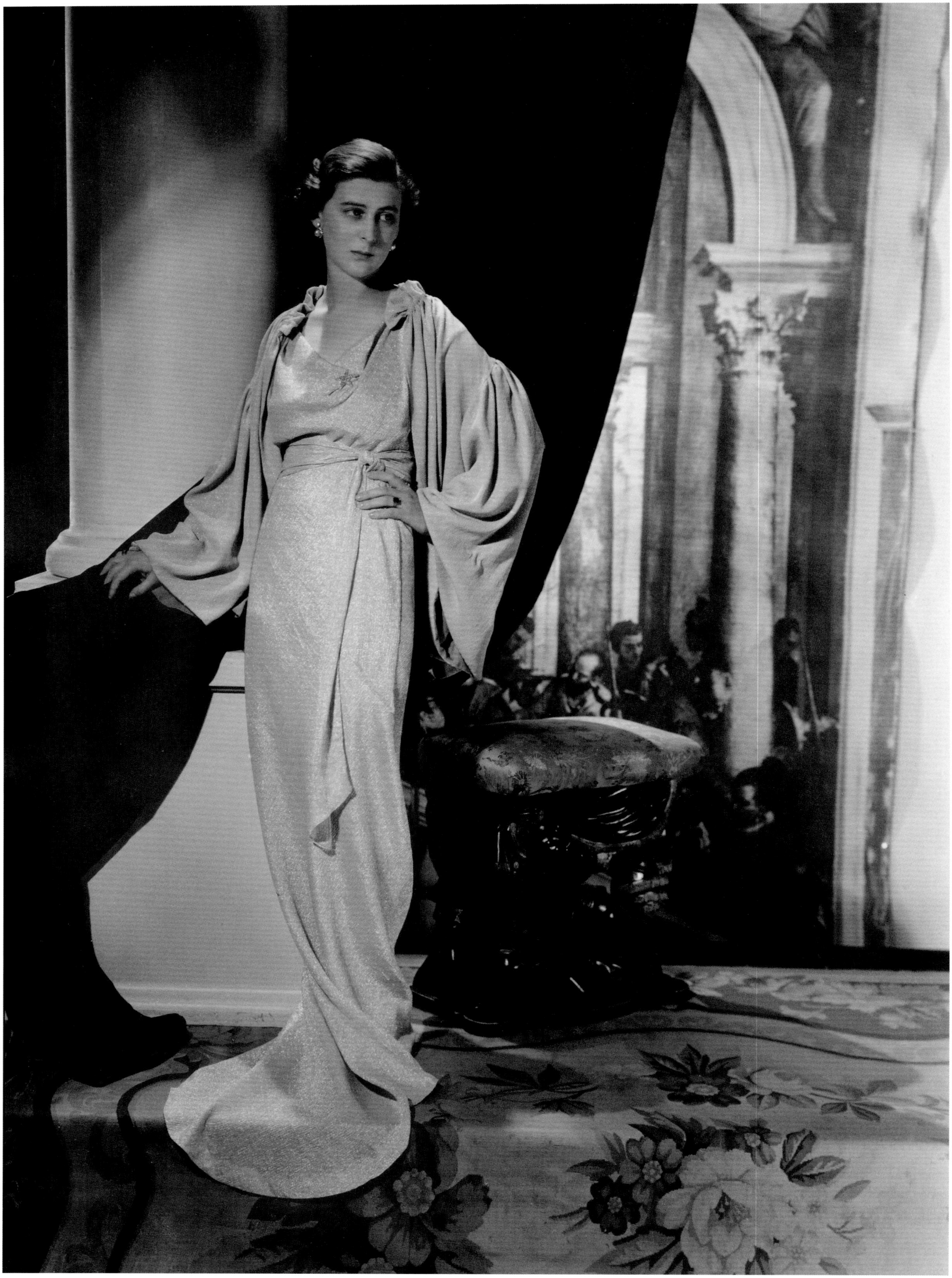

133. Princess Marina of Greece, 1934

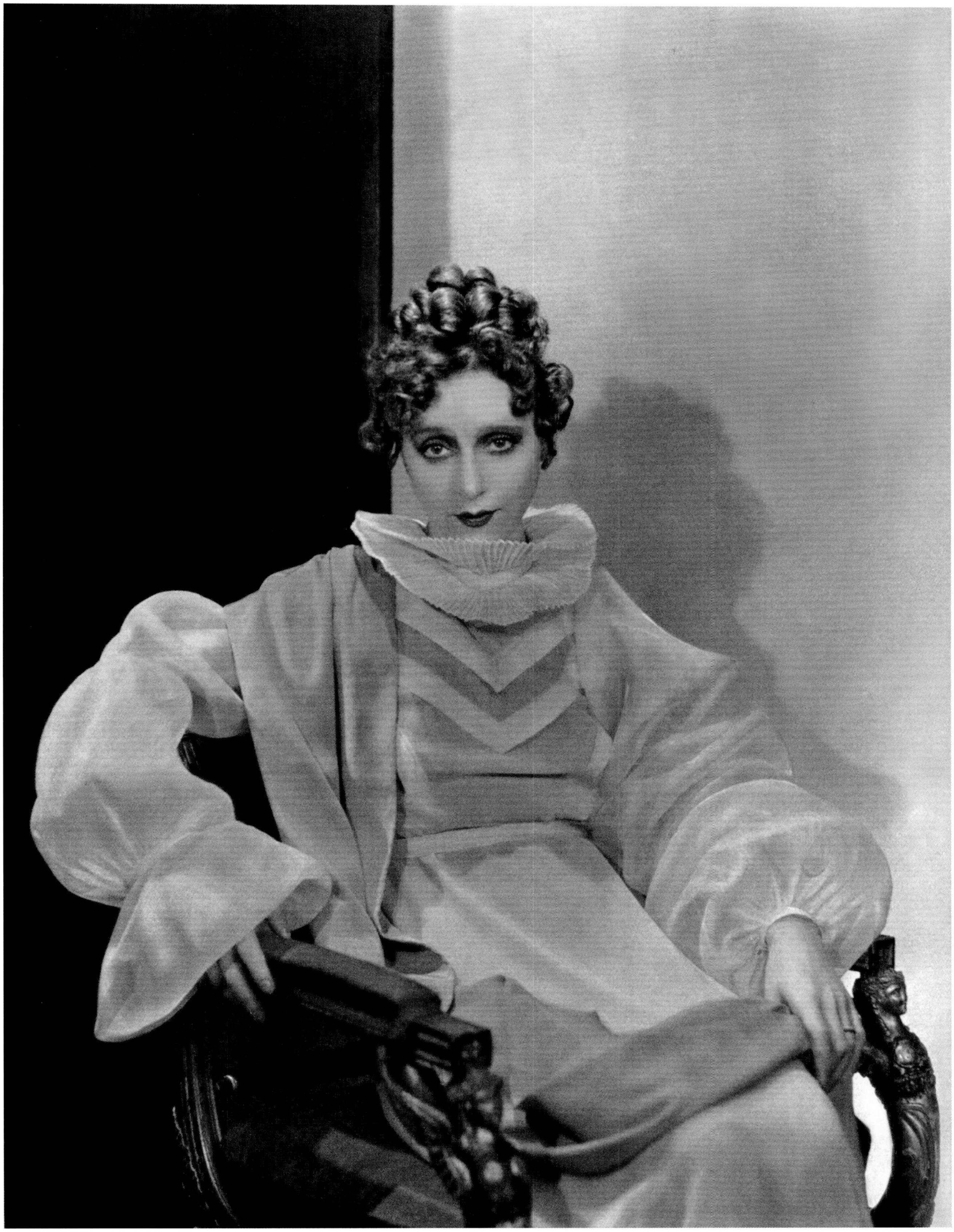

134. Yvonne Printemps as Mélanie in *Conversation Piece*, London, 1934

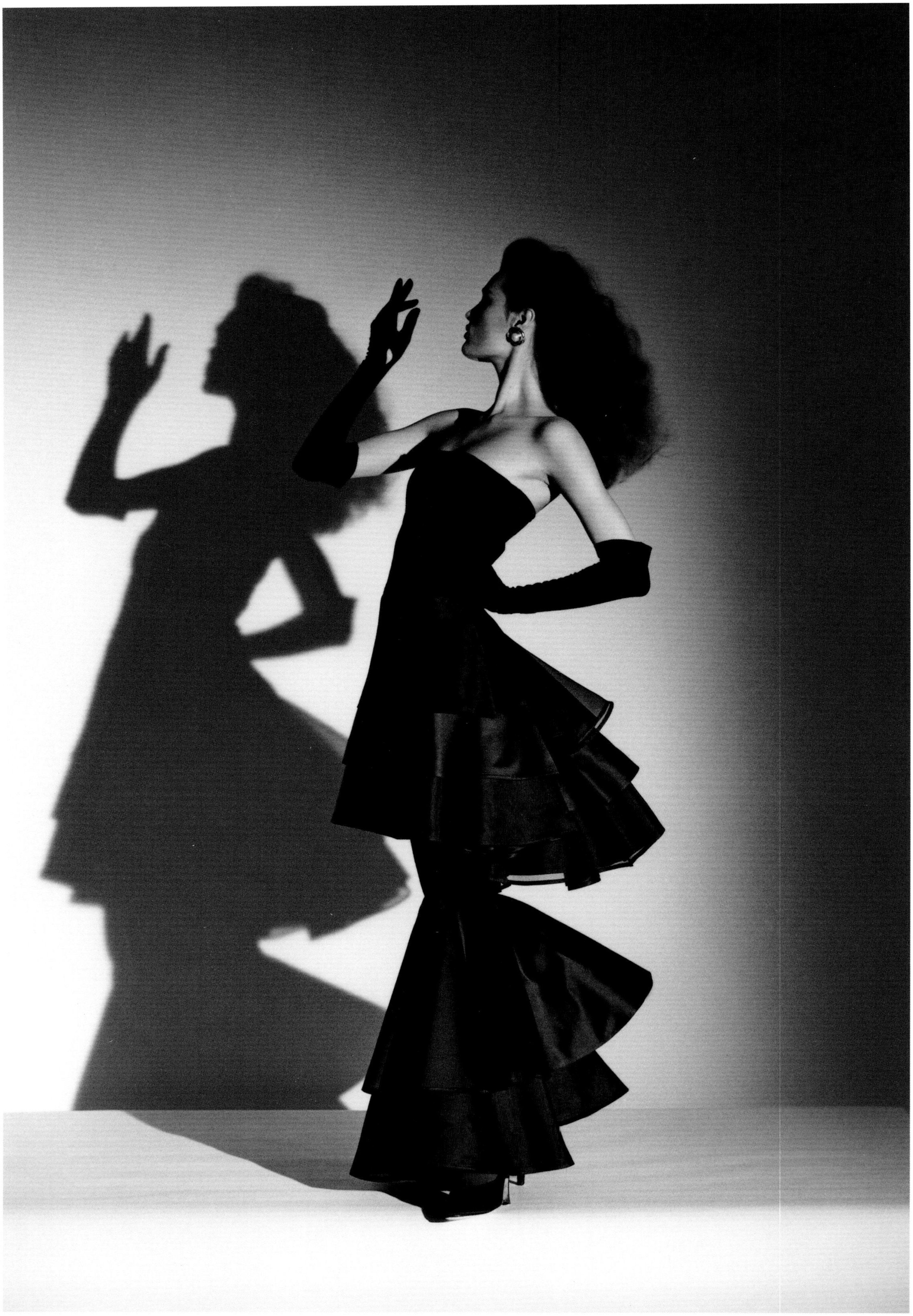

135. Dress by Versace, jewellery by Chanel, shoes by Manolo Blahnik, 1986

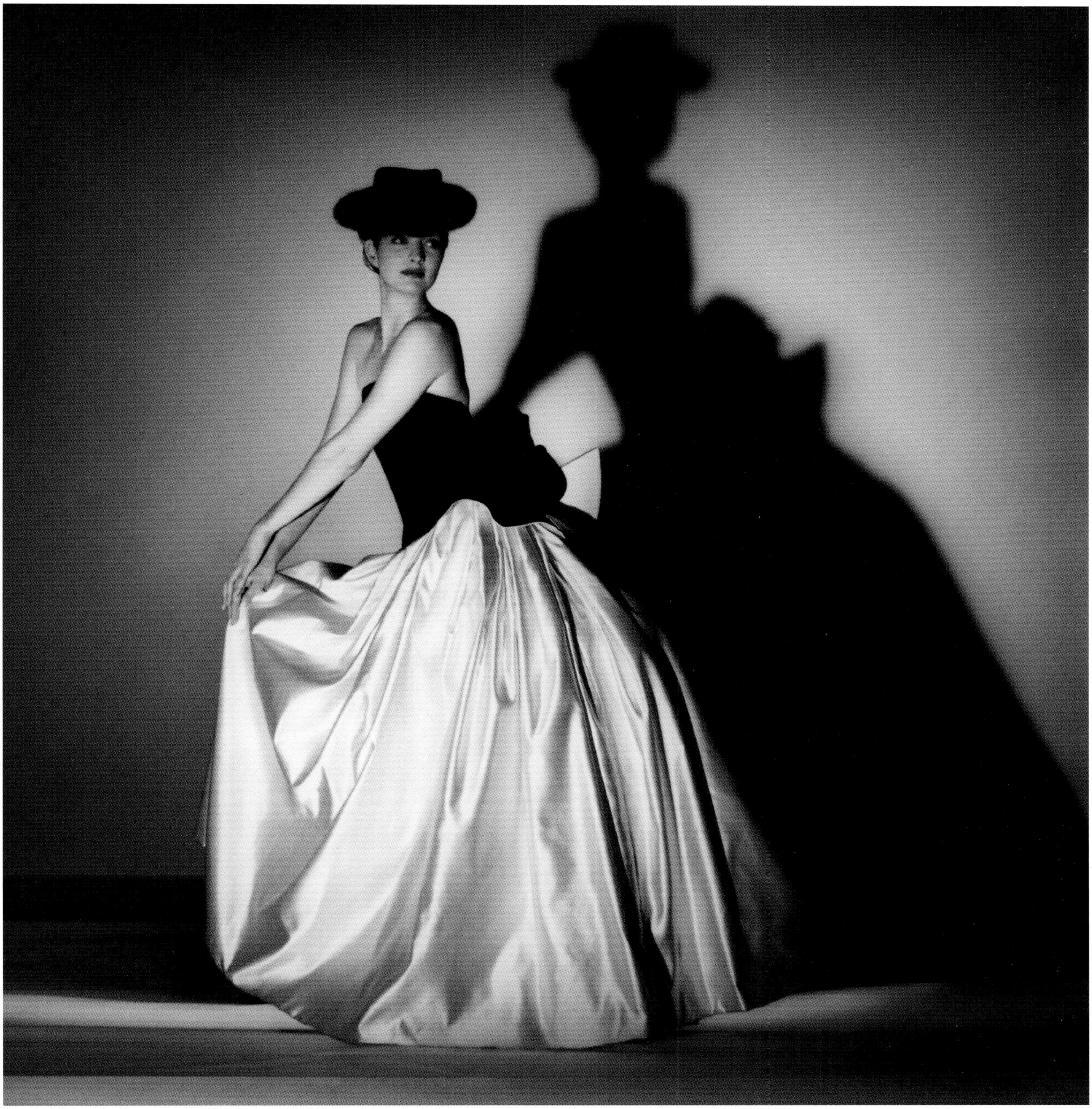

136. Catherine Bailey, ensemble by Anouska Hempel, hat by Stephen Jones, 1989

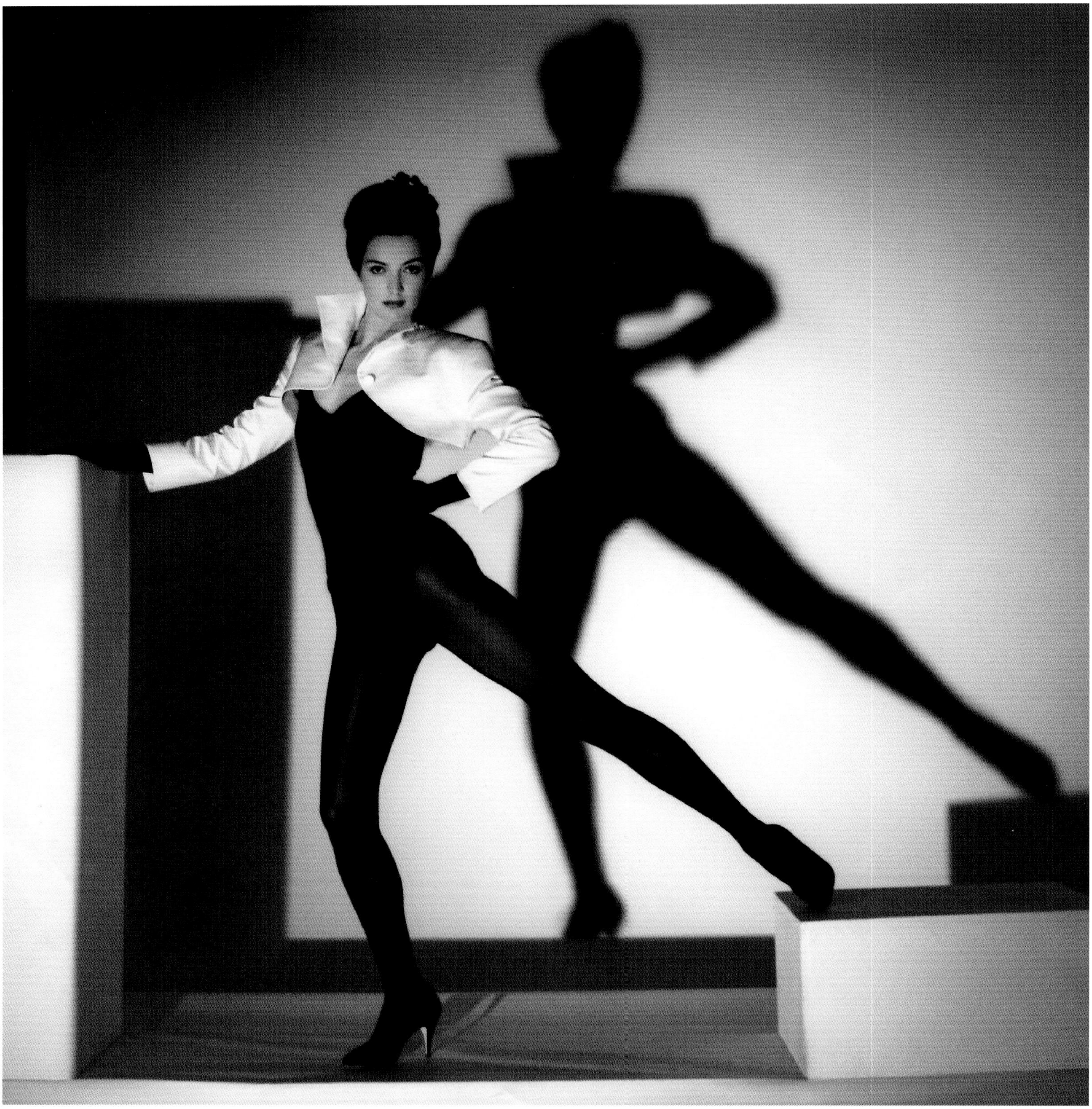

137. Catherine Bailey, ensemble by Jasper Conran, shoes by Manolo Blahnik, 1989

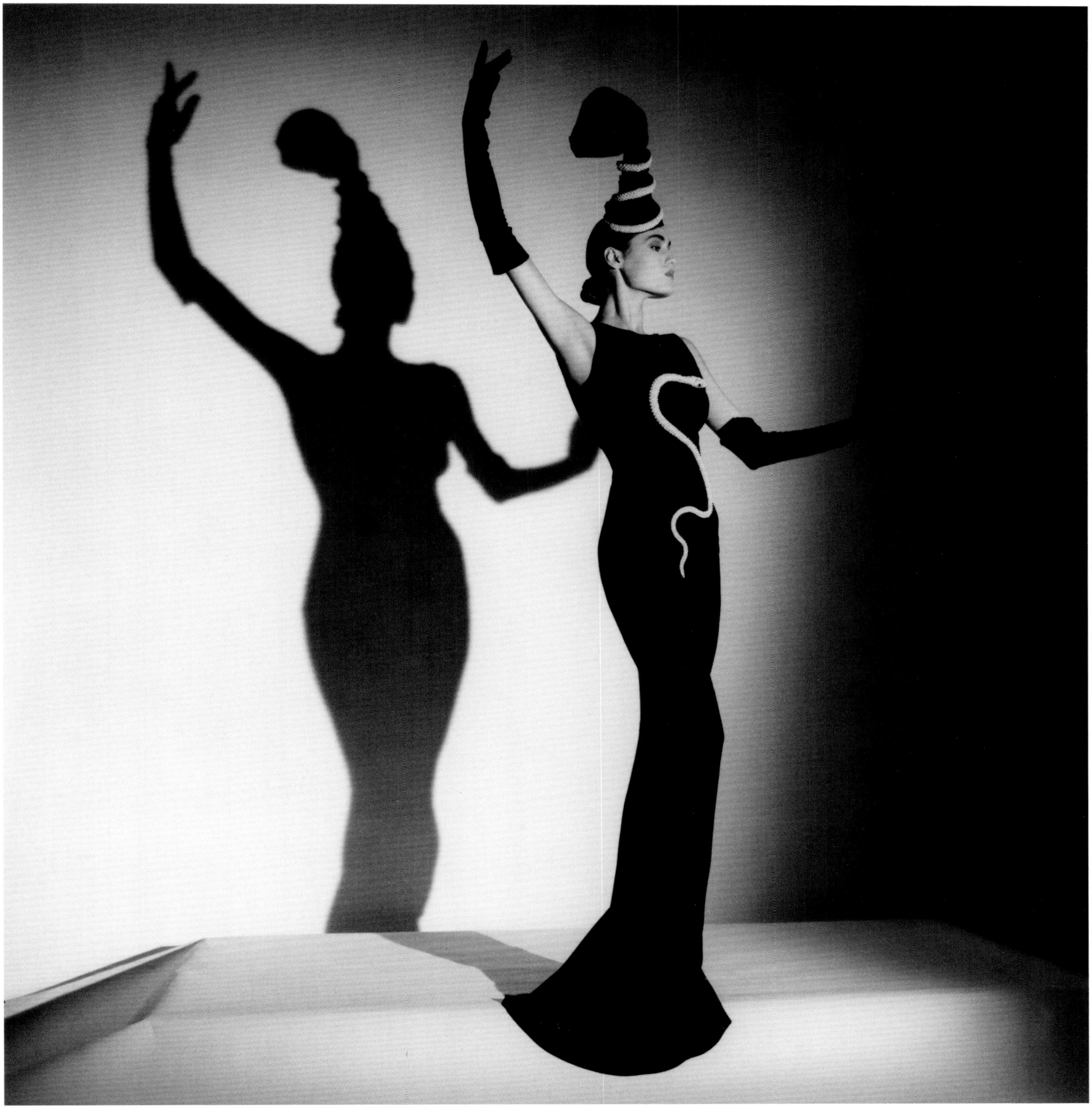

138. Ensemble by Chanel, 1986

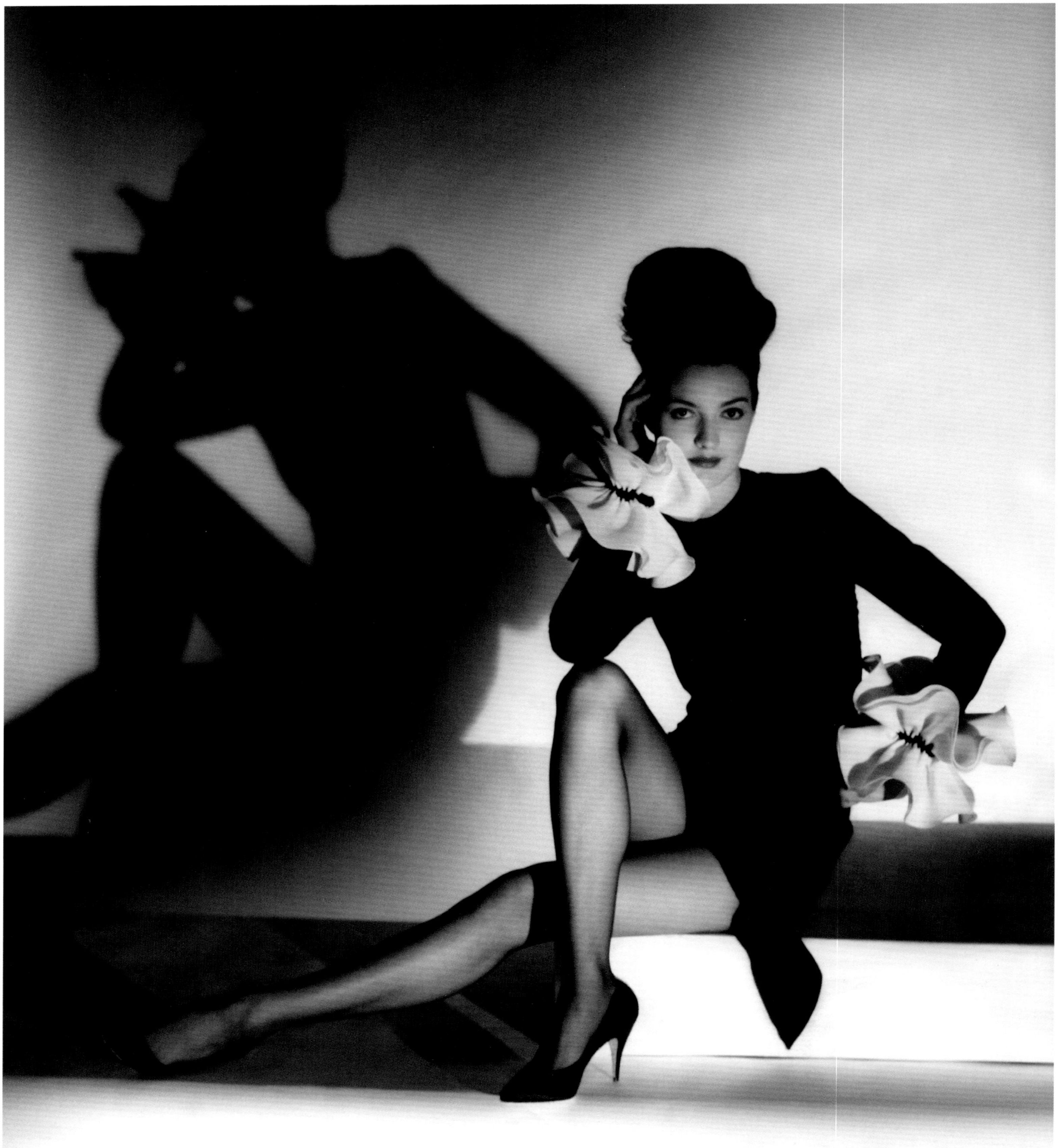

139. Catherine Bailey, dress by Alistair Blair, shces by Manolo Blahnik, 1989

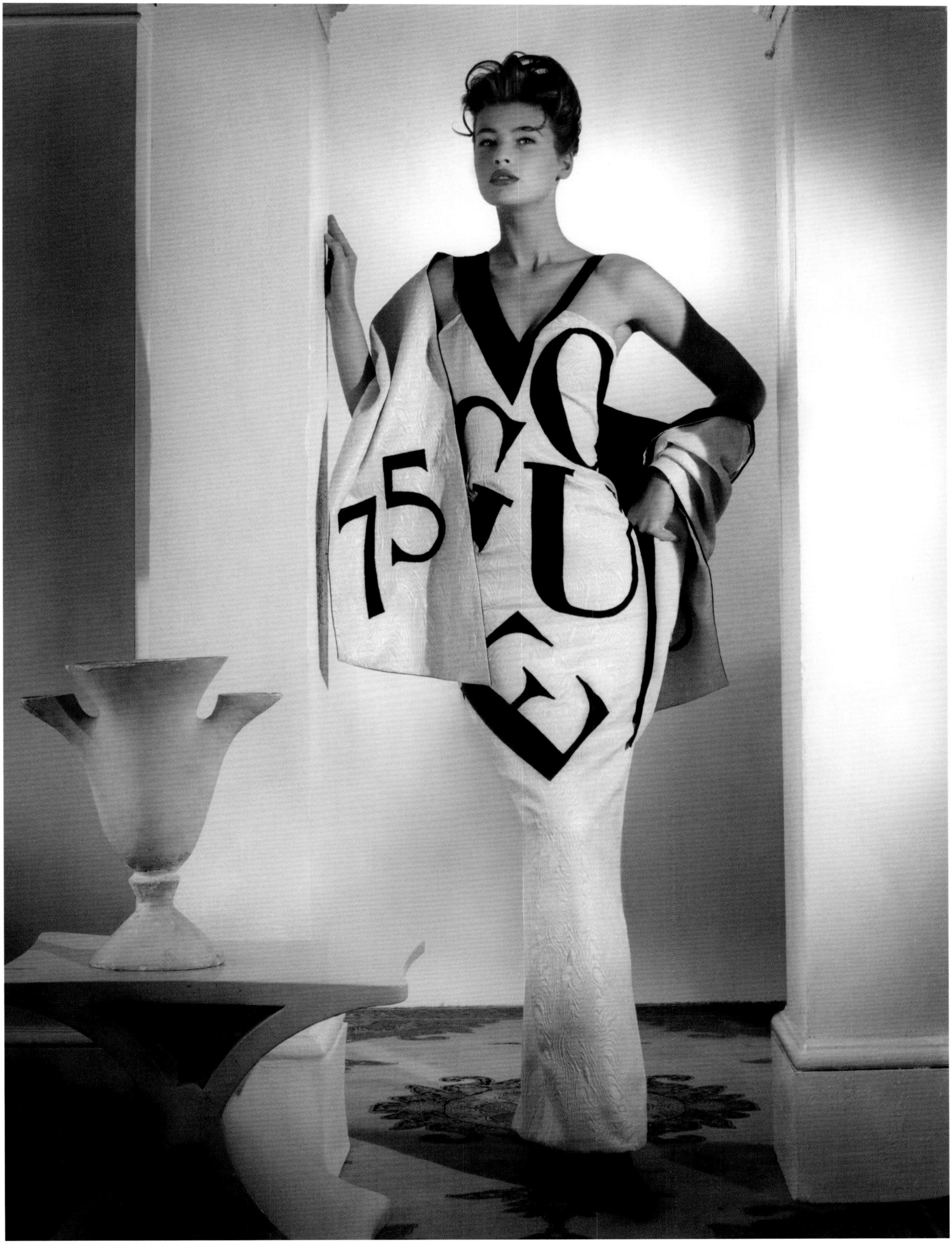

140. Daniella, dress and wrap by Antony Price, vase by Alberto Giacometti for Jean-Michel Frank, 1991

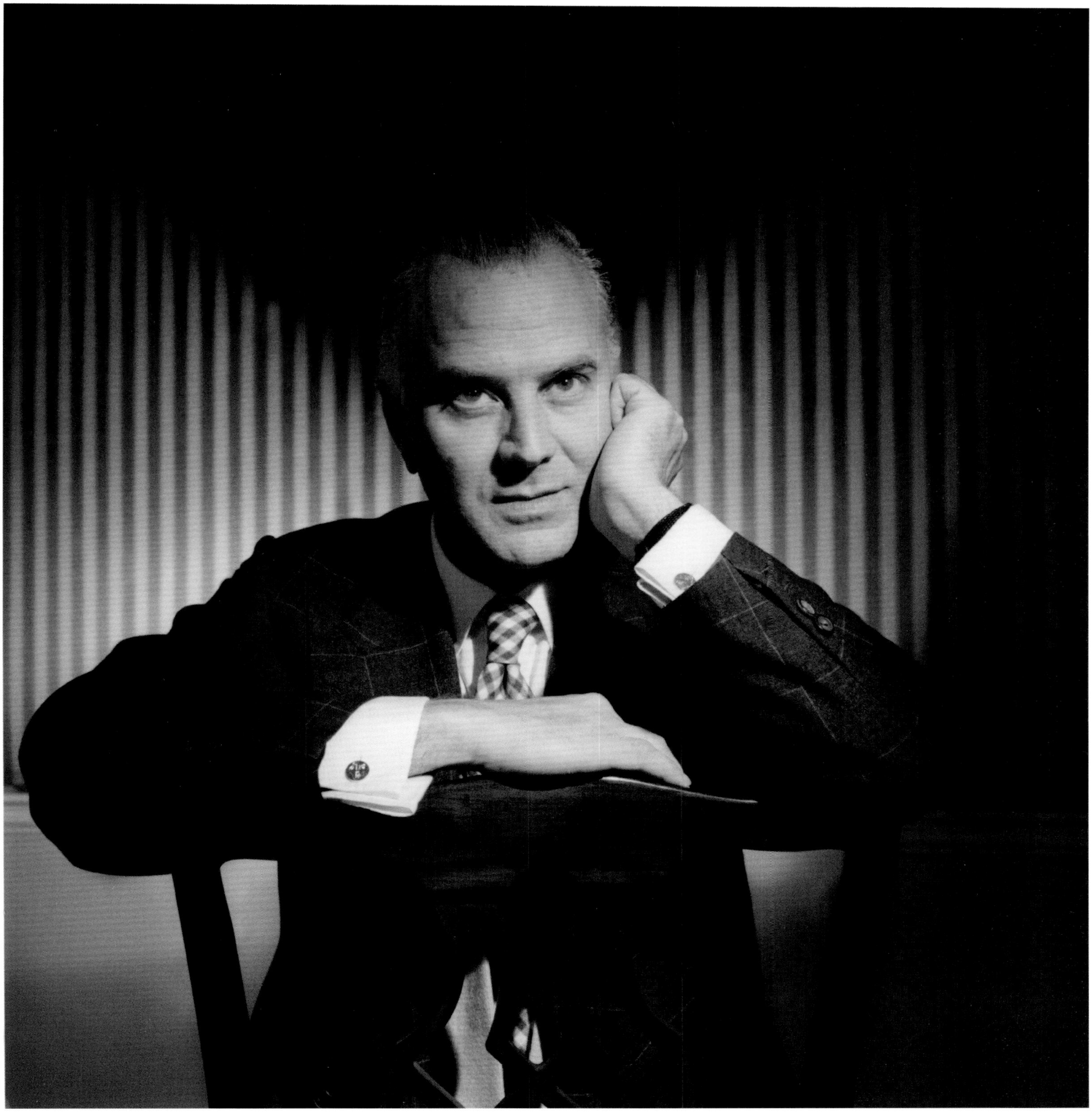

141. Manolo Blahnik, 1990

V

Fashion in Colour

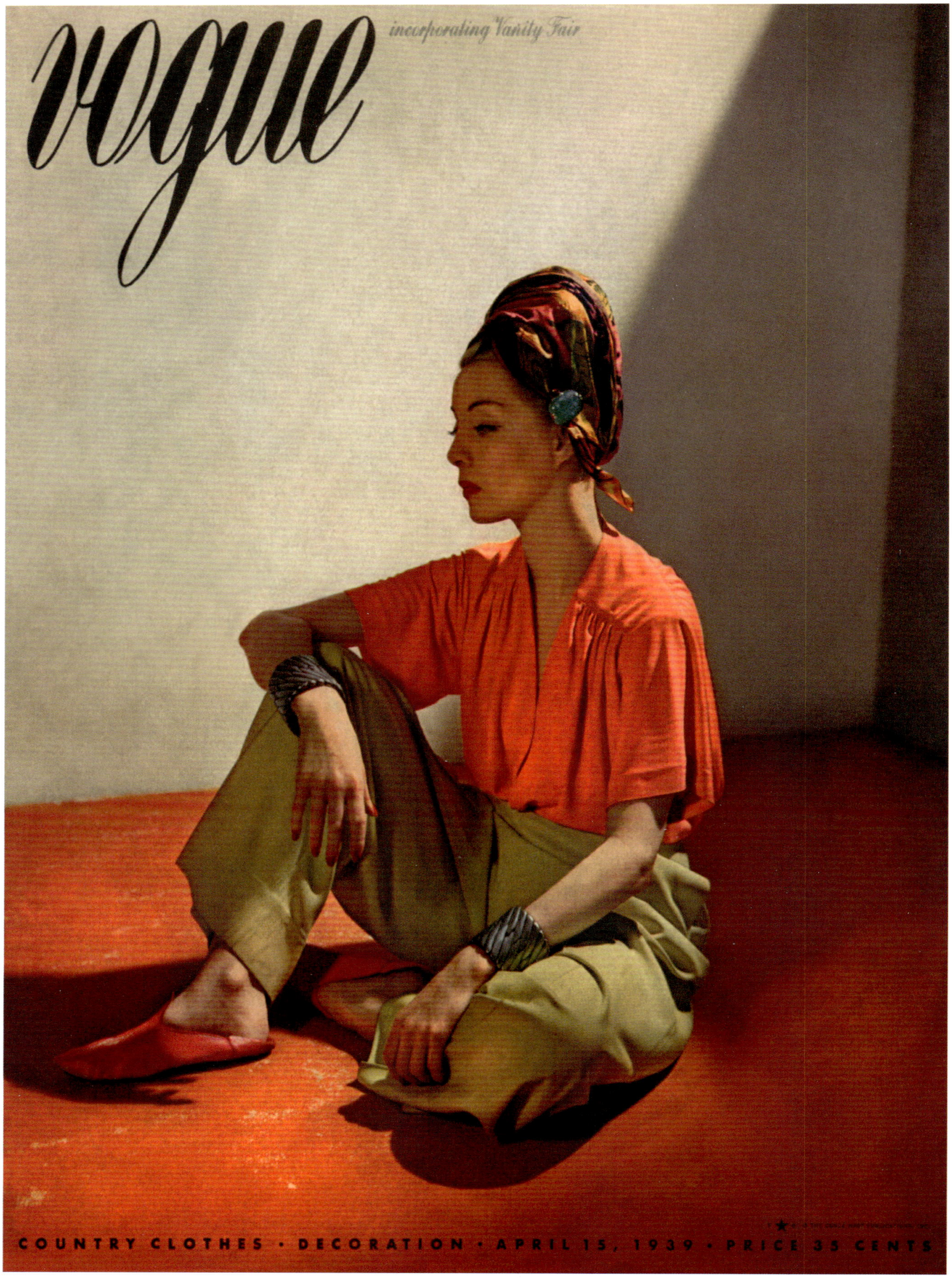

142. Helen Bennett,
American *Vogue* cover, 15 April 1939

HORST'S WORLD IN COLOUR

Shawn Waldron

In 1931, Horst began his incredible 60-year career with Condé Nast photographing still lifes in the company's Paris studio. In the same year, across the Atlantic, the American owner of the company was embarking on a quest to revolutionize colour reproduction in the pages of *Vogue, Vanity Fair* and *House & Garden*. The next 15 years witnessed great personal and professional growth for Horst, major changes at the Condé Nast empire, and the blossoming of the American fashion industry. The period also ushered in huge technical advancements in colour photography. The photographic historian Pamela Roberts has described the 1930s as perhaps 'the most formative and dynamic decade in a century of colour photography',[1] and Horst's success with the new medium was intrinsic to his ascendance at *Vogue*. Horst possessed a nuanced understanding of chromatic relationships and adapted quickly to the new visual vocabulary of the magazine.

Horst created some of *Vogue*'s most striking colour images, and more than 90 covers. However, his colour work has remained largely unseen in the museum and gallery setting for a simple reason: there are few vintage photographs to exhibit. Colour capture took place on a transparency, which could be plated and printed on the magazine page without the need to create a photographic print. It is only in the past few years that interest among curators and the public has brought some of these works to light through modern digital printing.[2] This essay explores Horst's approach to rendering the varied and vivid hues of fashions from the 1930s onwards. It also reveals how Mr Condé Nast transformed the quality of his publications through the research and development of cutting-edge colour reproduction, to produce magazines that were admired around the world.

The relationship between Horst and Mr Nast did not begin well. In the spring of 1932 Horst was invited to work for *Vogue* in New York for six months, at a salary of $75 per week.[3] Accustomed to the culture and beauty of Paris, it is perhaps not surprising that Horst found New York in the midst of the Great Depression a lonely, uninspiring city. He spent slow hours in the studio waiting for sittings and was instructed to emulate the style of Nast's star photographer, Edward Steichen, rather than refine his own aesthetic. Nast found Horst arrogant, and on 15 August 1932 he sent a telegram to *Vogue*'s editor-in-chief Edna Woolman Chase that read: 'fear horst's colossal vanity will always make him impossible collaborator and always disloyal either new york london or paris fear our training will go to benefit of some other organization stop am keeping him here for your observation'. When Horst dared to suggest to his employer that he could one day be as good as Edward Steichen, Nast flew into a rage and sent him back to Paris. Horst took an extended vacation and returned to the Paris studio a few months later. Ultimately, however, Horst's loyalty to *Vogue*, coupled with his prodigious output over the ensuing six decades, would prove Nast's initial impressions uncharacteristically misguided.

Mr Nast had purchased *Vogue* in 1905. He sought to transform the title (originally founded in 1892 by Arthur Turnure) into an international brand, the premier publication for wealthy, fashionable and cultured readers. In 1913, he employed Baron Adolph de Meyer as *Vogue*'s first contract photographer, knowing that in order for the magazine to thrive, he must improve the quality of the images on the printed page. In 1927, he moved the company's editorial and business operations into the Graybar Building, the understated Art Deco skyscraper located on Manhattan's Lexington Avenue. The company had been using a small New York City printing plant, but in an earlier move that was as much about quality as finance, Mr Nast decided to build a new printing plant outside the city. The resulting Condé Nast Press was a state-of-the-art facility on a manicured campus 35 miles from midtown Manhattan, in Greenwich, Connecticut, then a quiet suburb, easily reached by train from Manhattan.[4]

The press was fully operational by 1925. Mr Nast, an astute businessman, ran it as a separate and highly profitable company called Arbor Press. In addition to the Condé Nast titles (*Vogue, Vanity Fair, House & Garden* and, from 1926, *The American Golfer*), Arbor Press printed magazines by other publishers, including *Scientific American* and the fledgling title the *New Yorker*, which would be acquired by the Condé Nast company 60 years later. Nast was justly proud of his new jewel, and shortly after it opened, commissioned a local photographer to document every room in the facility. The resulting album shows the huge two-colour presses (pl.143), the layout rooms, type foundry, shipping rooms, even the boilers, cafeteria and employee parking garage – a wooden construction housing a gleaming line of Ford Model T automobiles.

With the impressive Greenwich press at his disposal, Nast turned his attention to improving the reproduction of colour photographs in his magazines. Although the accurate reproduction of colour illustration had been mastered for decades, a viable four-colour photographic printing process did not exist in the 1920s. The number of technical variables – lighting, lenses, filters, inks, engraving plates, press and paper – more often than not led to failure. In 1931 he hired the advertising photographer Anton Bruehl (1900–82), already well known for a 'sophisticated modernist style, characterized by geometric composition, oblique vantage points, close-ups, and a full tonal range'.[5] Between 1931 and 1936 Bruehl collaborated with the accomplished photo-engraver and technician Fernand Bourges to produce colour images of astounding quality, although true colour film would not be invented until later in the 1930s. The Bruehl-Bourges Process was partly based on the colour separation theory devised some 70 years earlier by James Clerk Maxwell. The pair worked closely: 'Bruehl designed the image, which Bourges took with the "one-shot" camera he had made: during the exposure, light passed through three thin acetate sheets with emulsions of different colour sensitivities. Condé Nast technicians then turned the composite transparency into a copper engraving for printing.'[6] The four colours of ink applied to the copper printing plate were cyan, magenta, yellow and black, a combination known in the print and publishing worlds as CMYK.

The output of the duo was nothing short of extraordinary: between May 1932 and December 1934 *American Vogue, Vanity Fair* and *House & Garden* ran a total of 195 editorial pages of colour photography. During that same period Bruehl and Bourges produced 479 photographs for the magazines' advertisers.[7] In the early 1930s, however, the Bruehl-Bourges Process of four-colour separations was not available in *Vogue*'s Paris studio, leaving simpler two-colour capture as the only option for Horst and his colleagues in France.

Horst's photograph for 'Chanel's Ode to Spring' was made in Paris and published in American *Vogue*, 1 March 1935 (pl.144). It reveals both the possibilities and the shortcomings of two-colour capture. The model wears a green wool knee-length jacket over a green-and-white patterned silk dress with white gloves, handbag and hat. A fern, lower right, provides a further splash of green. She stands before a plain stucco wall, against which a white lattice screen creates a right angle and echoes the print of the dress. The model is seen from the knees up, with one hand on her hip; she looks slightly off to the right and is evenly lit from the top left. The shadow of leaves and branches is cast horizontally across the back wall. The image is a perfect example of well-executed two-colour photography and printing. Using only cyan and yellow inks, Horst's composition accurately presents the fabrics and avoided Nast's most frequent complaint, directed towards his photographers: lack of detail. The reproduction's sole failure to the modern eye lies in the model's skin tone. The engravers were able to suggest red on the lips and blue-green make-up, but the skin tone overall falls flat in comparison to the Bruehl-Bourges Process.

Horst's first editorial pictures using the Bruehl-Bourges method were published across two pages of American *Vogue* on 1 May 1935. The spread featured three photographs of the latest evening slippers, stockings and shoes in vivid colours ranging from red to green, blue to orange, and black to white (pl.145). The most successful of the trio shows deep purple satin slippers and gold leather evening sandals against a black background. To the lower left of the image, the appearance of the corner of a maroon velvet settee grounds the feet in reality. The skin tones possess both depth and accuracy.

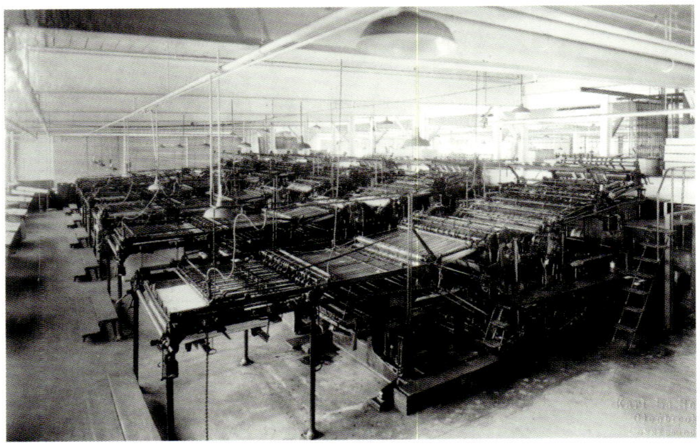

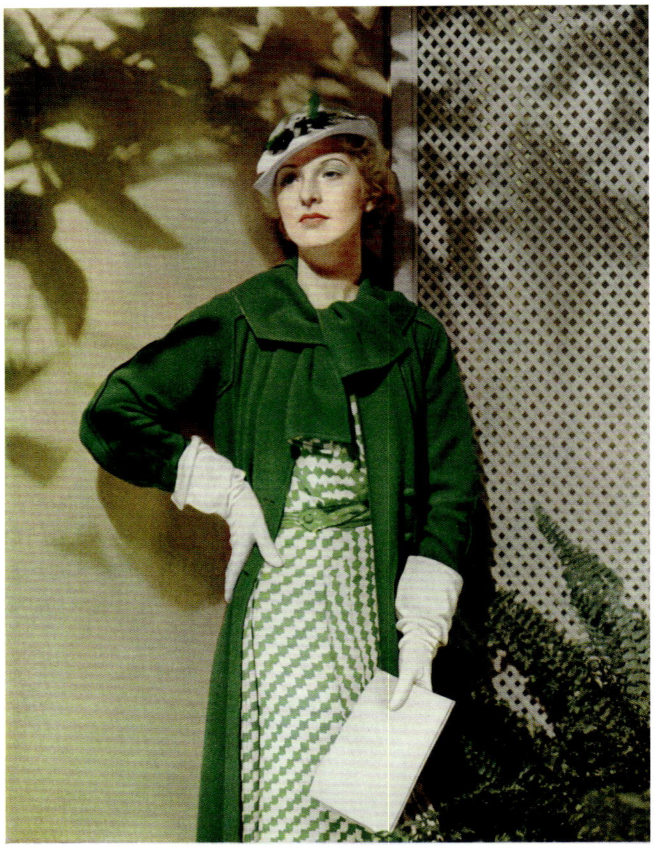

Above
143. The two-colour press room at the Condé Nast Press, Connecticut, late 1920s

Below
144. 'Chanel's Ode to Spring', American *Vogue*, 1 March 1935

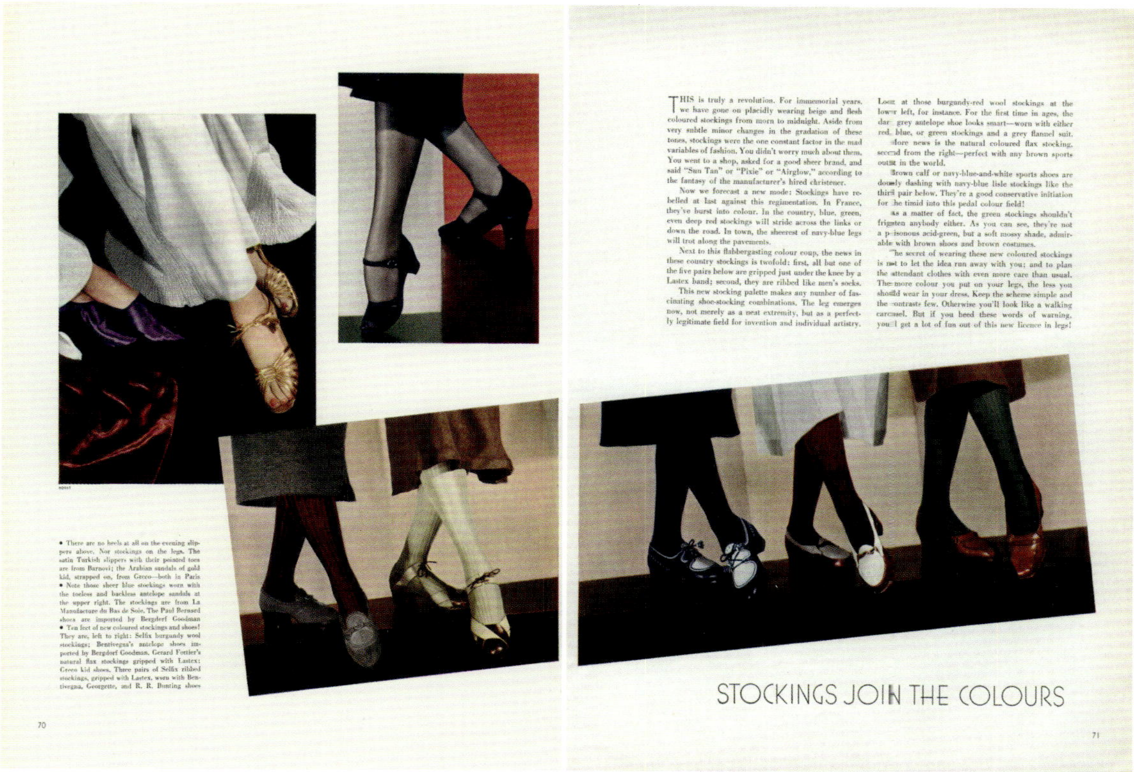

THIS is truly a revolution. For immemorial years, we have gone on placidly wearing beige and flesh coloured stockings from morn to midnight. Aside from very subtle minor changes in the gradation of these tones, stockings were the one constant factor in the mad variables of fashion. You didn't worry much about them. You went to a shop, asked for a good sheer brand, and said "Sun Tan" or "Pixie" or "Airglow," according to the fantasy of the manufacturer's hired christener.

Now we forecast a new mode: Stockings have rebelled at last against this regimentation. In France, they've burst into colour. In the country, blue, green, even deep red stockings will stride across the links or down the road. In town, the sheerest of navy-blue legs will trot along the pavements.

Next to this flabbergasting colour coup, the news in these country stockings is twofold: first, all but one of the five pairs below are gripped just under the knee by a Lastex band; second, they are ribbed like men's socks.

This new stocking palette makes any number of fascinating shoe-stocking combinations. The leg emerges now, not merely as a neat extremity, but as a perfectly legitimate field for invention and individual artistry.

Look at those burgundy-red wool stockings at the lower left, for instance. For the first time in ages, the dark grey antelope shoe looks smart—worn with either red, blue, or green stockings and a grey flannel suit.

More news is the natural coloured flax stocking, second from the right—perfect with any brown sports outfit in the world.

Brown calf or navy-blue-and-white sports shoes are doubly dashing with navy-blue lisle stockings like the third pair below. They're a good conservative initiation for the timid into this pedal colour field!

As a matter of fact, the green stockings shouldn't frighten anybody either. As you can see, they're not a poisonous acid-green, but a soft mossy shade, admirable with brown shoes and brown costumes.

The secret of wearing these new coloured stockings is not to let the idea run away with you; and to plan the attendant clothes with even more care than usual. The more colour you put on your legs, the less you should wear in your dress. Keep the scheme simple and the contrasts few. Otherwise you'll look like a walking carousel. But if you heed these words of warning, you'll get a lot of fun out of this new licence in legs!

• There are no heels at all on the evening slippers above. Nor stockings on the legs. The satin Turkish slippers with their pointed toes are from Barnovi; the Arabian sandals of gold kid, strapped on, from Greco—both in Paris • Note those sheer blue stockings worn with the toeless and backless antelope sandals at the upper right. The stockings are from La Manufacture du Bas de Soie. The Paul Bernard shoes are imported by Bergdorf Goodman • Ten feet of new coloured stockings and shoes! They are, left to right: Selfix burgundy wool stockings; Bentivegna's antelope shoes imported by Bergdorf Goodman. Gerard Fortier's natural flax stockings gripped with Lastex; Green kid shoes. Three pairs of Selfix ribbed stockings, gripped with Lastex, worn with Bentivegna, Georgette, and R. R. Bunting shoes

STOCKINGS JOIN THE COLOURS

70

71

145. Shoes by Barnovi, Bentivegna, Paul Bernard, Georgette, Greco and R.R. Bunting; stockings by Gerard Fortier, La Manufacture du Bas de Soie and Selfix, 'Stockings Join the Colours', American *Vogue*, 1 May 1935

More impressive, in terms of colour reproduction, is the curving and dynamic light reflected in the purple satin.

The cost of each page of *Vogue*'s striking colour editorial was subsidized by a corresponding page of colour advertising. To the reader, the colour photographs were the height of chic modernity; to advertisers, colour was a new, eye-catching way to promote products during the Depression. The importance of the advertising pages to Condé Nast Publications cannot be understated. In the 1920s photography had begun to outpace illustration as the preferred visual medium for advertisers; at the start of the decade fewer than 15 per cent of illustrated advertisements in mainstream magazines used photographs; 10 years later the figure was nearly 80 per cent.[8] Photographers including Steichen, Paul Outerbridge (1896–1958) and Ralph Steiner (1899–1986) launched successful commercial advertising careers that ran parallel to their editorial and fine art work. The development of Condé Nast's colour facilities was driven by the potential added value as perceived by Condé Nast's clients, their advertisers.

In 1935, to encourage more advertisers to invest in colour pages, Condé Nast published *Color Sells* (pl.146). The lavish promotional brochure featured 64 examples of the Bruehl-Bourges Process, both editorial spreads and advertisements from recent editions of *Vogue, Vanity Fair* and *House & Garden*. Its introductory text heralds 'The Launching of a New Art' and the two-page essay explains that Condé Nast could deliver colour images of a superior quality (pl.147). Bold quotations run alongside the images, including: 'Color photography: an accomplished fact' and 'Color is like dynamite – dangerous unless you know how to use it'. During the first half of the 1930s the Bruehl-Bourges Process dominated colour advertising and provided Condé Nast with 'a virtual monopoly on colour photography'.[9] In the second half of the decade, however, the monopoly would disintegrate.

The same year that Condé Nast published *Color Sells,* Eastman Kodak announced the development of Kodachrome, the world's first commercially viable colour film, bringing true single-capture colour photography to the mass market. This was followed, in 1938, by Kodachrome sheet film for professional use. Kodachrome's arrival soon rendered the Bruehl-Bourges additive process redundant. Condé Nast's years of investment, however, coupled with the refinement and expertise of the engraving division, put the plant in a very strong position to take advantage of the new film technology. The photographers in Condé Nast's stable were shooting increasing numbers of colour images for editorial use and advertising clients, but Bruehl and Bourges, previously seen as the specialists, were given fewer and fewer assignments in favour of more versatile photographers, including Horst, Toni Frissell (1907–88) and John Rawlings (1912–70). Horst's determination and talent became even more valuable to Condé Nast in the latter half of the 1930s, when several leading photographers left the company. In 1934 George Hoyningen-Huene defected to the Hearst-owned *Harper's Bazaar* after a dispute with Condé Nast's art director, Dr Mehemed F. Agha.[10] In 1937 Steichen, Condé Nast's chief photographer since the early 1920s, also announced his departure. Steichen was known around the company as 'The Colonel' on account of his work as an aerial photographer during the First World War and his revered position at Condé Nast. He had produced many of *Vogue*'s most iconic fashion studies, including the first colour photographic cover for the 1 July 1932 issue (pl.148), as well as glamorous portraits for *Vanity Fair*.

Steichen's exit was followed by Cecil Beaton's dismissal a year later, but the Englishman would be reinstated in 1940.

Although Horst's first experience of working in New York in 1932 had not been a positive one, his relationship with Mr Nast gradually improved, and in 1935, not long after Huene had joined *Harper's Bazaar*, Horst was invited to New York again. In the years leading up to the Second World War, Horst's status as a German national working in Paris became a cause for concern for both the photographer and his employer. The Condé Nast Archives contain a long series of correspondence between Mr Nast, Edna Woolman Chase and Iva Patcevitch,[11] revealing their commitment to protecting and helping the photographer. An agreement was reached that guaranteed Horst work in the New York studio, and the possibility of American citizenship, while also enabling him to photograph in Paris two or three times a year.

On arriving in New York in 1935, Horst took a room at the Gladstone Hotel on East 52nd Street, between Park and Lexington Avenues. By 1937, Horst had become one of Condé Nast's leading image-makers, with a salary that reflected his importance, and moved into an apartment at 2 Sutton Place, overlooking the East River on Manhattan's elegant Upper East Side. Horst paid a monthly rent of $200 for this comfortable home. He offered Huene the larger of the two bedrooms, in which Huene installed an unusual V-shaped bed designed by his fitness instructor, Joseph Pilates, and intended to support the body more effectively than a traditional bed. Horst furnished the rest of the apartment with items shipped from Paris: as much as he could afford from Jean-Michel Frank's workshop, including 'x-stools, an oak dressing table, parchment-covered tables, plaster lamps, and vases designed by Diego Giacometti' and the pieces Coco Chanel generously gave him later in 1937.[12] Paintings and drawings by Pavel Tchelitchew, Christian Bérard, Jean Cocteau and Pablo Picasso adorned the walls.[13]

As well as adapting to colour film, Horst created many of his most admired black-and-white fashion studies in the late 1930s, among them the Mainbocher Corset of 1939. This was the last photograph he made in Paris before fleeing for the safety of America aboard the SS *Normandie*. In the summer of 1940 Paris was captured, and the French *Vogue* offices were closed. Colleagues and friends from Europe who joined Horst and his fellow exiles in New York included Main Bocher himself, Jean-Michel Frank, the fashion illustrator Carl Erickson, Alexander Liberman and interior decorator Elsie de Wolfe. Horst would not visit France again until 1946.

The occupation of Paris brought about enormous change in the world of fashion: the majority of French ateliers closed and many couturiers and buyers left the country. The businesses that remained open struggled with extreme shortages of cloth and other supplies. The scarcity of French fashions in America, however, allowed American fashion designers to come into their own, and Mr Nast informed his employees that a new approach was required: 'The photographs were to reflect the qualities that he regarded as specifically "American". They must be "fresh and spontaneous"; and the models must not seem "remote", as in the past, but "friendly and relaxed", as in "real life".'[14] An image that seems to typify all these qualities is Horst's cover for American *Vogue*, 15 April 1939 (pl.142). It depicts the model Helen Bennett seated on the floor and wearing an ensemble from New York's luxury department store Lord & Taylor, with jewellery by Olga Tritt. Mr Nast wrote to Horst on 28 March 1940 to congratulate him on the picture: 'Dear Horst, Agha tells me that your cover (Miss Bennett in

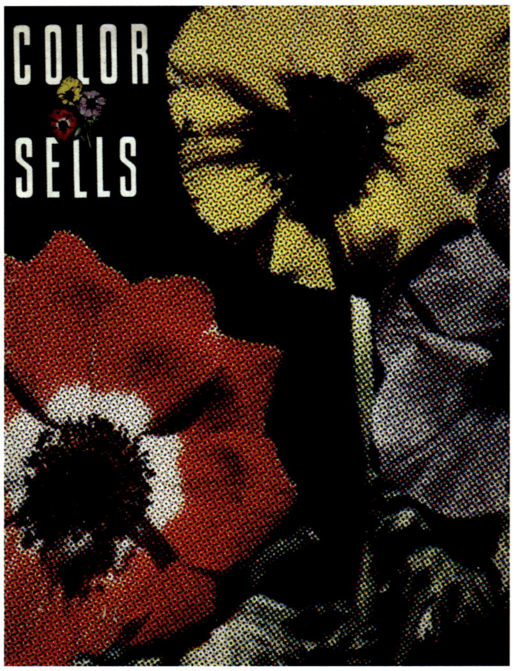

146. *Color Sells*, box cover, Condé Nast Publications, 1935

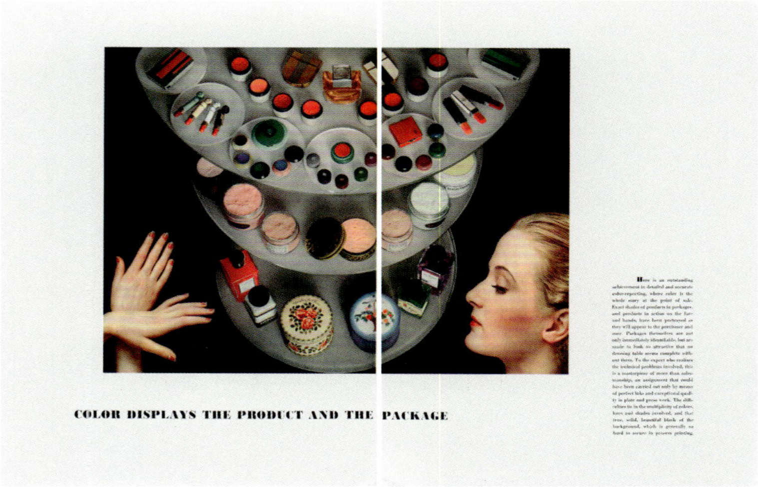

147. *Color Sells*, 'Color displays the product and the package', 1935

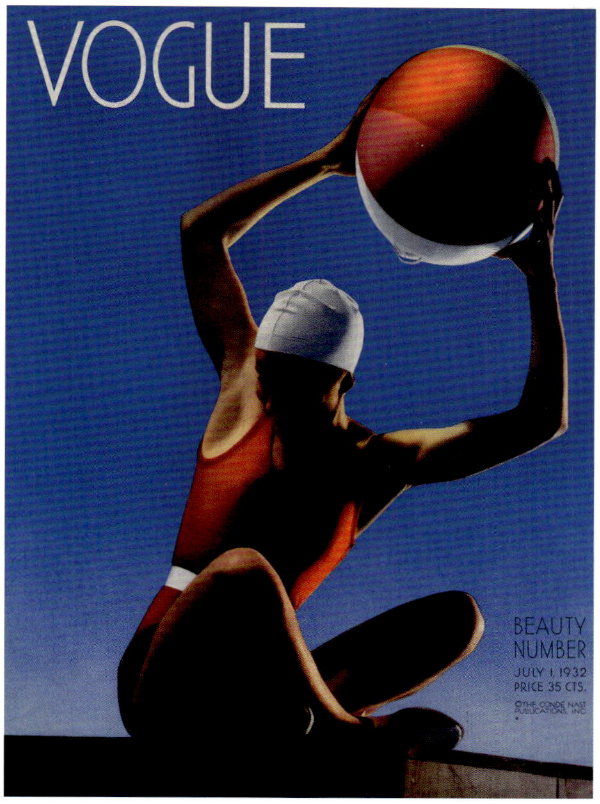

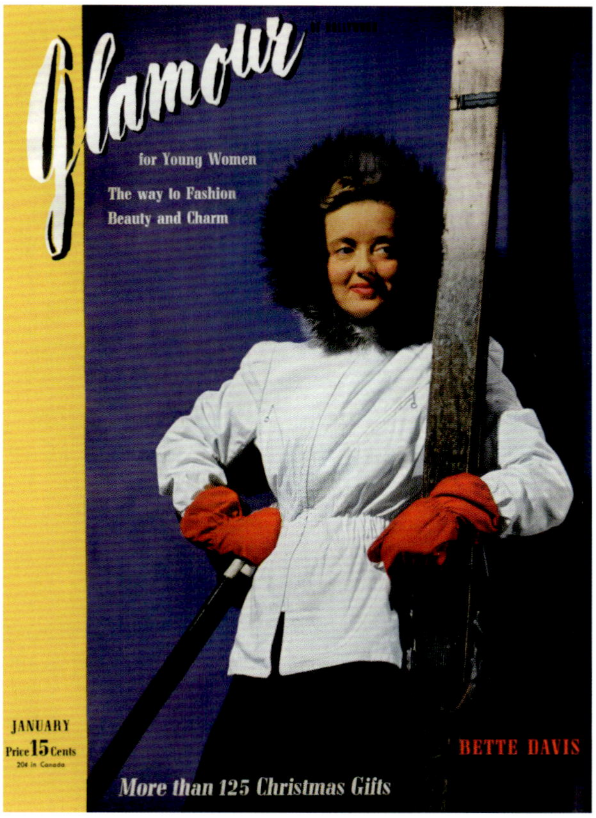

the green-and-red pyjamas) won for us again the first prize as the best magazine cover of the year. I was glad to hear this because I always felt that this cover was one of the most outstanding covers or perhaps even the most outstanding cover we ever had. Sincerely yours, Condé Nast'.[15]

During 1939 Horst produced more than 184 editorial pages for Condé Nast in New York alone. Dr Agha was flabbergasted, proclaiming it 'an extraordinarily high number, perhaps the highest number of pages produced by a single photographer in the history of the company'.[16] Horst continued to flourish in America and by 1941 his annual salary had risen to $16,000. That year he photographed more than 130 editorial pages and 61 advertising sittings. The advertising sittings earned an additional $8,714 for him, and $2,524 for the company, bringing down his overall cost to the company for the year to $13,476, or just over $100 per page.[17]

Between January 1939 and September 1942 Horst shot 34 covers for American *Vogue*, several of which are composed in the patriotic shades of red, white and blue. These include images of two of the era's leading models: Muriel Maxwell for the 1 July 1939 issue (pl.151), and Lisa Fonssagrives for 1 June 1940, for which she spelled out the letters V, O, G, U and E with her body (pl.152). One of Horst's most famous covers dates from 15 May 1941, and depicts a model balancing a beach ball on her feet (pl.150). This was the first cover produced in collaboration with the art director Alexander Liberman. Liberman, a Russian émigré, arrived at Condé Nast in 1941 and was placed in *Vogue*'s art department. His talents were quickly recognized and in 1943 he took over as the magazine's art director. From 1962 to 1994 Liberman was given the title editorial director and assumed editorial control over all of Condé Nast's titles.

As a master of studio photography, Horst sometimes struggled with the natural approach Mr Nast encouraged, and he reflected years later that, 'The new, "realistic" idea of how to sell a dress seemed to consist in having the models photographed in recognizable surroundings and everyday circumstances, not inside the studio but – still with the clumsy eight-by-ten studio camera – in people's houses or on the street ... For indoor shots, Helena Rubinstein's New York apartment, with its Picasso paintings and its dining room painted by Dalí, was considered eminently suitable by Mr Nast and Mrs Chase, as a background for fashion shots. Whether all this resulted in a greater realism struck me as an open question'.[18]

Yet Horst also noted that glamour and artifice remained important in the magazines: 'Looking today at my early wartime portraits, I am struck by the fact that many of the women I was told to photograph were movie actresses. Whatever may have been the editorial "final word" about realism, it is clear to me that Condé and Edna and Margaret Case [editor of *Vogue*] must privately have recognized that women in wartime needed glamour, just as soldiers needed pinups.'[19] Indeed, Mr Nast understood the economic power and cultural influence of the burgeoning motion picture industry,

Above
148. Edward Steichen,
American *Vogue* cover, 1 July 1932

Below
149. John Rawlings,
Bette Davis, *Glamour* cover,
January 1941

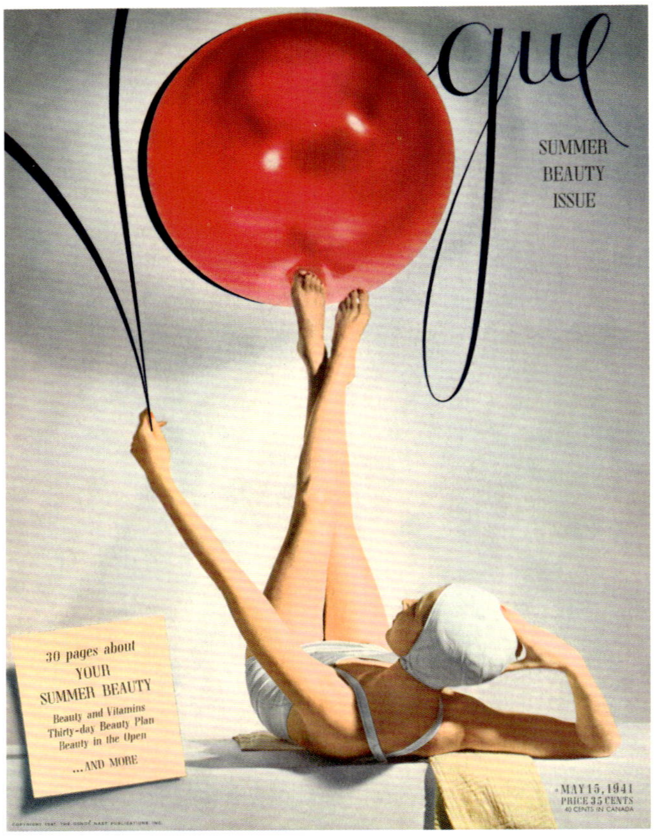

150. American *Vogue* cover, 15 May 1941

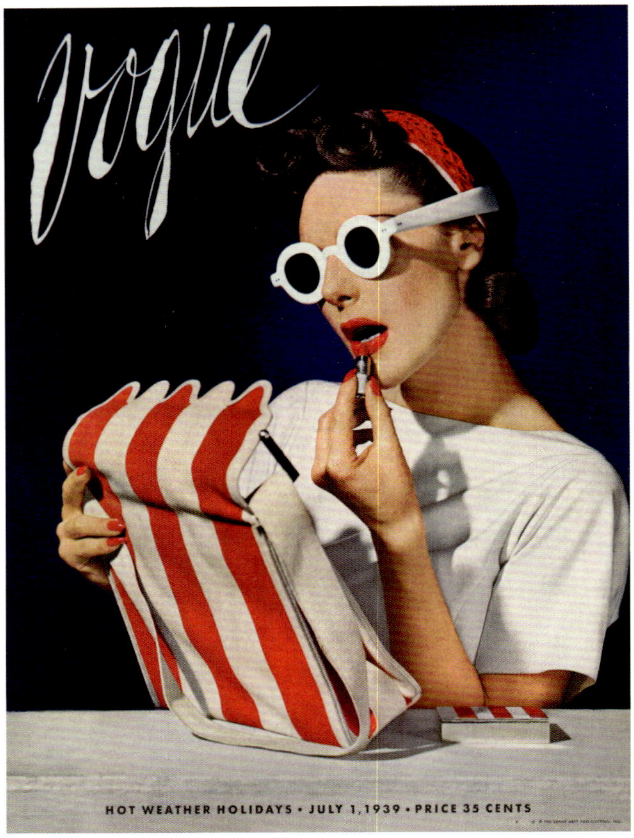

151. Muriel Maxwell, American *Vogue* cover, 1 July 1939

and in April 1939 he launched his first new magazine in two decades: *Glamour of Hollywood*, later shortened to simply *Glamour*. The new magazine featured celebrity profiles and portraits, many shot in colour on Kodachrome film. Though Nast began expanding his roster of photographers to fill the fledgling title's editorial needs in Hollywood, Horst and John Rawlings were given a number of the New York assignments for *Glamour* between 1939 and 1941, all of them in brilliant colour (pl.149).

Mr Nast employed his long-time friend and business partner, the Frenchman Lucien Vogel,[20] as an advisor, initially working on *Glamour*. But Vogel soon professed boredom and, in a memo to Mr Nast dated January 1941, requested permission to investigate the company's use of colour photography. In Vogel's opinion, the printing of colour photography had been made too perfect by the efforts of engravers, photographers and printers. The result, he believed, was that, 'all American magazine covers in colour are so uniformly like shop windows'.[21] He felt that in order for Condé Nast's magazines to stand out from the competition, it was necessary to manipulate the printing process to introduce a dominant tone back into the final product.

Later that year Vogel sent another long memo to Mr Nast, this time regarding *Vogue*'s in-house fashion illustrators. Vogel expressed the opinion that the 'drawings versus photographs' debate was becoming ever more important for the company due to the lack of 'extremely talented photographers we now have at our disposal. To tell the truth, we have only one – Horst.'[22] He went on to explain that John Rawlings had not developed beyond his original promise, except when it came to colour photography. Vogel places Horst in the top tier of the great photographers (alongside Steichen, Huene and Martin Munkácsi), with Rawlings in the second tier. Within a year, however, Vogel's opinion of the two photographers' talents would change.

In early September 1942 a memo labelled 'Private', on the subject of 'Studio Photographers', landed on Mr Nast's desk.[23] In the memo, Vogel discussed the work of Horst and Rawlings, and expressed his belief that there was 'not enough work to keep two first-class photographers busy'; his solution was to remove one. Vogel viewed Rawlings's recent work to be of a higher quality than Horst's, therefore Horst (the more expensive of the two photographers) should be let go. Vogel acknowledged, however, that both Dr Agha and Mr Nast were united in the opinion that Horst's colour work was better than Rawlings. Vogel agreed, with one important caveat: 'I am not in accord as far as the covers are concerned; I believe that in Alex Liberman, in addition to his other talents, we have an expert in covers. Thanks to him, in the last six months many of the best covers for *Vogue, Glamour,* and *Vogue Pattern Book* were those taken by Rawlings, because they were executed according to Liberman's dummies.'

Vogel's recommendation to end Horst's contract was not acted upon. Loyalty and hard work were always highly valued in Mr Nast's organization and Horst personified these two qualities. Through the defection of Huene, Beaton's dismissal and Steichen's retirement, Horst had continued to produce work at a high level and a feverish pace. Ultimately, the reason for Vogel's recommendation going unheeded may have had less to do with business and more to do with biology: Mr Nast's health was failing. He died a few weeks after receiving the memo. In what may be the ultimate barometer of the relationship between publisher and photographer, the formal,

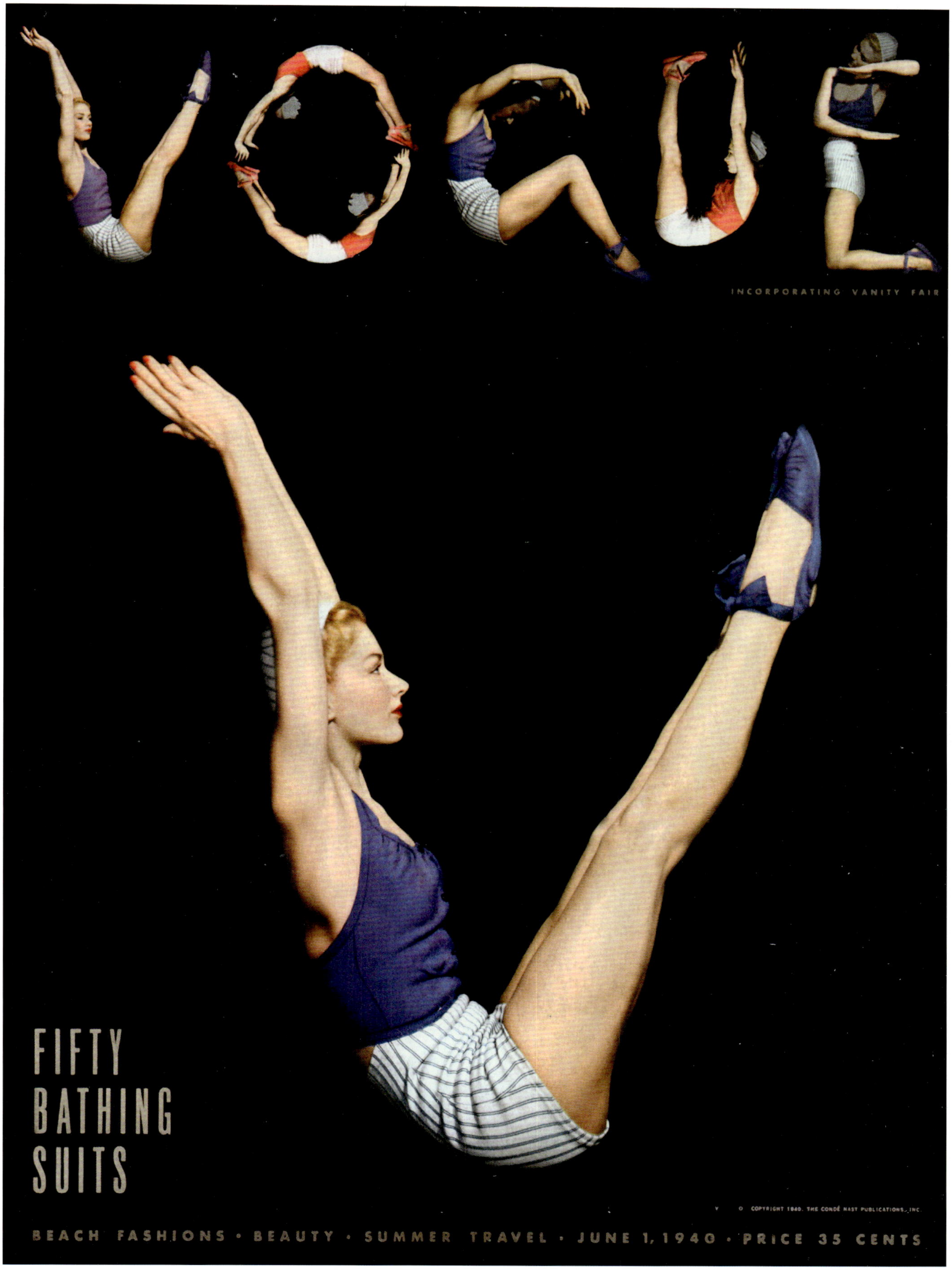

152. Lisa Fonssagrives,
American *Vogue* cover, 1 June 1940

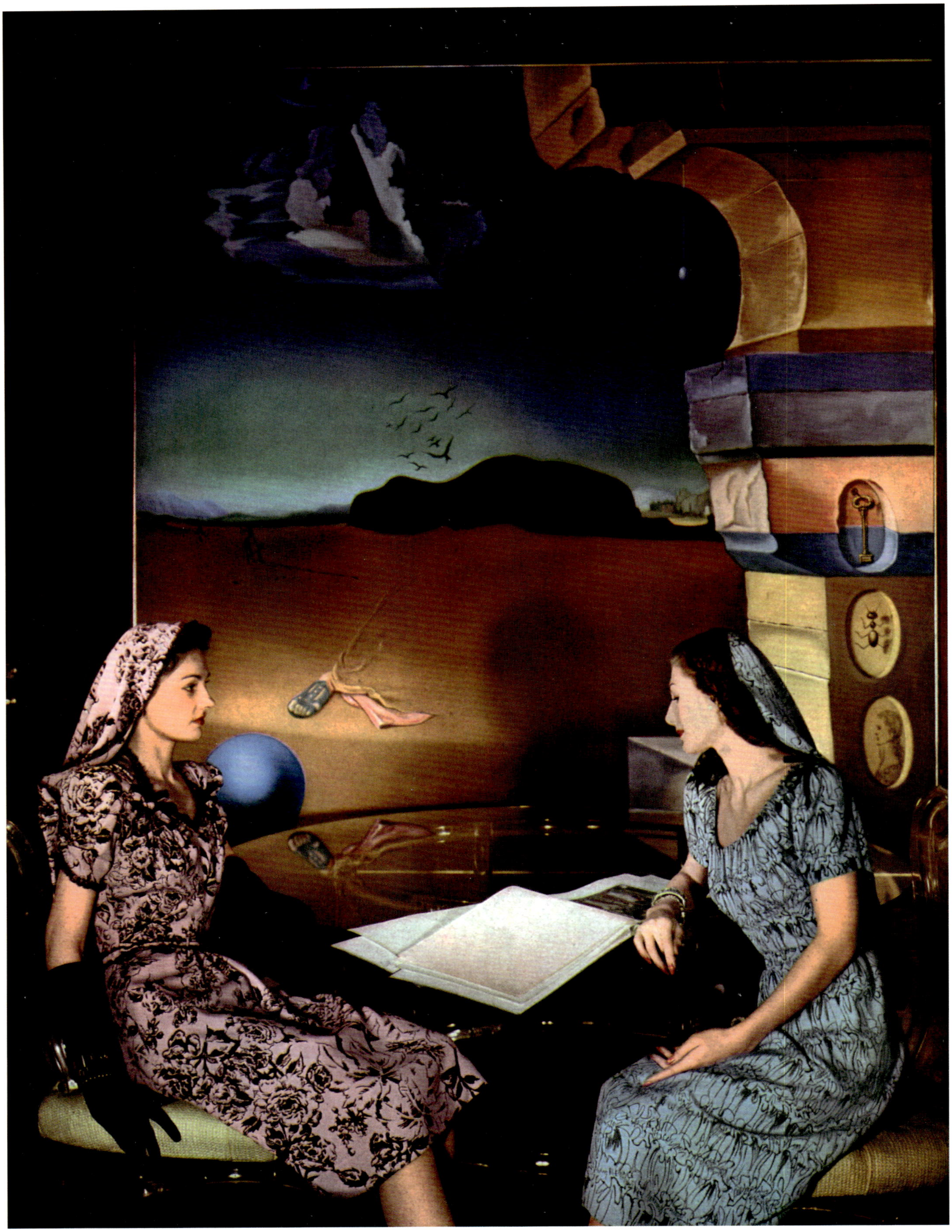

153. Dresses by Adele Simpson,
mural painting by Salvador Dalí, 1943

full-page portrait accompanying Nast's obituary notice in *Vogue* on 15 October 1942 bore a Horst credit (pl.154).

When the United States officially entered the Second World War in December 1941, Horst's work as a photographer became more difficult. He was still a German citizen and, therefore, officially an enemy alien. His travel was restricted and he had to surrender his photographic equipment: 'all of his cameras, lenses, filters, and light meters had been turned over to the *Vogue* studios for safekeeping.'[24]

However, largely thanks to the intervention of the Condé Nast lawyers, Horst managed to continue photographing. It was no doubt also due to the company's efforts that Horst's army induction was deferred by nine months. As Valentine Lawford noted, 'Mrs Chase held strongly to the view that the American fashion industry played an important part in the nation's wartime economy; and those were still the days when such opinions in such quarters, whether valid or not, carried weight.'[25]

It was during this period that Horst produced some of his most impressive colour images, including the cover for American *Vogue*, 15 June 1943. It depicts a model in a wide, deep, scoop bonnet in a shade of sunshine yellow, designed by John Frédérics, the millinery company run by John P. John. His show-stopping creations adorned the heads of Hollywood's biggest stars and were photographed by Horst for numerous other *Vogue* covers: Helen Bennett wore a vast, flower-decked straw hat for the 15 May 1938 issue and *Vogue*'s supremely elegant fashion editor Barbara 'Babe' Cushing donned a marten fur and feather hat, inspired by fashions of the 1870s, for the 1 August 1939 issue.

Horst finally undertook his army training in the summer of 1943. On 21 October of that year he officially became an American citizen, changing his surname from Bohrmann to Horst. He spent a physically gruelling three months at Fort Belvoir in Virginia and, according to the letters he exchanged with Edna Woolman Chase, found the structured army life tedious. Chase wrote to contacts in the military in an attempt to find Horst a better assignment. He eventually worked as a photographer for two army magazines: *Outfit* and *Yank*. Highlights included photographing President Truman at the White House and General Eisenhower, in 1945. Horst struck up a rapport with Eisenhower, and would later be invited to photograph Eisenhower's wife Mamie, when she became First Lady, one of a series of First Lady portraits Horst took for *Vogue* after the war.

The post-war years at Condé Nast mirrored those of post-war America – they boomed. The company, and its studios, were buzzing. The American fashion industry had found its footing and consumer product advertising soared. The Condé Nast studio went from a skeleton staff of two top photographers (Horst and Rawlings) to seven, with the addition of Cecil Beaton, André Kertész (1894–1985), Erwin Blumenfeld (1897–1969), Norman Parkinson (1913–90) and Irving Penn (1917–2009). The cast of supporting photographers in New York included the stroboscopic expert Gjon Mili (1904–84), Herbert Matter (1907–84), Clifford Coffin (1913–72) and Frances McLaughlin-Gill (b.1919), the first woman photographer employed under contract to *Vogue*.

In 1951, the best examples of the studio staff's colour work were compiled and published in *The Art and Technique of Color Photography*.[26] It is subtitled *A Treasury of Color Photography by The Staff Photographers*

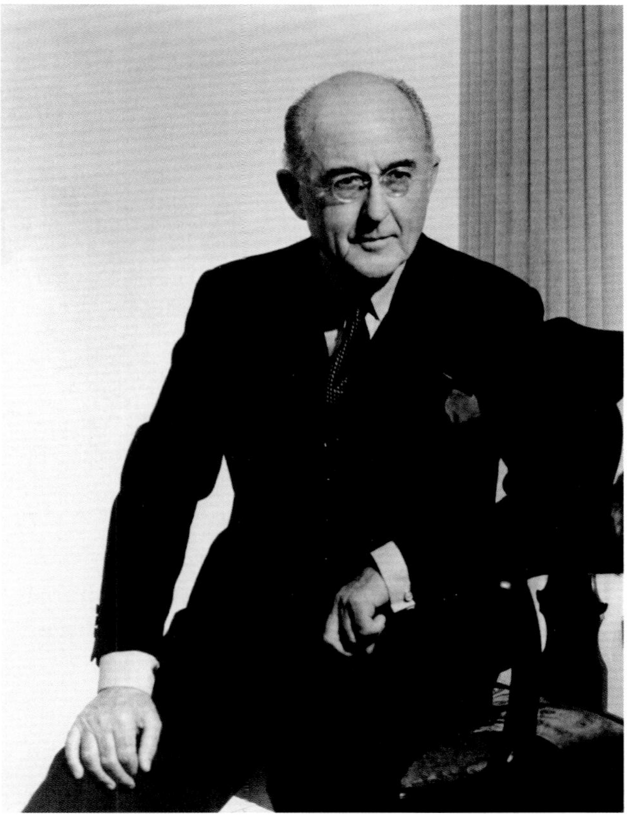

154. Mr Condé Nast, New York, 1942

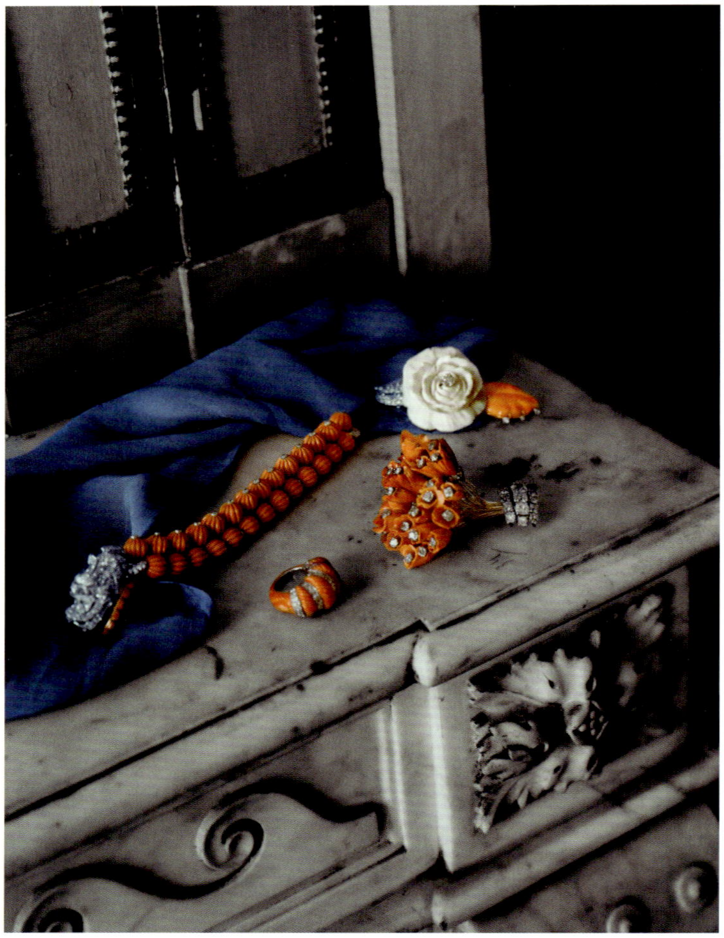

155. Still Life, 1949

of Vogue, House & Garden, and Glamour. The foreword, by Alexander Liberman, declares, 'The book comes out at the threshold of the colour era.' As well as praising the photographers' talents, Liberman acknowledges the efforts of Condé Nast's editors, studio staff, engravers and printers. Unlike *Color Sells* (1935), which had a strongly commercial message, this new publication features only editorial photography and celebrates the artistic quality of the images. The title of the book, Liberman's foreword and the individual image titles all seek to emphasize photography's close connection to historic art forms, particularly painting.

The book is divided into photographers' portfolios. The first belongs to Irving Penn, the company's rising star and a favourite of Liberman, the second to Horst, by then a senior member of the staff, followed by 15 others. Each portfolio begins with a short artist statement or essay by the photographer focusing on the use of colour. Horst opens with a common theme found in many of his texts and interviews: a love of photography, rooted in a love for mankind. For Horst photography is limitless, and, like the light it tries to capture, it is ever changing. He raises the subject of personal development, and the suggestion that his signature style has become passé. He writes, 'I used to be interested in dark subjects, with sharp, brilliantly-lit accents – subjects in which the shadows and dark colors blended into dark backgrounds. More recently, I have tried, in my color photographs, to make pictures in which every color shows distinctly, keeping the entire picture as light and clear and transparent as possible.'[27] Horst's portfolio reveals the breadth of his talent, featuring fashion studies, portraits, landscape, and two particularly strong still lifes (see pl.155). In a nod to the titular 'Technique', the back of the book contains an index of technical data for each photograph, information that would have been of use to other professional and amateur photographers. From this data we learn that Horst's photograph of coral jewels by Cartier, arranged on a mantelpiece in his studio, was taken with an 10 × 8 inch Ansco View camera. The lens was a 12 in Zeiss Tessar, f/6.3, and the film used was Ektachrome Daylight Type sheet film. The light was daylight through a window, at noon, and the exposure was 4 seconds at f/22.[28]

Horst's new approach to colour marked the next step in his development as a photographer. Throughout the second half of the 1940s his use of light had become softer and more refined, his colours more subtle, and his framing more experimental. His maturity and experience as a photographer allowed technical decisions to be shaped by the subject matter. In the 1960s, this new-found confidence would inform his series of colour shoots of spectacular homes and gardens, under the editorship of Diana Vreeland, and in so doing strike a new direction for *Vogue*.

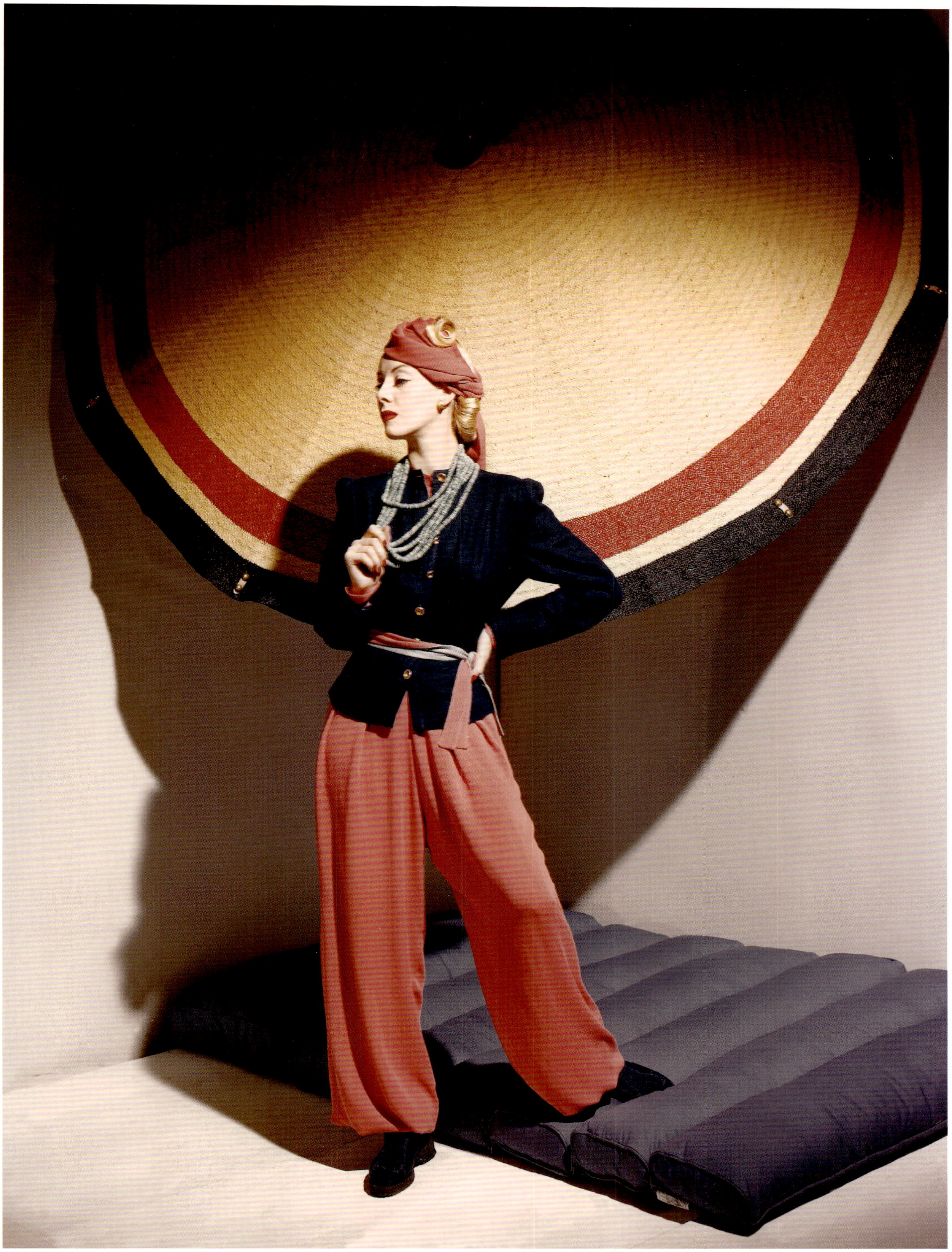

156. Helen Bennett, ensemble by Bergdorf Goodman, jewellery by Olga Tritt, 1939

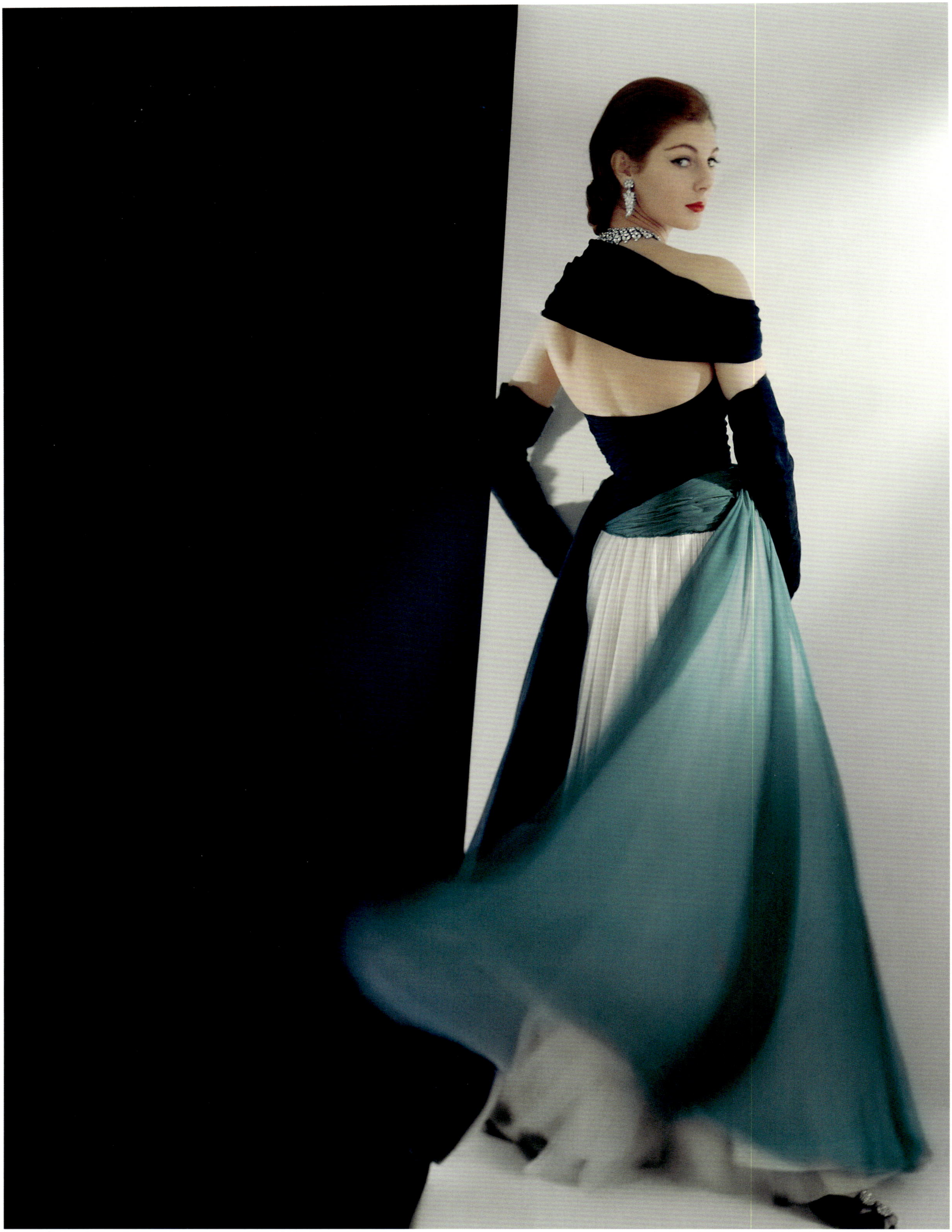

157. Dress by Jean Dessès, 1952

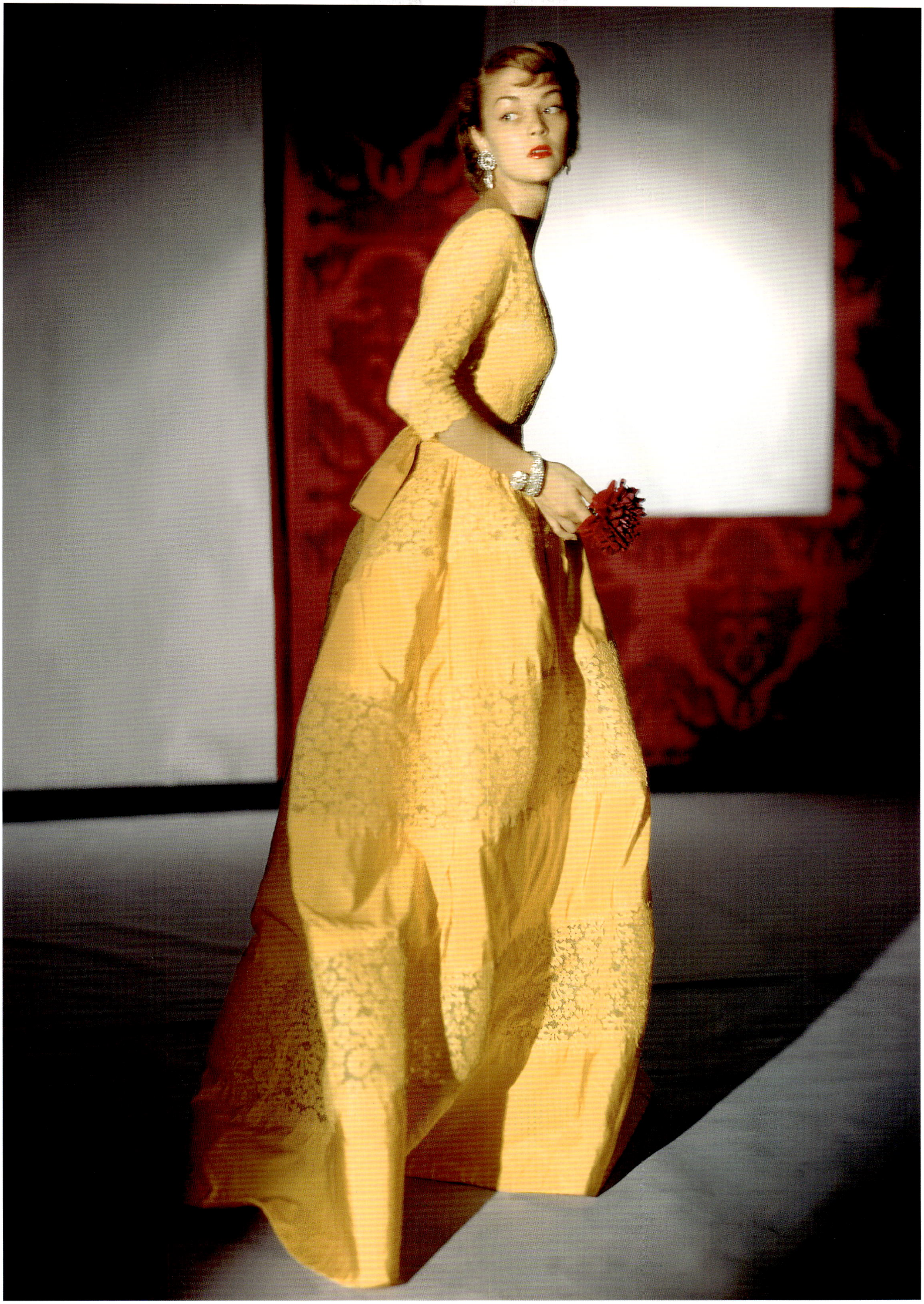

158. Dress by Henri Bendel, jewellery by Harry Winston, 1948

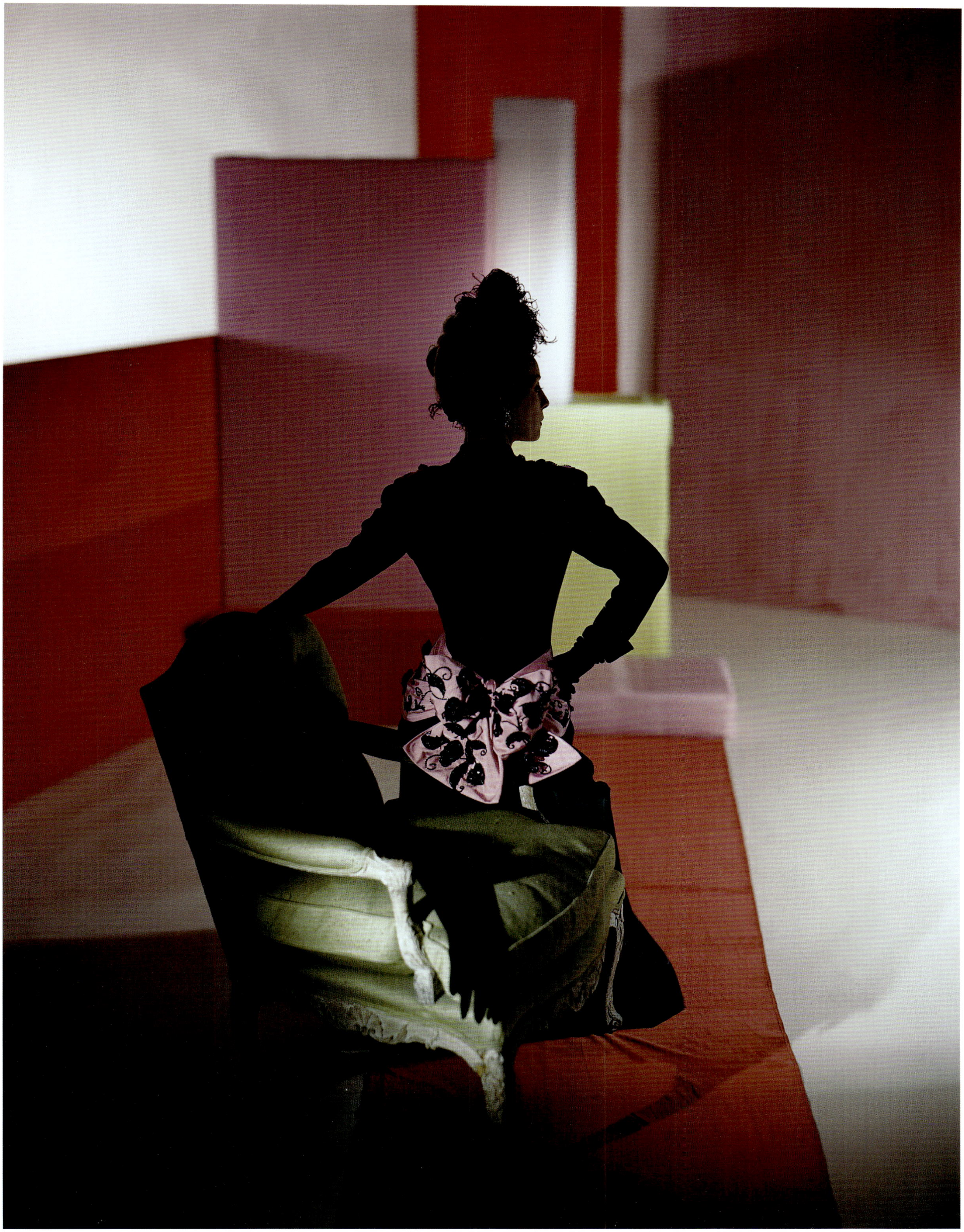

159. Suit and headdress by Schiaparelli, 1947

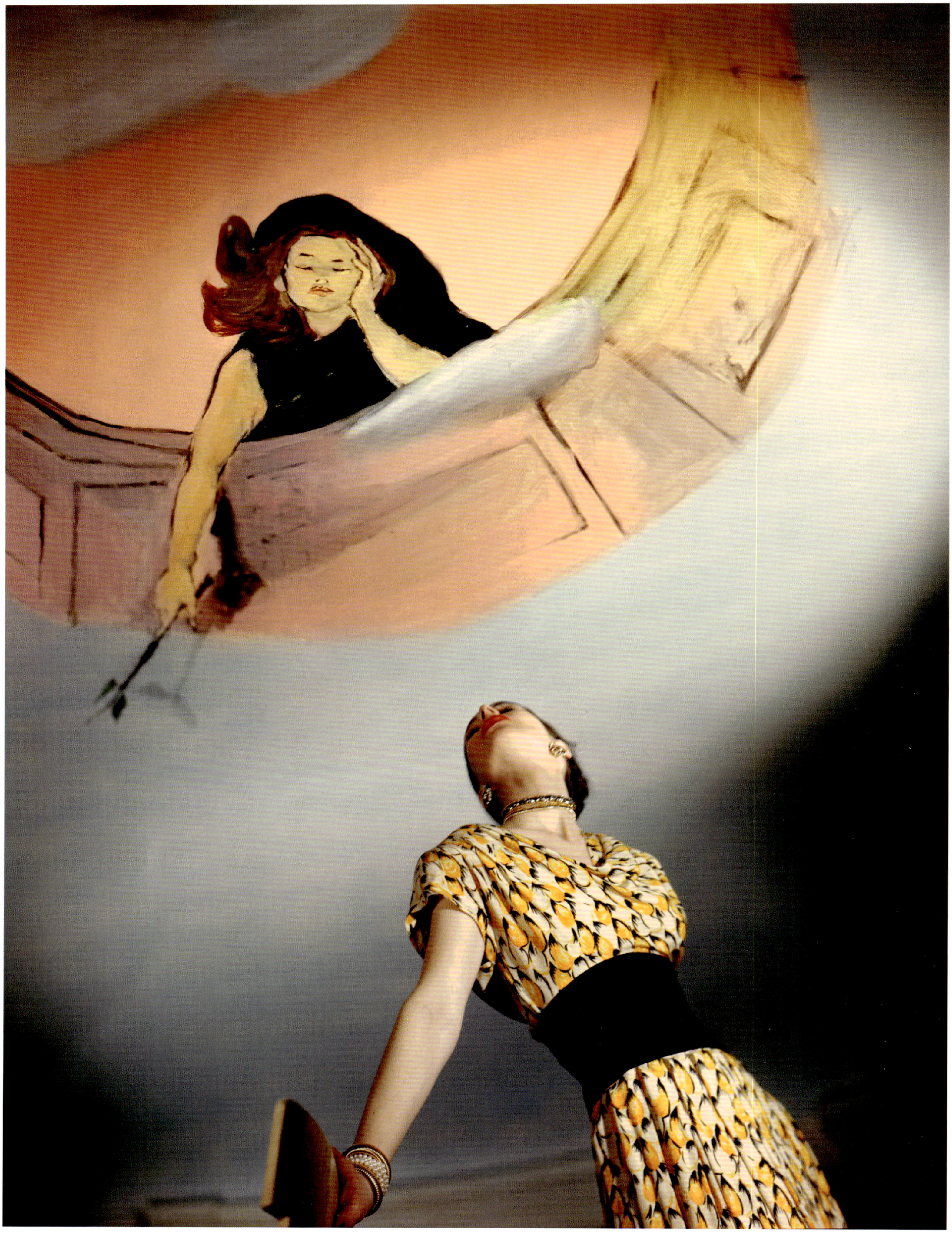

160. Dress by Jo Copeland, murals by Marcel Vertès, 1946

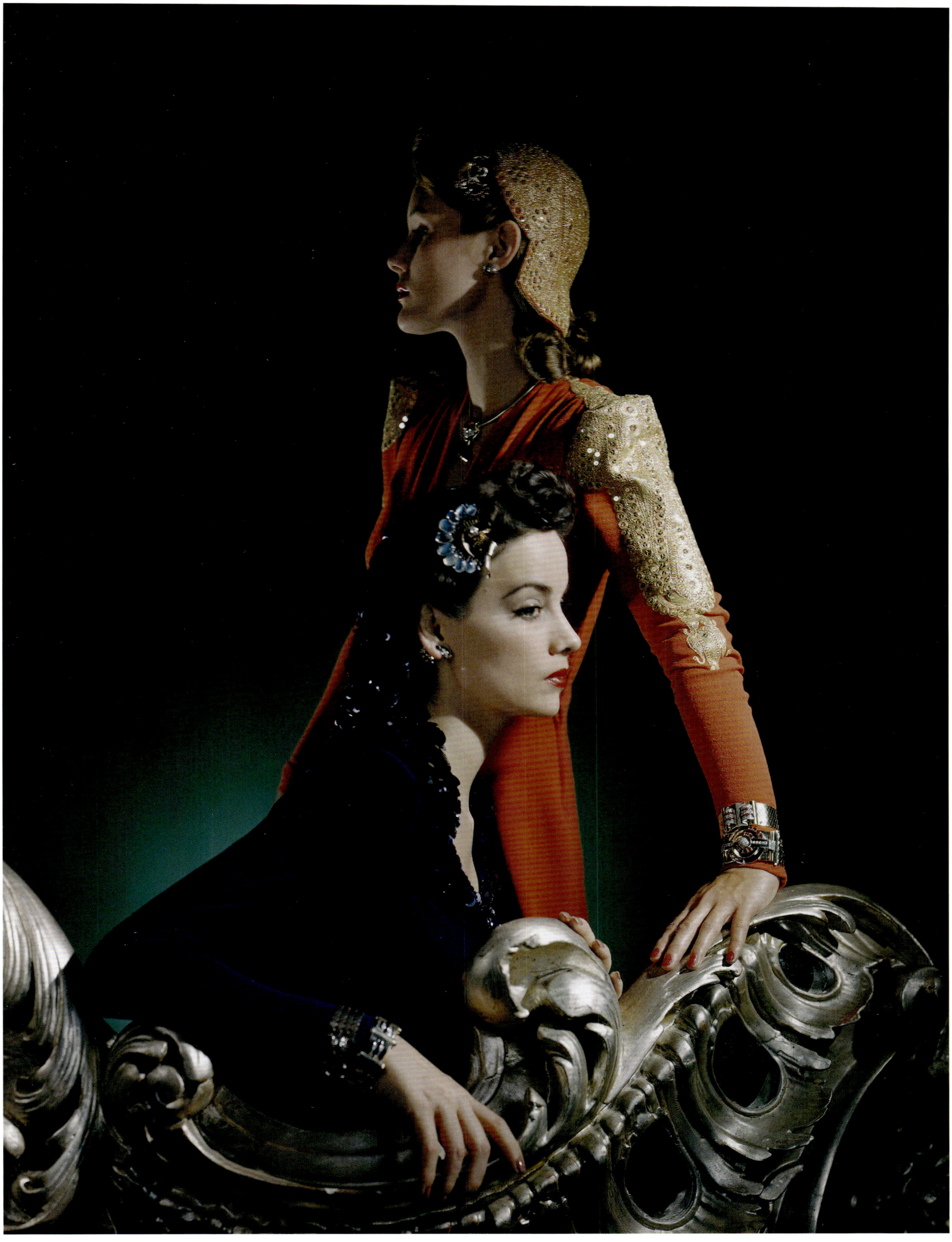

161. Ensembles by Nettie Rosenstein, jewellery by Tiffany and Company. 1940

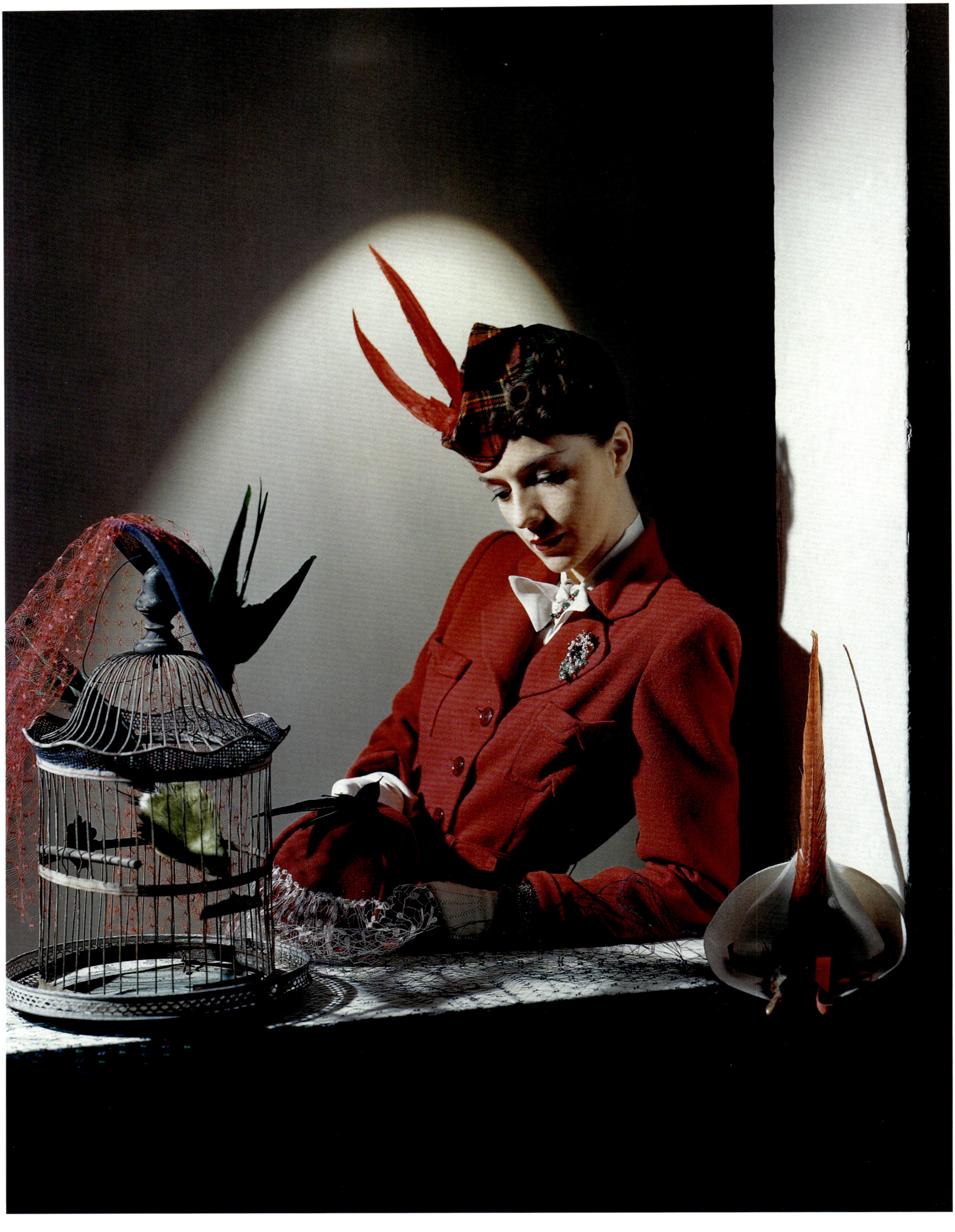

162. Ensemble by Bergdorf Goodman, jewellery by Cartier, 1939

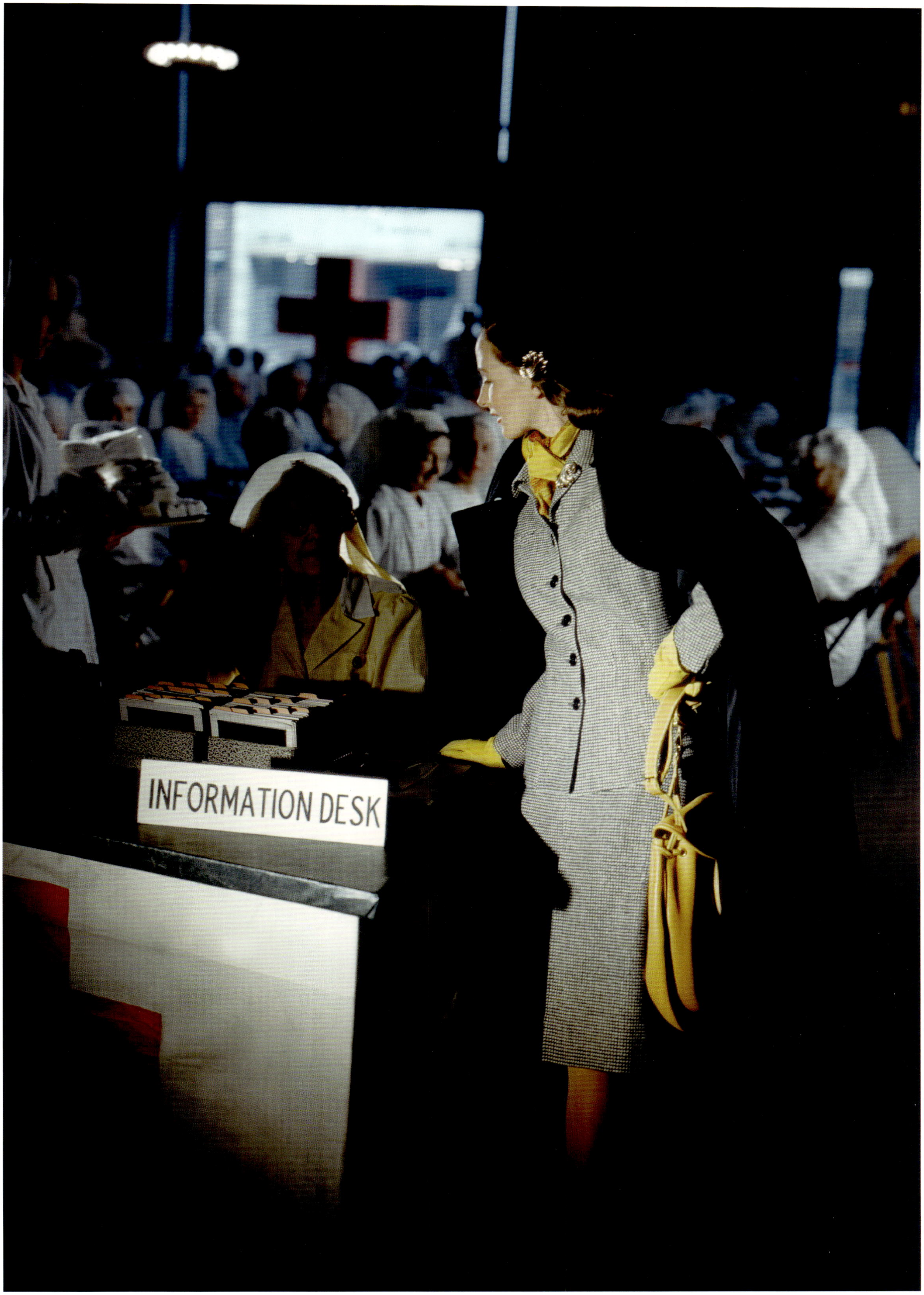

163. Suit and coat by Handmacher, 1943

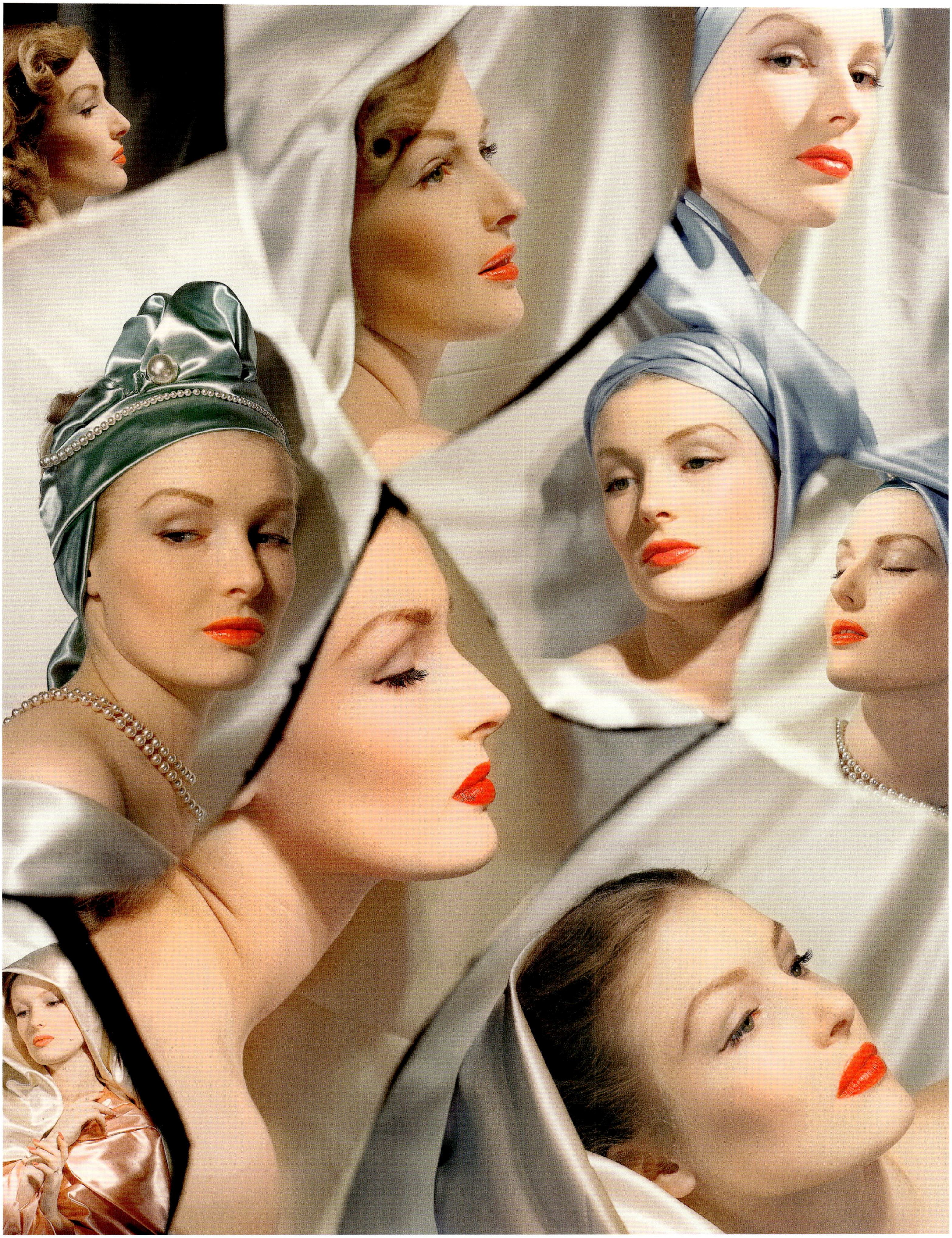

164. Susann Shaw, 1943

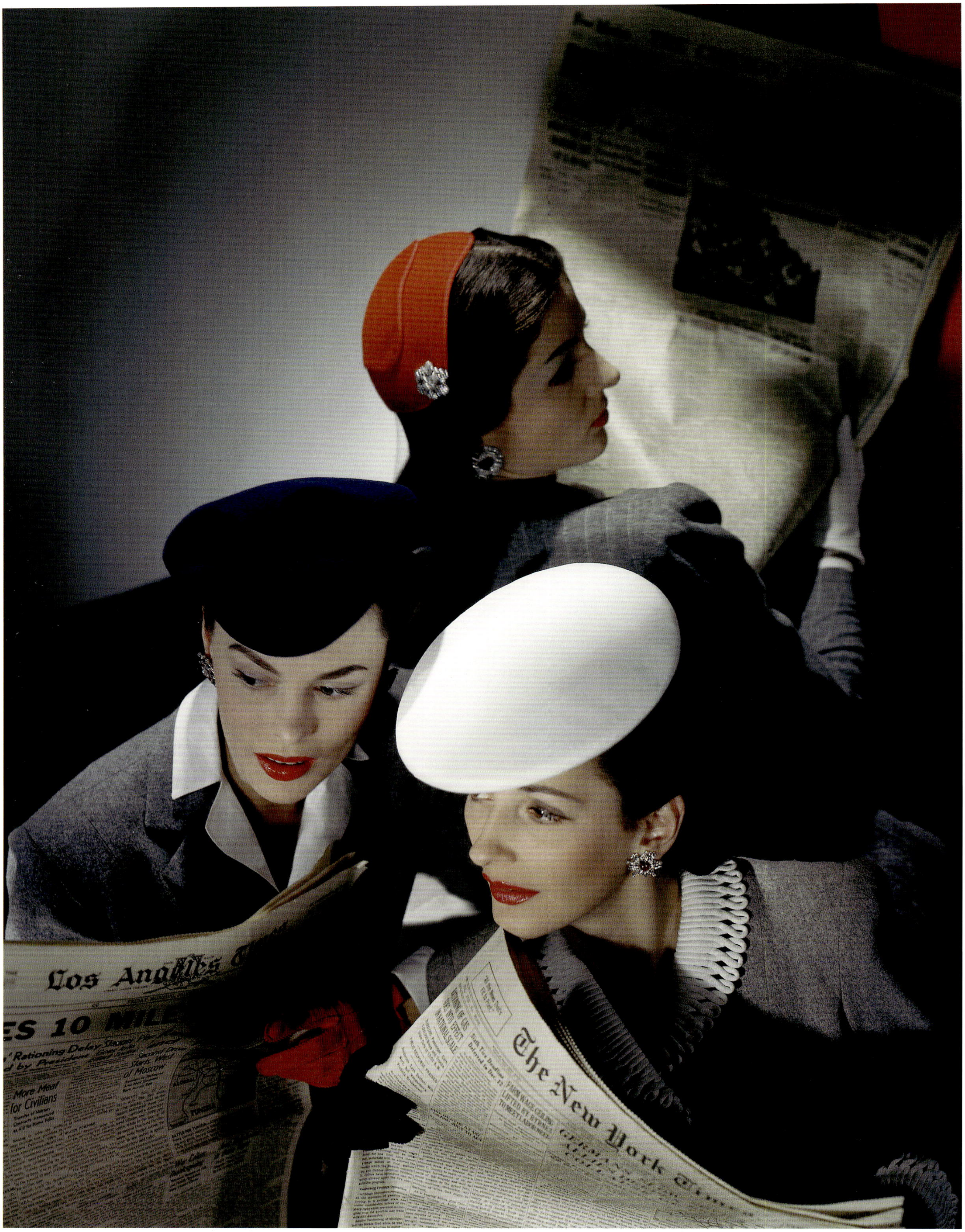

165. Hats by Best, Lord and Taylor and Mme Pauline, gloves by Dawnelle, 1943

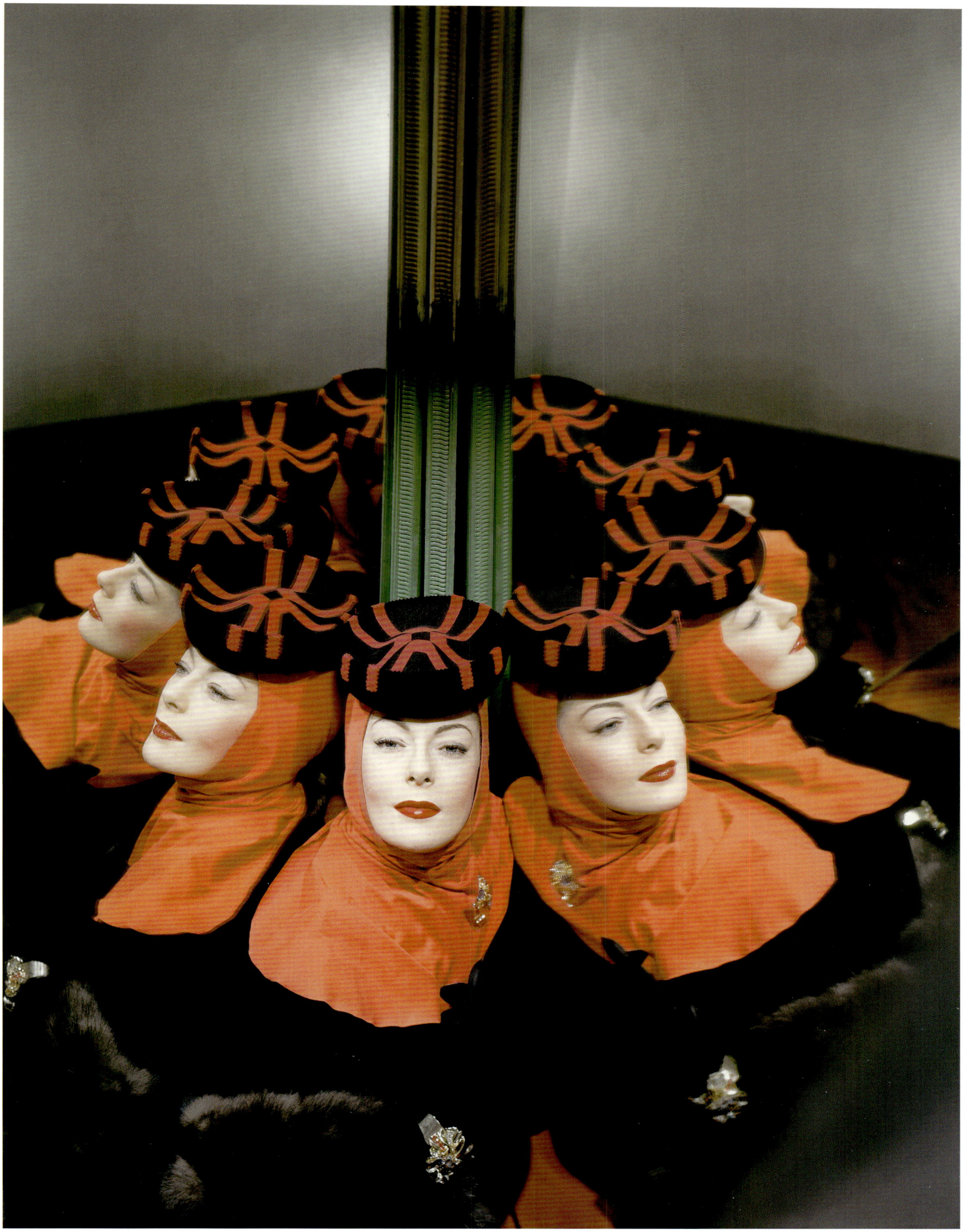

166. Muriel Maxwell, hat by Lilly Daché, jewellery by Trabert and Hoeffer-Mauboussin, 1940

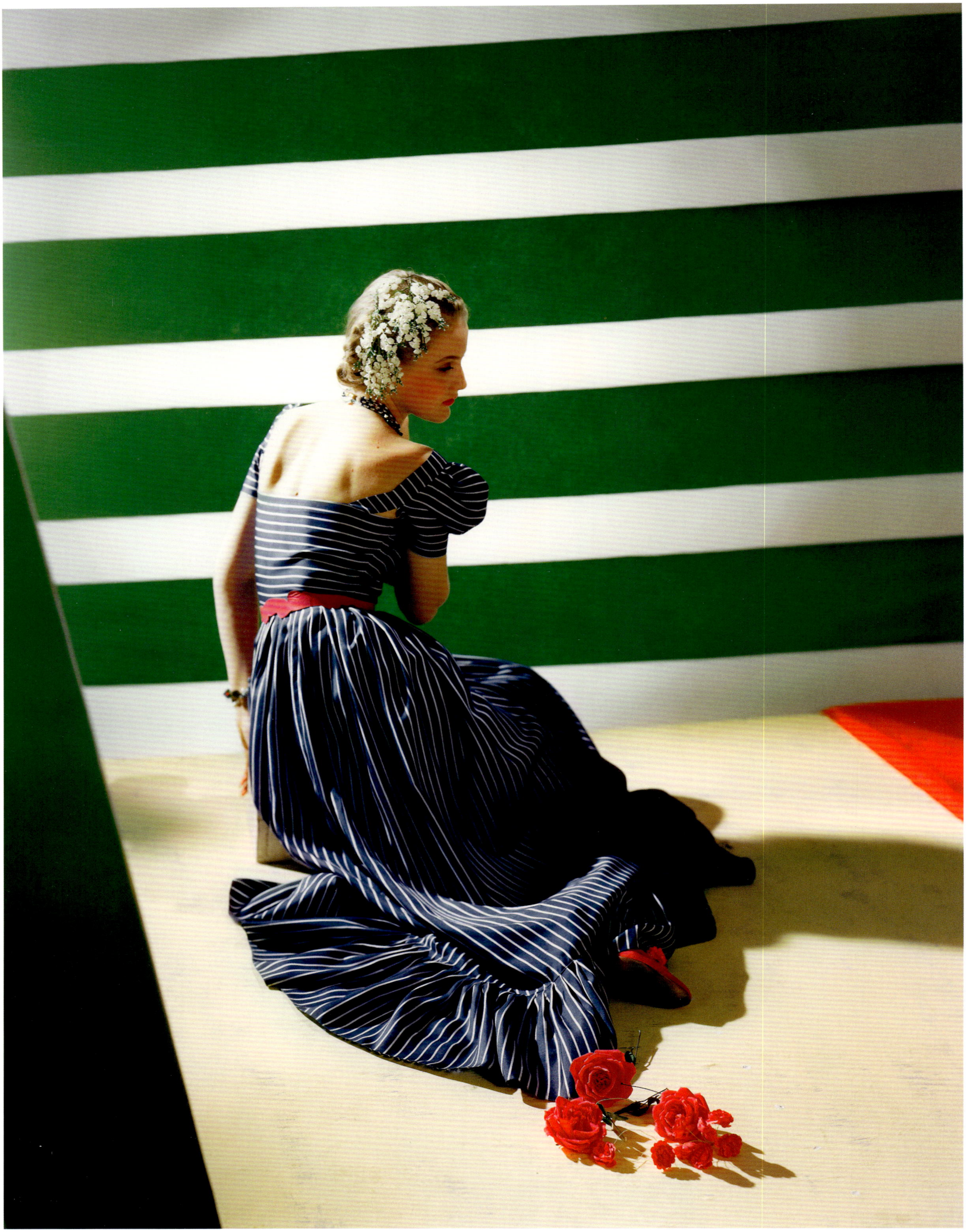

167. Dress by Hattie Carnegie, 1939

Vogue Covers

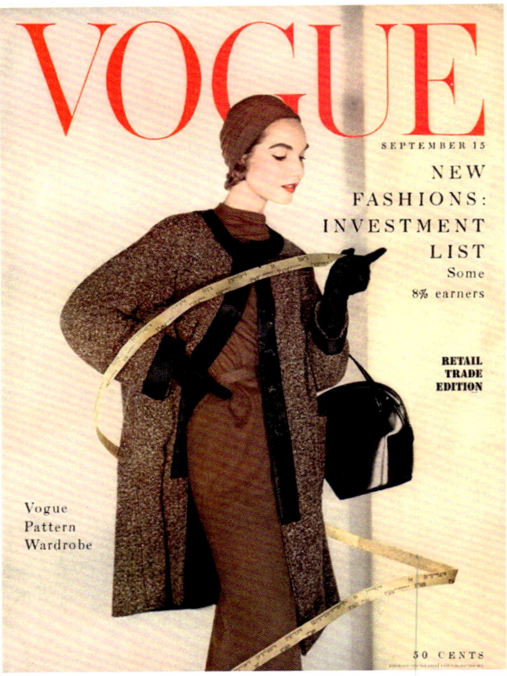
VOGUE
SEPTEMBER 15
NEW FASHIONS: INVESTMENT LIST
Some 8% earners
RETAIL TRADE EDITION
Vogue Pattern Wardrobe
50 CENTS

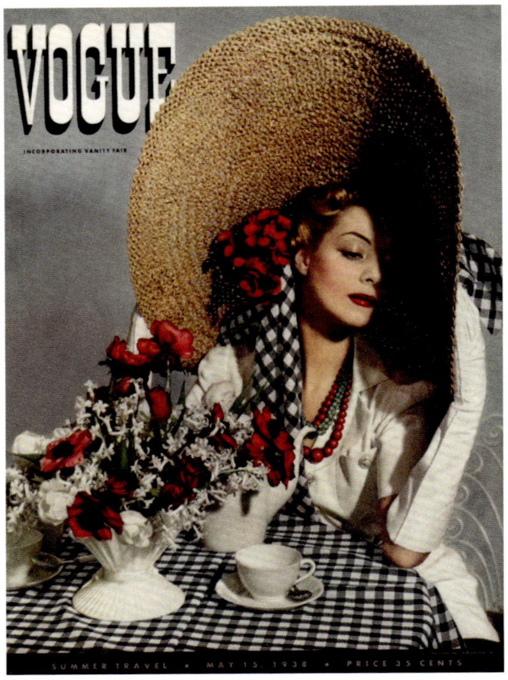
VOGUE
INCORPORATING VANITY FAIR
SUMMER TRAVEL • MAY 15, 1938 • PRICE 35 CENTS

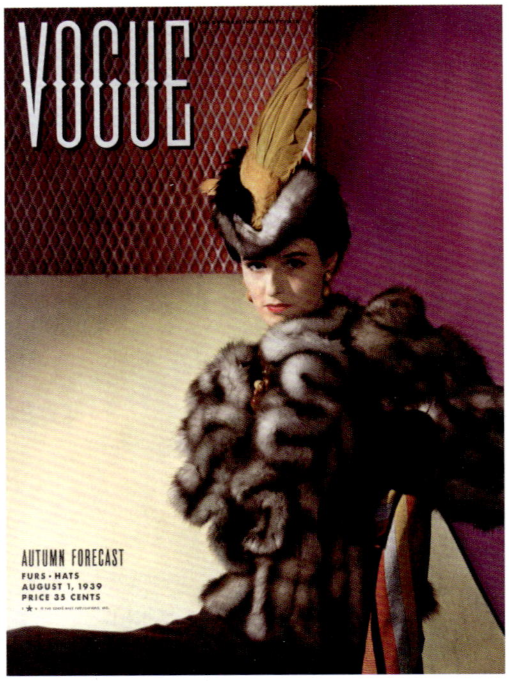
VOGUE
AUTUMN FORECAST
FURS • HATS
AUGUST 1, 1939
PRICE 35 CENTS

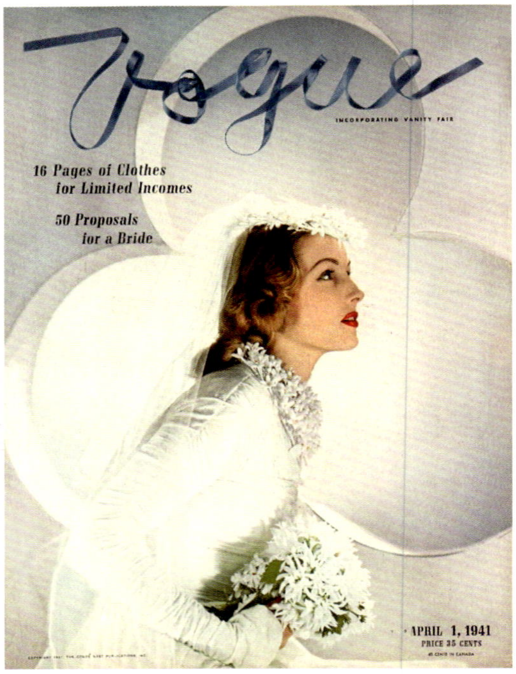
Vogue
INCORPORATING VANITY FAIR
16 Pages of Clothes for Limited Incomes
50 Proposals for a Bride
APRIL 1, 1941
PRICE 35 CENTS

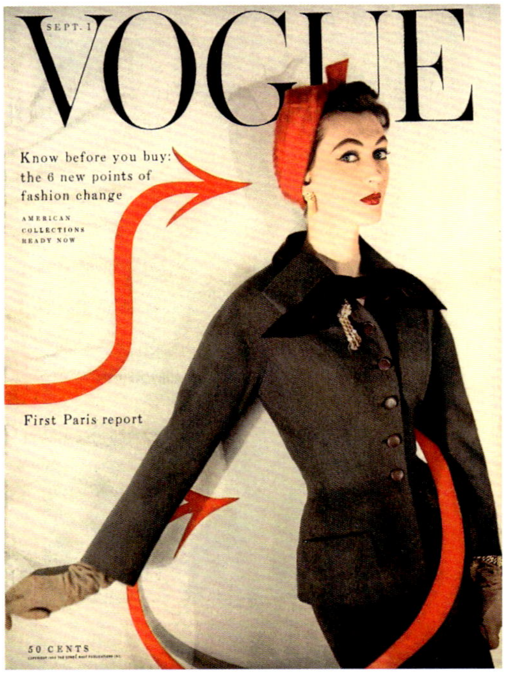
SEPT. 1
VOGUE
Know before you buy: the 6 new points of fashion change
AMERICAN COLLECTIONS READY NOW
First Paris report
50 CENTS

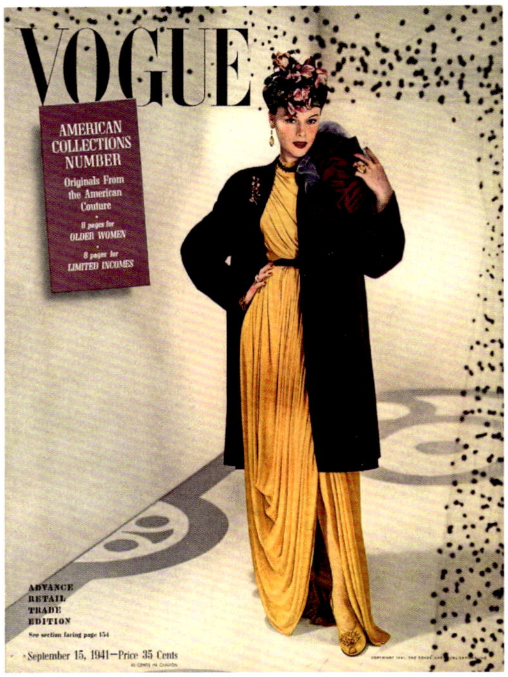
VOGUE
AMERICAN COLLECTIONS NUMBER
Originals From the American Couture
8 pages for OLDER WOMEN
8 pages for LIMITED INCOMES
ADVANCE RETAIL TRADE EDITION
See section facing page 154
September 15, 1941—Price 35 Cents

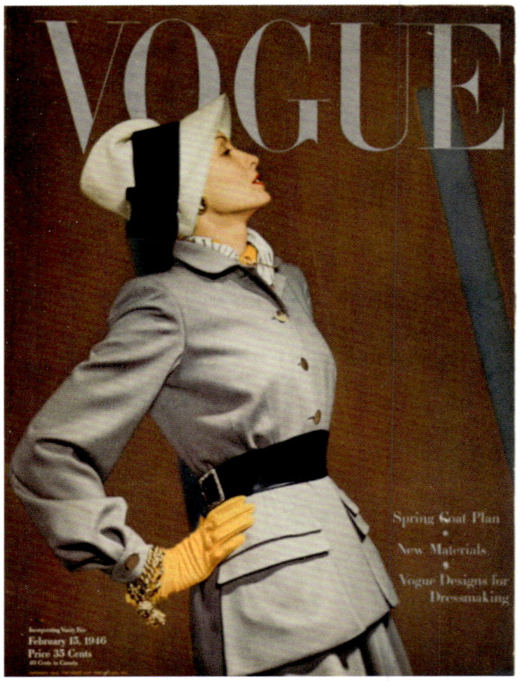
VOGUE
Spring Coat Plan
New Materials
Vogue Designs for Dressmaking
Incorporating Vanity Fair
February 15, 1946
Price 35 Cents

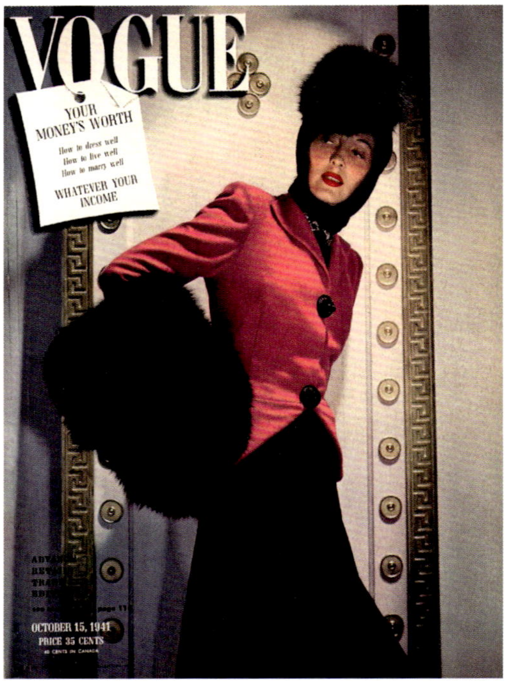
VOGUE
YOUR MONEY'S WORTH
How to dress well
How to live well
How to marry well
WHATEVER YOUR INCOME
OCTOBER 15, 1941
PRICE 35 CENTS

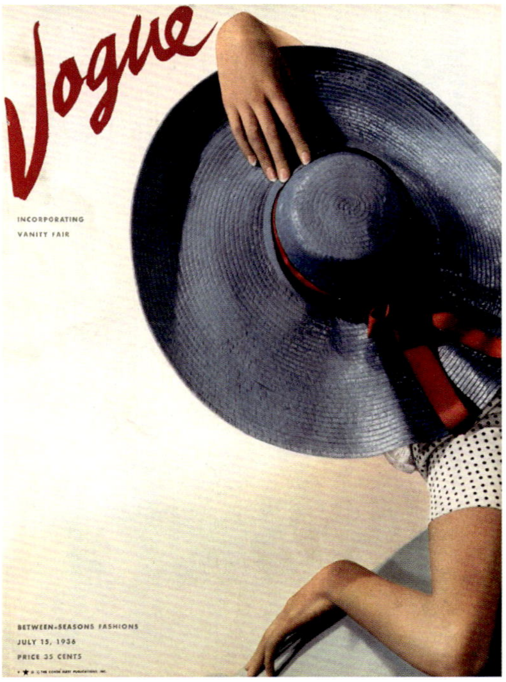
Vogue
INCORPORATING VANITY FAIR
BETWEEN-SEASONS FASHIONS
JULY 15, 1936
PRICE 35 CENTS

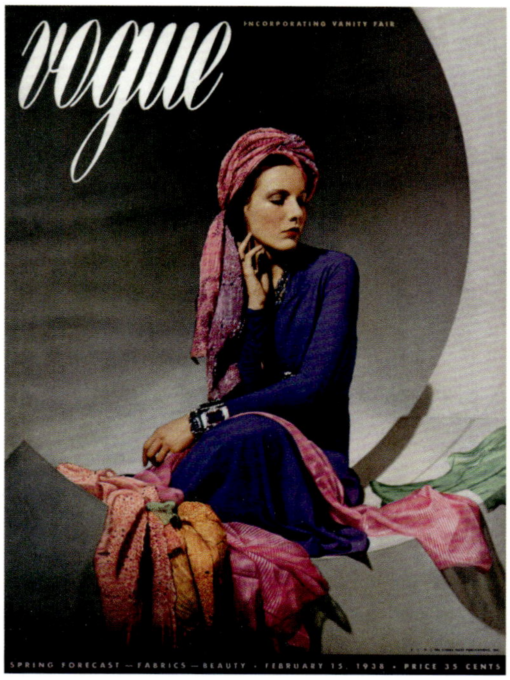
VOGUE
INCORPORATING VANITY FAIR
SPRING FORECAST — FABRICS — BEAUTY · FEBRUARY 15, 1938 · PRICE 35 CENTS

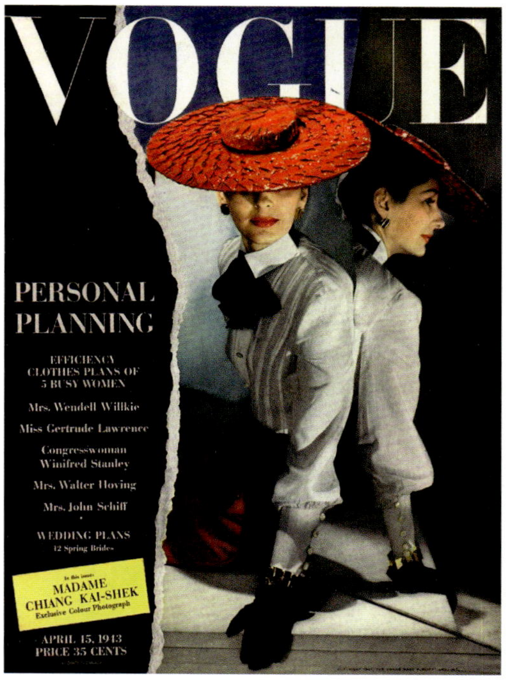
VOGUE
PERSONAL PLANNING
EFFICIENCY CLOTHES PLANS OF 5 BUSY WOMEN
Mrs. Wendell Willkie
Miss Gertrude Lawrence
Congresswoman Winifred Stanley
Mrs. Walter Hoving
Mrs. John Schiff
WEDDING PLANS
12 Spring Brides
In this issue:
MADAME CHIANG KAI-SHEK
Exclusive Colour Photograph
APRIL 15, 1943
PRICE 35 CENTS

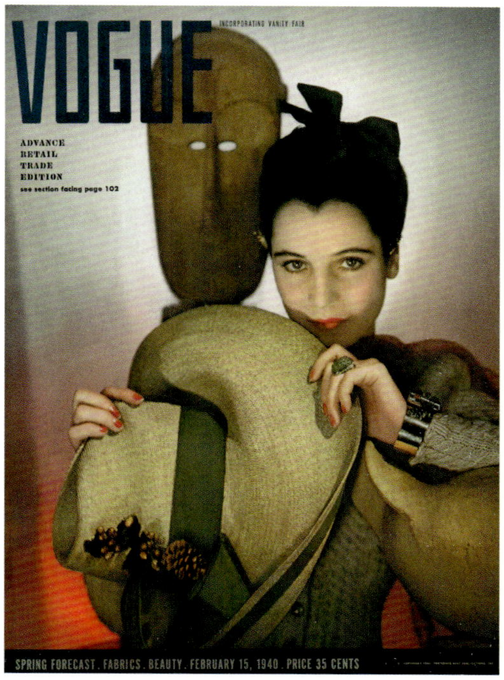
VOGUE
INCORPORATING VANITY FAIR
ADVANCE RETAIL TRADE EDITION
see section facing page 102
SPRING FORECAST. FABRICS. BEAUTY. FEBRUARY 15, 1940. PRICE 35 CENTS

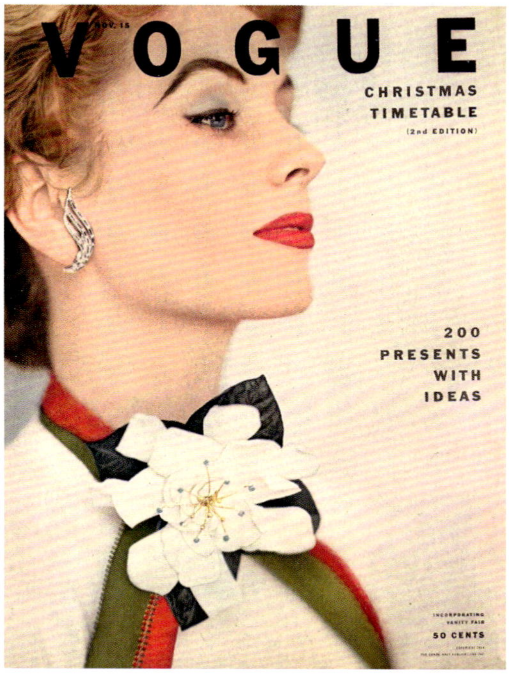
VOGUE
CHRISTMAS TIMETABLE
(2nd EDITION)
200 PRESENTS WITH IDEAS
INCORPORATING VANITY FAIR
50 CENTS

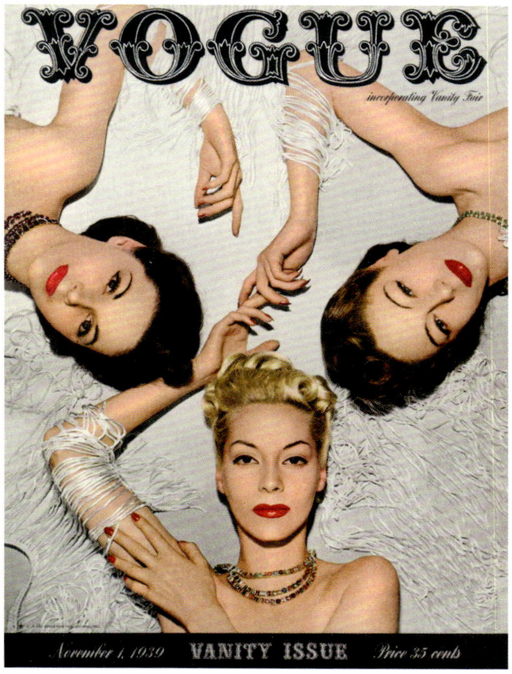
VOGUE
incorporating Vanity Fair
November 1, 1939
VANITY ISSUE
Price 35 cents

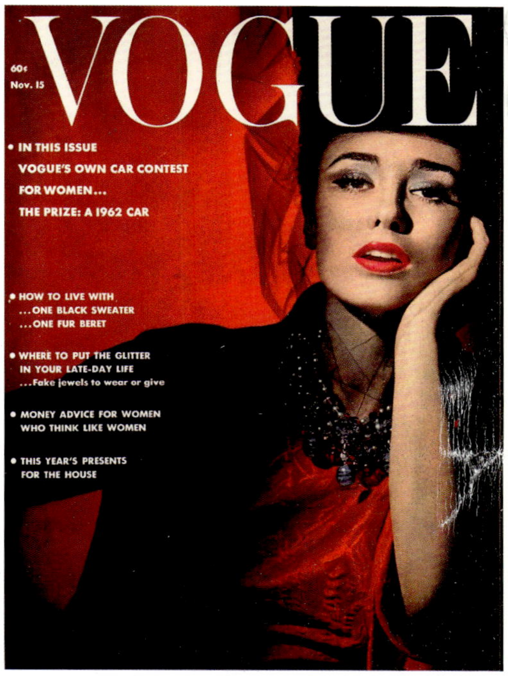
VOGUE
60¢
Nov. 15
IN THIS ISSUE
VOGUE'S OWN CAR CONTEST FOR WOMEN...
THE PRIZE: A 1962 CAR
HOW TO LIVE WITH
...ONE BLACK SWEATER
...ONE FUR BERET
WHERE TO PUT THE GLITTER IN YOUR LATE-DAY LIFE
...Fake jewels to wear or give
MONEY ADVICE FOR WOMEN WHO THINK LIKE WOMEN
THIS YEAR'S PRESENTS FOR THE HOUSE

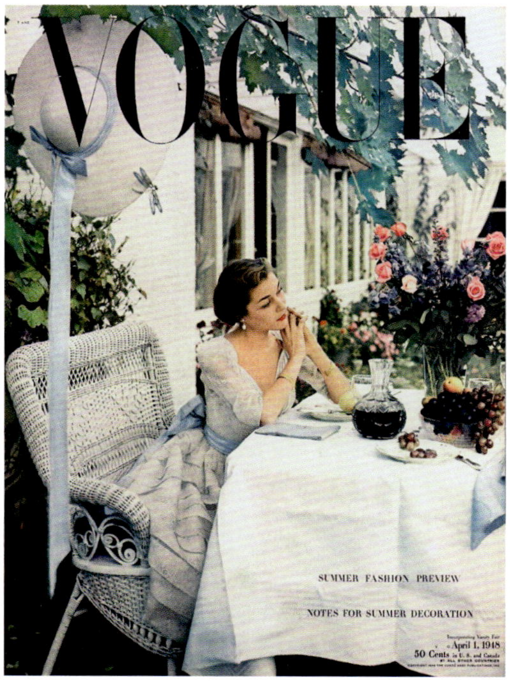
VOGUE
SUMMER FASHION PREVIEW
NOTES FOR SUMMER DECORATION
Incorporating Vanity Fair
April 1, 1948
50 Cents in U.S. and Canada

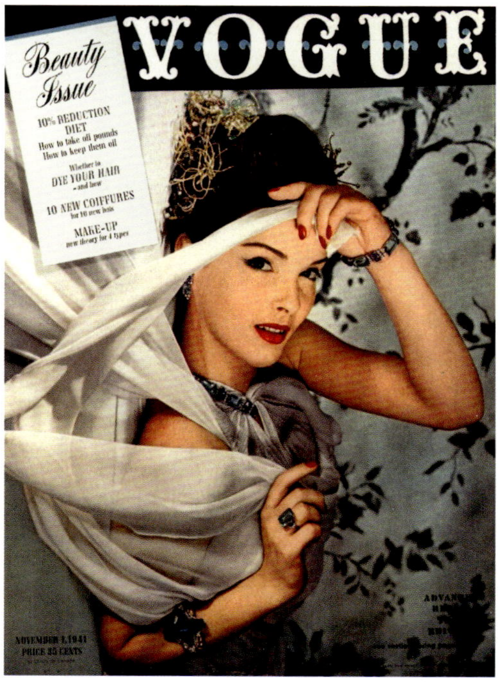
Beauty Issue
10% REDUCTION DIET
How to take off pounds
How to keep them off
Whether to
DYE YOUR HAIR
—and how
10 NEW COIFFURES
for 10 new hats
MAKE-UP
new theory for 4 types
VOGUE
NOVEMBER 1, 1941
PRICE 35 CENTS

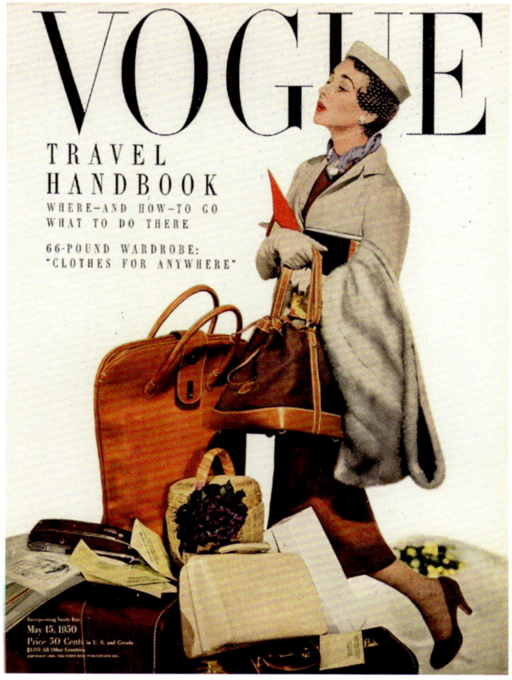
VOGUE
TRAVEL HANDBOOK
WHERE—AND HOW—TO GO
WHAT TO DO THERE
66-POUND WARDROBE:
"CLOTHES FOR ANYWHERE"
Incorporating Vanity Fair
May 15, 1950
Price 50 Cents in U.S. and Canada
$1.00 All Other Countries

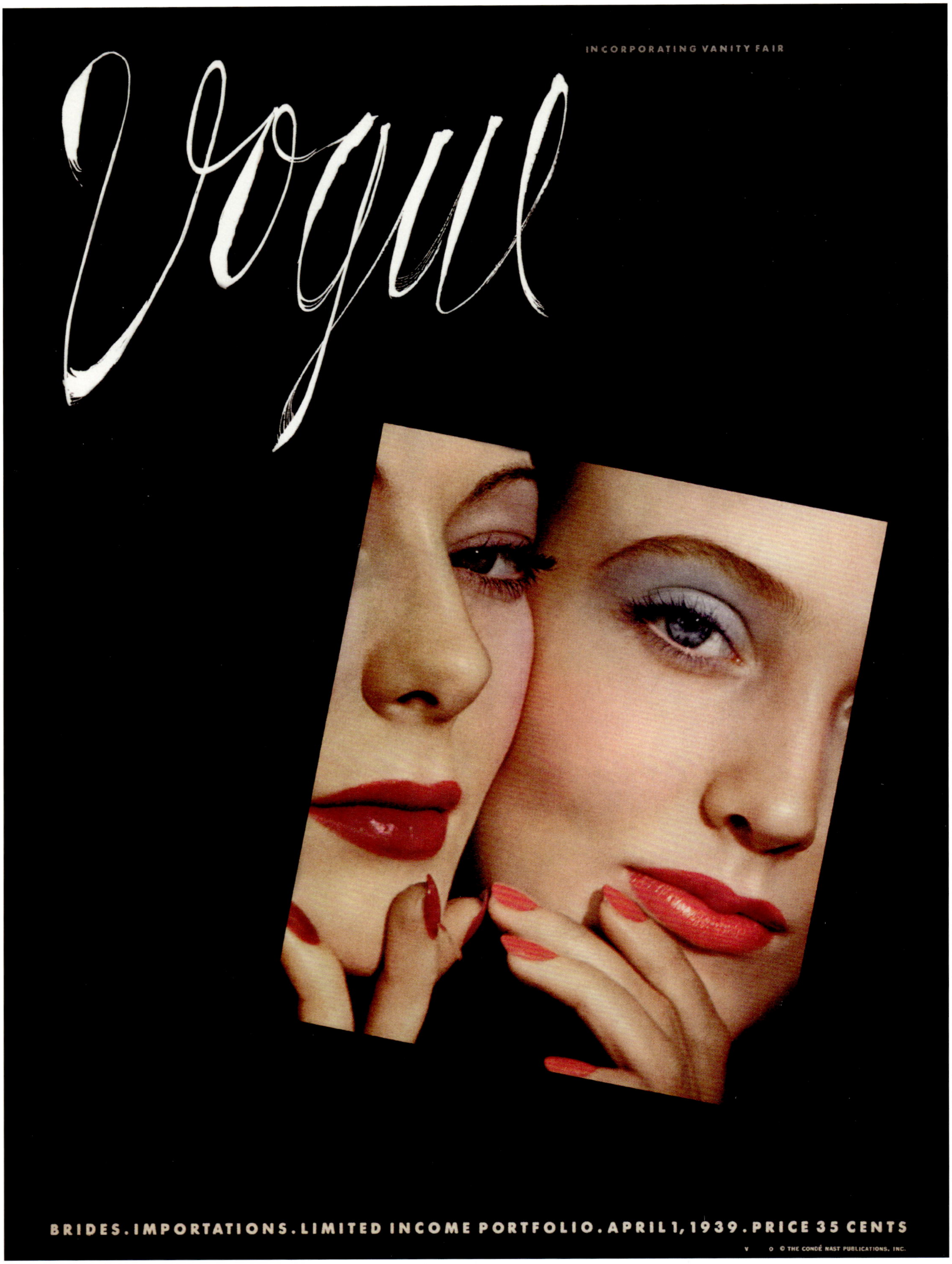
INCORPORATING VANITY FAIR
Vogue
BRIDES. IMPORTATIONS. LIMITED INCOME PORTFOLIO. APRIL 1, 1939. PRICE 35 CENTS
© THE CONDÉ NAST PUBLICATIONS, INC.

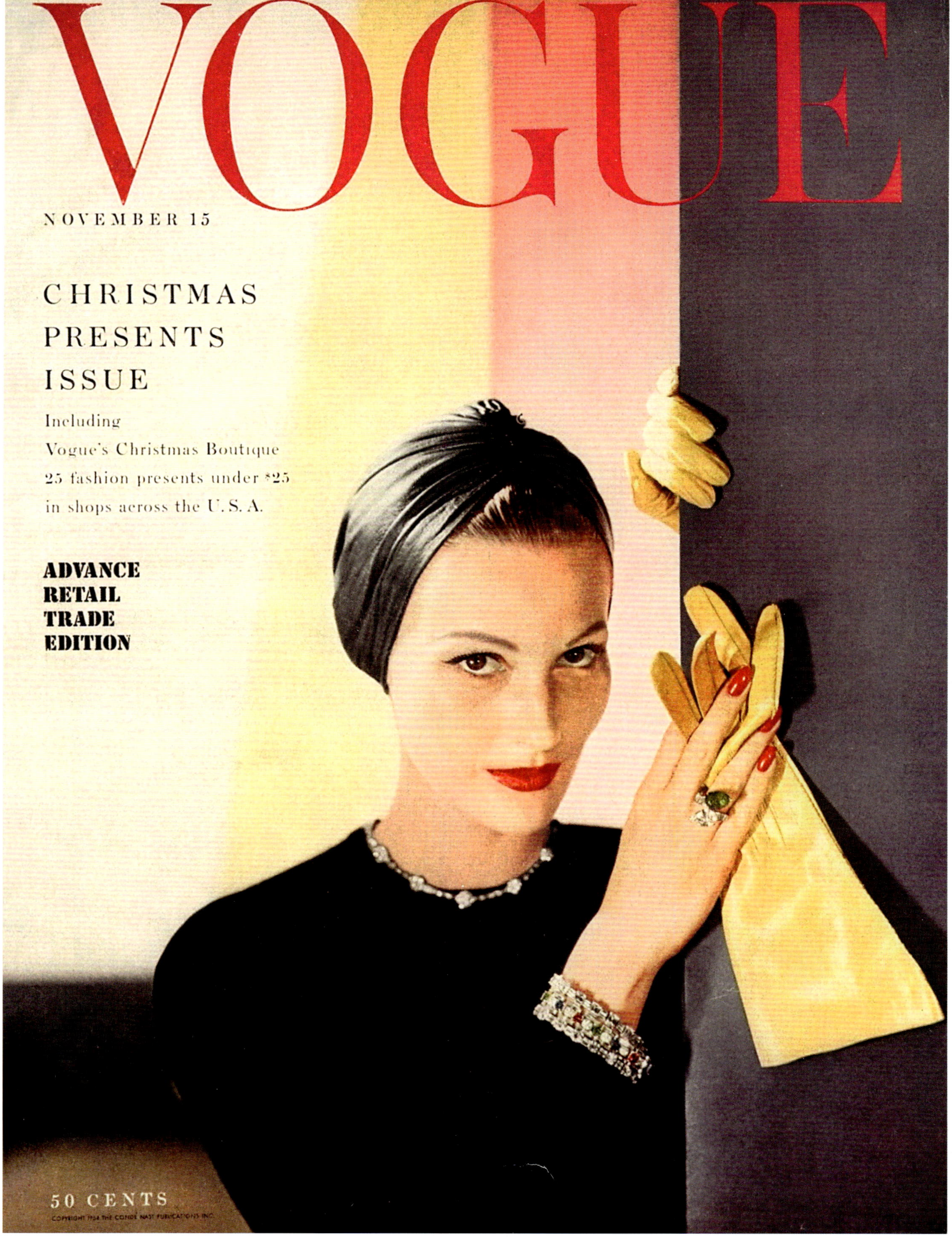
VOGUE
NOVEMBER 15
CHRISTMAS
PRESENTS
ISSUE
Including
Vogue's Christmas Boutique
25 fashion presents under $25
in shops across the U. S. A.
ADVANCE
RETAIL
TRADE
EDITION
50 CENTS

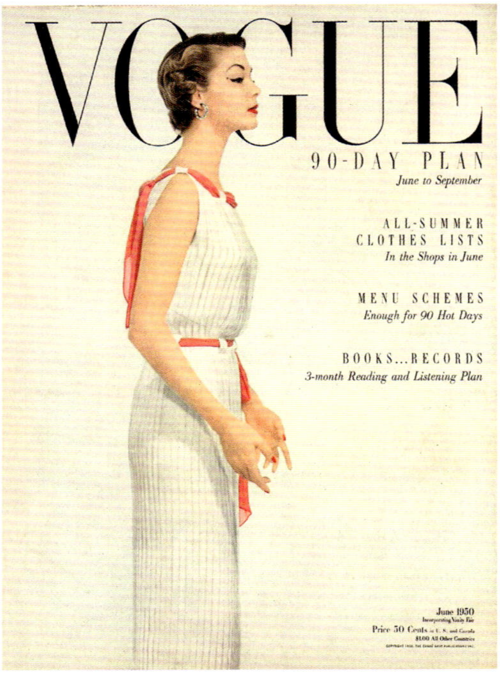
VOGUE
90-DAY PLAN
June to September
ALL-SUMMER CLOTHES LISTS
In the Shops in June
MENU SCHEMES
Enough for 90 Hot Days
BOOKS...RECORDS
3-month Reading and Listening Plan
June 1950
Price 50 Cents

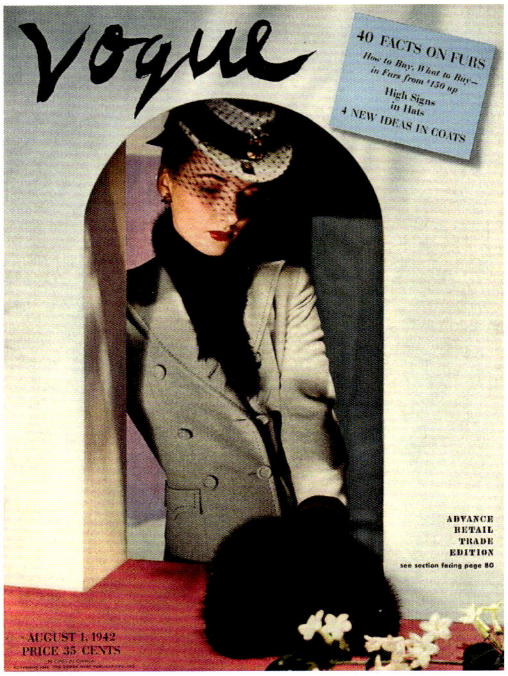
Vogue
40 FACTS ON FURS
How to Buy, What to Buy—in Furs from $150 up
High Signs in Hats
4 NEW IDEAS IN COATS
ADVANCE RETAIL TRADE EDITION
see section facing page 80
AUGUST 1, 1942
PRICE 35 CENTS

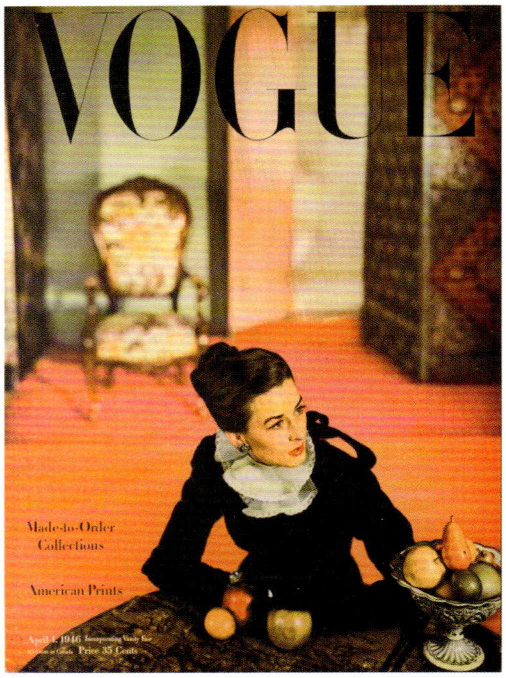
VOGUE
Made-to-Order Collections
American Prints
April 1, 1946
Price 35 Cents

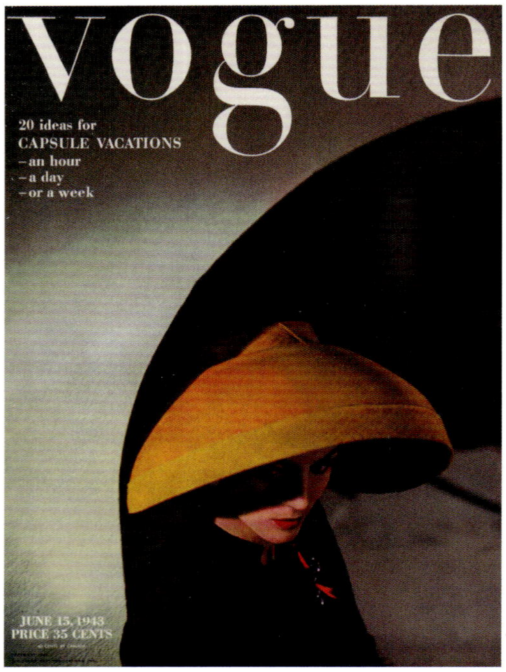
vogue
20 ideas for
CAPSULE VACATIONS
–an hour
–a day
–or a week
JUNE 15, 1943
PRICE 35 CENTS

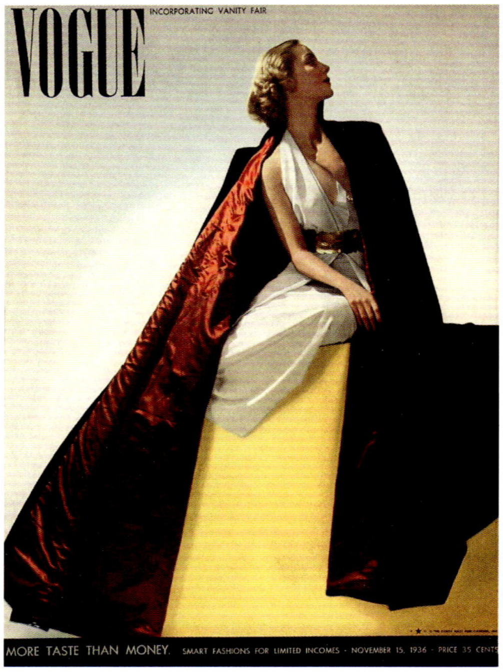
VOGUE
INCORPORATING VANITY FAIR
MORE TASTE THAN MONEY
SMART FASHIONS FOR LIMITED INCOMES · NOVEMBER 15, 1936 · PRICE 35 CENTS

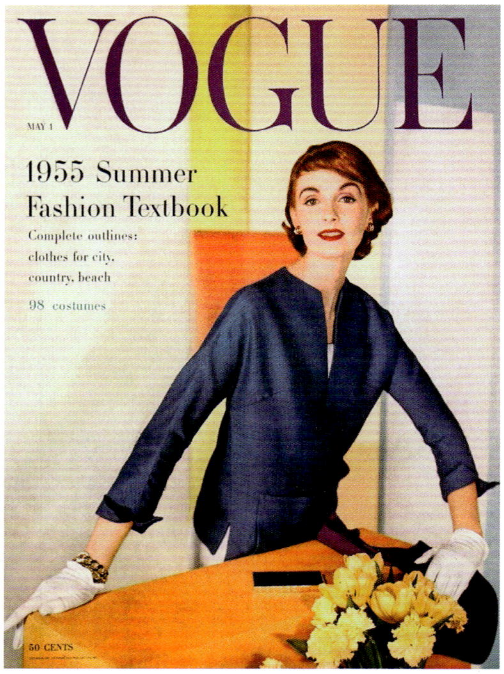
VOGUE
MAY 1
1955 Summer
Fashion Textbook
Complete outlines:
clothes for city,
country, beach
98 costumes
50 CENTS

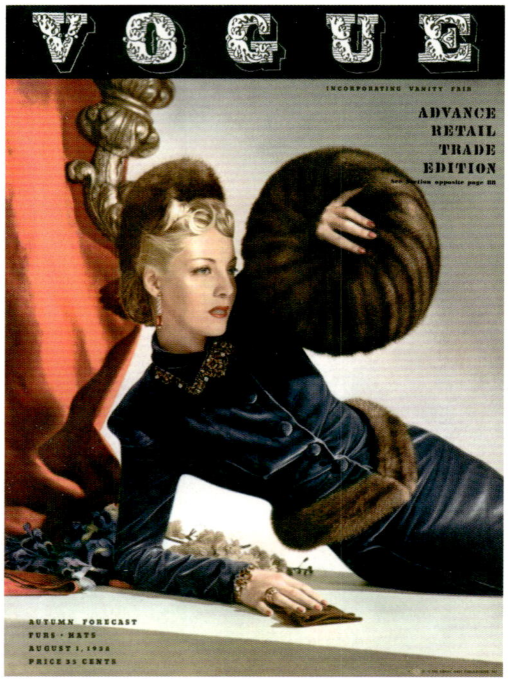
VOGUE
INCORPORATING VANITY FAIR
ADVANCE RETAIL TRADE EDITION
AUTUMN FORECAST
FURS · HATS
AUGUST 1, 1938
PRICE 35 CENTS

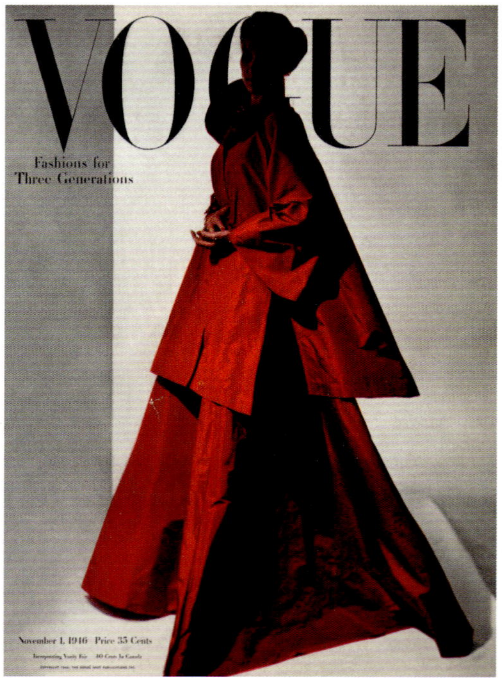
VOGUE
Fashions for
Three Generations
November 1, 1946
Price 35 Cents

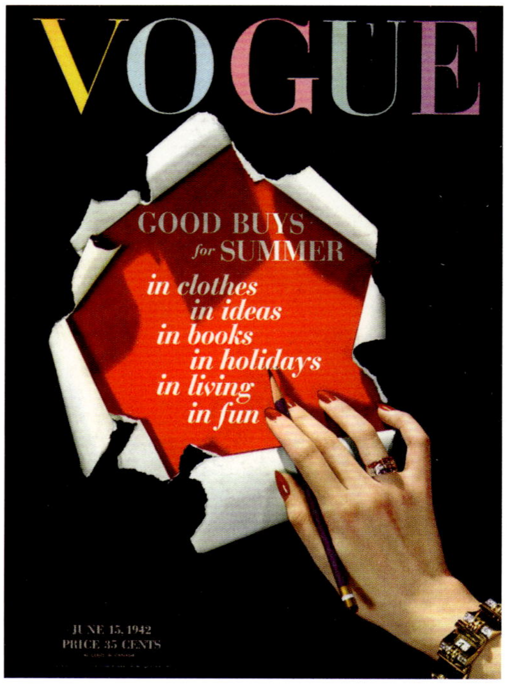
VOGUE
GOOD BUYS
for SUMMER
in clothes
in ideas
in books
in holidays
in living
in fun
JUNE 15, 1942
PRICE 35 CENTS

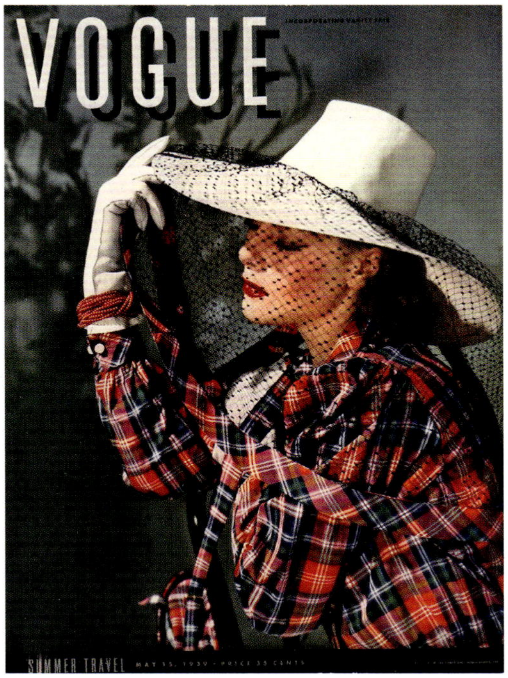
VOGUE
INCORPORATING VANITY FAIR
SUMMER TRAVEL
MAY 15, 1939 . PRICE 35 CENTS

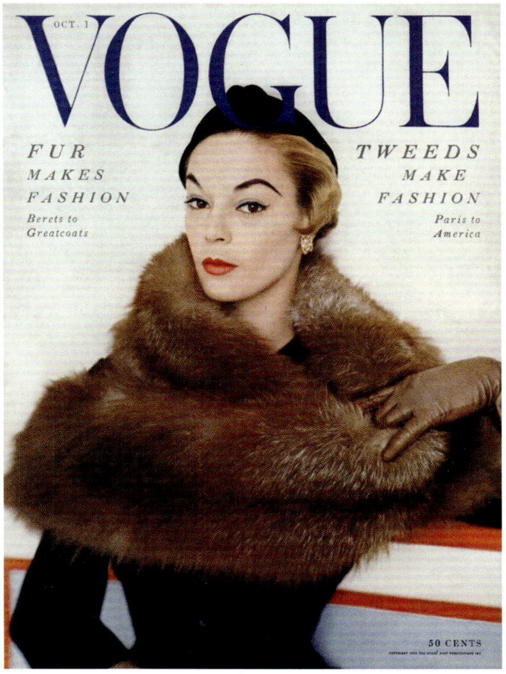
OCT. 1
VOGUE
FUR
MAKES
FASHION
Berets to
Greatcoats
TWEEDS
MAKE
FASHION
Paris to
America
50 CENTS

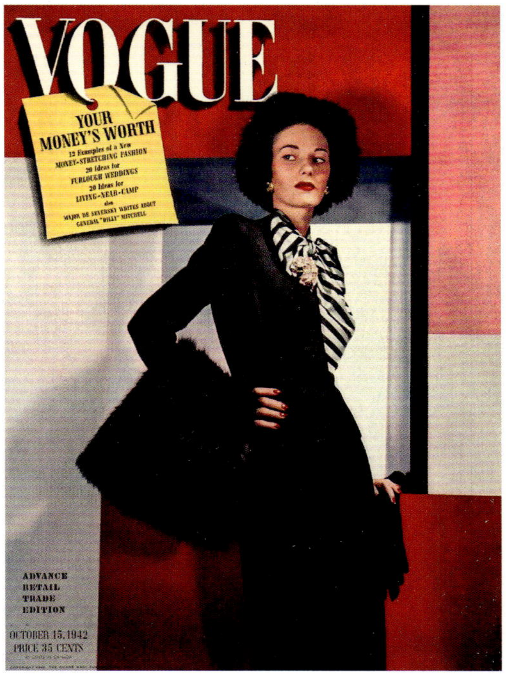
VOGUE
YOUR
MONEY'S WORTH
12 Examples of a New
MONEY-STRETCHING FASHION
20 Ideas for
FURLOUGH WEDDINGS
20 Ideas for
LIVING-NEAR-CAMP
also
MAJOR DE SEVERSKY WRITES ABOUT
GENERAL "BILLY" MITCHELL
ADVANCE
RETAIL
TRADE
EDITION
OCTOBER 15, 1942
PRICE 35 CENTS

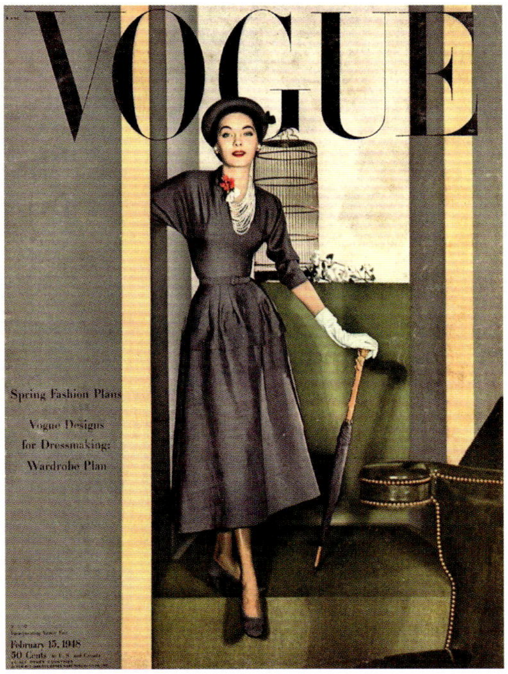
VOGUE
Spring Fashion Plans
Vogue Designs
for Dressmaking:
Wardrobe Plan
February 15, 1948
50 Cents

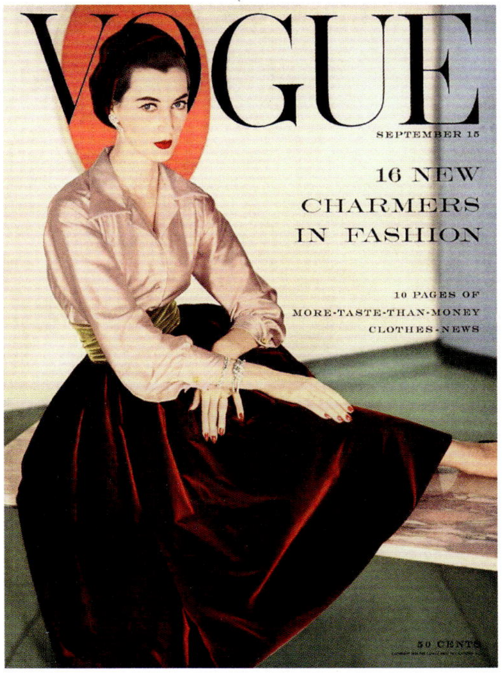
VOGUE
SEPTEMBER 15
16 NEW
CHARMERS
IN FASHION
10 PAGES OF
MORE-TASTE-THAN-MONEY
CLOTHES-NEWS
50 CENTS

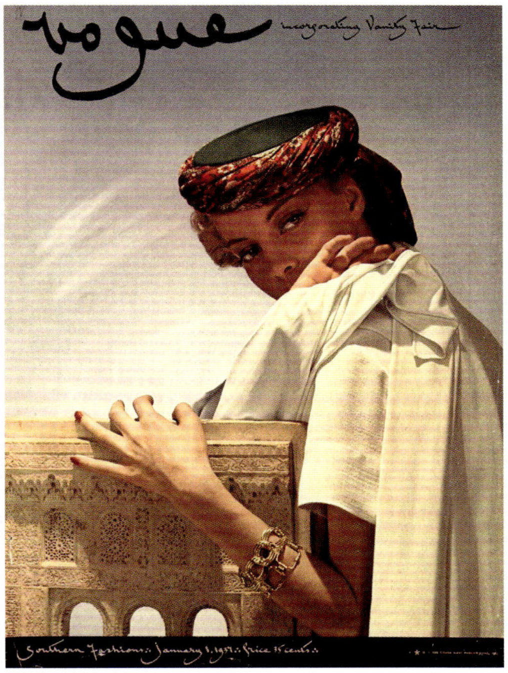
vogue
incorporating Vanity Fair
Southern Fashions
Price 35 cents

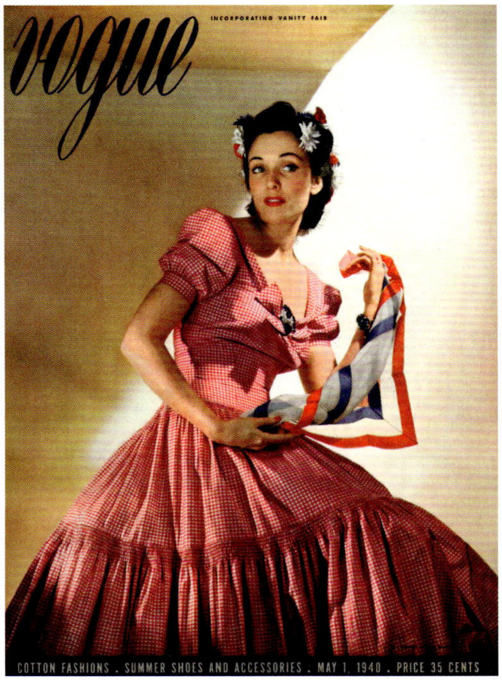
vogue
INCORPORATING VANITY FAIR
COTTON FASHIONS . SUMMER SHOES AND ACCESSORIES . MAY 1, 1940 . PRICE 35 CENTS

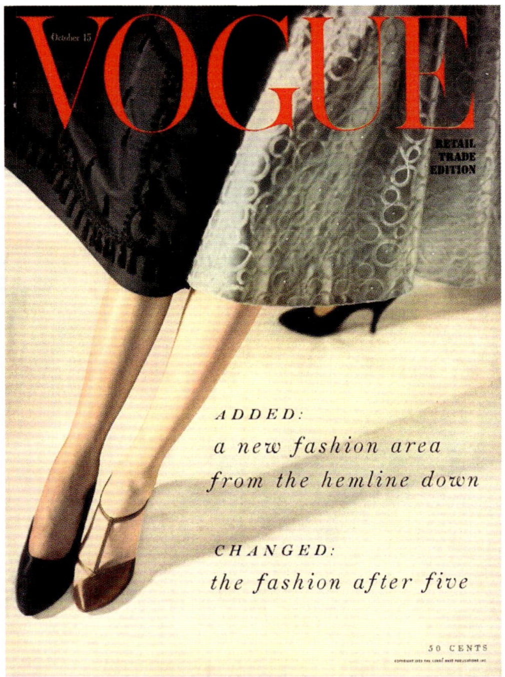
October 15
VOGUE
RETAIL
TRADE
EDITION
ADDED:
a new fashion area
from the hemline down
CHANGED:
the fashion after five
50 CENTS

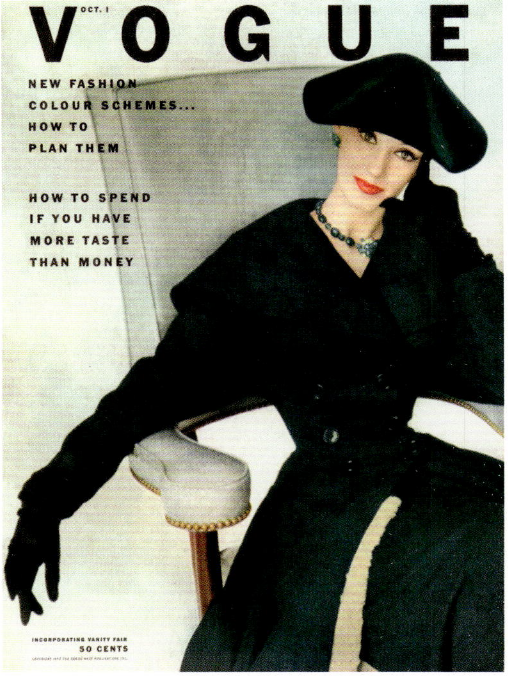
OCT. 1
VOGUE
NEW FASHION
COLOUR SCHEMES...
HOW TO
PLAN THEM
HOW TO SPEND
IF YOU HAVE
MORE TASTE
THAN MONEY
INCORPORATING VANITY FAIR
50 CENTS

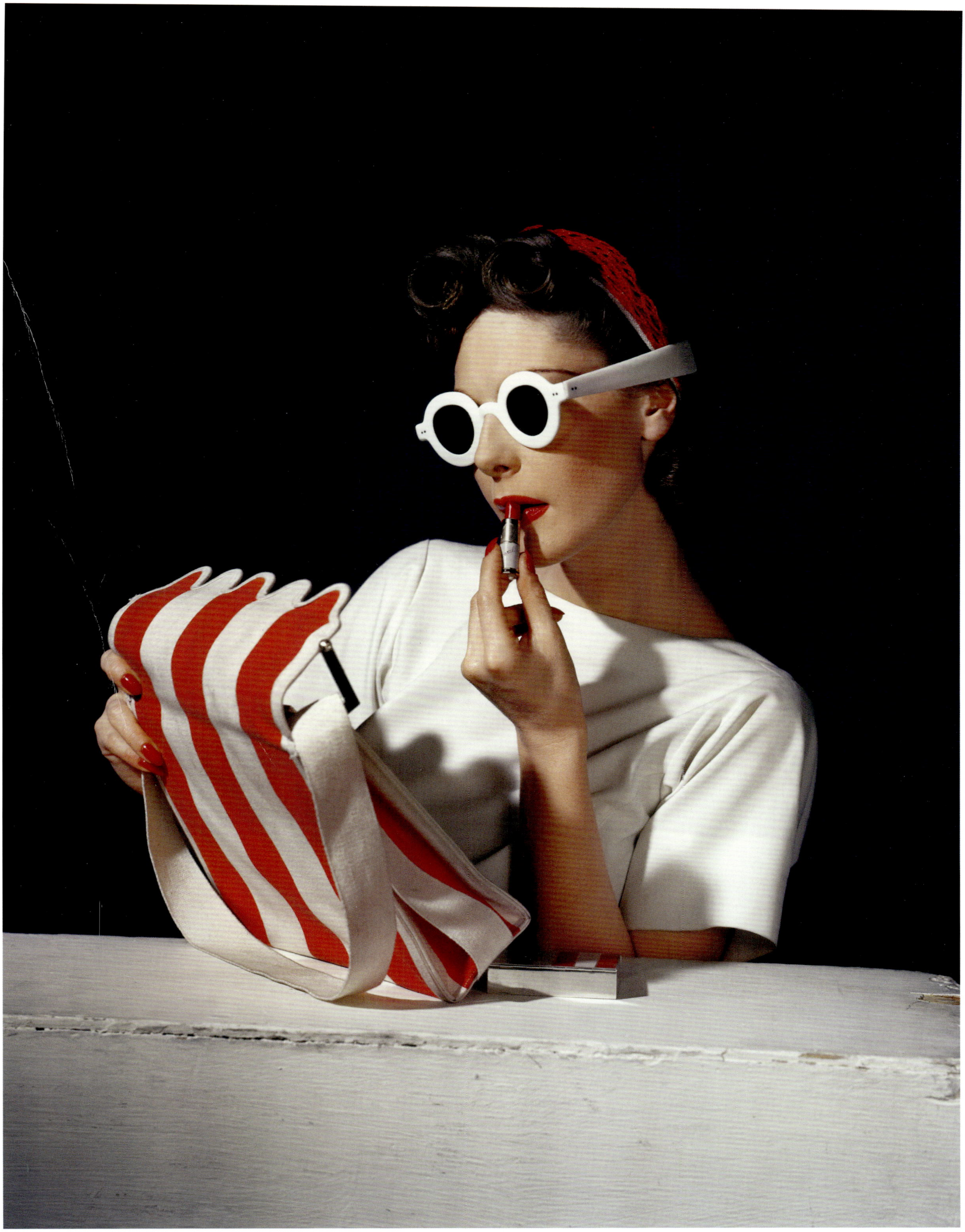

168. Muriel Maxwell, ensemble by Sally Victor, bag by Paul Flato, sunglasses by Lugene, 1939

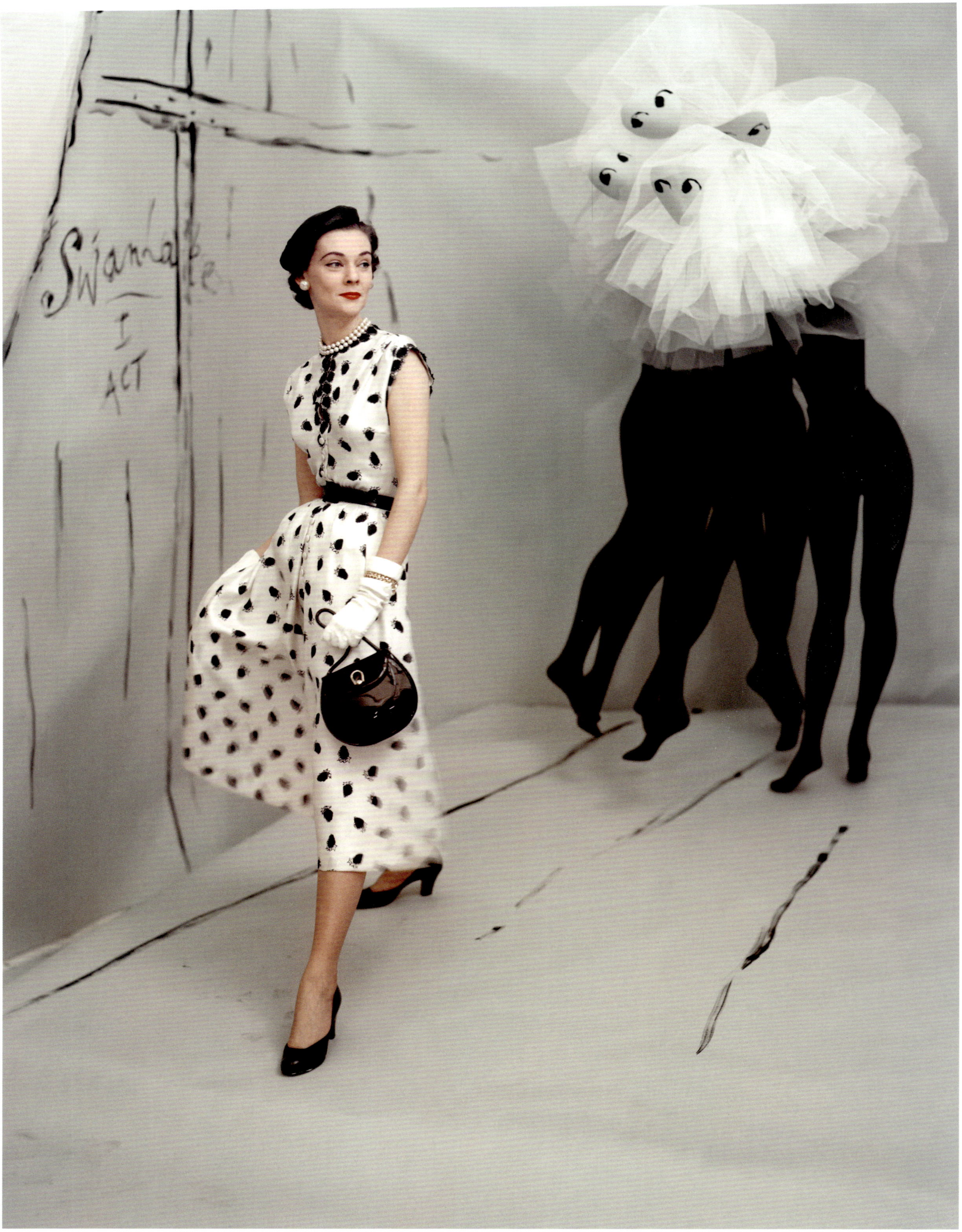

169. Dress by Mollie Parnis, background by Marcel Vertès, 1953

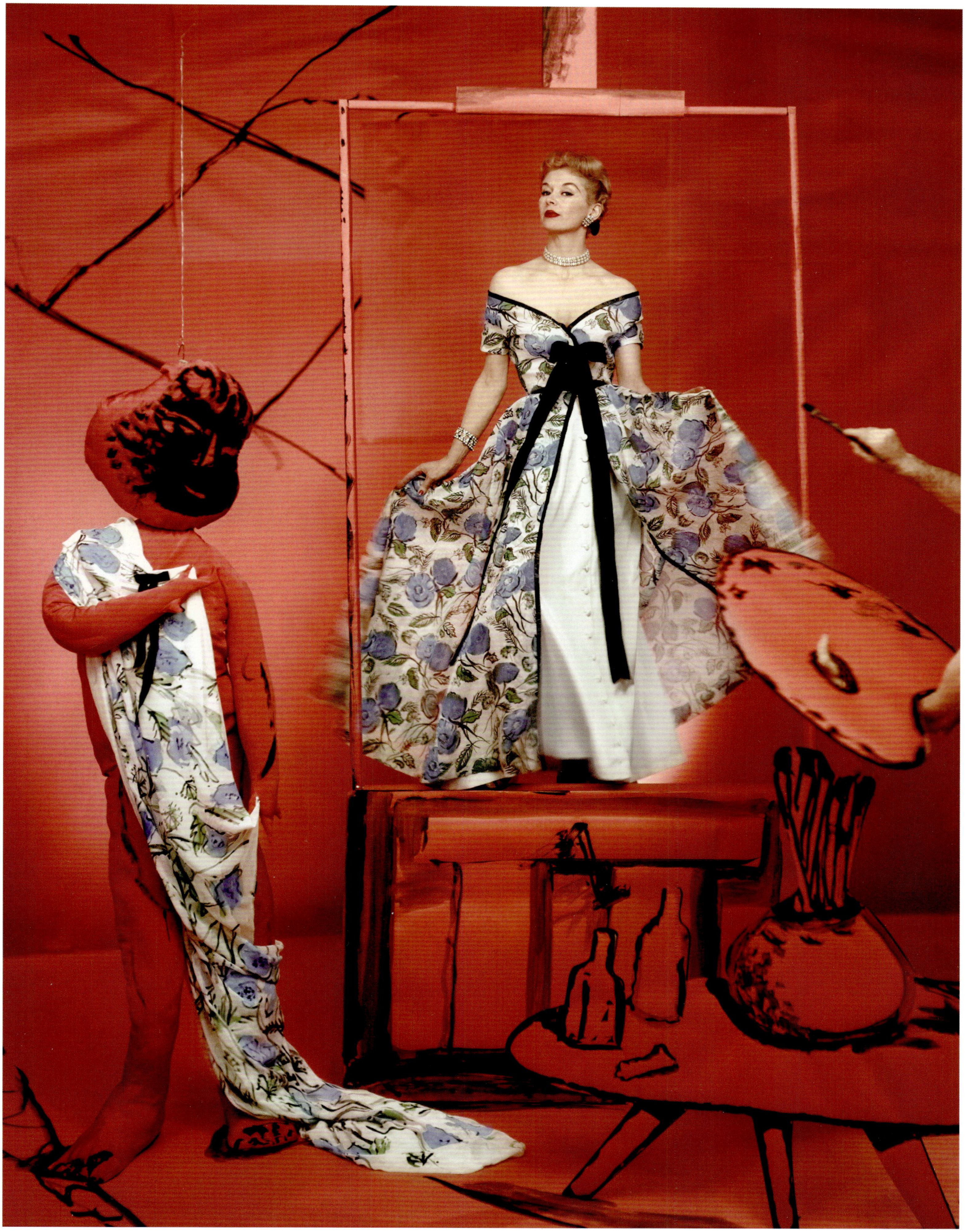

170. Andrea Johnson, dress by Pierre Balmain, background by Marcel Ve-tès, 1953

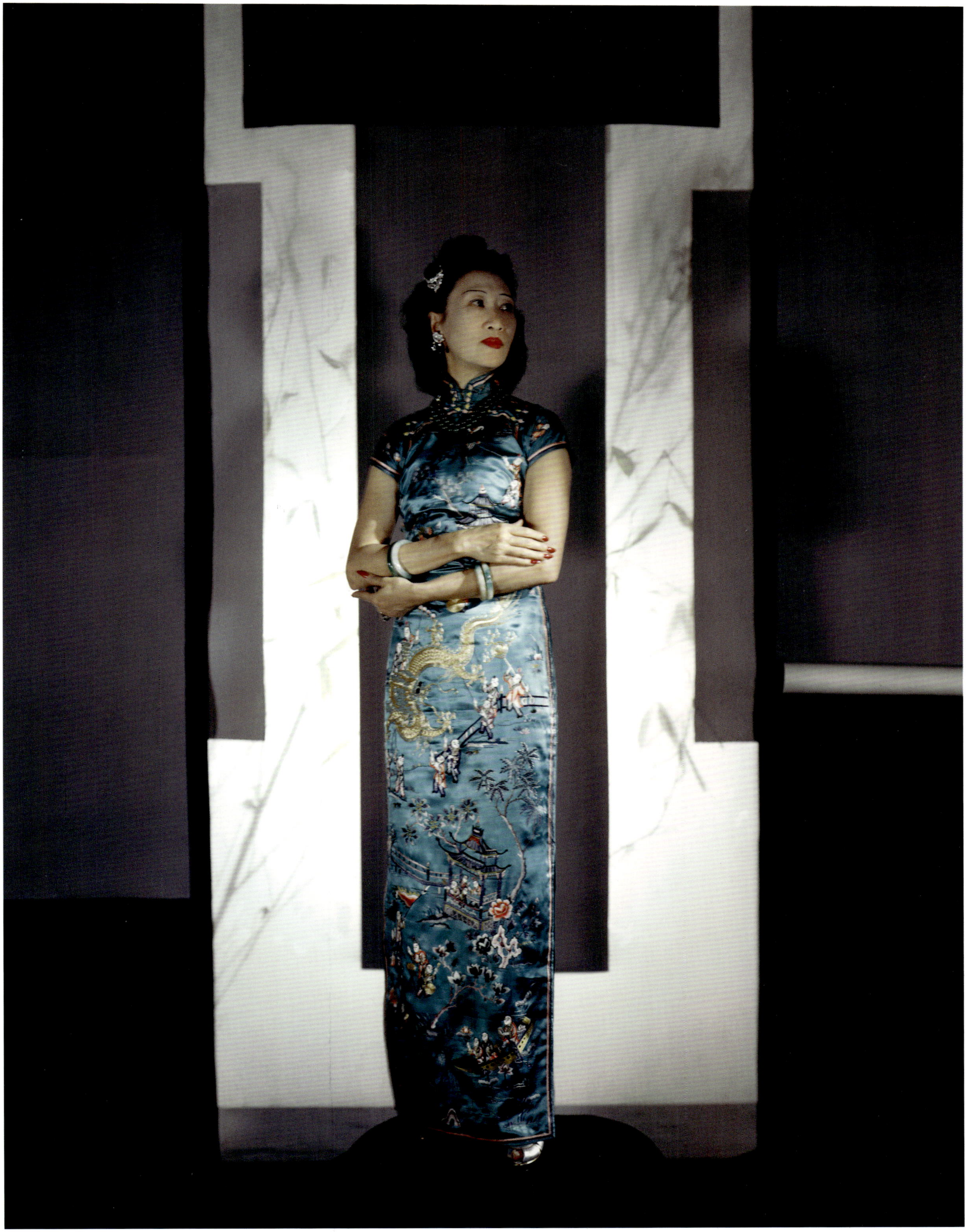

171. Madame Wellington Koo, New York, 1943

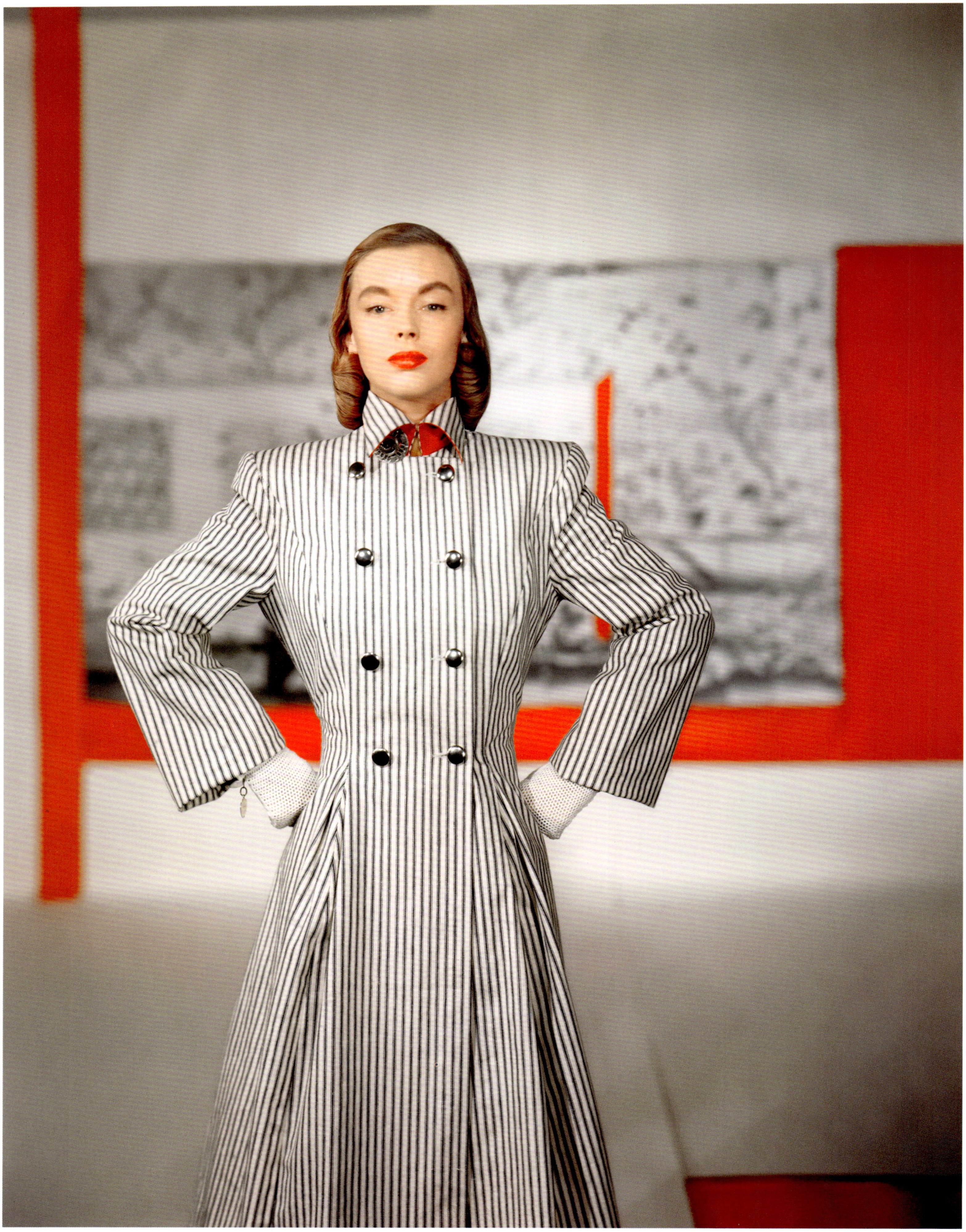

172. Coat by Connie Adams, 1946

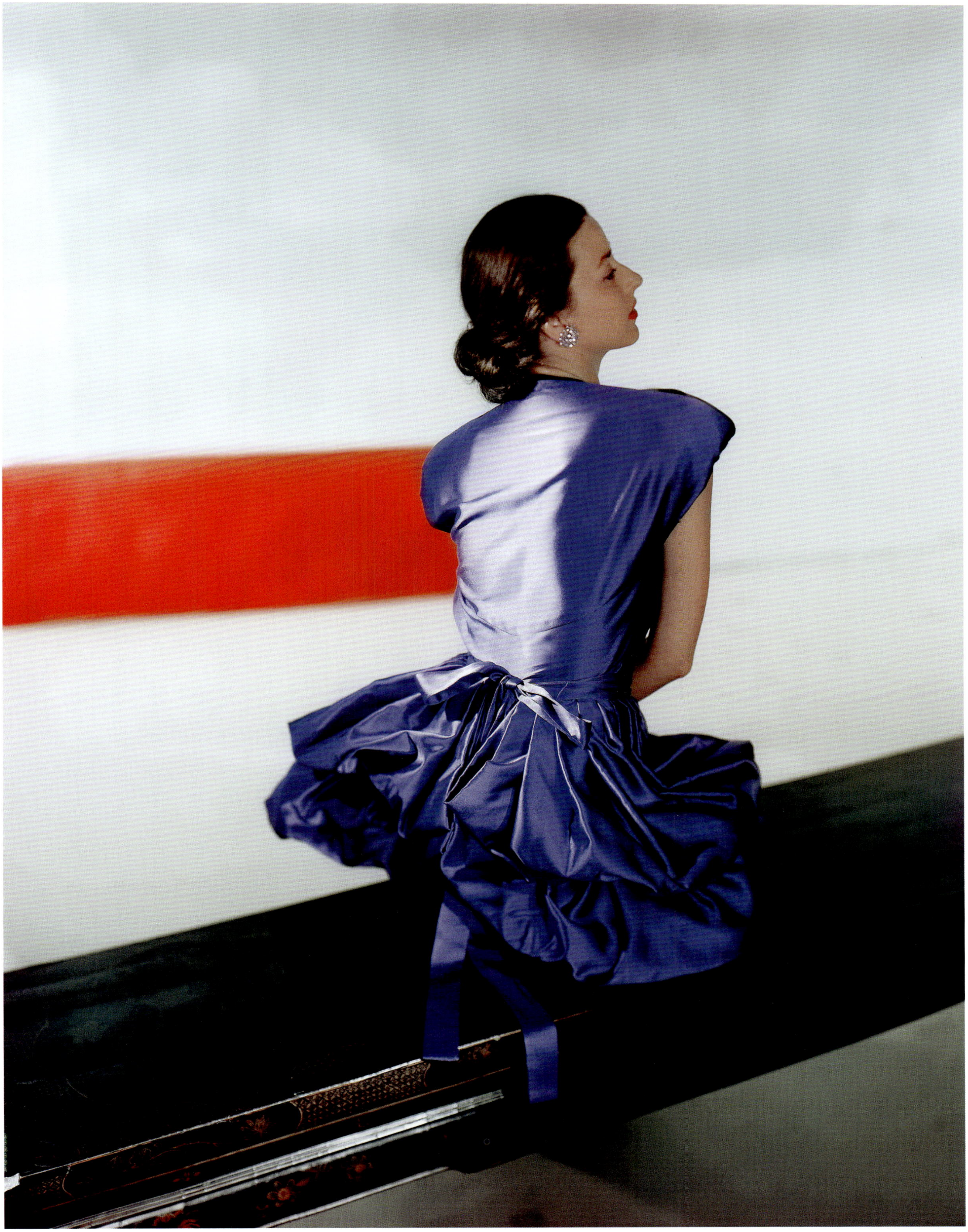

173. Dorian Leigh, dress by Henri Bendel, 1946

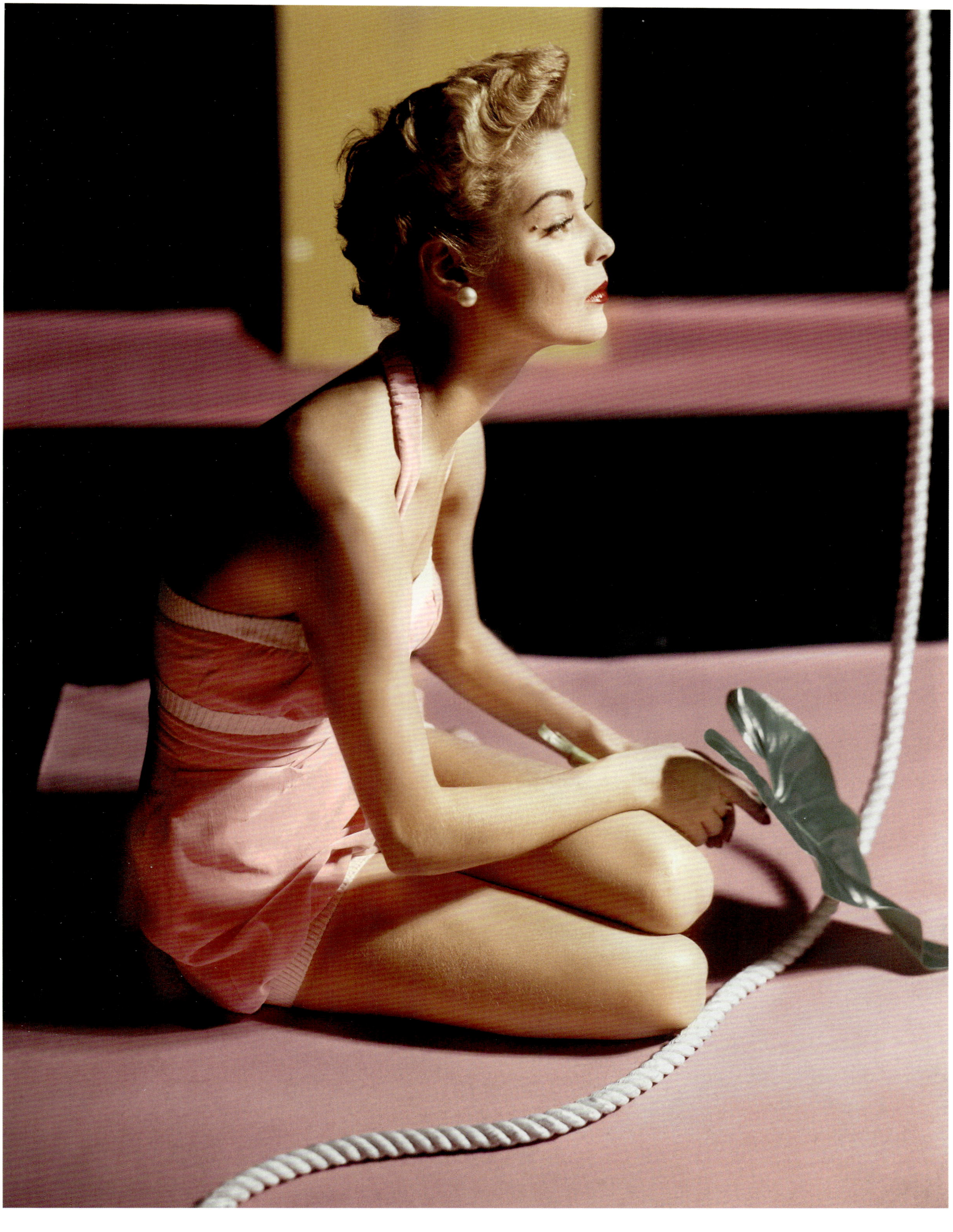

174. Jean Patchett, bathing suit by Brigance, 1951

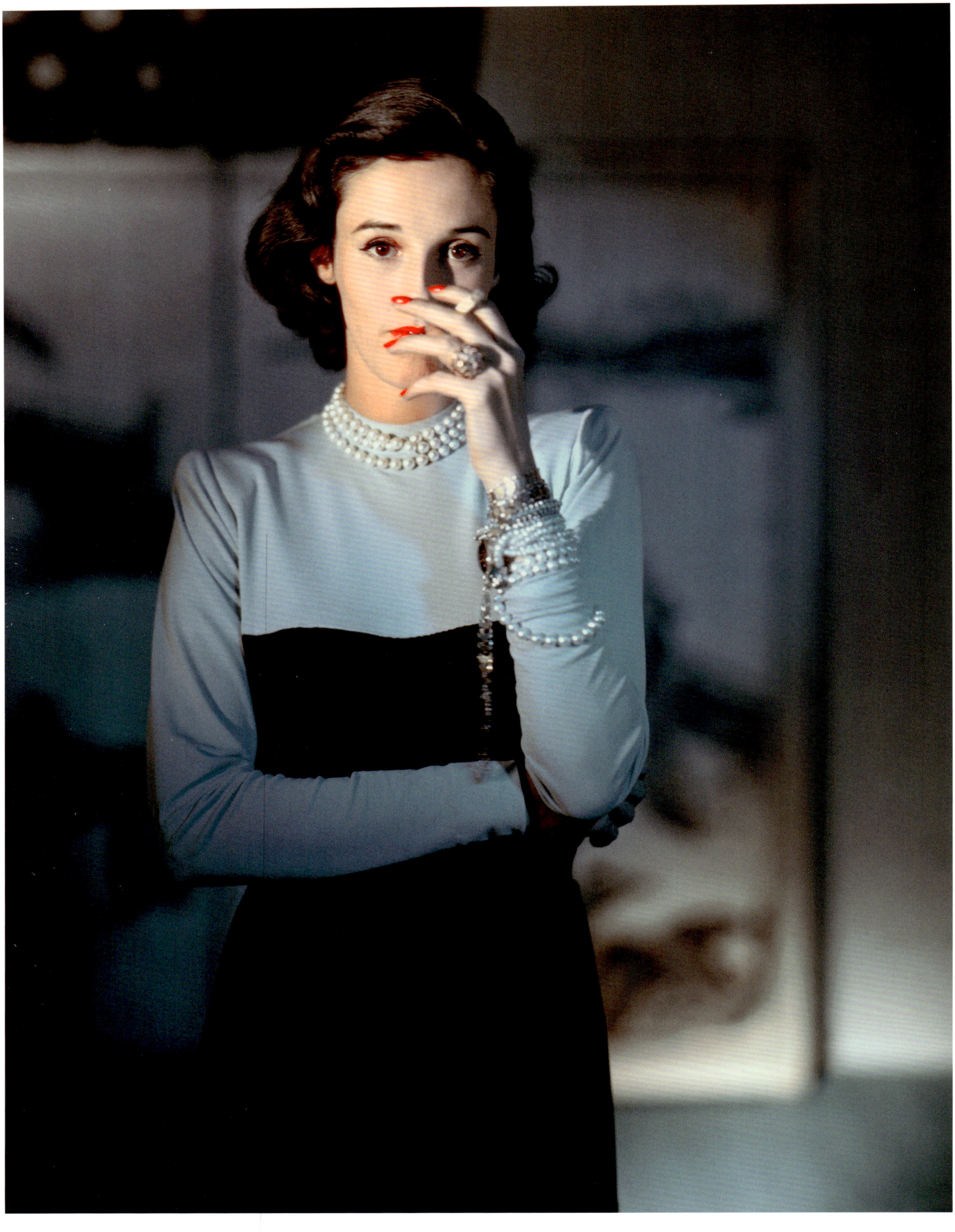

175. Babara 'Babe' Cushing Mortimer Paley, dress by Traina-Norell, 1946

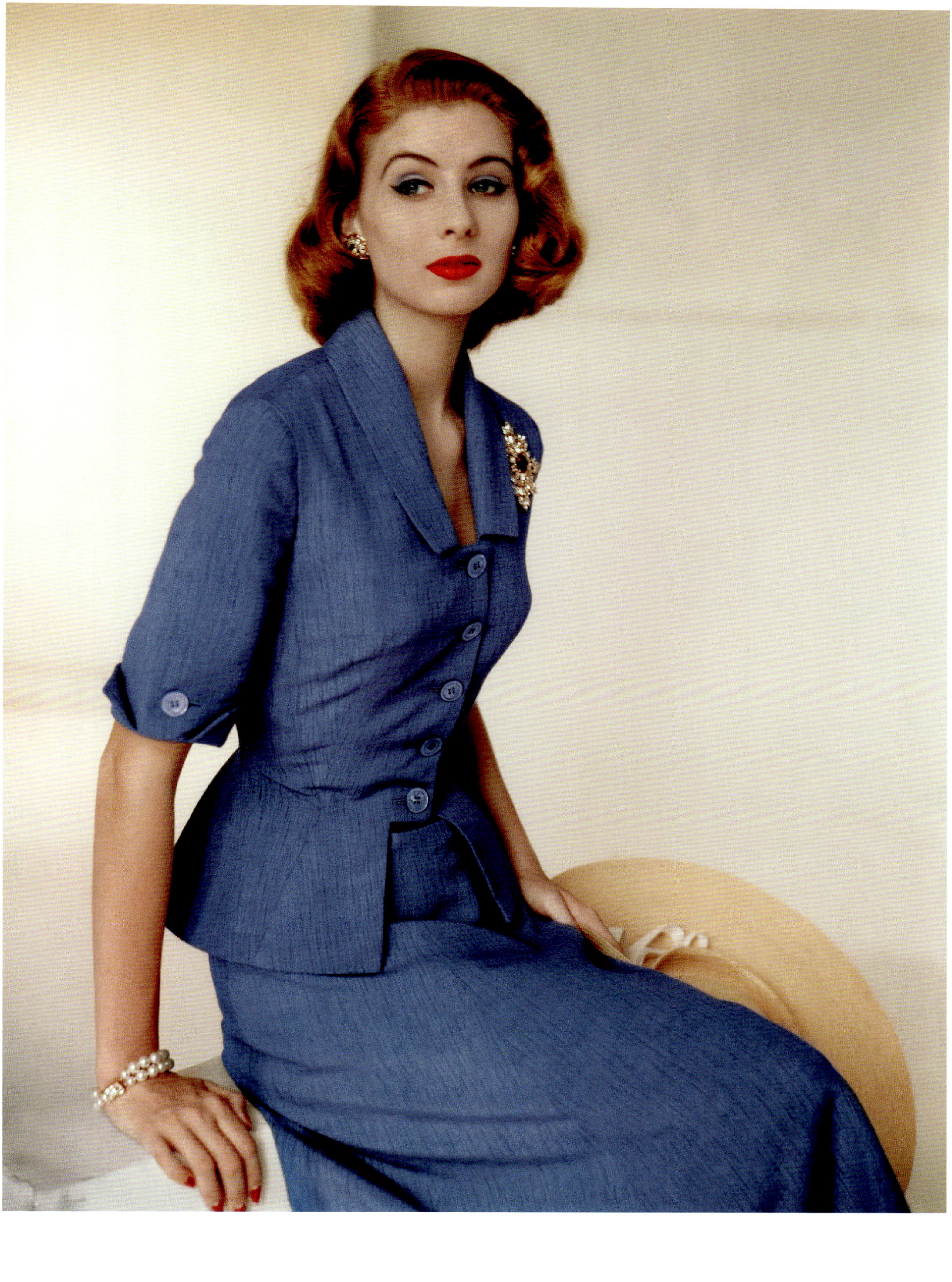

176. Suit by Brigance for Frank Gallant, jewellery by Schreiner, 1951

VI
Nature

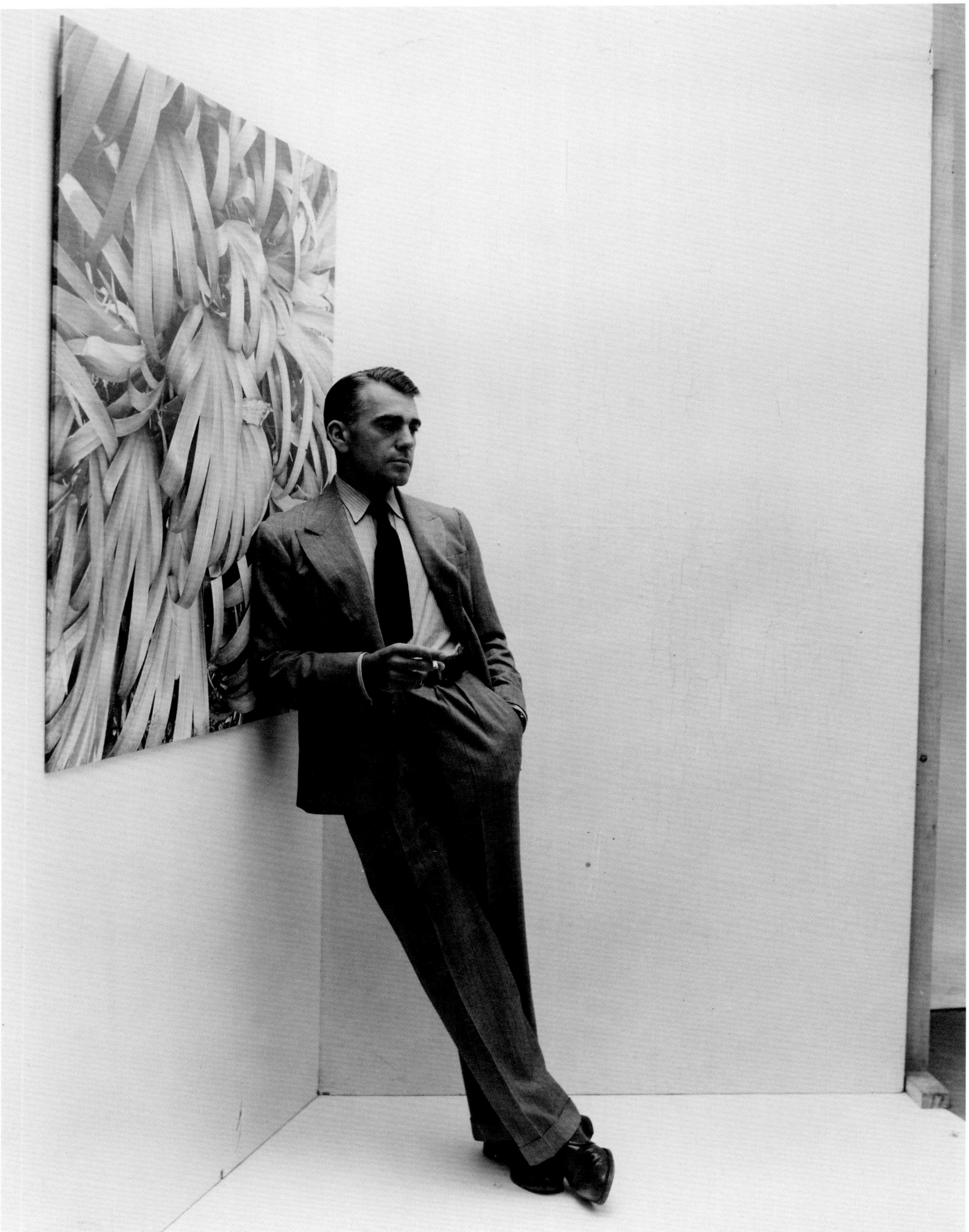

177. Irving Penn,
Horst, New York, 1946

PATTERNS FROM NATURE

Martin Barnes

At first glance, Horst's second book, *Patterns from Nature* (1946, pl.178), and the series of individual photographs from which it is derived, stands out as a curious diversion amid the high glamour of the fashion photographs, celebrity portraits and images of lavish interiors for which he is predominantly known. His usual signature style of strong directional studio lighting, theatrical sets and elegant human forms does not appear to be echoed in these close-up, black and white photographs of plants, shells and minerals. Even his poised, still life images of floral arrangements, taken in the studio, do not compare. In its subject matter, visual language and artistic ambitions, *Patterns from Nature* appears on the surface as if it is from the hand and sensibility of a different photographer altogether. However, the work can be seen to connect with his wider personal and professional interests in unexpected ways.

Throughout his career, Horst was not averse to adopting different styles suited to the subject and message he was commissioned to convey. Indeed, such flexibility was a prerequisite for survival and ongoing relevance amid the changing demands of the commercial world of fashion and magazines. Horst excelled at studio-based photography in the 1930s, 1940s and again in the 1980s when it became fashionable once more. His ability to control the environment and stage compositions was a necessity due to Condé Nast's house-style ruling for *Vogue* fashion photographers in the 1930s: a 10 × 8 inch negative and slow speed film had to be used to preserve maximum detail, no photograph could be cropped and images had to be contact-printed without any enlargement. It was only during the war years, when film became more expensive, that Horst was allowed to use smaller and more portable cameras, or as a result even consider capturing movement, by which time he had perfected his static and classical approach. His attempts during the 1960s at staying on trend by capturing the dynamism of moving fashion models outdoors are poor in comparison. In such cases, Horst was demonstrably willing to try other approaches but was simply out of his considerably refined visual comfort zone.

Perhaps surprisingly therefore, *Patterns from Nature* – with its images made outdoors using a Graflex Graphic View camera shooting 5 × 4 inch (12.5 × 10 cm) and a Rolleiflex shooting 2 ¼ inch (6 cm) square negatives – strikes a notably different yet harmonious chord alongside everything else in Horst's visual repertoire. It channels the more functionalist and Bauhaus-influenced visual world of his youth into photographic form, linked closely to the technical purity of 'photographic seeing' associated with the *Neue Sachlichkeit*, or New Objectivity, movement. It also connects with the modernist projects of Edward Weston (1886–1958), or with certain works by Paul Strand (1890–1976), by taking familiar forms of shells, rocks, wood or plants and examining them with such close attention that they become unfamiliar and revelatory (pl.182). Such revelations of natural forms under scrutiny exist alongside the demonstrably conscientious, scientific and classificatory in Horst's approach to *Patterns from Nature*. He is keen, for example, to list prominently in a technical index the type of film, developer, paper, camera and filters used to make each image.[1] If there is any connection to be made here with his fashion studio practice it is in an overarching sense of elegant monumentality.

One intriguing photograph by Horst, however, does make explicit the connection between his seemingly disparate worlds of fashion and nature photography (pl.179). Appearing in American *Vogue* in 1947, shortly after *Patterns from Nature* was published, the image shows a pattern of leaves superimposed (or double exposed) over a head and shoulders portrait of a woman. With her face uplifted and eyes closed, the photograph implies that the light, shadow and shapes of the leaves inhabit her inner vision as an after-image, or are perhaps the subject of her imagination. A poetic text, titled 'Vogue's eye view of summer beauty', links the image with new seasonal fashions: 'depending on pretty fabrics beautifully cut, on carefully calculated accessories, and on fragile pale colours in face and dress. A tribute to leafy coolness. A dappling of summer beauty, of summer fashion.'[2] Unusually for the time, Horst's photograph does not depict the fashions in question. Rather, in a way much more common in fashion photography today, it evokes without explicit illustration the aspirations and mindset of their potential wearer.

By 1946, having worked in the service of fashion and commercial photography for over 15 years, Horst was perhaps in need of the chance to exercise and demonstrate his visual imagination outside of his tested and successful *Vogue* studio parameters. *Patterns from Nature* provided him with that outlet in what would be described today as a photographer's 'personal project' – a self-directed study that is not generated by the needs of a commercial commission. (Its dedication to Edna Woolman Chase, *Vogue*'s editor-in-chief, indicates perhaps an acknowledgement of *Vogue*'s support for his need to recharge creatively.) The book is a demonstration of how Horst deliberately and refreshingly went back to basics, motivated by his own interests. In the book's introduction, he explained: 'For the most part, the pictures found here [are] of common objects daily

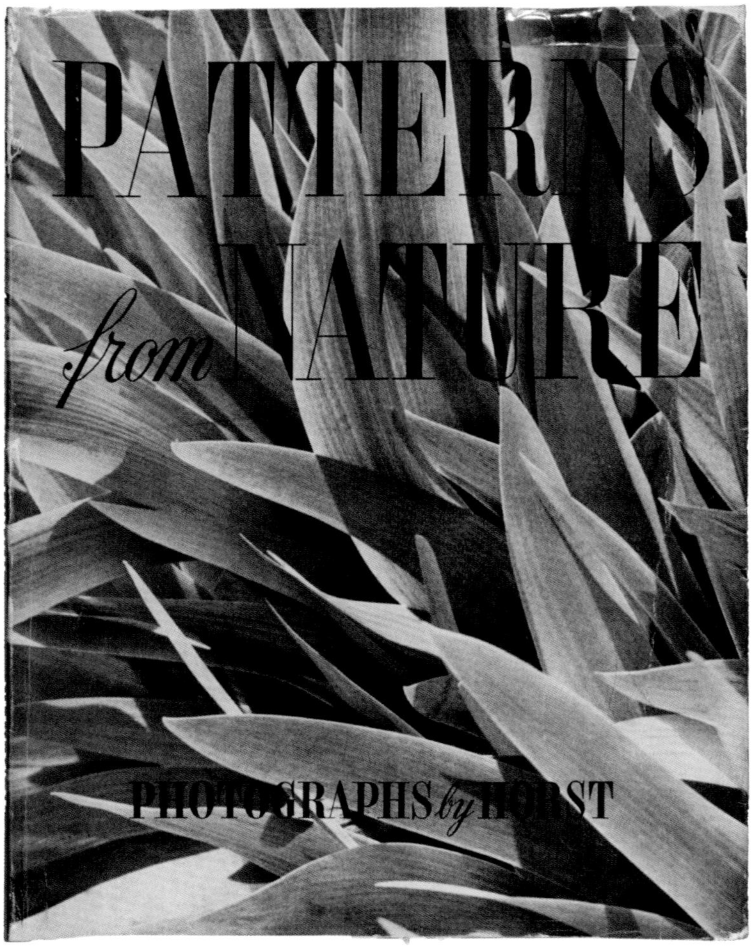

178. *Patterns from Nature*, 1946

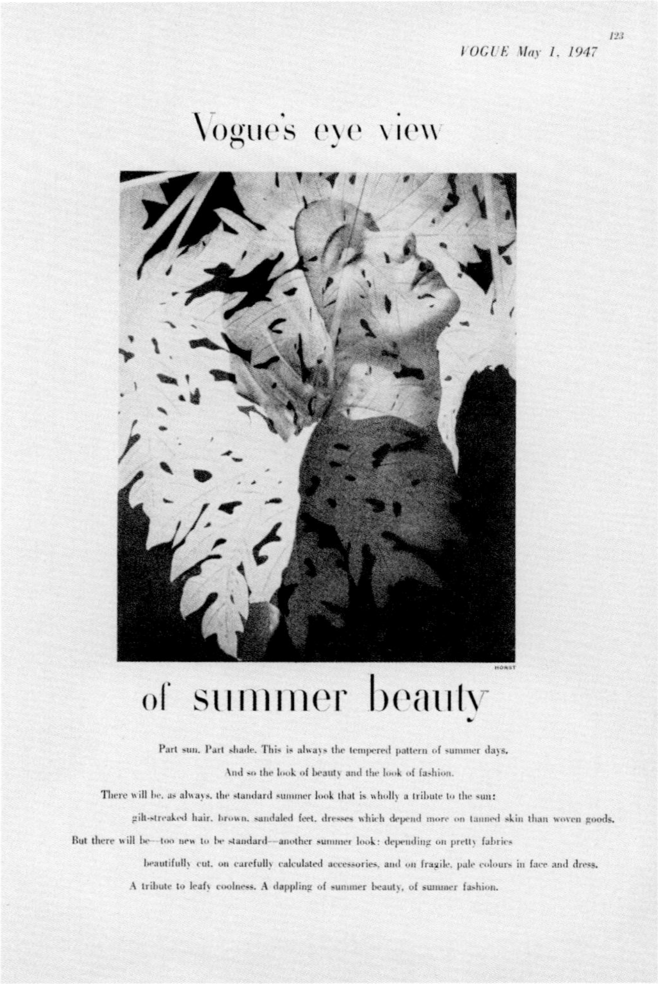

123

VOGUE May 1, 1947

Vogue's eye view

HORST

of summer beauty

Part sun. Part shade. This is always the tempered pattern of summer days.
And so the look of beauty and the look of fashion.
There will be, as always, the standard summer look that is wholly a tribute to the sun:
gilt-streaked hair, brown, sandaled feet, dresses which depend more on tanned skin than woven goods.
But there will be—too new to be standard—another summer look: depending on pretty fabrics
beautifully cut, on carefully calculated accessories, and on fragile, pale colours in face and dress.
A tribute to leafy coolness. A dappling of summer beauty, of summer fashion.

179. 'Vogue's eye view of summer beauty', American *Vogue*, 1 May 1947

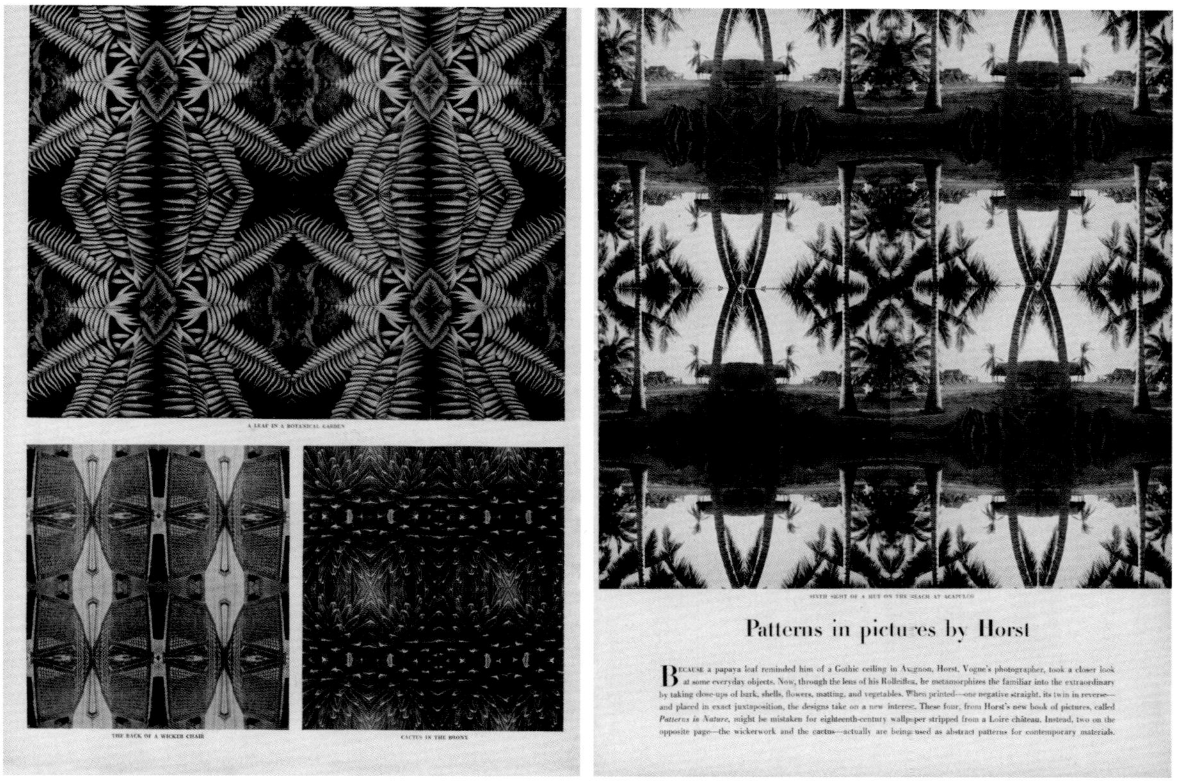
A LEAF IN A BOTANICAL GARDEN

THE BACK OF A WICKER CHAIR

CACTUS IN THE BRONX

SIXTH SIGHT OF A HUT ON THE BEACH AT ACAPULCO

Patterns in pictures by Horst

Because a papaya leaf reminded him of a Gothic ceiling in Avignon, Horst, Vogue's photographer, took a closer look at some everyday objects. Now, through the lens of his Rolleiflex, he metamorphizes the familiar into the extraordinary by taking close-ups of bark, shells, flowers, matting, and vegetables. When printed—one negative straight, its twin in reverse—and placed in exact juxtaposition, the designs take on a new interest. These four, from Horst's new book of pictures, called *Patterns in Nature*, might be mistaken for eighteenth-century wallpaper stripped from a Loire château. Instead, two on the opposite page—the wickerwork and the cactus—actually are being used as abstract patterns for contemporary materials.

180. 'Patterns in pictures by Horst', American *Vogue*, 15 October 1946

passing before our eyes. Nothing has been added to enhance them. They are photographed without artificial arrangements and special effects, in their own setting and in their proper light. Direct or diffused sunlight coming from above caresses their surface and in some instances dew or rain brings into relief their fine texture.'[3]

According to his biographer and partner, Valentine Lawford, Horst had been preparing ideas for *Patterns from Nature* in his spare time, 'before and since his discharge from the army', so presumably shortly before he was called up by the United States military in 1942 and after he was discharged in 1945.[4] He goes on to record, however, that most of the work 'was done in three months after his return to New York from Paris early in 1946'.[5] A short article in *Vogue* revealed the inspiration for the initial idea: 'Because a papaya leaf reminded him of a Gothic ceiling in Avignon, Horst, *Vogue*'s photographer, took a closer look at some everyday objects' (pl.180).[6] In the book's introduction Horst noted that, 'the pictures were taken in Mexico, in New York at the Botanical Gardens, in New England's forests and along the Atlantic and Pacific coasts'.[7] Clearly, some extensive travel in the years or months prior to the book's publication had helped him glean the variety of comparative images from various locations that he needed. Lawford traces Horst's first interest in natural phenomena to his childhood in the fields and forests of his native Thuringia. It was here, 'during World War I he had learned to appreciate the value of plants – even weeds – as food for his family and for their rabbits'.[8] Lawford goes on to quote Horst himself on the wider cultural ideas and influences in the book: 'It was all a typical old-fashioned German thing ... a combination of romanticism and realism and philosophy. Even Goethe entered into it, in terms of his recognition of the relationship between plant structure and animal structure, his longing to reduce the infinite variety of nature to unity, his faith in the value of comparison in interpreting the organic world. And of course I had known and admired Karl Blossfeldt's wonderful photographs of plants, and their revelation of the similarity of vegetable forms to art forms like wrought iron and Gothic architecture.'[9]

The book, then, is in part a consciously acknowledged homage to Horst's German heritage; one that allowed him, in the year immediately following the end of the Second World War, to make the implicit connection with untainted German pre-war cultural figures such as Goethe and Karl Blossfeldt (1865–1932). Stemming the waves of inevitable anti-German feeling during this time, it was one area in which Horst could both retain national pride and stake a claim within an elevated artistic and philosophical lineage. Alexander Liberman, art director of American *Vogue*, was also keen to invoke Goethe in the publicity text printed on the back flap of the dust jacket for *Patterns from Nature*: 'The return to Nature as a source of inspiration is a healthy sign in an age of weird manifestations of the ego. Horst in this book has had the humility to search for the abstract and the eternally beautiful within reality, and successfully makes Goethe's definition of Art come true: "Art is Nature seen through a temperament." Horst and his camera help us all to see.'[10]

It is tempting to speculate that, for Liberman, Horst's nature studies were an eye-opening corrective, a kind of antidote to the ego-driven world of fashion and celebrity in which both of them had been immersed. Horst's publication followed in an established Germanic line of popular picture books that combined scientific inquiry with artistically rendered plant and nature forms: *Kunstformen der Natur*

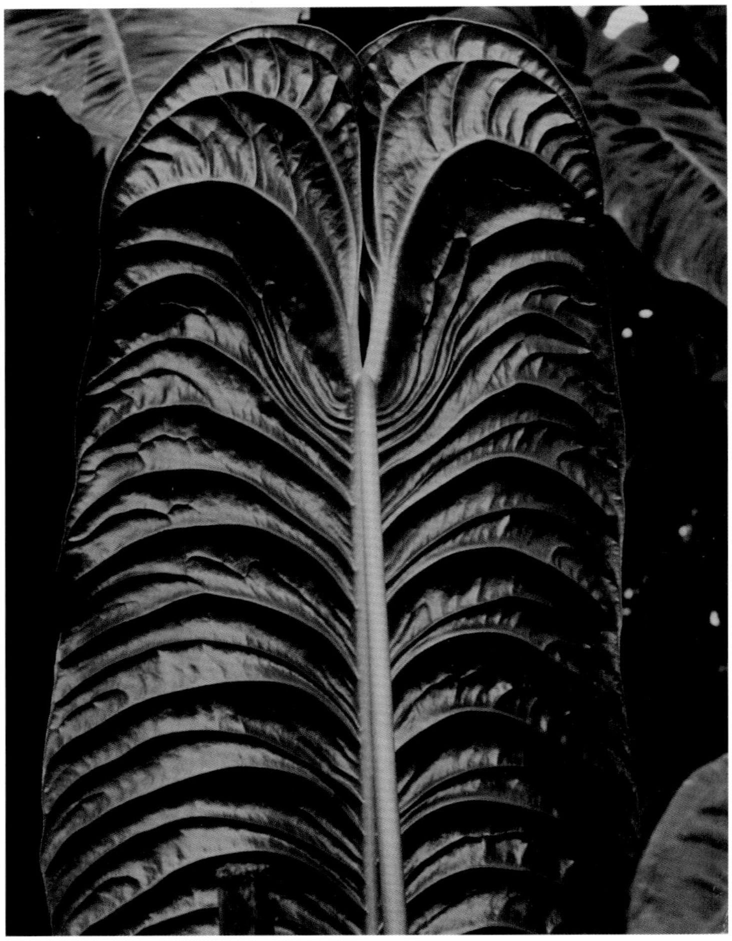

181. *Anthurium*, 1946

(Art Forms in Nature; 1899–1904), a compendium of coloured lithographs by Ernst Haeckel (1834–1919), and most notably, as Horst himself acknowledged, Blossfeldt's seminal *Urformen der Kunst* (Art Forms of Nature; 1928) and its follow-up *Wundergarten der Natur* (Wonder Garden of Nature; 1932). Like Haeckel and Blossfeldt before him, Horst was carrying out in pictorial form elements of Goethe's search for the 'Urpflanze' – an ideal prototype that contains all the natural forms of the past and the future – and by implication the more abstract idea of the 'Urform', the primary forming archetype of all matter.

Blossfeldt's work, however, specifically posits a connection between natural plant forms and man-made architectural and designed structures. By dissecting, arranging and enlarging specimens, Blossfeldt's images allowed, for example, a cross-section of 'Rough Horse Tail' to appear like a Doric column, or ferns and pumpkin tendrils to be easily recognised as the natural precursors of the whiplash forms favoured by Art Nouveau (pl.183). Blossfeldt's training as a sculptor may account for his interest in more isolated, sculptural forms. His photographs are often like individual portraits of plants, gathered together like an alphabet. Only occasionally do his images deal with mass repetition and all-over pattern. With Horst, the emphasis is rather about repeated structures, not only in individual images, but also in the comparative pairing of images. Horst travels further into abstracted pattern, and also into making explicit visual connections between matching forms in contrasting natural materials. For example, his pairing of the *Pyrite, Mineral* and *Prunus Pennsylvania, Bark* draws attention to their repetition of horizontal lines (pl.184); *Quartz* and *Betula Lenta, Bark* have similar vertical building blocks (pl.185); sun-baked *Clay* and the *Boehmeria Argenta* leaf exhibit matching reticulated patterns (pl.186); *Petrified Wood* echoes *Brachet* [*sic*] *Fungus* (pl.187); the *Agave Rupicola* plant and the *Wing of Ornithoptera Cellularis, Butterfly* (pl.188) share camouflage stripes of light and shade. In Horst's game of matching patterns, even coral and a cauliflower can be compared with each other.

The exactitude of classification in the book is due to Jamie Caffery, whom Lawford noted was 'a young American friend ... who worked for *Fortune* magazine but was also a knowledgeable amateur botanist. (Caffery later became a well known garden designer in Europe).' Caffery accompanied Horst on the trip to Mexico and California gathering images. However, it is neither as a botanical guide, nor as a notable addition to the modernist photographic quest for the 'Urform' that *Patterns from Nature* leaves its most enduring and creative mark. It is in the unexpected step that Horst takes with the book's closing nine collaged images, which he prefaces as follows: 'The ten following pages are photographs shown in simple repeat. The resulting patterns are immediately applicable to industrial fields such as textiles, wall-paper, carpets, plastics, glass, ceramics, china, leather, book-binding, and jewelry. It is also a demonstration of how modern design can be achieved through modern means.'[11] If any of these patterns were indeed put into production for the myriad design uses that Horst envisaged, the actual results remain tantalizingly yet to be traced.

Lawford again notes a collaborator who assisted Horst with this idea: 'Another American friend, Warren Stokes, who afterwards worked in the art department of *Vogue*, did the layout of the book, and helped Horst produce nine photographic patterns for potential use as textile designs, each made from a detail of one of the photographs.'[12]

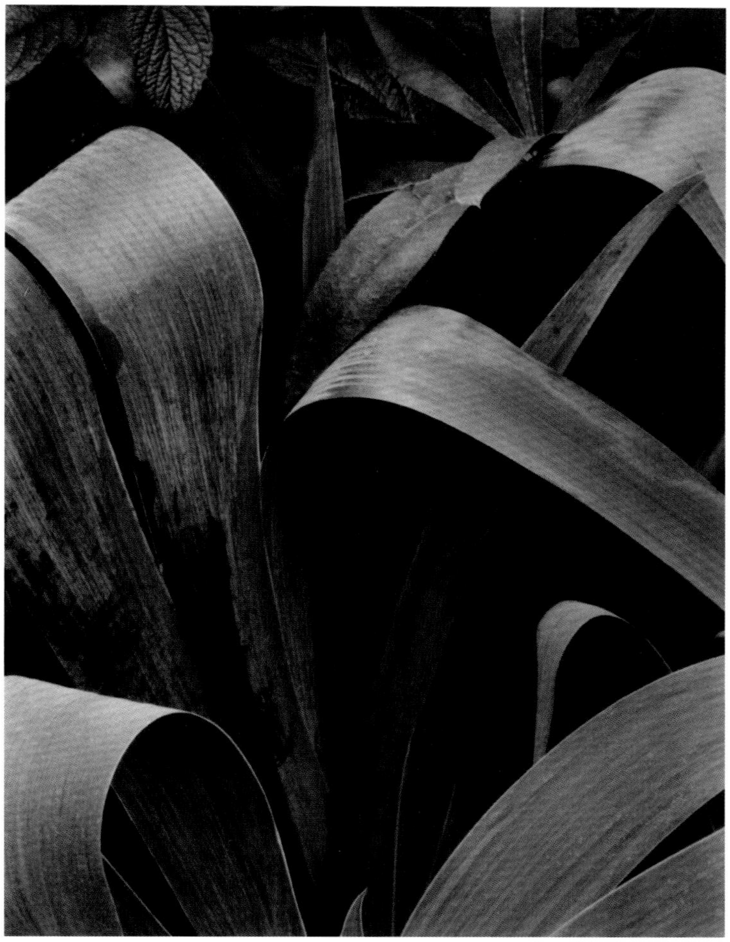

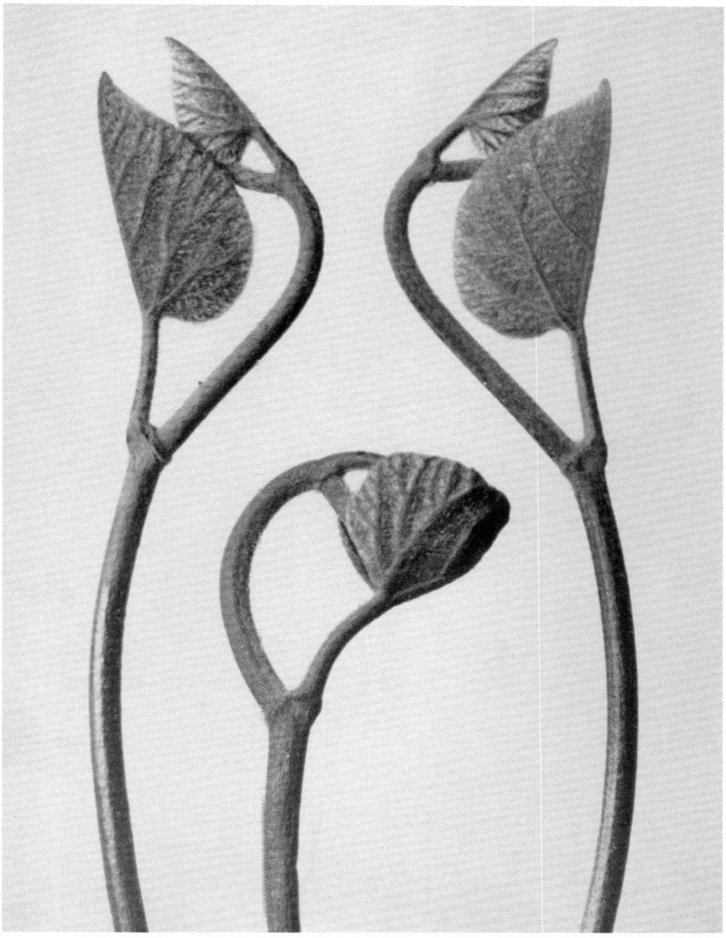

In fact, Horst did not strictly use 'details' from the photographs. Some of the original collages – or rather tessellated or mosaic-like photographs – survive in the photographer's archive. Comparing them with the plates as printed in the book shows that Horst made four contact prints from one of his 2 ¼ square or 5 × 4 inch negatives, two the correct way round and two flipped in the printing to produce a mirror image. These he arranged in a square or rectangle with the 'straight' images the right way up at top left, and then upside down at bottom right, and the 'flipped' images in the same manner at top right and bottom left. He then repeated this grid of four, joining each arrangement edge to edge. The plates in the book simply reproduce these mosaics to scale.

Though the process is simple, the effect is striking, making abstracted and kaleidoscopic patterns that appear to oscillate between three-dimensional photographic images and complex flat patterns. While Horst was open about how these patterns might be applied, one of the original photo-mosaics is specifically annotated 'silk', and others, not published, are designated 'wallpaper' and 'scarf'.[13] The 1946 article in *Vogue* (pl.180). 'Patterns in pictures by Horst', remarked that the collages 'might be mistaken for eighteenth-century wallpaper stripped from a Loire chateau' and continues that they were, 'actually being used as abstract patterns for contemporary materials'.[14] A more specific reference, suggesting that Horst's designs were actually used in production, is given in another article, 'Nature turns Designer', in *House & Garden*, which makes explicit that 'These photographs will be translated into an interesting and arresting group of decorative textiles by Wesley Simpson Inc.'[15] A notice in the *New York Times* (10 June 1947) confirms that fabrics were indeed produced and offered for sale:

Above left
182. Paul Strand, *Iris*, c.1928, V&A: PH.375-1982

Above right
183. Karl Blossfeldt, *Aristolochia spec. Birthwort, Shoots of Tendrils*, undated

> Photographs of a Mexican scene and still-life subjects have inspired a new group of decorative fabrics by Wesley Simpson just introduced at Macy's. Based on photographs by Horst, the designs feature a cross-like arrangement of motifs, as well as unusual color combinations.
>
> A view of a Mexican archway has been transplanted into a strong plaid pattern. In the photograph, three sunlit pillars in a row, plus the deep horizontal shadows they cast, form a striped right-angle design. This has been printed in four directions to create a large pattern stressing vertical lines. One version combines blue terra cotta on a brown background.
>
> A photogenic pot of ivy has been repeated similarly to form a rough square. For a summery effect, it comes in deep green and bright yellow on a gray ground. A design of large shells is shown in navy and peach on a pale blue ground accented by scrolls in olive green.
>
> A plant resembling a cabbage in appearance forms an abstract design. Three different colorings combine rose, green and pink, blue, pink and white, or lime with gray and white ... the fabrics are a combination of cotton and rayon thirty-nine inches wide.

The variety of coloured patterns into which the black and white photographs were translated is striking, as well as Horst's deviation from plant forms to include architectural motifs. A recent search of the extensive Wesley Simpson archive of sample books, now held at the New York Public Library, revealed none of the fabrics themselves, although two original Horst collages were discovered.[16]

Wesley Simpson produced decorative textiles in New York. The company operated from the 1930s until the late 1940s, printing modern patterns on rayon and crêpe grounds and supplying fabrics to some of the better Seventh Avenue design and dress houses, including Davidow, Mary Lee, David Crystal, Hattie Carnegie and Townley Frocks. Simpson also commissioned original scarf and drapery designs by artists including Salvador Dalí, costume designer Marcel Vertès (1895–1961) and illustrator Ludwig Bemelmans (1898–1962). Advertisements for the company offer a line of inexpensive furnishing fabrics.[17] Photography had been used previously for textile design, most notably Edward Steichen's abstractions of weeds, pins, sugar cubes and thread for the Stehli Silks Corporation's Americana Prints collection (a series of artist-designed textiles produced between 1925 and 1927) and images by Steichen, Charles Sheeler (1883–1965) and others for Mallinson Fabrics' Camera Prints collection in the 1930s. However, Horst appears to have been the first to use photo-mosaics for this purpose, and also to publish his designs alongside their originating images, suggesting their wider design application. As historian Dilys Blum has pointed out, the trend for artist-designed textiles grew in a receptive climate after the Second World War for several reasons: the willingness of artists, galleries and the textile industry to work together to revitalize their market in the face of renewed French competition; the continuation of government war-time fabric restrictions resulting in unadorned dresses where the pattern made the fashion; and a greater aesthetic awareness in the American people, generated by the public art programmes of the Works Progress Administration.[18] Horst's foray into photography's potential physical overlap with fashion is part of a wider movement to make such endeavours possible. Yet it also naturally coalesces with his personal interests and professional experience.

Patterns from Nature gains its full meaning through the pairing and repetition of images, and thus makes sense best of all in book form. However, Horst also made a fine set of 12 × 10 inch (30.5 × 25.5 cm) exhibition prints on a slightly textured, opalescent paper. As individual works of fine art photography these prints have continued to have an afterlife independent from the book when shown in a gallery context. Horst showed these prints at a gallery in New York as late as 1977.[19] Yet the full life cycle of Horst's project may still remain to be discovered. It is possible that garments, furnishings and other designed items embellished with Horst's *Patterns from Nature* photo-collages may one day come to light. This potential circularity between photography, fashion, design and interiors would surely have pleased Horst, whose open-minded aspirations for applied photography he made so explicit and so innovatively in *Patterns from Nature.*

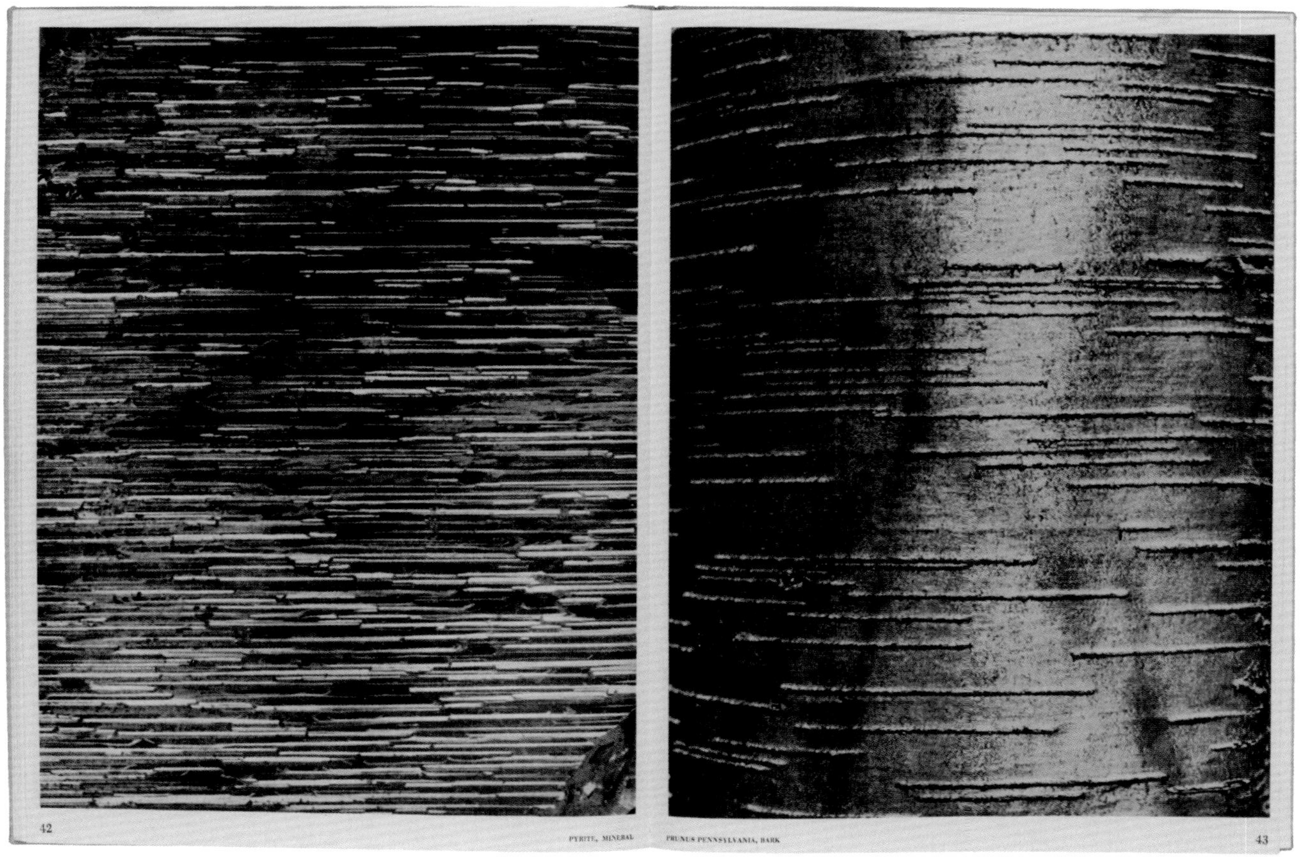

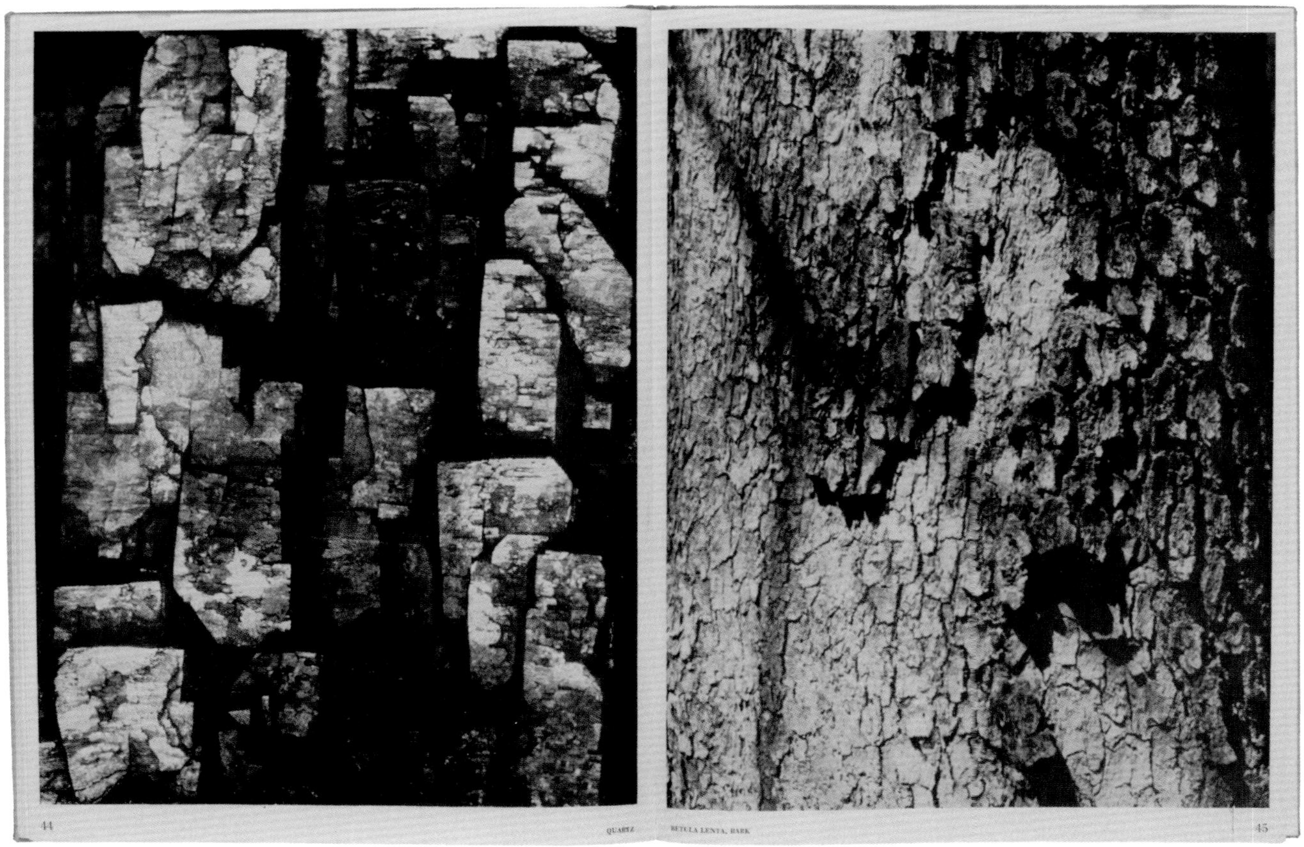

184. *Pyrite, Mineral* and
Prunus Pennsylvania, Bark, 1946

185. *Quartz* and *Betula Lenta, Bark*, 1946

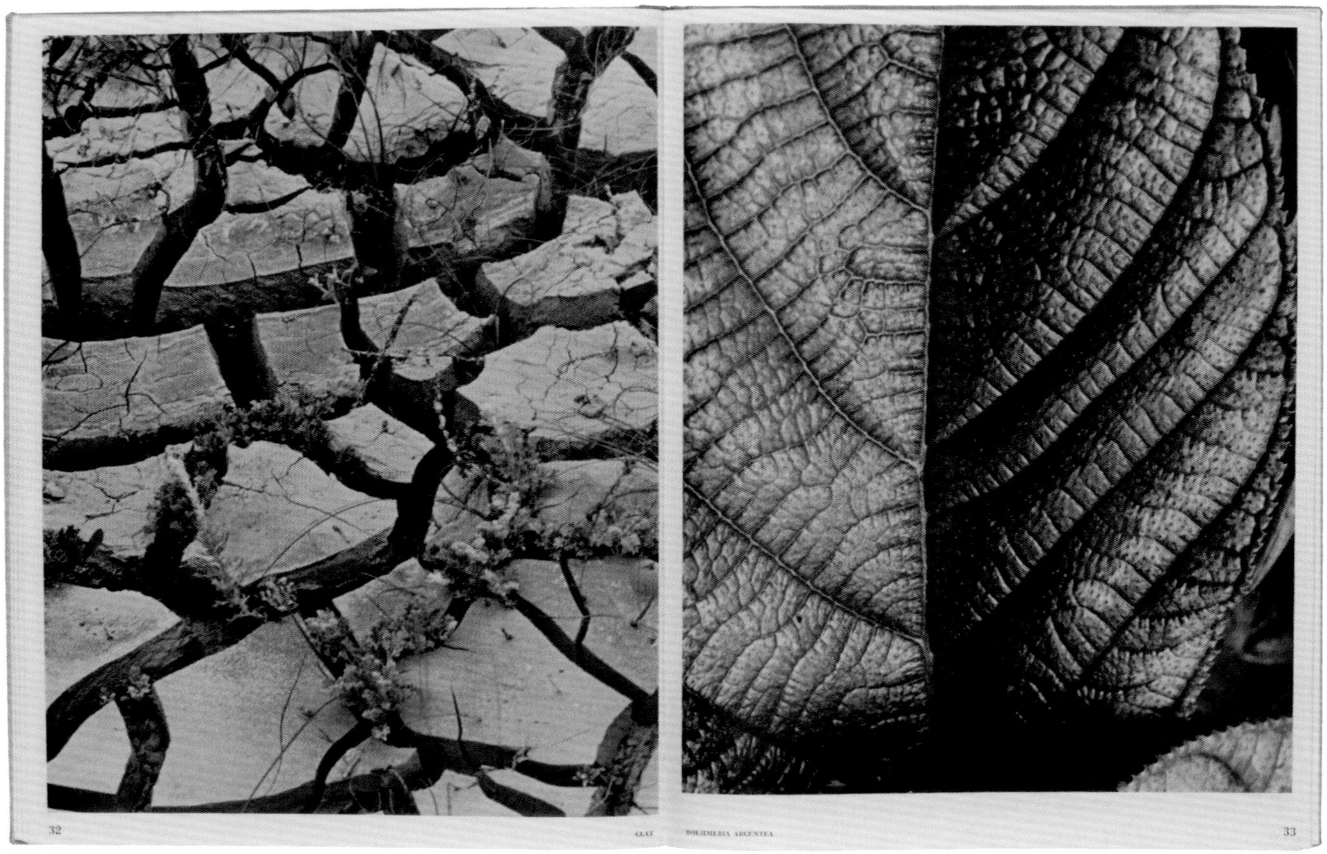

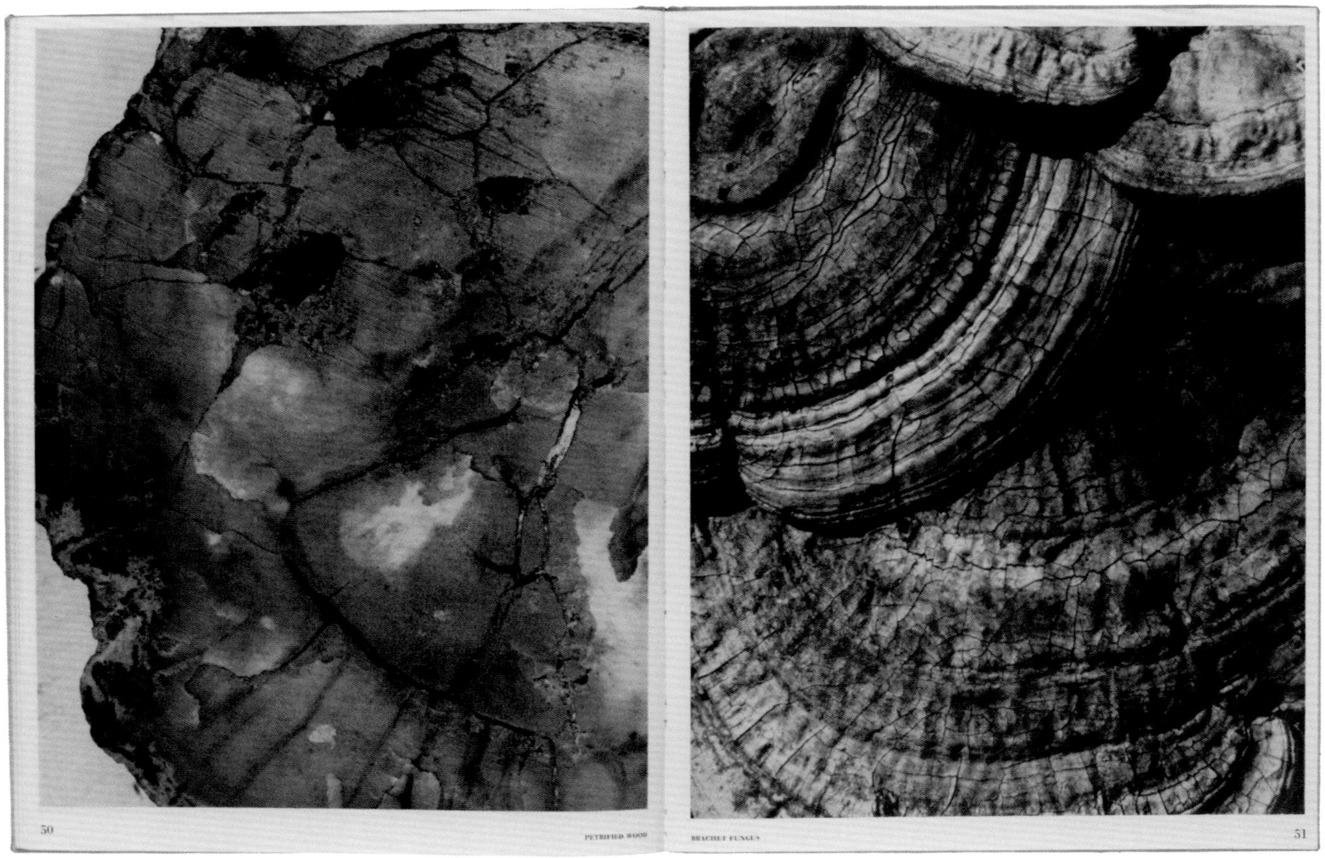

186. *Clay* and *Boehmeria Argenta*, 1946

187. *Petrified Wood* and *Brachet Fungus*, 1946

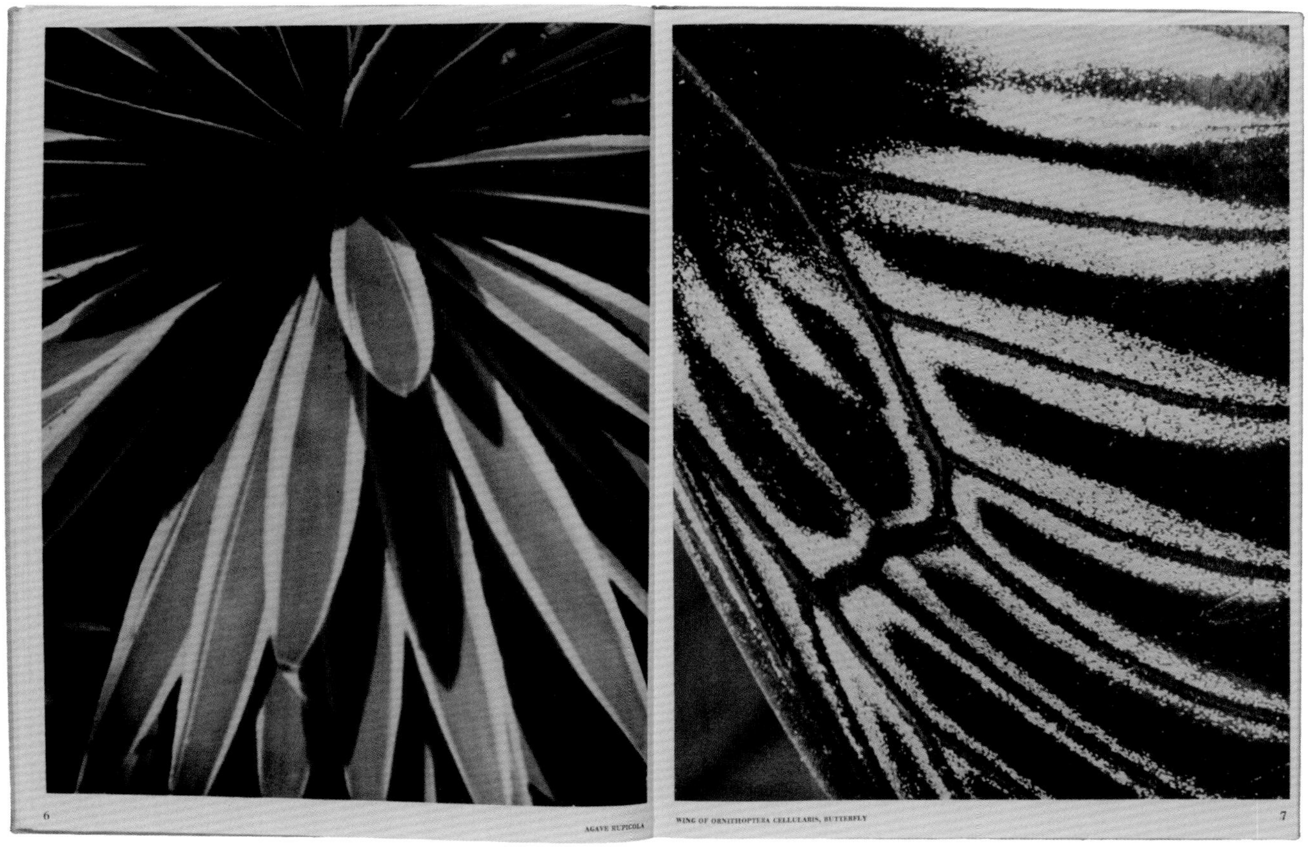

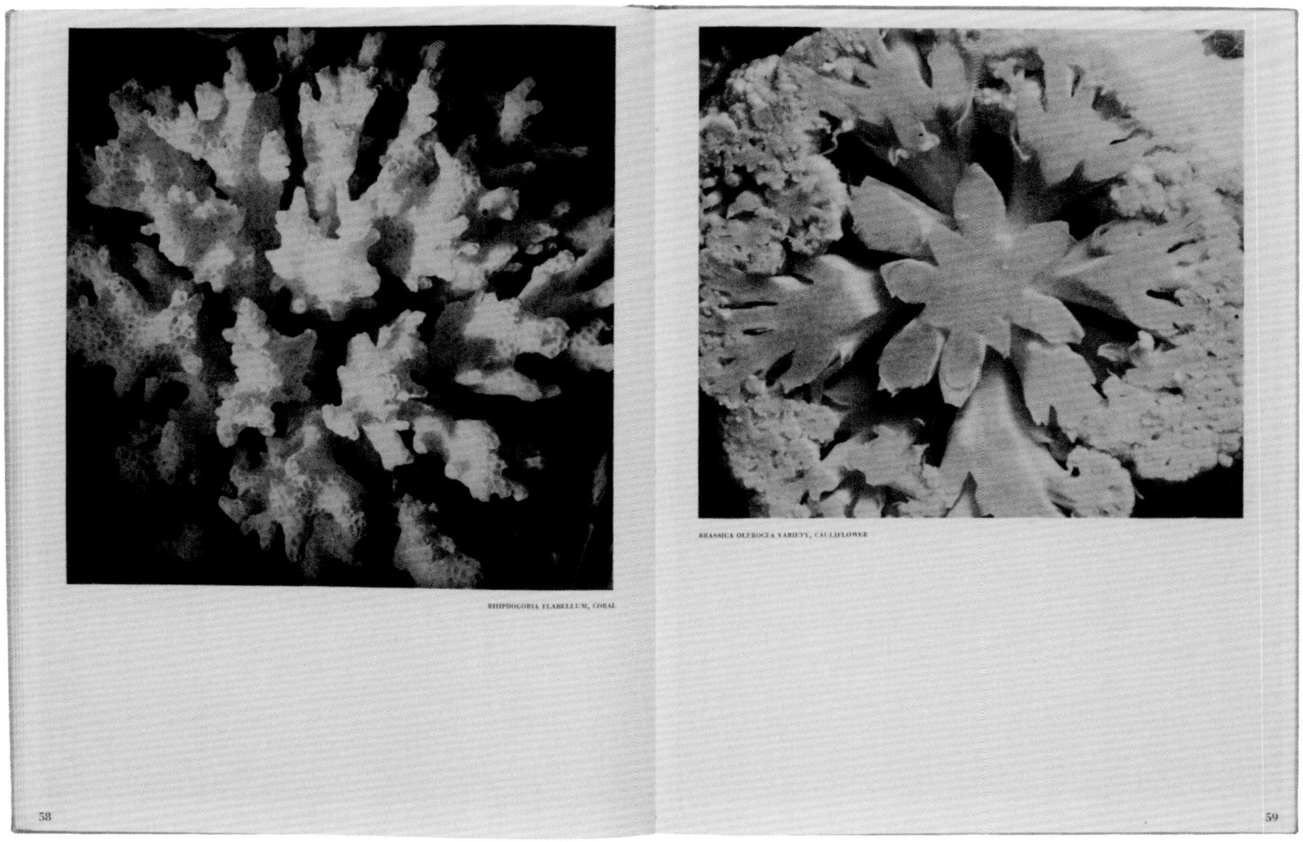

188. *Agave Rupicola* and *Wing of Ornithoptera Cellularis, Butterfly*, 1946

189. *Rhipdogorin Flabellum, Coral* and *Brassica Olerocea variety, Caulifower*, 1946

Kodak Negative Album

A Lilliputian album with golden letters embossed on its spine contains negatives and prints from Horst's *Patterns from Nature* project. The album fits in the palm of one's hand and is specifically designed to protect square format Rolleiflex negatives, measuring 2 ¼ × 2 ¼ inches (6 × 6 cm). It fastens with a press stud and begins with six lined pages for listing the contents, followed by 100 numbered paper folders, or folios, to hold negatives. As the text on the inside cover explains, 'The folders in this album are made of transparent paper. Negatives stored in them can be readily identified without removal, by holding the folders separately to the light and viewing the negatives through them.' As Horst filled the album with negatives and their corresponding contact prints, he wrote the subject of each image in careful, tiny script on the contents pages: 'Chinese Fan Palm ... Tourmaline ... Allium Cepa ...'. The order of the images in the album matches the order in which they were reproduced in the 1946 publication *Patterns from Nature*. The album also includes a small number of photographs – of subjects such as lily pads on a pond – that were not reproduced in the book.

Many of the contact prints include Horst's crop marks in thick black or red lines, to indicate which section of an image was to be used in the final publication. These uncropped prints harbour surprising details and occasionally a human presence, giving them a character very different to their more purist, published counterparts. For example, the uncropped image of Hechtia Glomerata, photographed directly from above in the Bronx Botanical Gardens, includes Horst's shiny shoe (pl.192). We discover that he photographed bamboo leaves, Bambusa, through a greenhouse window, and positioned the field mushroom, Agaricus Campestris, on a wooden table top.

As Martin Barnes has discussed, *Patterns from Nature* connects with well-known photographs by Karl Blossfeldt, Edward Weston and Paul Strand. Horst's project is also reminiscent of the 1930s work of another German, Elsa Thiemann (1910–81). She studied under Walter Peterhans (1897–1960) at the Dessau Bauhaus from 1929 to 1931 and her photographic studies of various everyday objects were published in magazines such as *Rätselbilder* (*Mystery Images*). Horst's photographs of an onion and red cabbage are particularly similar in style to Thiemann's close-up images of vegetables, though the parallels should not be surprising given Horst's strong interest in the teachings of the Bauhaus.

The forensic detail of the published photographs and the inclusion of Latin names gives *Patterns from Nature* a scientific quality, yet, for Horst, plants and flowers were highly emotive: 'We think of Easter when we talk of Lillies; dogwood conjures up a warm sunny day in Spring, and our visual conception of a rose is inextricably connected with its scent and with its color, be it a glowing crimson or a gentle white, and with tenderness and love.'[1] The book opens with a quote from William Shakespeare's pastoral comedy *As You Like It*:

> And this our life exempt from public haunt
> Finds tongues in trees, books in the running brooks,
> Sermons in stones and good in everything.

These lines (spoken by Duke Senior in act 2, scene 1) are part of a longer speech which contrasts the city and countryside; the 'painted pomp' of court life is juxtaposed with the sanctuary and simple pleasures to be found in the woods. The sentiment resonated with Horst's own feelings about the power and beauty of the natural world. *Patterns from Nature* and this miniature album represent a break in the photographer's career from the artifice of high fashion, conveying both his respect for nature and his versatility as a photographer.

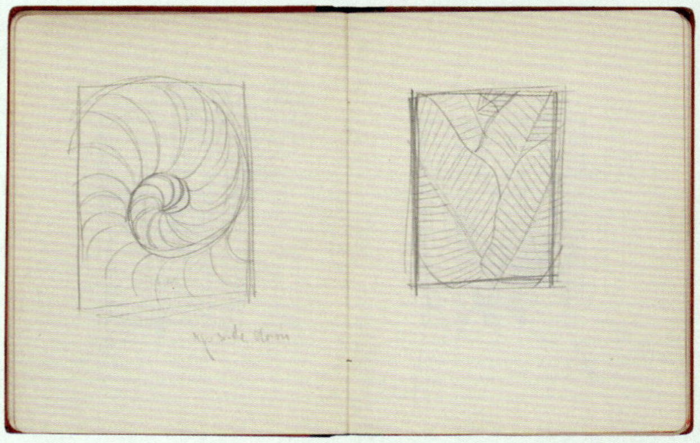

190. Horst's sketchbook, 1940s

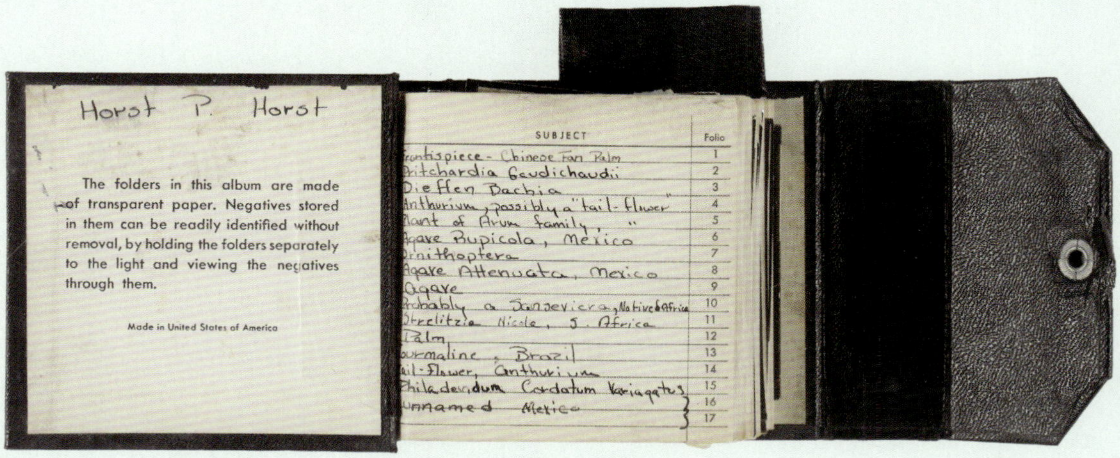

191. Kodak negative album, 1946

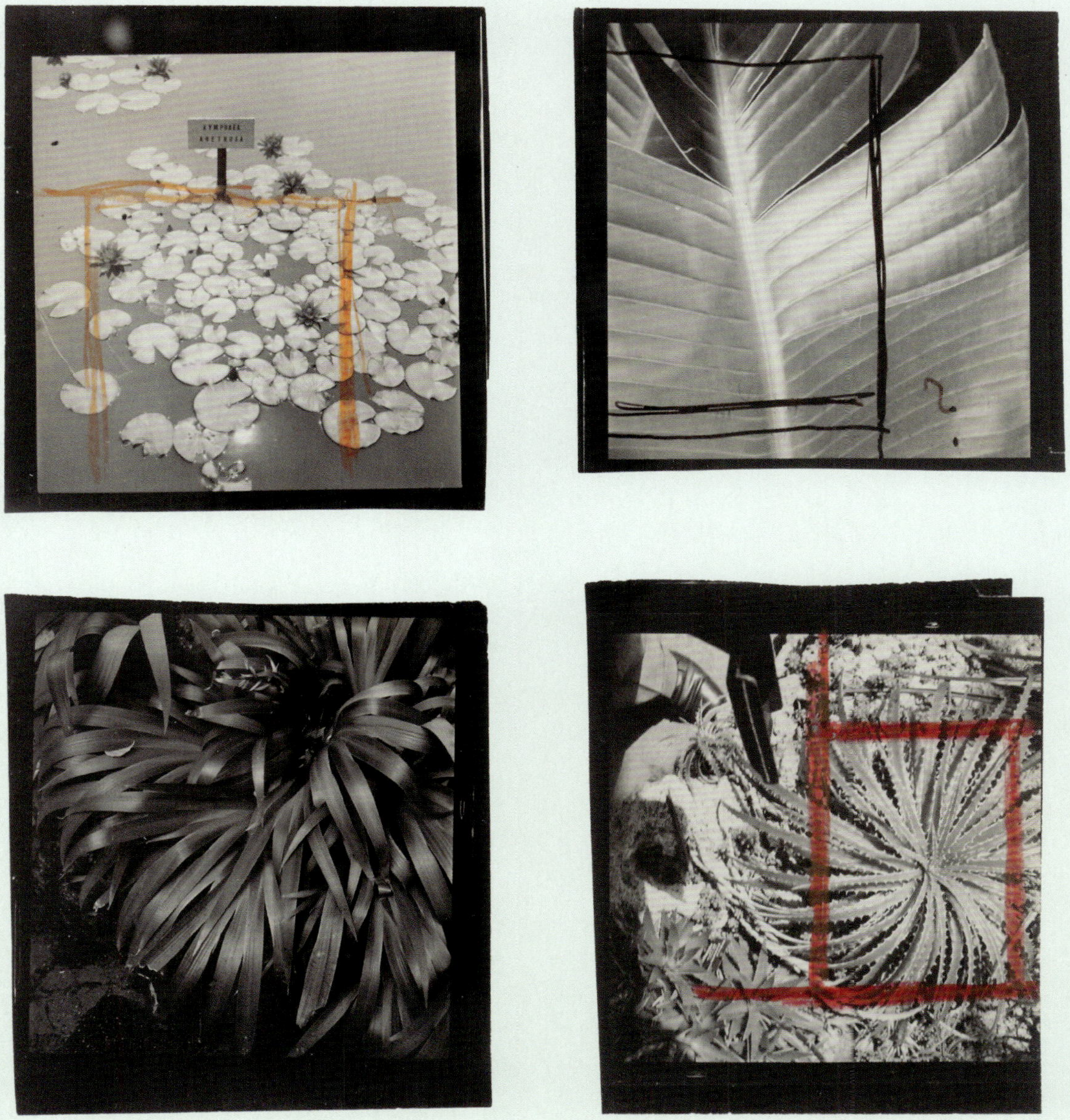

192. Four contact prints from the Kodak negative album, 1946

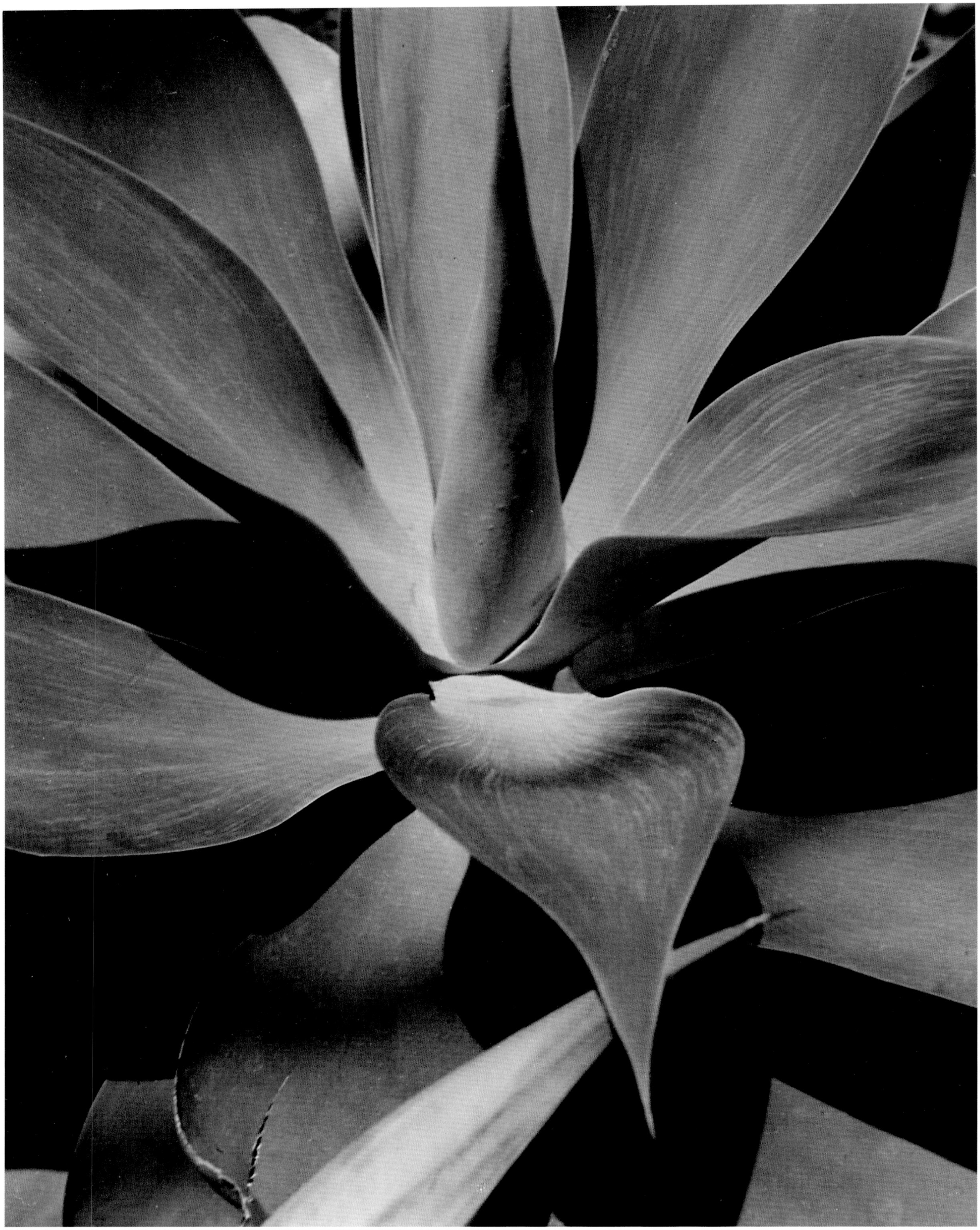

193. *Agave Attenuata*, 1946

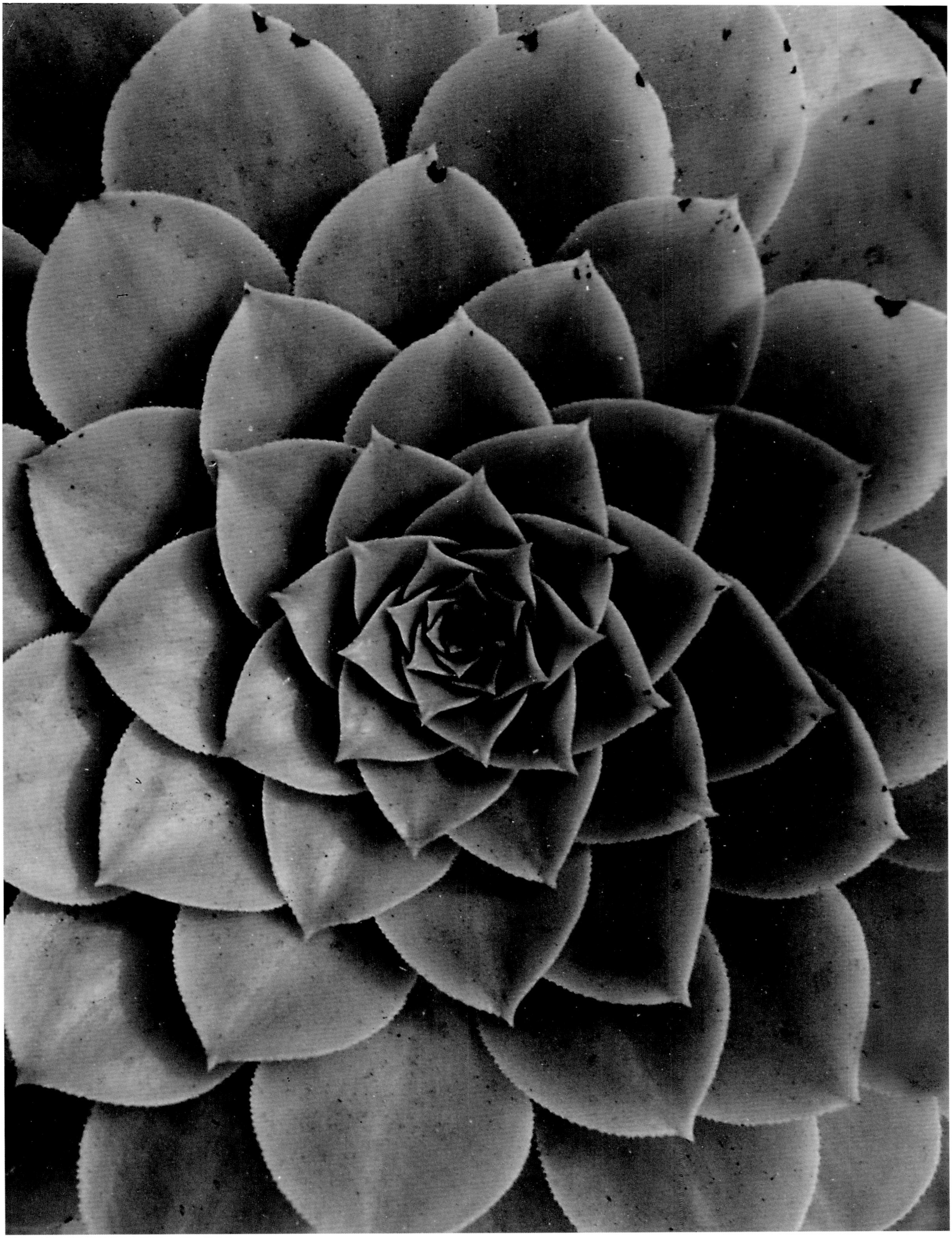

194. *Aednium Holochrrysum*, 1946

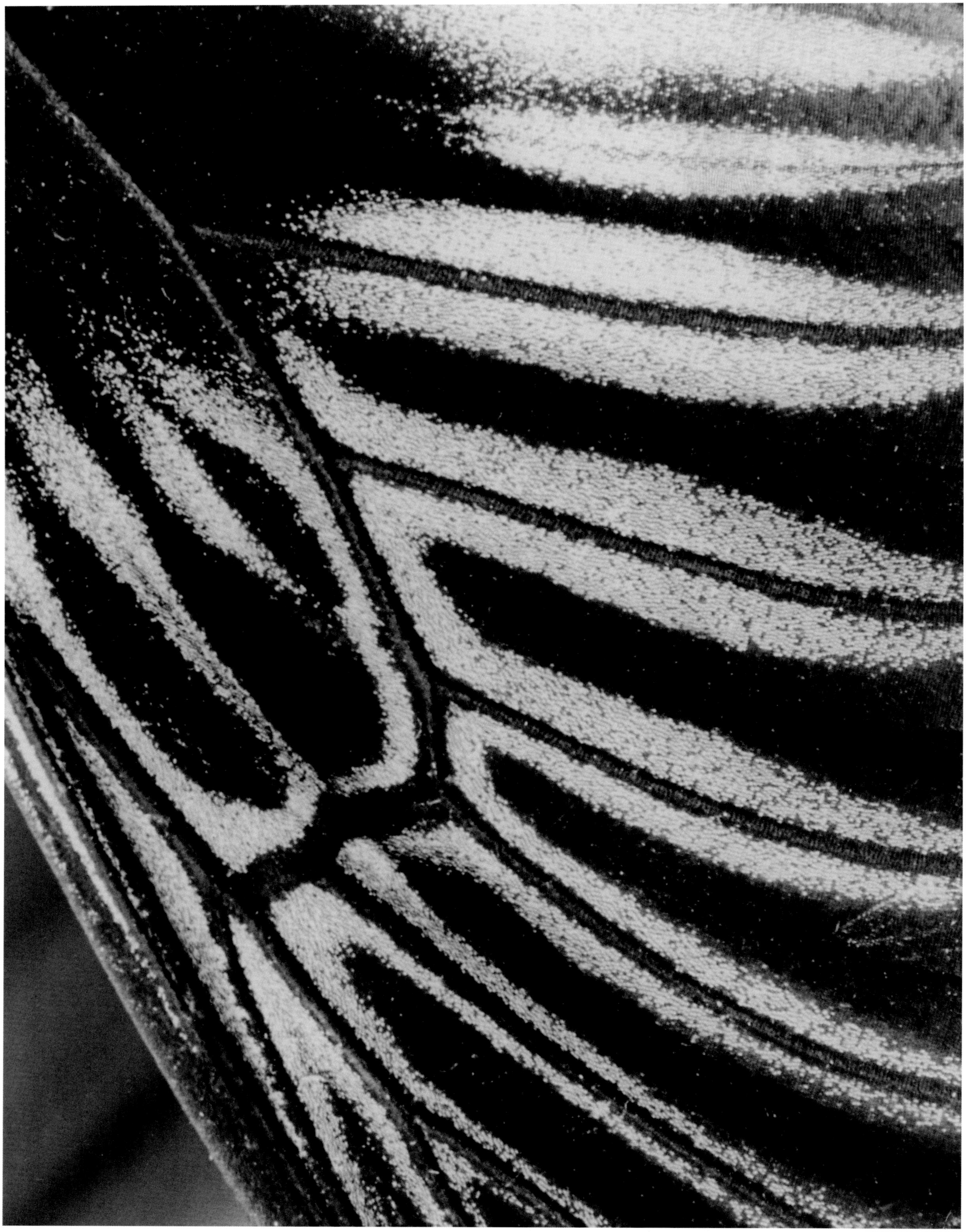

195. *Wing of Ornithoptera Cellularis, Butterfly*, 1946

196. *Pyrite, Mineral*, 1946

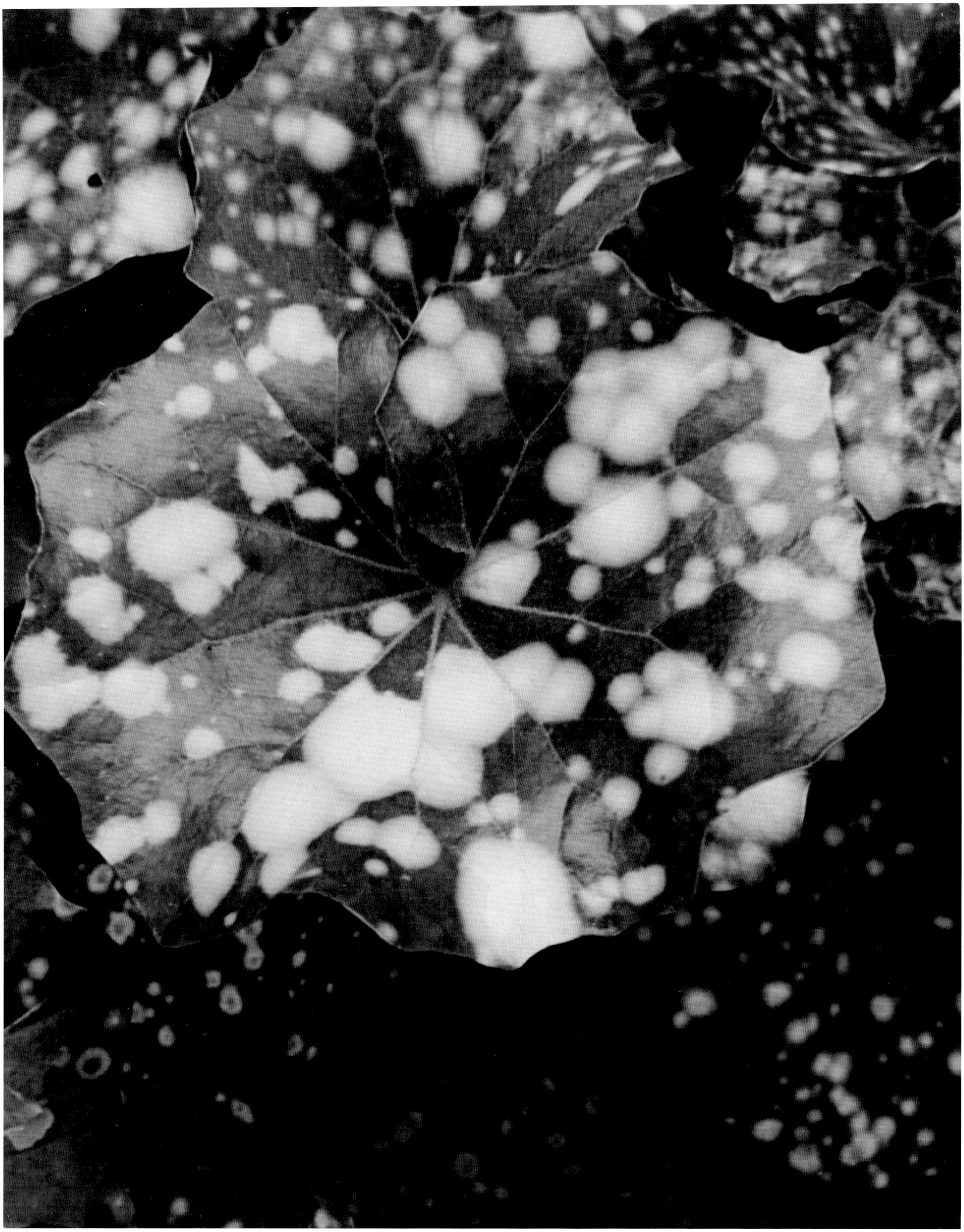

197. *Ligularia Kaempferi*, 1946

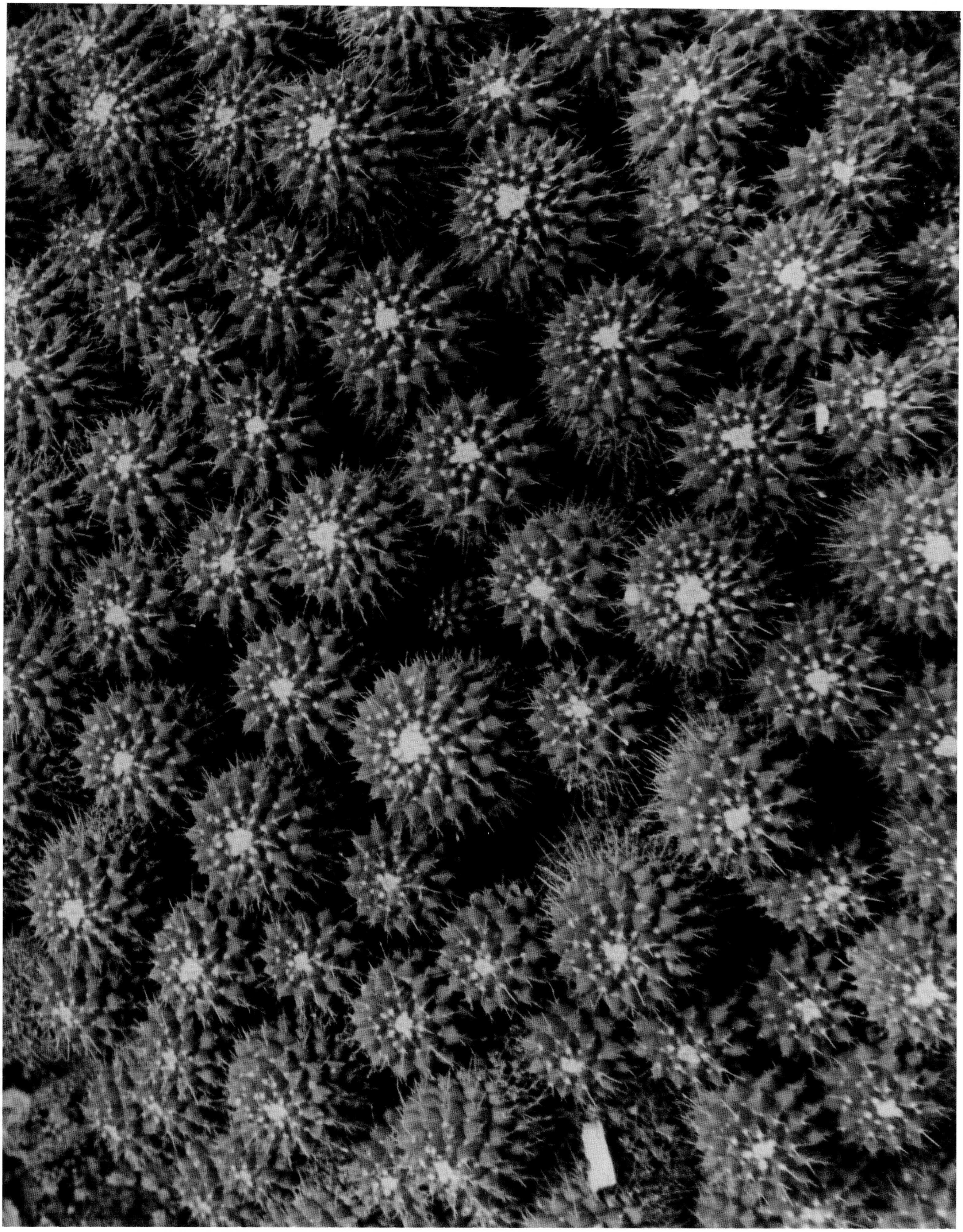

198. *Trichocereus Candicans*, 1946

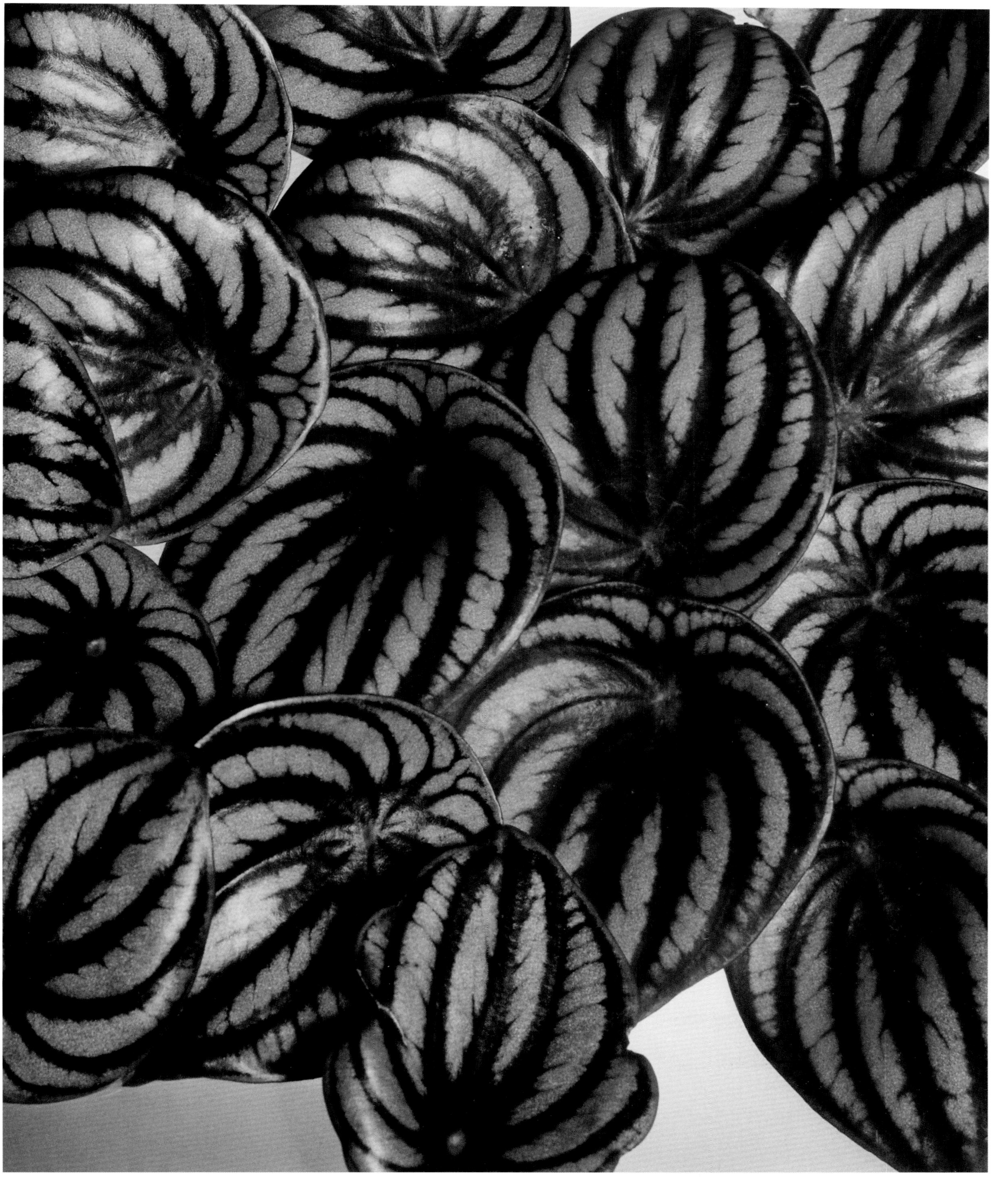

199. Photogrcphic collage, made from *Peperomia Sandersii*, 1946

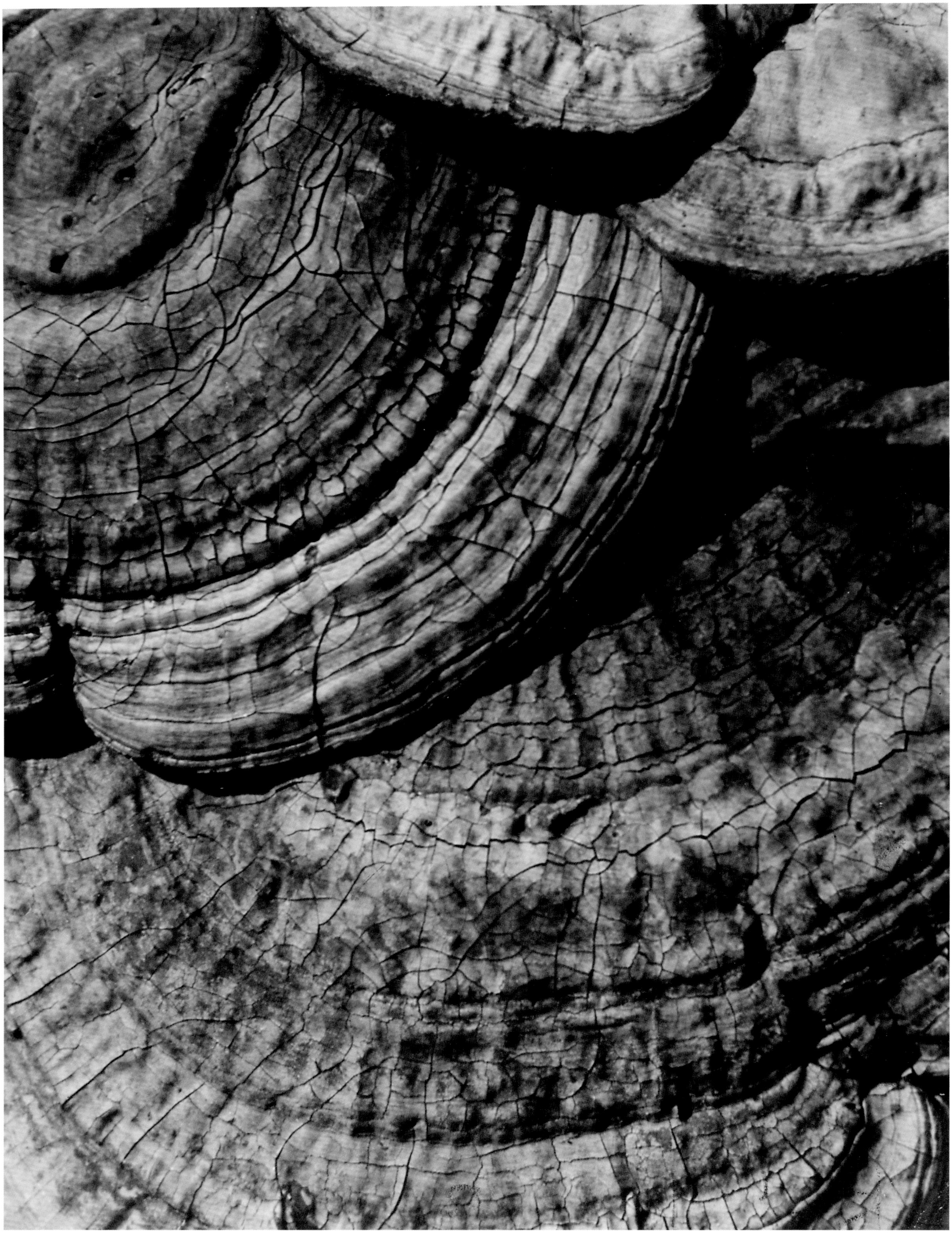

200. *Brachet* [sic], *Fungus*, 1946

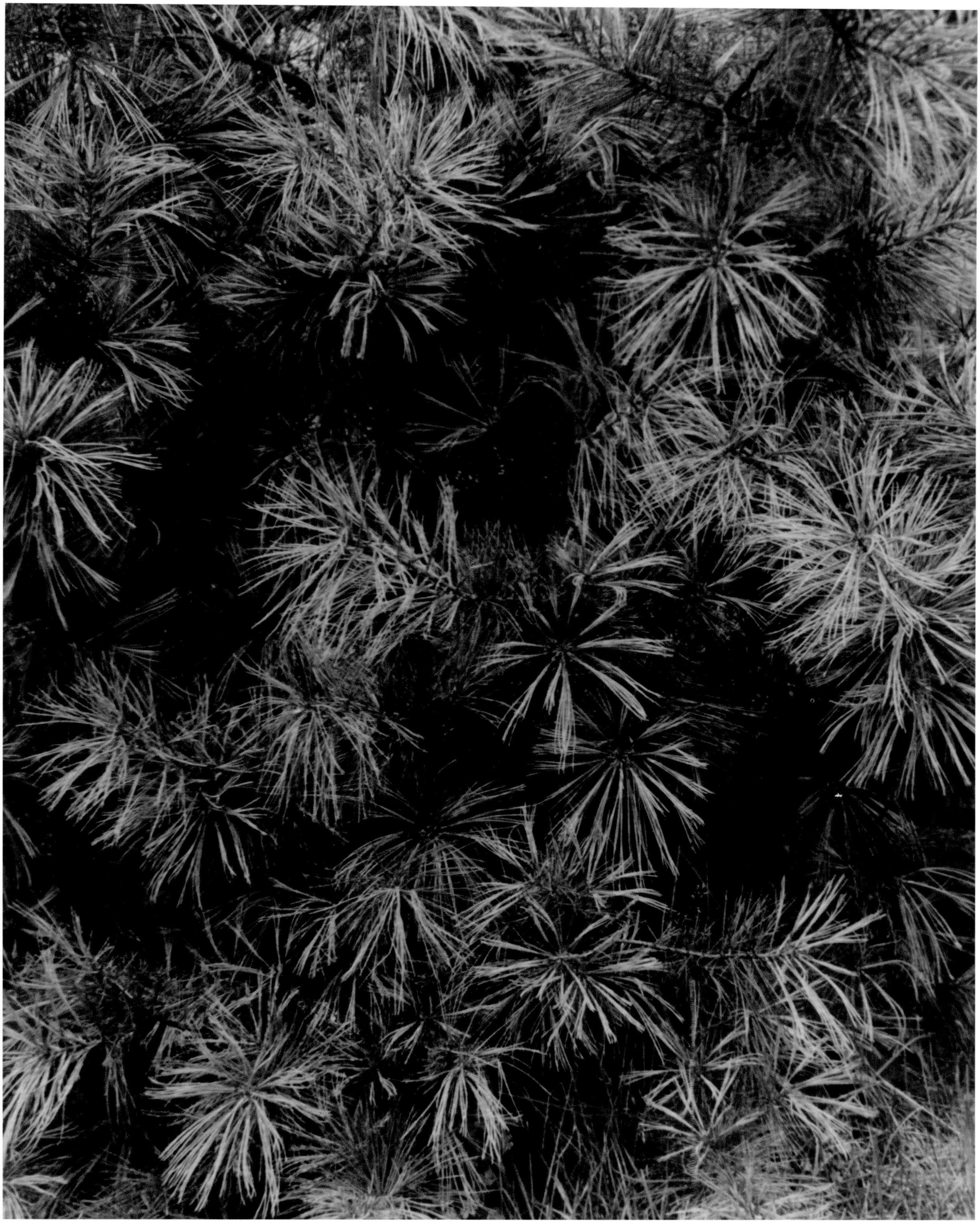

201. *Pinus Strobus*, 1946

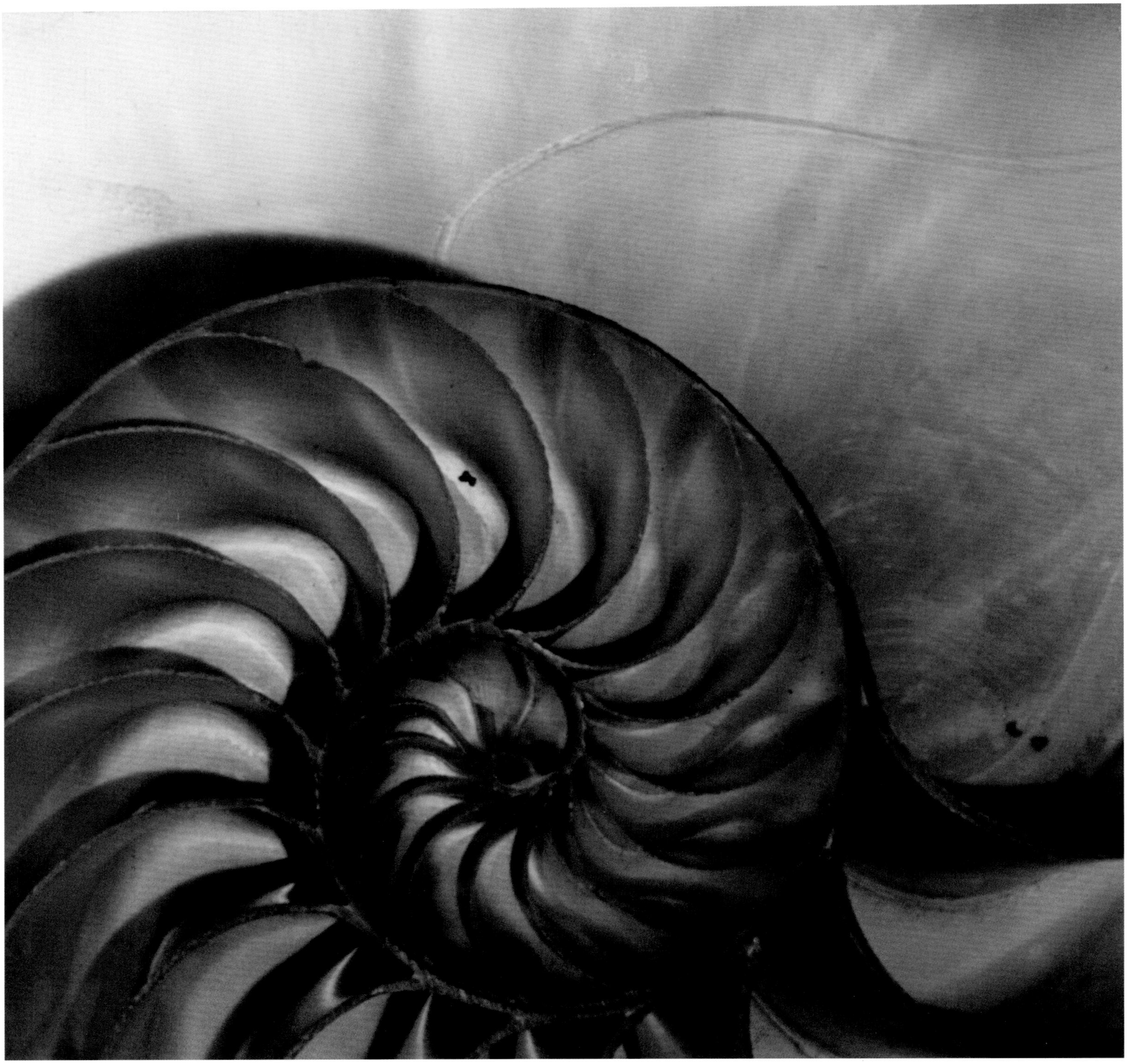

202. *Nautilus Pompileus, Shell*, 1946

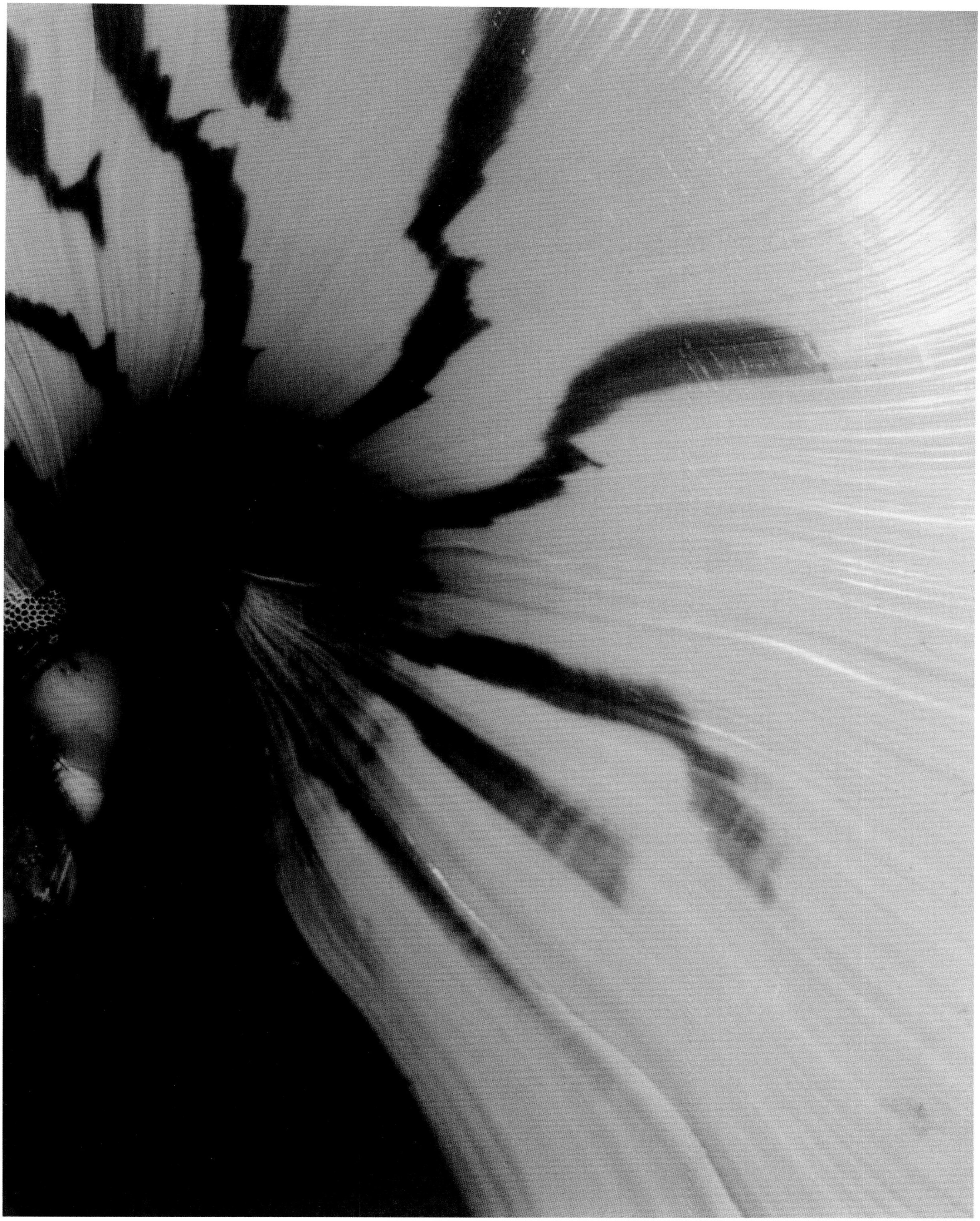

203. *Nautilus Pompileus, Shell*, 1946

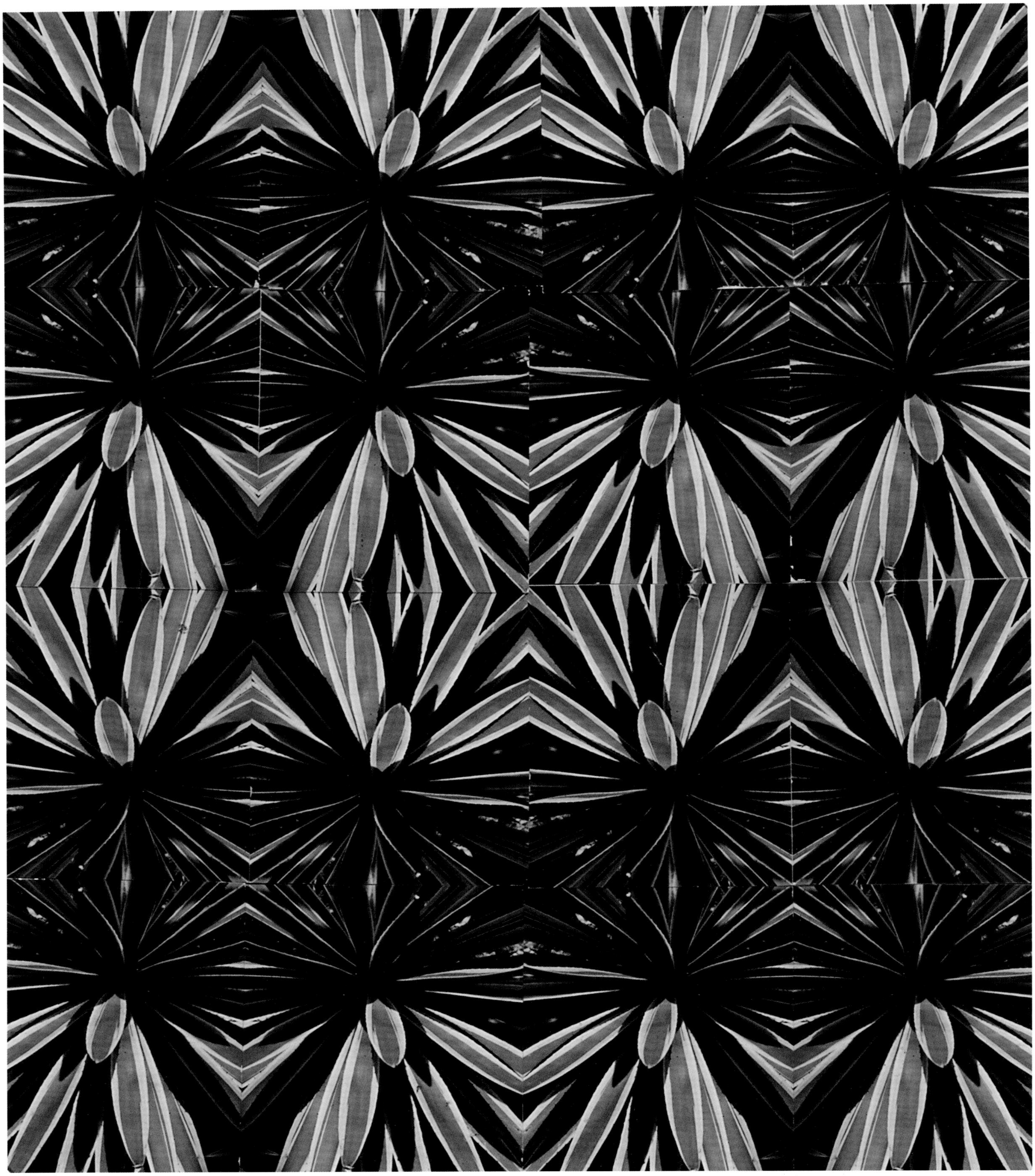

204. Photographic pattern, *Agave Rupicola*, 1946

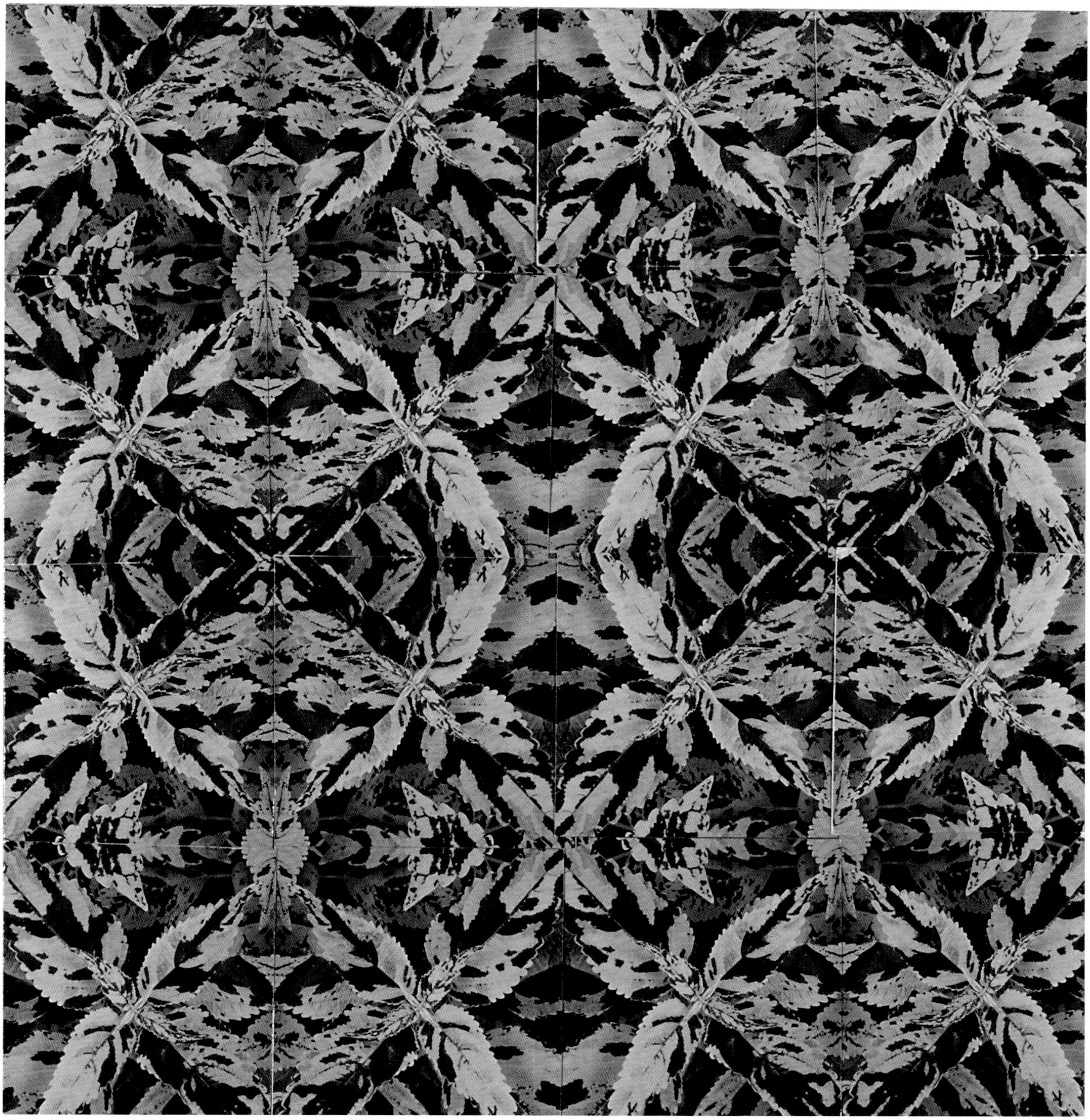

205. Photographic pattern, *Coleus Blumei*, 1946

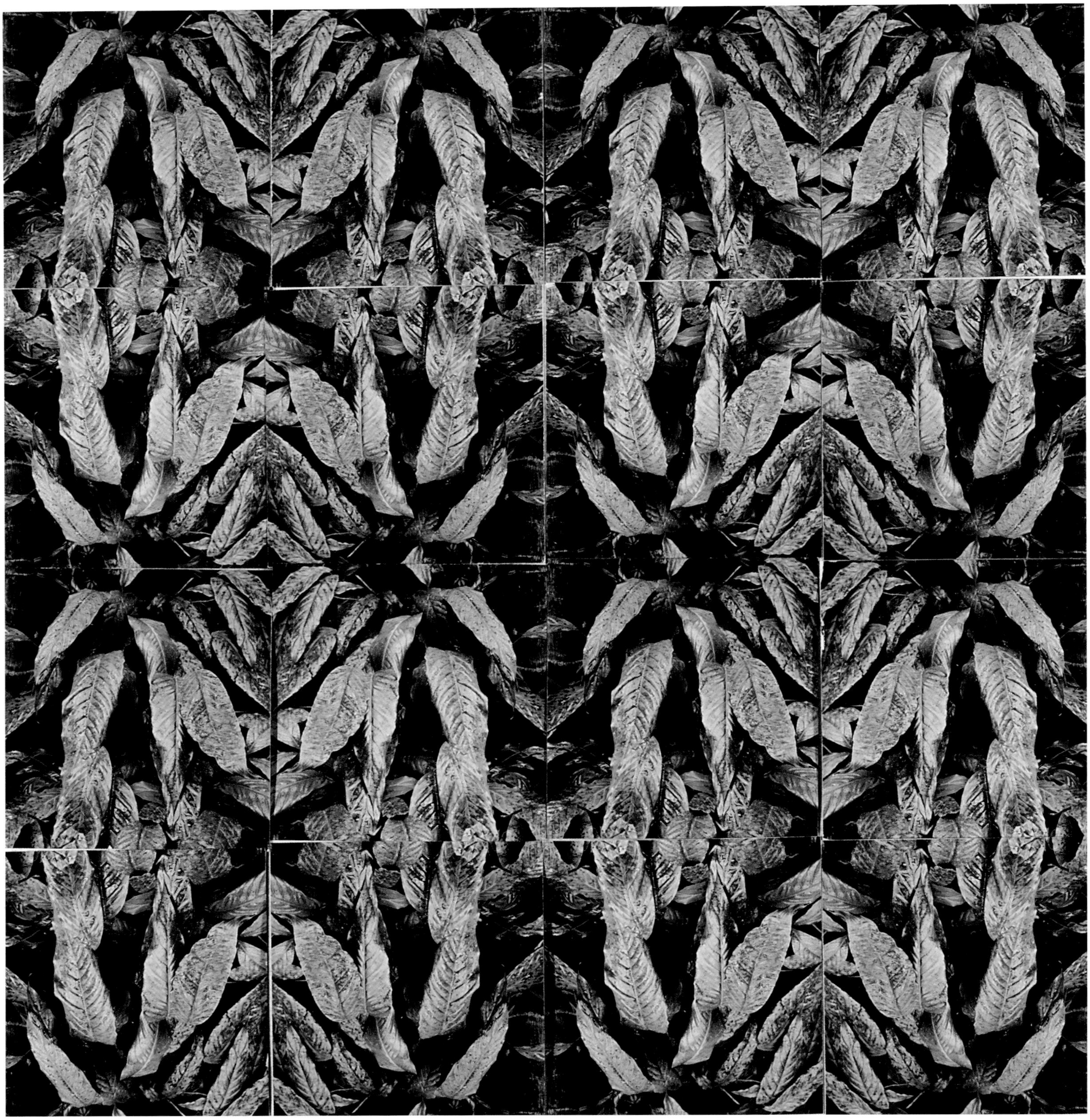

206. Photographic pattern, *Spathiphyllum Wallisi*, 1946

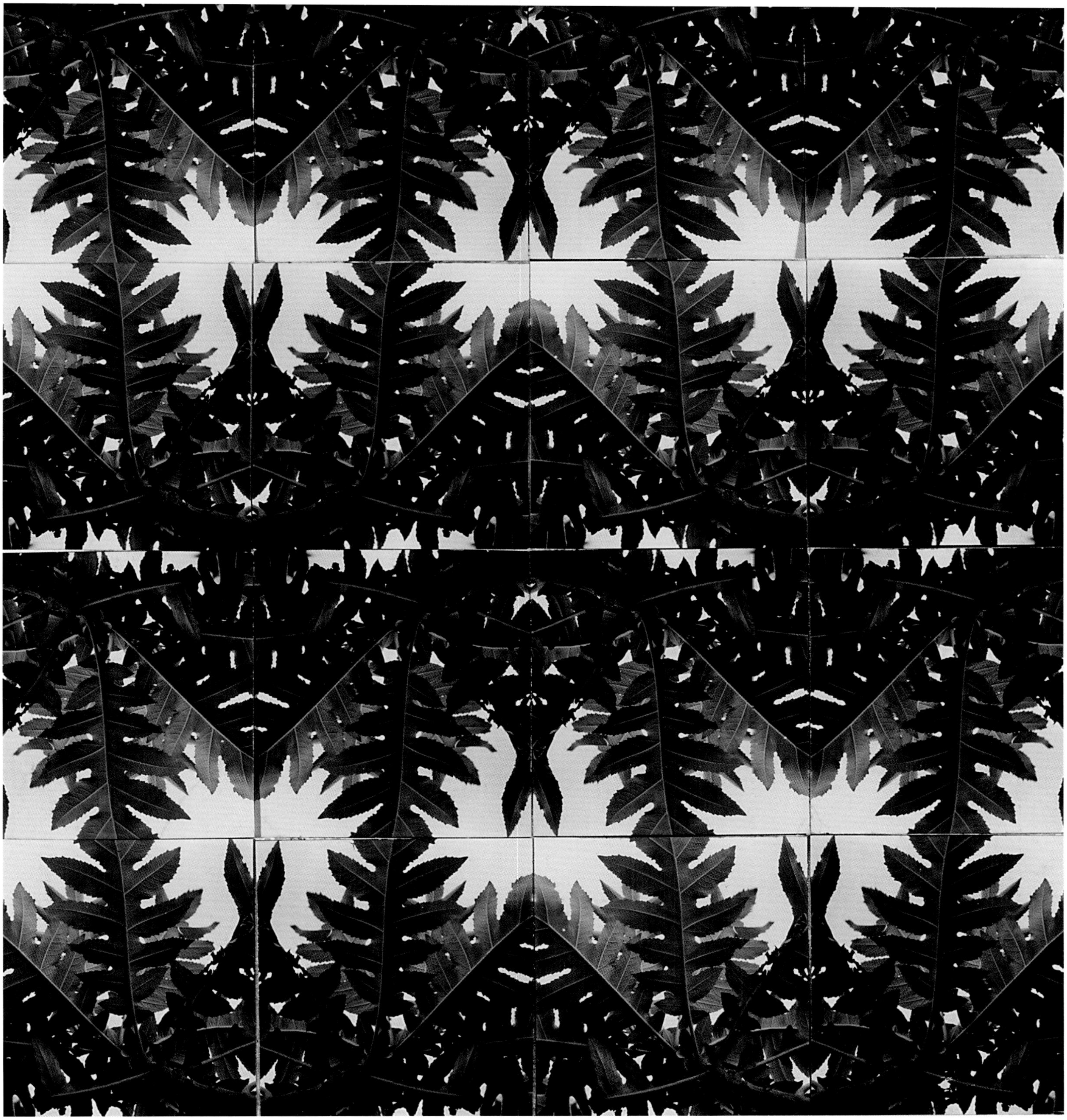

207. Photographic pattern, 1946

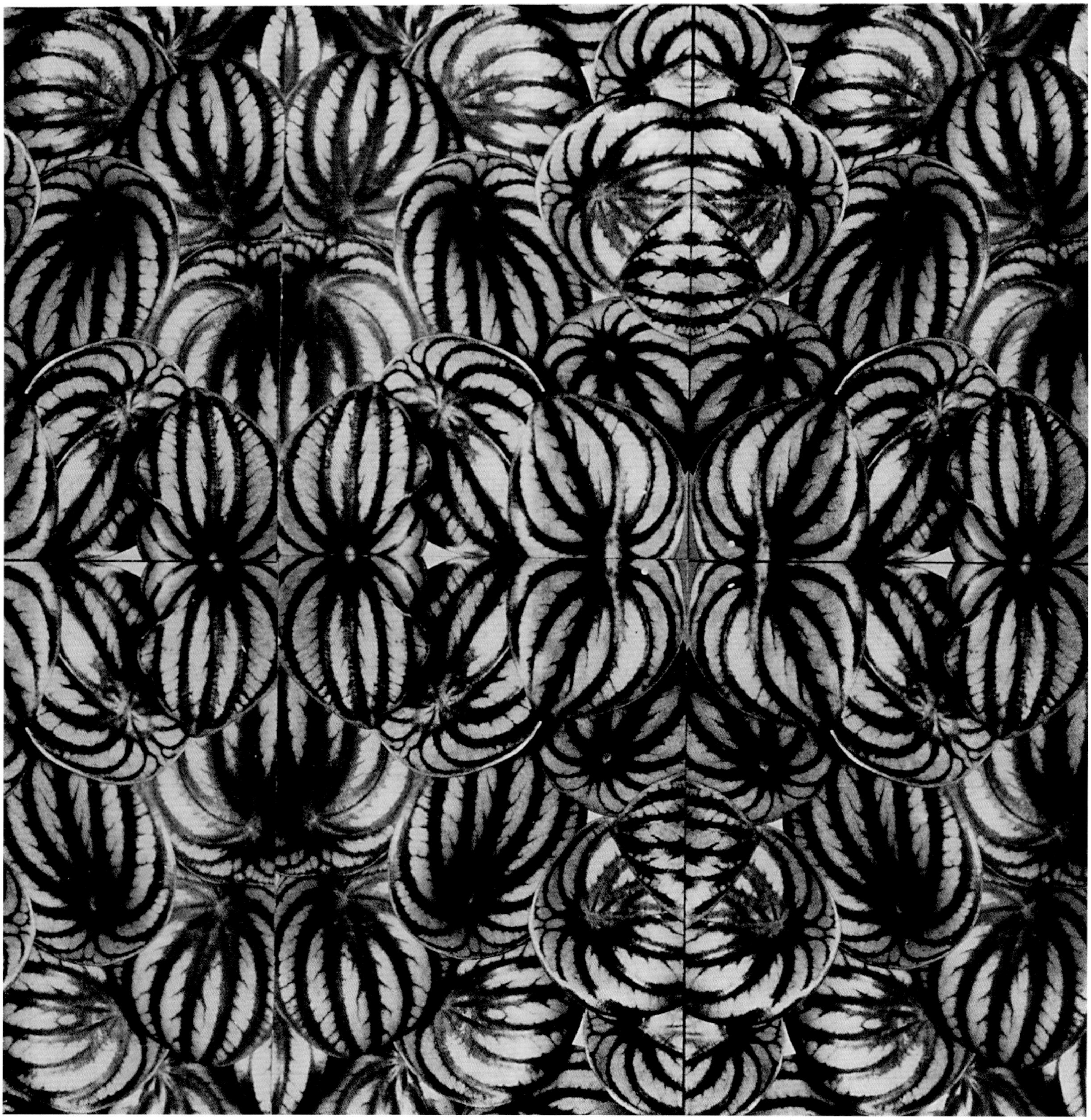

208. Photographic pattern, *Peperomia Sandersii*, 1946

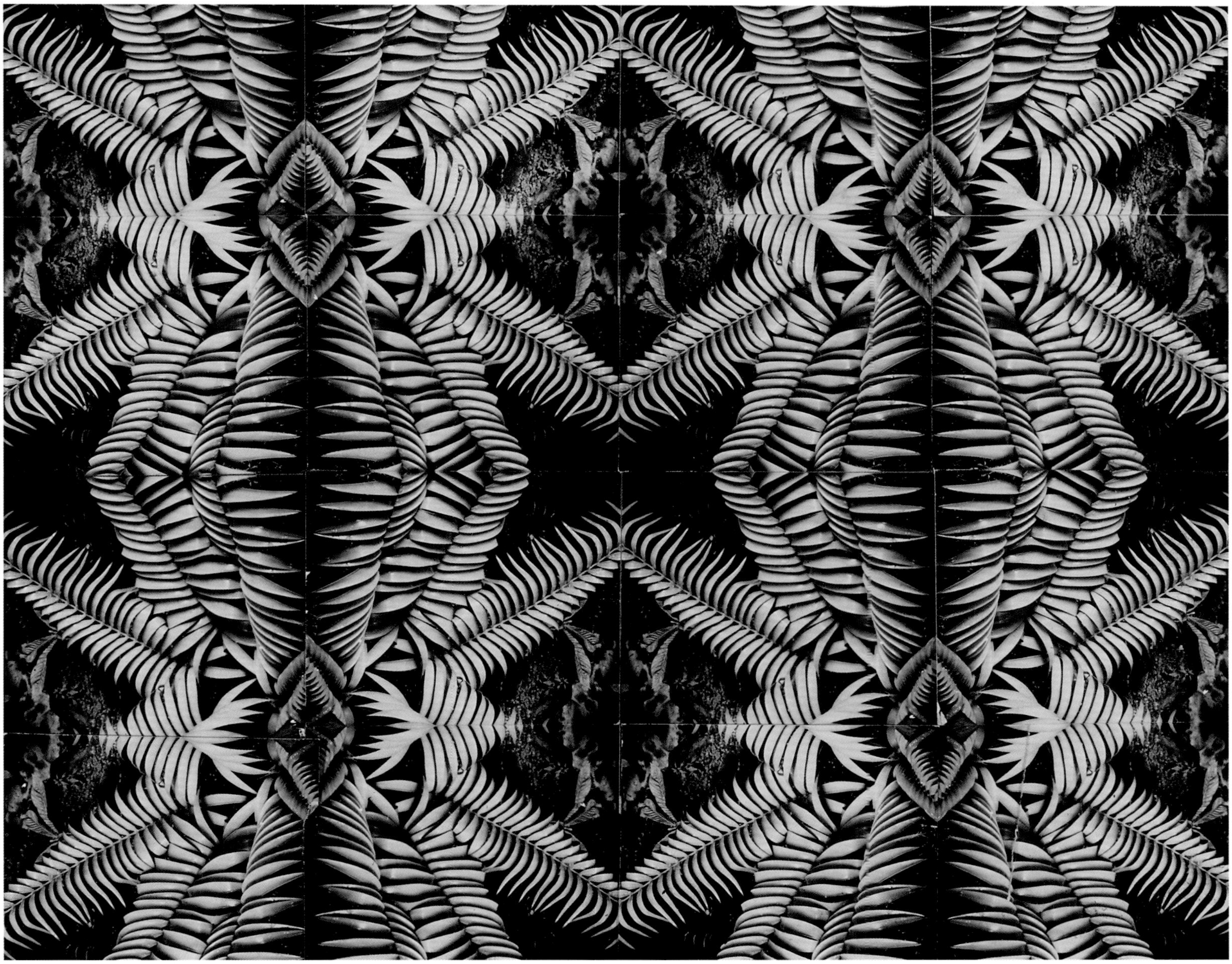

209. Photographic pattern, 1946

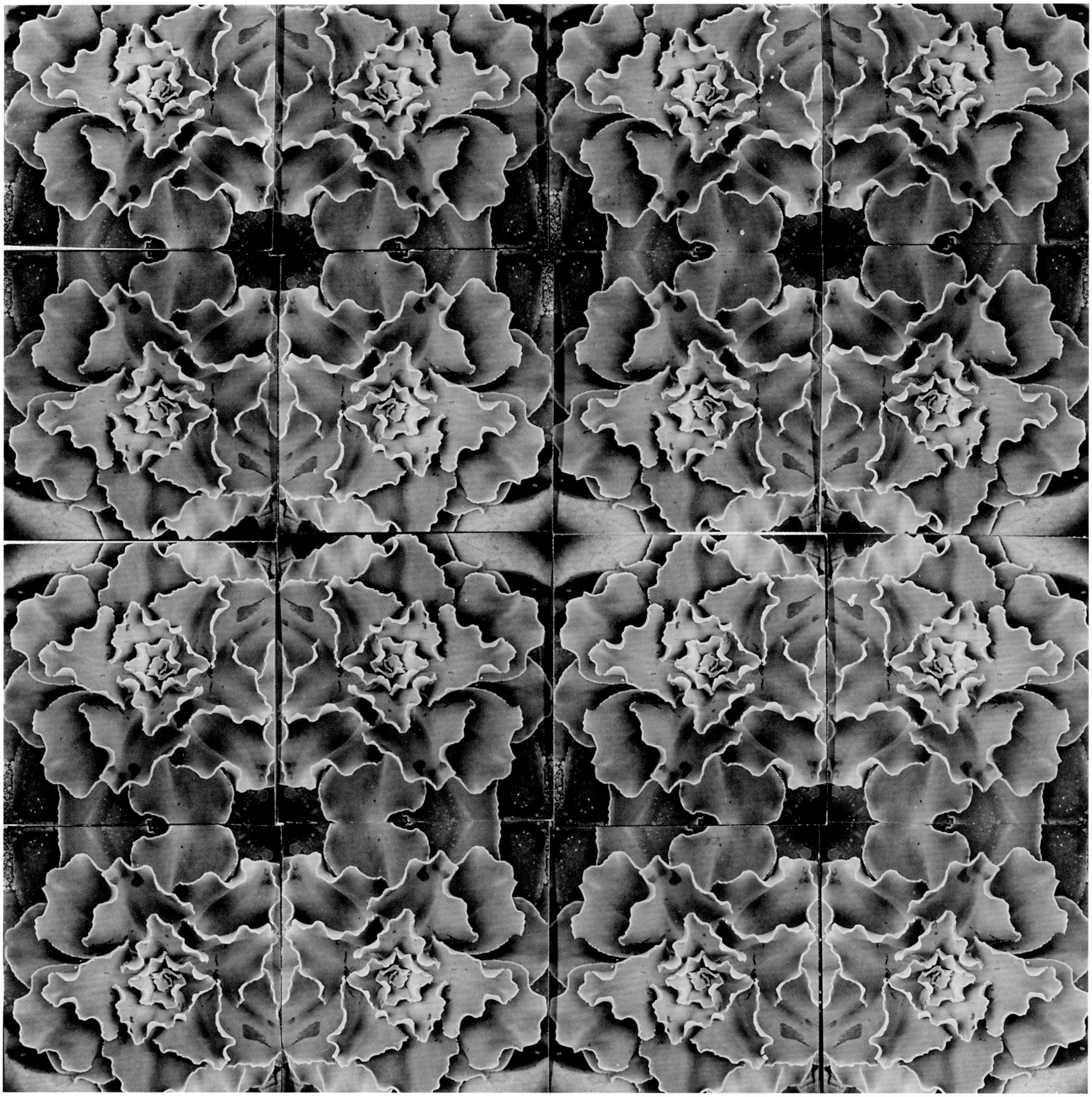

210. Photographic pattern, *Echeveria Gibbiflora Crispa*, 1946

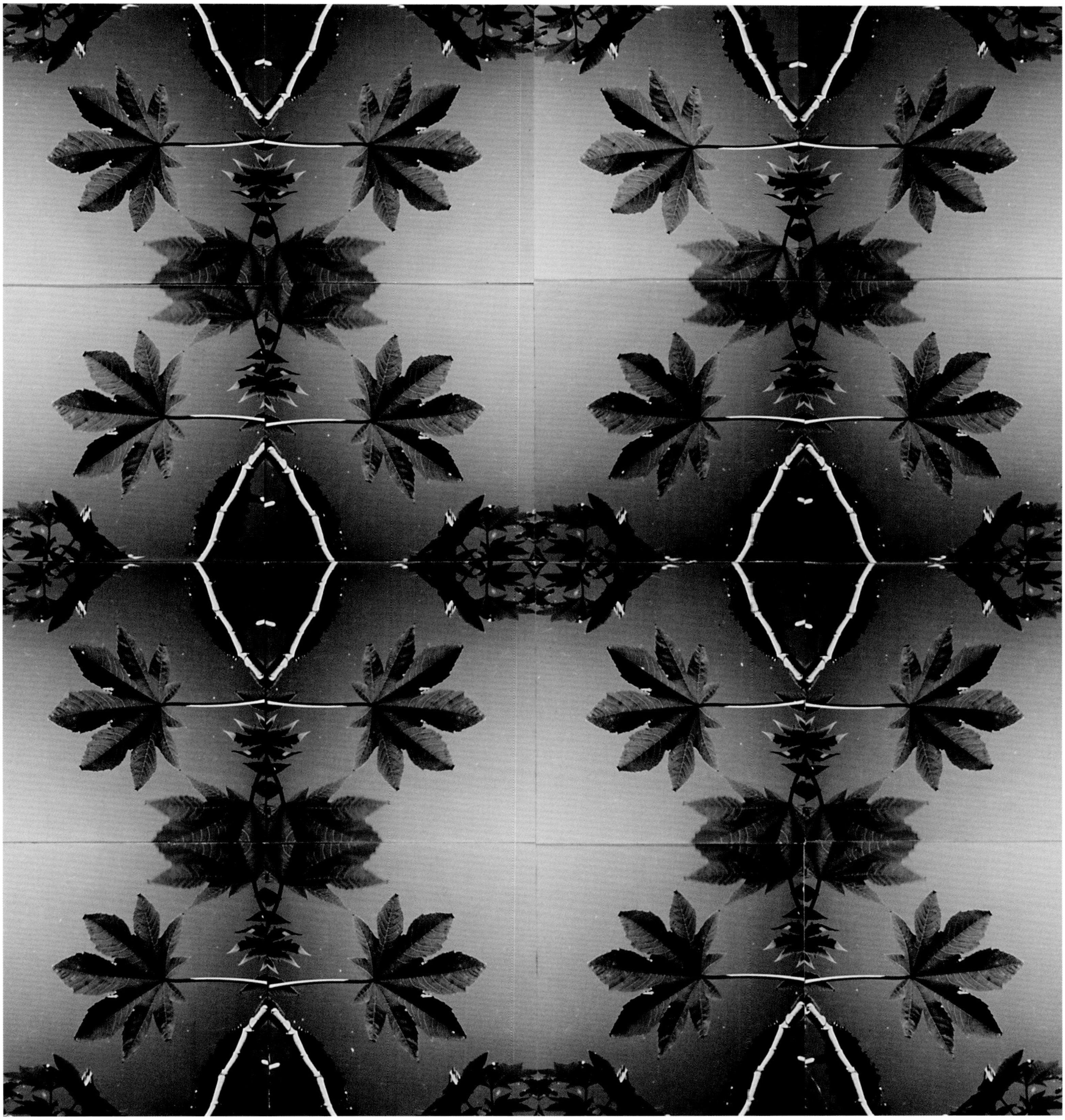

211. Photographic pattern, 1946

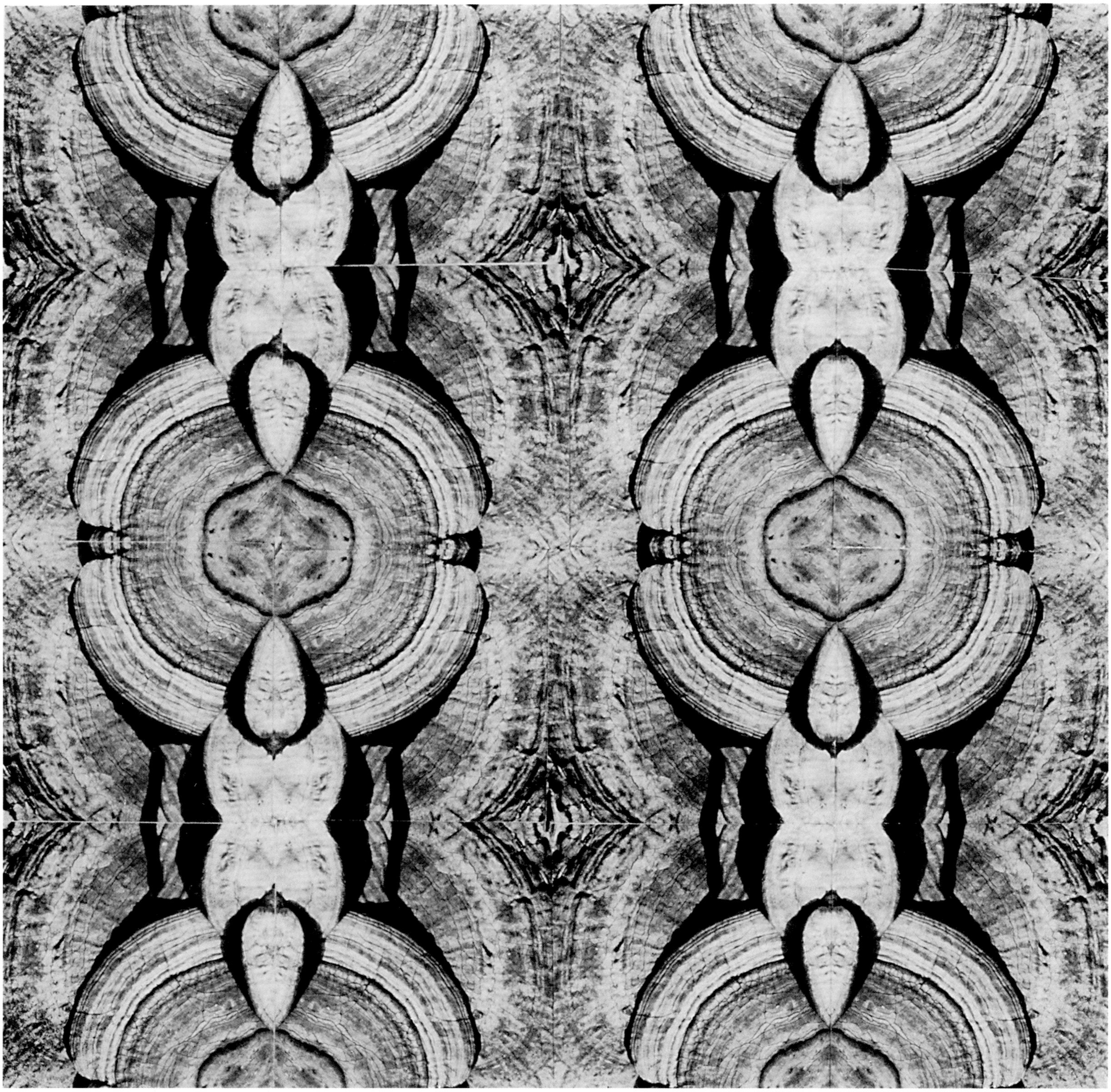

212. Photographic pattern, *Brachet [sic] Fungus*, 1946

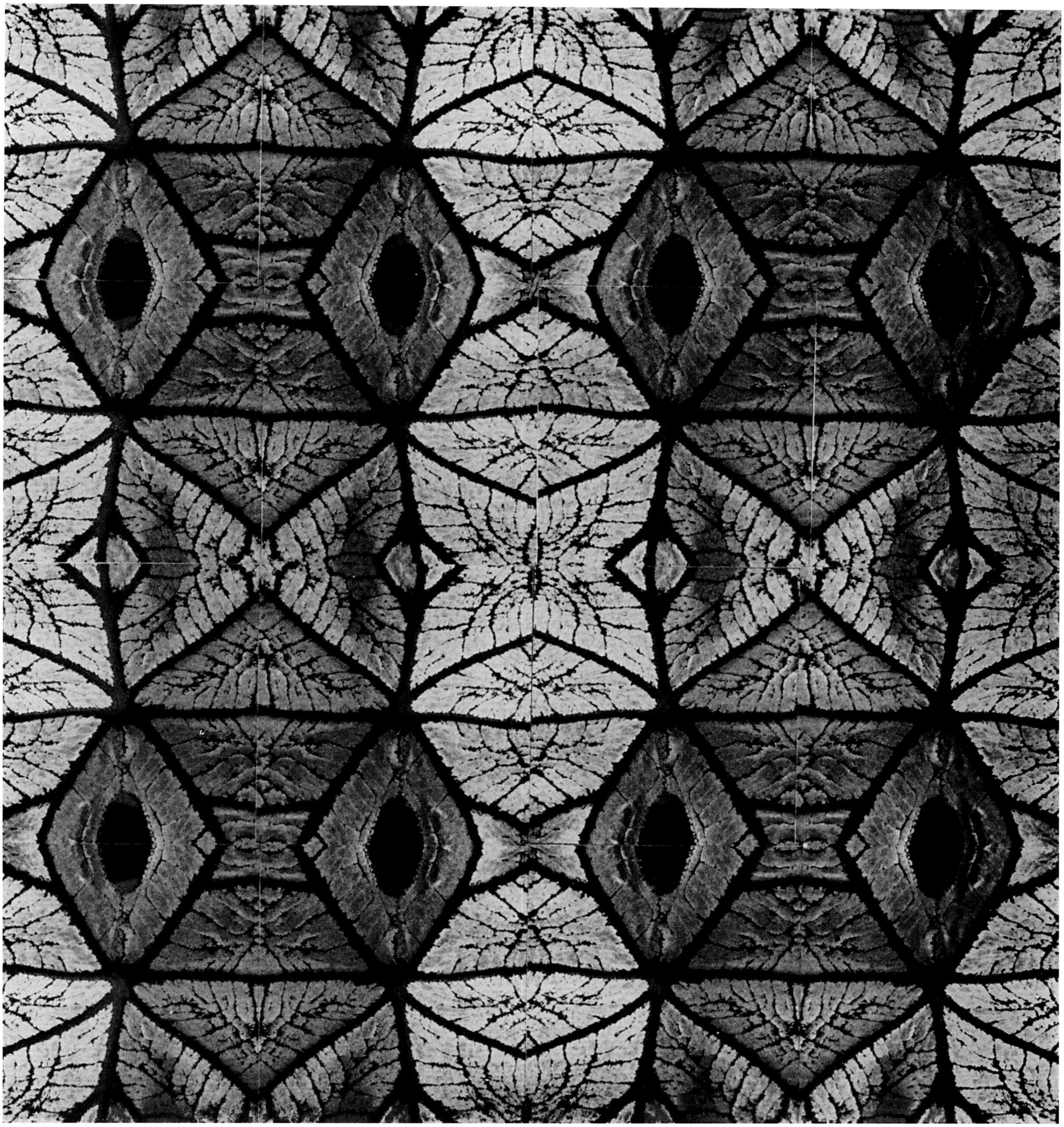

213. Photographic pattern, *Calladium*, 1946

VII
Travel

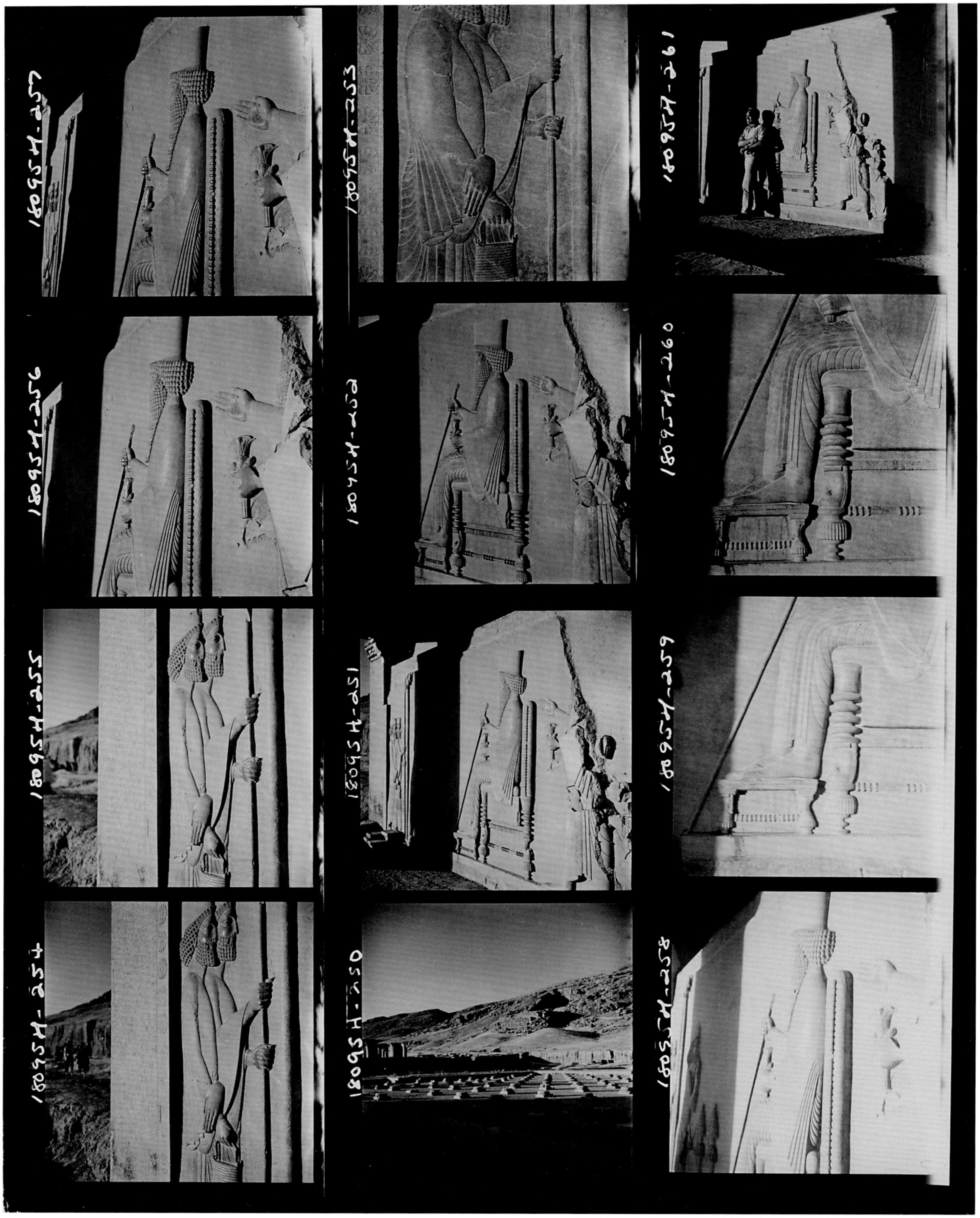

214. Contact sheet, Persepolis, 1949

MIDDLE-EASTERN DIARIES

Horst P. Horst and Valentine Lawford

In the summer of 1949, Horst undertook a month-long journey to the Middle East with his partner Valentine Lawford, who had been appointed political counsellor at the British Embassy in Tehran. Lawford explained Britain's relationship with Iran:

> Its vast oilfields were still largely exploited by the Anglo-Iranian Oil Company; but it was recognized as inevitable that the Iranian Government must eventually be given a far greater degree of control over their country's main source of natural wealth. ... The youthful shah, European educated and widely credited with enlightened views, was attempting to bring his countrymen belatedly into the twentieth century, by instituting a series of reforms destined, as he hoped, to lead to eventual material prosperity and social progress. Horst took a month's vacation to accompany me to my new post, welcoming this unexpected opportunity to visit and photograph a famously beautiful part of Asia before it had been modernized beyond recognition. In the summer of 1949 the U.S. Ambassador in Tehran was John C. Wiley, whose Polish-born wife, Irena, had been so hospitable to Horst in wartime Washington. She presented Horst to the shah's twin sister, Princess Ashraf, who arranged for him to take photographs in Isfahan and Persepolis.[1]

Horst kept a diary during his travels and filled it with evocative descriptions, and occasional sketches, of scenes unlike anything he had previously encountered. The extracts that follow are taken from that diary.[2]

28 JUNE 1949
DAMASCUS AND BEIRUT

The mountains and hills seen from the air have formations like certain old shells burned by the sun and the wind; others are rounded like half globes of all sizes with light yellow-green shapes where they meet. The variety of beiges, light yellows and greys seems endless. In the city, the bazaars are messy and some streets resemble medieval European architecture like Rothenburg. Under those streets are Roman remains, some being dug up. What appears to be an ancient mosque is near a warehouse and is like an Arabian Piranesi etching.

To Beirut by hired car. Beirut, backed by mountains, busy, typically Mediterranean town. Then off into the unknown, in a Buick convertible. ... Drove to Damascus, down a steep serpentine road, saw Baalbek in the late afternoon at sunset. Granite pillars from Egypt, which were later used by Emperor Constantine to build St. Sophia. Wonderful colours, gigantic scale, decadent sculpture reminiscent of the late Renaissance. The evening was beautiful, with a new moon, and Mozart on the car radio. Dinner with British Ambassador Broadmead, our host at Damascus.

PERSEPOLIS

Baghdad with its unhealthy wind and the dry steep passes, the primitive hovels and the filth seemed already far away but they are all outside the gate of the compound. Dust, mud hovels in the process of becoming dust again, reminding me too clearly of the human 'footprints in the sand of time.' Everyone cries water if there were water, but there is water but no-one lifts a finger to halt its flow, to build dams, it trickles into the sand and disappears under the impotent eyes of the staring. Even the reservoirs which made the plains of Persepolis wealthy enough to become the goal of Alexander's ambition lie unused in the desert, a few months of labour could apparently restore prosperity to the few thousand, once it held millions of inhabitants.

Darius' Palace with portals and square windows seems small, the Apadana Stairs well preserved under the sand. Only the bases of the columns, Hall of hundred columns,

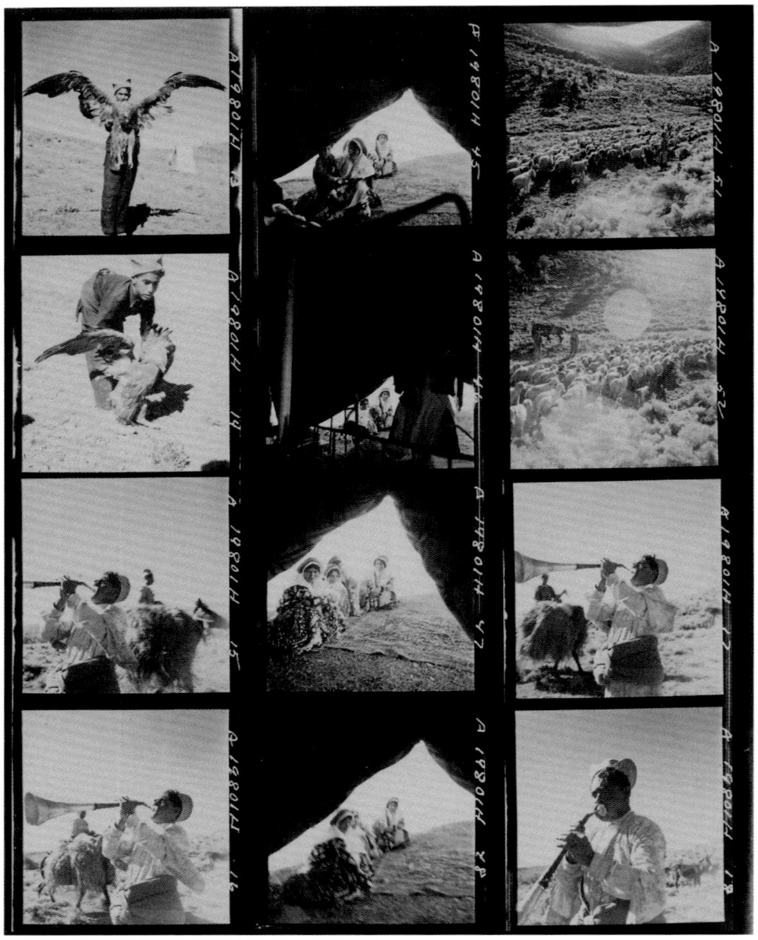

215. Contact sheet, Qashqa'i tribe, c.1949

should have been most impressive. The style of Persepolis has not changed in the 150 years while being built. The longest period of art without undergoing change in style. Excavations are slow but fruitful. Repeating sculptures depicting Darius enthroned receiving tributes, all over the staircases men bringing gifts, Xerxes standing in back of throne or elevating higher the common men reaching out for throne but not touching it. Men paying tribute to Darius, bowing, holding breath in front of mouth so not to pollute the majesty of the King with his breath. ... Figures all of same heights bringing animals, vases, rugs, furniture, different dress denoted their origin as well as accompanying animals, sheep, camels, horses, horse drawn chariots, bulls, lions. Columns are tall and thin, fluted, ornament on top with scrolls and above two bulls heads, which carried the wooden beams, the bases stylized leaf. Animal sculpture is lifelike and graceful, realistic expression and movement. Completely stylised human faces, except for one small head of lapis lazuli of Darius recently found now in the museum in Teheran.

Horst's first journey to the Middle East left a strong impression and he was compelled to visit Iran again in the spring of 1950. He spent a week with Valentine Lawford at the relatively remote south-eastern shore of the Caspian Sea before documenting with his Rolleiflex the annual migration of the Qashqa'i clan. Horst and Lawford were invited by Malik Mansur Khan Qashqa'i to spend ten days with his tribe, who had their own territory in the mountains of south Iran, as they travelled by camel and horse in search of vegetation for their flocks. Horst was surprised to discover that 'the chief of the tribe spoke perfect English and perfect German.'[3] Horst's photograph of a huge bird bears witness to the chief's skill as a hunter: he had shot the bird from a galloping horse, and Horst recalled, 'The eagle was so high up I hadn't even seen it.'[4] The extracts that follow are Valentine Lawford's recollections of their journey with the tribe.

TRAVELS WITH THE QASHQA'I CLAN, 1950

Since the tribe's means of locomotion were horse and camel, and Horst was anything but an expert rider of either animal, the chieftain provided him with a sure-footed, broad-backed mule (named Jeep) to convey him across the rivers and up and down the mountains, and an armed and mounted tribesman to carry his bags of film and cameras. For ten days we lived and moved with the tribe. Every noon we picnicked, sitting cross-legged on carpets spread on the grass. Every evening we dined in the chieftain's tent of woven goat's hair, waited on by tribesmen on their knees, bearing silver platters of rice and herbs and lamb and game. Whenever we needed a bath, we sat naked on mats of plaited palm fronds, while hot and cold water was poured over our backs through a gap in the roof of our tent. On our last evening, Malik Mansur Khan's servants laid out dozens of gilims – the handwoven, vegetable-dyed rugs for which the tribe was famous – on the floor of the chieftain's tent; and we asked to take our pick, by the light of hurricane lanterns.[5]

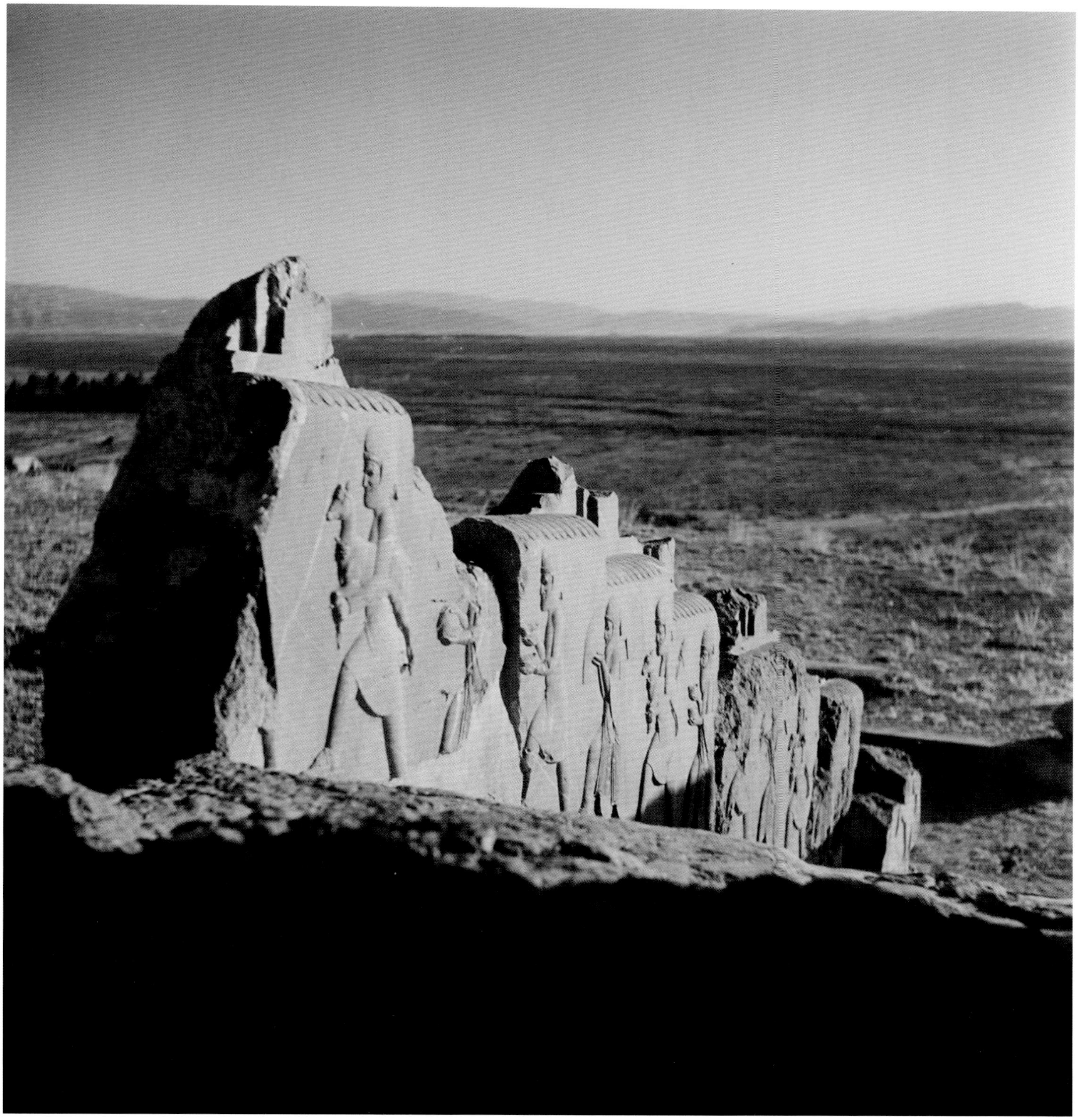

216. Staircase wall, Persepolis, 1949

Persepolis Bull
1949

Persepolis was once the magnificent ceremonial capital of the Persian Empire, which stretched from Greece to Afghanistan and from Libya and Egypt to western India. The building of the terrace and gigantic palaces began under the rule of Darius the Great (521–485 BCE), but the city was captured, looted and left in ruins by the army of Alexander the Great in 331 BCE. Throughout the 1930s, archaeologists conducted excavations at the site, uncovering parts of the city that had lain buried for over two thousand years.[1] Horst photographed Persepolis in the summer of 1949, during a month-long journey to the Middle East, which also covered the cities of Beirut, Damascus, Baghdad, Tehran and Isfahan. Afterwards, he travelled to the newly established State of Israel on a photographic assignment for *Vogue*.[2]

One of Horst's most poignant images from his Middle Eastern visit is *Persepolis Bull*, which depicts the head of a colossal stone bull in ceremonial dress. This elaborately carved creature was one of a pair that had flanked the northern portico of the 100-columned Throne Hall.[3] Guardian figures such as these were a common architectural feature of important buildings in ancient Persia. The bull's head measured over two metres high, and Horst's photograph conveys both the awe-inspiring scale and melancholy beauty of the ruined city. The rough texture of the ground beneath provides a contrast to the smooth grey limestone of the carving and the bright desert sun illuminates one side of the head, leaving the more damaged area and missing eye in shadow. Horst kept a diary during his travels and filled it with evocative descriptions, and occasional sketches, of scenes unlike anything he had previously encountered. He was especially struck by the quality of light and its effects at different times of day:

> Persepolis facing west, situated on terraced grounds on the foot of a hill overlooks a vast plateau surrounded by strangely shaped mountains, one of them in the shape of a giant tree trunk with root, others have wild leafy looking silhouettes. The rivers are still flowing but the dams are in disrepair and the plains dry. Before sunset the scene comes alive with dusk shadows and light colours ranging from dusty yellows and greens to innumerable shades of beiges and greys, touches of orange accentuated by occasional blue of the local inhabitants passing by on donkeys. ... The flat relief comes to life in the evening sun, outlining the figures with a sharp line and highlighting the polished stone.[4]

A variant of Persepolis Bull, showing a more face-on view, was published in American *Vogue* on 15 November 1949 alongside Horst's pictures of the bas-relief carvings, the ruins of the great treasury building, and a fragment of the capital of the tripylon (or triple gate).[5]

The publishing of the photographs coincided with the Shah of Persia's first visit to the United States. On seeing the article, Diana Vreeland – then fashion editor for *Harper's Bazaar* – was compelled to write a letter to Horst from her Madison Avenue office. Vreeland's typically exuberant prose reveals that, regardless of the supposed rivalry between the two magazines, she believed in commending talent: 'I cannot tell you how perfectly beautiful I think your pictures of Persia are. They are the most exciting and thrilling things that any of us have had to look at for years and years and years! Your trip must have been extraordinary. Millions of congratulations on these superb pictures.'[6]

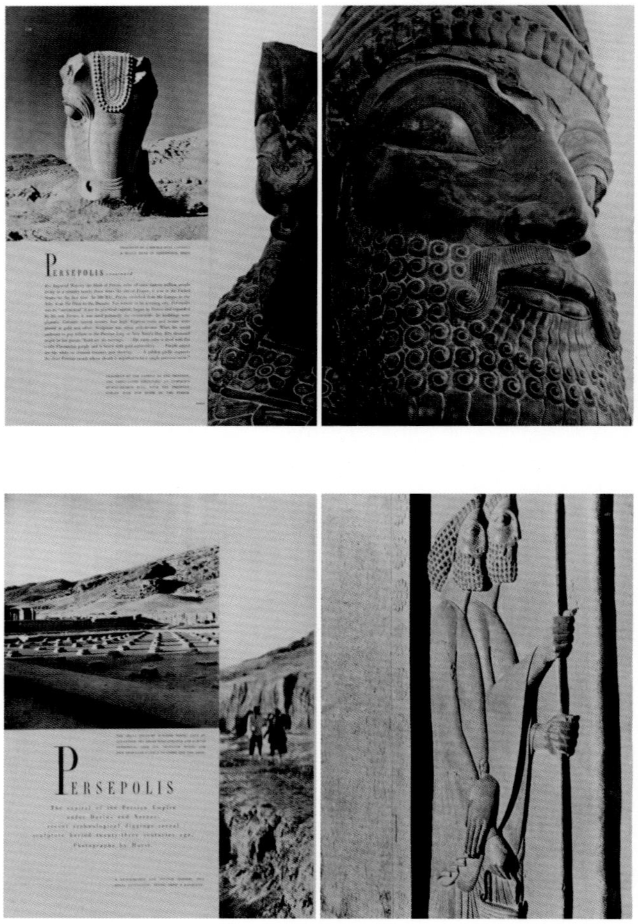

217. 'People and Ideas: Persepolis', American *Vogue*, 15 November 1949

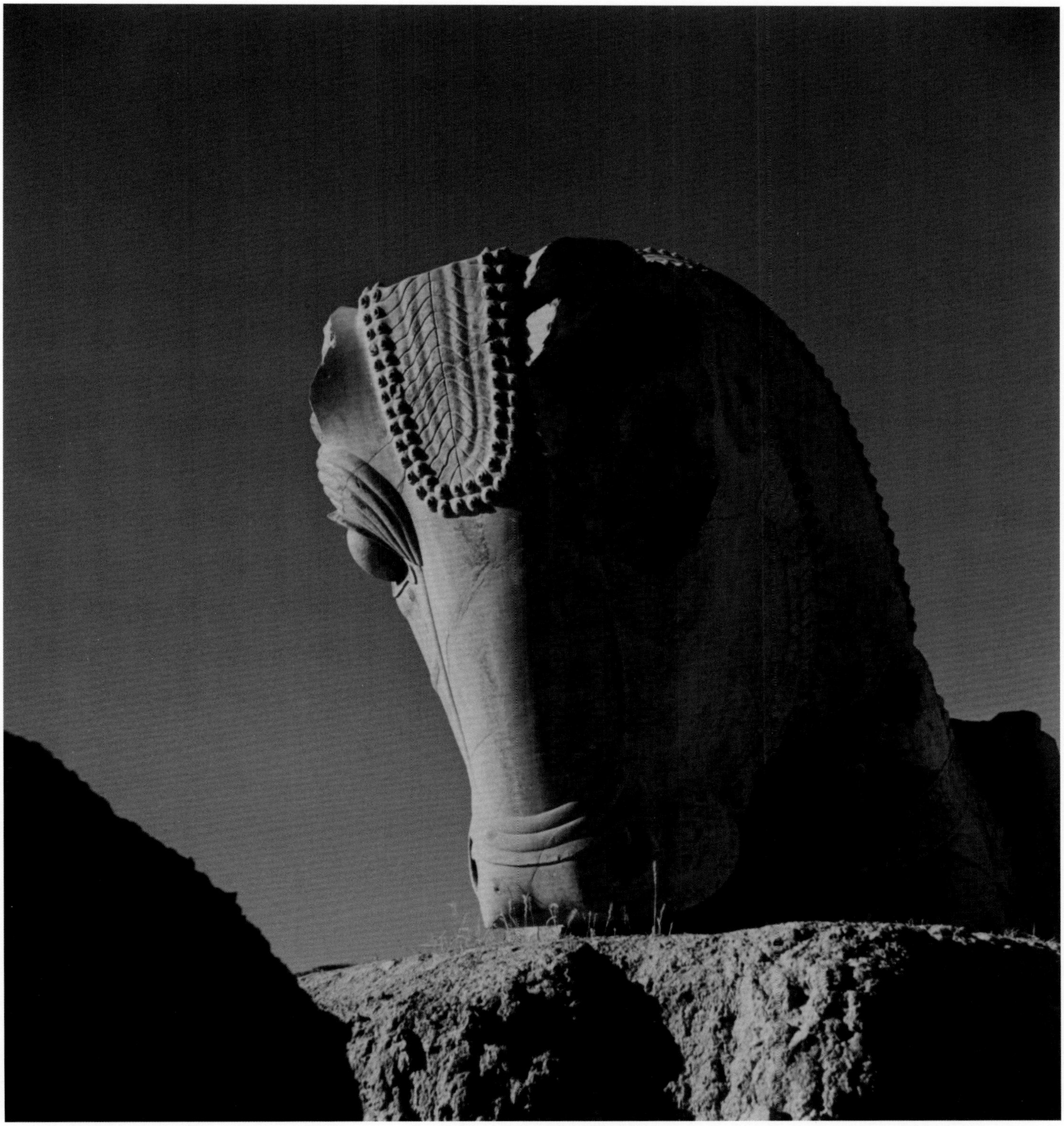

218. *Persepolis Bull*, 1949

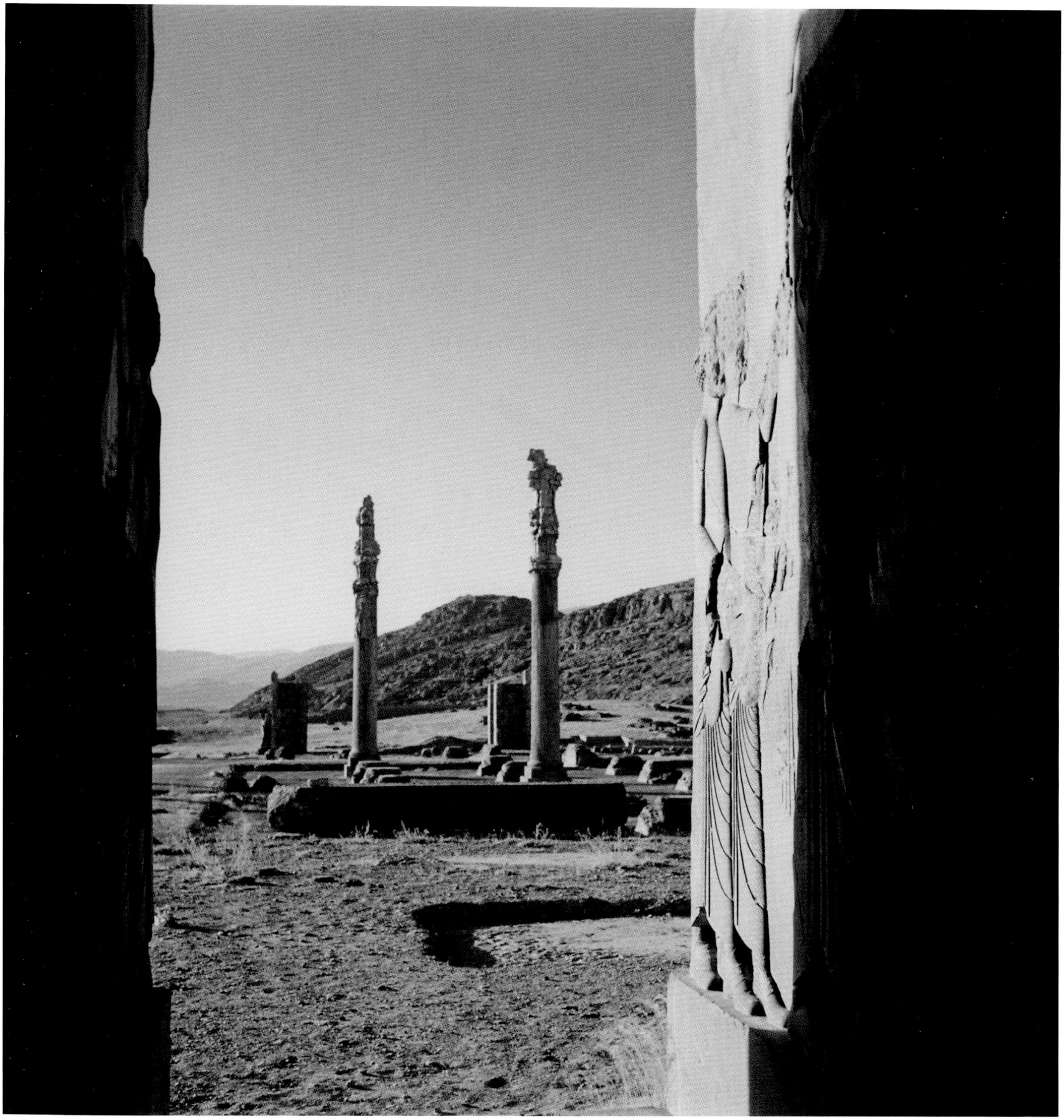

219. Palace of Persepolis, 1949

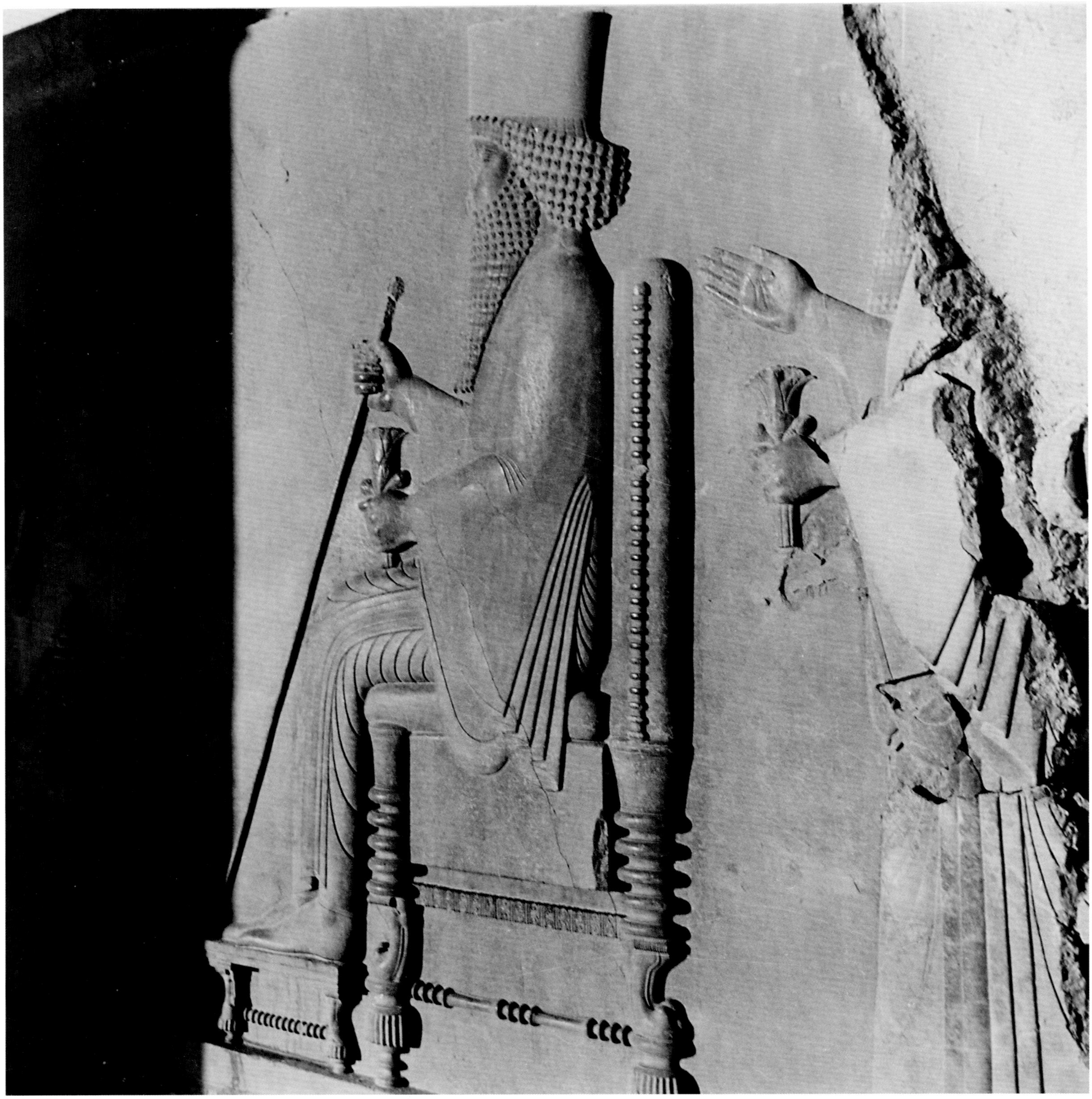

220. Bas-relief from the Palace of Xerxes, Persepolis, 1949

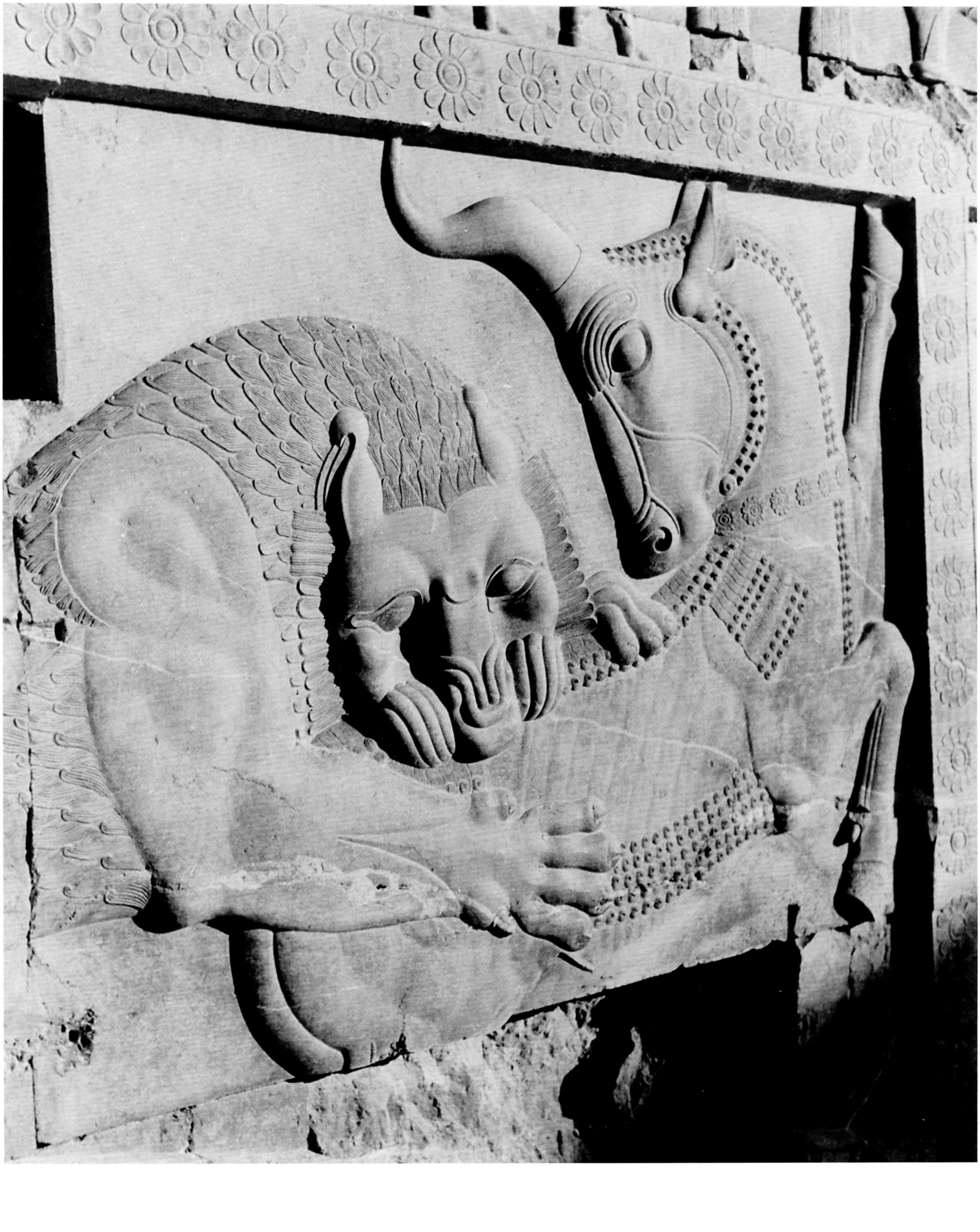

221. Bas-relief from the Palace of Xerxes, Persepolis, 1949

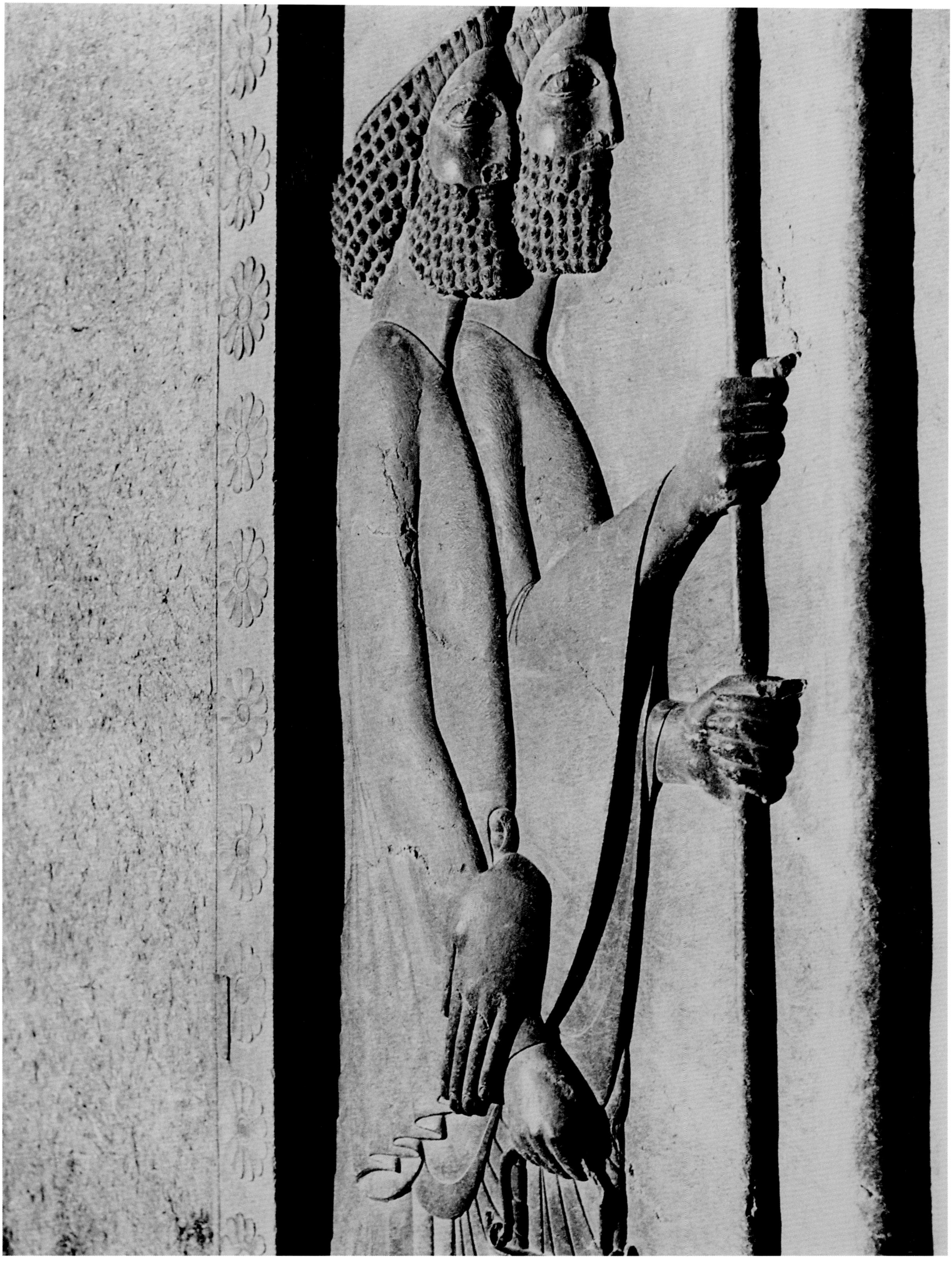

222. Bas-relief from the Palace of Xerxes, Persepolis, 1949

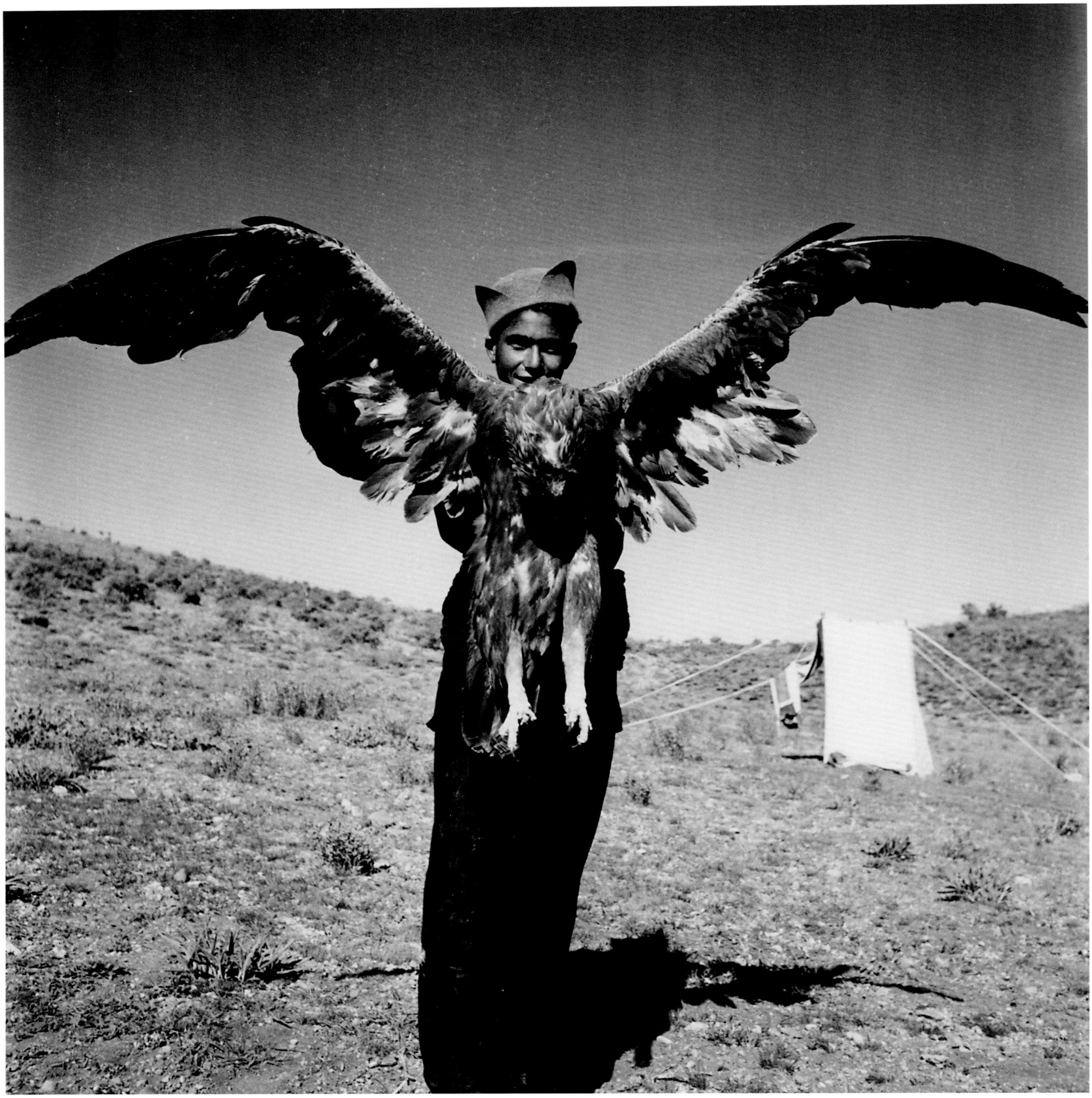

223. Boy with eagle, c.1949

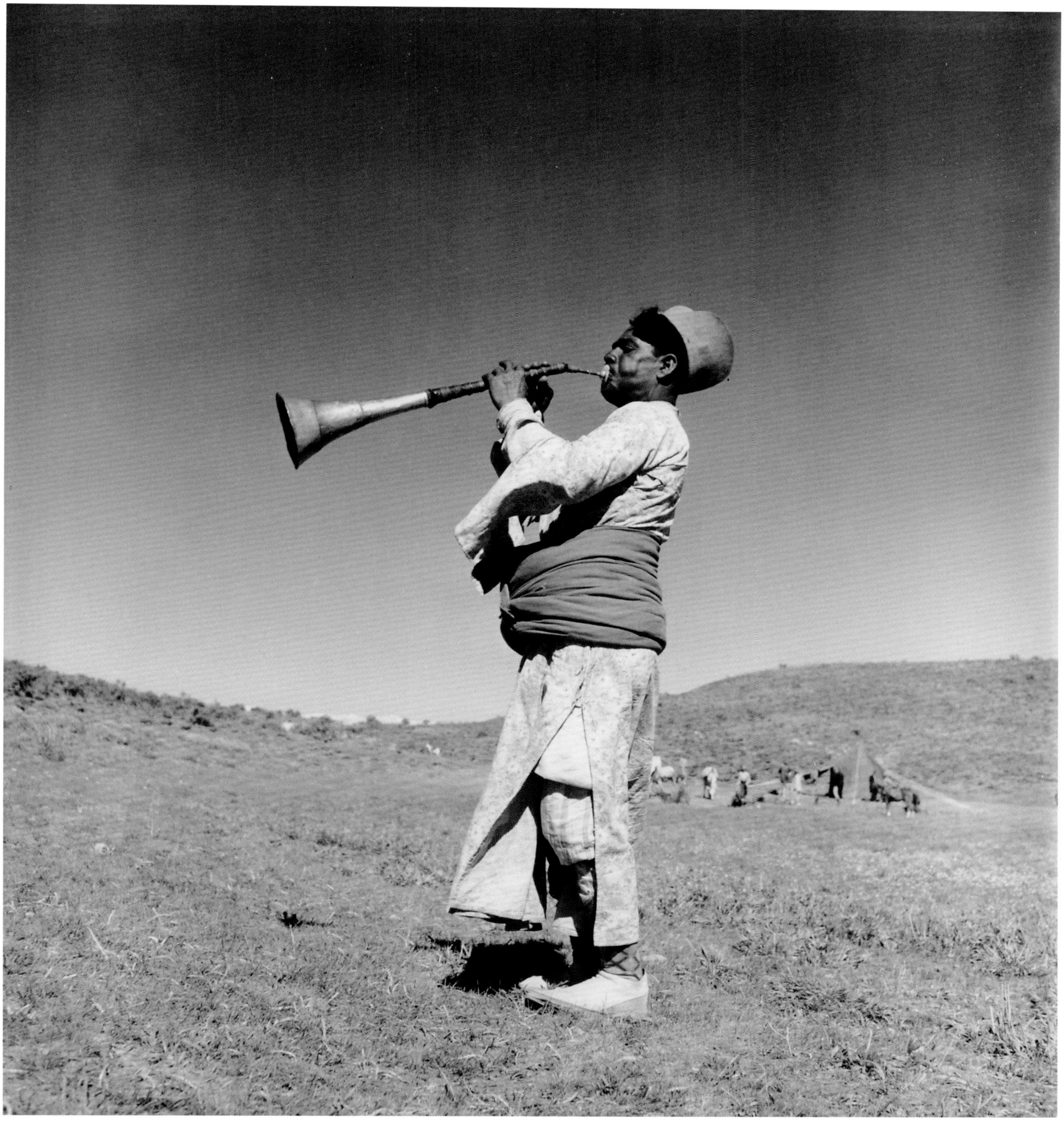

224. Qashqa'i trumpeter, c.1949

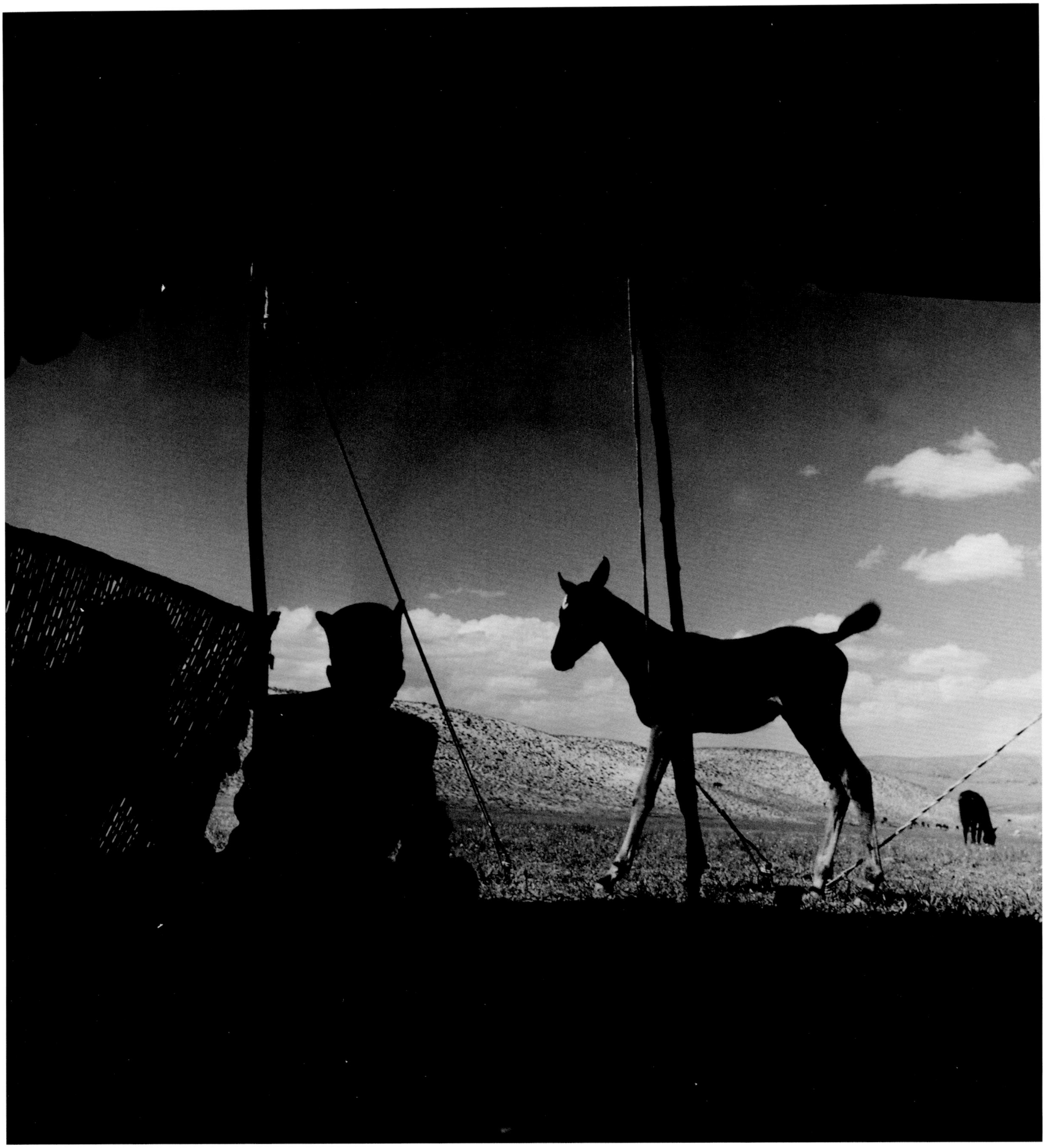

225. Colt and Qashqa'i tribesmen, c.1949

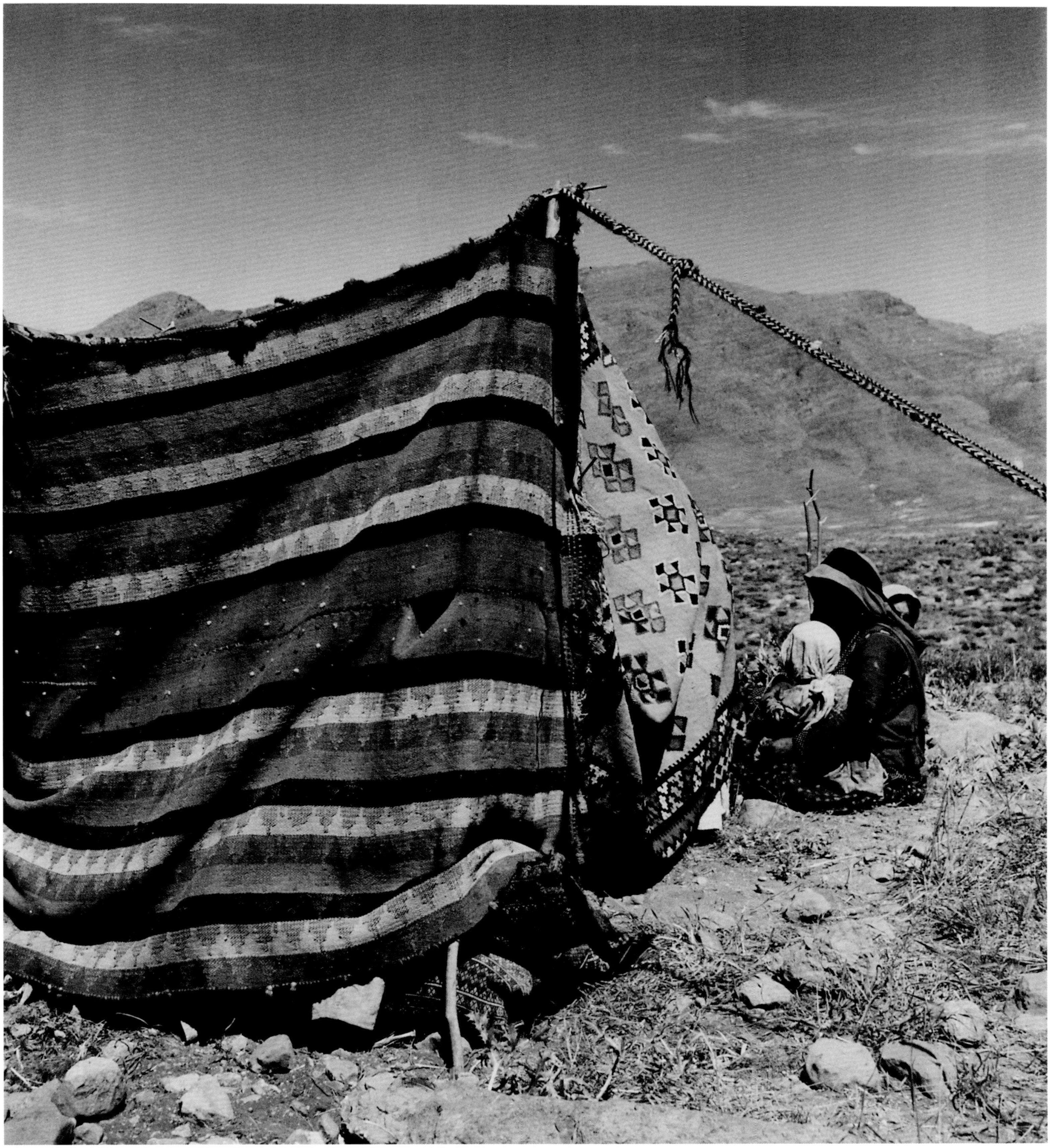

226. Qashqa'i camp, 1950

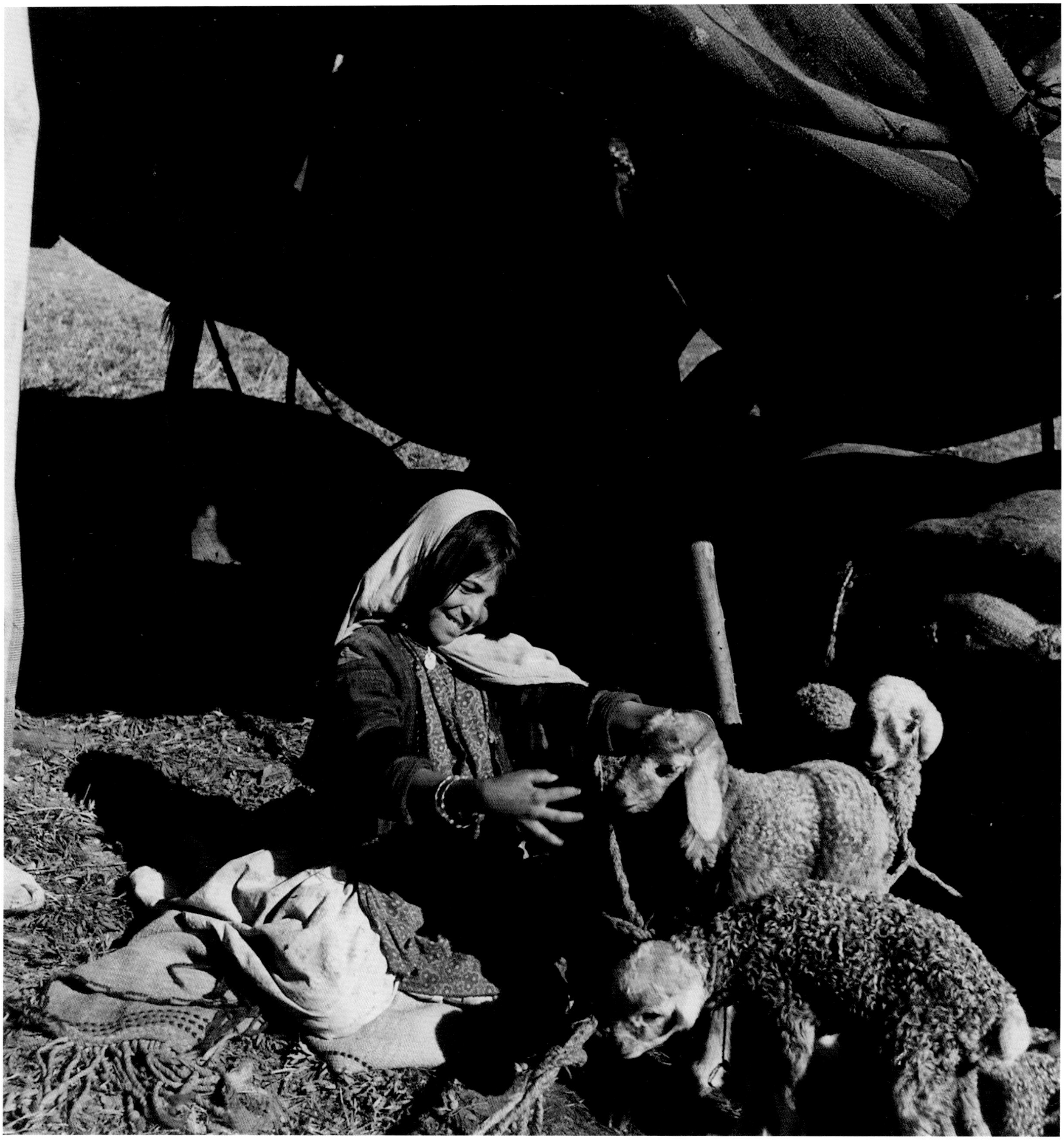

227. Young girl with sheep, 1950

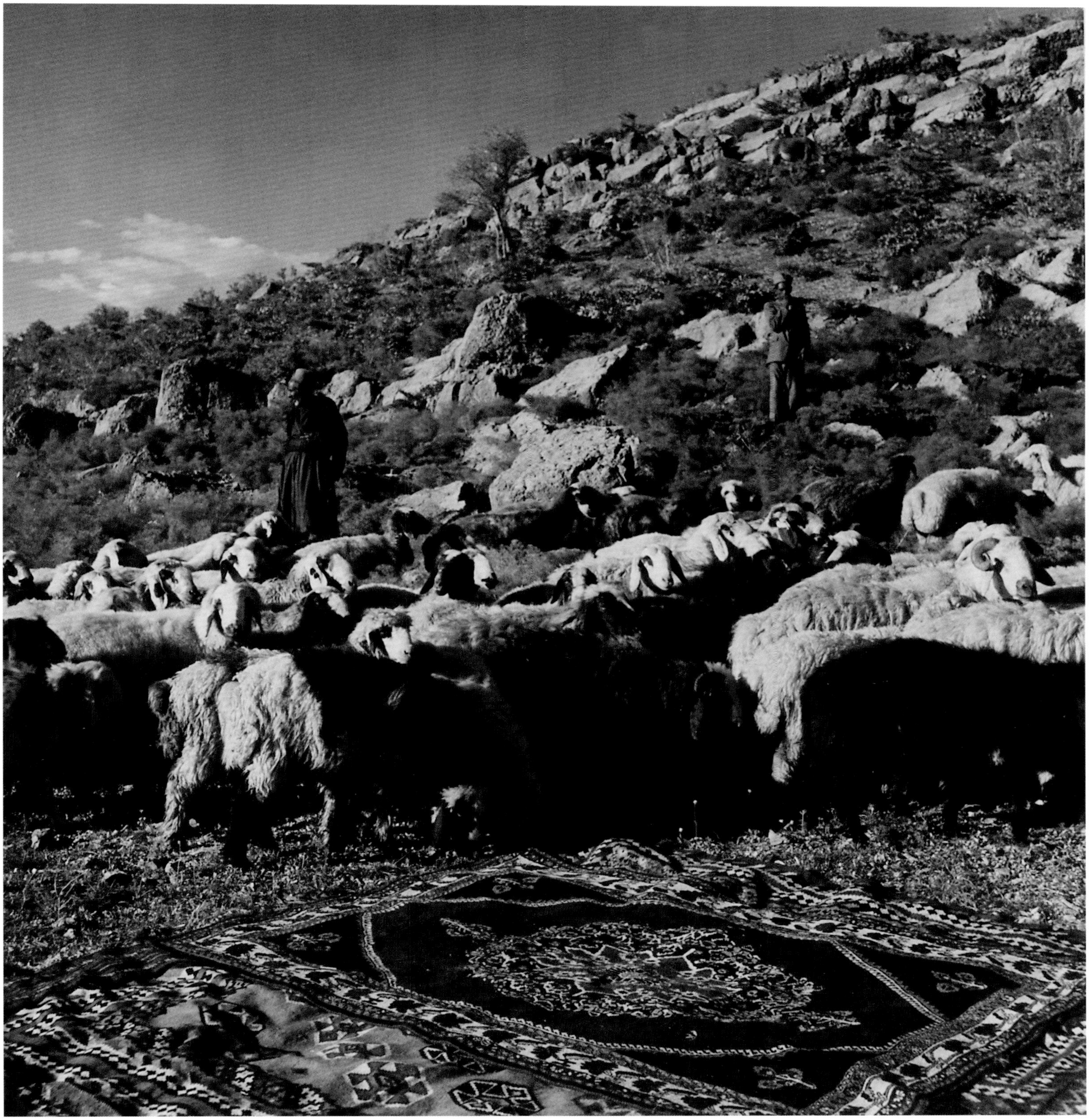

228. A Qashqa'i shepherd and his son, 1950

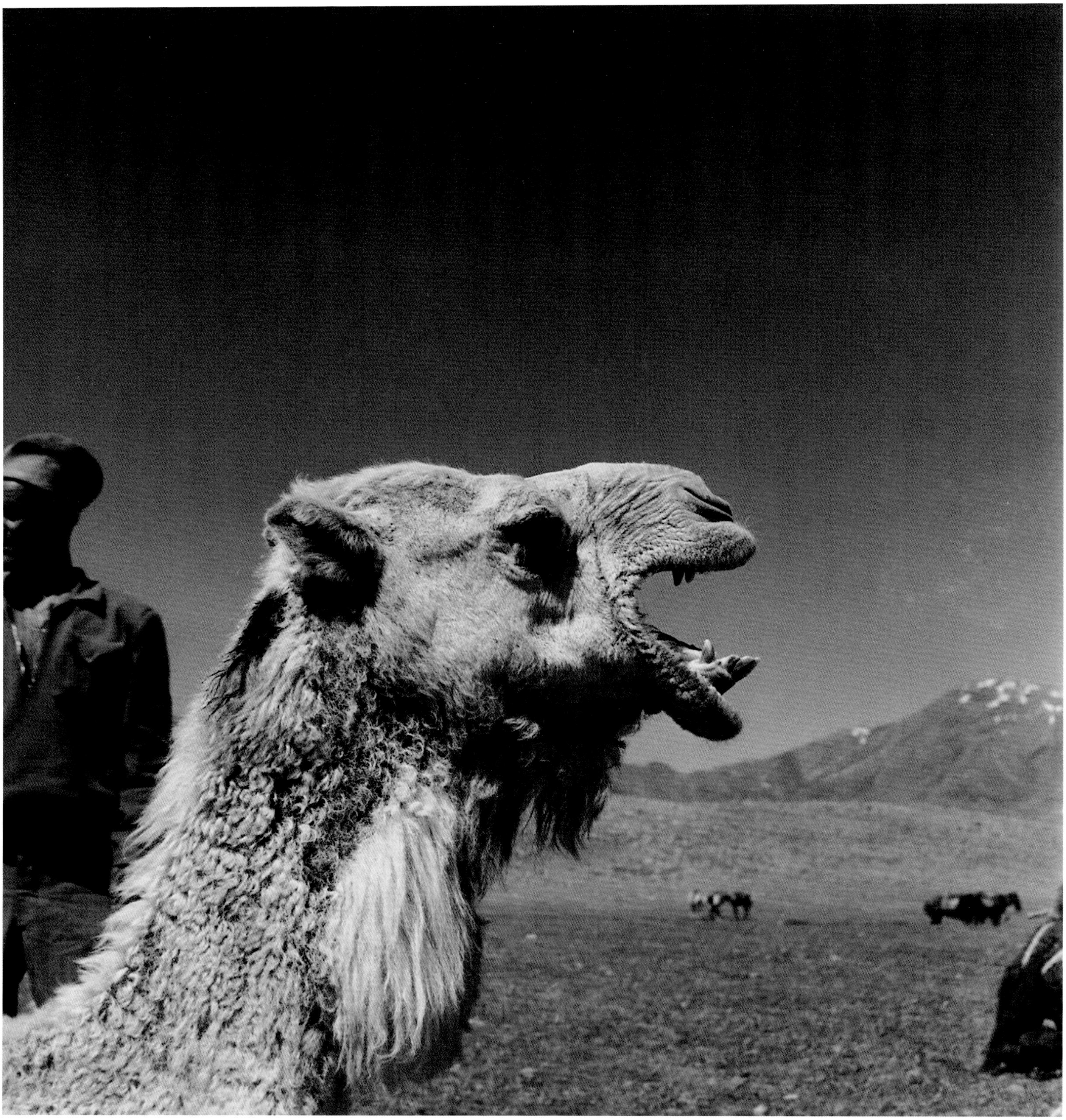

229. Camel, 1950

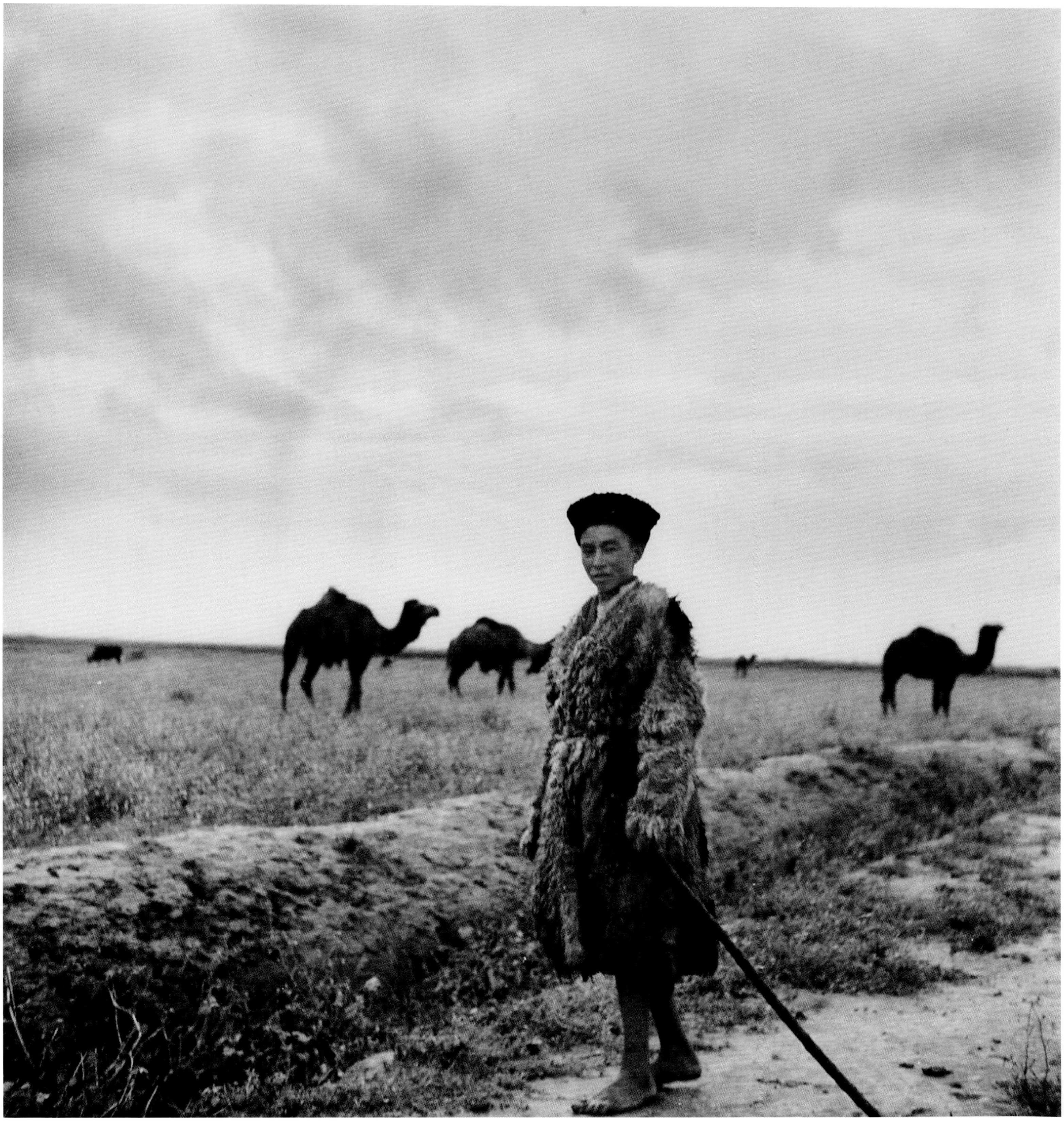

230. Turkoman boy on steppe, c.1949

VIII
The Male Nude

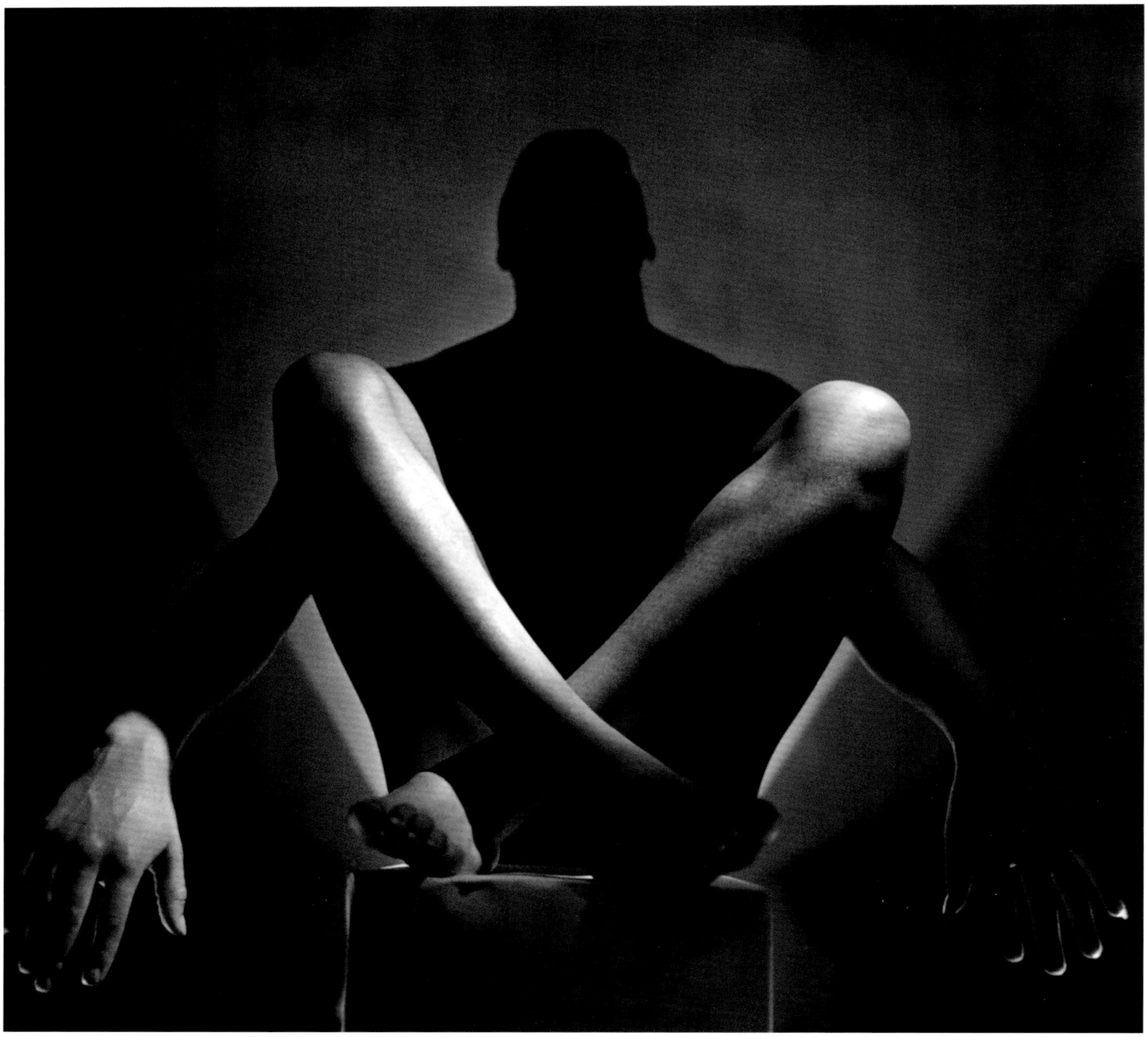

231. Male Nude, 1950

HARD BODIES: MALE NUDES

Oliver Winchester

Horst really was the twentieth century.

Eric Borman, 1999[1]

In the early 1950s Horst produced a set of distinctive photographic prints the subject of which was quite unlike much of his previous output. A series of male nudes with coolly detached titles, this set of figure studies was exhibited in Paris in 1953. Yet Horst's richly illustrated biography, written by his long-term partner Valentine Lawford and published in 1984, reproduces only one of these images and makes no reference to it in the main text. Full details regarding this exhibition remain stubbornly difficult to trace. Such an exclusion suggests, one might therefore assume, that this seemingly uncharacteristic suite of works might be of less significance than Horst's widely appreciated fashion photography.

Yet the impact of these images can clearly be seen in the work of many later photographers who turned their attentions to the male body, most notably Robert Mapplethorpe (1946–89), the controversial *enfant terrible* of the 1980s New York art world. The auction catalogue for the sale of Horst's estate following his death in 1999 contains a series of quotes relating to the photographer, including one by art historian Martin Kazmaier, who declares that 'Mapplethorpe ... learned so much from Horst.'[2] Indeed, in 1989 Mapplethorpe produced a portrait of Horst, who cuts a dashing bronzed figure, sunglasses in hand, leaning against one of Mapplethorpe's Mission-style chairs. What then links Horst, a photographer who spent his career working at *Vogue* producing images of elegance and glamour, with an artist whose brutal images of black nudes and homosexual sadomasochist practices were reviled by Senator Jesse Helms as 'promoting homosexuality'?[3] Perhaps Horst's small series of male nudes packs a far weightier punch than might first appear?

Horst was a homosexual and as such the opening chapters of Lawford's biography are lightly spiced with barely coded amusing anecdotes. Living briefly in Frankfurt as a youth, Horst, we are told, modelled for a 'Herr Professor who painted him in oils as Saint Sebastian, nude and tied to a post'. But 'in the middle of a sitting a woman whom [Horst] took to be the professor's wife arrived unexpectedly; and [Horst] never saw the painter, or the portrait, again.'[4] These descriptions are generally couched in terms of innocent 'chance encounters [and] stray smiles', many of which were politely rebuffed by Horst.[5] Upon his arrival in Paris for the first time in 1930, for example, 'sex beckoned from every sidewalk and life waited to be discovered down every street' providing 'the pleasure of *just looking* [that] kept [Horst] happily occupied for several weeks'.[6] Horst's subsequent and long-lasting relationships, first to his mentor George Hoyningen-Huene, followed by the aristocratic Count Luchino Visconti (pl.234) and later Valentine Lawford himself, are expressed as an intimate mutual support of like-minded aesthetes. Yet the cautious openness of this biography was only possible from the position of the 1980s. Prior to the seismic shift achieved by the gay liberation movement of the early 1970s, Horst's sexuality, whilst an open secret that is undeniably present as a stylistic subtext in much of his photographic work, was at most inferred and certainly did not constitute his subject matter.[7]

Yet as art historian Allen Ellenzweig has written, 'the homoerotic photograph is not a separate stylistic category. Rather, as an area of inquiry into feeling between men, the homoerotic photograph reveals social conventions of a given period while being open to the stylistic influences of the time'.[8] In other words, homoerotic images constitute a double trace, holding within themselves evidence of both an aesthetic style and social meaning. Such images do not simply capture reality in photographic emulsion but are part of a social process in themselves. Horst's images are thus as much an active social document as they are part of his wider *oeuvre*.

Horst's working life spanned the history of the homosexual as an identifiable category. In 1930 he embarked on a short-lived and unsatisfactory career as an architectural draftsman for Le Corbusier prior to picking up a camera for the first time. At this same moment Brassaï (1899–1984) was documenting the Parisian demi-monde, work that was later published as *Paris de Nuit* (1933) and included some of the very first images of homosexual social networks. Horst's death came only a few years after the emergence of Queer theory, a strident iconoclastic academic concept that 'reflected the loss of faith in the coherence of "gay" or "lesbian" identity' and that problematized conventional notions of sexuality and gender as a whole.[9] It was midway between these poles, during the 1950s, at a moment famously described by Marxist historian Eric Hobsbawm as 'the great transformation', that Horst photographed his male nudes.[10]

In the early 1950s McCarthyism was it its height in the United States and the associated 'lavender scare' asserted that the 'enemy within' was not merely communist but included homosexuals. In fact a policy of exclusion resulted in a far higher number of dismissals from public office for homosexual men than suspected communists.[11] In France, President de Gaulle's administration retained the repressive policies of the Vichy government and

France would, by the end of the 1950s, characterize homosexuality together with tuberculosis and alcoholism as a 'social plague'.[12] Any sexualized public expression of homosexuality would therefore have been of great professional risk to a photographer of international fame. Indeed, George Platt Lynes (1907–55), a contemporary of Horst who shared a similar sensibility, was subject to the same social pressures. Platt Lynes, too, photographed the male body, most famously the dancers who performed in the 1950 New York Ballet production of *Orpheus*. The choreographer George Balanchine, describing the work of his long-time friend in terms that could equally apply to Horst, noted that 'Lynes's secret was his sense of plasticity, his genius for lighting in space so that his bodies seemed to exist in an actual aery ambience, akin to the three dimensional vitality in sculpture.'[13] Yet Platt Lynes's published work, despite its homoeroticism, was able to rebuff accusations of egregious sexual content due to its anchoring within the culture of dance. The use of Homeric allusion and the trappings of the classical past acted as a weak foil, both moral and sexual, to the depictions of youthful beauty. Yet whilst dance and the images that surrounded it permitted 'gay men to believe that beauty has a primary legitimacy', Platt Lynes's starkly sexualized photographs of men remained hidden, were circulated privately or published in European magazines under a pseudonym.[14] At the end of his life Platt Lynes destroyed the negatives of his commercial and exhibition photographs, handing over the negatives and prints of this private work to the sexologist Alfred Kinsey, forming a record of 'the homosexual aesthetic'.[15]

Clearly Platt Lynes's work was subject to an artificial and imposed division between his public face and private desire. Indeed, such a division and carefully controlled response can be seen in two images of the young Horst taken by Huene, which are reproduced on opposite pages of Lawford's biography of Horst (pl.235). The first, more conventionally acceptable, image captures Horst at a low eye level in a heroic pose in bright sunlight, an image that clearly references classical statuary. The second, captures a seemingly private moment of enjoyment as a naked Horst sits astride a cast of a classical horse's head, riding the sculpture with his right arm pulled back, fist clenched. Both captions attempt to deflect accusations of impropriety through reference, one to the classical past, the other to professional photographic experimentation. Horst astride a horse is captioned 'The lighting here was brand new. We had tried to duplicate the lighting of the Acropolis at sunset', thereby linking this image to technique rather than any possible sexualized interpretation.[16] The statuesque image is captioned 'Both George and I had this extraordinary feeling about Greece. The physical beauty of the men and women, the sun and the fresh air and the sea.'[17] In both cases, and through different mechanisms and references, the private is to some degree or other eschewed in favour of something veiled, coded and complex. As *Vanity Fair*'s Ingrid Sischy has noted, in reference to homosexual men and their difficult relationship with secrecy, 'privacy is a choice; it's about living your life the way you want to. Secrecy is usually a form of protection, but the safety if affords has the same relationship to freedom as being locked in an isolation chamber.'[18] Horst's biography retains a residual spectre of the closet, which hangs uncomfortably over two of the most erotically suggestive images of the youthful and beautiful photographer.

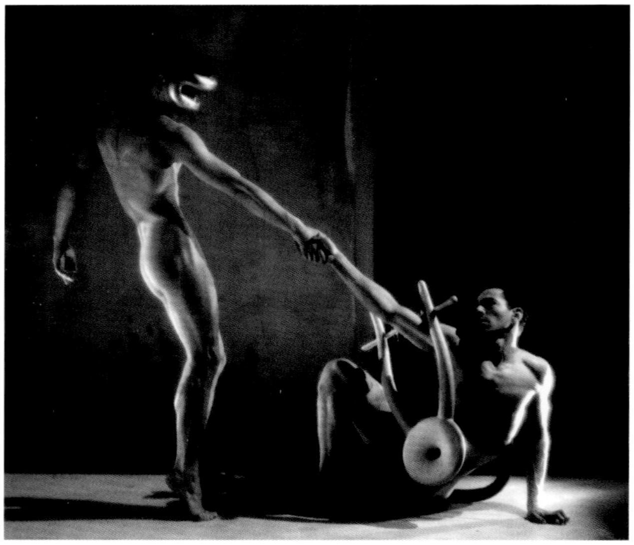

232. George Platt Lynes,
New York Ballet production
of *Orpheus*, 1950

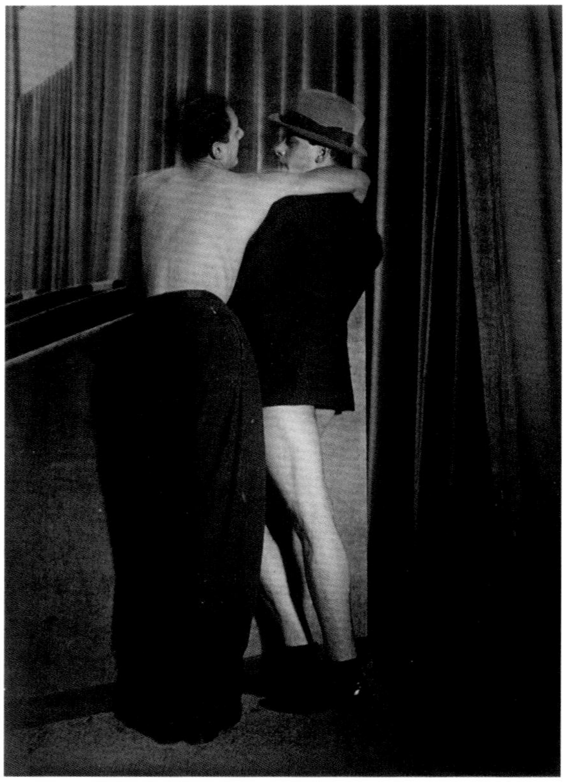

233. George Brassaï,
Young couple wearing a Two-In-One-Suit,
Bal de la Montagne, Sainte-Genevieve, Paris, c.1931

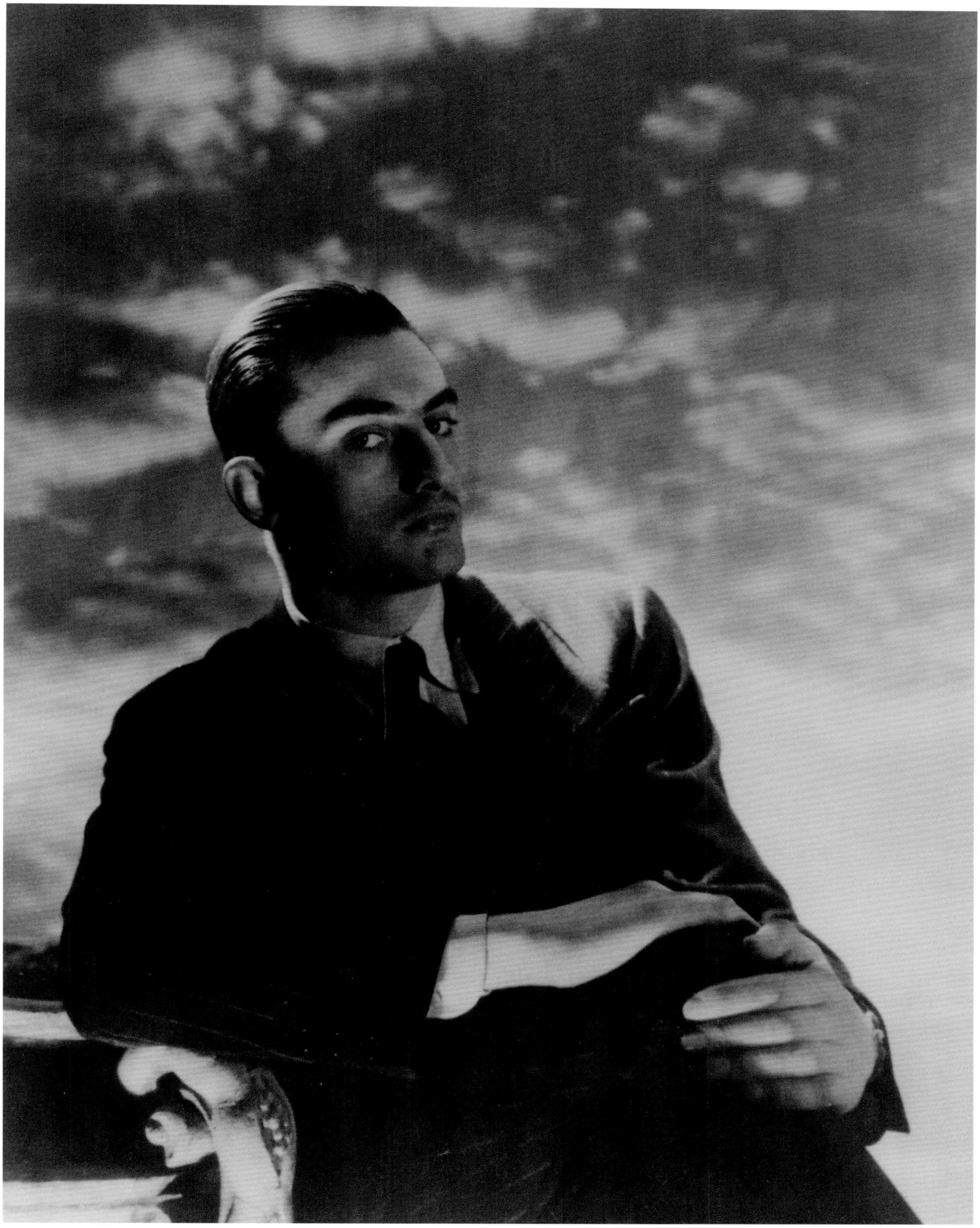

234. Luchino Visconti, Paris, 1936

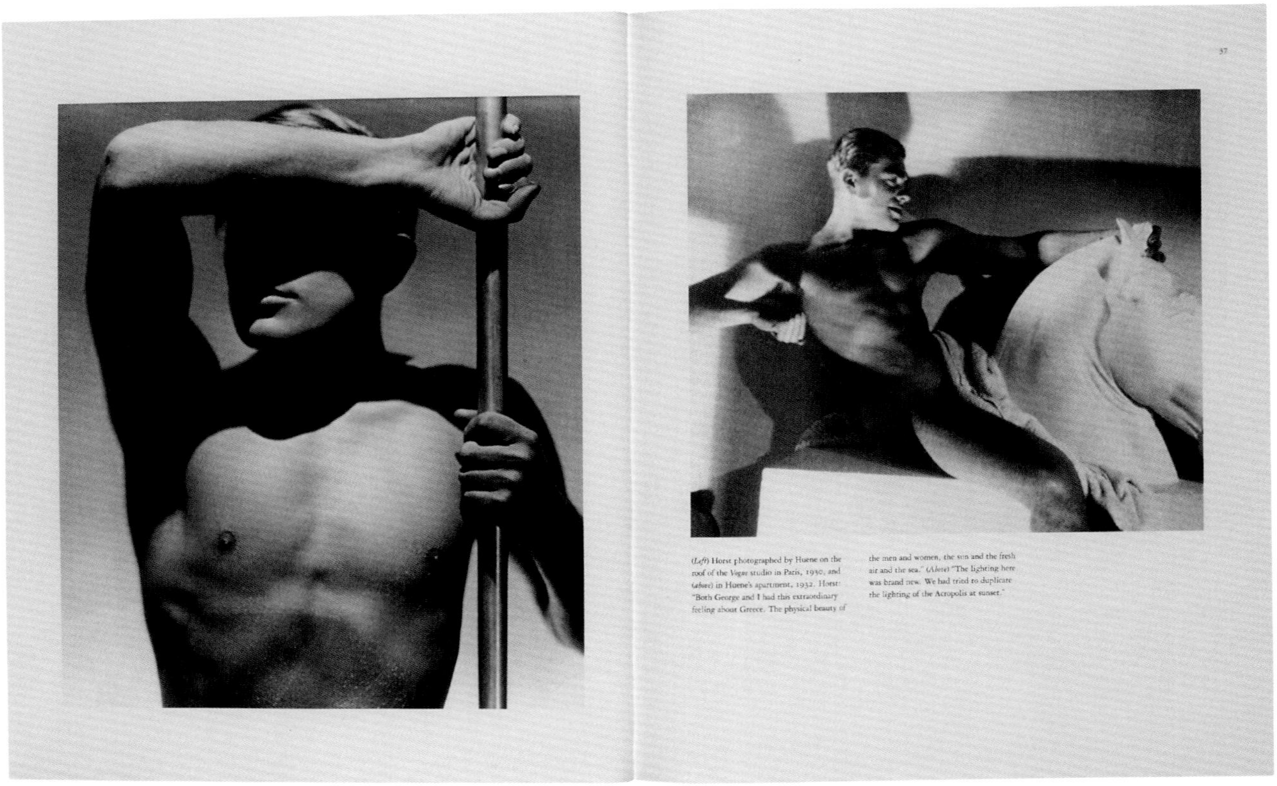

235. George Hoyningen-Huene,
Horst in 1930 and 1932, published in
Horst: His Work and His World, 1984

Yet the images Horst shot in the 1950s capture monumental and anonymous bodies in a sparse, dramatically lit studio setting, using an economy of form far beyond that employed by Huene or Horst's later contemporaries. These images are seemingly without allusion, pared down to the very minimum of association, using the techniques of commercial photography that Horst had developed at *Vogue* before the war and which constituted his aesthetic signature. Horst preferred to use spots rather than floodlights, which gave a greater tonal range, and his early use of cumbersome 10 × 8 inch cameras demanded that models pose for a number of seconds to ensure a clear focus, a stillness that remains visible in Horst's later work. Dr Mehemed Agha of American *Vogue* declared that through these techniques Horst 'takes the inert clay of human flesh and models it into the decorative shapes of his own devising. Every gesture of his models is planned, every line controlled and coordinated to the whole of the picture. Some gestures look natural and careless, because carefully rehearsed; the others, like Voltaire's god, were invented by the artist because they did not exist.'[19] As Horst himself declared of his stylistic development, 'my first pictures were loaded with background. Finally I realised the incongruous effect and began a series of strong black compositions that made a big splash on the magazine page ... I was still evading the issue ... so by elimination, I arrived at a clarity and simplification – which believe me, is harder to accomplish than the murky romanticism of yesteryear.'[20]

This clarity and simplification, as Horst acknowledges, was part of a wider turn towards the 'spectacle of modernity' that filled the pages of fashion and art magazines, using photography to describe modern dress, socialites, artists, performers and furnishings, 'all in a modern way'.[21] Readers were offered imagery of indistinct meaning that blurred modernity, aesthetics and sexuality to produce pictures the interpretation of which was heavily contingent on a particular viewer's reading of the signs. Isolating his subjects in space using only the simplest of studio props, Horst captures these men with a hard, sculpted intensity, achieved through the careful manipulation of light. He creates an image that is heavily formalized, abstracted and focused on geometry, in turn reducing the body to an object for contemplation as solid as the table or plinth on which it is posed. The desiring gaze is folded in upon the disinterested lens of the aesthetic.

Sigmund Freud wrote that 'the love of beauty seems a perfect example of an impulse inhibited by its aim. "Beauty" and "attraction" are originally attributes of the sexual object.'[22] Writing on the decadents of the early twentieth century, Ellenzweig notes that 'the reverence for beautiful things and people functions as a kind of asocial confirmation of the "outlaw" homosexual conditions. To be able to experience the world aesthetically sets in motion a conscious disregard for the "civilized" world's moral injunctions.'[23] Jean-Paul Sartre, writing of Jean Genet (himself a friend of Horst), stated that the aesthete's aim is to 'reduce the universe and man himself to the simple play of an imagination ... aestheticism does not derive from an unconditional love of the Beautiful: it is born of resentment. Those whom Society has placed in the background ... subtly attempt to reject a world which rejects them.'[24] Using the same eye that he employed for his fashion subjects, Horst disinterestedly crafts images of beauty, flattening out any implied homoerotic content and thereby sidestepping the conventions of allusion or classical reference employed by Platt Lynes. Where Platt Lynes's images were doubly hobbled, first by a need

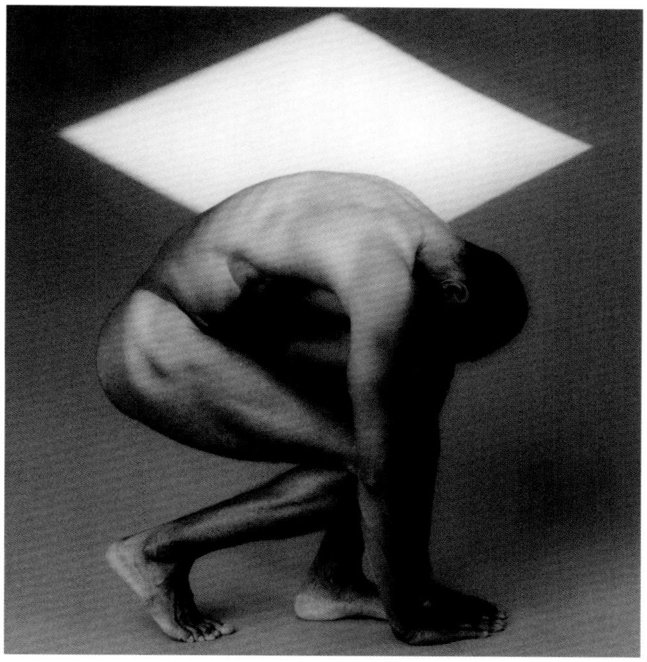

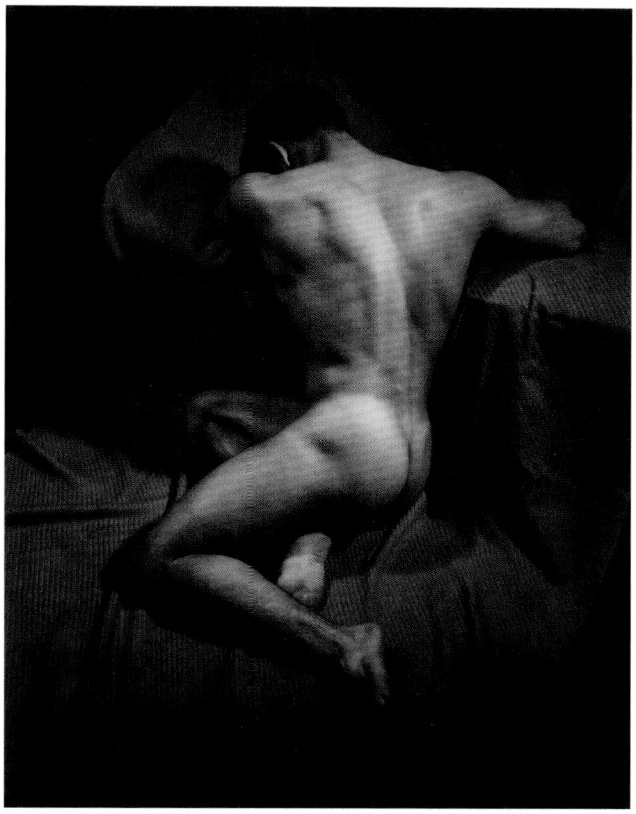

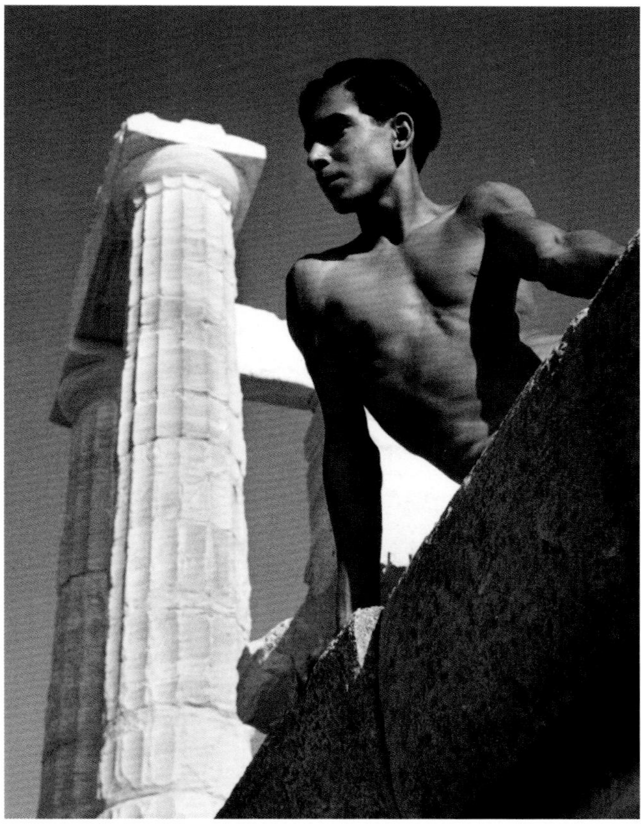

Top left
236. Robert Mapplethorpe,
Thomas, 1987

Above
237. Minor White,
Gino Cipolla, Portland, Oregon, 1940
Minor White Archive,
Princeton University Art Museum

Left
238. Herbert List,
Athens, 1938

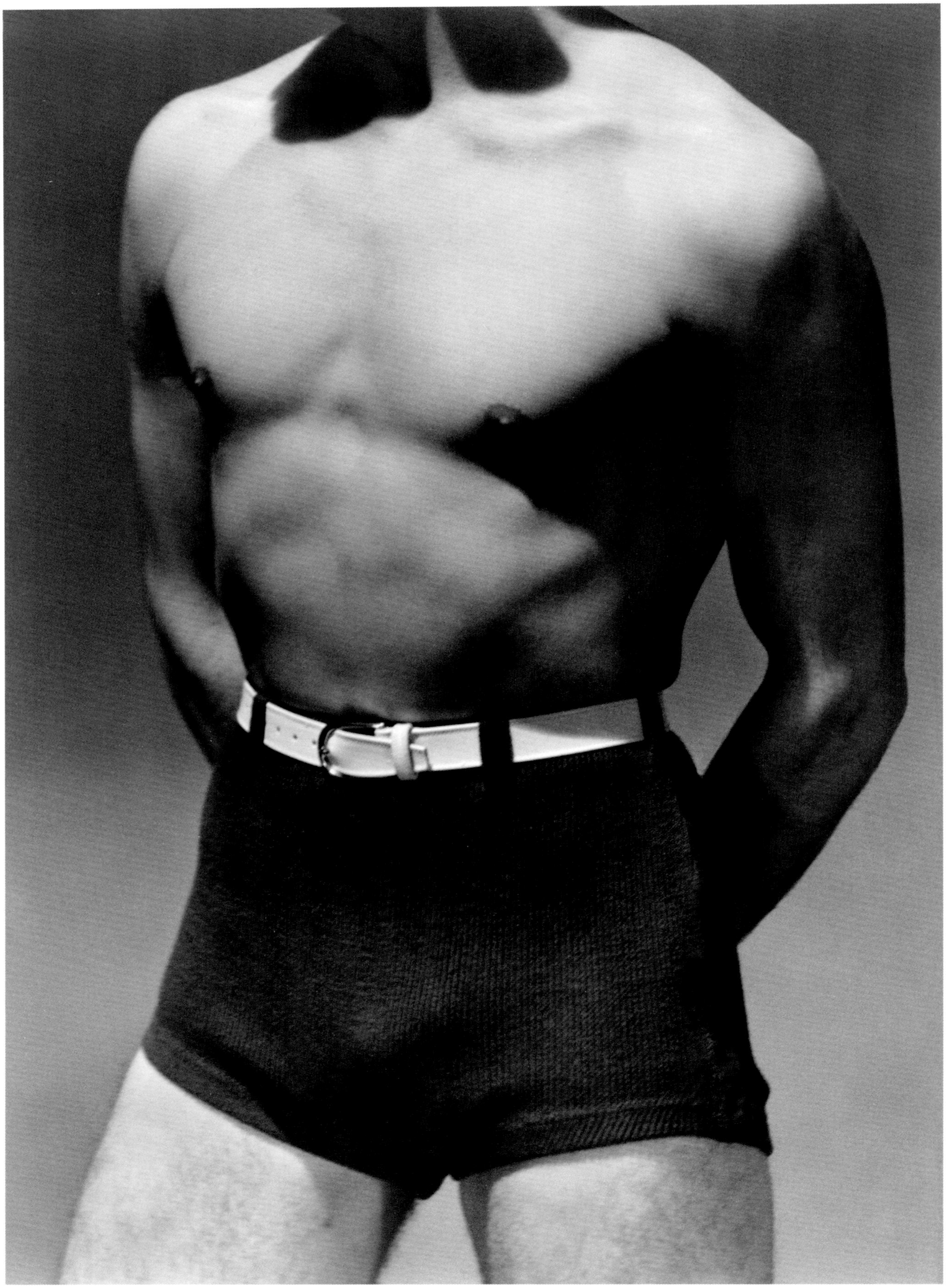

239. George Hoyningen-Huene,
Horst, 1931

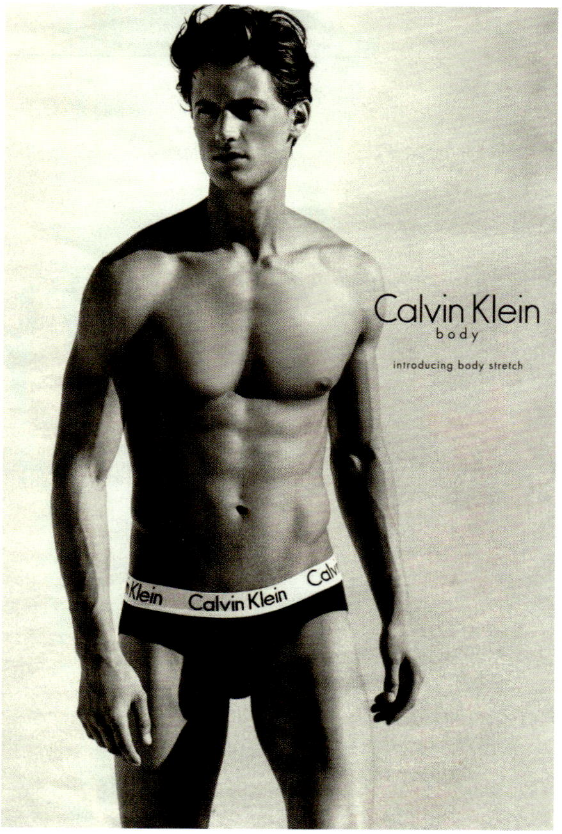

240. Bruce Weber,
Calvin Klein advertisement

to avoid homosexual reference and, second, by using a set of visual strategies that makes this avoidance explicit, Horst employed principles that were firmly rooted in commerce. Horst was thereby able to remove all allusion to the social content of these pictures, paring the photographs down by focusing on form alone. As such these images engage with a tradition of an appreciation of beauty for its own sake, a tradition that reached back to the close of the nineteenth century, a moment that coincided with the original naming of homosexual man himself. In this sense, then, the most significant aspect of Horst's suite of nudes is the way in which they deftly apply the foil of asocial commercial fashion photography to the socially charged arena of the male body. This is the use of allusion through its absence, crafted seemingly by technical means alone. And it is here that the link between Horst and subsequent photographers of the male body is most apparent.

Robert Mapplethorpe's work is distinctive for its lack of erotic subtext. Whilst Mapplethorpe said of his own photographs, 'I hope there's a certain kind of sensuality that goes through all of them', clearly the images he captures are highly stylized to the point of anaesthesia.[25] Form becomes content as Mapplethorpe points his camera at bodies that become objects par excellence, a style that led the critic Janet Kardon to suggest he 'might well be holding a chisel instead of a camera'.[26] With Mapplethorpe detachment has reached its natural conclusion, 'translated into a full blown moral vacuum'. Yet as Ellenzweig has pointed out, at the very moment of his infamy during the culture wars in the United States, 'it is an irony ... that Robert Mapplethorpe, of all people, should come to symbolize "gay photography" for he was the least involved in any realpolitik, gay or otherwise.' Ellenzweig pithily comments that 'a Mapplethorpe photograph may not be artless – just heartless.'[27]

Fashion-photography-as-style has now fully consumed itself and become a marketing strategy used by the unblinking eye of postmodern capitalism. This is best seen in the work of Mapplethorpe's contemporary, Bruce Weber (b.1946), who rose to fame with his luxurious and highly sexually charged images for Ralph Lauren and Calvin Klein. Weber's images are 'fully exploited to sell not merely a line of clothes, but an attitude, an aspiration, a dream of a way of living'.[28] With Weber, the gates were opened to 'physical and emotional desire [as] an analogue of consumer desire, and their images are calibrated to conflate the two'.[29] Indeed, in 1992 Weber described his response to Horst in a television documentary, stating that 'the elegance of his photographs ... took you to another place ... the untouchable quality of the people is really interesting as it gives you something of a distance ... it's like seeing somebody from another world ... and you wonder who that person is and really want to know that person and really want to fall in love with that person.'[30] It is in the untouchable nature of much of the photography that employs the male body in the service of fashion that one finds the true legacy of Horst's small suite of images. Whilst the bodies of 1953 were untouchable thanks to techniques that revelled in beauty for its own sake, safely distanced from the polluting complexities of social context, today these images function more as mementos from a time when desire was imagined in a manner more nuanced than it is today. After all, desire is a 'human event, not a stylistic quality'.[31]

The Classical Torso, Paris, 1932

This photographic study of a sculpted torso by Horst predates his male nudes by 20 years, but it might be described as the antecedent to that series, sharing an emphasis on idealized human form, minimal set and expressive use of light and shadow. Like the nudes of 1952–3, it represents 'an appreciation of beauty for its own sake.'[1] This inanimate figure is brought to life by dynamic lighting, while Horst's later faceless and monumental living nudes resemble marble sculptures. As Roxana Marcoci discusses in *The Original Copy: Photography of Sculpture, 1839 to Today*, the notion that a photographic image could be 'animated' is almost as old as the medium itself: 'With the transition from the daguerreotype, which is borne on a metal plate, to photographs on paper, the image became more vibrant, instilled with interiority and movement.'[2]

One of the earliest uses of photography was to document sculpture. For example, in the mid-nineteenth century, at the South Kensington Museum (later renamed the Victoria and Albert Museum), Charles Thurston Thompson and a team of Royal Engineers photographed artworks from both the Museum's collection and important pieces from other collections. Today, many of the photographs Thurston Thompson and his colleagues produced are prized not only as records, but also as works of art in their own right. Towards the end of the nineteenth century, cinema began to influence the manner in which sculptures were documented: 'photographs of portions of objects (close-ups) were most uncommon before the moving picture.'[3] In the 1920s and 30s, photographers became increasingly preoccupied with this mode of animist thinking: 'whether relatively independent or associated with schools or movements such as Dada, Surrealism, and the Bauhaus, [photographers] staged scenarios or captured situations in which either lifeless objects appeared as animate things or live models seemed petrified into statues.'[4] This photograph might be seen, therefore, to connect with Surrealism and the Bauhaus, as well as Horst's early fascination for classical forms and Mediterranean sunlight.

Handwritten text on the back of the vintage print provides some clues as to the photograph's original purpose; the pencil inscription reads:

> Classical Greek Statue, Paris, 1932
> Photo by Horst
> Made in France
> Sent on approval to Dr Agha

These short lines suggest that the picture was sent as an early sample of Horst's work from *Vogue*'s Paris office to the magazine's art director in New York, Dr Agha, a champion of photography, who wrote: 'The desire to make pictures is one of the very fundamental elements in human makeup, and satisfying this desire plays an important part in the pursuit of happiness to which we are all entitled.'[5]

The statue in Horst's photograph is a Diadoumenos, which literally translates as 'man binding his head'. It depicts a youth tying a ribbon around his head after a victory in an athletic competition. He appears calm and contemplative, standing in contrapposto with his head inclined to the right. The original ancient Greek Diadoumenos was crafted in bronze by the sculptor Polykleitos, in around 420 BCE. Numerous Roman copies exist, most carved in marble, but the version in Horst's photograph closely resembles a smaller terracotta statuette, dating from the first century BCE, which is more slender and graceful in its form than the bronze original. The terracotta was purchased by New York's Metropolitan Museum of Art at the end of 1932, and before then it was displayed in the Louvre, as an article in the *American Journal of Archaeology* explains:

> The Metropolitan Museum has acquired a terracotta copy of the Diadumenos of Polykleitos, 11 ½ inches high as preserved, dating from the late Hellenistic or early Roman period. The statuette was for a long time on loan at the Louvre in Paris where it aroused the admiration of visitors. It was probably found at Smyrna and belongs to the same group as a number of fragments found there which copy famous works of Greek sculpture. Like others of the group it shows traces of gilding and of yellow paint, which formed a basis for the gilding. It is one of the most beautiful versions of the Diadumenos which have come down to us ... The terracotta is a freehand reproduction on a small scale in which the artist embodies his own taste and conceptions.'[6]

Since Horst was a frequent visitor to the Louvre, he likely saw the statuette there and possibly bought a modern plaster copy of the famous work, in order to practise his lighting technique. Perhaps it was the strength of this image that led Horst to be invited by Dr Agha and Mr Nast to work in *Vogue*'s New York studio for six months. And so both the ambitious, handsome young photographer, and the victorious athlete he had photographed, travelled from Paris to New York for the first time in 1932.

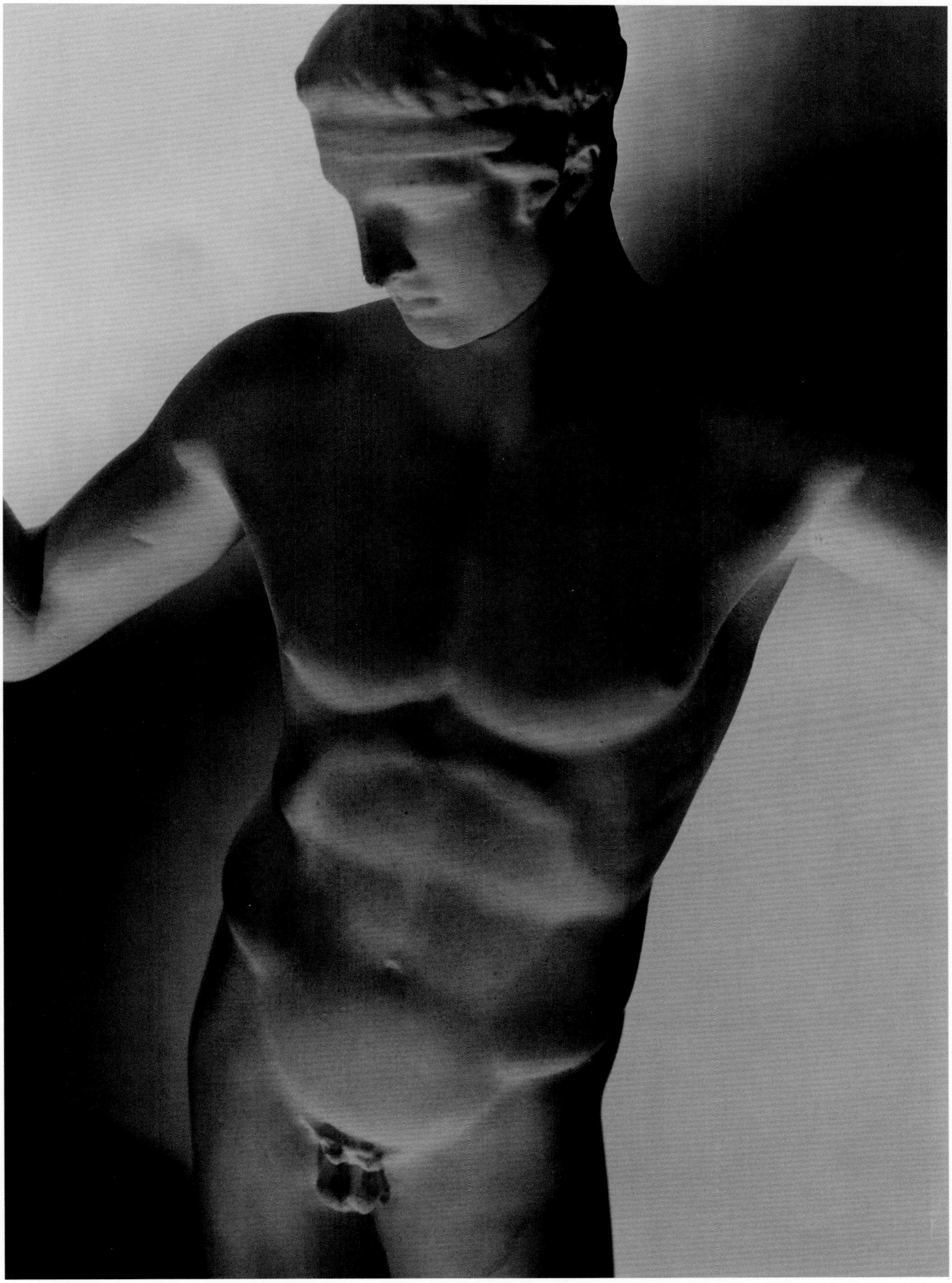

241. Classical Torso, Paris, 1932

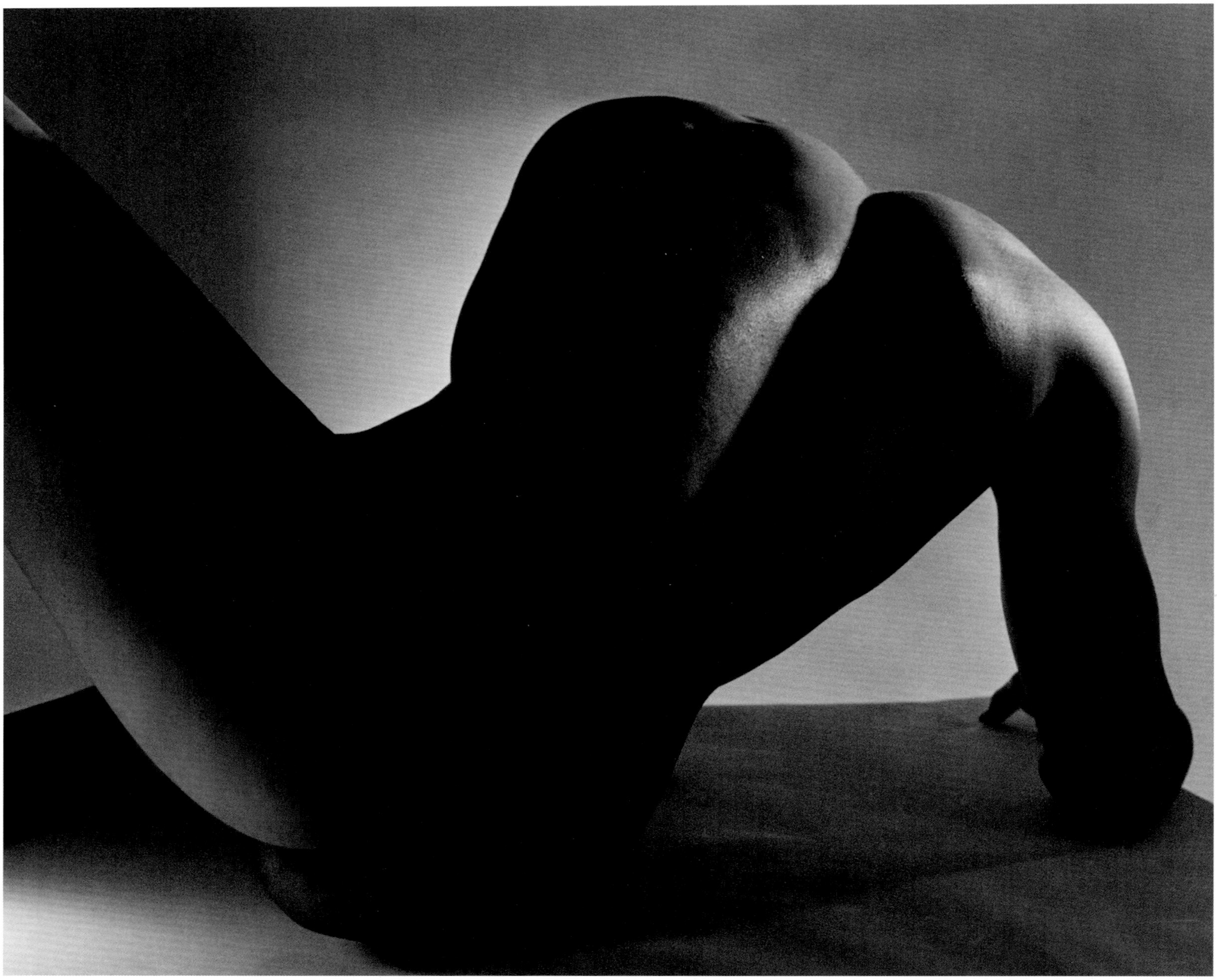

242. Male Nude, 1953

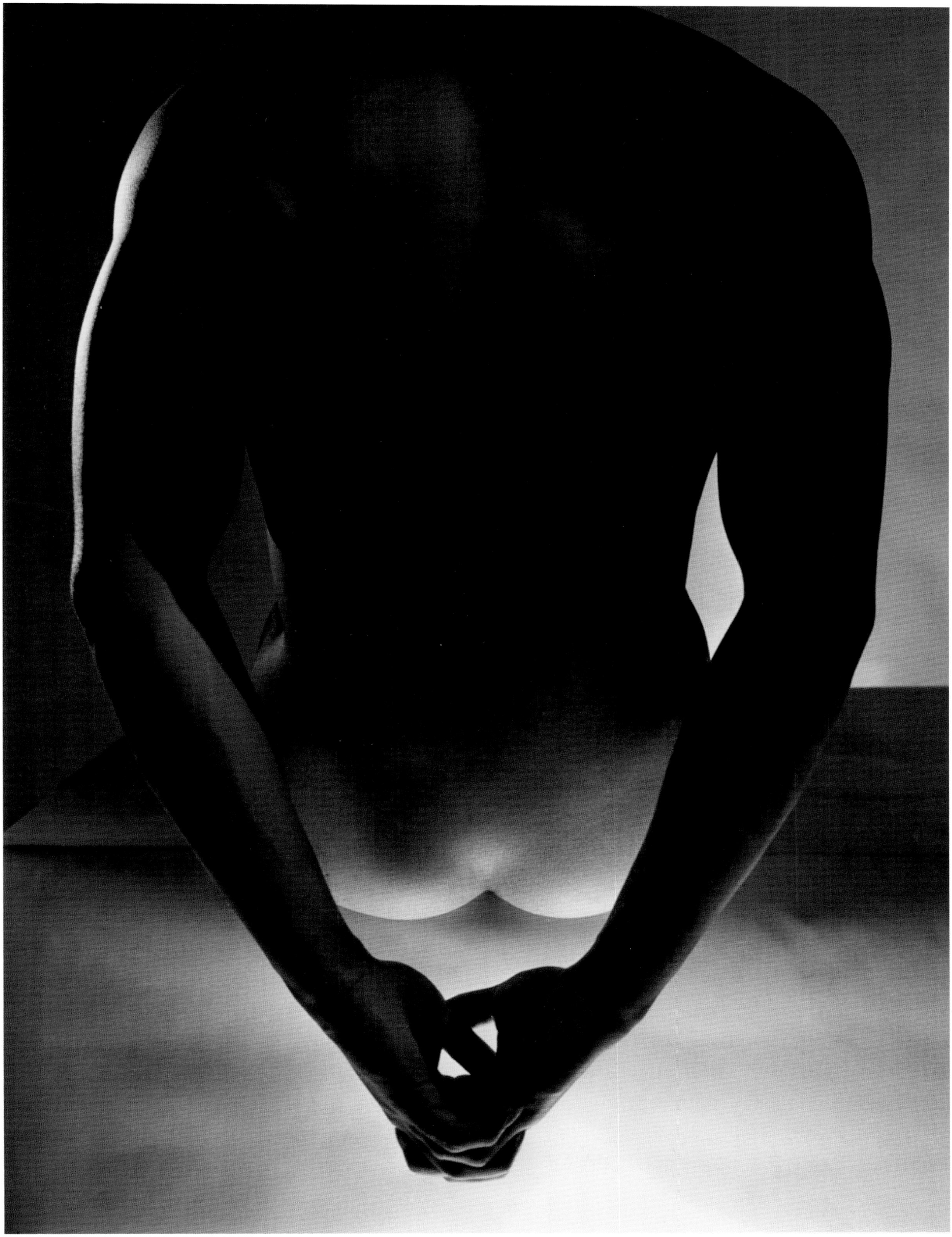

243. Male Nude, 1952

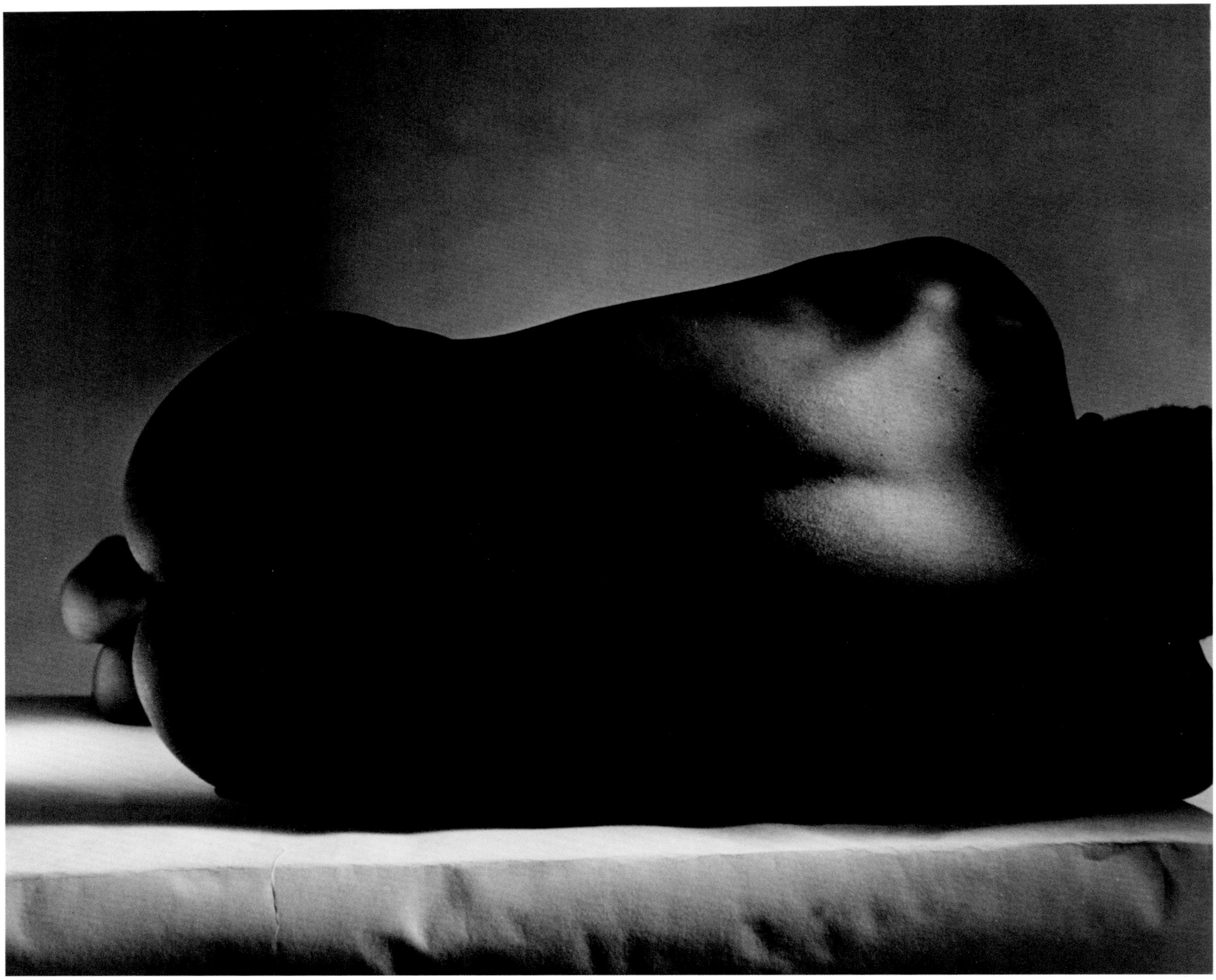

244. Male Nude, 1952

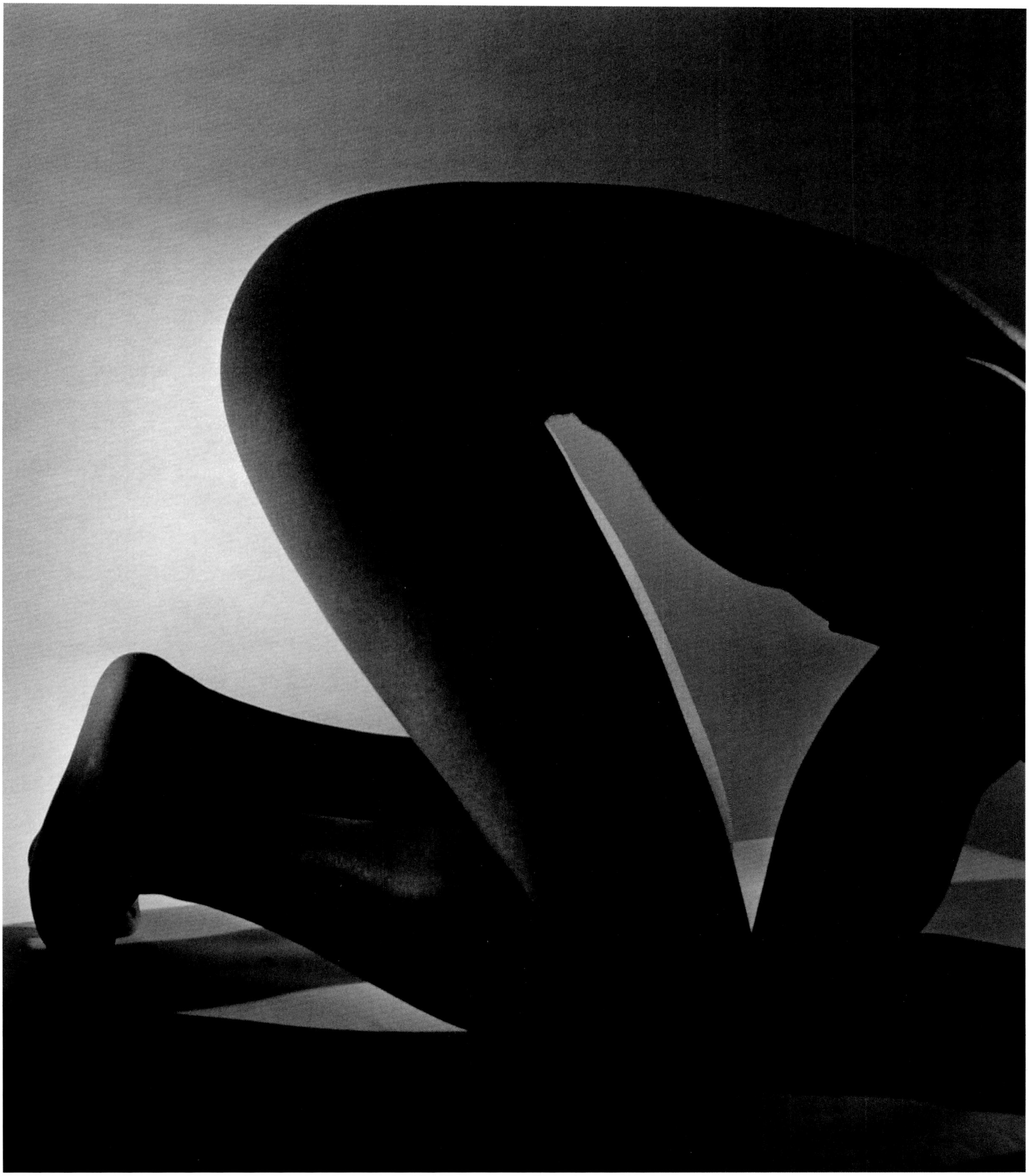

245. Male Nude, 1953

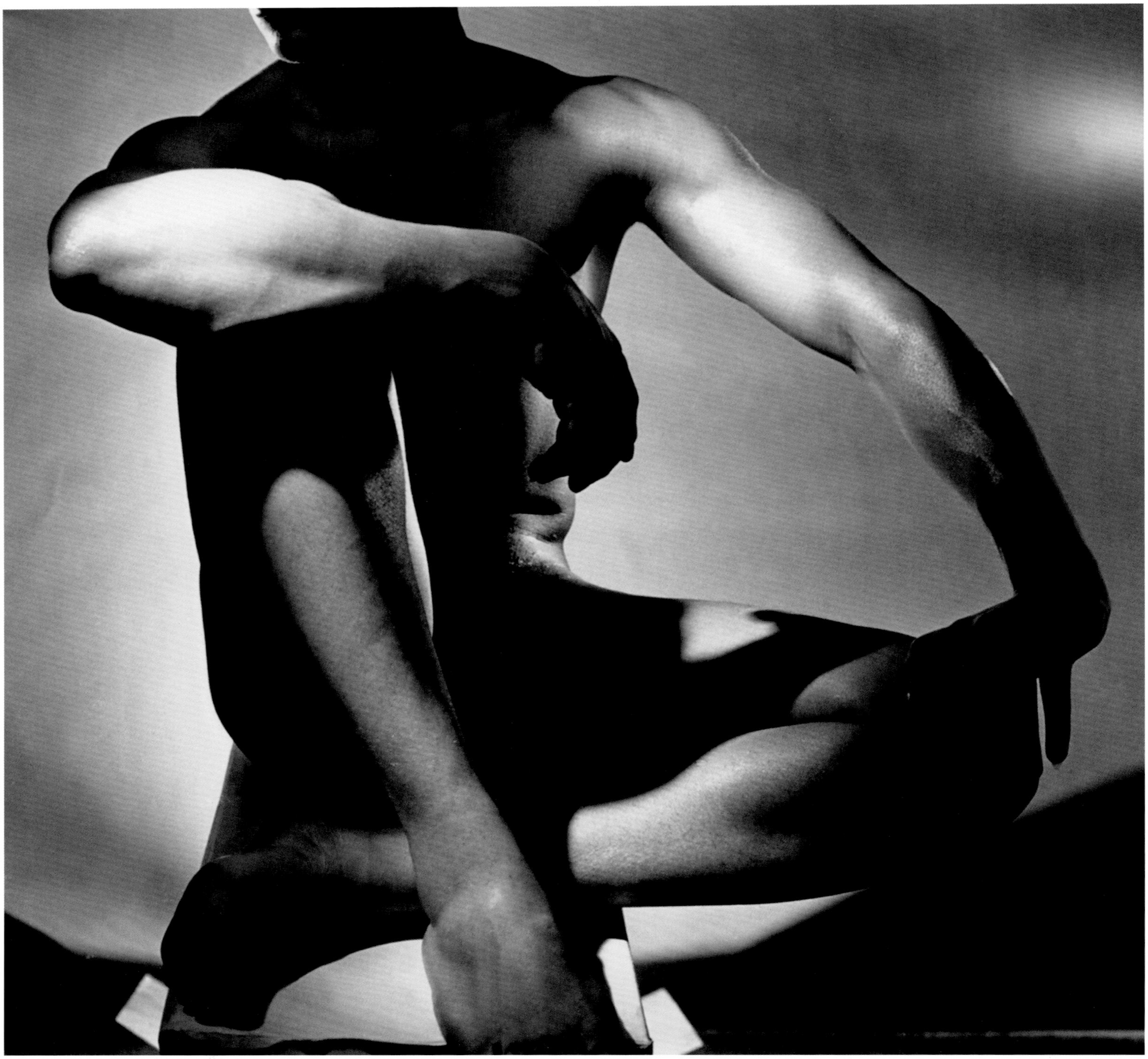

246. Male Nude, 1952

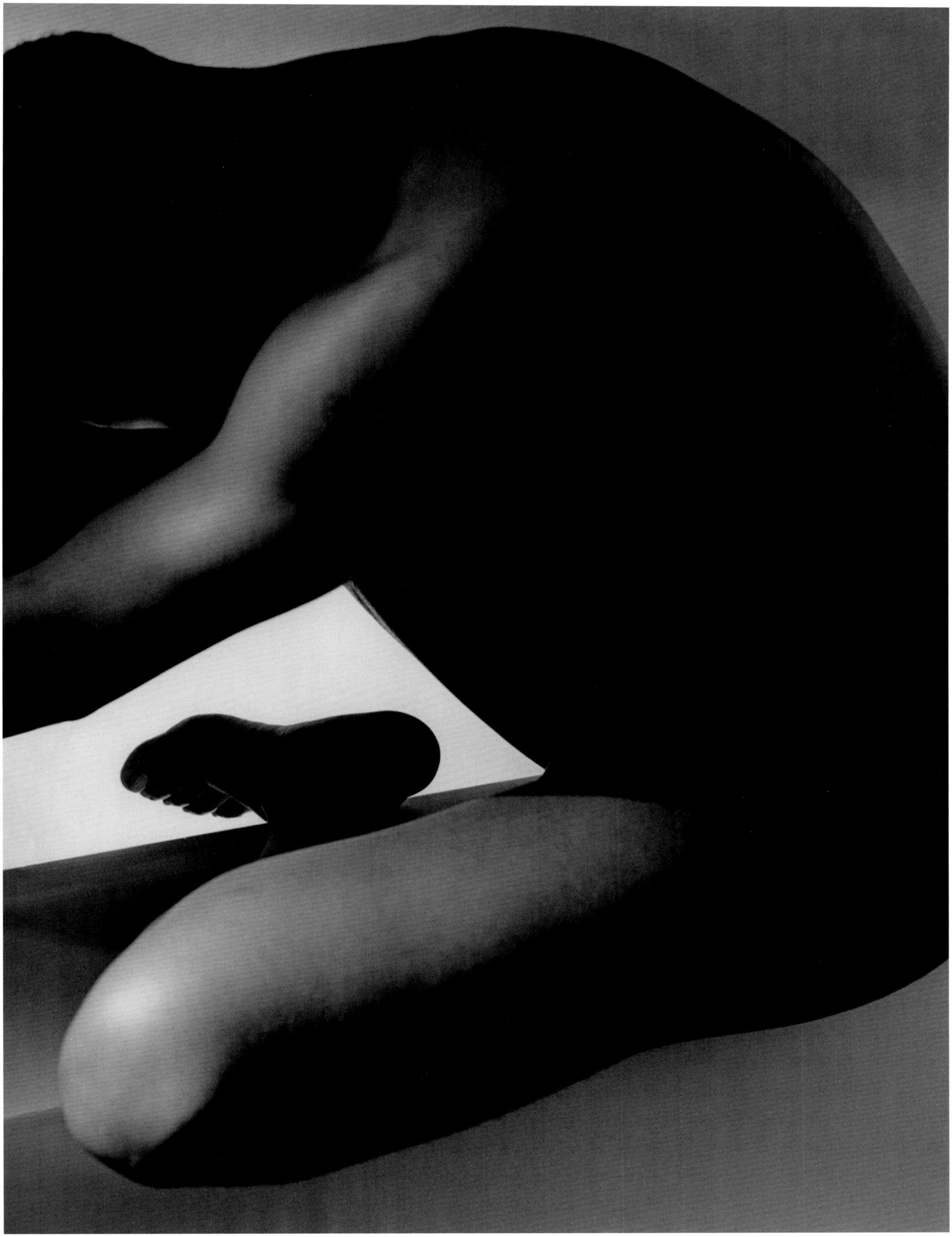

247. Male Nude, 1952

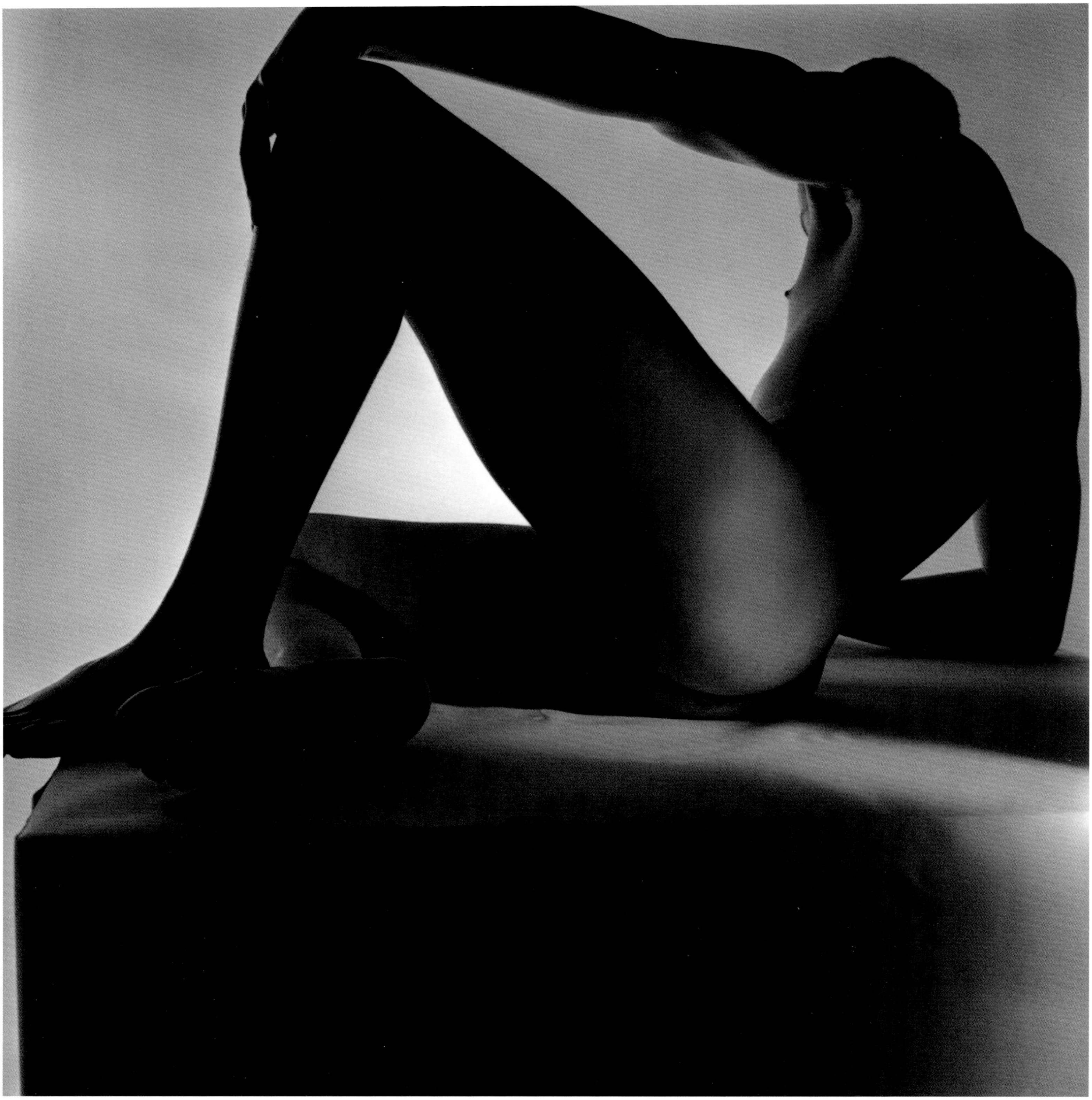

248. Male Nude, 1953

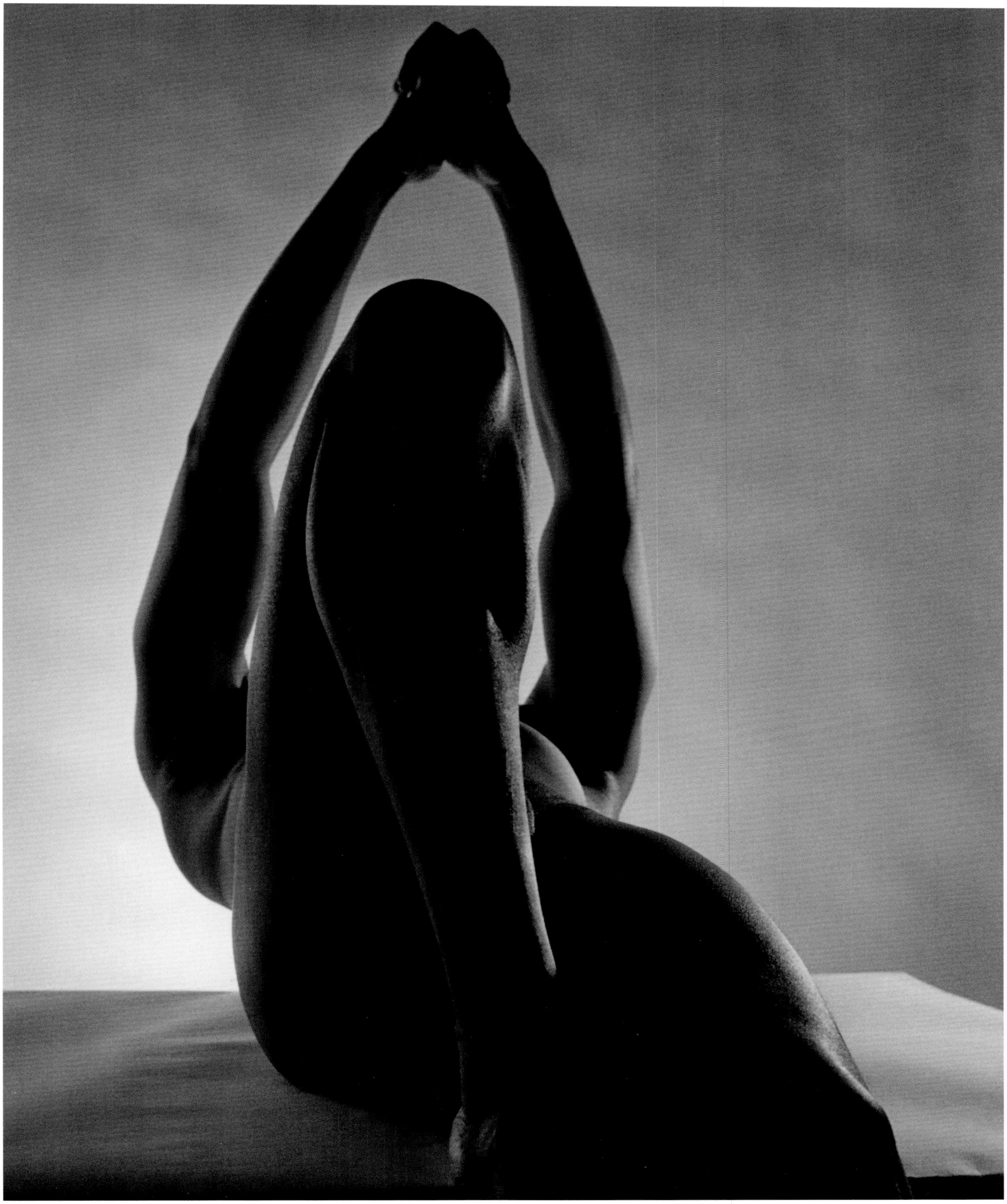

249. Male Nude, 1952

IX
Living in Style

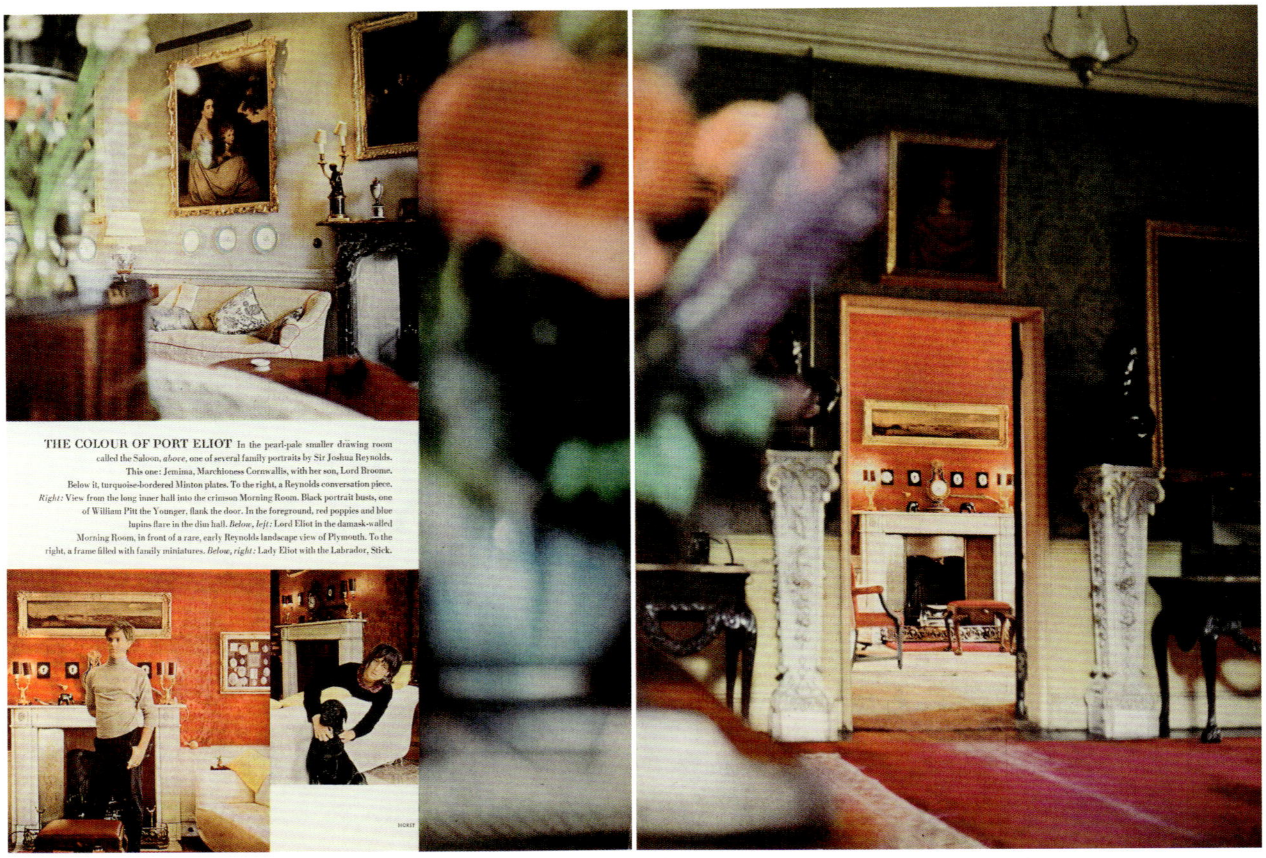
THE COLOUR OF PORT ELIOT In the pearl-pale smaller drawing room called the Saloon, *above*, one of several family portraits by Sir Joshua Reynolds. This one: Jemima, Marchioness Cornwallis, with her son, Lord Broome. Below it, turquoise-bordered Minton plates. To the right, a Reynolds conversation piece. *Right:* View from the long inner hall into the crimson Morning Room. Black portrait busts, one of William Pitt the Younger, flank the door. In the foreground, red poppies and blue lupins flare in the dim hall. *Below, left:* Lord Eliot in the damask-walled Morning Room, in front of a rare, early Reynolds landscape view of Plymouth. To the right, a frame filled with family miniatures. *Below, right:* Lady Eliot with the Labrador, Stick.

HORST

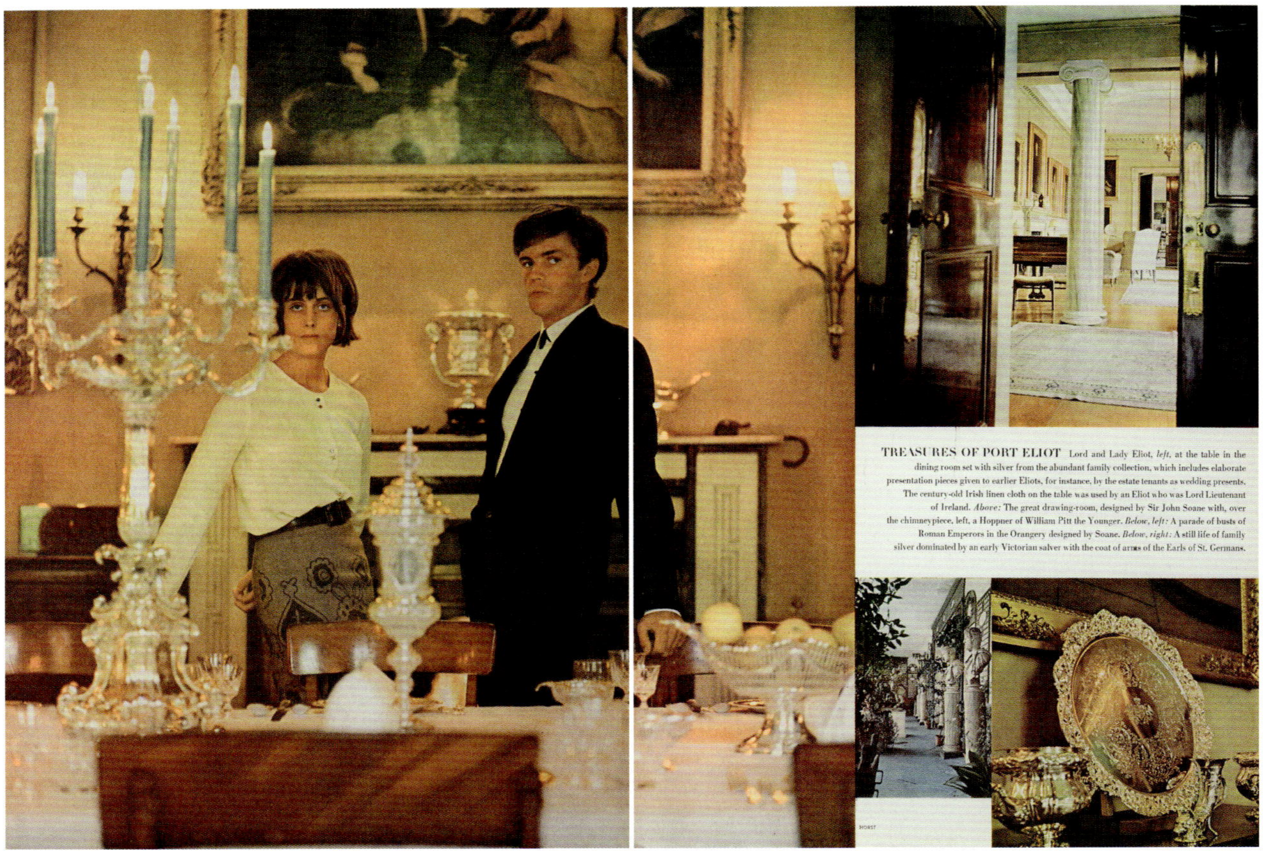
TREASURES OF PORT ELIOT Lord and Lady Eliot, *left*, at the table in the dining room set with silver from the abundant family collection, which includes elaborate presentation pieces given to earlier Eliots, for instance, by the estate tenants as wedding presents. The century-old Irish linen cloth on the table was used by an Eliot who was Lord Lieutenant of Ireland. *Above:* The great drawing-room, designed by Sir John Soane with, over the chimneypiece, left, a Hoppner of William Pitt the Younger. *Below, left:* A parade of busts of Roman Emperors in the Orangery designed by Soane. *Below, right:* A still life of family silver dominated by an early Victorian salver with the coat of arms of the Earls of St. Germans.

HORST

250 and 251.
Lord and Lady Eliot, Port Eliot, Cornwall, 1966

CONVERSATION PIECES: INTERIORS OF HORST AND LAWFORD[1]

Glenn Adamson

'Everything about such a house as this cries out to be described.'[2] So wrote Valentine Lawford of Port Eliot, an ancient manse in Cornwall, in 1966. Lawford and his partner Horst had gone to the house on assignment for British *Vogue*, to produce one of their collaborative features for their Fashions in Living series. The resulting article is indeed richly descriptive of Port Eliot's historic appointments: portraits by Joshua Reynolds, a drawing room designed by John Soane, a vase of red poppies and blue lupins (pl.250). But the stars of the show are Lord and Lady Eliot, the youthful owners of the house. Horst's lead image shows them at a remove, gazing at the camera across a linen-covered dining table, through a screen of glittering silver and glass (pl.251). The picture drips with hauteur and fashionable élan.

How should we assess this image – and the many other exclusive interiors that Horst documented in the pages of *Vogue* in the 1960s and 1970s? Today, it may seem difficult to take these pictures seriously. They present the fashionable rich as a breed apart, whose upscale decorating choices are inherently deserving of lavish, even fawning, attention. In this sense they are manifestly reactionary images, and even escapist. In Horst's pictures and Lawford's text alike, it is as if the Eliots have just stepped out of a book or a painting. They are 'more than good-looking enough for fiction', Lady Eliot's 'delicate face as pale as an Ingres against the crimson walls'.[3] It all seems unreachably posh, almost too good to be true.

On the other hand, Horst and Lawford were clearly aware that their portrayal of these cosseted 25-year-olds had a trace of the ridiculous. Lawford readily conceded that their family background 'seems to have about as little relevance to real life as the opening of a nineteenth-century three-decker novel',[4] and in one photograph, Horst showed Lord Eliot clambering like an overgrown child (in trainers and cufflinks) over the books and high-backed Jacobean chairs in the library (pl.120). 'Among his unexpected finds,' Lawford dryly noted, were 'a thirteenth-century illuminated French missal and a manuscript by Charles I.'[5] This image has the appeal of both the old guard and the latest thing, and indeed the whole article was published under the title 'The Upswing Young', suggesting some mysterious connection between this ultra-privileged young couple and the London scene that was then indeed in full swing. As Lawford put it in his conclusion to the article: 'true continuity is the natural ally, never the rigid enemy, of evolution, fashion, change.'[6]

Horst's interior photographs, and the dashing prose that Lawford wrote to accompany them, generally attempted to strike a balance. On the one hand, they were disconcertingly sanguine about the trappings of immense wealth. They were, after all, members of an elite class themselves, and in many cases were on friendly terms with the subjects they portrayed. According to his colleague at *Vogue*, the photographer Karen Radkai (1919–2003), Horst often rearranged and redecorated the interiors as he shot them, further blurring the boundary between himself and his well-to-do subjects.[7] On the other hand, as men of the fashion industry, they were exquisitely aware that the world was moving on, and that class was not the settled, hierarchical affair it once had been. It can even be tempting to see their collaboration as an application of camp taste, given Susan Sontag's famous definition of that aesthetic as 'the sensibility of failed seriousness, of the theatricalization of experience'.[8] But while Horst and Lawford certainly saw the home as a stage set, well stocked with attractive *dramatis personae*, for them the style of the patrician class was by no means a failure. It was a source of inspiration, and something to which they themselves aspired personally. Yet they also knew this world of closed, cosmopolitan refinement was not built to last. At its best, their work captured that fragility. A light shines through it – as if through the cracks in the edifice of aristocracy.

Thus, for all the breathless enthusiasm that Horst and Lawford brought to *Vogue*'s pages, they are tinged with melancholy. It is possible to see these images as a late, elegiac variation upon a tradition of image-making that extends back to the Renaissance, in which the well-to-do were depicted in their domestic surroundings as paragons of quality. Such images included individual portraits, of course, but also group portrayals, sometimes called 'conversation pieces' in the British context.[9] It seems to me that Horst and Lawford looked back at this tradition with considerable longing, and a degree of self-consciousness. Take their handling of Samuel Reed (a wealthy financier) and his family. Horst photographed them in a way strongly reminiscent of John Singer Sargent, and pointedly juxtaposed them with a historical portrait in the couple's collection by the minor Italian painter Pietro Rotari (pl.253).[10] Lawford underlined the message, writing that while the Reeds 'live in the rapids of a fast-running life – 1966 to the last drop', they nonetheless 'manage to look as if they had time to sit for eighteenth-century portraits'. Elsewhere in the article, he came close to mocking the American and his wife for their Old World class pretensions, noting that Mrs Reed's profile 'once might have fetched its possessor to the guillotine', and informing the reader that the couple lived out their evenings exclusively by candlelight, with a ban on use of the telephone.

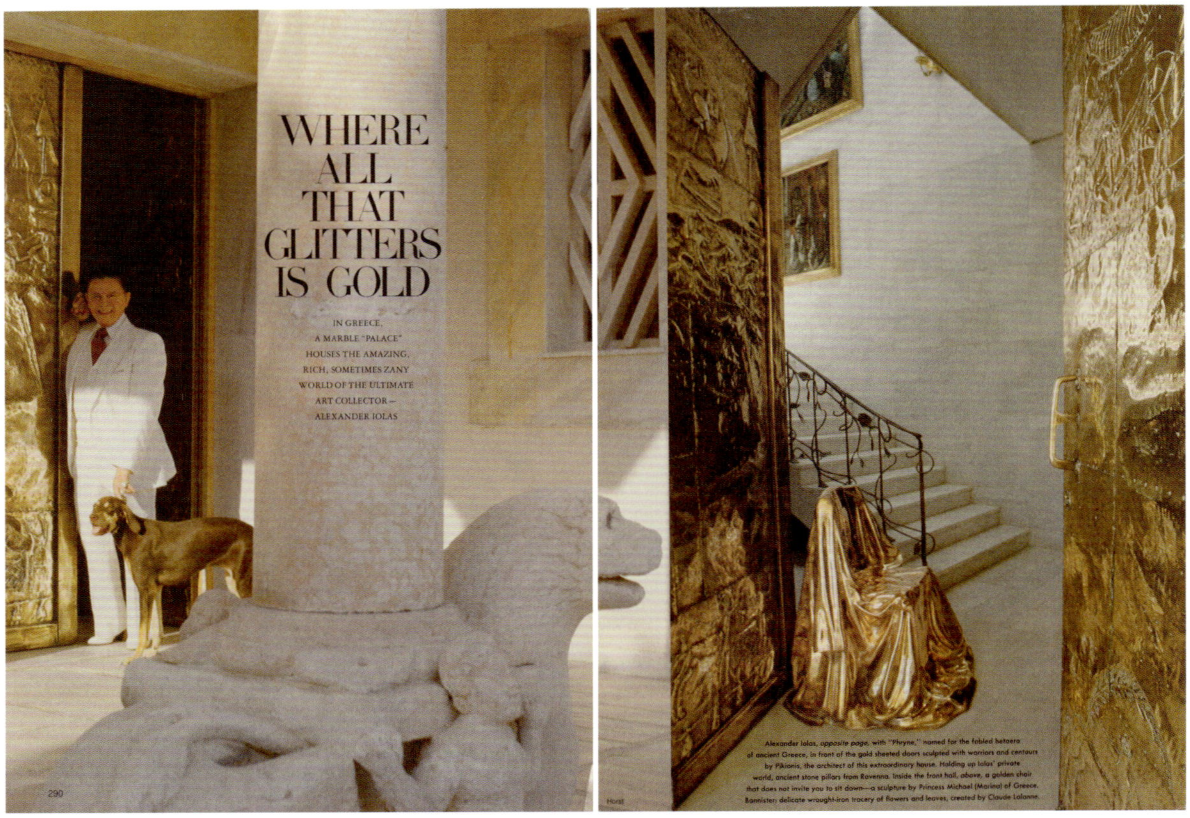

252. Alexander Iolas, Athens, 1963

The overall effect is sympathetic, but there is no doubt in the reader's mind that the Reeds are living in a fantasy world. It is an aesthetic that bears close comparison to that of the Italian film director Luchino Visconti, a friend (and former lover) of Horst's, whose 1963 film *The Leopard*, set in the nineteenth century, depicted the Italian aristocracy's losing battle with modernity. Horst and Lawford had accompanied Visconti to the New York premiere of that movie (in the company also of Jean Seberg, Claudia Cardinale and Warren Beatty, which certainly gives one a flavour of the times) and were impressed by 'the atmosphere, the ambience, the unforgettable beauty of certain incidental details'.[11] These were exactly the qualities that Horst sought to achieve in his own interiors, which were indeed cinematic – like stills from gorgeous but unrealized films.

The first commission that the two received from American *Vogue* was in 1963 – thanks to Diana Vreeland, who had taken over as editor – and it was to portray the Long Island home of Consuelo Vanderbilt Balsan in New York State.[12] She was an apt inaugural subject: author of an autobiography entitled *The Glitter and the Gold: The American Duchess* (1953), and a woman of impeccable upper-class credentials with a fascinating, operatic, life story.[13] Lawford set the scene, beginning with the line 'the long neck is justly famous', then noting that the 17-year-old Consuelo's marriage to the 9th Duke of Marlborough 'had been the outstanding social event in New York in 1895', before detailing her progress – an itinerary that included residential stints at Marble House (Newport, Rhode Island) and Fifth Avenue (New York) in America and Blenheim Palace in Britain.[14] The final line is charm itself: 'Here is admittedly a woman on whom life has lavished the best it has to give. But how beautifully she returns the compliment.'[15]

The house, as depicted in Horst's golden-hued photographs, is packed with finery: a crystal chandelier by Baguès, a Savonnerie rug, paintings by Fragonard, Pissarro, Renoir and Cézanne; Meissen and Chinese porcelain; and a rich complement of Louis Quinze furniture ('extremely comfortable', in the owner's judgment).[16] Yet modern life impinges. The house may be a 'terrestrial paradise' but it is also 'within hearing of the increasing traffic on Route 25A and the massed bulldozers preparing for the invasion and devastation of East Norwich and Syosset'.[17] More to the point, like the Sicilian nobles in *The Leopard*, Madame Balsan herself is the personification of faded glory (she was in fact in the last year of her life, although none of the participants knew this). Horst's lead image shows her as the tiny centre of a vast room, vulnerable despite her riches (pl.255). Swathed in a gown of eighteenth-century cut, she perches on a sofa and perhaps dreams of yesteryear. 'She can sit,' the caption notes poignantly, 'as if she were in a sunlit garden.'

The sense of time's inexorable passing is enhanced by the inclusion of a portrait of Madame Balsan in her glamorous youth, and also still life images that recall both the traditional *vanitas* theme (cut flowers clustered in a bowl, pl.254) and more recent surrealist art (a garden sculpture with a deathly veil of plastic sheeting). On publication, Balsan wrote to Vreeland from her second home in Palm Springs, expressing her satisfaction: '[it] could not have been better done, nor with greater tact … hating publicity as I do, you must take this as a compliment.'[18] This is testimony to Lawford's and Horst's skill (and indeed, 'tact' may have been their most useful trait).[19] While creating a compassionate portrait of this grand lady, they had also managed to capture the moment when she passed into history.

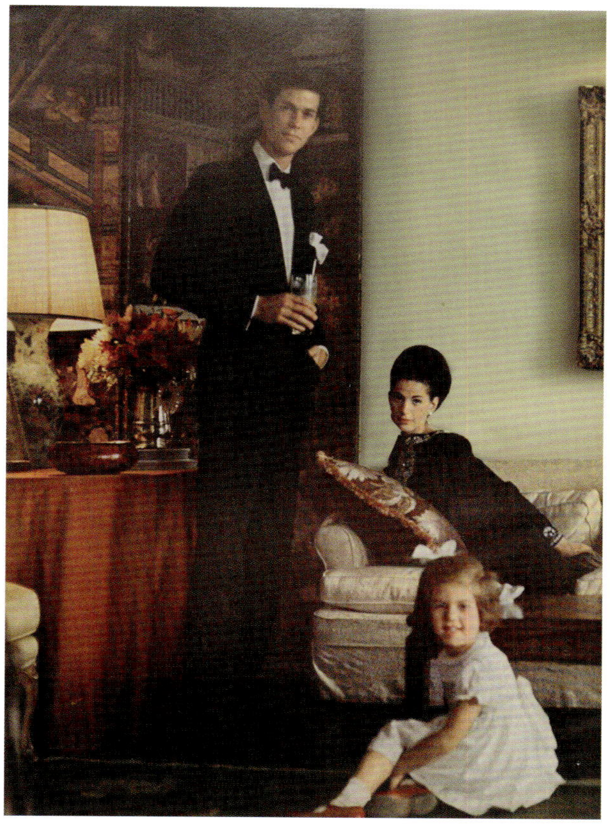

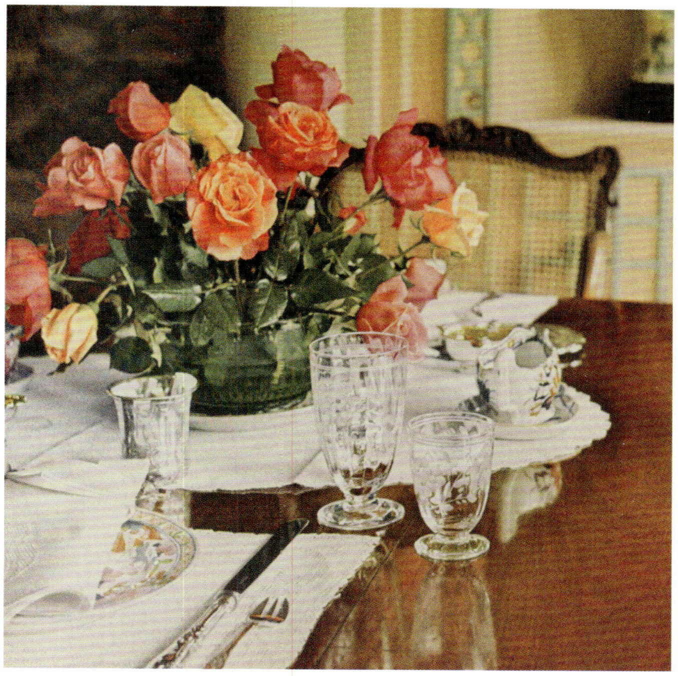

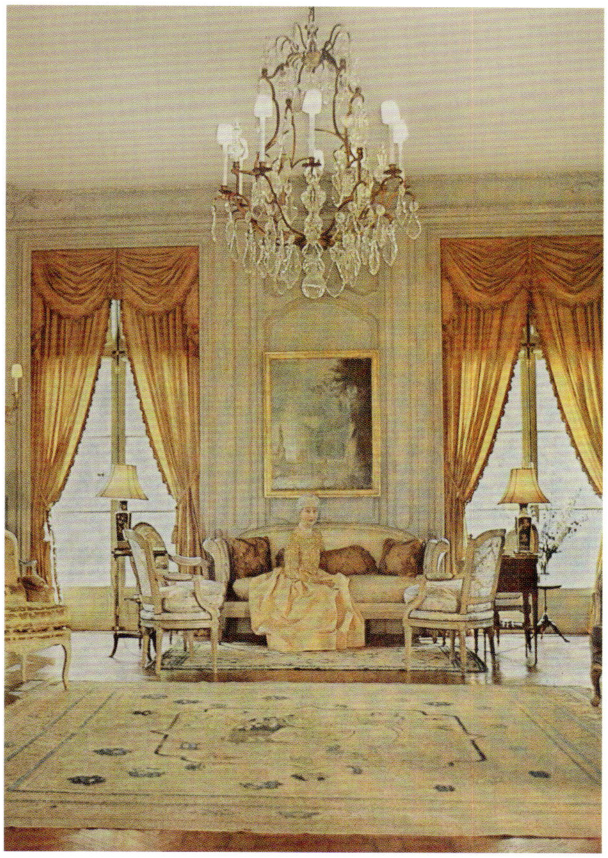

Top left
253. Samuel Reed and family, New York, 1966

Above
254. Cut flowers, Consuelo Vanderbilt Balsan's home, Southampton, New York, 1963

Left
255. Consuelo Vanderbilt Balsan, Southampton, New York, 1963

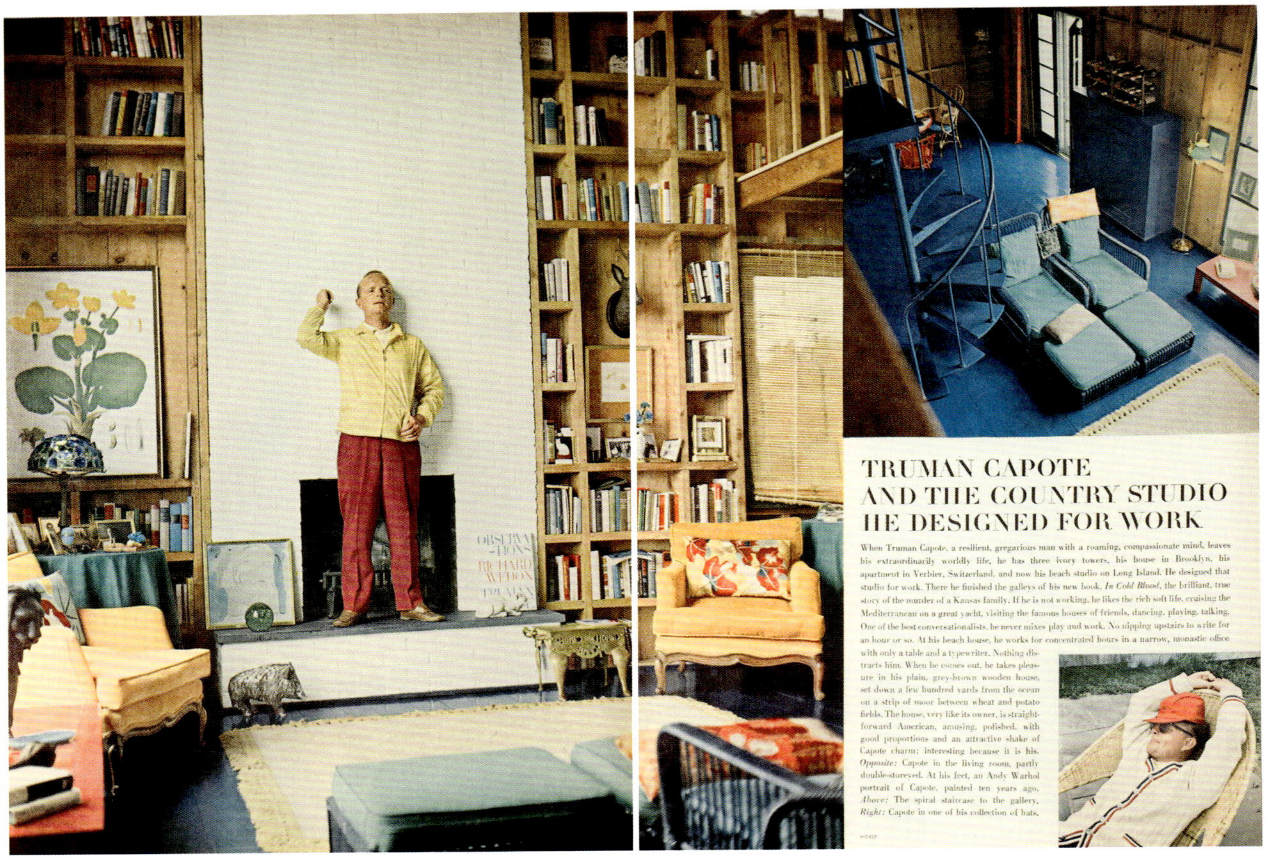

TRUMAN CAPOTE AND THE COUNTRY STUDIO HE DESIGNED FOR WORK

When Truman Capote, a resilient, gregarious man with a roaming, compassionate mind, leaves his extraordinarily worldly life, he has three ivory towers, his house in Brooklyn, his apartment in Verbier, Switzerland, and now his beach studio on Long Island. He designed that studio for work. There he finished the galleys of his new book, *In Cold Blood*, the brilliant, true story of the murder of a Kansas family. If he is not working, he likes the rich soft life, cruising the Mediterranean on a great yacht, visiting the famous houses of friends, dancing, playing, talking. One of the best conversationalists, he never mixes play and work. No nipping upstairs to write for an hour or so. At his beach house, he works for concentrated hours in a narrow, monastic office with only a table and a typewriter. Nothing distracts him. When he comes out, he takes pleasure in his plain, grey-brown wooden house, set down a few hundred yards from the ocean on a strip of moor between wheat and potato fields. The house, very like its owner, is straightforward American, amusing, polished, with good proportions and an attractive shake of Capote charm; interesting because it is his. *Opposite:* Capote in the living room, partly double-storeyed. At his feet, an Andy Warhol portrait of Capote, painted ten years ago. *Above:* The spiral staircase to the gallery. *Right:* Capote in one of his collection of hats.

HORST

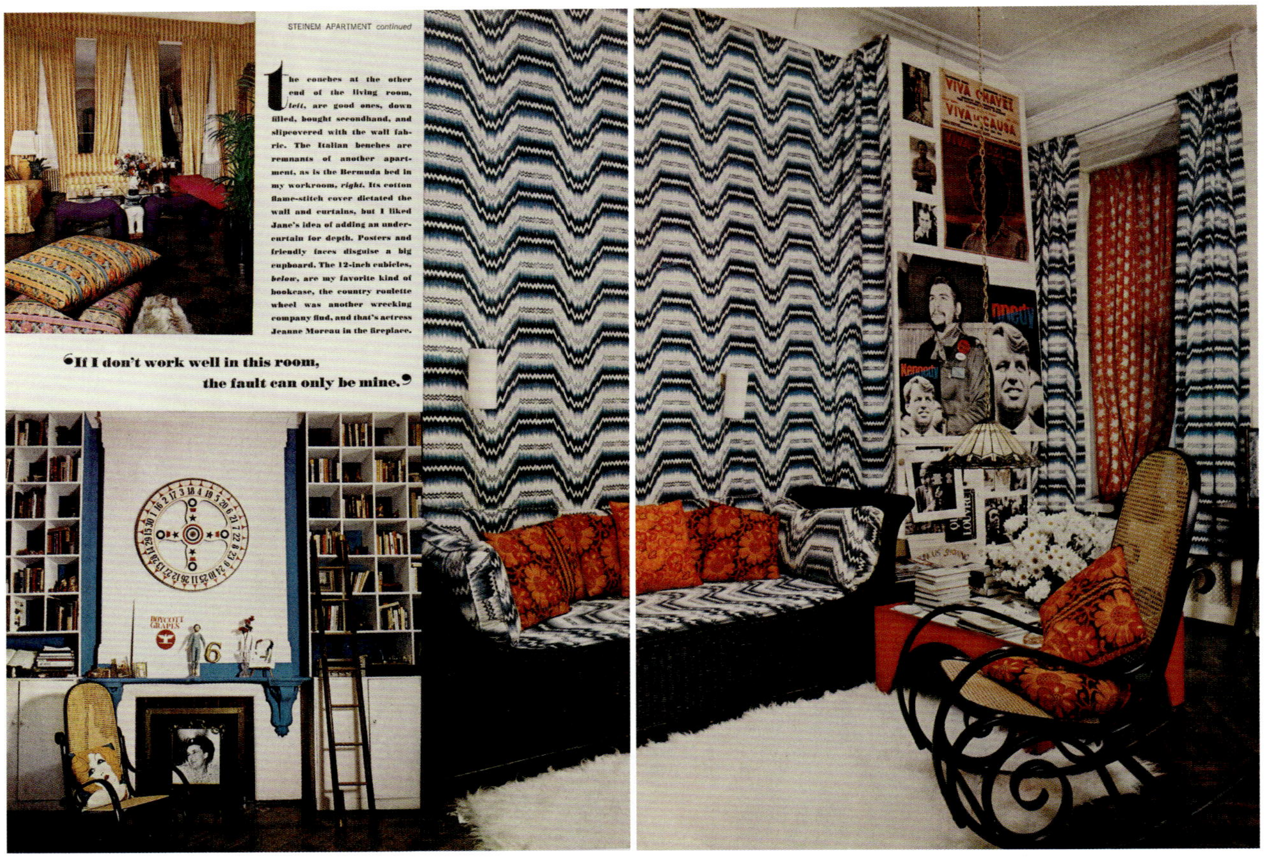

STEINEM APARTMENT *continued*

The couches at the other end of the living room, *left*, are good ones, down filled, bought secondhand, and slipcovered with the wall fabric. The Italian benches are remnants of another apartment, as is the Bermuda bed in my workroom, *right*. Its cotton flame-stitch cover dictated the wall and curtains, but I liked Jane's idea of adding an undercurtain for depth. Posters and friendly faces disguise a big cupboard. The 12-inch cubicles, *below*, are my favorite kind of bookcase, the country roulette wheel was another wrecking company find, and that's actress Jeanne Moreau in the fireplace.

'If I don't work well in this room, the fault can only be mine.'

256. Truman Capote at home, Long Island, 1965

257. Gloria Steinem's home, New York, 1971

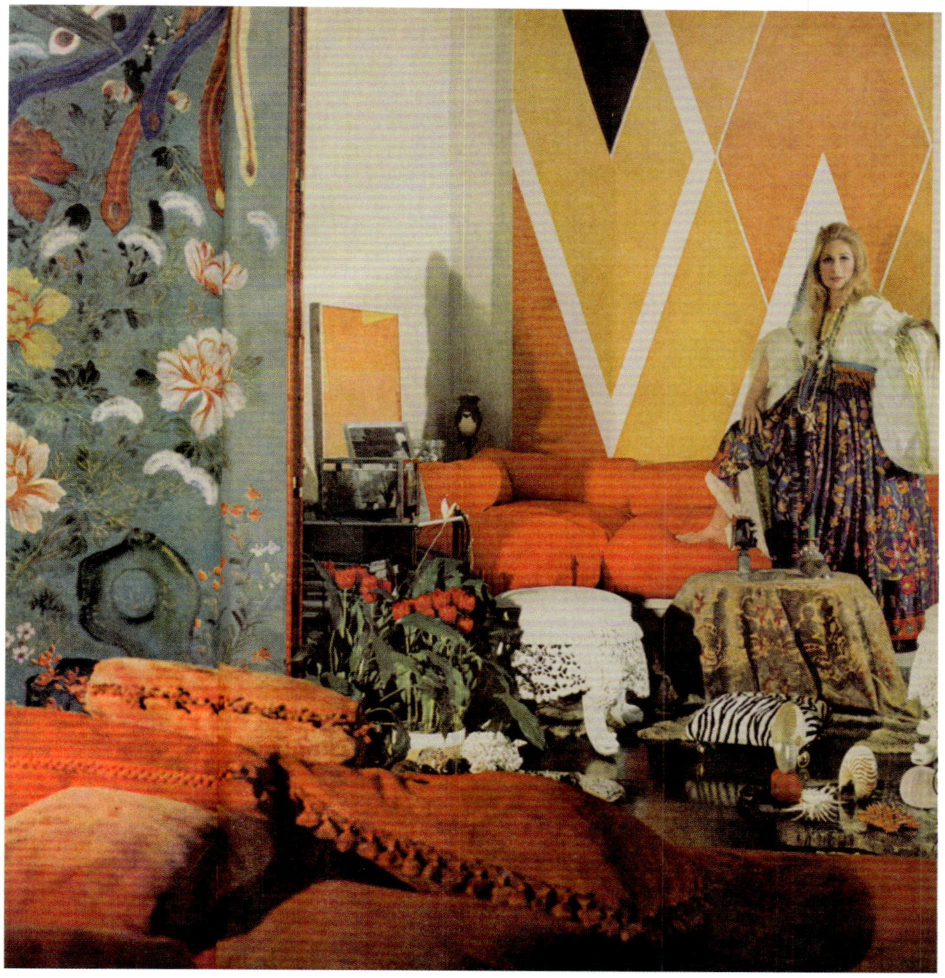

258. 'Baby Jane' Holzer, New York, 1969

An instructive contrast can be made with a feature from almost a decade later – 1971 – entitled 'A Reflection of Now', which profiled the art collector Jan Gardner Cowles (née Hochstraser, pls 259, 260).[20] By this time, Horst and Lawford had charted quite a few figures who did not fit the mould of the traditional aristocracy: Truman Capote, standing cocksure in the Long Island farmhouse where he finished *In Cold Blood* (pl.256); the Warhol 'Superstar' 'Baby Jane' Holzer, resplendent in a Sant'Angelo gypsy dress, surrounded by Pop Art and 'masses of pillows in suede thrown accurately in the most superb positions' (pl.258); the feminist activist Gloria Steinem, whose political posters and flame-stitch draperies Horst duly photographed (pl.257).[21] In this pantheon of Pop celebrity, Cowles may not seem particularly lustrous; but she was a power broker par excellence, and therefore of great interest. Her husband was the founder of *Look* magazine, trustee of four universities, a director of the *New York Times*, Macy's and United Airlines, and a trustee of New York's Museum of Modern Art. Her son, Charles Cowles, was publisher of *Artforum*, the leading art journal at the time, and would later become one of the most powerful gallerists in New York.

And Jan Cowles herself? Perhaps she seemed to Horst and Lawford the latest incarnation of the type that Madame Balsan represented so well. Horst's unforgettable portrait shows her with a 100-watt smile, almost disappearing into the reflection of a Protractor painting by Frank Stella (b.1936), her tensed form echoed by a tumbling, gently vertiginous sculpture by Beverly Pepper (b.1922). The apartment, occupying the entire upper floor of a building on Fifth Avenue, was designed by modernist architect Paul Rudolph (1918–97), and was decorated by François Catroux and Mark Hampton (1940–98) – the former suggesting deep aubergine for the walls. In addition to Stella, the feature shows the depth and currency of Cowles' collection: paintings by Andy Warhol (1928–87), Cy Twombly (1928–2011), Roy Lichtenstein (1923–70), Morris Louis (1912–62); furniture by Eero Saarinen (1910–61) and Verner Panton (1926–98) ('arranged with tender austerity' in a child's bedroom); and a luxurious bathroom sheathed in miniature mirrors and a white shag rug, with a tub set into floor and a lithograph by Jim Dine (b.1935).

What Horst and Lawford have captured here, with astonishing frankness, is the uncomfortable proximity of money and art. The modernist avant-garde is shown to have a taste that is as 'correct' as Old Master paintings and antiques had been for previous generations, and which Horst and Lawford also documented. This is a tacit, but nonetheless provocative theme in their work: contemporary art is just another property for the interior decorator to manage, no more (or less) expressive than any other expensive object. Horst's and Lawford's most revealing project in this regard was their feature on the painter Cy Twombly, whose house in Rome, as Lawford wryly noted, 'happens to be in a palazzo' (pl.261).[22]

As writer Pierre Alexandre de Looz has commented, the article

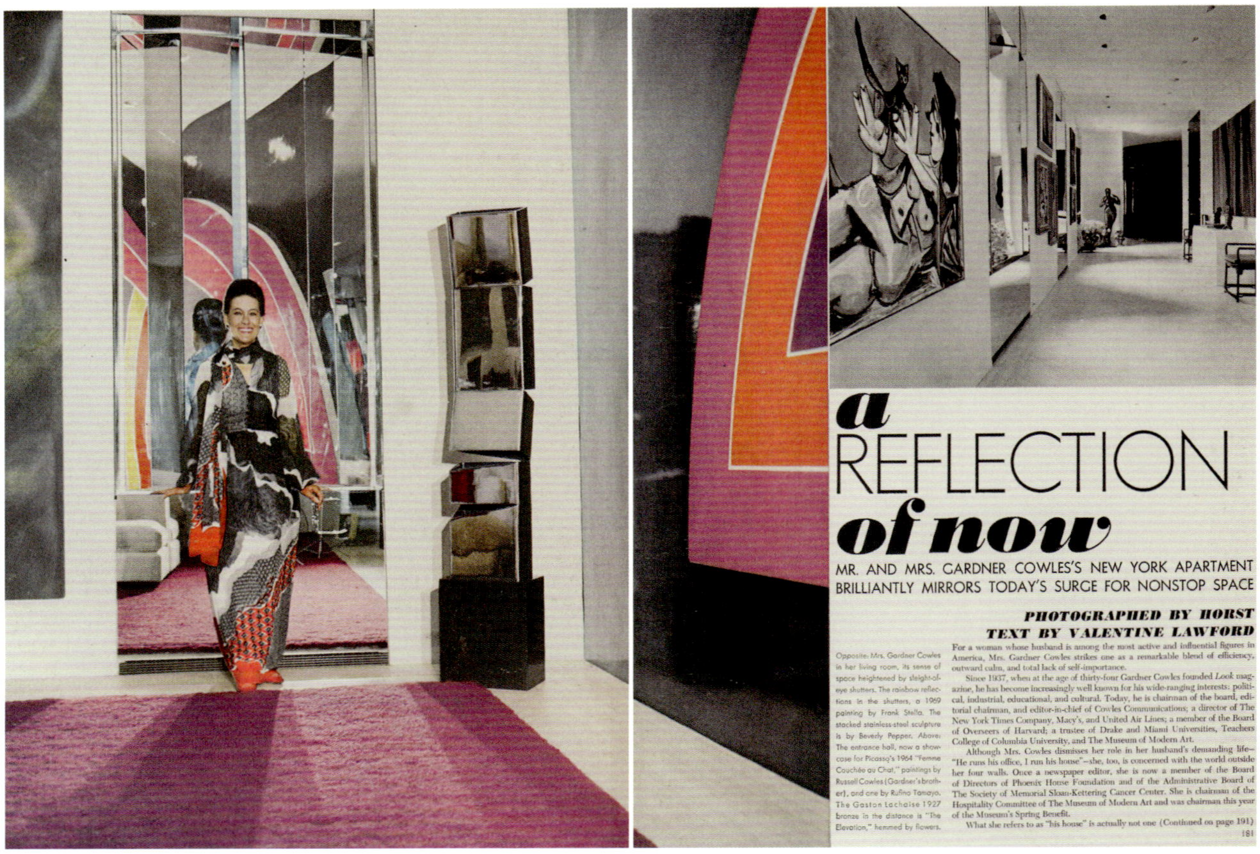

a REFLECTION of now

MR. AND MRS. GARDNER COWLES'S NEW YORK APARTMENT BRILLIANTLY MIRRORS TODAY'S SURGE FOR NONSTOP SPACE

PHOTOGRAPHED BY HORST
TEXT BY VALENTINE LAWFORD

Opposite: Mrs. Gardner Cowles in her living room, its sense of space heightened by sleight-of-eye shutters. The rainbow reflections in the shutters, a 1969 painting by Frank Stella. The stacked stainless-steel sculpture is by Beverly Pepper. *Above:* The entrance hall, now a showcase for Picasso's 1964 "Femme Couchée au Chat," paintings by Russell Cowles (Gardner's brother), and one by Rufino Tamayo. The Gaston Lachaise 1927 bronze in the distance is "The Elevation," hemmed by flowers.

For a woman whose husband is among the most active and influential figures in America, Mrs. Gardner Cowles strikes one as a remarkable blend of efficiency, outward calm, and total lack of self-importance.

Since 1937, when at the age of thirty-four Gardner Cowles founded *Look* magazine, he has become increasingly well known for his wide-ranging interests: political, industrial, educational, and cultural. Today, he is chairman of the board, editorial chairman, and editor-in-chief of Cowles Communications; a director of The New York Times Company, Macy's, and United Air Lines; a member of the Board of Overseers of Harvard; a trustee of Drake and Miami Universities, Teachers College of Columbia University, and The Museum of Modern Art.

Although Mrs. Cowles dismisses her role in her husband's demanding life—"He runs his office, I run his house"—she, too, is concerned with the world outside her four walls. Once a newspaper editor, she is now a member of the Board of Directors of Phoenix House Foundation and of the Administrative Board of The Society of Memorial Sloan-Kettering Cancer Center. She is chairman of the Hospitality Committee of The Museum of Modern Art and was chairman this year of the Museum's Spring Benefit.

What she refers to as "his house" is actually not one (Continued on page 191)

181

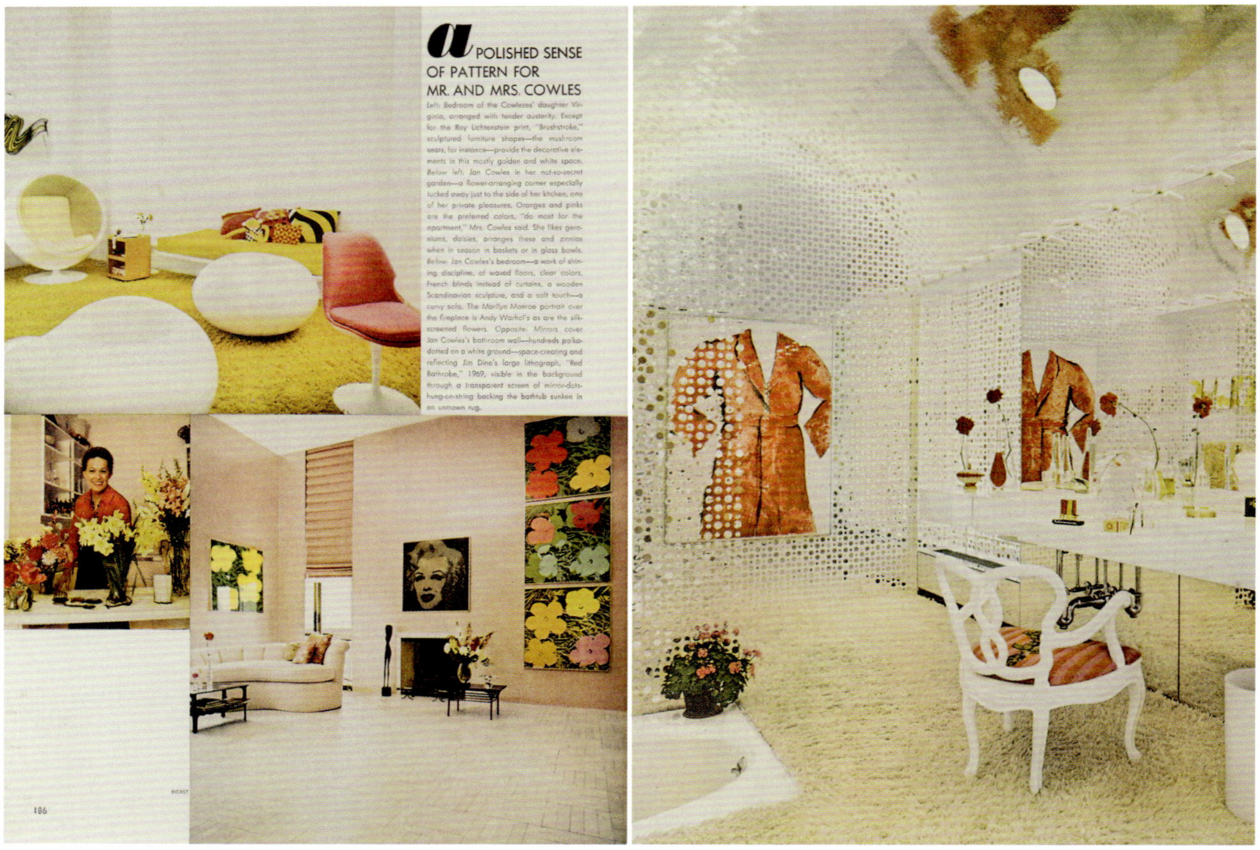

a POLISHED SENSE OF PATTERN FOR MR. AND MRS. COWLES

Left: Bedroom of the Cowleses' daughter Virginia, arranged with tender austerity. Except for the Roy Lichtenstein print, "Brushstroke," sculptured furniture shapes—the mushroom seats, for instance—provide the decorative elements in this mostly golden and white space. *Below left:* Jan Cowles in her not-so-secret garden—a flower-arranging corner especially tucked away just to the side of her kitchen, one of her private pleasures. Oranges and pinks are the preferred colors, "do most for the apartment," Mrs. Cowles said. She likes geraniums, daisies, arranges these and zinnias when in season in baskets or in glass bowls. *Below:* Jan Cowles's bedroom—a work of shining discipline, of waxed floors, clear colors, French blinds instead of curtains, a wooden Scandinavian sculpture, and a soft touch—a curvy sofa. The Marilyn Monroe portrait over the fireplace is Andy Warhol's as are the silk-screened flowers. *Opposite:* Mirrors cover Jan Cowles's bathroom wall—hundreds polka-dotted on a white ground—space-creating and reflecting Jim Dine's large lithograph, "Red Bathrobe," 1969, visible in the background through a transparent screen of mirror-dots-hung-on-string backing the bathtub sunken in an unmown rug.

186

259 and 260. Jan Gardner Cowles
at home, New York, 1971

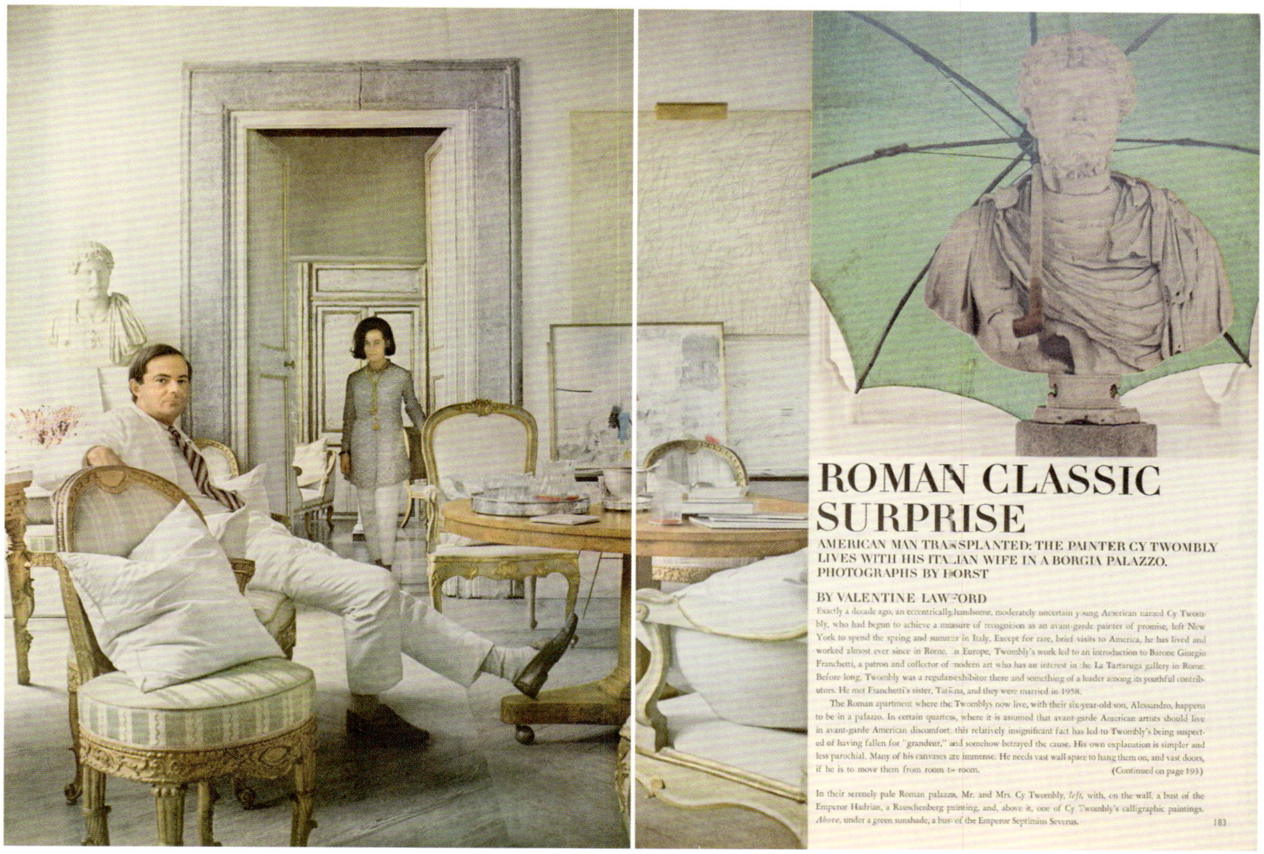

ROMAN CLASSIC SURPRISE

AMERICAN MAN TRANSPLANTED: THE PAINTER CY TWOMBLY LIVES WITH HIS ITALIAN WIFE IN A BORGIA PALAZZO. PHOTOGRAPHS BY HORST

BY VALENTINE LAWFORD

Exactly a decade ago, an eccentrically handsome, moderately uncertain young American named Cy Twombly, who had begun to achieve a measure of recognition as an avant-garde painter of promise, left New York to spend the spring and summer in Italy. Except for rare, brief visits to America, he has lived and worked almost ever since in Rome. In Europe, Twombly's work led to an introduction to Barone Giorgio Franchetti, a patron and collector of modern art who has an interest in the La Tartaruga gallery in Rome. Before long, Twombly was a regular exhibitor there and something of a leader among its youthful contributors. He met Franchetti's sister, Tatiana, and they were married in 1958.

The Roman apartment where the Twomblys now live, with their six-year-old son, Alessandro, happens to be in a palazzo. In certain quarters, where it is assumed that avant-garde American artists should live in avant-garde American discomfort, this relatively insignificant fact has led to Twombly's being suspected of having fallen for "grandeur," and somehow betrayed the cause. His own explanation is simpler and less parochial. Many of his canvases are immense. He needs vast wall space to hang them on, and vast doors, if he is to move them from room to room. (Continued on page 193)

In their serenely pale Roman palazzo, Mr. and Mrs. Cy Twombly, *left*, with, on the wall, a bust of the Emperor Hadrian, a Rauschenberg painting, and, above it, one of Cy Twombly's calligraphic paintings. *Above*, under a green sunshade, a bust of the Emperor Septimius Severus.

183

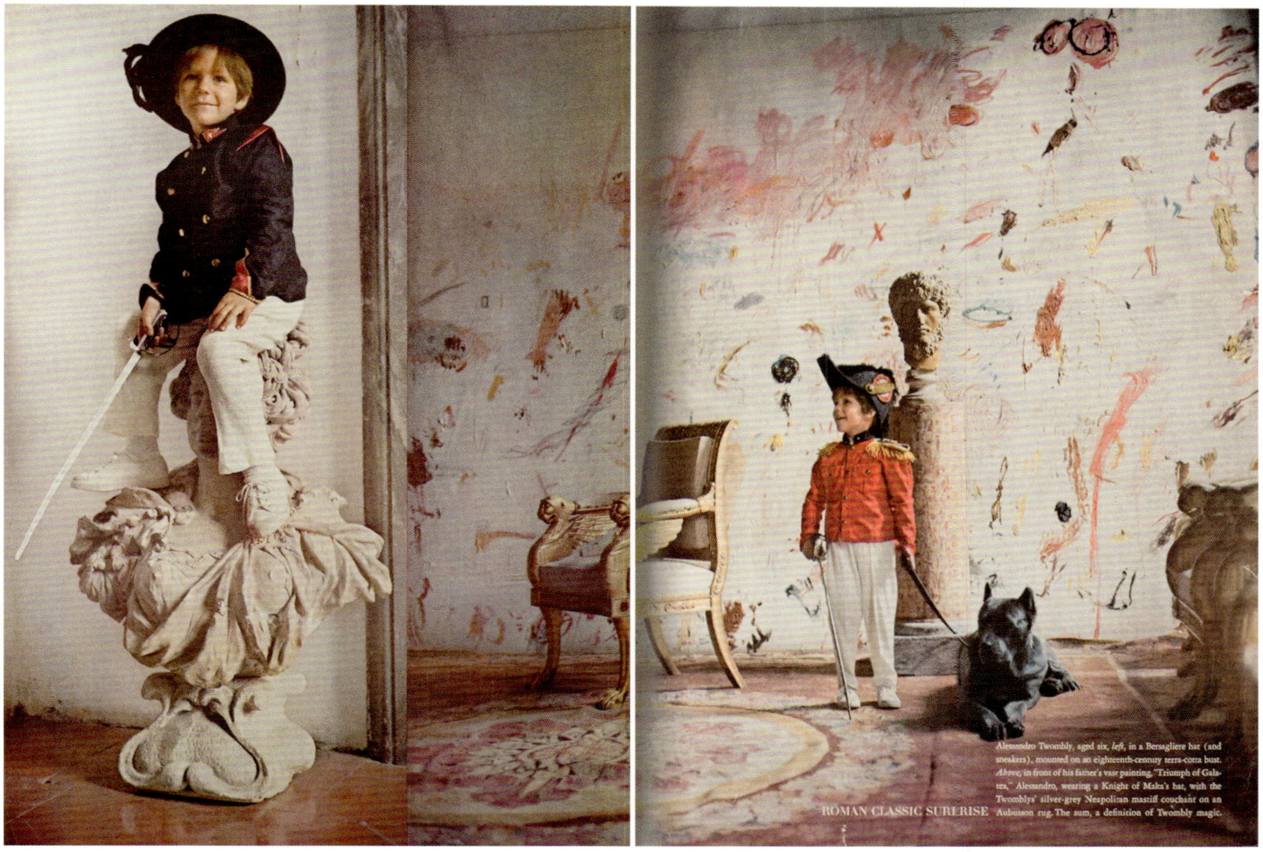

ROMAN CLASSIC SURPRISE

Alessandro Twombly, aged six, *left*, in a Bersagliere hat (and sneakers), mounted on an eighteenth-century terra-cotta bust. *Above*, in front of his father's vast painting, "Triumph of Galatea," Alessandro, wearing a Knight of Malta's hat, with the Twomblys' silver-grey Neapolitan mastiff couchant on an Aubusson rug. The sum, a definition of Twombly magic.

261 and 262. Cy Twombly and family at home, Rome, 1966

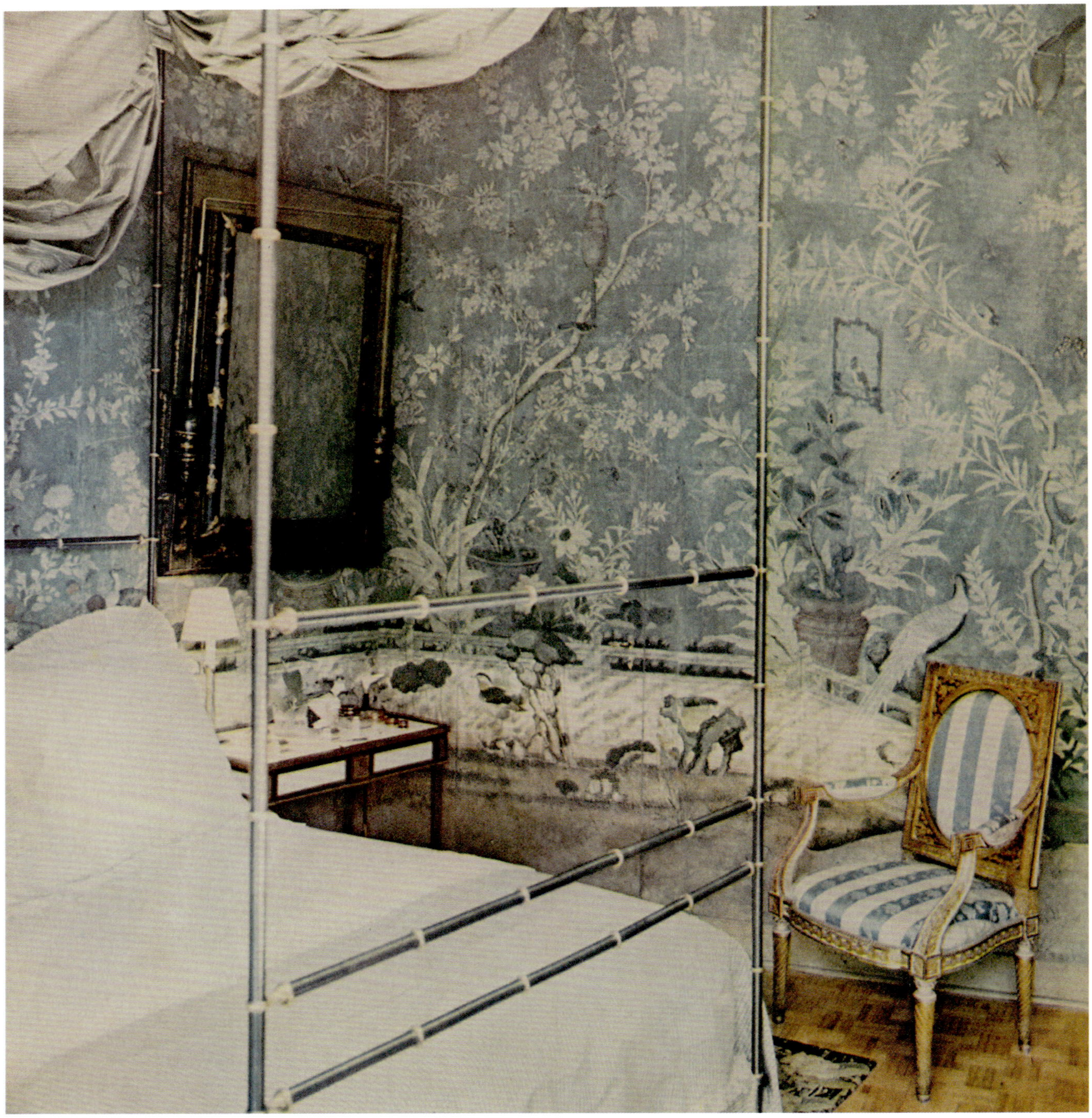

263. Baroness Pauline de Rothschild's
bedroom, Paris, 1969

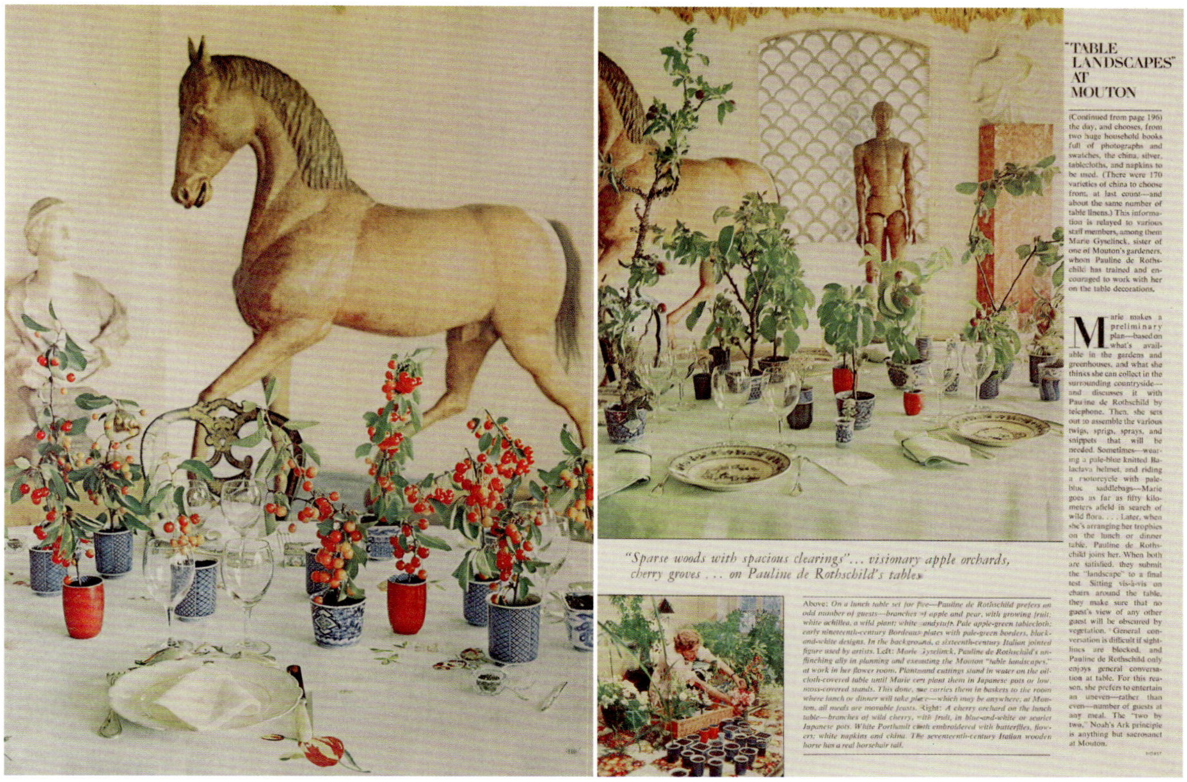

"TABLE LANDSCAPES" AT MOUTON

(Continued from page 196) the day, and chooses, from two huge household books full of photographs and swatches, the china, silver, tablecloths, and napkins to be used. (There were 170 varieties of china to choose from, at last count—and about the same number of table linens.) This information is relayed to various staff members, among them Marie Gyselinck, sister of one of Mouton's gardeners, whom Pauline de Rothschild has trained and encouraged to work with her on the table decorations.

Marie makes a preliminary plan—based on what's available in the gardens and greenhouses, and what she thinks she can collect in the surrounding countryside—and discusses it with Pauline de Rothschild by telephone. Then, she sets out to assemble the various twigs, sprigs, sprays, and snippets that will be needed. Sometimes—wearing a pale-blue knitted Balaclava helmet, and riding a motorcycle with pale-blue saddlebags—Marie goes as far as fifty kilometers afield in search of wild flora. . . . Later, when she's arranging her trophies on the lunch or dinner table, Pauline de Rothschild joins her. When both are satisfied, they submit the "landscape" to a final test. Sitting vis-à-vis on chairs around the table, they make sure that no guest's view of any other guest will be obscured by vegetation. "General conversation is difficult if sightlines are blocked, and Pauline de Rothschild only enjoys general conversation at table. For this reason, she prefers to entertain an uneven—rather than even—number of guests at any meal. The "two by two," Noah's Ark principle is anything but sacrosanct at Mouton.

"Sparse woods with spacious clearings"... visionary apple orchards, cherry groves . . . on Pauline de Rothschild's tables

Above: *On a lunch table set for five—Pauline de Rothschild prefers an odd number of guests—branches of apple and pear, with growing fruit; white achillea, a wild plant; white candytuft. Pale apple-green tablecloth; early nineteenth-century Bordeaux plates with pale-green borders, black-and-white designs. In the background, a sixteenth-century Italian jointed figure used by artists.* Left: *Marie Gyselinck, Pauline de Rothschild's unflinching ally in planning and executing the Mouton "table landscapes," at work in her flower room. Plants and cuttings stand in water on the oil-cloth-covered table until Marie can plant them in Japanese pots or low, moss-covered stands. This done, she carries them in baskets to the room where lunch or dinner will take place—which may be anywhere; at Mouton, all meals are movable feasts.* Right: *A cherry orchard on the lunch table—branches of wild cherry, with fruit, in blue-and-white or scarlet Japanese pots. White Porthault cloth embroidered with butterflies, flowers; white napkins and china. The seventeenth-century Italian wooden horse has a real horsehair tail.*

264. Table landscapes, Baron and Baroness Philippe de Rothschild's Home, Château de Mouton, Pauillac, France, 1963

marked a brave departure from the usual depiction of Abstract Expressionism as a macho boys' club. Horst and Lawford all but outed Twombly as a gay man, portraying him (not without admiration) as an indolent sybarite, and also implying that his painting and his interior decorating were more or less a single, continuous activity.[23] The article bristles with fascinating detail. A feminist theorist would have much to say, for example, about the description of Twombly's wife, a descendant of the Borgias: 'Slight and self-effacing, almost imperceptible yet frankly indispensable, Tatiana Twombly is the painter's wife personified. A painter herself – a sensitive and successful portraitist of children – she is reticent about her own productions.'[24] And any museum educator, fatigued with the task of explaining why a child could *not* have produced Twombly's work, will note with interest the fact that the painter's son Alessandro 'has been allowed to draw, within defined limits, on certain walls'.[25] Horst's portrait of the boy, wearing a *bersagliere* hat and tennis shoes, and standing in front of Twombly's painting *The Triumph of Galatea* (1961) with a sleepy dog at his side, comes across as a parody of Velázquez's *Las Meninas* (1656) (pl.262).[26]

In the Cowles and Twombly features, Horst and Lawford demonstrated, better than innumerable doctoral dissertations have since, the fact that contemporary art is more a matter of conspicuous consumption than most would care to admit. Again, it should be stressed that their attitude to this reality was not critical. They were devotees of extravagance for its own sake, and blissfully untroubled by any concern about snobbery. In actual fact, they preferred figures who were more patrician than Twombly. Their aesthetic pole stars were people like Madame Balsan, or Baroness Pauline de Rothschild, reputedly Horst's favourite subject, whose Chinese wallpapers and 'table landscapes' they returned to again and again in an attempt to capture that elusive quotient, *le style Pauline* (pls 263, 264).[27] (Vreeland later commented, 'We could have gone on and on producing articles about Pauline forever, don't you think?')[28]

The joy Horst and Lawford found in the delightful absurdities of individual taste is, paradoxically, precisely what makes their work together so politically revealing: they traced the lineaments of stylized power with a forthrightness that has been in short supply in more recent years. While it is common enough for contemporary art to point the finger at its own collector-based support system – witness the still-life interiors of Louise Lawler (b.1947, pl.265), the adopted guises of Cindy Sherman (b.1954, pl.266), or the abstracted society portraits of Julian Opie – we rarely have an unvarnished view into this system of patronage. A growing sense that it is inappropriate to flaunt avant-garde works as if they were Baroque paintings, perhaps combined with a heightened emphasis on privacy (given the escalating values of fine art works), has since rendered the portrayal of elite interiors somewhat less frank. There are certainly photographers who have assumed Horst's mantle – such as Fritz von der Schulenburg, Eric Boman, and François Halard – but the view that they supply in publications such as *World of Interiors* and *House & Garden*, while equally gorgeous, lacks the unguarded quality of Horst's work.

It is a measure of Horst's and Lawford's serenely guileless approach that when they turned their attention to their own house in Oyster Bay – not far from Madame Balsan's place – there was no perceptible shift in tone. The feature, titled 'The House that Horst Grew', published in American *Vogue* in 1966, might have been a profile of yet another

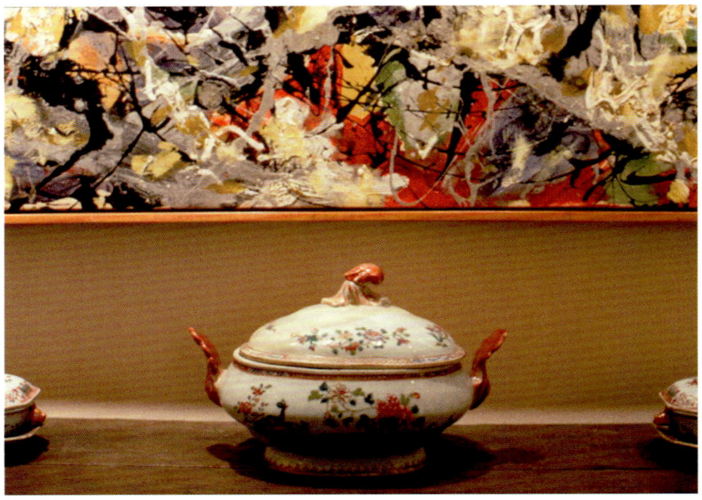

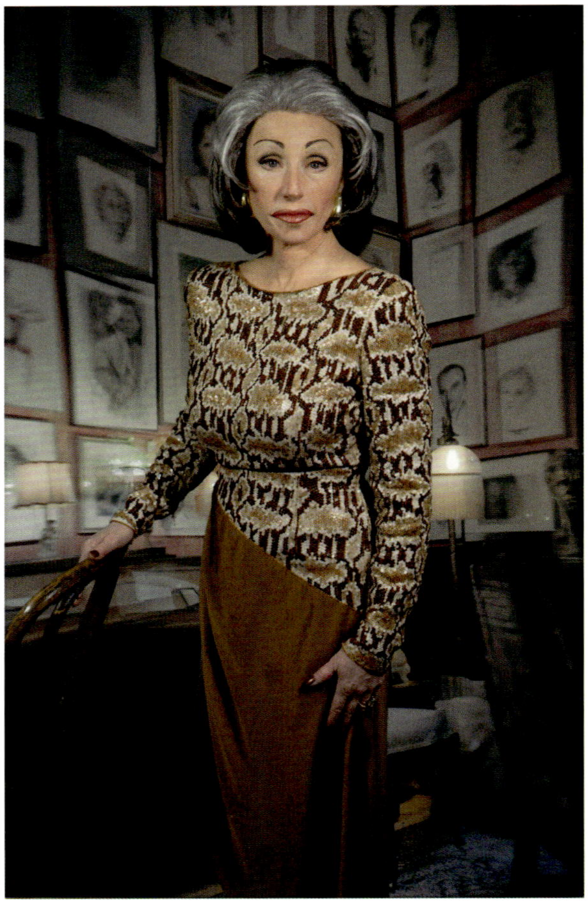

gentry estate (pl.270). Given the attitudes to homosexuality prevalent at the time, the two men's relationship was certainly not made clear, and Lawford wrote about his partner in a polite, even distant manner. Even so, he stated their joint aesthetic as clearly as if he had been writing a manifesto: 'As a one-time assistant to Le Corbusier, and admirer of Philip Johnson, Horst had tastes that were scarcely conservative. But with the passage of time, his house has assumed the elegance and distinction of an eighteenth-century hunting lodge.'[29] In fact, the house was, by Lawford's own admission, 'almost barbarically mixed'. Built up over the course of years, it ended up as a complicated sprawl, complete with a sunbathing courtyard and a pigeon house. Blindingly white on the outside, the interiors were furnished with an eclectic collage of colour, patterns and treasures: antique silver, Polynesian screens (their fabric among the furnishings spontaneously given to Horst by Coco Chanel after he made the mistake of admiring it in her stores) and designs by the brilliant French exponent of Art Deco, Jean-Michel Frank.

The impression given, as the article's strapline put it, was 'intensely individual', the reflection of a lifetime of looking. Lawford was not wrong when he wrote that these interiors felt like 'notes for an autobiography, or studies for a self-portrait'.[30] It is undeniable that there is something precious, even cloying, in this approach, and the same can be said of the atmosphere that Horst and Lawford created at Oyster Bay, and in the many features they published. But we should not visit upon these two inspired men the dreadful posterity of hindsight. Here in their own private space, as in all their work together, they created a sense of belonging, and did so entirely on their own terms. Nearly 50 years later, it is an accomplishment that is still worth talking about.

265. Louise Lawler,
Pollock and Tureen, Arranged by Mr. and Mrs. Burton Tremaine,Connecticut, 1984

266. Cindy Sherman,
Untitled #474, 2008

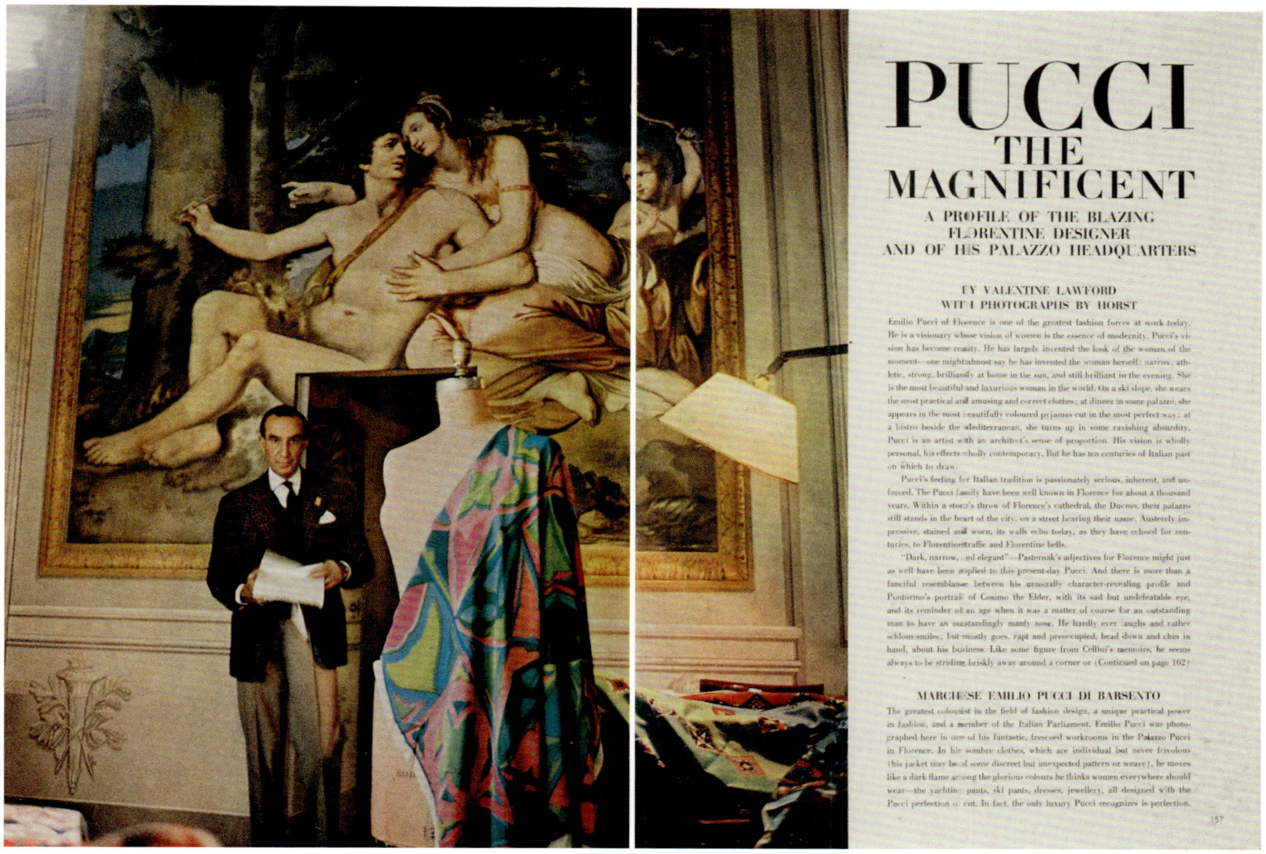

PUCCI THE MAGNIFICENT

A PROFILE OF THE BLAZING FLORENTINE DESIGNER AND OF HIS PALAZZO HEADQUARTERS

BY VALENTINE LAWFORD WITH PHOTOGRAPHS BY HORST

Emilio Pucci of Florence is one of the greatest fashion forces at work today. He is a visionary whose vision of women is the essence of modernity. Pucci's vision has become reality. He has largely invented the look of the woman of the moment—one might almost say he has invented the woman herself: narrow, athletic, strong, brilliantly at home in the sun, and still brilliant in the evening. She is the most beautiful and luxurious woman in the world. On a ski slope, she wears the most practical and amusing and correct clothes; at dinner in some palazzo, she appears in the most beautifully coloured pyjamas cut in the most perfect way; at a bistro beside the Mediterranean, she turns up in some ravishing absurdity. Pucci is an artist with an architect's sense of proportion. His vision is wholly personal, his effects wholly contemporary. But he has ten centuries of Italian past on which to draw.

Pucci's feeling for Italian tradition is passionately serious, inherent, and unforced. The Pucci family have been well known in Florence for about a thousand years. Within a stone's throw of Florence's cathedral, the Duomo, their palazzo still stands in the heart of the city, on a street bearing their name. Austerely impressive, stained and worn, its walls echo today, as they have echoed for centuries, to Florentine traffic and Florentine bells.

"Dark, narrow, and elegant"—Pasternak's adjectives for Florence might just as well have been applied to this present-day Pucci. And there is more than a fanciful resemblance between his unusually character-revealing profile and Pontormo's portrait of Cosimo the Elder, with its sad but undefeatable eye, and its reminder of an age when it was a matter of course for an outstanding man to have an outstandingly manly nose. He hardly ever laughs and rather seldom smiles; but mostly goes, rapt and preoccupied, head down and chin in hand, about his business. Like some figure from Cellini's memoirs, he seems always to be striding briskly away around a corner or (Continued on page 162)

MARCHESE EMILIO PUCCI DI BARSENTO

The greatest colourist in the field of fashion design, a unique practical power in fashion, and a member of the Italian Parliament, Emilio Pucci was photographed here in one of his fantastic, frescoed workrooms in the Palazzo Pucci in Florence. In his sombre clothes, which are individual but never frivolous (his jacket may be of some discreet but unexpected pattern or weave), he moves like a dark flame among the glorious colours he thinks women everywhere should wear—the yachting pants, ski pants, dresses, jewellery, all designed with the Pucci perfection of cut. In fact, the only luxury Pucci recognizes is perfection.

157

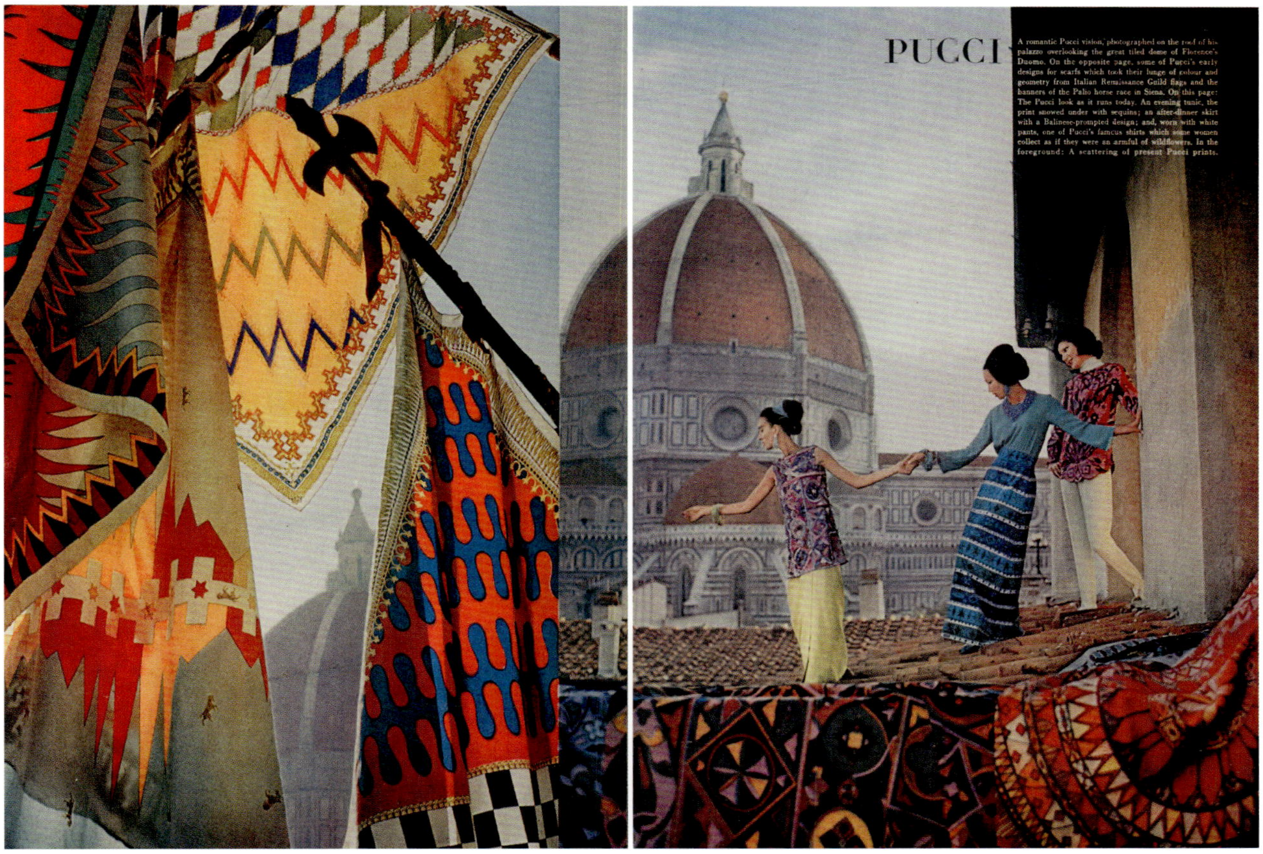

PUCCI

A romantic Pucci vision, photographed on the roof of his palazzo overlooking the great tiled dome of Florence's Duomo. On the opposite page, some of Pucci's early designs for scarfs which took their lunge of colour and geometry from Italian Renaissance Guild flags and the banners of the Palio horse race in Siena. On this page: The Pucci look as it runs today. An evening tunic, the print snowed under with sequins; an after-dinner skirt with a Balinese-prompted design; and, worn with white pants, one of Pucci's famous shirts which some women collect as if they were an armful of wildflowers. In the foreground: A scattering of present Pucci prints.

267 and 268. Emilio Pucci at home, Florence, 1964

The House that Horst Grew

In 1947 Horst acquired five acres of land in Oyster Bay Cove, Long Island, part of the estate once owned by the belle époque designer Louis Comfort Tiffany. At a cost of 500 dollars per acre, Horst's purchase included a pond, two streams, a wood and a field alive with wildflowers, rabbits, pheasants and raccoons. On the land he described as 'everything I had ever dreamed of', he built a unique house and landscaped garden with the help of the architect Ed Tauch, whom he had known in Paris, and builder David Murchison.[1] The single-storey white stucco building was built primarily of wood, brick and cement-block, painted white or plastered and whitewashed. The design took inspiration from myriad sources, including the modernist ideals of the Bauhaus and the simplicity of George Hoyningen-Huene's white villa in Tunisia, where Horst had spent many happy days in the 1930s. From the outset the plan for the garden was as significant as the house itself. Adjoining the building Horst created a series of individual gardens, planted to suit their prevailing sunshine or shade. Outside his study a pergola became the summer living room filled with fig trees, hibiscus and oleanders, while *allées* of evergreen trees and shrubs in contrasting shades fanned out from the house.

To finance the costly project, Horst sold two of his favourite artworks: the Picasso gouache of a clown and boy, given to him by the cellist and art collector Francesco von Mendelssohn, and the Toulouse-Lautrec portrait of May Belfort, purchased from Germain Seligman's gallery in the 1930s. But other treasured possessions were carefully combined in each room: pictures by Bérard, Braque and Dalí; Persian rugs from the chieftain of the Qashqa'i tribe; Coco Chanel's baroque mirror; Jean-Michel Frank furniture and Giacometti plaster lamps and vases – all reflective of the owner's international life, personal style and passions. Horst frequently entertained at Oyster Bay, arranging lunches and dinners for his wide circle of friends and *Vogue* colleagues. Among the very first invited visitors were the designer Valentina, Alexander Liberman and Edna Woolman Chase, who lived close by. Other notable early guests included Huene, Dalí, Beaton, Chanel and Dior. When Valentine Lawford visited for the first time in 1947 (along with Noël Coward, Christopher Isherwood and Greta Garbo) it was the beginning of a relationship with Horst that would last until Lawford's death in 1991.[2] Their shared love of interior and garden design would later lead to the magnificent Fashions in Living series for *Vogue*. A snapshot taken in 1949 exemplifies the couple's broad social circle and shows Lawford, Greta Garbo, Edith Sitwell and Mab Moltke (a former *Vogue* editor) conversing in the garden.[3] This intimate gathering was the only occasion on which Horst photographed Garbo.

Even before it was complete, the house became the location for fashion shoots, and occasional pictures for *House & Garden*. These tend to appear more casual than Horst's studio photographs of earlier years, taking full advantage of the daylight and variety of textures within the house. One of his favourites was titled *Bombay Bathing Fashion*, 1950 (pl.269), of which he commented, 'I always loved sunlight and shadow and straw mats. The picture is simple, relaxed. It is human.'[4] As well as memorable fashion studies, Horst created many still lifes at Oyster Bay. He combined crafted and natural forms in table settings suffused with light, or delicately arranged sculptures from his collection with fruits, plants and flowers such as roses and tulips. The still lifes dating from the 1980s are darkly toned and evoke the classicism of Horst's 1930s studies. Some incorporate his prints from earlier decades; portraits and nudes are grouped with sculptural fragments and treasured *objets* to produce studies that are intensely personal and contemplative.

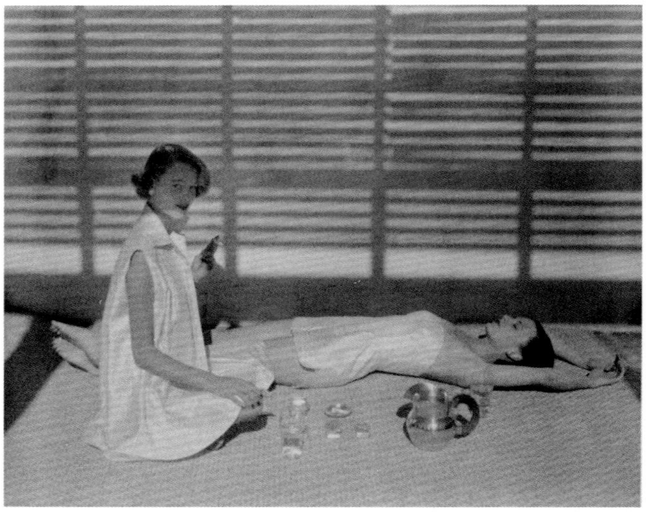

269. *Bombay Bathing Fashion*, 1950

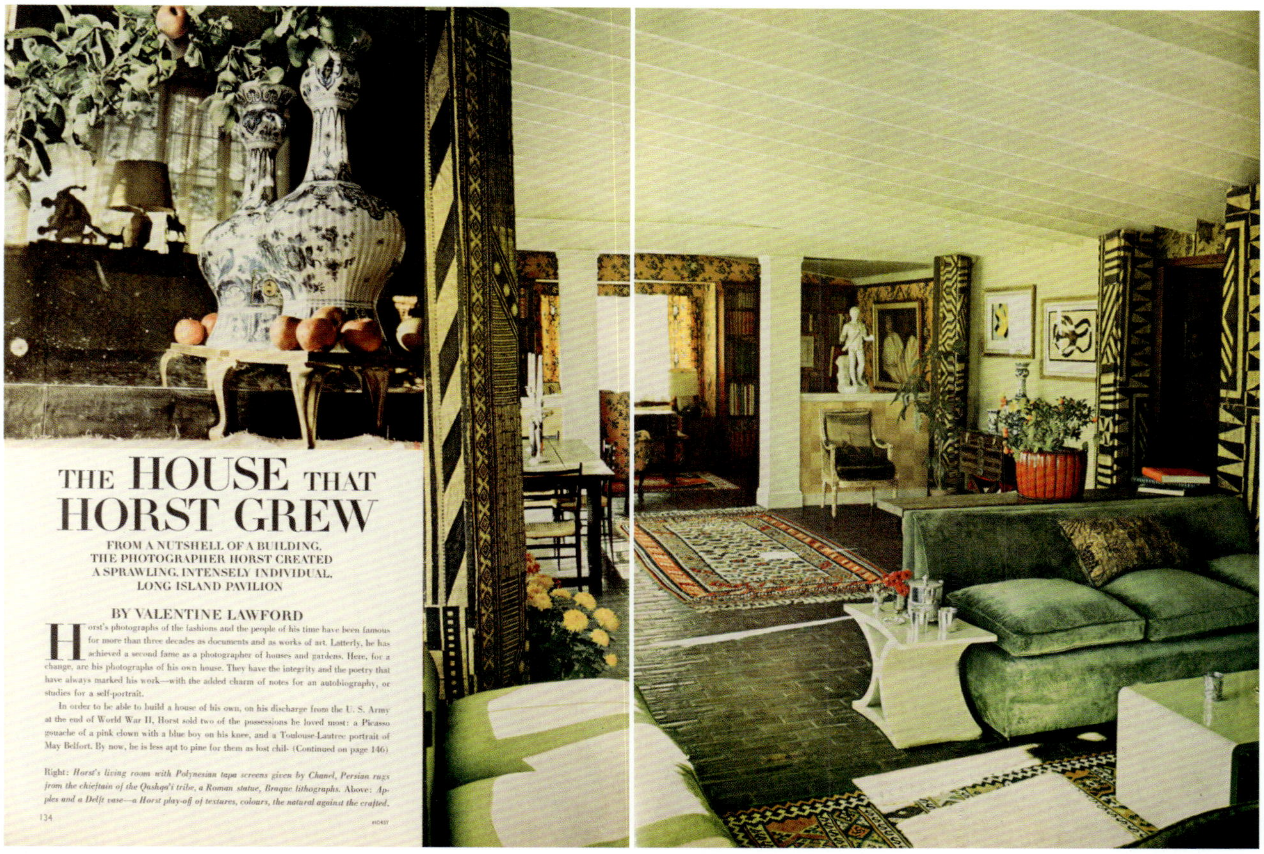

THE HOUSE THAT HORST GREW

FROM A NUTSHELL OF A BUILDING, THE PHOTOGRAPHER HORST CREATED A SPRAWLING, INTENSELY INDIVIDUAL, LONG ISLAND PAVILION

BY VALENTINE LAWFORD

Horst's photographs of the fashions and the people of his time have been famous for more than three decades as documents and as works of art. Latterly, he has achieved a second fame as a photographer of houses and gardens. Here, for a change, are his photographs of his own house. They have the integrity and the poetry that have always marked his work—with the added charm of notes for an autobiography, or studies for a self-portrait.

In order to be able to build a house of his own, on his discharge from the U. S. Army at the end of World War II, Horst sold two of the possessions he loved most: a Picasso gouache of a pink clown with a blue boy on his knee, and a Toulouse-Lautrec portrait of May Belfort. By now, he is less apt to pine for them as lost chil- (Continued on page 146)

Right: *Horst's living room with Polynesian tapa screens given by Chanel, Persian rugs from the chieftain of the Qashqa'i tribe, a Roman statue, Braque lithographs.* Above: *Apples and a Delft vase—a Horst play-off of textures, colours, the natural against the crafted.*

134

HORST

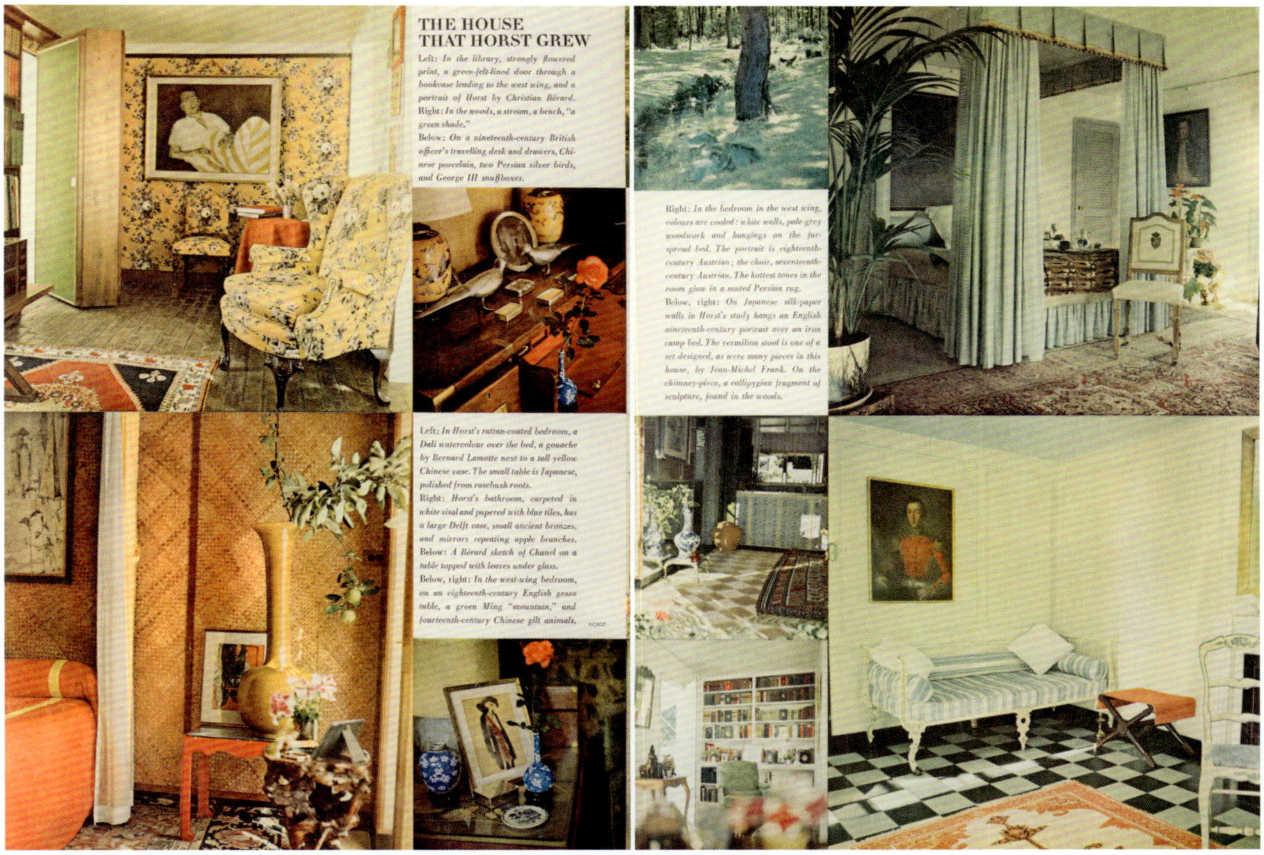

THE HOUSE THAT HORST GREW

Left: *In the library, strongly flowered print, a green-felt-lined door through a bookcase leading to the west wing, and a portrait of Horst by Christian Bérard.*
Right: *In the woods, a stream, a bench, "a green shade."*
Below: *On a nineteenth-century British officer's travelling desk and drawers, Chinese porcelain, two Persian silver birds, and George III snuffboxes.*

Right: *In the bedroom in the west wing, colours are cooled: white walls, pale-grey woodwork and hangings on the fur-spread bed. The portrait is eighteenth-century Austrian; the chair, seventeenth-century Austrian. The hottest tones in the room glow in a muted Persian rug.*
Below, right: *On Japanese silk-paper walls in Horst's study hangs an English nineteenth-century portrait over an iron camp bed. The vermilion stool is one of a set designed, as were many pieces in this house, by Jean-Michel Frank. On the chimney-piece, a callipygian fragment of sculpture, found in the woods.*

Left: *In Horst's rattan-coated bedroom, a Dali watercolour over the bed, a gouache by Bernard Lamotte next to a tall yellow Chinese vase. The small table is Japanese, polished from rosebush roots.*
Right: *Horst's bathroom, carpeted in white sisal and papered with blue tiles, has a large Delft vase, small ancient bronzes, and mirrors repeating apple branches.*
Below: *A Bérard sketch of Chanel on a table topped with leaves under glass.*
Below, right: *In the west-wing bedroom, on an eighteenth-century English gesso table, a green Ming "mountain," and fourteenth-century Chinese gilt animals.*

HORST

270. Interior of Horst's Oyster Bay house, Long Island, 1966

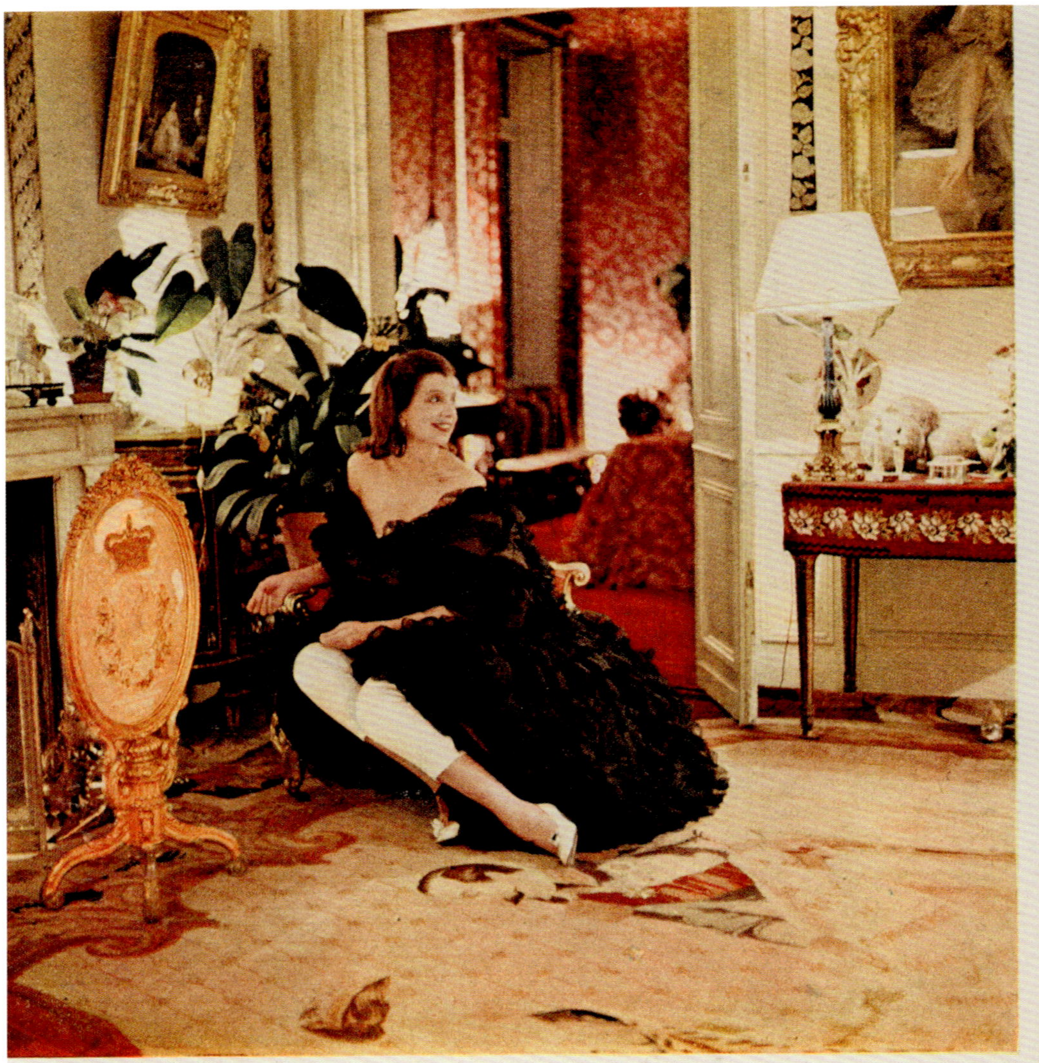

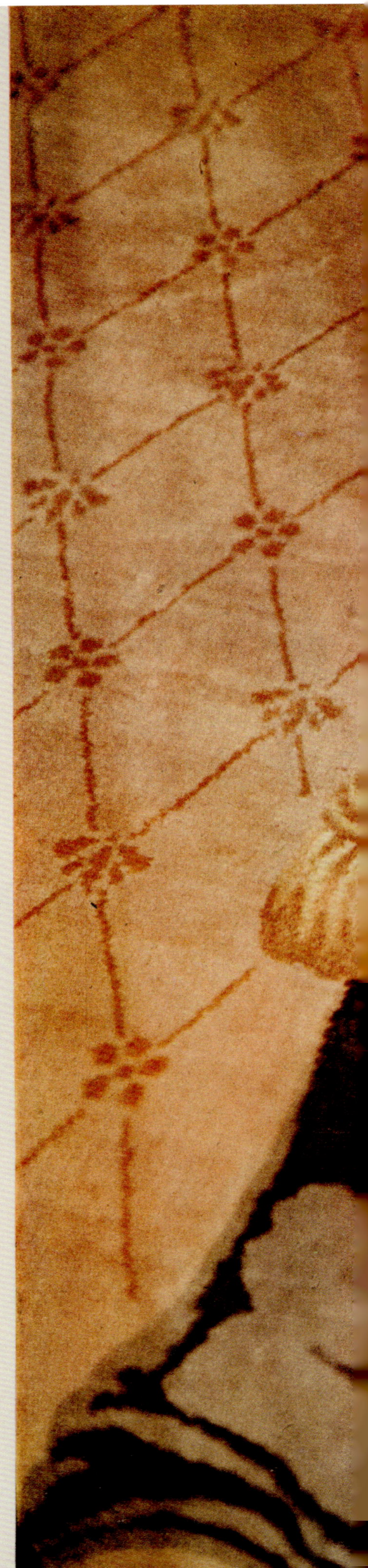

CHÂTEAU DE MOUTON
Continued

Above: Baroness de Rothschild in the Second Empire fantasy drawing room; on the ornamented silk fire screen, a portrait of Queen Victoria and crown. *Opposite:* The Baron de Rothschild's tapestry evening slipper on a mid-nineteenth-century carpet (with an over-life-size figure of Napoleon III) commemorating a Franco-British Treaty of Commerce. *Below:* On the same carpet: Napoleon III's boots, a beadwork Victorian footstool, and another evening slipper, this one of beadwork like the stool. This extraordinary room is dominated by a great portrait of Baron Philippe's mother. Painted about 1900 by Flameng, the portrait hung there throughout the war, and departing Germans and the *Maquis* in turn placed in front of it large vases of flowers.

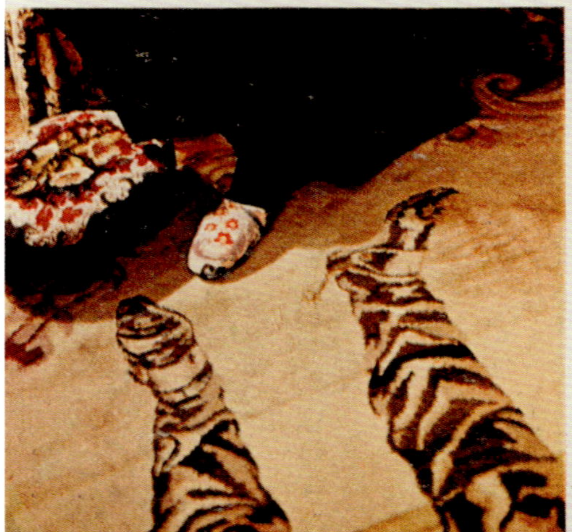

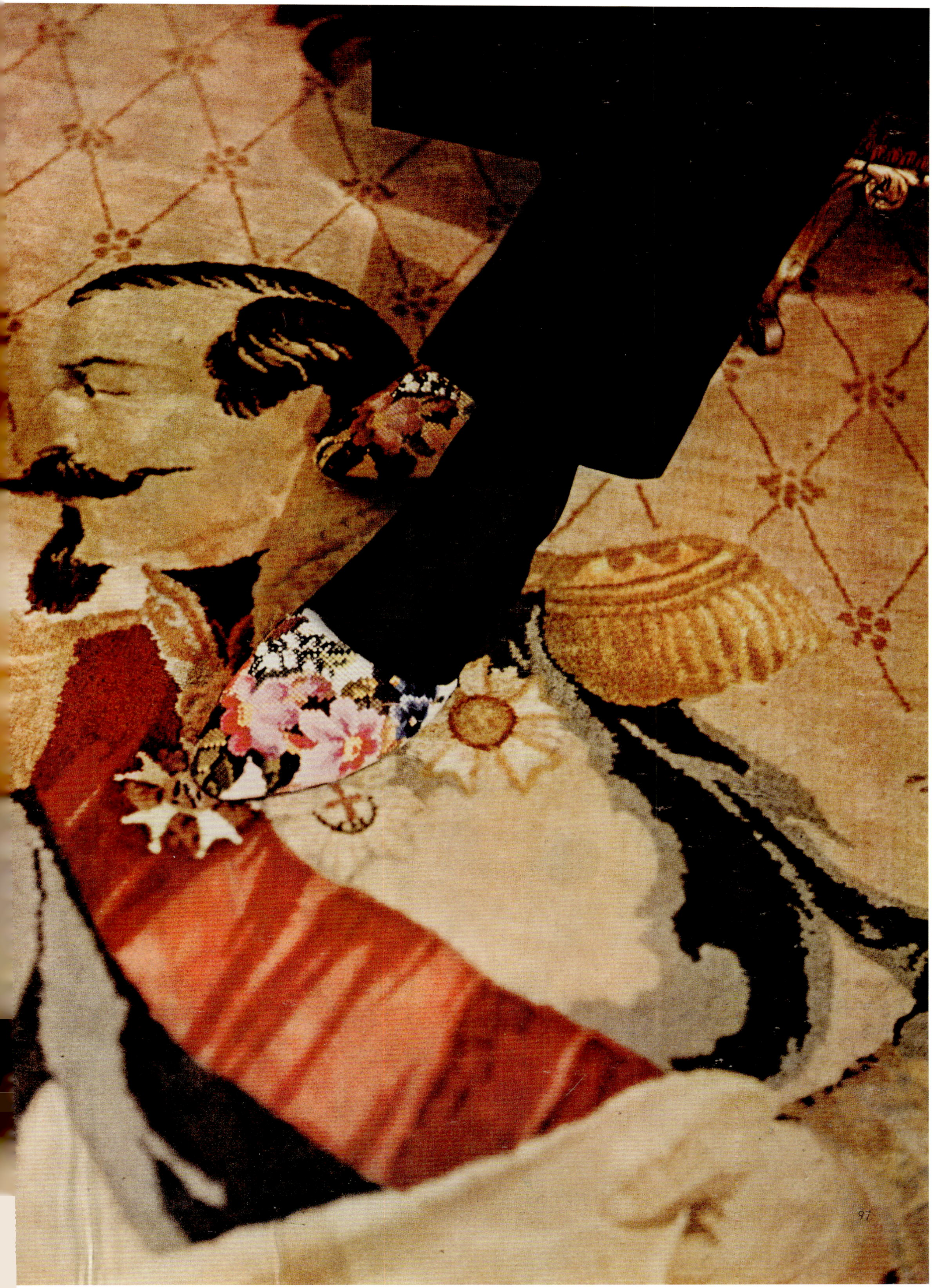

271. Baron and Baroness Philippe de Rothschild's home, Château de Mouton, Pauillac, France, 1963

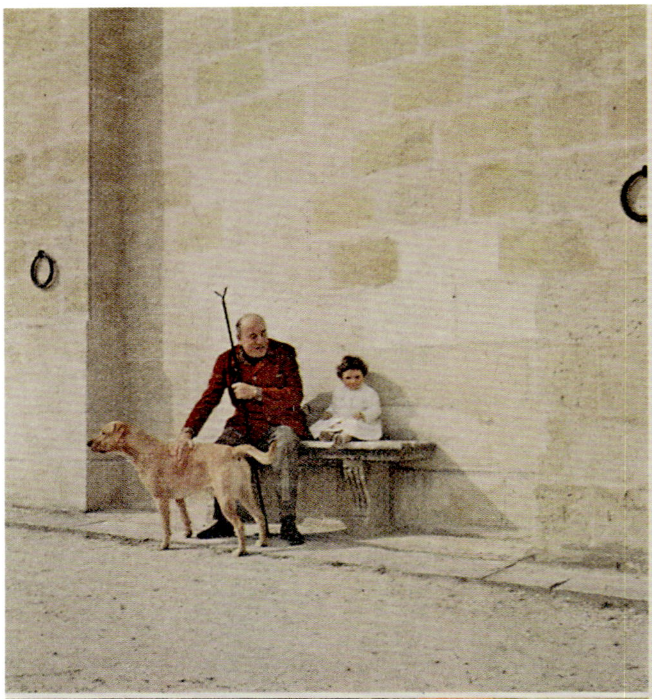
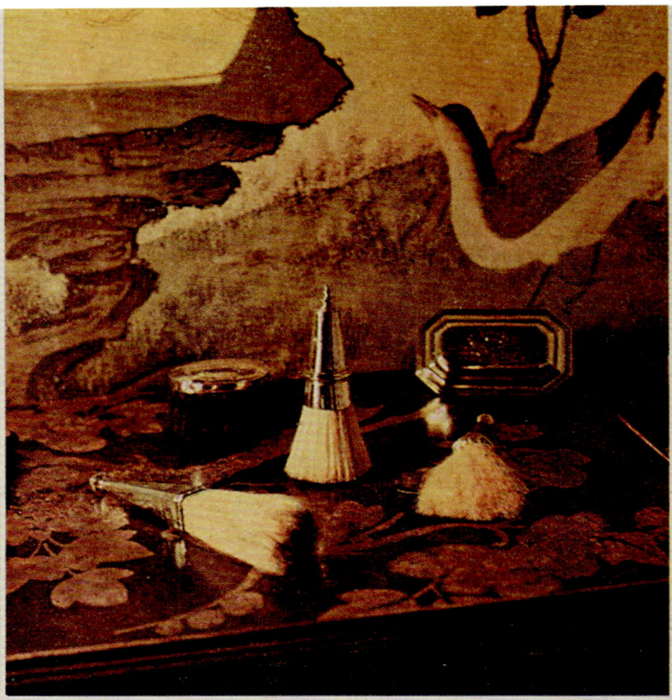
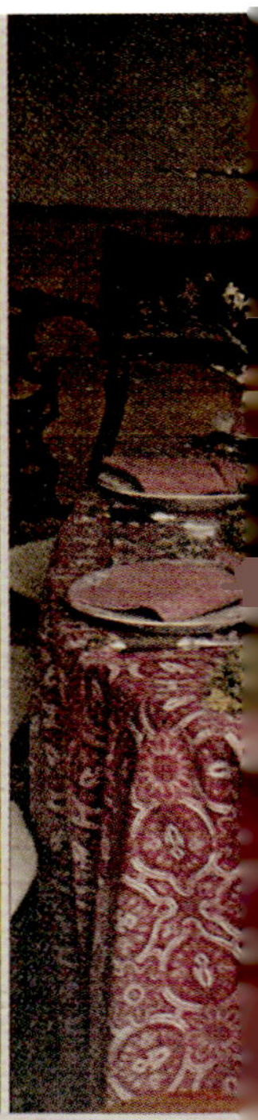
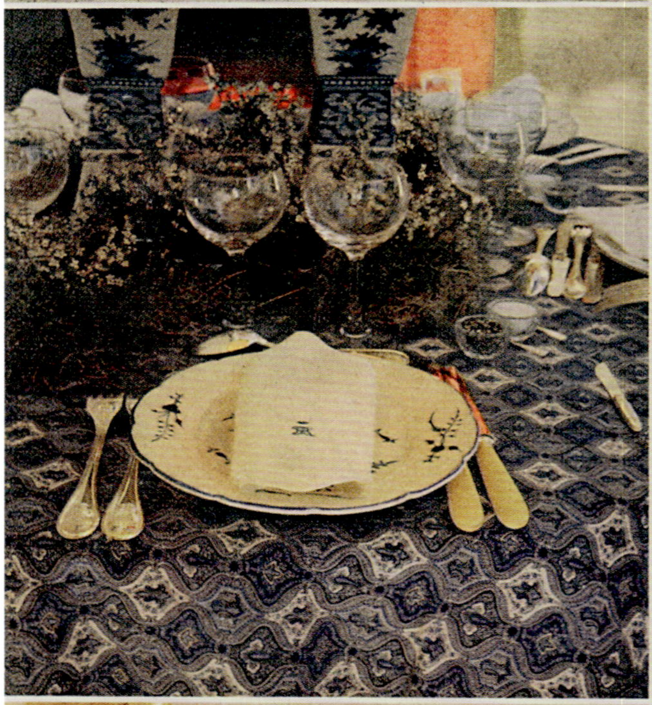
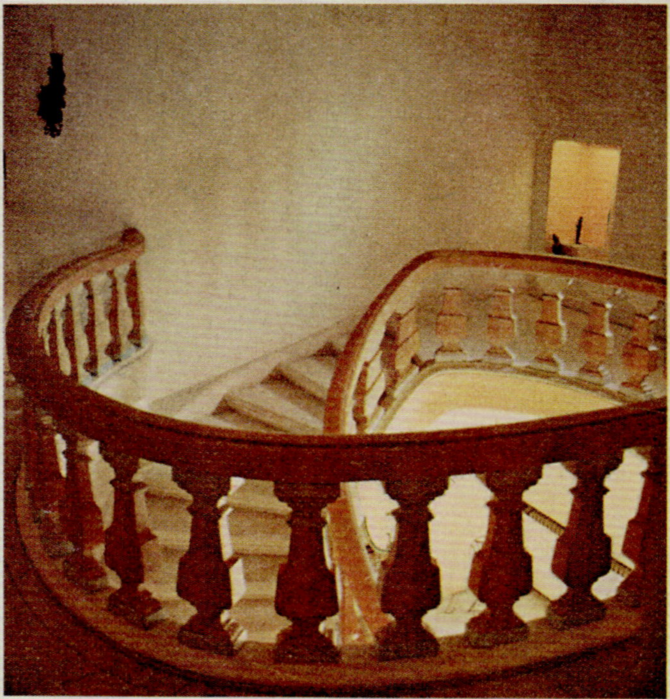
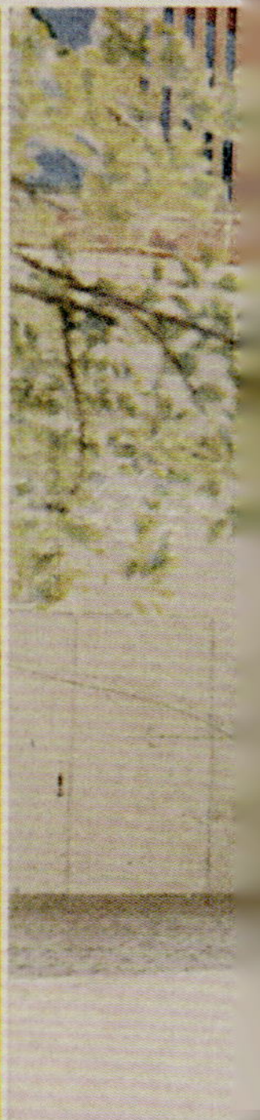
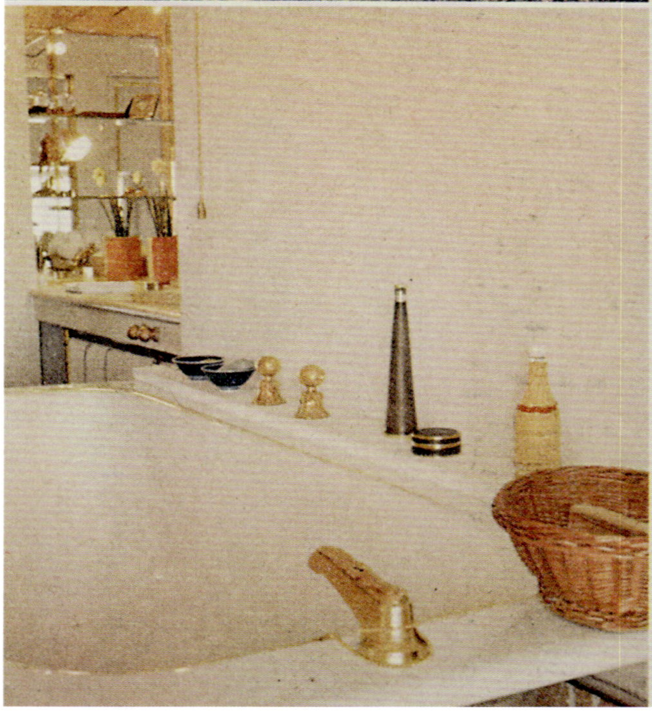
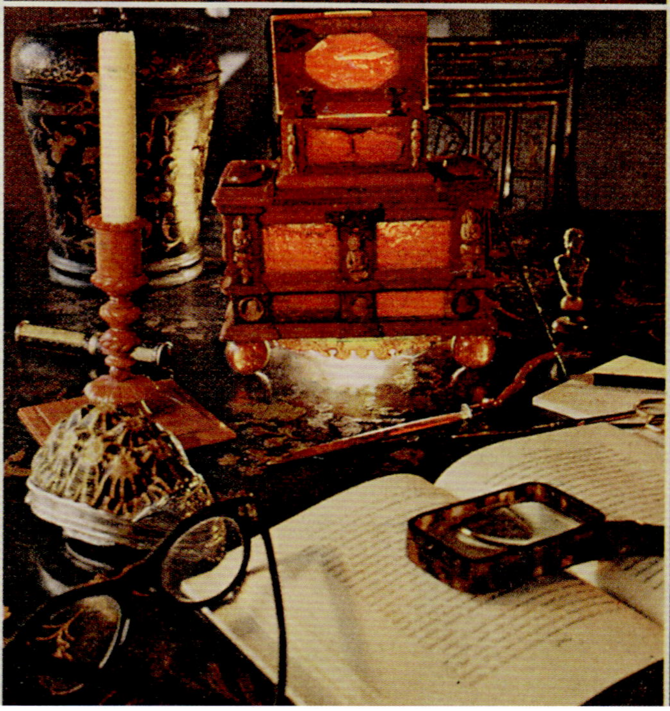
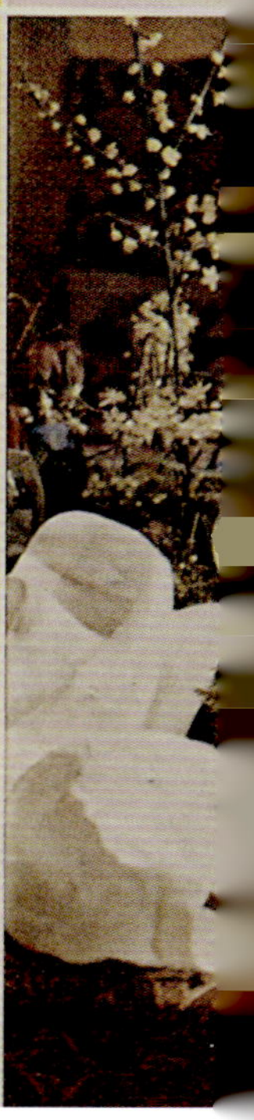

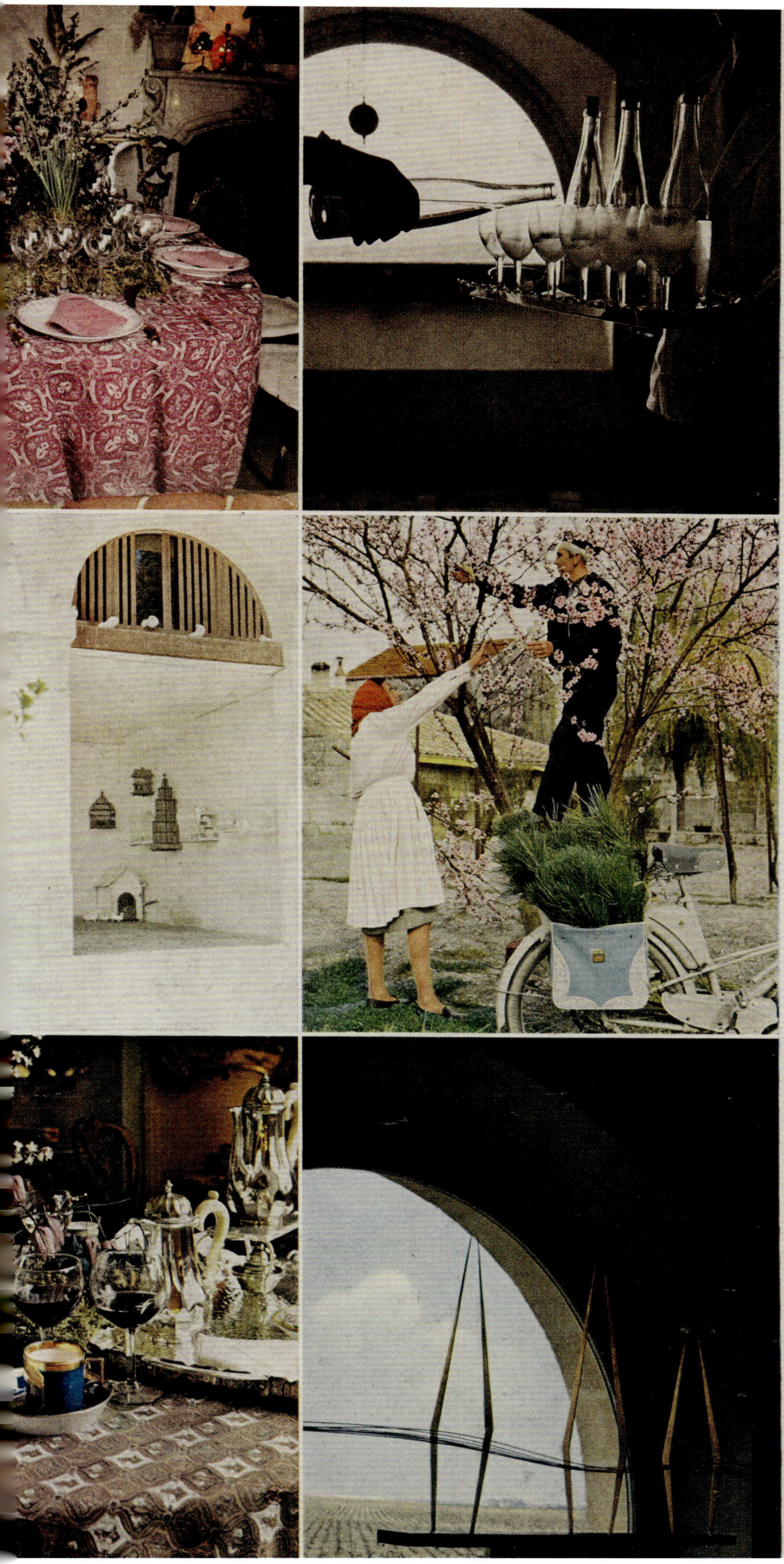

CHÂTEAU DE MOUTON Continued

Top row, left to right:
Baron de Rothschild with his small granddaughter, Camille, and Gogo the golden retriever, outside the Château.
Still life of English and Dutch seventeenth-century silver brushes, against a background of an eighteenth-century Chinese paper panel in the new bedroom of the Baroness de Rothschild.
Table setting for luncheon: in centre, peach blossoms, jonquils, whitethorn, and sea sage on a moss foundation.
Butler's white-gloved hand pouring liqueurs: Framboise, Mirabelle, Kirsch.

Second row, left to right:
For luncheon on outdoor terrace: white heather and blue-and-white Delft vases.
Balustrade—trompe-l'oeil red-ochre, white-grey marble; reverse stairway.
Doves and watchdogs at the entrance.
Marie, the flower-arranger, taught by the Baroness, gathering peach blossoms and pine for one of her masterpieces.

Third row, left to right:
Still life in bathroom: vermeil boxes, wicker baskets, gilt handles like lemons.
Tortoiseshell still life: including a seventeenth-century Dutch miniature cabinet and candlestick, a tortoise snuffbox, all on a Chinese black lacquer table.
After luncheon: speckled tulips, brown Paisley-patterned cloth, with one of a vast collection of different coffee cups.
Lippold's "Cortège" in the living room.

93

272. Baron and Baroness Philippe de Rothschild's home, Château de Mouton, Pauillac, France, 1963

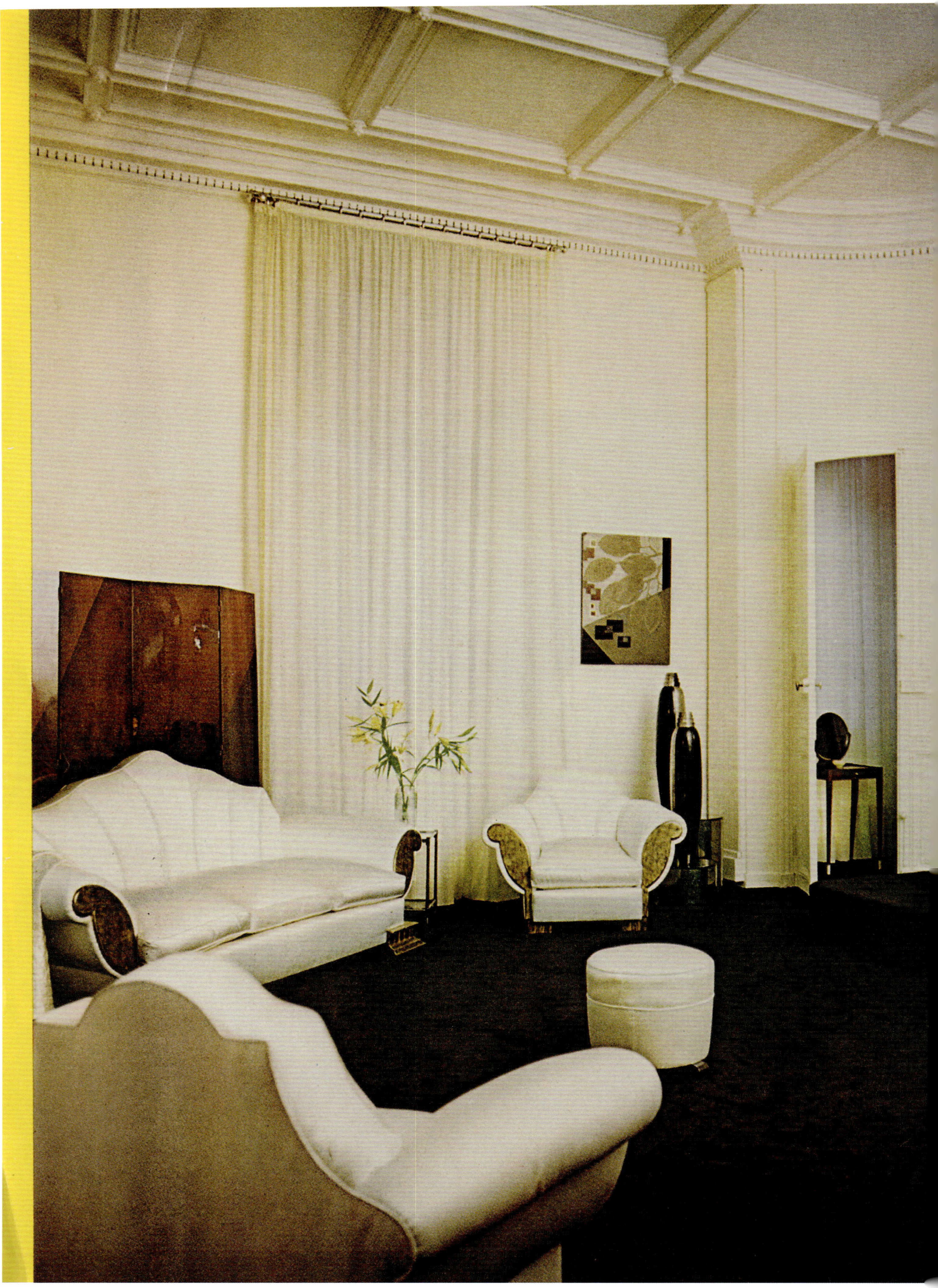

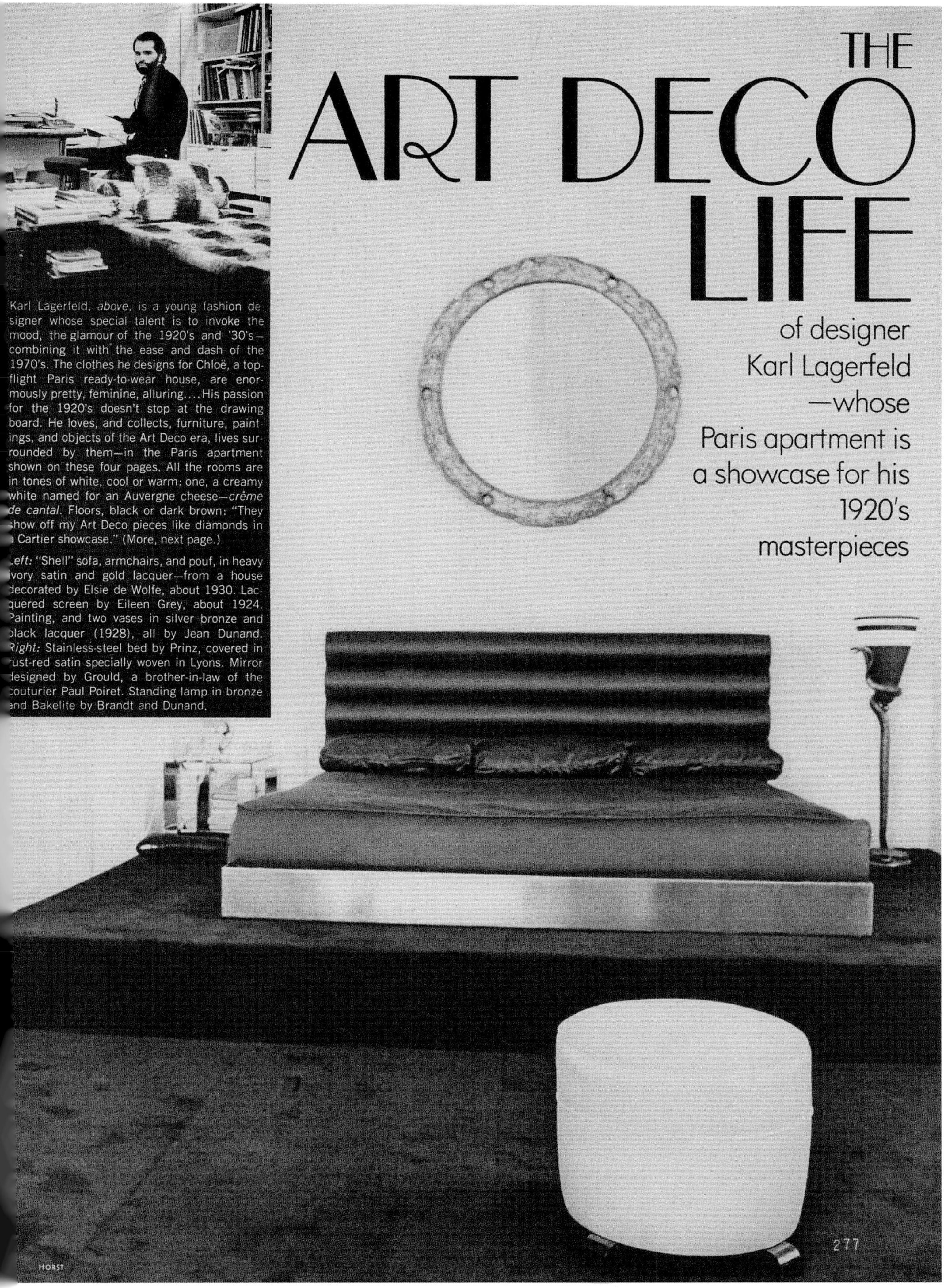
THE ART DECO LIFE

of designer Karl Lagerfeld —whose Paris apartment is a showcase for his 1920's masterpieces

Karl Lagerfeld, *above*, is a young fashion designer whose special talent is to invoke the mood, the glamour of the 1920's and '30's—combining it with the ease and dash of the 1970's. The clothes he designs for Chloë, a top-flight Paris ready-to-wear house, are enormously pretty, feminine, alluring.... His passion for the 1920's doesn't stop at the drawing board. He loves, and collects, furniture, paintings, and objects of the Art Deco era, lives surrounded by them—in the Paris apartment shown on these four pages. All the rooms are in tones of white, cool or warm: one, a creamy white named for an Auvergne cheese—*crême de cantal*. Floors, black or dark brown: "They show off my Art Deco pieces like diamonds in a Cartier showcase." (More, next page.)

Left: "Shell" sofa, armchairs, and pouf, in heavy ivory satin and gold lacquer—from a house decorated by Elsie de Wolfe, about 1930. Lacquered screen by Eileen Grey, about 1924. Painting, and two vases in silver bronze and black lacquer (1928), all by Jean Dunand. *Right:* Stainless-steel bed by Prinz, covered in rust-red satin specially woven in Lyons. Mirror designed by Grould, a brother-in-law of the couturier Paul Poiret. Standing lamp in bronze and Bakelite by Brandt and Dunand.

HORST

277

273. Karl Lagerfeld's apartment, Paris, 1974

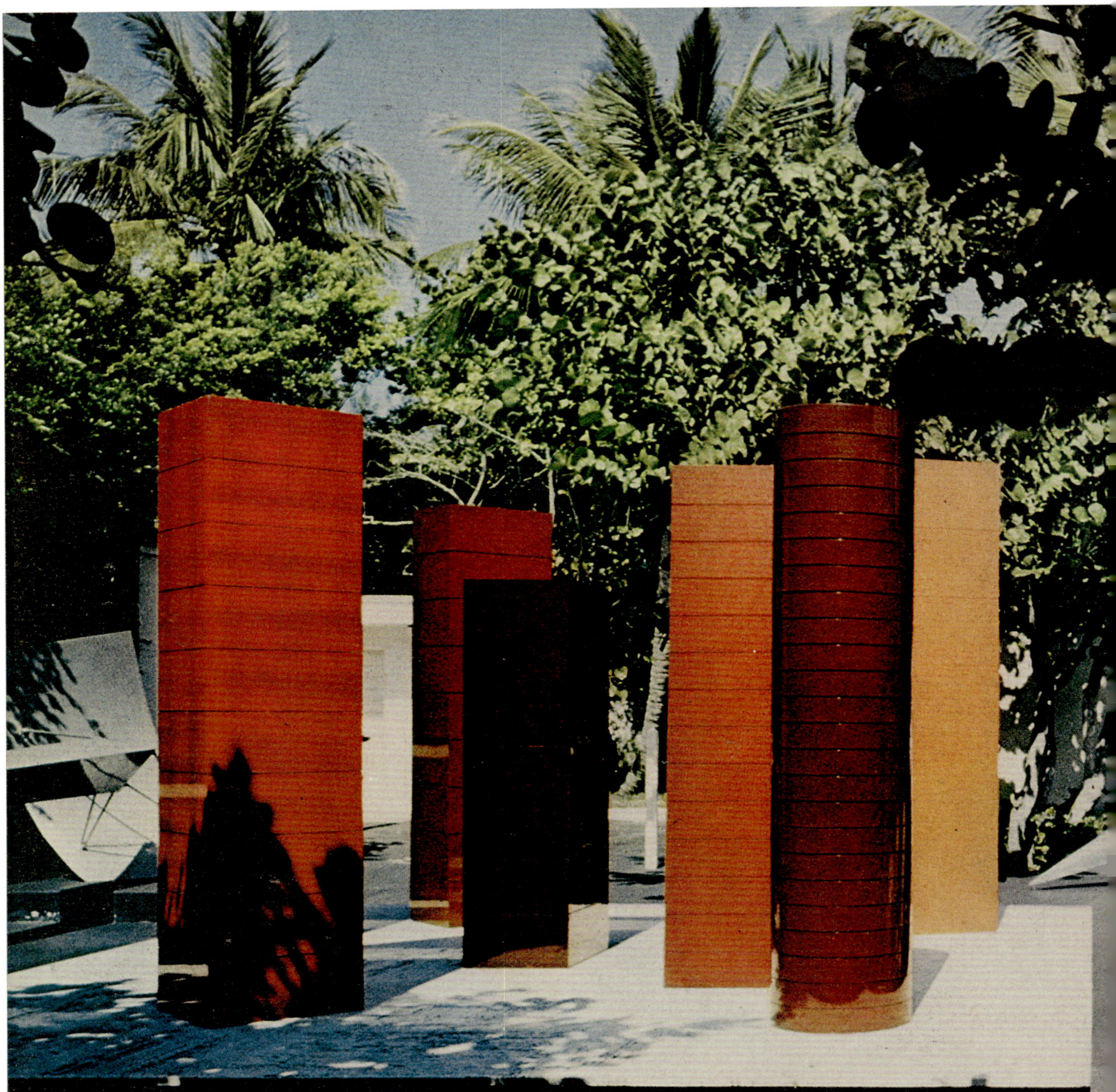

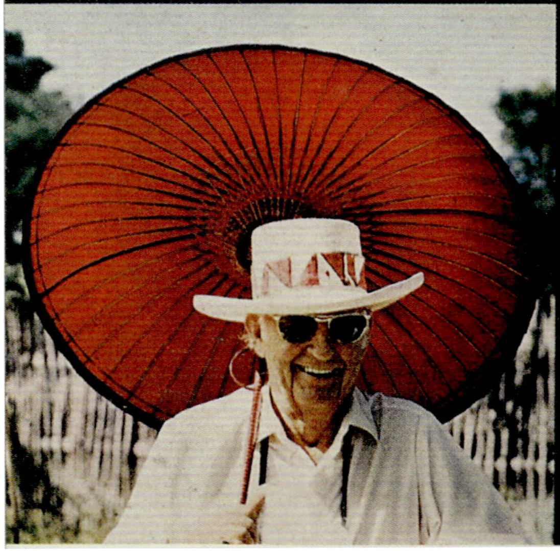

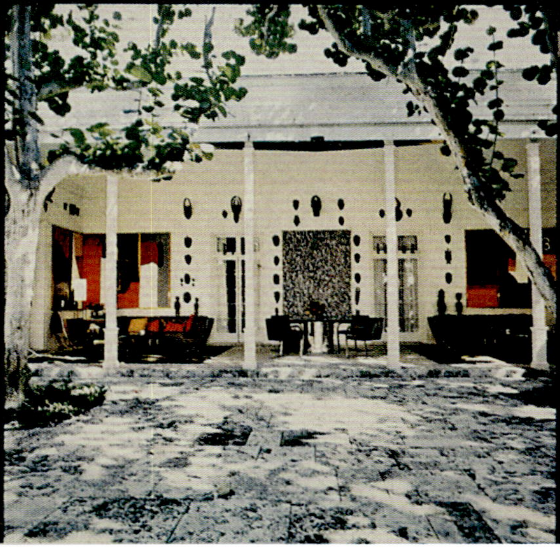

Art should be lived with, not just looked at, Patrick Lannan *(far left)* believes. Tall, white-haired, with shrewd blue eyes and a natural flamboyance, Mr. Lannan has turned "Four Winds," his house in Palm Beach, into a picture gallery and his grounds into a sculpture garden. The major aim of his collecting has always been to encourage young artists by buying and displaying their work. Patrick Lannan's early, and continuing, interest in electrical engineering and physics, coupled with an instinct for art, led him into the Buckminster Fuller group and on to kinetic art. He has built an outstanding

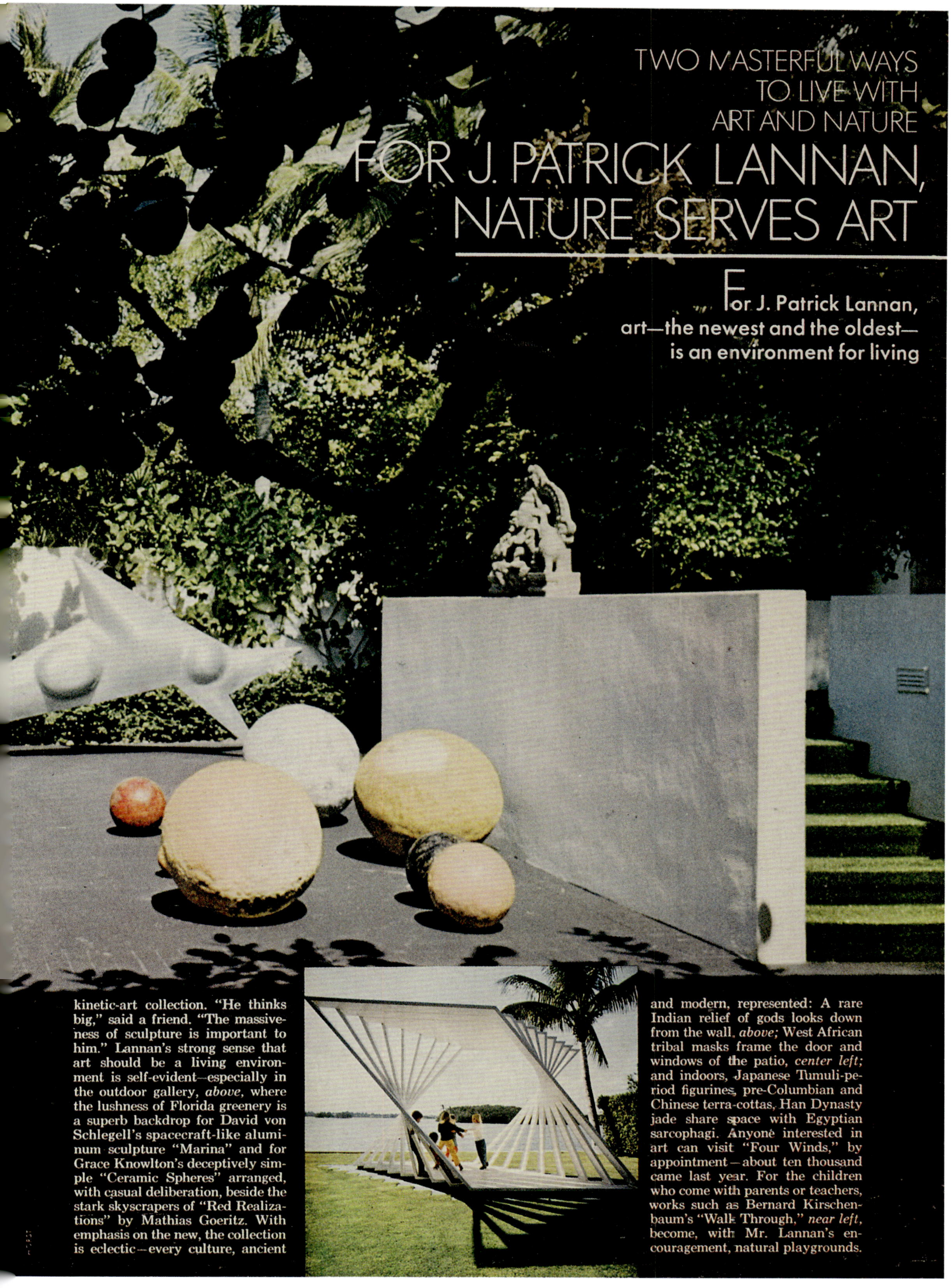

TWO MASTERFUL WAYS TO LIVE WITH ART AND NATURE

FOR J. PATRICK LANNAN, NATURE SERVES ART

For J. Patrick Lannan, art—the newest and the oldest—is an environment for living

kinetic-art collection. "He thinks big," said a friend. "The massiveness of sculpture is important to him." Lannan's strong sense that art should be a living environment is self-evident—especially in the outdoor gallery, *above*, where the lushness of Florida greenery is a superb backdrop for David von Schlegell's spacecraft-like aluminum sculpture "Marina" and for Grace Knowlton's deceptively simple "Ceramic Spheres" arranged, with casual deliberation, beside the stark skyscrapers of "Red Realizations" by Mathias Goeritz. With emphasis on the new, the collection is eclectic—every culture, ancient and modern, represented: A rare Indian relief of gods looks down from the wall, *above;* West African tribal masks frame the door and windows of the patio, *center left;* and indoors, Japanese Tumuli-period figurines, pre-Columbian and Chinese terra-cottas, Han Dynasty jade share space with Egyptian sarcophagi. Anyone interested in art can visit "Four Winds," by appointment—about ten thousand came last year. For the children who come with parents or teachers, works such as Bernard Kirschenbaum's "Walk Through," *near left,* become, with Mr. Lannan's encouragement, natural playgrounds.

274. J. Patrick Lannan's home, Palm Beach, 1973

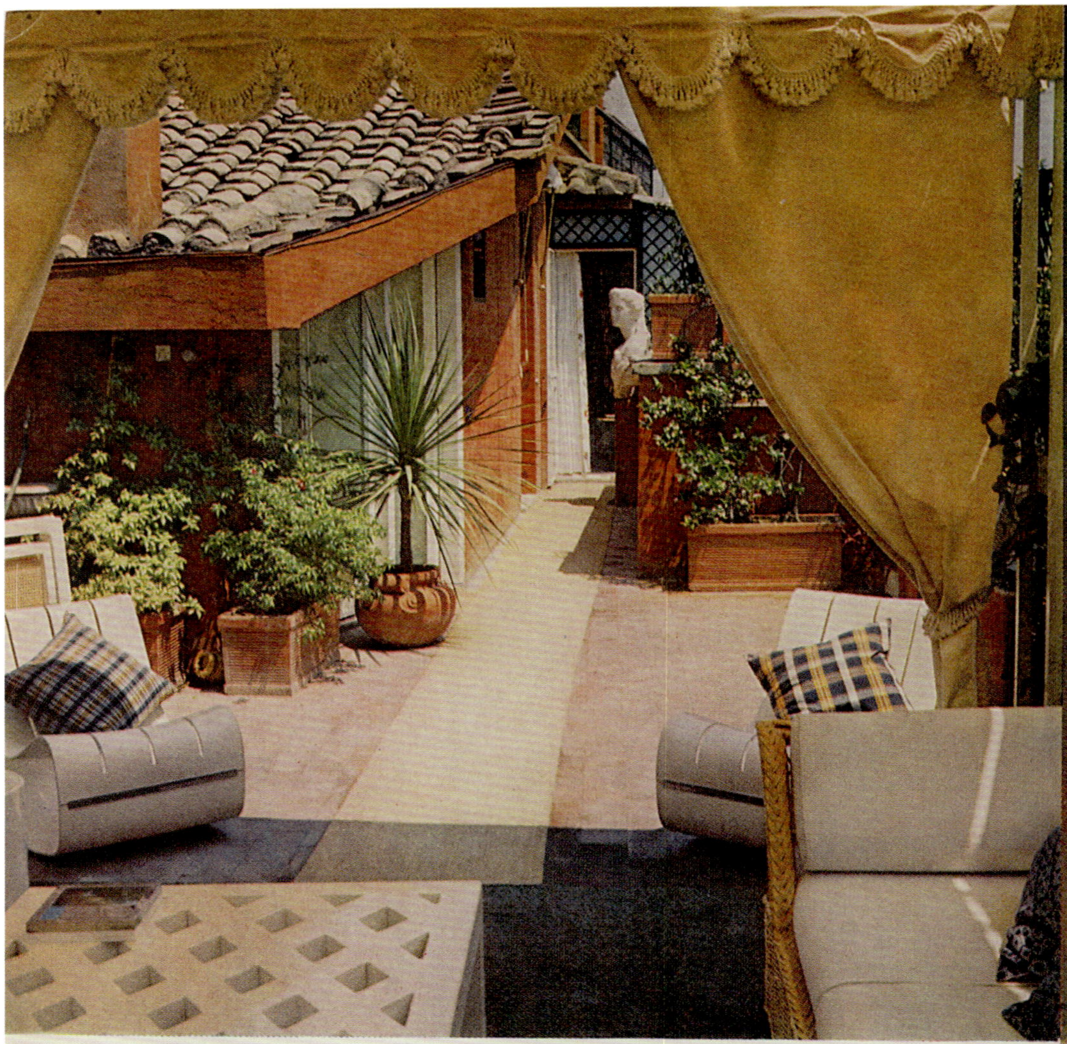

Well ordered, exact, superbly detailed, and alive with fantaisie

Valentino's ROMAN ROOF-TOP

To his two-storey penthouse on top of a small palazzo in Rome, Valentino, the Italian designer whose soft-spoken perfectionist clothes are as noted in this country as they are in his, has brought the best of Italian workmanship to shape a place of romantic surprises and no accidents. From the fit of fabrics on walls and cushions to the metal bindings on doors, the rooms have a correctness, an authority of detail that raise voluptuous outbursts of fantasy to a new order. Valentino's challenge was to beat, inside his apartment, the unbeatable outside: the view—the splendid, stretching red-ochre view of the roofs of Rome, the amazing sky with its starts of swallows. Working with the architects-designers of Studio GS, taking from the old, the new, the bold, the muted, setting no limits but the strictness of his eye, Valentino designed a live-in Valentino. IN A ROOF-TENT, above, Valentino has summer lunches and dinners. Against the roof's terra-cotta colours he played yellow sailcloth, a green splurge of potted plants and vines, the sharp whites of a classic sculpture and geometrically precise furniture, the chairs copied from Oriental ones. IN A TURQUERIE TENT, right, forming a glowing alcove off the coolly white and brown living room, the swathes of linen are printed with a design copied from a book of Persian art, the colours Valentino's choosing. Shining metal tables, square white planting boxes edged with chrome sharpen the opulence of pillows in linen and Indian silk, of leopard-skin rugs.

HORST

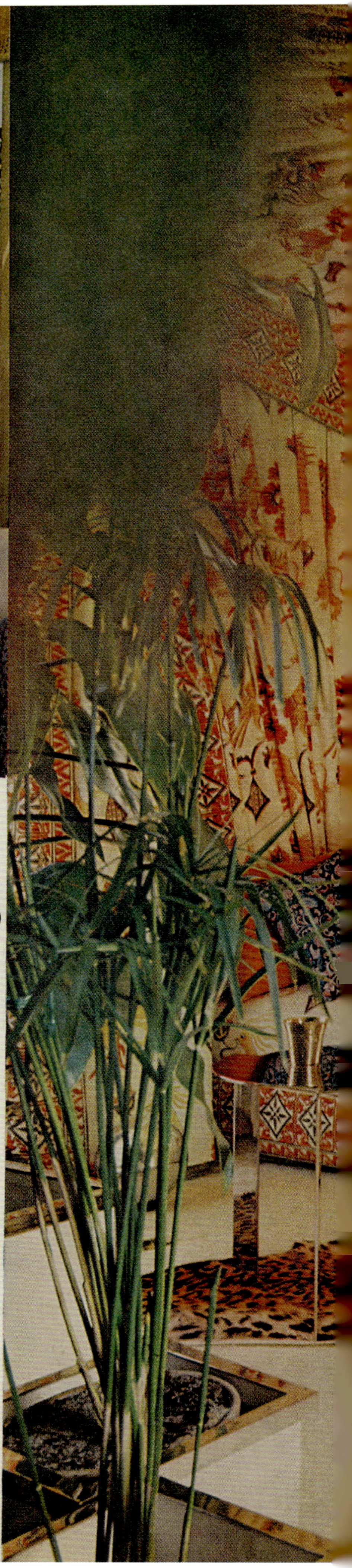

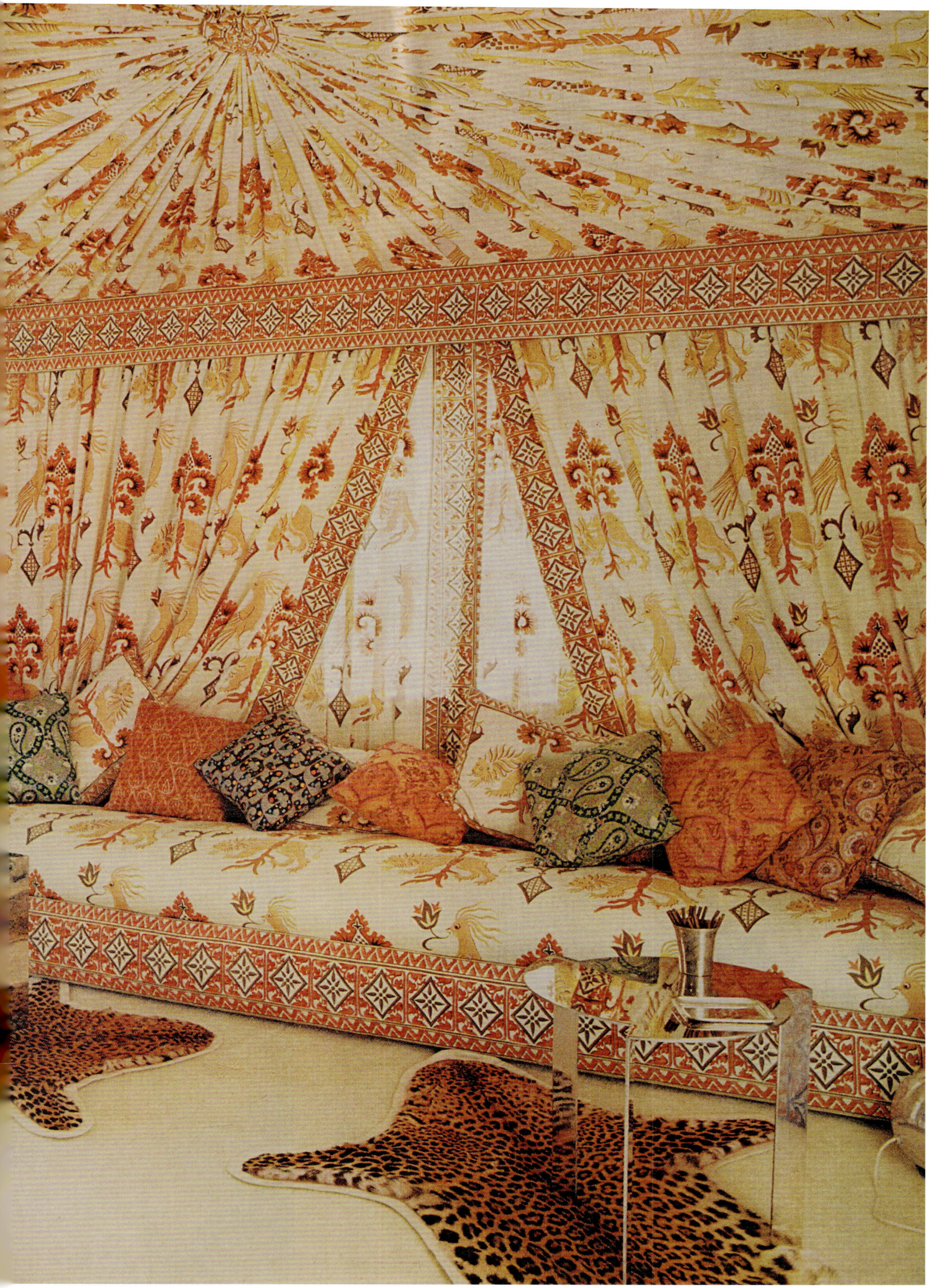

275. Valentino's penthouse, Rome, 1970

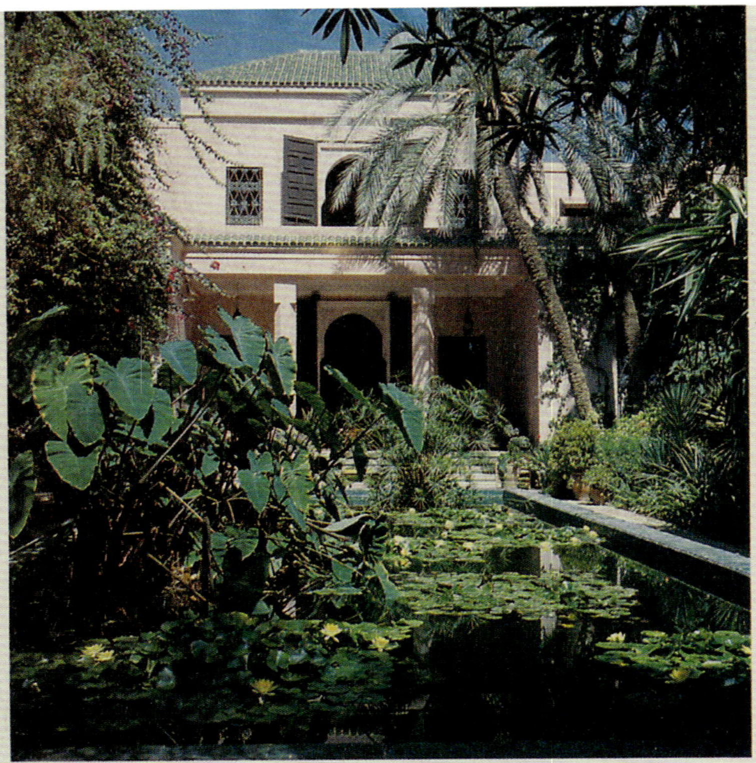

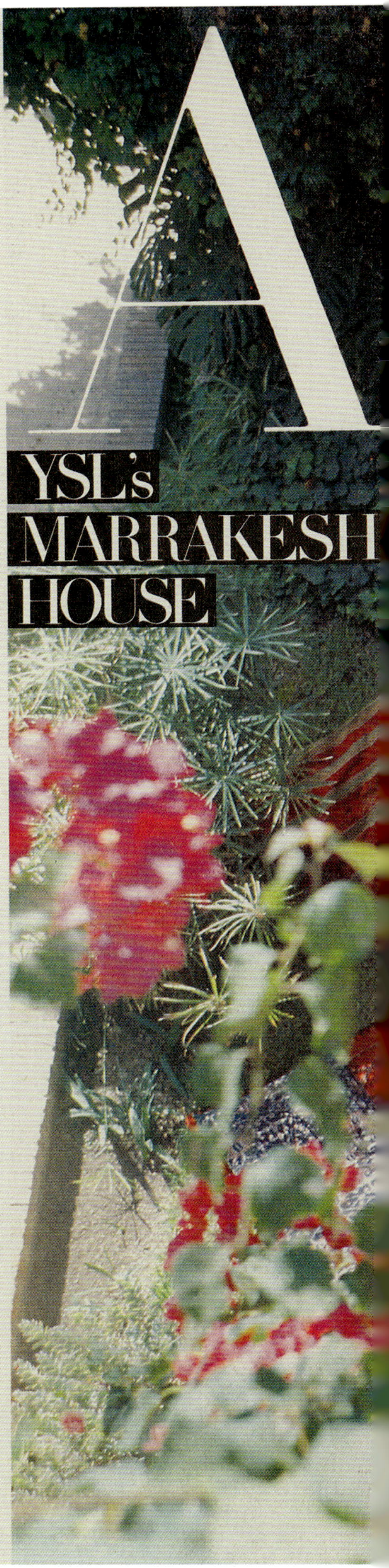

A YSL's MARRAKESH HOUSE

BEHIND A WALLED GARDEN LUSH WITH ROSES, ORANGE TREES, PALMS, STANDS DAR ES SAADA, "THE HOUSE OF HAPPINESS," YVES SAINT LAURENT'S NEW MARRAKESH RETREAT. MORE THAN A VACATION REFUGE—HIS REAL HOME

BY G. Y. DRYANSKY

To visit Yves Saint Laurent in the pink city of Marrakesh, you ask your driver to take you to "the house of happiness," in the quarter called "Serenity." (Dar Es Saada and La Zahia in Arabic.) Behind a high wall are a house and gardens laid out with a gentle order.

It's also very French, Cartesian, this geometry of vistas—of mini-vistas: in the way rooms of Saint Laurent's house give on to other rooms, and the garden path, for example, that leads to a vine-covered kiosk where Saint Laurent and Pierre Bergé, his partner in life and business, take mint tea on Oriental rugs, waited on by boys in harem pants. But there's nothing like a poor-man's Versailles here, just a spine of order; and the hedonism, if luxurious, is without pomp. Dar Es Saada is neither a French palace nor a local, Arab one. "The last thing I wanted was a palace," Saint Laurent said, "I'm against ultra-splendor."

The coziness of the flea-market furniture inside has an English colonial feeling, but there are more emotional ripples to the place than you'd associate with Victorian polo players.

From nearly every window of the house, Saint Laurent points out, "Linear perspectives convey a sense of calm." Wherever you are inside, landscapes seem to radiate like spokes whose center is yourself. Remember, Saint Laurent is a shy person and an intensely curious one at the same time, and he often uses as a metaphor for his way of life the image of a man beside a window. Remember, as well, that in a desert climate—Marrakesh is a walled oasis—a house has the same crucial sense of shelter that a chalet does in the Alps. The windows are barred at Dar Es Saada, screened with an elegant grillwork inspired by a still from a Hollywood silent film—Saint *(Continued on page 238)*

Yves Saint Laurent, *right*, in his Moroccan garden—as much an outdoor living room as a natural splendor—strewn with rugs, pillows from the bazaar—a peaceful place to drink mint tea offered by houseboys costumed in harem pants. *Above:* The house with its rosy stucco and polished limestone walls, seen from water-lily pond.

Horst

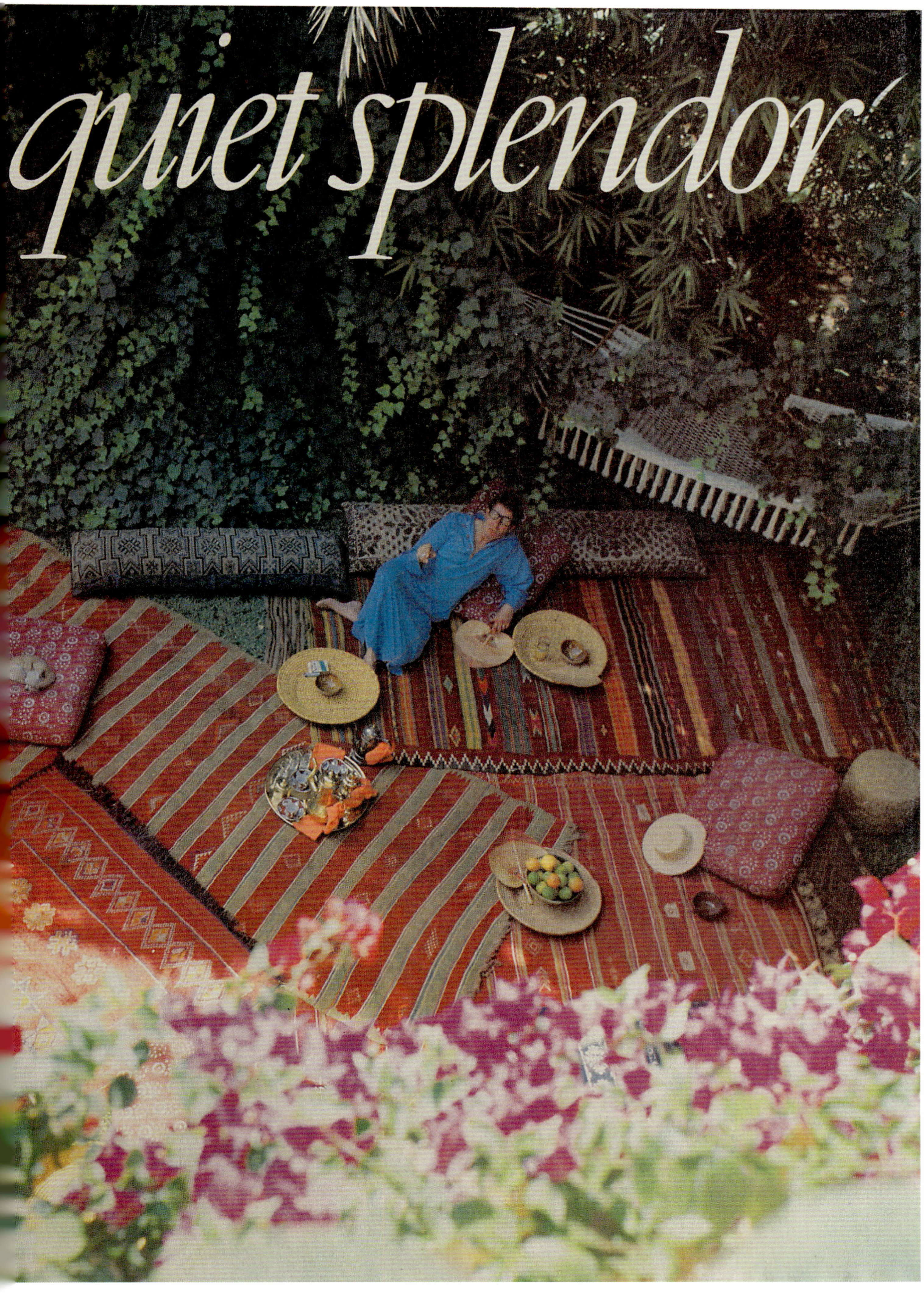

276. Yves Saint Laurent's home, Marrakesh, 1980

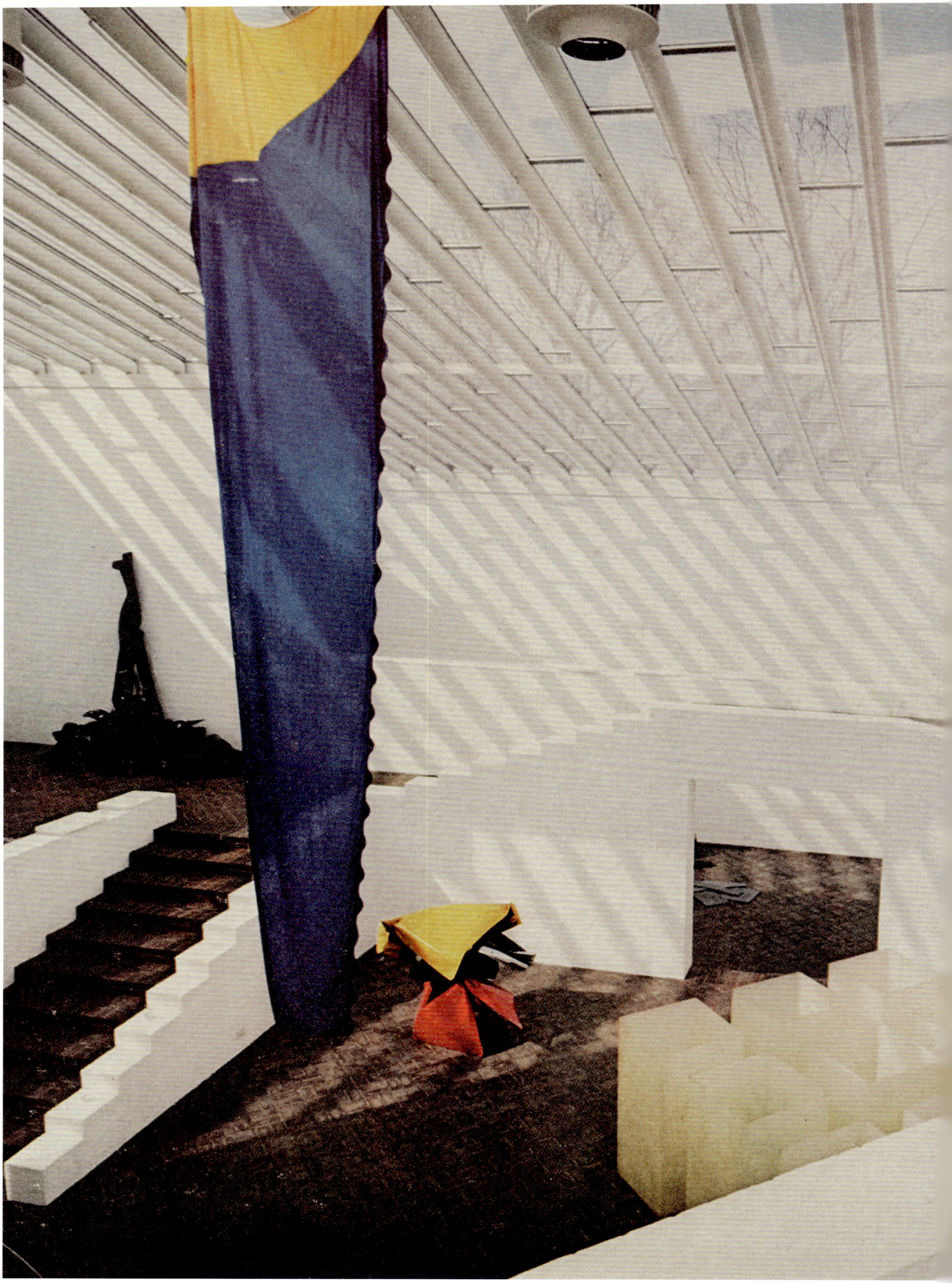

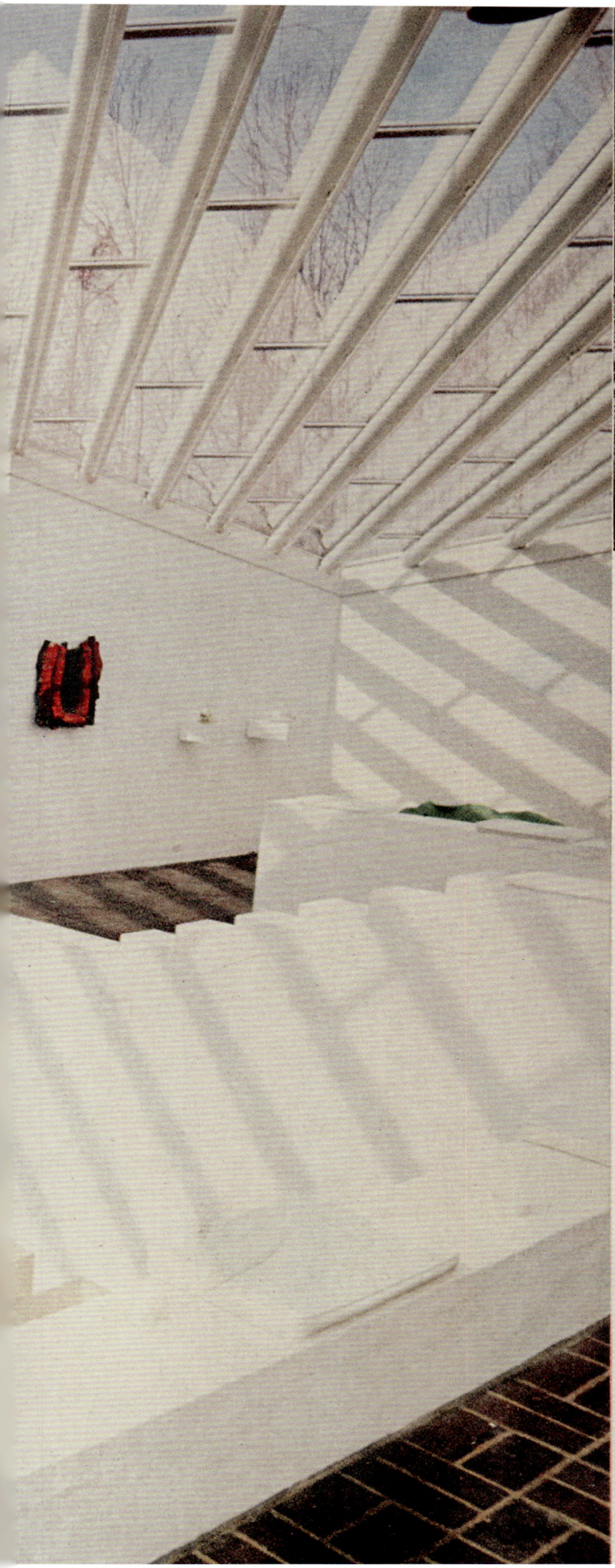

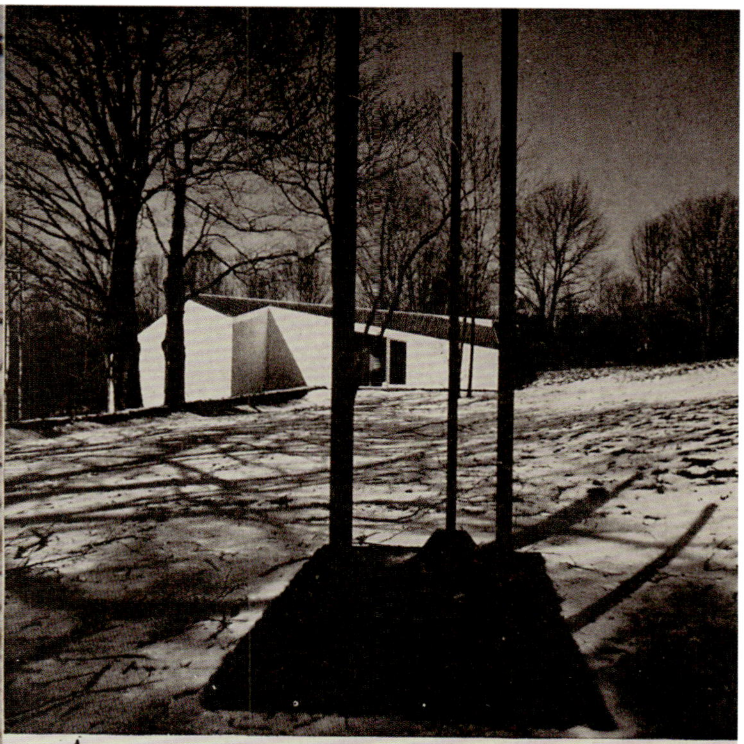

ART UNDER GLASS

Philip Johnson's new gallery: a sculpture to hold sculpture

Since 1949, when his precedent-making Glass House was completed, Philip Johnson—an architect's architect—has made his thirty-two acres near New Canaan, Connecticut, a proving ground for his ideas about architecture. What has resulted is a series of some of the most beautiful modern buildings in America: the main house, a guesthouse, a pavilion, a subterranean paintings gallery, and now a many-leveled sculpture gallery, *above,* painted white, built into a hillside, that combines Johnson's extraordinary and unique patronage of contemporary artists with his definite sense of how sculpture should be seen. (Over the years, Johnson has designed ten art galleries across America.) (Continued)

a sweep of the sculpture gallery, *left,* the sun pouring into the many-leveled room, with its works by American artists. From the left: a 1967-68 black felt sculpture by Robert Morris; hanging from the glass-and-pipe ceiling, Claes Oldenburg's "Soft Saw"; in one of the corner niches, a John Chamberlain sculpture made in the early 'sixties from junked automobiles; through the wall opening, metal plates—part of a 1969 Richard Serra; in front, Robert Morris's 1968 serial sculpture of nine fiber-glass forms; upper right in this photograph, Oldenburg's soft sculptures on two small shelves and hanging on the wall. *Above:* Outside the gallery, the soaring steel columns of a 1965 sculpture, 112 inches high, by Barnett Newman.

HORST

103

277. Philip Johnson's sculpture gallery, New Canaan, Connecticut, 1971

HAPPY Rockefeller now

BY KATE LLOYD

When Margaretta Fitler Murphy was married to Nelson Aldrich Rockefeller, for fifteen years Governor of New York State and now Vice President of the United States, and the nation agawp with curiosity, a man who knew her said, "A woman would say she was well-scrubbed; a man would say she was glowing." If there has been a change since then, this is it: a woman, too, would say she is glowing. Either Happy Rockefeller has been ridiculously presented in the press, or she has changed (some close friends believe she has changed, especially since her mastectomies). You can't step in the same river twice, Heraclitus pointed out—the truth is now, and in Happy Rockefeller it now presents itself thus: A handsome country woman, who seems taller than fact; forthright, funny, quick-minded, kind, in charge of her scene. She aims opinions as directly as headlights: "The condition of the American Woman," she said, getting right to the heart of the issue at hand, "is the subject of endless discussion, pro and con—I think the American Woman is so much better off than women in other countries, that we ought to be accentuating the positive and eliminating the negative." She looks at the person she is talking to with intense attention. It would be hard to deliver white lies to those brown eyes.

Happy Rockefeller's voice is appetizing and non chi-chi, her laugh delicious. She draws people out. A man meeting her for the first time said: "I had expected to meet Mrs. Nelson Rockefeller; instead, I met *her*." The impression is that this reputedly shy, withdrawn, unsure woman would be a smash on a lecture platform and win any office she ran, or just plain strolled, for. She has put a lot of complex years, sorry events, and major surgery behind her and come out whole. "There were times in the past when you weren't sure whether you were talking to Happy Rockefeller, Happy Murphy, or Happy Fitler," a friend said. "Now she is her own woman."

Few things are more confusing than truth. Untruths, myths require clear-cut structure, pilings to shore up rationale. For centuries American women have been turned into packaged untruths: The Flower of Southern Womanhood; the Little Women's "Marmee"; the Gibson Girl, full of incipient twentieth-century naughtiness; Mrs. Stationwagon waiting for Betty Friedan to fix her suburban machines. Untrue, except at the level of polemics and cartoon. Mrs. Rockefeller is right: the truth about the American Woman is that for two centuries she has had the greatest opportunities of any woman anywhere, ever, in developed or undeveloped countries, to be whatever she blooming well *is*. And that's never the same twice. How confusing, how downright confounding of Happy Rockefeller to be her *self*, and how probable that if she flinches or puts people off, it might be because we want her to play a packaged role . . . and she won't, or can't, or both. Elemental forces, childbirth, life-and-death decisions don't seem to scare her much; "sappy" requests do. (Continued)

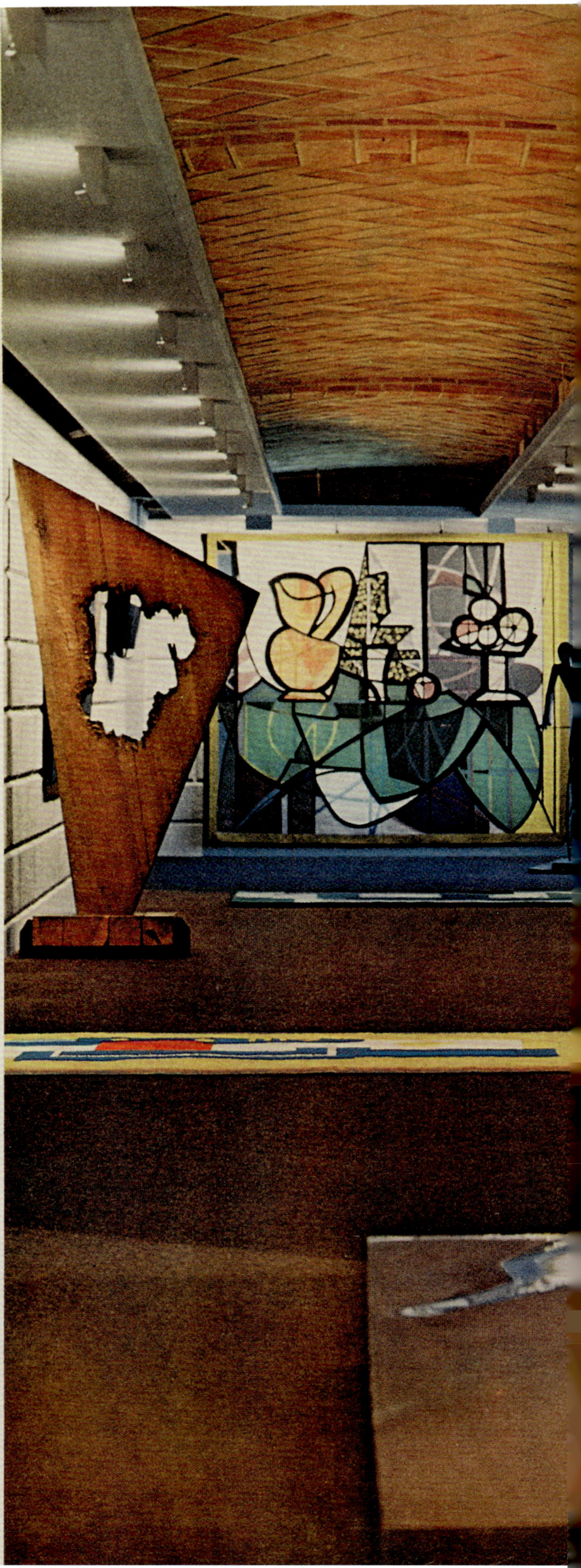

Mrs. Nelson A. Rockefeller

In the gallery her husband created in the cellar of the family house at Pocantico Hills, the real Happy Rockefeller with her acrylic, silkscreen portrait done in 1968 by Andy Warhol. Reconstructing basement corridors into a beautifully lighted, climate-controlled place for a daring collection of avant-garde art, Nelson Rockefeller created a vibrant, comfortable, modern hideaway in a 1908 house. Shown here, on the rear wall, one of a series of magnificent tapestries that extend down other corridors of the gallery, all made after Nelson Rockefeller's favorite paintings by Picasso with the artist's cooperation. "Picasso," Mrs. Rockefeller said, "chose the colors of the yarns himself." This one, woven in 1970 after Picasso's 1931 "Pitcher and Bowl of Fruit."

HORST

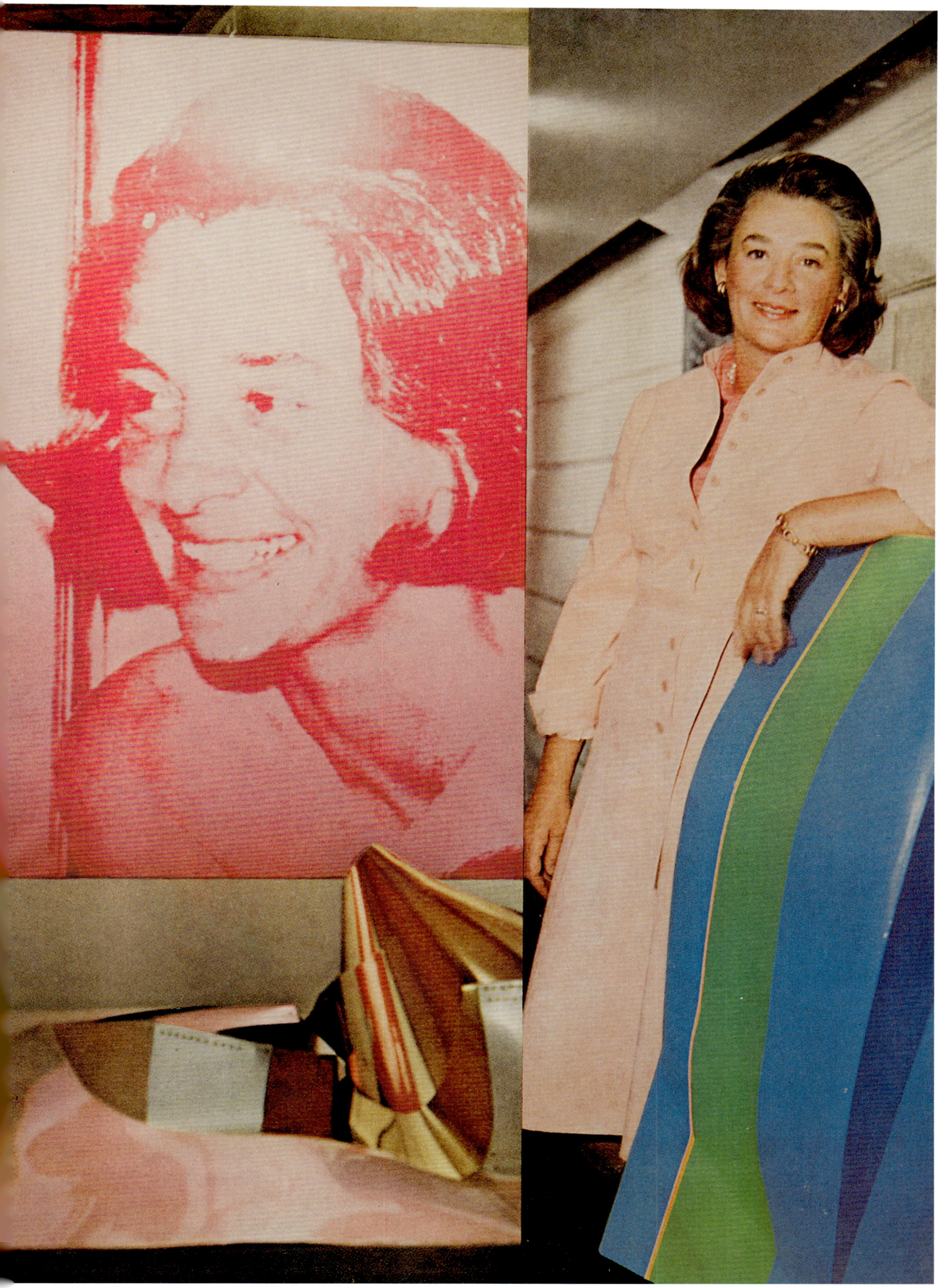

278. Margaretta Fitler Murphy (Mrs Nelson A. Rockefeller) at home, Pocantico Hills, New York, 1975

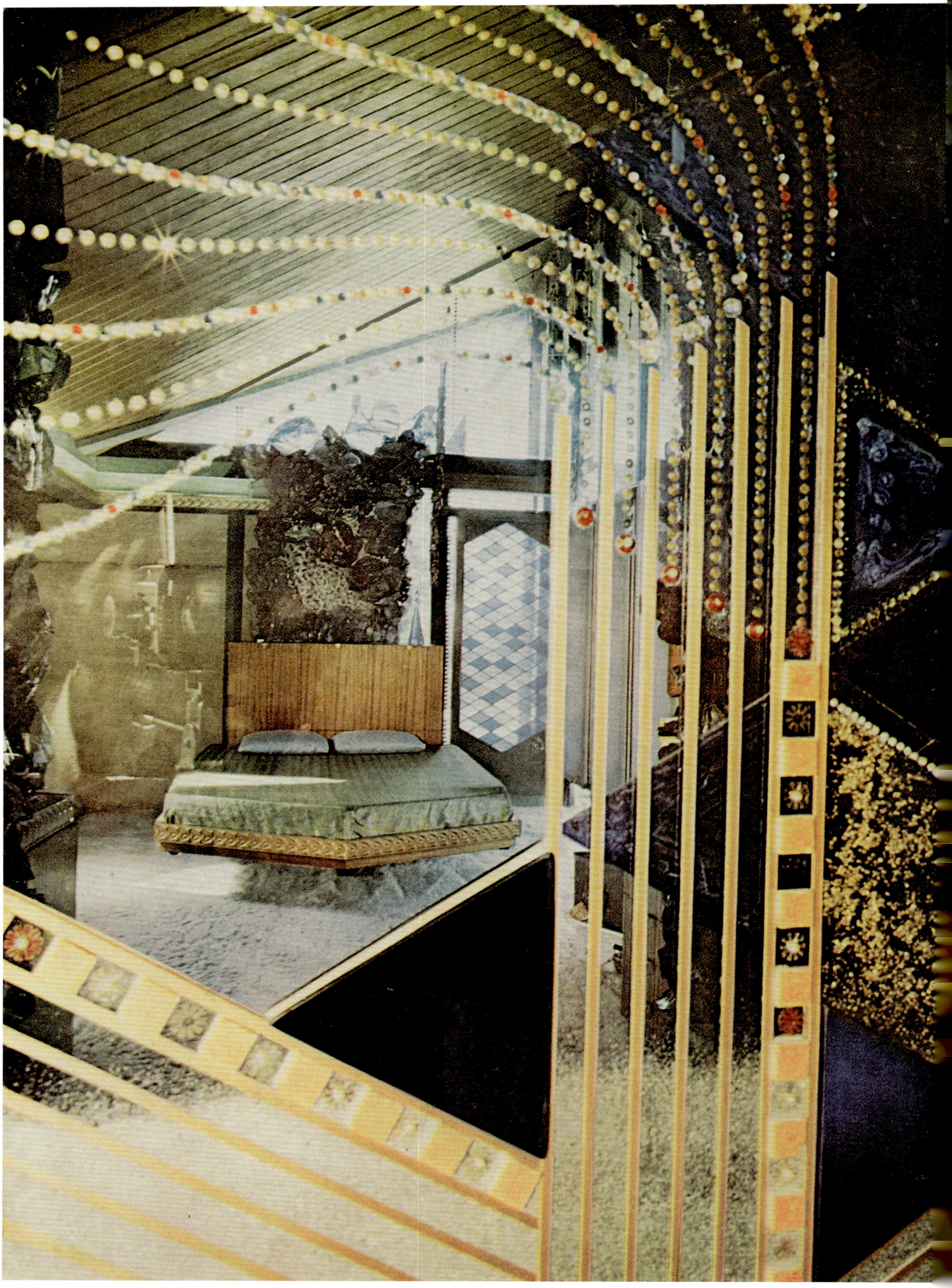

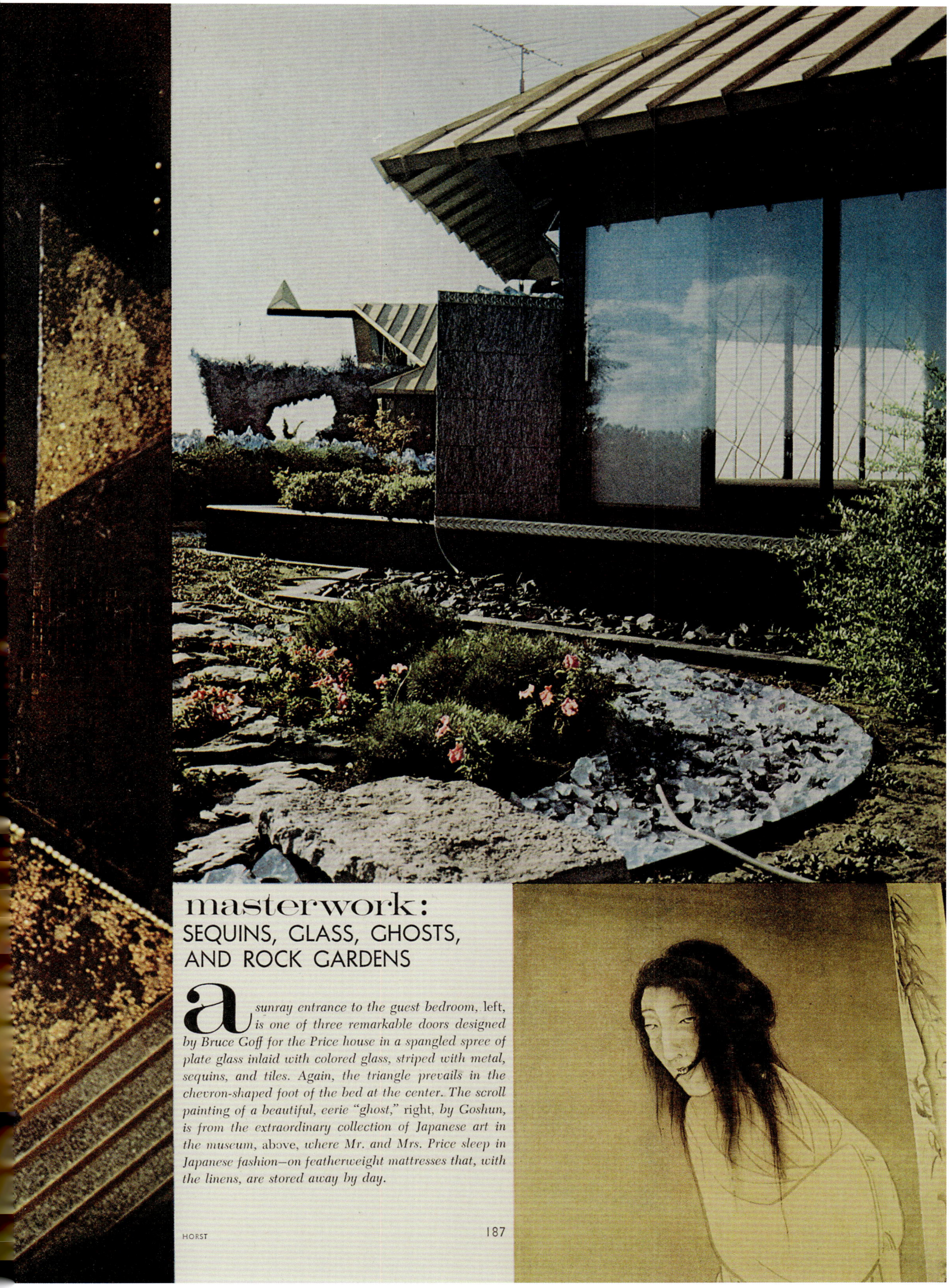

masterwork:
SEQUINS, GLASS, GHOSTS, AND ROCK GARDENS

a sunray entrance to the guest bedroom, left, *is one of three remarkable doors designed by Bruce Goff for the Price house in a spangled spree of plate glass inlaid with colored glass, striped with metal, sequins, and tiles. Again, the triangle prevails in the chevron-shaped foot of the bed at the center. The scroll painting of a beautiful, eerie "ghost,"* right, *by Goshun, is from the extraordinary collection of Japanese art in the museum,* above, *where Mr. and Mrs. Price sleep in Japanese fashion—on featherweight mattresses that, with the linens, are stored away by day.*

HORST

187

279. Mr and Mrs Joe D. Price's home, Oklahoma, 1972

NOBLE AL

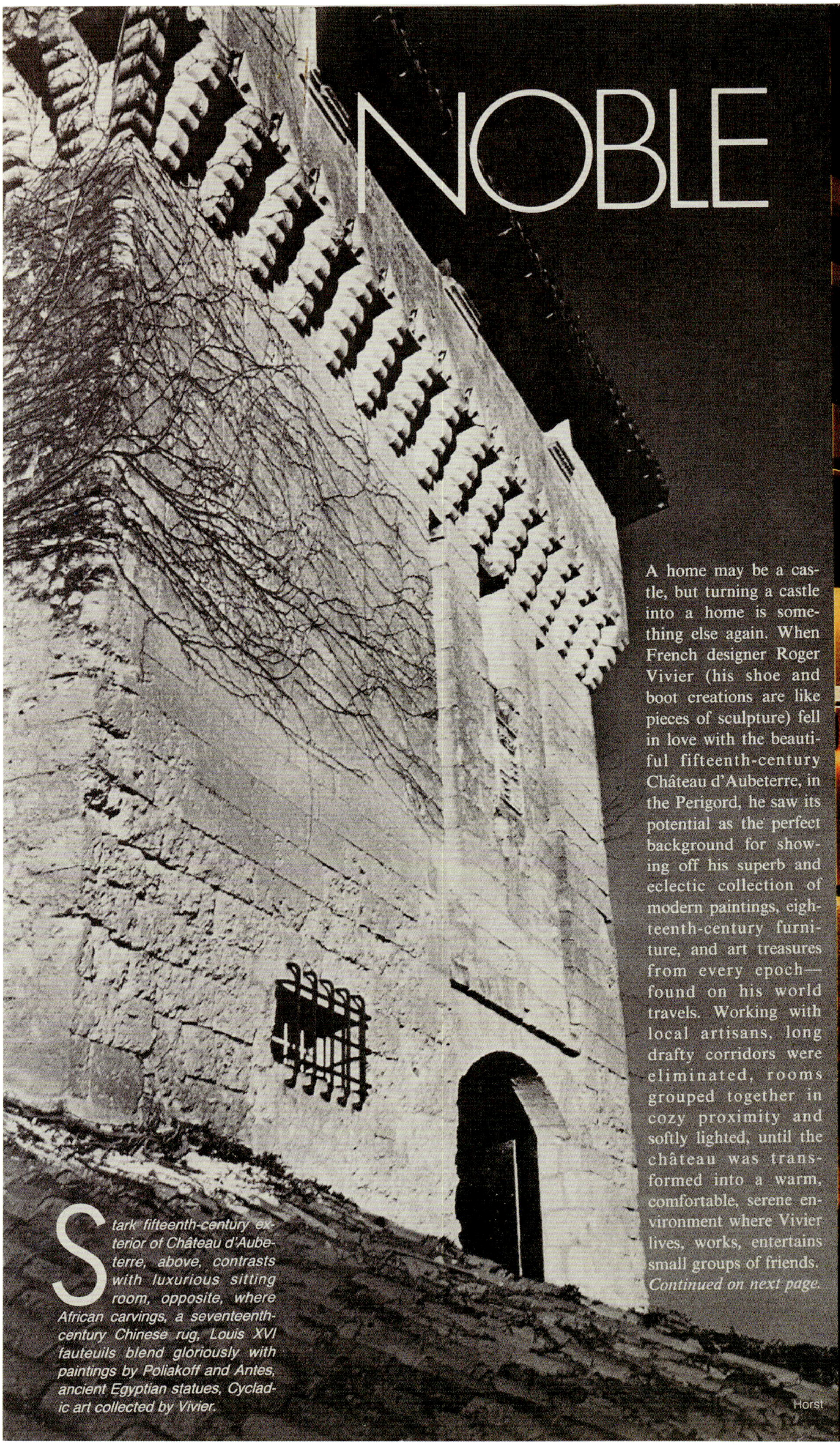

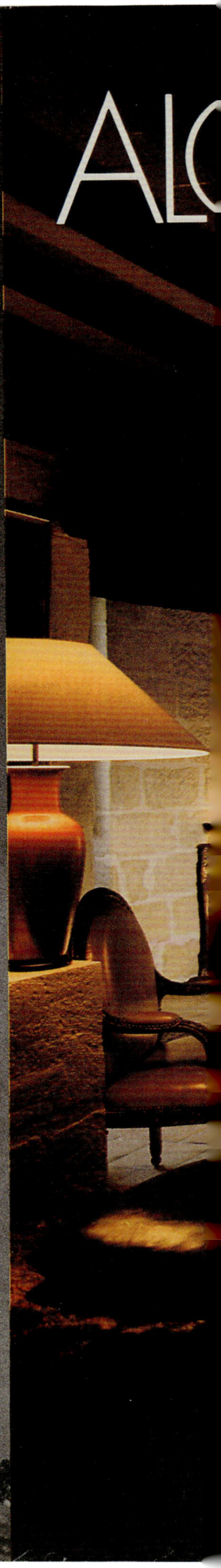

A home may be a castle, but turning a castle into a home is something else again. When French designer Roger Vivier (his shoe and boot creations are like pieces of sculpture) fell in love with the beautiful fifteenth-century Château d'Aubeterre, in the Perigord, he saw its potential as the perfect background for showing off his superb and eclectic collection of modern paintings, eighteenth-century furniture, and art treasures from every epoch—found on his world travels. Working with local artisans, long drafty corridors were eliminated, rooms grouped together in cozy proximity and softly lighted, until the château was transformed into a warm, comfortable, serene environment where Vivier lives, works, entertains small groups of friends.

Continued on next page.

Stark fifteenth-century exterior of Château d'Aubeterre, above, contrasts with luxurious sitting room, opposite, where African carvings, a seventeenth-century Chinese rug, Louis XVI fauteuils blend gloriously with paintings by Poliakoff and Antes, ancient Egyptian statues, Cycladic art collected by Vivier.

Horst

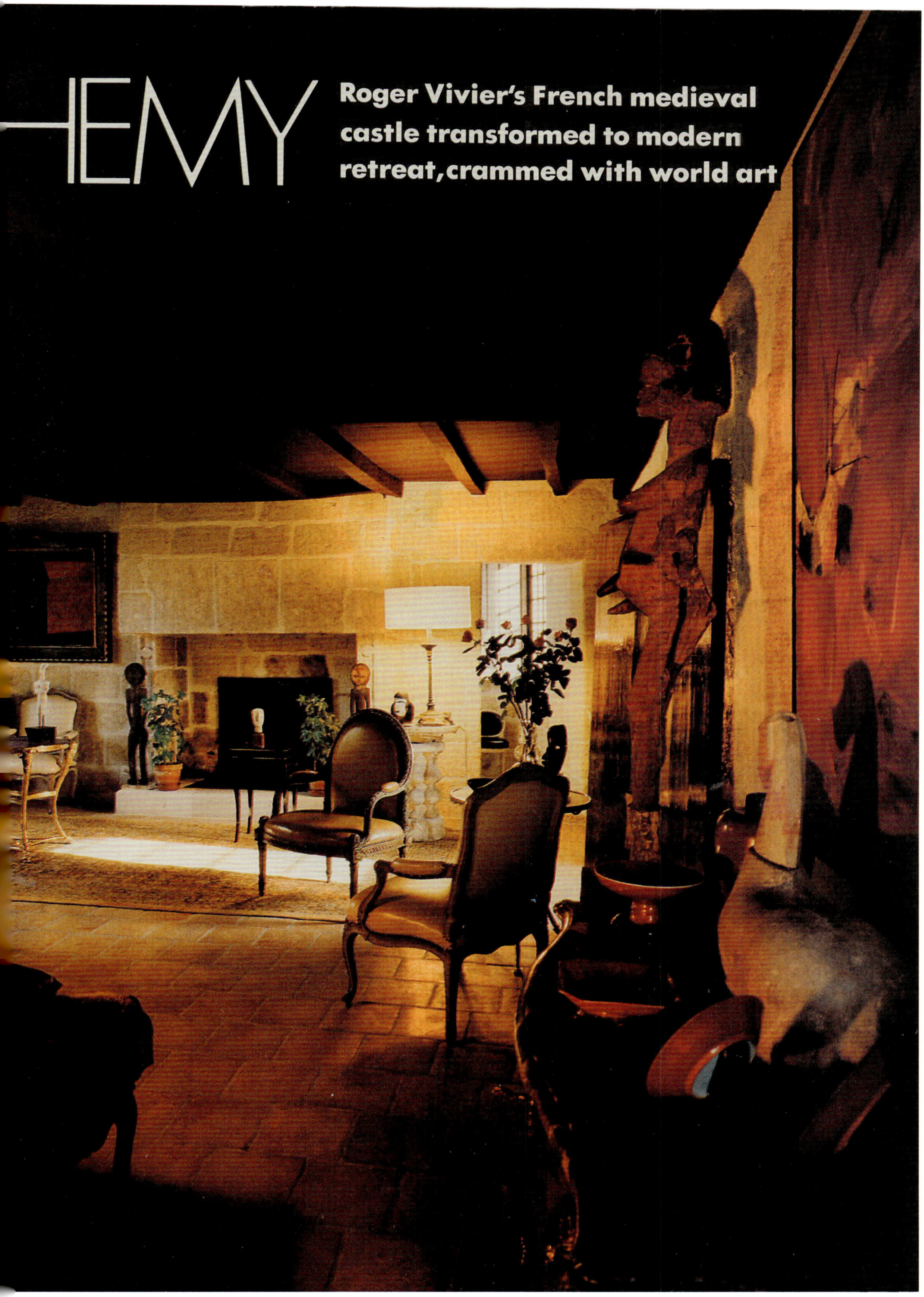

280. Roger Vivier's home, Château d'Aubeterre, Périgord, France, 1980

X

Carmen: An Interview

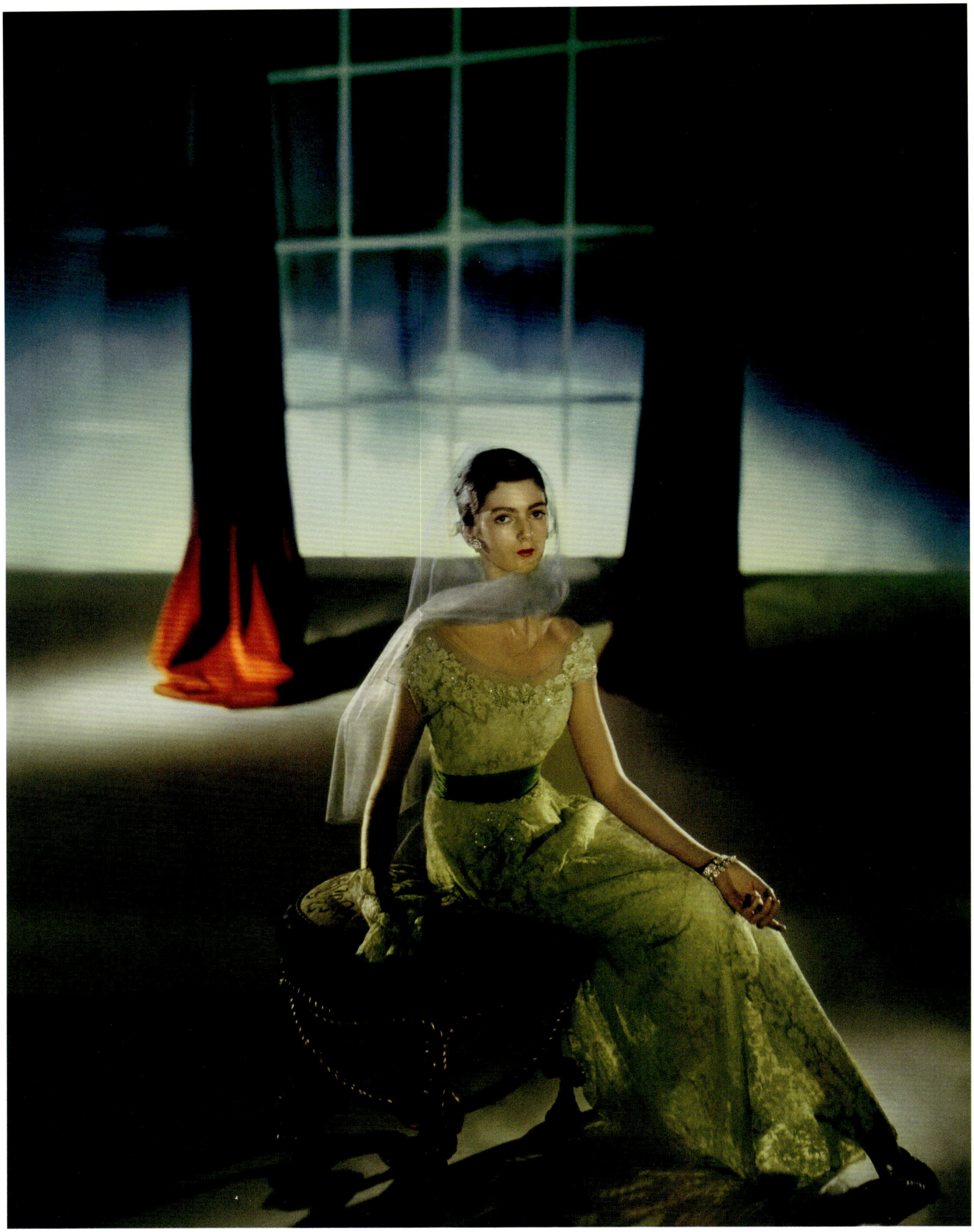

281. Carmen Dell'Orefice,
dress by Hattie Carnegie, 1947

CARMEN: AN INTERVIEW

Interview by Susanna Brown with Carmen Dell'Orefice at Hôtel Plaza Athénée, New York, December 2013

'My career as a model was an accident; it just happened. I was born in 1931. I started working just after the Second World War ended, in November 1945. The next step was not accidental: through my godparents[1] I met Carol Phillips, *Vogue*'s beauty editor. The following year she brought me to Vogue Studios, 480 Lexington Avenue, New York. The first shoot was with Clifford Coffin, the second week was Irving Penn, then Horst. In the subsequent weeks Cecil Beaton, Constantin Joffé and Serge Balkin also photographed me. Last but not least, Erwin Blumenfeld, who was responsible for my first *Vogue* cover in 1947. In retrospect, I realize how privileged I was. What I knew then was that I was lucky, lucky, lucky! Here were these creative, courageous expatriates of the war, who were smart enough to escape when they could. When they arrived in the US, Alexander Liberman, who had preceded them, provided a safe haven for their talents at Condé Nast. In 1946 I was well aware of the power of money. We had very little, but it became clear that, if I was doing the job well, I could bring home much needed money to my mother.

'The first pictures Horst took of me were published in 1946. Just after the war ladies were beginning to look at themselves differently, although many didn't know *how* to look at themselves, including myself back then. But I had the guidance of Horst. I had the great good fortune to meet a gentleman who made me feel like a person, not a 15-year-old child. Horst knew my background, as did all the other photographers, but he was the most gentle and affirming. He became one of the custodians of my youth and gave me a glimpse of my future, speaking to me as a surrogate parent. I realize now how young and handsome he was, with the most sensual voice that communicated to me that I was beautiful, intelligent and valuable.

'Horst's intellect and aesthetic sense were so integrated, his lifetime's appreciation of all art forms and nature clearly reflected in all his photography. Horst appreciated the discipline I had acquired in my extensive ballet and swimming training, which made it possible to instinctively respond to him, as partners do with each other on a dance floor. I was happily, totally, obedient to the exposure of his 10 × 8 inch bellows camera. I'd sit in a dress by Jean Dessès or Hattie Carnegie, stone still in an attitude, trying not to blink for thirty, sometimes sixty, seconds.

'Horst was one of my mentors. I think I was married and already had a child when he asked me: "Why are the corners of your mouth always turned down?" That question made me realise I no longer had braces on my teeth, and could smile. Every time I smile, in my heart I'm thanking Horst.

'That was my banner year – 1946. Of course, as a young teenager, I didn't really know what I was representing in a fashion picture; Horst did, as every picture would ultimately show. He would give me perfect instructions, and a witness to all of that was fashion editor Scully Montgomery, who was a steady partner with Horst on many of his sittings, which appeared in American, British and French *Vogue*. I had hair almost down to my waist, which I thought was the only good thing about me, and was terribly disappointed when she carefully pulled my hair back, and put the famous white band on my head. I felt very ugly.

'Horst would explain what we were doing, that I was to pretend to be a grown up lady, "which you will be one day Carmen ...". I had no idea about time, or age. It was always about sharing vibrations, doing a silent dance, making a picture happen. He was very much a part of my early education in observing and understanding silent communication. He really understood me, although he had no children of his own. He was a great teacher, enormously patient and a taskmaster for detail when he had to be. I learned so much from how he communicated with his assistants and with the fashion editors. That was my school, the school of life – I have a PhD in living and Horst was one of my teachers.

'Before I even arrived at the studio, Horst, Liberman and the fashion editor would plan the photographs – they shared a creative vision which I was going to be a part of. Horst understood how light falls on an object. He saw me as a living sculpture to be projected through his photographs.

'It was really because of Horst I started painting as a hobby. He made me think about light on the body, and the idea of being outside my body, looking at myself and being aware of the surrounding environment, which included the people in it. That meant a great deal to me as a young girl. He kept helping me to expand my sense of self through the decades; he was such a good friend. I didn't even know I was absorbing his lessons; that's the beauty of it. Horst, Penn and Blumenfeld helped me look at myself. I am lucky that I came into the world with this surrogate brotherhood, my extended family. An interesting observation – these artists all supported each other, it was very fine fraternity of gentlemen.

'Horst knew his craft, he knew when black and white suited the drama of what he wanted to create. You see, he was an artist.

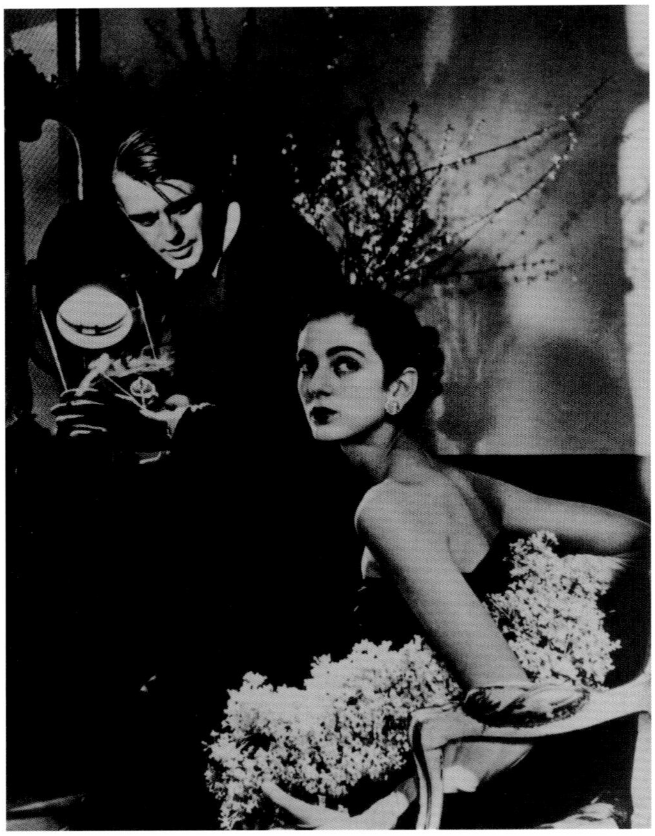

282. Leonard McCombe,
Carmen and Horst photographed
for *LIFE* magazine, 1947

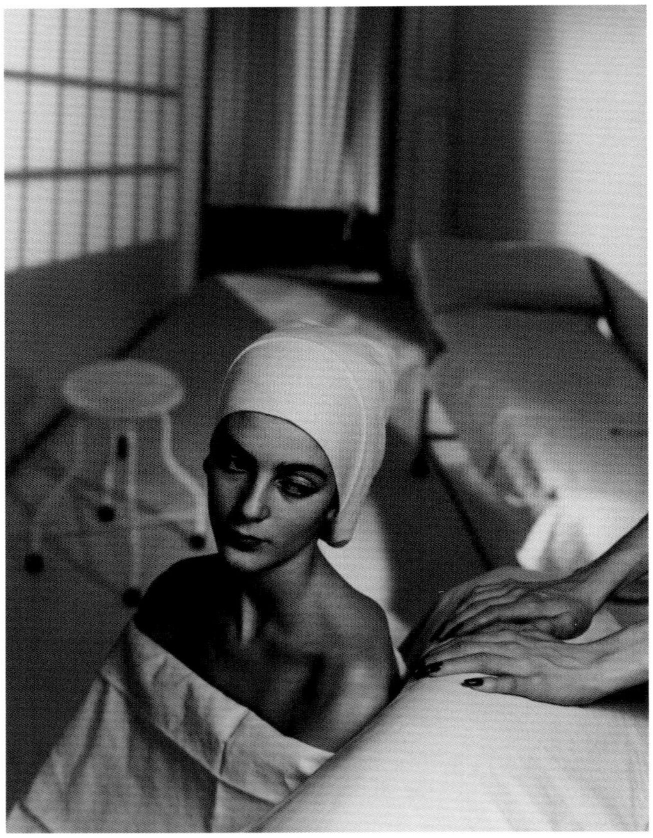

283. *Carmen, Face Massage*
(unpublished variant), 1946

Few photographers worked in colour as early or as successfully as Horst and Beaton. Black and white photography talks one language and colour speaks another. He made me feel like a princess in a Hattie Carnegie beaded dress for a colour shoot for American *Vogue* in February 1947 (pl.281). I remember that day particularly well, and I adored the dress. The secret is that I had two boxes of Kleenex in the top of the dress because at the time my chest was so flat it was almost concave! In those days I had dark eyebrows and long, thick, dark lashes. I didn't wear much make up, but Scully Montgomery put a little red lipstick on me. Horst had a picture in his head and he always achieved the elements of the composition because he knew precisely what he was after. He just took my wrist and turned my hand around – at that moment he was his own art director.

'In 1947 *LIFE* magazine commissioned a story about me, photographed by Leonard McCombe (pl.282).[2] Horst agreed to appear in the photographs, acting out his role as a photographer to show what a fashion sitting was like. I love one picture in particular because Horst is looking down at me very affectionately. The black strapless dress that I wore was one I had made myself from black silk taffeta, which the milliner John Frédérics had given to me. I was a great seamstress, taught by my Hungarian mother. Horst loved the fact that I sewed, and was so supportive of my hobbies. He helped to build my confidence by booking me as a model until he retired – I call that loyalty – and he made me look like the person I dreamt of becoming at the most awkward times of my life.

'The world has changed so much since the 1940s: it was a time when America's skill at marketing was just emerging and when fashion photography and modelling as a profession was just being born. Today, the business is so commercialized and compartmentalized. In one way it's great, the fashion industry has grown as the population has grown; it can't be a boutique industry any more. In another way, sadly, for the models it's so depersonalized; they don't have the nurturing care and education that I was fortunate enough to have from those creative geniuses, as they are called now – though to me they were just my buddies. Beaton was a playmate. He invited me to the opening when he appeared in *Lady Windermere's Fan*. I wore my fedora hat, and I roller-skated to Broadway. That was in 1946. In those days people slept in Central Park because it was before air conditioning, to put that time in perspective!

'I am honoured to have known Horst and to be part of the V&A's retrospective of his beautiful work, along with Marlene Dietrich and the wonderful Lisa Fonssagrives Penn. I'm rather thrilled to have been born when I was, to be part of history, and it was such fun! But nothing remains the same. Later in his life, when Horst was retired and living in Florida, we would chat. I spoke to him one day shortly before he died. Richard, his assistant, handed him a phone, so he could speak to me from the swimming pool. He said, "Carmen, you sound like you're smiling. I'm happy to hear that, I'm smiling too. I'm feeling the warm sun on my face, I can't see a thing any more,[3] but it feels good and the water is warm." And I said, "Dear Horst, that sounds wonderful." Horst said: "Let's keep smiling." I can't *stop* smiling and laughing even now. Horst's legacy to me is the smile he put in my heart.'

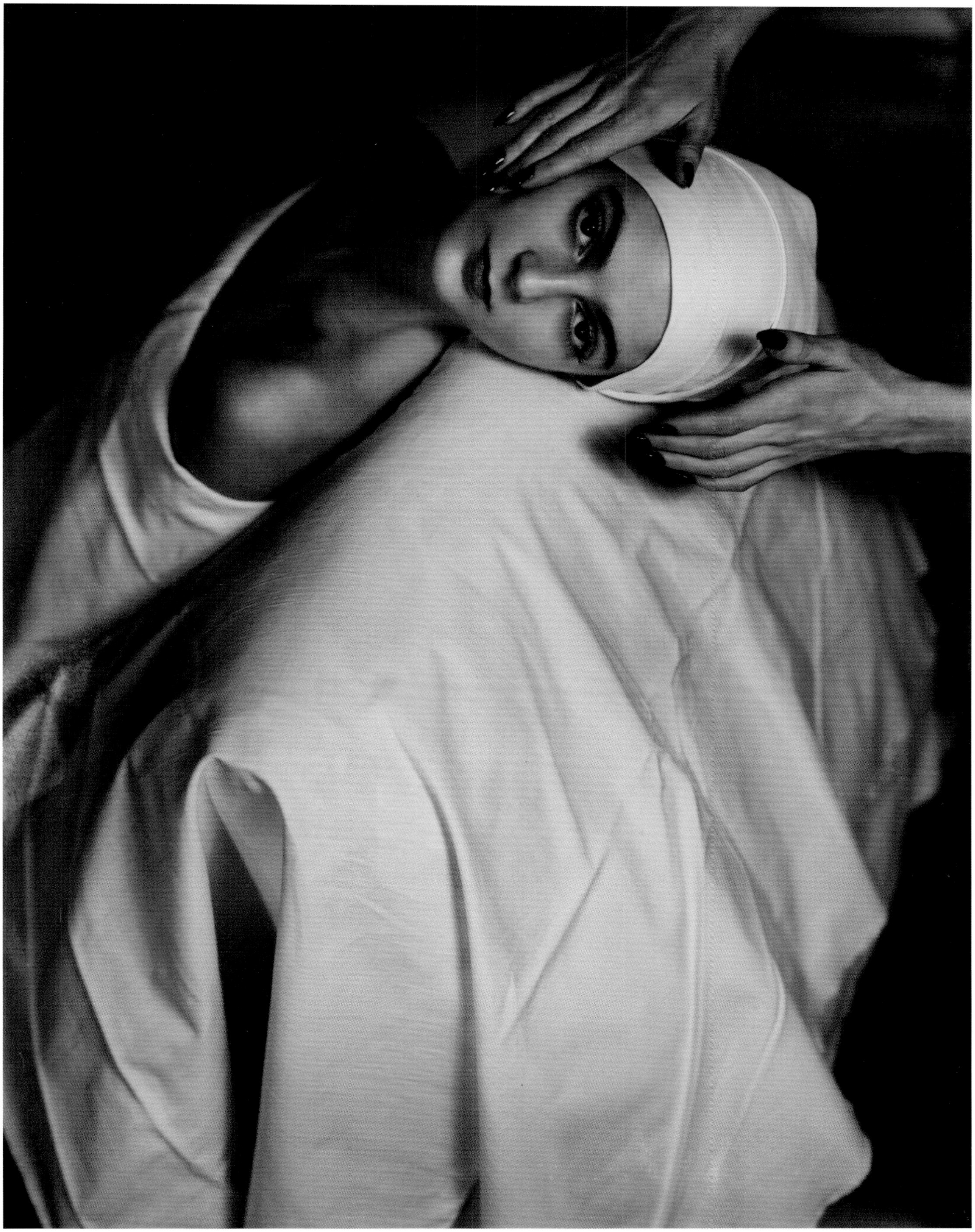

284. *Carmen, Face Massage*, 1946

NOTES

Introduction: Inventing Elegance
Susanna Brown

1. Horst quoted in Valentine Lawford, *Horst: His Work and His World* (New York, 1984), p.392.
2. Lawford (cited note 1), pp.392–6.
3. For examples of photographs of Horst by Hoyningen-Huene see French *Vogue*, July 1931, pp.32–5. Huene's well-known photograph of a man and woman in Izod bathing suits is said to depict Horst, but curator Terence Pepper notes in *Horst: Portraits* (London, 2001), p.39, that the image was published in June 1930, several months before Horst and Huene first met.
4. William Ewing, *Horst* (New York, 1984), p.6.
5. Bettina Ballard, *In My Fashion* (Philadelphia, 1960), p.18.
6. Ballard (cited note 5), p.43.
7. American *Vogue*, 1 February 1947, p.165.
8. Lawford (cited note 1), p.114.
9. Lawford (cited note 1), p.63.
10. Lud (1913–90). For more information on these models, and other fashionable Russian émigrés in Paris, see Alexandre Vassiliev, *Beauty in Exile* (New York, 2000).
11. Lawford (cited note 1), p.225.
12. Ballard (cited note 5), p.44.
13. Lisa Fonssagrives (1911–92).
14. Lisa Fonssagrives interview, http://bombsite.com/issues/12/articles/645 (accessed January 2013).
15. Article by Barbara Rose, American *Vogue*, 1 May 1976, pp.174, 175 and 208.
16. Letter from Lisa Fonssagrives Penn to Horst, dated 16 June 1976. Collection of R.J. Horst.
17. Lisa Fonssagrives Penn interview for the television documentary *Horst: Sixty Years and Still in Vogue*, produced by Gerald Scarfe, Omnibus, 1992.
18. Toto Koopman (1908–91).
19. Ballard (cited note 5), p.45.
20. Helen Bennett (1911–2001).
21. *Horst: Salute to the Thirties*, foreword by Janet Flanner, photographs by Horst and George Hoyningen-Huene (New York, 1971), p.13, Horst Introduction.
22. Susann Shaw (1920–2009); Barbara 'Babe' Cushing Mortimer Paley (1915–78); Carmen Dell'Orefice (b.1931).
23. New York model agent Patty Sicular interview with former model Lillian Marcuson, 22 February 2014.
24. Lawford (cited note 1), p.303.
25. Dovima (1927–90, full name Dorothy Virginia Margaret Juba); Sunny Harnett (b.1924, as Annemarie Margot Harnett); Jean Patchett (1927–2002); Dorian Leigh (1917–2008); Suzy Parker (1932–2003).
26. Author interview with Johann Mayr (known as Hans), Soho House, New York, January 2013.
27. Author interview with Richard J. Horst, 21 March 2014. Richard became Horst's manager, archivist and adopted son.
28. Author interview with Johann Mayr (known as Hans), Soho House, New York, January 2013.
29. Letter from Emilio Pucci to Horst, dated 24 March 1964, Florence. Collection of R.J. Horst.
30. Letter to Horst from Richard Avedon. Collection of R.J. Horst. The letter is dated 10 November 1966. The feature that Avedon refers to is titled 'Roman Classic Surprise', American *Vogue*, 15 November 1966, pp.182–7, 193–6.
31. Author interview with model Carol Alt, 19 February 2014.
32. Author interview with model Eva Malmstrom, 2 December 2013.
33. The platinum prints were printed by Salvatore Lopes in America, and Martin Axon in England.
34. Introduction, *Platinum* (London, 2006), unpaginated.
35. Letter from Main Bocher to Horst, 22 October 1963. Collection of R.J. Horst.

I
1930s Paris – Fashion, Art, Elegance and Imagination
Philippe Garner

1. Valentine Lawford, *Horst: His Work and His World* (New York, 1984), p.82.
2. Lawford (cited note 1), p.185.
3. Lawford (cited note 1), p.13.
4. Translation: naturism.
5. Lawford (cited note 1), p.12.
6. Lawford (cited note 1), p.163.
7. Lawford (cited note 1), p.15.
8. Cecil Beaton, *The Glass of Fashion* (London, 1954), p.277.
9. 'Sur les toits de Paris le jardin enchanté de M. Charles de Bestegui', French *Vogue* (October 1932), pp.54–5.
10. Beaton (cited note 8), p.220.
11. Amy Fine Collins, 'A Snapper-up of Considered Trifles', *The Times Saturday Review* (2 February 1991), p.28.
12. *Horst: Salute to the Thirties*, foreword by Janet Flanner, photographs by Horst and George Hoyningen-Huene (New York, 1971), p.11.
13. French *Vogue*, (March 1930) p.74; French *Vogue* (April 1930), p.88; French *Vogue* (December 1930), pp.70-1.
14. 'A la manière de...', French *Vogue* (August 1930), pp.48–9, 82–3.
15. French *Vogue* (July 1931), p.29.
16. *Hoyningen-Huene Meisterbildnisse* (Berlin, 1932), unpaginated.
17. *Vu* (February 1931), cover.
18. 'La folie de l'Acropole', *Voilà* (9 June 1934), no.168, cover and pp.8–9.
19. Lawford (cited note 1), p.37.
20. Ibid.
21. *Horst: Photographs of a Decade*, introduction by Dr M. Agha, edited by George Davis (New York, 1944), pp.6–7.
22. *Horst: Photographs of a Decade* (cited note 21), p.7.
23. Lawford (cited note 1), p.388.
24. Marcel Rochas (ed.), *Vingt-cinq ans d'élégance à Paris 1925-1950* (Paris, 1951), p.53.
25. 'Dans les montagnes et les îles de la Grèce', French *Vogue* (September 1930), p.39.
26. *Horst: Salute to the Thirties* (cited note 12), p.145.
27. Boris Kochno, *Christian Bérard* (London, 1988), p.34.
28. Fine Collins (cited note 11), p.28.
29. *Important 20th Century Decorative Art & Design*, Christie's, New York (7 December 2005), lots 358-82.
30. *Photographic Images and Related Material*, Sotheby's, London (8 May 1992), lot 342 (and lots 343–53 for other relevant photographs from the Kochno estate).
31. Beaton (cited note 8), p.192.
32. *Horst: Sixty Years and Still in Vogue*, a television documentary by Gerald Scarfe, Omnibus, 1992.
33. *Horst: Salute to the Thirties* (cited note 12), p.4.
34. 'Un Bal 1900', French *Vogue* (November 1932), p.28.
35. 'De fêtes en fêtes', French *Vogue* (August 1935), pp.26-7.
36. 'Une Nuit d'Art Vivant', French *Vogue* (August 1935), pp.30-3.
37. 'Carnets de bals – images d'une belle saison', French *Vogue* (August 1939), pp.12–17.
38. *Horst: Salute to the Thirties* (cited note 12), p.12.
39. Elsa Schiaparelli, *Shocking Life* (London, 1954), p.75.
40. Beaton (cited note 8), p.192.
41. Schiaparelli (cited note 39), p.71.
42. Schiaparelli (cited note 39), p.42.
43. Beaton (cited note 8), p.176.
44. 'Les Arts à Paris Activités de ce Printemps', French *Vogue* (May 1935), p.61.
45. *Horst: Salute to the Thirties* (cited note 12), p.12.
46. French *Vogue* (August 1935), p.16.
47. French *Vogue* (October 1935), p.28.
48. *Important 20th Century Decorative Art & Design*, Christie's, New York (7 December 2005).
49. Martin Battersby, *The Decorative Thirties* (London, 1971), p.193.
50. Battersby (cited note 49), p.137.

Electric Beauty, Paris, 1939
Susanna Brown

1. Many new cosmetics companies were launched in the early years of the twentieth century. Among the most successful were Elizabeth Arden, Helena Rubinstein, Max Factor and L'Oréal (originally named Société Française de Teintures Inoffensives pour Cheveux).
2. Geoffrey Jones, *Beauty Imagined: A History of the Global Beauty Industry* (Oxford, 2010), unpaginated.
3. French *Vogue* (June 1937), p.148.
4. French *Vogue* (June 1937), p.134.
5. 'Mask Your Face', American *Vogue* (1 June 1939), p.79. The full caption reads: 'This is the Inspiré Mask, which utilizes electricity (thermostatically controlled) and infrared ray to cleanse and refresh your skin. You may use it with or without a cream, for the mask is lined with medical silk that can be washed with alcohol – either way, your facial tissues will tell a tale! The heat is so gentle and even that there is no sudden rush of blood to the surface, endangering the tiny blood-vessels.' The photograph is credited to 'Hirsch', along with a photograph on the facing page of a foot masque treatment, available at Helena Rubinstein's Fifth Avenue salon. However, a close examination of these two pages, the model's hair, limbs, and the crisply folded cloth on which her feet rest, indicate that the photographs were probably taken at the same sitting as Horst's *Electric Beauty* and were likely taken by Horst himself.
6. The electric massage device is the 'Gilbert Vitalator', depicted in a photograph by Baker in 'Discoveries in Beauty', American *Vogue* (1 March 1939), p.108.

II
The Aura of Glamour: Couture Fashion
Claire Wilcox

1. British *Vogue* (16 January 1938), p.35.
2. Paris fashion correspondent, 'The Glass of Fashion', *The Times*, 19 July 1938.
3. Olivier Saillard and Anne Zazzo, *Paris Haute Couture* (Paris, 2013), p.151.
4. Edna Woolman Chase and Ilka Chase, *Always In Vogue* (New York, 1954), p.166.
5. Alexander Liberman and Polly Devlin, *Vogue Book of Fashion Photography* (London, 1979), p.8.
6. Célia Bertin, *Paris à la Mode: A Voyage of Discovery* (London, 1956), p.42.
7. *Time* magazine, 18 August 1947, quoted in Claire Wilcox, *The Golden Age of Couture: Paris and London 1947–1957* (London, 2008), p.21.
8. *Horst: Salute to the Thirties*, foreword by Janet Flanner, photographs by Horst and George Hoyningen-Huene (New York, 1971), p.12.
9. 'Horst P. Horst, 1906–1999, The Legendary Photographer Who Died Last November, Was A Guiding Light At *Vogue* For Six Decades. Talking To Horst's Friends And Subjects Hamish Bowles Reveals A Man As Elegant, Charming, And Glamorous As His Work...', American *Vogue* (1 February 2000), pp.149, 150, 154.
10. http://bombsite.com/issues/12/articles/645; accessed 27 November 2013.
11. American *Vogue* (15 March 1935), p.56.
12. Pamela Golbin (ed.), *Madeleine Vionnet* (New York, 2009), p.16.
13. Bertin (cited note 6), p.172.
14. Golbin (cited note 12), p.282.
15. Bettina Ballard, *In My Fashion* (Philadelphia, 1960), p.75.
16. I'd like to thank Oriole Cullen for making me aware of this publication: J.P.P. Higgins, *Cloth of Gold: a history of metallised textiles* (London, 1993), p.81.

17. The material was in fact Rhodophane, made by the French fabric house Colcombet. See 'Glass and Schiaparelli', American *Vogue* (15 January 1935), pp.54–5.
18. Diana Vreeland, 'People Are Talking About: Photographers in *Vogue*: Horst – The Aura of Glamour', American *Vogue* (1 October 1984), p.702.
19. Chase and Chase (cited note 4), p.260.
20. *Horst: Photographs of a Decade*, introduction by Dr M. Agha, edited by George Davis (New York, 1944), p.10.
21. Valentine Lawford, *Horst: His Work and His World* (New York, 1984), p.129.
22. Ballard (cited note 15), p.75.
23. Diana Vreeland, American *Vogue* (1 October 1984), p.702.
24. Ibid.
25. Caroline Seebohm, *The Man Who Was Vogue: The Life and Times of Condé Nast* (new York, 1982), p.138.
26. Chase and Chase (cited note 4), p.229.
27. *Horst: Salute to the Thirties* (cited note 6), p.12.
28. Diana Vreeland, American *Vogue* (1 October 1984), p.703.
29. Jessica Krick. 'Gabrielle "Coco" Chanel (1883–1971) and the House of Chanel' in Heilbrunn Timeline of Art History. New York: The Metropolitan Museum of Art, 2000–; http://www.metmuseum.org/toah/hd/chnl/hd_chnl.htm(accessed October 2004).
30. 'Fancy-Dress and Fashion', American *Vogue* (1 August 1935), pp.34–5.
31. Lawford (cited note 21), p.176.
32. Ballard (cited note 15), p.72.
33. Bertin (cited note 6), p.174.
34. 'Now Everything's Zippers', *LIFE* (8 November 1937), quoted in Robert Friedel, *Zipper: An Exploration in Novelty* (New York, 1994), p.192.
35. 'High Spirits at the Paris Openings', American *Vogue* (15 September 1938), pp.67–78, 157–160.
36. 'The Autumn Forecast', American *Vogue* (1 August 1938), p.29.
37. Ballard (cited note 15), p.68.
38. Ballard (cited note 15), pp.96–7.
39. Ballard (cited note 15), p.96.
40. Francine du Plessix Gray, *Them: A Memoir of Parents* (New York, 2005), p.47.
41. Seebohm (cited note 25), p.245.

Mainbocher Corset, 1939
Susanna Brown

1. Valentine Lawford, *Horst: His Work and His World* (New York, 1984), p.185.
2. *Horst: Photographs of a Decade*, introduction by Dr M. Agha, edited by George Davis (New York, 1944), p.7.
3. Cathy Horyn, 'Horst P. Horst', *New York Times*, 19 November 1999.
4. Horst created numerous subsequent corset photographs for *Vogue* and most echo elements of this image, employing spotlighting to bring a luminous effect to the skin and accentuate the form of the neck and back. For Horst's other photographs of corsets, see American *Vogue*, 15 March 1940, p.80; American *Vogue*, 15 May 1946, pp.152–3; American *Vogue*, 1 February 1948, p.228; American *Vogue*, 1 October 1950, pp.182–3.
5. American *Vogue*, 1 September 1939, p.43.
6. *LIFE* magazine, 28 August 1939, pp.16–17.
7. In French *Vogue*, the shape was termed '*la taille-diabolo*' ('the diabolo waist'), a reference to the shape of the spool used in the spinning game of the same name. French *Vogue*, December 1939, p.35.

III
From Limelight to Starlight: Portraits of Stage and Screen Stars
Terence Pepper

1. The book included notes on the plates by Valentine Lawford and a foreword by Janet Flanner, the American-born Paris correspondent of the *New Yorker*, herself the subject of one of Horst's earliest portraits, taken in Paris in 1932.
2. *Horst Portraits: 60 Years of Style* was held at the National Portrait Gallery, London, from 1 March to 3 June 2001, and toured to the Museum of Fine Arts, Boston, from 21 October 2001 to 6 January 2002.
3. American *Vogue* (15 May 1943).
4. Uncredited portrait of Agnetha Fischer, French *Vogue* (November 1931), p.59. First credited photographs appear in French *Vogue*, (December 1931), pp.56–7.
5. The context of the image of Gertrude Lawrence is 'Six Plays and their Players' by Christine Jope-Slade, from the regular 'Seen on Stage' series, which also included a portrait of Diana Wynyard by Steichen (British *Vogue* [27 April 1932], p.65).
6. Portrait of Bette Davis, *Vanity Fair* (November 1939).
7. Published in French *Vogue* (February 1934), p.33.
8. Published in British *Vogue* (28 June 1933), p.46.
9. Published in British *Vogue* (18 April 1934), p.82.
10. British *Vogue* (31 October 1934), p.82: 'Seen on the Stage' by G.B. Stern.
11. See *Theatre World* (May 1936).
12. Published in American *Vogue* (November 1936), pp.62–3. The series also appeared in British *Vogue* (20 January 1937), pp.56-7.
13. Published in British *Vogue* (8 February 1939), p.46.
14. Published in British *Vogue* (18 August 1937), p.51.
15. American *Vogue* (15 January 1941), p.63: 'People and Ideas: Paulette Goddard: Actress-wife of Charles Chaplin'.
16. Variant from this shoot published in American *Vogue*, (1 March 1967), p.135, 'Men in *Vogue*: Steve McQueen'.
17. Published in *LIFE* (25 December 1944).

Marlene Dietrich, New York, 1942

1. It was a style of lighting favoured by George Hurrell (1904-92), who photographed many of Hollywood's brightest stars for Paramount Pictures. The effect is also known as 'Paramount lighting'. Horst's contemporaries, including Edward Steichen and Nickolas-Muray as well as Hurrell, also used the approach in their captivating portraits of Dietrich.
2. Valentine Lawford, *Horst: His Work and His World* (New York, 1984), p.236.
3. Lawford (cited note 2), p.236. Such was the success of this portrait that when Dietrich was in Hollywood making *Kismet* (1944), Horst received a telegram asking how the lighting could be recreated for the film.
4. Lawford (cited note 2), p.236.
5. A needlepoint cushion, based on the same still life photograph, features in the book *Needlepoint Design* by Louis J. Gartner (New York, 1970). Gartner was a designer, special projects editor and creative crafts editor of *House & Garden* magazine. Horst personalized a similar chair by making a needlepoint panel based on a 1930s drawing of Coco Chanel by Christian Bérard, and also added a needlepoint seascape to a green-painted Louis XVI chaise. See *Important 20th Century Decorative Art & Design*, Christie's, New York (7 December 2005), pp.82–4 and pp.104–5.
6. Translation: a painting or sculpture of a human figure with the skin removed to reveal the musculature.
7. *Photographs*, Phillips, New York (4 October 2011), lot 53.
8. American *Vogue* (1 July 1942), p.35.
9. Ibid.
10. Lawford (cited note 2), p.236.
11. Published in American *Vogue*, 'People and Ideas: Marlene Dietrich and Her Daughter Maria' (1 January 1948), p.144, and French *Vogue*, 'Marlene Dietrich et sa fille', May 1949, p.40.

IV
An English Interlude
Robin Muir

1. British and American *Vogue* ran it in September 1935, and the French edition in November 1935. The model was the Princess Kyril Scherbatow.
2. Drusilla Beyfus, 'Horst Sense', British *Vogue* (May 1987), p.98.
3. Valentine Lawford, 'Reflections: Stylish Times, Stylish Men Captured by Horst', *Esquire* (September 1984), p.146. Horst misremembered the year of his first visit as 1931.
4. J. McMullin, 'The London Collections Seen with a Parisien [*sic*] Eye', British *Vogue* (4 April 1934), p.70.
5. The portrait of Printemps was subsequently reproduced in the July 1934 issue of *Vanity Fair* with an erroneous credit line reading, 'Photographed by Horst in Paris for *Vanity Fair*', *Vanity Fair* (July 1934), p.20. It was also reproduced in Horst's first book *Horst: Photographs of a Decade*, introduction by Dr M. Agha, edited by George Davis (New York, 1944), p.48.
6. Cecil Beaton and Gail Buckland, *The Magic Image* (London, 1975) p.190.
7. Covers were regularly duplicated and none of the photographs that appeared in British *Vogue* by the two progenitors of *Vogue* fashion photography, Baron Adolph de Meyer (1868–1946) and Edward Steichen, ever originated there.
8. Maurice Beck and Helen Macgregor (1886–1960) were prolific during the early to mid-1920s but by the end of the decade had disappeared from *Vogue*'s pages. Shaw Wildman (1900–83) and Peter Rose Pulham (1910–56) were also exceptions, but the former was underused while the latter was engaged by *Harper's Bazaar*.
9. H.W. Yoxall, *A Fashion of Life* (London, 1966), p.183.
10. Coster, one of the few London portrait photographers who made a successful transition to fashion, was put under contract to British *Vogue* from 1928 to 1931 under a shared credit with his wife as 'Howard and Joan Coster'. On his infrequent trips to London, George Hoyningen-Huene had a similar arrangement with the Costers and is likely to have introduced his protégé on their 1930 visit. An early credit line read 'Horst at Howard Coster's Studio'.
11. Valentine Lawford, *Horst: His Work and His World* (New York, 1984), p.60.
12. Genêt' [Janet Flanner], 'Paris Letter', *New Yorker* (27 February 1932), p.54.
13. *Horst, Photographs of a Decade* (New York, 1944), p.10.
14. Lawford (cited note 11), p.60. 'Miss Lawrence in Widow's Crape', American *Vogue* (1 July 1932), p.40.
15. He enjoyed at a charity ball the spectacle of the younger son of the Earl of Pembroke and the daughter of the future Prime Minister, Winston Churchill, performing a nightclub act *en déshabillé*.
16. Lawford (cited note 11), p.71. He was referring to the business suit of his employer Mr Condé Nast.
17. Lawford (cited note 3), p.146. Taken in 1963, the set of pictures was published in 1964.
18. Lawford (cited note 3), p.148.
19. '*Vogue*'s Eye View of the Mode', British *Vogue* (17 October 1934), p.61.
20. British *Vogue* (28 November 1934), pp.74-9. Terence Pepper notes that Horst retained a small framed print of Princess Marina at his home in Oyster Bay, one of only three photographs on

display there; see Terence Pepper, *Horst Portraits* (London, 2001), p.18. Horst also contributed a crepuscular colour interpretation of a peeress with coronet to *Vogue*'s 'Coronation Issue' (28 April 1937), celebrating the ascension in May 1937 of King George VI.
21. Valentine Lawford was educated at Repton and Cambridge, where he earned a double first in modern and mediaeval languages. He was fluent in French and German, having completed his studies at the Sorbonne and in Strasbourg, and later Vienna. From 1939 to 1946 Lawford was private secretary to three successive Foreign Secretaries. During the Second World War he was the official interpreter for the British at a number of war councils with the French and regularly served as interpreter for Churchill in his conversations with President Charles de Gaulle. From 1946 to 1949, he was the alternate British delegate to the United Nations Security Council. From 1949 to 1950, he was political counsellor and chargé d'affaires at the British Embassy in Teheran, Iran. In 1950, he resigned from the diplomatic service and settled in Oyster Bay with Horst. I am indebted to Lawford's nephew Herry Lawford for his insights into his uncle's life. See also Valentine Lawford, *Bound for Diplomacy* (London, 1963).
22. Hugo Vickers (introduction), *The Unexpurgated Beaton. The Cecil Beaton Diaries as he wrote them* (London, 2002), p.35.
23. Robert Rhodes James (ed.), *Chips. The Diaries of Sir Henry Channon* (London, 1967), pp.249 and 418. Lawford gives a glimpse of what he might have revealed in 'Three Ministers', *Cornhill Magazine* (Autumn 1956), pp.73–99.
24. For a fuller account of the fateful weekend, one that demanded more than passing reference, see Lawford (cited note 11), pp.41–3. Cecil Beaton's nephew (Sir John Smiley), in conversation with Susanna Brown (Curator of Photographs, V&A) and drawing on Beaton's Visitors Books from Ashcombe, has confirmed that Horst and Huene visited Ashcombe on 28 December 1930 and again in November 1933 (presumably staying for a weekend on each occasion).
25. Cecil Beaton letter to Horst, 30 December 1971, quoted in Hugo Vickers, *Cecil Beaton, The Authorized Biography* (London, 1985), pp.559–60. The review appeared in *Books and Bookmen*.
26. Lawford (cited note 11), p.203. Lady Mountbatten was married to Lord Mountbatten, son of a German prince, Prince Louis of Battenberg, and a German princess, Princess Victoria of Hesse. Despite the difficult sitting, Horst liked the portrait enough to include it in his earliest compilation of photographs *Horst, Photographs of a Decade* (cited note 13), p.125.
27. Amanda Mackenzie-Stuart, *Diana Vreeland, Empress of Fashion* (London, 2012), p.219.
28. Diana Vreeland, 'Horst – the Aura of Glamour', American *Vogue* (October 1984), p.703.
29. Frank Crowninshield, '*Vogue* ... Pioneer in Modern Photography', American *Vogue* (15 June 1941), p.72. Horst continued into the 1980s as a contributor to American *House & Garden*.
30. Lawford (cited note 11), p.356.
31. Valentine Lawford, 'An English Dream', American *Vogue* (July 1965), pp.113–21 *et seq*.
32. Valentine Lawford, 'The Duke and Duchess of Windsor in Paris', American *Vogue* (1 April 1964), pp.176–87 *et seq*.
33. Polly Devlin, 'Country House in Flower', American *Vogue* (July 1971), pp.100–07 *et seq*. and British *Vogue* (1 September 1971), pp.128–31 *et seq*. The best would be collected for *Vogue's Book of Houses, Gardens and People* (New York, 1968). Other features would be added for Barbara Plumb, *Horst Interiors* (New York, 1993).
34. Valentine Lawford, 'The House that Horst Grew', American *Vogue* (1 June 1966), pp.134–9 *et seq*. See also Amy Fine Collins, 'Reflections of Horst', *Vanity Fair* (December 1990), vol.53, no.12, pp.188–93 *et seq*.
35. Vreeland (cited note 28), p.703.
36. Nicholas Haslam, *Redeeming Features. A Memoir* (London, 2009), p.184.
37. The lamps were admired by Cecil Beaton, who described them as 'among the most beautiful of modern household objects' (Cecil Beaton, *The Glass of Fashion* [London, 1954], p.176). For further examples, see *Important 20th Century Decorative Art & Design*, Christie's, London (7 December 1995), pp.62–111.
38. Cecil Beaton came for lunch in 1947 but never returned. 'There was nothing in the house grand enough for him,' recalled Lawford, quoted in Amy Fine Collins, 'A Snapper-up of Considered Trifles', *The Times Saturday Review* (2 February 1991), p.28. Their stylish friend Baron Nicolas 'Niki' de Gunzburg, then a fashion editor for *Harper's Bazaar*, considered the landscaping 'less Versailles than Idlewild', quoted in Lawford (cited note 34), p.147.
39. Leo Lerman, *The Grand Surprise* (New York, 2007), pp.296–7.
40. Lawford (cited note 34), p.146.
41. Alan Pryce-Jones, 'The Country Life', American *House & Garden* (February 1983), pp.50–63. Pryce-Jones, a man of letters and former editor of *The Times Literary Supplement*, had sat for Horst in the *Vogue* studio, Paris, in 1931.
42. John Bowes-Lyon, 'Arundel Park', American *House & Garden* (October 1985), pp.172–81.
43. 'New Pillars of Society', British *Vogue* (November 1986), pp.226–9.
44. *Tatler* (April 1988), pp.100–1. The Duchess was flanked by the Countess of Woolton and Isabel Goldsmith. The cover model wearing a hat by Kirsten Woodward (b.1961) was Evgenia Citkowitz.
45. Lucinda Chambers, 'Horst on Horst', British *Vogue* (August 1989), pp.142–7.
46. Sarajane Hoare, 'Footnotes from Manolo Blahnik', British *Vogue* (September 1990), pp.348–50. Princess Michael of Kent, 'Courtesans and Kings', British *Vogue* (October 1991), p.36.
47. 'Great Images, Great Dresses', British *Vogue* (June 1991), p.113.

Royal Still Lifes
Susanna Brown

1. Author interview with Johann Mayr (known as Hans), Soho House, New York, January 2013. Mr Mayr lived with Horst and Valentine Lawford at Oyster Bay and recalled how Horst often enjoyed photographing still lifes after lunch.
2. The author would like to express particular thanks to Andrew Cowan for sharing his thoughts on this fascinating series of images.
3. *Horst: Salute to the Thirties*, foreword by Janet Flanner, photographs by Horst and George Hoyningen-Huene (New York, 1971), p.11.

V
Horst's World in Colour
Shawn Waldron

1. Pamela Roberts, *A Century of Colour Photography* (London, 2007), p.78.
2. For an excellent treatise on this trend, see Katherine A. Bussard and Lisa Hostetler, *Color Rush: American Color Photography from Stieglitz to Sherman* (New York, 2013).
3. The average salary in 1932 was US$1,368 per annum; a loaf of bread cost $.05; and dinner at the Waldorf Astoria Hotel was $2.00.
4. The turreted building still stands, but the printing plant was closed in 1966 and it is now a hotel and event space. Two stone pillars at the entrance, which bear the name of the company and its three publications – *Vogue, Vanity Fair* and *House & Garden*, are the only evidence of the building's history.
5. Robin Lenman (ed.), *The Oxford Companion to the Photograph* (Oxford, 2005), p.89.
6. *The Oxford Companion to the Photograph* (cited note 5), p.89.
7. Anton Bruehl and Fernand Bourges (eds), *Color Sells* (New York, 1935), unpaginated.
8. *The Oxford Companion to the Photograph* (cited note 5), p.5.
9. *Anton Bruehl*, exh. cat., Howard Greenberg Gallery, New York, 1998. Reference found in *New York Times* review of the exhibition, 20 February 1998.
10. Dr Agha was originally hired as art director for the ill-fated German *Vogue*. When the magazine was closed just a few years after its launch, Mr Nast brought Dr Agha to New York in 1929, promoting him to the role of art director for the American titles. Agha oversaw a successful Art Deco-inspired redesign of *Vogue, Vanity Fair* and *House & Garden*. His new approach included the introduction of full-bleed pages, sans-serif type, clean and graceful lines, and more white space in the magazines.
11. Iva Patcevitch (1901–93) was first employed as personal assistant to Mr Nast in 1928. He was a troubleshooter at various Condé Nast publications in the 1930s, including French *Vogue*. As specified in Mr Nast's will, he became chairman of Condé Nast's executive committee in 1942, retiring in 1971.
12. Valentine Lawford, *Horst: His Work and His World* (New York, 1984), p.118.
13. Lawford (cited note 12), pp.146–7. Valentine Lawford explains how Horst came to be in possession of the Picasso. Such was Horst's natural generosity and positive financial situation by 1936 that he did not hesitate in making an unconditional loan of $5,000 to his friend Francesco von Mendelssohn. Francesco insisted that Horst accept as collateral the Stradivarius cello that had once belonged to Felix von Mendelssohn-Bartholdy. This family heirloom remained in Horst's room at the Gladstone Hotel until Francesco required it for a recital, and gave Horst instead a Picasso gouache depicting a red clown with a blue boy on his knee.
14. Lawford (cited note 12), p.198.
15. Lawford (cited note 12), p.194.
16. Memo, Agha to Nast, 17 January 1940. Condé Nast Archive MC001 3/20.
17. Memo, I. Patcevitch to Dr Agha, 28 November 1941, Condé Nast Archive MC001 3/21.
18. Horst quoted in Lawford (cited note 12), p.198.
19. Lawford (cited note 12), p.198.
20. Lucien Vogel (1886–1954) was a French publisher, editor and art director for a number of magazines including *Art et Decoration, La Gazette du Bon Ton* and *Vu*; with regard to the last two he was also a founder. Mr Condé Nast was a publishing partner on *Bon Ton* and Alexander Liberman served as art director under Vogel at *Vu*.
21. Memo, Vogel to Nast, 10 January 1941. Condé Nast Archive MC001 11/23.
22. Memo, Vogel to Nast, 2 September 1941. Condé Nast Archive MC001 11/25.
23. Memo, Vogel to Nast, 2 September 1942. Condé Nast Archive MC001 11/24.
24. Lawford (cited note 12), p.207.
25. Lawford (cited note 12), p.210.
26. *The Art and Technique of Color Photography: A Treasury of Color Photography by The Staff Photographers of Vogue, House & Garden, and Glamour* (New York, 1951).
27. *The Art and Technique of Color Photography* (cited note 26), p.28.
28. *The Art and Technique of Color Photography* (cited note 26), p.200.

VI
Patterns from Nature
Martin Barnes

1. Horst records: 'All photographs are taken on Super XX Film. 120 Films developed in Defender 777. 4 x 5 Films developed in Kodak Developer DK 50. All enlargements on Opal G paper. Paper developer Kodak # 52'. *Patterns from Nature. Photographs by Horst* (New York, 1946), p.ix. His negatives and prints survive in the Horst Archive.
2. American *Vogue* (1 May 1947), p.123. Horst made another version, using the same image of the woman but with a different leaf background. A 10 x 8 in print is part of the Horst Archive.
3. *Patterns from Nature* (cited note 1), p.viii.
4. Valentine Lawford, *Horst: His Work and his World* (New York, 1984), p.264.
5. Lawford (cited note 4), pp.264–6.
6. 'Patterns in pictures by Horst', American *Vogue* (15 October 1946), pp.192–3.
7. *Patterns from Nature* (cited note 1), p.viii.
8. Lawford (cited note 4), p.264.
9. Lawford (cited note 4), pp.264–6.
10. *Patterns from Nature* (cited note 1), text on dust jacket.
11. *Patterns from Nature* (cited note 1), p.95.
12. Lawford (cited note 4), p.266.
13. The original photo-mosaic reproduced on page 100 of *Patterns from Nature* is annotated 'silk'. A further 20 collages survive that were not reproduced in *Patterns from Nature*. Three of these were produced from the images on pages 4, 27 and 67 of the book, and two others, which it does not reproduce, are annotated 'wallpaper'.
14. 'Patterns in pictures by Horst' (cited note 6), pp.192–3.
15. 'Nature turns Designer', *House & Garden* (November, 1946), vol.LXXX, p.188.
16. These included the 'Mexican archway', mentioned in the *New York Times* article and the collage reproduced on page 99 of *Patterns from Nature*. The Wesley Simpson Custom Fabrics, Inc. Swatch Book Archive, 1898-1950, New York Public Library, call number JSN 08-2.
17. See Lynn Felsher, 'Wesley Simpson; Designer, Stylist and Entrepreneur', in *Silk Roads, Other Roads: Textile Society of America 8th Biennial Symposium* (26–8 September 2002), Smith College, Northampton, Massachusetts.
18. See Dilys Blum, 'Painting by the Yard: American Artist Designed Textiles 1947–57', in *Disentangling Textiles: Techniques for the study of designed objects*, Mary Schoeser and Christine Boydel (eds) (London, 2002), pp.109–18.
19. *Horst: Patterns from Nature*, Andrew Crispo Gallery, 41 East 57th Street, New York, 31 March – 26 April 1977.

Kodak Negative Album
Susanna Brown

1. *Patterns from Nature* (New York, 1946), p.vii.

VII
Middle-Eastern Diaries
Horst P.Horst and Valentine Lawford

1. Valentine Lawford, *Horst: His Work and His World* (New York, 1984), p.283.
2. Diary, collection of R.J. Horst. Diary extracts have been edited to read more easily.
3. Lawford (cited note 1), p.301.
4. Ibid.
5. Lawford (cited note 1), p.299.

Persepolis Bull, 1949
Susanna Brown

1. The scientific excavations at Persepolis were led by archaeologists from the Oriental Institute of the University of Chicago.
2. Valentine Lawford, *Horst: His Work and His World* (New York, 1984), pp.283-4: 'In the summer of 1949, after more than three years at the United Nations, I was appointed political counsellor at the British Embassy in Teheran. Iran was at that time generally regarded in the West as one of the more promising and potentially important nations of the Middle East. ... Horst, who had seldom been much farther east than his native Thuringia, took a month's vacation to accompany me to my new post, welcoming this unexpected opportunity to visit and photograph a famously beautiful part of Asia before it had been modernised beyond recognition. In order to make his journey even more worthwhile, professionally, he suggested to Mrs Chase and Mr Liberman – who accepted the suggestion – that he should visit Israel, too, and take photographs there for an article about that country in *Vogue*.'
3. The head of the other limestone bull is displayed at the Oriental Institute of the University of Chicago, OIM A24065. Both bulls were carved c.486–424 BCE.
4. Handwritten notebook with cover label: 'Horst: Diary of Middle East Trip, 1949', unpaginated. Collection of R.J. Horst.
5. American *Vogue*, 15 November 1949, pp.132–5.
6. Letter from Diana Vreeland to Horst, dated 5 December 1949. Typed on *Harper's Bazaar* letterhead, handwritten signature. Collection of R.J. Horst.

VIII
Hard Bodies: Male Nudes
Oliver Winchester

1. Eric Boman, quoted in Terence Pepper, 'Always in *Vogue*', *Horst Portraits*, exh.cat., National Portrait Gallery, London, 2001, p.35.
2. Valentine Lawford, *Horst: His Work and His World* (New York, 1984), p.66.
3. Allen Ellenzweig, *The Homoerotic Photograph: Male Images from Durieu/Delacroix to Mapplethorpe* (New York, 1992), p.205.
4. Lawford (cited note 2), p.16.
5. Ibid.
6. Lawford (cited note 2), p.23; author's parentheses.
7. See Christopher Reed, *Art and Homosexuality: A History of Ideas* (Oxford, 2011), pp.142–8. Notably the reference to the scrapbooks of Carl Van Vechten.
8. Ellenzweig (cited note 3), p.168.
9. Reed (cited note 7), p.231.
10. Quoted in Domenico Rizzo, 'Public Spheres and Gay Politics since the Second World War' in *Gay Life and Culture: A World History*, ed. Robert Aldrich (London, 2006), p.197.
11. See John D'Emilio, *Sexual Politics, Sexual Communities: The Making of a Homosexual Minority in the United States, 1940–1970* (Chicago, 1983), pp.40-53.
12. Quoted in Rizzo (cited note 10), p.205.
13. Ellenzweig (cited note 3), pp.98–104.
14. Ibid., p.104.
15. Ibid.
16. Lawford (cited note 2), p.37.
17. Ibid.
18. Ellenzweig (cited note 3), p.121.
19. *Important 20th Century Decorative Art & Design*, Christie's, New York (7 December 2005), p.42.
20. Ibid.
21. Reed (cited note 7), p.145.
22. Ellenzweig (cited note 3), p.39.
23. Ibid.
24. Ibid.
25. Ellenzweig (cited note 3), p.127.
26. Ellenzweig (cited note 3, p.133.
27. Ellenzweig (cited note 3, p.140.
28. Ellenzweig (cited note 3, p.163.
29. Ellenzweig (cited note 3, p.167.
30. Christie's sale catalogue (cited note 19), pp.36–7.
31. Ellenzweig (cited note 3), p.204.

The Classical Torso, Paris, 1932
Susanna Brown

1. Oliver Winchester, 'The Male Nude', *Horst: Photographer of Style* (London, 2014), p.255.
2. Roxana Marcoci, *The Original Copy: Photography of Sculpture, 1839 to Today* (New York, 2010), p.16.
3. Beaumont Newhall, 1937, quoted in David Campany, *Photography and Cinema* (London, 2008), p.64.
4. Marcoci (cited note 2), p.16.
5. Mehemed Fehmy Agha, 'Raphaels Without Hands', American *Vogue*, (15 June 1941), p.19.
6. 'Editorial Comment', *American Journal of Archaeology*, vol.36, no.4, October-December 1932, p.381.

IX
Conversation Pieces:
Interiors of Horst and Lawford
Glenn Adamson

1. The author would like to express his thanks to Susanna Brown and Emily Marshall Orr for assistance in preparing this essay. For overviews of the Living in Style series, see Barbara Plumb, *Horst Interiors* (Boston, 1993), and Valentine Lawford, *Vogue's Book of Houses, Gardens, People, Photographed by Horst* (London, 1968).
2. Valentine Lawford, 'The Upswing Young', American *Vogue* (1 August 1966), pp.140–7, 153, 157, 160-1: 160.
3. Lawford (cited note 2), pp.147, 153.
4. Lawford (cited note 2), p.141.
5. Lawford (cited note 2), p.147.
6. Lawford (cited note 2), p.161.
7. Undated letter from Karen Radkai to Willard Seymour, collection of R. J. Horst.
8. Susan Sontag, 'Notes on Camp', *Partisan Review* (January 1964).
9. Kate Retford, 'From the Interior to Interiority: The Conversation Piece in Georgian England', *Journal of Design History* (2007), 20/4, pp.291–307.
10. 'The Reed Team', American *Vogue* (15 January 1966), pp.114–17.
11. Valentine Lawford, *Horst: His Work and His World* (New York, 1984), p.372. Yves Saint Laurent was another figure in Horst's circle who took inspiration from Visconti's 'incomparably stylish evocation of upper-class life'. See John Richardson, 'Yves Saint-Laurent's Château Gabriel: A Passion for Style', American *Vogue* (1 December 1983), pp.302–15, 395: 309. This was one of several features the magazine ran on the houses of the great fashion designer with photographs by Horst. See also Valentine Lawford, 'Oasis in Paris', American *Vogue* (1 November 1971), pp.158–63; 'Saint Laurent Surprise', American *Vogue* (1 May 1979), pp.258–63, 293; and G.Y. Dryansky, 'A Quiet Splendor: YSL's Marrakesh House', American *Vogue* (1 August 1980), pp.232–9, 283.
12. Valentine Lawford, 'Consuelo Vanderbilt Balsan: Portrait of a Unique American', American *Vogue* (1 February 1963), pp.124–33, 164–8.
13. Consuelo Vanderbilt Balsan, *The Glitter and the Gold: The American Duchess* (London, 1953).
14. Lawford (cited note 11), p.353.
15. Lawford (cited note 12), p.168.
16. Lawford (cited note 12), p.164.

17. Lawford (cited note 12), p.126.
18. Letter from Consuelo Balsam to Diana Vreeland, January 1963. Collection of R.J. Horst.
19. No less than Jacqueline Onassis commented that Horst had been the 'most generous of men' when he visited her to take a picture. Undated letter from Jacqueline Onassis to Horst, collection of R.J. Horst.
20. Valentine Lawford, 'A Reflection of Now', American *Vogue* (1 October 1971), pp.180–7, 191. See also Horst's portrayal of art collectors Alexander and Elizabeth Vagliano, who lived in high-tech interiors rather reminiscent of Stanley Kubrick's *2001: A Space Odyssey* (1968) and *Clockwork Orange* (1971), in 'Line-and-Form', American *Vogue* (1 February 1971), pp.178–9.
21. 'Truman Capote and the Country Studio He Designed for Work', American *Vogue* (1 November 1965), pp.208-11; 'Jane Holzer the Lion-Hearted', American *Vogue* (1 November 1969), pp.210-15: 210; Gloria Steinem, British *Vogue* (January 1971), pp.104–5.
22. Valentine Lawford, 'Roman Classic Surprise', American *Vogue* (15 November 1966), pp.182–7, 193–6: 183.
23. Pierre Alexandre de Looz, 'Cy Twombly 1966', *O32c* (Summer 2010), 19, pp.101–19.
24. Lawford (cited note 22), p.194.
25. Lawford (cited note 22), p.195.
26. Lawford (cited note 11), following p.370.
27. Valentine Lawford, 'Le Style Pauline', American *Vogue* (1 June 1969), pp.150–3, 159–60.
28. Quoted in Lawford (cited note 11), p.364.
29. Valentine Lawford, 'The House that Horst Grew', American *Vogue* (1 June 1966), pp.134–9. See also the sale catalogue of objects from Horst's estate, *Important 20th Century Decorative Art & Design*, Christie's, New York. (7 December 2005).
30. Lawford (cited note 29), p.134.

The House that Horst Grew
Susanna Brown

1. Valentine Lawford, *Horst: His Work and His World* (New York, 1984), pp.269–70.
2. Lawford describes the first months of his relationship with Horst in Lawford (cited note 1), p.283.
3. Lawford (cited note 1), p.314. The photograph also includes George Schlee, a financier who was Valentina's husband and Garbo's friend.
4. Lawford (cited note 1), p.242.

X
Carmen: An Interview

1. Carmen Dell'Orefice's godparents were Gregory D'Alessio and his wife, Hilda Terry.
2. The story was never published as an article on Haile Selassie took priority.
3. Horst suffered from failing eyesight in later years.

SELECT BIBLIOGRAPHY

MONOGRAPHS

Davis, George (ed.), preface by Dr M. Agha, *Horst, Photographs of a Decade* (J.J. Augustin, New York, 1944)

Horst, Horst P., *Patterns from Nature; Photographs by Horst* (J.J. Augustin, New York, 1946)
—*Horst: fotografie 1931–1984* (Idea Books, Milan, 1985)
—*Form: Horst* (Twin Palms Publishers, Santa Fe, New Mexico, 1992)

Lawford, Valentine, *Horst: His Work and His World* (Alfred A. Knopf, New York, 1984)

Plumb, Barbara, *Horst: Interiors* (Little, Brown, Boston & London, 1993)

Salute to the Thirties, foreword by Janet Flanner, photographs by Horst P. Horst and George Hoyningen-Huene, notes on the plates by Valentine Lawford (Viking Press, New York; Bodley Head, London, 1971)

Siemens, Jochen, David Parker, *Horst* (Stern Gruner + Jahr AG & Co., Hamburg; TeNeues, New York, 2002)

Tardiff, Richard J., Lothar Schirmer (eds), with text by Martin Kazmaier, *Horst: Sixty Years of Photography* (Thames & Hudson, London, 1991; Schirmer/Mosel, Munich & London, 1995)

Tardiff, Richard J., Filippo Passigli, *Horst: Images of Elegance* (Idea Books, Milan, 1993)

BOOKS AND JOURNALS

Aletti, Vince, Richard Avedon, Carol Squiers (eds), *Avedon Fashion* (Harry N. Abrams, Inc., New York, 2009)

Ballard, Bettina, *In My Fashion* (Secker & Warburg, London, 1960)

Battersby, Martin, *The Decorative Thirties* (Studio Vista, London, 1971)

Beaton, Cecil, *The Glass of Fashion* (Weidenfeld & Nicolson, London, 1954)

Beaton, Cecil, Gail Buckland, *The Magic Image: The Genius of Photography from 1839 to the Present Day* (Weidenfeld & Nicolson, London, 1975)

Bertin, Célia, translated by Marjorie Deans, illustrated by Mariel Deans, *Paris à la Mode: A Voyage of Discovery* (Victor Gollancz, London, 1956)

Blum, Dilys, 'Painting by the Yard: American Artist Designed Textiles 1947–57', in Mary Schoeser and Christine Boydel (eds), *Disentangling Textiles: Techniques for the Study of Designed Objects* (Middlesex University Press, London, 2002)

Bussard, Katherine A., Lisa Hostetler, *Color Rush: American Color Photography from Stieglitz to Sherman* (Aperture, New York, 2013)

Campany, David, *Photography and Cinema* (Reaktion, London, 2008)

Cartier: *Innovation through the 20th Century*, forewords by Elena Gagarina, Bernard Fornas; texts by Michel Aliaga et al. (Flammarion, Paris; distributed in North America by Rizzoli, 2007)

Chase, Edna Woolman, Ilka Chase, *Always In Vogue* (Victor Gollancz, London, 1954)

Chermayeff, Catherine (ed.), *Fashion Photography Now* (Harry N. Abrams, New York, 2000)

Cooper, Emanuel, *The Sexual Perspective: Homosexuality and Art in the Last 100 Years in the West* (Routledge, London & New York, 1994, 2nd ed.)

D'Emilio, John, *Sexual Politics, Sexual Communities: The Making of a Homosexual Minority in the United States, 1940–1970* (University of Chicago Press, Chicago, 1983)

Demornex, Jacqueline, *Madeleine Vionnet* (Thames & Hudson, London, 1991)

Derrick, Robin, Robin Muir (eds), *Vogue Covers: On Fashion's Front Page* (Little, Brown, London, 2007)

Devlin, Polly, Alexander Liberman (eds), *Vogue Book of Fashion Photography* (Thames & Hudson, London, 1979)

Du Plessix Gray, Francine, *Them: A Memoir of Parents* (Penguin Press, New York, 2005)

Ellenzweig, Allen, *The Homoerotic Photograph: Male Images from Durieu / Delacroix to Mapplethorpe* (Columbia University Press, New York, 1992)

Ewing, William A., *The Photographic Art of Hoyningen-Huene* (Thames & Hudson, London, 1986)
—*The Idealizing Vision: The Art of Fashion Photography* (Aperture Foundation, New York, 1991)

Felsher, Lynn, 'Wesley Simpson; Designer, Stylist and Entrepreneur', in *Silk Roads, Other Roads: Textile Society of America 8th Biennial Symposium*, 26–8 September 2002 (Smith College, Northampton, Massachusetts, 2002)

Friedel, Robert, *Zipper: An Exploration in Novelty* (W.W. Norton, New York & London, 1994)

Gartner, Louis J., *Needlepoint Design* (William Morrow, New York, 1970)

Golbin, Pamela (ed.), *Madeleine Vionnet* (Rizzoli, New York, 2009)

Haslam, Nicholas, *Redeeming Features. A Memoir* (Alfred A. Knopf, New York, 2009)

Herschdorfer, Nathalie, *Coming into Fashion: A Century of Photography at Condé Nast* (Thames & Hudson, London, 2012)

Higgins, J.P.P., *Cloth of Gold: a history of metallised textiles* (Lurex Co., London, 1993)

Hoyningen-Huene, George, introduction by H.K. Frenzel, *Hoyningen-Huene. Meisterbildnisse. Frauen. Mode. Sport.Kunstler* (Dietrich Reimer, Berlin, 1932)

Jones, Geoffrey, *Beauty Imagined: A History of the Global Beauty Industry* (Oxford University Press, Oxford, 2010)

Kazanjian, Dodie, foreword by Hamish Bowles, *Vogue: the Covers* (Harry N. Abrams, New York, 2011)

Keenan, Brigid, *The Women We Wanted to Look Like* (St Martin's Press, New York, 1978)

Kirke, Betty, *Madeleine Vionnet* (Chronicle Books, San Francisco, 1998)

Kochno, Boris, *Christian Bérard* (Herscher, Paris, 1987)

Lawford, Valentine, *Bound for Diplomacy* (Little, Brown, London, 1963)
—introduction by Diana Vreeland, photographs by Horst, *Vogue's Book of Houses, Gardens, People* (Viking Press, New York; Bodley Head, London, 1968)

Lenman, Robin (ed.), *The Oxford Companion*

to the Photograph (Oxford University Press, Oxford, 2005)

Leo, Lerman, *The Grand Surprise* (Alfred A. Knopf, New York, 2007)

Liberman, Alexander, *Greece, Gods and Art* (Collins, London, 1968)
—*Then: Photographs, 1925–1995*, preface by Calvin Tomkins, selected and designed by Charles Churchward (Random House, New York, 1995)

Liberman, Alexander (ed.), documentation compiled by Jonathan Tichenor, introduction by Aline B. Louchheim, *The Art and Technique of Color Photography: A Treasury of Color Photography by The Staff Photographers of Vogue, House & Garden, and Glamour* (Simon & Schuster, New York, 1951)

Mackenzie-Stuart, Amanda, *Diana Vreeland, Empress of Fashion* (Thames & Hudson, London, 2013)

MacSweeney, Eve (ed.), *Vogue: The Editor's Eye* (Harry N. Abrams, New York, 2012)

Martin, Richard (ed.), *Contemporary Fashion* (St James Press, London, 1995), vol.III

Rachline, Sonia, *Paris Vogue: Covers 1920–2009* (Thames & Hudson, London, 2009)

Reed, Christopher, *Art and Homosexuality: A History of Ideas* (Oxford University Press, Oxford, 2011)

Rennolds Milbank, Caroline, *Couture: the great fashion designers* (Thames & Hudson, London, 1985)

Rhodes James, Robert (ed.), *Chips. The Dairies of Sir Henry Channon* (Weidenfeld & Nicolson, London, 1967)

Rizzo, Domenico, 'Public Spheres and Gay Politics since the Second World War', in Robert Aldrich (ed.), *Gay Life and Culture: A World History* (Universe, New York, 2006)

Roberts, Pamela, *A Century of Colour Photography: from the autochrome to the digital age* (Andre Deutsch, London, 2007)

Rochas, Marcel (ed.), *Vingt-cinq ans d'élégance à Paris 1925–1950* (Pierre Tisné, Paris, 1951)

Saillard, Olivier, Anne Zazzo, *Paris Haute Couture* (Flammarion, Paris, 2012)

Schiaparelli, Elsa, *Shocking Life* (J.M. Dent, London, 1954)

Scottish Arts Council and Victoria and Albert Museum, *Fashion, 1900–1939* (Idea Books, London, 1975)

Seebohm, Caroline, *The Man Who Was Vogue: The Life and Times of Condé Nast* (Weidenfeld & Nicolson, London, 1982)

Seidner, David, Martin Harrison and Diana Edkins (eds), *Lisa Fonssagrives: Three Decades of Classic Fashion Photography* (Thames & Hudson, London, 1996)

Silver, Cameron, *Decades: A Century of Fashion* (Bloomsbury, London, 2012)

Steele, Valerie (ed.), *Encyclopedia of Clothing and Fashion* (Scriber Library of Daily Life, Detroit; Thomson Gale, London, 2005)

Vanderbilt Balsan, Consuelo, *The Glitter and the Gold: The American Duchess* (George Mann Ltd, London, 1953)

Vickers, Hugo, *Cecil Beaton, The Authorized Biography* (Weidenfeld & Nicolson, London, 1985)

Vickers, Hugo, introduction, *The Unexpurgated Beaton. The Cecil Beaton Diaries as he wrote them* (Weidenfeld & Nicolson, London, 2002)

Watters, James, with new photographs by Horst, *Return Engagement: Faces to Remember, Then & Now* (Clarkson N. Potter, Inc: Crown Publishers, New York, 1984)

Yochelson, Bonnie, *Anton Bruehl* (Howard Greenberg Gallery, New York, 1998)

Yoxall, H.W., *A Fashion of Life* (Heinemann, London, 1966)

MAGAZINES AND ARTICLES

Vogue – in its British, French and American editions – from 1932, the year Horst's work first appeared in the magazine, until 1999, the date of his death, has been an invaluable source of reference for this publication.

Horst: Spezial Fotografie (Portfolio No.24; 28 October 2001)

LIFE (28 August 1939; 25 December 1944)

Tatler (April 1988)

Voguepedia, various articles, http://www.vogue.com/voguepedia/; accessed 2013

Voilà (9 June 1934), no.168

Vu (February 1931)

Bowes-Lyon, John, 'Arundel Park', American *House & Garden* (October 1985), pp.172–81.

Boxer, Sarah, 'Bodies Doubled: The Art of Being Horst P. Horst', *New York Times*, 19 April 1996

Collins, Amy Fine, 'Reflections of Horst', *Vanity Fair* (December 1990), vol.53, no.12
—'A Snapper-up of Considered Trifles', *The Times*, Saturday Review, 2 February 1991

Deal, Jo, interview with Horst, *Image*, vol.18, no.3, (September 1975), pp.1–11

Dowd, Maureen, 'Horst: A Man of Style', *New York Times*, 28 February 1988

Flanner, Janet, 'Letter from Paris', *New Yorker*, 27 February 1932

Flood, Richard, review of Horst exhibition at Sonnabend Gallery, New York, *Artforum*, vol.19, no.2 (October 1980), pp.80–1

'Genêt' [Janet Flanner], 'Paris Letter', *New Yorker*, 27 February 1932

Hochswender, Woody, 'He is the Camera that Captured Glamour: Images of Horst', *New York Times*, 5 September 1991

Lawford, Valentine, 'Three Ministers', *Cornhill Magazine* (Autumn 1956)
—'Reflections: Stylish Times, Stylish Men Captured by Horst', *Esquire* (September 1984)

'Nature turns Designer', American *House & Garden* (November 1946), vol.LXXX

Paris fashion correspondent, 'The Glass of Fashion', *The Times*, 19 July 1938

'Photographed by Horst in Paris for Vanity Fair', *Vanity Fair* (July 1934)

Pryce-Jones, Alan, 'The Country Life', American *House & Garden* (February 1983), pp.50–63

Retford, Kate, 'From the Interior to Interiority: The Conversation Piece in Georgian England', *Journal of Design History* (2007), 20/4

Seidner, David, 'Lisa Fonssagrives-Penn', BOMB 12 / Spring 1985, ART, http://bombsite.com/issues/12/articles/645; accessed 2013

Sontag, Susan, 'Notes on Camp', *Partisan Review* (January 1964)

FILMS AND DOCUMENTARIES

Horst: Sixty Years and Still in Vogue, a television documentary by Gerald Scarfe for Omnibus, 1992

EXHIBITION CATALOGUES / EXHIBITION-RELATED PUBLICATIONS

Chorus of Light: Photographs from the Sir Elton John Collection (High Museum of Art, Atlanta, 2000); edited by Ned Rifkin

Fashion: An Anthology by Cecil Beaton, exh. cat., Victoria and Albert Museum, London, 1971; text by Madeleine Ginsburg

Fashion and Surrealism (Rizzoli, New York, 1987; Thames & Hudson, London, 1988); text by Richard Martin; published to accompany an exhibition at the Metropolitan Museum of Art, New York, 1987, and at the Victoria and Albert Museum, London, 1988

Horst, exh. cat., International Center of Photography, New York, 1984

Horst: 60 Ans de Photographie, exh. cat., Musee des Arts de la Mode, Paris, 1991

Horst P. Horst, exh. cat., Museum Ludwig, Cologne, 1992 edited by Reinhold Misselbeck, Rainer Wick and Richard J. Tardiff

Horst: Magier des Lichts, exh. cat., Staatliche Galerie Moritzburg, Halle, Germany, 1997; Josef Albers Museum Quadrat, Bottrop, Germany, 1997; Frankfurter Hof, Mainz, Germany, 1997; and other locations; edited by Reinhold Misselbeck, text by Herbert Locher

Horst Portraits: Paris, London, New York (National Portrait Gallery, London, 2001); published to accompany the exhibition *Horst Portraits: 60 Years of Style*, National Portrait Gallery, London, 2001, text by Terence Pepper, notes on plates and chronology by Robin Muir

Madeleine Vionnet, 1876–1975: L'art de la Couture (Musées de Marseille, Marseille, 1991); published to accompany an exhibition at the Centre de la Vieille Charité, Marseille, 1991

Original Copy: Photography of Sculpture, 1839 to Today (Museum of Modern Art, New York, 2010); texts by Roxana Marcoci, Geoffrey Batchen and Tobia Bezzola

Platinum (Jefferies Cowan, London, 2006); published to accompany an eponymous exhibition at Hamiltons, London, 2006

Schiaparelli & Prada: Impossible Conversations (Yale University Press, New Haven CT & London, in association with the Metropolitan Museum of Art, New York, 2012)

The Golden Age of Couture: Paris and London 1947–1957 (Victoria and Albert Museum, London, 2007); edited by Claire Wilcox

The Model as Muse: Embodying Fashion (Yale University Press, New Haven CT & London, in association with the Metropolitan Museum of Art, New York, 2009); texts by Harold Koda and Kohle Yohannan

Underwear: Fashion in Detail (Victoria and Albert Museum, London, 2010); published to accompany the V&A touring exhibition *Undressed: 350 Years of Underwear in Fashion*, 2010; text by Eleri Lynn

AUCTION CATALOGUES

Photographic Images and Related Material
Sotheby's, London, 8 May 1992

Important 20th Century Decorative Art & Design: properties from John Getty ... estate of Horst P. Horst ... Barbara Jakobson ... estate of Lucy Kennedy Miller (Mrs. J. O. Miller) ... City of New London, Connecticut ... estate of Ruth Phillips
Christie's, New York, 7 December 2005

Antiquities : properties from ... Evelyn Annenberg Hall ... estate of Horst P. Horst ... John W. Kluge Morven ... Los Angeles County Museum of Art ... Leo Mildenberg Collection of Ancient Animals ... Henry E. Owsley III and Alexa Van de Walle ... Nathan Mark Schulman ... William Suddaby
Christie's, New York, 9 December 2005

Horst, photographs from the collection of Gert Elfering
Christie's, New York, 23 April 2007

Photographs, Phillips, New York, 4 October 2011

OBITUARIES

Bowles, Hamish, 'Horst P. Horst, 1906–1999', American *Vogue*, (1 February 2000)

Core, Philip, 'Horst P. Horst', *Independent*, 20 November 1999

Hopkinson, Amanda, 'Horst P. Horst: From stylish fashion shoots to glamorous portraits of the famous', *Guardian*, 20 November 1999

'Horst P. Horst', *The Times*, 22 November 1999

'Horst P. Horst, Photographer who lent elegance to the most striking society figures from the Thirties to the Nineties', *Daily Telegraph*, 23 November 1999

Horyn, Cathy, 'Horst P. Horst', *New York Times*, 19 November 1999

'Light fades for Horst, aged 93', *British Journal of Photography*, 24 November 1999

Muir, Robin, 'Strike a Pose', *Independent*, Magazine, 19 June 1999

ARCHIVES AND COLLECTIONS

Collection of R.J. Horst

Condé Nast Archive, New York, Correspondence files MC001

Condé Nast Publications Library and Archive, London

Les Archives de *Vogue*, Paris

The Horst Estate, www.horstphorst.com

The Wesley Simpson Custom Fabrics, Inc. Swatch Book Archive, 1898–1950, New York Public Library, call number JSN 08-2

APPENDIX TO ILLUSTRATIONS
Anisa Hawes

All photographs by Horst, unless otherwise stated. Titles in italics were assigned by the photographer. Photographs by Horst are reproduced courtesy of the Condé Nast Archive, New York; Collection Condé Nast, France; and the Horst Estate.

Dimensions, where known, are given in centimetres, height precedes width. The following exceptions have been made throughout the book: references to 10 x 8 plate cameras, film or negatives; 12 x 10 prints; or 5 x 4 or 2 ¼ square negatives. Here inches are retained as accepted terminology. Conversions are as follows: 12 x 10 in (30.5 x 25.5 cm); 10 x 8 in (25.5 x 20 cm); 5 x 4 in (12.5 x 10 cm); 2 ¼ in square (6 cm square).

Unnumbered gatefold: between 1935 and 1963 Horst photographed over 90 covers for *Vogue*. The selection of images shown are American *Vogue* covers. Many of these photographs were also published on the British and French editions of the magazine.

Plate 181 and plates 193–203: the technical index from *Patterns from Nature*, p.ix, gives the following information: 'All photographs are taken on Super XX Film. 120 films developed in Defender 777. 4 x 5 Films developed in Kodak Developer DK 50. All enlargements on Opal G paper. Paper-developer Kodak #52'.

Frontispiece
Helen Bennett, Paris, 1936
Platinum-palladium print, printed later
Horst Estate

Plate 1
Still Life, 1942
Gelatin silver print
25.4 x 20.3 cm
Horst Estate

Plate 2
Estrella Boissevain, hat and coat-dress by Bergdorf Goodman, 1938
Gelatin silver print
25.4 x 20.5 cm
V&A: E.221-2014, Given by Gert Elfering

Published:
American *Vogue*, November 1938, p.78:
'Fashion: Your Better Self'
Caption reads: 'Beauty by day – direct, fresh, a subject for a modern canvas. Hat and original black wool coat-dress; Bergdorf Goodman'.

British *Vogue*, 30 November 1938, p.70:
'Your Better Self'
Caption reads: 'Beauty by day – direct, fresh, a fitting subject for a modern canvas'.

Plate 3
Roy Stevens
Horst and Lisa Fonssagrives in the studio, New York, 1949
Gelatin silver print
24.6 x 19.7 cm
Horst Estate
Time & Life Pictures / Getty Images

Plate 4
Helen Bennett, nightgown by Dubrulle, 1938
Gelatin silver print
16.2 x 22.5 cm
Paris *Vogue* Archive

Photographed: 18 February 1938

Published:
American *Vogue*, 15 April 1938, p.120:
'Features: A Wave of Pink for the Bride's Linen'
Caption reads: 'Shades of pink for the bride's linen – that's a fresh, charming departure. On this page, some of the new pinks. Opposite: Dubrulle's nightgown of sheerest pink crêpe'.

Variant, British *Vogue*, 2 November 1938, p.78:
'A Wave of Pink for the Bride's Linen'
Caption reads: 'Shades of pink for the bride's linen – that's a fresh, charming departure. Opposite: Dubrulle's nightgown of sheerest pink crêpe. Debenham and Freebody have it'.

Plate 5
Preparatory sketch for a fashion photograph, 1930s
Ink and pencil on paper
21.7 x 28.2 cm
Collection of R.J. Horst

Plate 6
Gloria Vanderbilt, New York, 1941
Gelatin silver print
25.3 x 20.1 cm
V&A: E.216-2014, Given by Gert Elfering

Published:
Variant, American *Vogue*, 15 January 1942, p.48:
'People and Ideas: Miss Gloria Vanderbilt Marries Mr. Pasquale di Cicco'
Caption reads: 'When Miss Gloria Laura Vanderbilt married Mr. Pasquale di Cicco in California last month, she wore a wedding-dress by Howard Greer, who also designed her trousseau. She is dark and beautiful, seventeen years old, daughter of the late Reginald C. Vanderbilt and Mrs. Vanderbilt, and great-great granddaughter of the famous Commodore Vanderbilt, founder of the clan'.

Plate 7
Lud, suit and hat by Schiaparelli, jewellery by Mauboussin, 1937
Gelatin silver print
24 x 18 cm
Horst Estate

Photographed: 1 February 1937

Published:
American *Vogue*, 1 March 1937, p.79:
'Fashion: More from the Paris Openings'
Caption reads: 'Schiaparelli, flirting with baroque throughout her Collection, puts white gingerbread scrolls on a black woollen suit. With it, a frothy blouse. And her black felt Napoleonic hat, flaring boldly off the face; imported by Bergdorf Goodman. Mauboussin jewels'.

Variant, British *Vogue*, March 1937, p.68:
'Sparks from Paris'
Caption reads: 'Baroque Art: Schiaparelli flirts lightly with Viennese baroque in this black woollen suit, its wide collar and jacket-hem outlined with patent leather painted with white gingerbread scrolls. The turned-up felt hat has a faintly Napoleonic, and wholly conquering air'.

French *Vogue*, March 1937, p.53: 'Arabesques Décoratives'
Caption reads: 'Schiaparelli s'inspire de baroque viennois en peignant des volutes blanches sur un galon de cuir verni. Grande feutre noir'.

Plate 8
Helen Bennett, 1936
Gelatin silver print
25.4 x 20.1 cm
Horst Estate

Plate 9
Lyla Zelensky, dress by Jean Patou, jewellery by Boucheron, 1938
Gelatin silver print
27.3 x 16.2 cm
Paris *Vogue* Archive

Photographed: 2 August 1938

Published:
American *Vogue*, 15 September 1938, p.83:
'Fashion: More from the Paris Openings'
Caption reads: 'Lace frills in Patou's collection. Ruffles of black lace cascade in panels down this black silk velvet evening dress. The waist is shaped like an hour-glass. The décolletage shaped like a heart. (Jay-Thorpe). Jewels on both pages from Boucheron'.

British *Vogue*, 24 August 1938, p.27:
'Paris Collections Focus On: Lace and Velvet'
Caption reads: 'Lace and Velvet – Godets of black-over-white ruffle pointing up the moulded waist, piling the heart-shaped neckline'.

Plate 10
Marquise de Montesquiou-Fezensac, accessories by Molyneux, 1938
Gelatin silver print
24.1 x 18 cm
V&A: E.213-2014, Given by Gert Elfering

Photographed: 12 February 1938

Published:
American *Vogue*, 15 March 1938, p.86:
'Fashion: Paris Collections – Inside Out'
Caption reads: 'In praise of Molyneux's Toulouse-Lautrec fashions, Horst composed these memorable still lifes. His portrait of the Marquise de Montesquiou-Fezensac is re-photographed, surrounded by the dramatic accessories: huge black straw hat, taffeta fan, rose-trimmed dog-collar'.

French *Vogue*, April 1938, p.66
Caption reads: 'La Marquise de Montesquiou notre le soir ce canotier de paille noire accompagné d'une rose rouge et d'un éventail de tulle. Molyneux'.

British *Vogue*, 27 April 1938, p.76: 'Trompe L'œil'
Caption reads: 'In praise of Molyneux's Toulouse-Lautrec fashions, Horst composed these memorable still lifes. His portait of the Marquise de Montesquiou-Fezensac is re-photographed, surrounded by the dramatic accessories: huge black straw hat, taffeta fan, rose-trimmed dog-collar'.

Plate 11
Suzy Parker, dress by Balenciaga, 1951
Platinum-palladium print, printed later
35.6 x 27.9 cm
Horst Estate

Plate 12
Miss Lane and Lisa Fonssagrives, dresses and hats by Saks-Fifth Avenue, 1940
Gelatin silver print
29.4 x 22.8 cm
V&A: E.207-2014, Given by Gert Elfering

Published:
American *Vogue*, 15 June 1940, p.27:
'Fashion: Shadow-Weights'
Caption reads: 'One thin layer of black over one thin layer of white silk marquisette – a filmy dress for afternoons all summer. $45. The brim of that horse-hair hat comes off to leave a cap. Saks-Fifth Avenue / To make you look – and feel – ten degrees cooler, for garden-lunching or roof-dining – a crisp black silk marquisette dress with a full circular skirt. $45. Hat of black pleated net, Saks-Fifth Avenue'.

Plate 13
Round the Clock, 1987
Platinum-palladium print, printed later
35.6 x 27.9 cm
Horst Estate

Published:
American *Vogue*, 1 November 1987, p.110:
'Pantyhose for Men', advertisement for RoundTheClock hosiery

Plate 14
George Hoyningen-Huene (1900–68)
Horst, 1931
Gelatin silver print
25.4 x 20.5 cm
Collection of R.J. Horst
© Estate of George Hoyningen-Huene

Plate 15
George Hoyningen-Huene, 1933
Gelatin silver print
14.8 x 12.1 cm
Collection of R.J. Horst

Plate 16
Martin Munkácsi (1896–1963)
Leni Riefenstahl, cover of *Vu*, February 1931
© Martin Munkácsi, Courtesy Howard Greenberg Gallery, New York

Plate 17
Count de Beistegui's apartment, 136 Champs Elysées, Paris, designed by Le Corbusier, 1930s
Illustrated in *Vingt-cinq ans d'élégance à Paris 1925-1930*, Editions Pierre Tisné, France, 1951
P. Garner

Plate 18
Nelly (Elli Souyioultzoglou-Seraïdari, 1899–1998)
Nikolska, Parthenon, Athens, 1929
Gelatin silver print
20.8 x 27.9cm
P. Garner

Plate 19
Unknown photographer
Winged Victory of Samothrace c.220–185 BCE, Musée du Louvre, Paris, after its reinstallation in the summer of 1885
Albumen print
28 x 22.3 cm
P. Garner

Winged Victory of Samothrace, c.220–185 BCE
Parian and Rhodian marble
Musée du Louvre, Paris, MA 2369

Plate 20
George Hoyningen-Huene
Horst, 1932
Gelatin silver print
13 x 11.8 cm
P. Garner
© Estate of George Hoyningen-Huene

Plate 21
George Hoyningen-Huene
Horst, 1930
Gelatin silver print
Collection of R.J. Horst
© Estate of George Hoyningen-Huene

Plate 22
Christian Bérard (1902–49)
Horst, 1933–4
Oil on canvas
78.8 x 105.4 cm
© ADAGP, Paris and DACS, London 2014.
Photo © Christie's Images / The Bridgeman Art Library

Plate 23
Gloves by Chanut, Alexandrine, Nicolet, Dina and Molyneux, 'New Chic on Hand', American *Vogue*, 1 January 1933

Published:
American *Vogue*, 1 January 1933, pp.52–3:
'New Chic on Hand'
Captions read: 'Prepare to throw your old inhibitions about gloves overboard, for, this year, gloves are made of all sorts of materials and have a hint of novelty. Not too much, of course, since nothing is worse than an over fancy glove, but a compromise as simple as the glove shown just above. It is medium length and made of light coloured suède, with a side opening at the wrist, held by a pearl button. Chanut glove; Jay-Thorpe. / The first glove at the lower right, from Dina, is of rosy-beige kid with a stitched cuff pleated at the wrist and held at the side by metal buttons. / Beyond it, at the lower right is a sports glove made of very soft tanned leather, in brown, with hand-stitched seams and with four rows of pin tucking on the cuff; from Chanut. / The gloves just above are woollen ones shading faintly from brown to beige, to wear for daytime on chilly days, with rough woollens. The large cuffs fasten at the side with metal buttons and braided brown suède loops. Alexandrine made them: from Saks-Fifth Avenue. / At the left are some sports gloves – a type which may be a bit more novel than gloves for street wear. These are made of dark green leather and have contrasting cuffs of silk with a tiny, tailored design in yellowish-green and red – very effective with harmonizing country clothes. Molyneux designed these antelope gloves in Paris. / [p.53]. The Chanut glove at the top is of light brown suède with a tiny cording and a pinked edge; Jay-Thorpe / Next is Alexandrine's beige suède glove; sunburst design in black; Saks-Fifth Avenue. / The white glove, left, is for morning wear, and its back is of braided felt, its palm of suède, all lined with silk jersey. Alexandrine model; Saks-Fifth Avenue. / Nicolet's hand-stitched wool jersey glove, with straight cuffs, may be had in dark colours; George Baring, Inc.

'Fabrics you would never have dreamed could be used for gloves, as well as new forms and treatments in leathers, are adding fresh chapters to glove history this year. Felt, jersey, and angora woollen are among them, and, if you look at the photographs on these two pages, you will see how smart and practical these ideas are. The principle of all the new gloves is to maintain the appearance of a small hand, no matter what the material. In the majority of cases, you have a slender wrist, as well, by means of one or two metal or pearl buttons fastening a slit on the outer edge [...]'.

Plate 24
Raoul Barbà
Cotillon, Ballet Russe de Monte Carlo, sets and costumes by Christian Bérard, 1932
Gelatin silver print
16.4 x 11.6 cm
P. Garner

Plate 25
Pavel Tchelitchew (1898–1957)
Set design for *L'Errante*, at the Théâtre des Champs Elysées, Paris, 1933
Watercolour and gouache with pen and sepia on cartridge paper
21.5 x 30 cm
V&A: S.2092-1986

Plate 26
Madame José-Maria Sert, 'Bal Oriental', 1935

Published:
American *Vogue*, 1 August 1935, p.35:
'Fancy-Dress and Fashion'
Caption reads: 'Three brilliant costumes at the Hon. Mrs. Reginald Fellowes' Bal Oriental [...] Madame José-Maria Sert straight out of the Arabian Nights [...] in Ira Belline Pyjamas'.

French *Vogue*, August 1935, p.27 : 'De Fêtes en Fêtes – Texte et dessins de Vertès'
Caption reads: 'The Hon. Mrs. Reginald Fellowes avait pris pour theme de son bal: "Une soirée chez le Gouverneur". Süe, charge de la décoration, créa l'atmosphère au moyen de palmiers en stuc blanc. C'était un Orient de lègende et de rêve'.

Plate 27
Still from the original version of *Le Sang d'un Poète*, by Jean Cocteau, 1930
Illustrated in *Vingt-cinq ans d'élégance à Paris 1925–1930*, Editions Pierre Tisné, France, 1951
P. Garner

Plate 28
Dress and cape by Lanvin, sandals by Bally Bottier, stool by Jean-Michel Frank, vase by Giacometti, 1935

Published:
French *Vogue*, August 1935, p.16
Caption reads: 'La tombée calme et noble de cette ample cape de Lanvin, autant que le bleu intense du velours, rappelle les robes d'anges de Fra Angelico. La robe, également de Lanvin, est en lamé argent. Sandales de Bally Bottier. Décor de J.-M. Frank. Vase de Giacometti'.

Plate 29
Costume designed by Salvador Dalí for his World's Fair installation, Dream of Venus, New York, 1939
Gelatin silver print
24.2 x 19.2 cm
Collection of R. J. Horst

Plate 30
Décor for a *Vogue* fashion set, designed by Emilio Terry, 1936
Gelatin silver print
22.6 x 16.3 cm
Paris *Vogue* Archive

Photographed: 12 February 1936

Published:
French *Vogue*, April 1936, p.31: 'Le Point de Vue de *Vogue*'
Caption reads: 'Une grotte, si vous êtes sensible au merveilleux, ou si vos souvenirs d'enfance ont quelque vivacité, un grotte, c'est la promesse d'un trésor'.

Plate 31
Electric Beauty, Paris, 1939, and three variant poses

All:
Gelatin silver prints
25.4 x 20.4 cm
Horst Estate
Main image, V&A: E.209-2014
Centre image, below, V&A: E.210-2014

Plate 32
Lisa Fonssagrives, *Lisa with Harp*, 1939
Gelatin silver print
25.4 x 20.3 cm
A. Cowan

Plate 33
Lisa Fonssagrives, *Lisa on Silk*, 1940
Gelatin silver print
25.3 x 20.4 cm
Horst Estate

Plate 34
Hands, Hands, Hands, 1941
Gelatin silver print
24.1 x 16.7 cm
Horst Estate

Plate 35
Barefoot Beauty, 1941
Gelatin silver print
25.1 x 20 cm
V&A: E.208-2014, Given by Gert Elfering

Published:
British *Vogue*, August 1941, p.36: 'Portfolio of Wartime Beauty – Basic Beauty'
Caption reads: 'Your hands and feet, given equal care, can be equally beautiful. On your feet depends your poise. By your hands your grooming will be judged. We hope the photograph opposite will move you to take a critical look at your own bare feet. Because from now on you're going to be foot-conscious all year round, for the rational reason that, during war winters, we'll save our stockings and shoes for outdoors, wear sandal-slippers at home [...] Before you set about prettifying your feet, please check up on their general fitness, bearing in mind, too, that prevention is not only better than cure, but easier and less expensive. Putting these platitudes into practice, here's a brief outline of common foot faults to help you tread from health to beauty.'

Plate 36
Odalisque II, 1943
Gelatin silver print
25.3 x 20.4 cm
Horst Estate

Plate 37
Comtesse Gérard de Moustier, 'Bal de Valses', 1934
Gelatin silver print
22.6 x 16 cm
Paris *Vogue* Archive

Photographed: 4 July 1934

Published:
American *Vogue*, 15 August 1934, p.20: 'Features: Paris Under the French'
Caption reads: 'Comtesse Gérard de Moustier at the Baron de Gunzburg's "1860 Ball"'.

French *Vogue*, August 1934, p.15: 'Le Bal de Valses'
Caption reads: 'Qui sont ces ravissantes apparitions? Celle-ci est vêtue d'une robe organdi blanc crée par Ira Beline – la nièce du compositeur Stravinsky – une résille retient ses cheveux'.

British *Vogue*, 3 October, 1934, p.62: 'Autumn Collections'
Caption reads: 'Comtesse Gérard de Moustier impersonates a Viennese beauty of the 1860s'.

Plate 38
Madame Edouard Baurdet, 'Bal de Valses', 1934
Gelatin silver print
22.4 x 14.8 cm
Paris *Vogue* Archive

Photographed: 5 July 1934

Published:
French *Vogue*, August 1934, p.15: 'Le Bal de Valses'
Caption reads: '[...] Tragique, oh! Tragique Marie Veczera (Madame Edouard Baurdet). Habillée, d'aprés un dessin de Bérard, par Madame Karinska qui execute tous les costumes des Ballets Russes, votre destin était déjá inscrit dans votre robe, dans ce tulle pâle comme une plaque tombale, brodé de couronnes mortuaires, de têtes d'angelots (priez pour nous), d'oiseaux expirants, dans ce diadème qui semblait fait de perles funéraires'.

Photograph not published, American *Vogue*, 15 August 1934, p.23: 'Features: Paris Under the French'
Caption reads: '[...] Madame Edouard Bourdet (the wife of the dramatic author) came as Marie Veczera in a fascinating, if slightly macabre, costume designed by Bérard, the painter. It was made with stone-white tulle adorned with funeral crowns, angel heads, black tulle, and expiring birds.'

Plate 39
Count Charles de Beistegui, 'Bal de Valses', 1934
Gelatin silver print
21.7 x 16.5 cm
Paris *Vogue* Archive

Photographed: 4 July 1934

Published:
French *Vogue*, August 1934, p.15: 'Bal de Valses'
Caption reads: 'Voici, parmi les hôtes royaux le Roi de Bavière Louis II, qui finit fou (M. Charles de Beistegui qui donna un grand dîner avant le bal). Il bâtit un palais l'imitation de Versailles pour lui, un théâtre – Bayreuth pour Wagner, son ami, et se noya dans le lac de Starnberg'.
Photograph not published, American *Vogue*, 15 August 1934, p.23: 'Features: Paris Under the French'
Caption reads: '[...] Monsieur Charles de Beistegui represented the mad King Ludwig of Bavaria, who built the famous fairy-like castles, a theatre at Bayreuth for Wagner, and finally drowned himself in the lake of Starnberg'.

Plate 40
Baron Nicolas de Gunzburg, 'Bal de Valses', 1934
Gelatin silver print
22.3 x 16.5 cm
Paris *Vogue* Archive

Photographed: 5 July 1934

Published:
American *Vogue*, 15 August 1934, p.23: 'Features: Paris Under the French'
Caption reads: 'This season, Baron Nicolas de Gunzburg revived for a night the splendour of the last century when he received his guests at an 1860 "Bal des Valses". The romantic setting of the little island in the Bois, surrounded by trees and water, was a perfect background for the glittering, billowy costumes of the women and the rich uniforms of the men. The guests, who were to portray important personages in Vienna at that time, arrived through the woods and were ferried across to the island, where their host greeted them as the Archduke Rodolph, wearing a green velvet uniform designed by Valentine Hugo. [....] Despite the gloom that had befallen most of these dramatic personalities, their impersonators dined gaily in Monsieur de Beistegui's flat overlooking the Arc de Triomphe. There were no electric lights in the room, but candles burning in every corner gave soft brilliance. The long tables were magnificent, lighted with huge gold and silver dinner-plates and the pyramid of blue porcelain from Bavaria that was used as a centrepiece, the men in their rich uniforms and decorations and the women in their diaphanous costumes, glittering jewels, and diadems – the whole scene was reminiscent of the grandeur of Vienna in 1860'.

Plate 41
Lyla Zelensky, dress by Jean Patou, jewellery by Mauboussin, 1937
Gelatin silver print
24.1 x 18 cm
Horst Estate

Photographed: 1 February 1937

Published:
American *Vogue*, 1 March 1937, p.64: 'Fashion: Sparks from the Paris Openings'
Caption reads: 'In Patou's Collection: the wings of a dream moth hovering over a white chiffon dress pleated this way and that, and bound at the waist with leaves in spring green. Mauboussin jewellery'.

Variant, British *Vogue*, 3 March 1937, p.66: 'Sparks from Paris'
Caption reads: 'Moth's wings on Patou's ravishing white chiffon gown, intricately pleated, breathing a spirit at once classic and gay'.

French *Vogue*, March 1937, p.29: 'Premiers Echos des Collections'
Caption reads: 'Cette robe de Patouen mousseline blanche à un movement d'ailes. Les plis sont tantôt verticaux, tantôt en diagonale. Bijoux de Mauboussin'.

Plate 42
Lud, dress by Alix, 1938
Gelatin silver print
25.8 x 18.8 cm
Horst Estate

Published:
American *Vogue*, 15 March 1938, p.75: 'Fashion: Sugar and Spice in the Paris Collections – Second Report on the Spring Openings'
Caption reads: 'Alix's marble statue in white jersey – an immortal dress with, surprisingly, long sleeves and a stab of black in a plume-like head-dress of braid and jet bracelet. (Dress imported by Bergdorf Goodman)'.

British *Vogue*, 13 April 1938, p.71
Caption reads: 'Alix's marble statue in white jersey – an immortal dress with surprising long sleeves, heavy drapery clutched to the front, and a stab of black in a headdress of braid and a jet bracelet. Marie José'.

French *Vogue*, April 1938, p.55:
'Grâce de tous les drapés'
Caption reads: '[....] La robe drapée s'accommode fort bien de manches longues qui la rendent d'un usage encore plus facile, et en font la robe idéale de tous le soir. Alix en a réussi une merveilleuse version qui pourrait être attribuée au ciseau de Phidias: tout en jersey mat blanc, avec de longues manches très simples, toute l'ampleur est ramenée légèrement sur un côté, d'où elle tombe – plis profonds de la taille jusqu'á terre'.

Plate 43
Cora Hemmet, dress by Worth, jewellery by Mauboussin, 1935
Gelatin silver print
25.4 x 16.6 cm
Paris *Vogue* Archive

Photographed: 28 August 1935

Published:
French *Vogue*, October 1935, p.32: 'Nuits Blanches'
Caption reads: 'Worth crêpe "amusade" de Ducharne, Bijoux Mauboussin'.

Plate 44
Cora Hemmet, dress by Lucien Lelong, jewellery by Cartier, console by Jean-Michel Frank, 1935
Gelatin silver print
24 x 18 cm
Horst Estate

Photographed: 6 August 1935

Published:
American *Vogue*, 15 September 1935, p.50: 'Fashion: Hellenic Drapery'
Caption reads: 'Lucien Lelong's beautiful goddess drapery in shirred white rayon jersey'.

British *Vogue*, 18 September 1935, p.58: 'Paris White Magic'
Caption reads: 'Hellenic Caryatid – Lelong's fine white silk jersey, horizontally shirred and trailing: Lilian Lawler'.

French *Vogue*, October 1935, p.28: 'Nuits Blanches'
Caption reads: 'D'une grâce tout hellénique, cette robe merveilleusement drapée de Lucien Lelong est en crêpe "Faribole" blanc de Ducharne. Les bijoux sont Cartier. Console J. M. Frank'.

Plate 45
Classical Still Life, 1937
Platinum-palladium print, printed later
55.9 x 43.8 cm
Horst Estate

Plate 46
Houdon Still Life, 1939
Platinum-palladium print, printed later
54 x 42.6 cm
Horst Estate

Plate 47
Set designed by Salvador Dalí, dresses by Hattie Carnegie, 1947
Gelatin silver print
25.2 x 20 cm
Horst Estate

Photographed: 16 March 1948

Published:
Variant American *Vogue*, 15 May 1948, p 88: 'People and Ideas: Dalí Composes a Photograph'
Caption reads: 'At *Vogue*'s invitation, Sa vador Dalí, levitation expert among artists, applied his sense of detachment to a fashion photograph. The suspension motif which marked his latest exhibition (at the Bignou Gallery) appears here in the picture which he arranged, Horst photographed. The models, without visible means of support, wear evening dresses with a new summer sparkle: one, glitter-veined organdie with a black bolero; one, sequin-sewn chiffon, black over white. Both dresses, made-to-order at Hattie Carnegie'.

Liberman, Alexander (ed.), documentation compiled by Jonathan Tichenor, introduction by Aline B. Louchheim, *The Art and Technique of Color Photography: A Treasury of Color Photography by The Staff Photographers of Vogue, House & Garden, and Glamour*, Simon & Schuster, New York, 1951, p.40: 'Composition by Salvador Dalí'.
Caption reads: 'A trick photograph. The idea was Dalí's and he composed the picture. Camera: 8 x 10 Ansco View. Lens: 12" Zeiss Tassar, f/6.3. Film: Kodachrome Type B sheet film. Light: Two 5000-watt floods, two 750-watt spots, 1500-watt spot overhead, 1500-watt flood. Exposure: ½ second at f/16'.

Plate 48
Costumes designed by Salvador Dalí for Leonid Massine's ballet, *Bacchanale*, 1939
Gelatin silver print
25.6 x 20.3 cm
Horst Estate

Published:
Variant, British *Vogue*, 6 September 1939, p.57: 'Spotlight on the Ballet'
Caption reads: 'Crutches prop Dalí's coryphées'.

French *Vogue*, December 1939, p.35: 'C'était Hier'
Caption reads: 'Un ballet de Dalí'.

Plate 49
Louise Sheldon, dress by Vionnet, jewellery by Mauboussin, 1936
Gelatin silver print
24 x 18 cm
Horst Estate

Published:
American *Vogue*, 15 March 1936, p.66: 'Fashion: "I Dress as I Please", from the Paris Collections'
Caption reads: 'Vionnet's white rayon satin dress: one shoulder bared of glistening folds, one ankle draped with them. Up one side, a row of rhinestone bows and in back, a wealth of train (Salon de Couture, Bonwit Teller)'.

Variant, British *Vogue*, 18 March 1936, p.78: 'Collection Fever'
Caption reads: 'Vionnet's shining white satin stalagmite, with bows of brilliants from bare shoulder to lifted hem: Marie José'.

Plate 50
Lud, dress by Jean Patou, jewellery by Mauboussin, 1936
Gelatin silver print
23.9 x 18 cm
Horst Estate

Photographed: 10 February 1936

Published:
American *Vogue*, 15 March 1936, p.69: 'Fashion: "I Dress as I Please", from the Paris Collections'
Caption reads: 'Patou's famed pink-mauve is used for this dress in his collection. Shirring makes panel, yoke, collar. Thousands of stitches were pressed into the crêpe; then broken to give this effect. All jewels from Mauboussin'.

Variant, British *Vogue*, 18 March 1936, p.81: 'Collection Fever'
Caption reads: 'In Patou's workrooms they are doing a new kind of shirring, the stitches broken so that it is elastic. He uses panels of it in this gown. Mauboussin's Indian ruby necklace brings out the undertones of the heavy clinging mauve-pink crêpe. It's at Vanité, Sloane Street'.

French *Vogue*, April 1936, p.35:
'Le Point de Vue de *Vogue*' / 'Pour le Soir'
Caption reads: 'Un travail – l'aiguille, nervures et fronces, décoré une robe de Jean Patou en Fleursoir mauve. Bijoux Mauboussin'.

Plate 51
Coco Chanel, Paris, 1937
Gelatin silver print
20.3 x 19.1 cm
V&A: E.220-2014, Given by Gert Elfering

Published:
Variant, American *Vogue*, 1 December 1937, p.86: 'Fashion: Mid-Season Prophecies'.

Plate 52
Curtis Moffat (1887–1949)
Mirror staircase at the House of Chanel, 31 rue Cambon, Paris, 1925–30
Gelatin silver contact print
6.4 x 5.8 cm
V&A: E.838-2007, Gift of Penelope Smail
© Victoria and Albert Museum, London / Estate of Curtis Moffat

Plate 53
Marie-Laure, Vicomtesse de Noailles, Paris, 1935

Published:
American *Vogue*, 1 July 1935, p.28: 'Vive L'Italie'
Caption reads: 'More Renaissance lines – in the costumes on these pages. In the photograph, the Vicomtesse de Noailles, with her sombre Florentine beauty, looks like a Medici youth in a stiff Suzy pill-box, ornamented with velvet pastilles; Bergdorf Goodman. Her coiffure, hair parted in the middle and docked straight below the ears, adds to the illusion. Schiaparelli's heavily corded suit has the richness of detail to make it a perfect complement; from Bonwit Teller'.

French *Vogue*, July 1935, p.28: 'Adaptations'
Caption reads: 'Toque en feutre de Suzy. Ensemble de Schiaparelli'.

Plate 54
Albert Seeburger
Madeleine Vionnet's Grand Salon, 50 avenue Montaigne, Paris, c.1930
Stained glass ceiling by Lalique, decorative scheme by George de Feure

Plate 55
Cora Hemmet and Lud, dresses by Schiaparelli and Alix, 'Close-up of the Paris Collections', American *Vogue*, 15 March 1935

Published:
American *Vogue*, 15 March 1935, pp.56–7: 'Close-up of the Paris Collections'

Caption reads: 'Schiaparelli's dress of black satin draped to turn you into a human column; from the Salon de Couture at Bonwit Teller. Jewellery from Herz; [p.57]: Alix turns sculptor to make a Roman toga of white rayon jersey with a separate cape that leaves your back bare; Milgrim'.

French *Vogue*, April 1935, pp.44–5
Caption reads: 'De Schiaparelli, ce fourreau de satin drapé. Bijoux Herz. (Modèles déposés P.A.I.S) / Drapé a l'antique cet ensemble d'Alix en jersey d'albène'.

Plate 56
George Hoyningen-Huene
Left: Madame Vittorio Crespi, ensemble by Schiaparelli
Horst
Centre and right: hat, bag and slippers by Suzanne Talbot
'Glass and Schiaparelli', American *Vogue*, 15 January 1935

Published:
American *Vogue*, 15 January 1935, pp.54–5:
'Glass and Schiaparelli'
Caption reads: 'Madame Vittorio Crespi in a Schiaparelli dress with a glass tunic. Hoyningen-Huene, Paris. Three photographs by Horst, Paris. Talbot uses glass for a hat, a bag and a slipper. No one took Schiaparelli very seriously, last autumn, when she brought out a dress of glass. People smiled sceptically and dismissed it as one of those mad whims of genius. But, unruffled, Schiaparelli went on, and, in her Mid-Season Collection, made three or four more glass dresses, a couple of glass evening jackets, and any number of glass belts. The scepticism melted noticeably. A few of the more daring spirits saw fun in this glass, bought, wore, and liked the dresses. And everyone begged to know what it was made of. Was it honestly glass? Just what it is is one of those deep dark trade secrets. It isn't Cellophane. It probably hasn't an iota of silica and lime and potash in it, as real glass has. It manages to have most of the transparency of glass, but doesn't shatter like a window-pane. The technicians call it Rhodophane, which leaves you as much in the dark as ever. It is a brittle, fragile, transparent substance – you must handle it with care – and it appears in flat, ribbon-like strips interwoven with silk, rayon, or metal threads. The fabric house, Colcombet, is its chief exploiter, and most of the exciting bolts are cornered by Schiaparelli. Lest you think that it is something only a movie queen might wear, we are showing you some of its uses, in the photographs on these two pages. Witness, first, Madame Vittorio Crespi, a beautiful young Italian from Milan, who bought, wears, and is mad about her Schiaparelli glass dress. Only the front of the tunic is glass – the rest is of stiff pale blue satin. Mrs. Harrison Williams wears it, too, and so does Madame Jean Dupuy. You can see it at the left on the opposite page. On the same page, we show a glass hat from Suzanne Talbot – like a crystalline halo. Enchanting for a bridesmaid! Colcombet's glass fabrics form the background. The evening bag at the top of this page is of glass, too, bound with silver braid. Talbot made it. And shades of Cinderella – above is a modern glass slipper, also from Talbot and banded with silver braid. It's charming with a tea-gown. The shimmering material shielding the mannequin's foot is another Colcombet glass fabric'.

Plate 57
George Hoyningen-Huene, self-portrait with Lee Miller in the *Vogue* studio, Paris, 1931
Gelatin silver print
P. Garner
© Estate of George Hoyningen-Huene

Published:
British *Vogue*, 18 March 1931, p.45:
'Paris Fashions As Seen by the Camera'
Caption reads: 'A scene in *Vogue*'s studio while posing a fashion photograph'.

French *Vogue*, May 1931, p.23:
'Le Point de Vue de *Vogue*'

Plate 58
Cora Hemmet, dress by Jean Patou, jewellery by Boucheron, 1935
Gelatin silver print
24 x 17.9 cm
Horst Estate

Photographed: 6 August 1935

Published:
American *Vogue*, 15 September 1935, p.53:
'Fashion: Hellenic Drapery'
Caption reads: 'Patou ... pours you into a sylph sheath of shimmering sea-green and silver lamé. Below the close drapery of the thighs – a fish-tail train, slightly offside. And again, the revealing décolletage'.

British *Vogue*, 18 September 1935, p.62:
'Paris White Magic'
Caption reads: 'Shimmering sea-green and silver lamé wraps Patou's modern mermaid. Below the close drapery of the thighs, a fish-tail train. Note the revealing décolletage, that we predicted, caught up in the sideway movement of the gown: from Ella Wells'.

Variant, French *Vogue*, October 1935, p.30:
'Nuits Blanches'
Caption reads: 'Cette robe de Jean Patou évoque la légendaire sirêne, tant par sa ligne prolongée en traîne que par l'éclat miroilant du lamé d'argent "Ninive" de Bianchini. Bijoux Boucheron'.

Plate 59
Sonia Colmer, dress by Vionnet, jewellery by Mauboussin, 1937
Gelatin silver print
22.9 x 16.7 cm
Paris *Vogue* Archive

Photographed: 11 August 1937

Published:
American *Vogue*, 15 September 1937, p.82:
'Fashion: Woman of the World: the Spirit of the Paris Openings'
Caption reads: 'Gold and Glitter – Vionnet's magnificent Directoire dress – sheerest gold lamé tucked and pleated and held only by a rhinestone necklace clipped to the bodice (Bergdorf Goodman). Mauboussin jewellery'.

British *Vogue*, 15 September 1937, p.51:
'High Points from Paris'
Caption reads: 'Revealed in Vionnet's Directoire masterpiece of chiffon-fine lamé, draped to define the breasts. Divided by the high source of the skirt. Suspended from a necklace, it falls, a torrent of molten gold, in pleats which record every motion of the body. Lydia Moss has it'.

French *Vogue*, November 1937, p.33
Caption reads: 'La magnifique robe de Madeleine Vionnet reproduite ci-contre est faite d'un très fin lamé d'or. Sa souplesse permet de la travailler de nervures tout autour de la taille haute, d'oú il retombre plissé jusqu'á terre. Un collier remplace les épaulettes. Bijoux de Boucheron'.

Plate 60
Madame Buchardt and Lisa Fonssagrives, dresses by Chanel, 1938
Gelatin silver print
21.8 x 16.2 cm
Paris *Vogue* Archive

Photographed: 29 July 1938

Plate 61
Lyla Zelensky, hat and dinner suit by Schiaparelli, 1938
Gelatin silver print
26.7 x 16.3 cm
Paris *Vogue* Archive
Photographed: 6 August 1938

Published:
American *Vogue*, 15 September 1938, p.68:
'Fashion: High Spirits at the Paris Openings'
Caption reads: 'Schiaparelli's ostrich hat, mirror-studded dinner-suit. Coiffures by Paul of "Charles of the Ritz"'.

French *Vogue*, October 1938, p.50:
'Haut les têtes ...'
Caption reads: 'Velours Vizir de Ducharne. Touffe d'autruche dorée et glycérinée'.

Plate 62
Andrée Lorain, hat by Schiaparelli, 1938
Gelatin silver print
27 x 16 cm
Paris *Vogue* Archive

Photographed: 14 June 1938

Published:
American *Vogue*, 1 August 1938, p.29:
'*Vogue*'s Eye View: The Autumn Forecast'
Caption reads: 'Significant things are beginning to emerge from behind the wall of the future. First to come into sight are the new hats. Hats laden with parrot-bright plumage – above is Schiaparelli's ostrich-tipped one [...]'.

Plate 63
Elsa Schiaparelli, Paris, 1937
Gelatin silver print
21 x 13.6 cm
A. Cowan

Published:
American *Vogue*, 1 September 1937, p.97:
'Four Couturiers Wear Models From Their Own Collections'
Caption reads: 'Schiaparelli designs with her own chic in mind, and no one wears Schiaparelli models better. From her new Collection, she chose this tailored evening ensemble and fantastic hat – the wine velvet jacket embroidered with gold and blue glass, the wine felt hat sweeping high'.

British *Vogue*, 29 September 1937, p.85:
'Four Couturiers Wear Models From Their Own Collections'
Caption reads: 'Schiaparelli designs with her own chic in mind, and no one wears Schiaparelli models better. From her new Collection, she chose this tailored evening ensemble and fantastic hat – the wine velvet jacket embroidered with gold and blue glass, the wine felt hat sweeping high'.

Plate 64
Lisa Fonssagrives, hat by Suzy, jewellery by Boucheron, 1938
Gelatin silver print
23.8 x 17.9 cm
Horst Estate

Photographed: 13 June 1938

Published:
American *Vogue*, 1 August 1938, p.54:
'Fashion: Mammoth Tricorn, Miniature Tricorn'
Caption reads: 'Large tricorns and little tricorns are edging over the autumn horizon. This is Suzy's black felt "D'Artagnan", folded obliquely, trimmed with Brandenburg braid, worn sideways with musketeer bravado. Boucheron jewels'.

British *Vogue*, 3 August 1938, p.32:
'Mammoth Tricorne, Miniature Tricorne'
Caption reads: 'Large tricornes and little tricornes

are edging over the autumn horizon. This is Suzy's black felt "D'Artagnan", folded obliquely, trimmed with Brandenburg braid, worn sideways with the bravado of the original mousquetaire himself. Santa has this'.

Plate 65
Mary Belevsky, beret and cape by Lanvin, jewellery by Boucheron, 1938
Gelatin silver print
24 x 17.9 cm
Horst Esate

Photographed: 13 June 1938

Published:
American *Vogue*, 1 August 1938, p.35:
'Fashion: Hats-and Furs: Silhouette Hats'
Caption reads: 'Lanvin's huge pie-pan beret of black felt, with a triangle nicked out of the upturned side. Its outlines show clearly above Lanvin's finger-tip winter cape of beaver with no actual collar, only two deep folds thrusting forward at each side of the neck-line'.

British *Vogue*, 3 August 1938, p.35:
'Mammoth Tricorne, Miniature Tricorne'
Caption reads: 'Lanvin's huge cake-tin beret of black felt, with a slice nicked out of the upturned side. Its outlines show clearly above Lanvin's "Alaska", a winter cape of beaver with no actual collar, only deep folds each side of the neckline. Lillian Lawler has the hat'.

French *Vogue*, August 1938, p.22: 'Avec et Sans Col'
Caption reads: 'La souplesse du castor a permis – Lanvin de réaliser cette belle cape avec deux plis profonds – l'encolure. Grand béret encoché de feutre noir'.

Plate 66
Lisa Fonssagrives, dress by Chanel, 1939
Gelatin silver print
25.8 x 16.4 cm
Paris *Vogue* Archive

Photographed: 11 May 1939

Published:
Variant, American *Vogue*, 1 July 1939, p.56:
'Fashion: Chanel's Slim, Tiered Mummy-Dress / Alix's Willowy Statue-Dress'
Caption reads: 'Chanel's slim, tiered mummy-dress – slim dresses are sliding in among the bouffants. Yards of blue crêpe wrap spirally, end in a scarf. Gold necklace'.

Variant, British *Vogue*, 12 July 1939, p.26:
'Chanel's Slim, Tiered Mummy-Dress'
Caption reads: 'Chanel's slim, tiered mummy-dress – slim dresses are sliding in among the bouffants. Yards of blue crêpe wrap spirally, end in a scarf. At Lilian Lawler'.

Variant, French *Vogue*, August 1939, p.29:
'Premiers mouvements de la mode d'hiver'
Caption reads: '[...] draperies antiques ou souple spirale d'une écharpe s'enroulant en robe'.

Plate 67
Dress by Robert Piguet, 1936
Gelatin silver print
26.1 x 16.6 cm
Paris *Vogue* Archive

Photographed: 23 January 1936

Plate 68
Constant, dress by Chanel, jewellery by Boucheron, 1937
Gelatin silver print
23.9 x 18 cm
Horst Estate

Photographed: 2 August 1937

Published:
American *Vogue*, 1 September 1937, p.83:
'Fashion: Paris Collections Stress Full bosoms, tiny waists'
Caption reads: 'Chanel's famous tiny waist influences her whole Collection – these three evening dresses are typical of her new wide-hipped, flat-diaphragmed line [...] The long, closely fitted basque bodice is a favourite Chanel method for achieving the coveted, negligible waist-line. This one is of silver brocade, reaching well down on the hips; the skirt is of widely ribbed crêpe, gathered in folds. All jewels: Boucheron'.

British *Vogue*, 1 September 1937, p.71:
'Chanel Silhouette'
Caption reads: 'A waist you can span with your hands, the flattest of flat diaphragms – this is the figure Chanel herself possesses; this is the figure she is intent on giving you. Left: She makes you look paper-thin from the side, by running flat faille panels down front and back and puffing full tulle ones at the sides. Above: Her white moiré – a seam curving across the body, accentuated by a flight on silver sequin birds (her pet motif); a heavily shirred bodice; another full-sided skirt. Opposite: A silver brocade bodice moulded almost to the hipbone; a heavy ribbed crêpe skirt, its gathered fullness springing from the self-same spot – this is Chanel's favourite formula for fining down your torso'.

French *Vogue*, September 1937, p.33:
'Grâce de la taille fine'
Caption reads: 'Chanel fait merveilleusement valoir la finesse de la taille, par d'intéressantes variations dans l'ampleur de la jupe. Par exemple, des panneaux de tulle s'échappent d'une robe de faille noire au corsage pincé. Ou bien des paillettes d'argent accentuent la diagonale coupant l'ampleur d'une jupe de moiré blanche. Ci-contre, un long corsage ajusté affin la taille, la jupe en lourd crêpe côtelé est montée au-dessus des hanches. Bijoux de Boucheron'.

Plate 69
Horst's sketchbook, undated
Pencil on paper, black hard cover sketchbook
Collection of R.J. Horst

Plate 70
Madame Bernon, corset by Detolle for Mainbocher, 1939
Platinum-palladium print, printed later
Horst Estate

Photographed: 11 August 1939

Published:
American *Vogue*, 15 September 1939, p.76:
'Fashion: Paris Openings - Variety Show'
Caption reads: 'Waist-lines Ltd., Paris, France – From Paris – The Detolle corset with back lacing – Paris puts you back in laced corsets – and here they are. Detolle made the extreme, back-lacing corset, opposite and first above, to bind you in for the Velázquez silhouette. This corset is specifically for evening. [...] These are the corsets that established the tiny waist as the theme of the Paris Openings. You'll notice that the tighter the waist, the more leeway you're allowed for hips. You'll notice a firm, high, smoothly laced corset is comfortable, and never rides up. You'll notice that your posture is completely changed for the better by the persuasion of well-placed bones. One thing to remember (in addition to tying your stay laces firmly) is that you can not have the idealized willow-wand figure unless you start with a naturally small waist – and that means exercise and corrected posture – not merely a constricting corset. Let your corset emphasize a waist that you have whittled down to its lowest possible denominator'.

French *Vogue*, December 1939, p.35: 'C'était Hier'
Caption reads: 'La taille-diabolo'.

Plate 71
Louise Sheldon, dinner suit by Robert Piguet, top hat by Louise Bourbon, 1936
Gelatin silver print
25 x 16.3 cm
Paris *Vogue* Archive

Photographed: 29 January 1936

Published:
American *Vogue*, 1 March 1936, p.65:
'Fashion: Extremes Meet at Paris Spring Collections'
Caption reads: 'Robert Piguet's Mephistophelian dinner-suit [...] goes to extremes; enormous shirred shoulders on the swallow-tailed satin cape, slick straightness in an ankle-length black wool dress and Louise Bourbon top-hat'.

British *Vogue*, 4 March 1936, p.57:
'Extremes Meet in Paris'
Caption reads: 'Parisian mephisto: Piguet's tail-coated cape over a sinuous dress; Christabel Russell. Louise Bourbon's top hat; Santa'.

French *Vogue*, March 1936, p.44:
'Contrastes, ce Printemps'
Caption reads: 'Robert Piguet: Cape de satin, hautes épaules froncées, sur robe longue de lainage noir. Haut de forme de Louise Bourbon'.

Plate 72
Louise Sheldon, dress by Lucien Lelong, 1936
Gelatin silver print
25.3 x 16.1 cm
Paris *Vogue* Archive

Photographed: 29 January 1936

Published:
American *Vogue*, 1 March 1936, p.52:
'Fashion: Extremes Meet at Paris Spring Collections'
Caption reads: 'Lelong's defiant contrast of white crêpe, cinnamon scarf, black patent leather belt (Bergdorf Goodman)'.

British *Vogue*, 4 March 1936, p.54:
'Extremes Meet in Paris'
Caption reads: 'Lelong's defiant contrast of white crêpe, cinnamon scarf, black patent leather belt'.

French *Vogue*, March 1936, p.45:
'Contrastes, ce Printemps'
Caption reads: 'Lucien Lelong: du crêpe Marsala de Ducharne posé en transparent sur un pyjama; grande écharpe caramel formant empiècement. Ceinture en cuir'.

Plate 73
Lyla Zelensky, dress by Mainbocher, jewellery by Herz, 1936
Gelatin silver print
24 x 18 cm
Horst Estate

Photographed: 30 January 1936

Published:
American *Vogue*, 1 March 1936, p.54:
'Extremes Meet at Paris Spring Collections'
Caption reads: 'Mainbocher, turning his eyes to the Near East, had visions of the traditional Moscow ballerina when he designed this dress. The stiff taffeta tunic, flower-shadowed, juts bravely out – fullest in back, balanced in front by a bunch of flowers that matches the print of the tunic. Matching, too, is the chiffon slip (from Wanamaker, New York, Philadelphia). Herz jewels'.

British *Vogue*, 4 March 1936, p.58:
'Extremes Meet in Paris'
Caption reads: 'The fastidious beauty of the deer (José-Maria Sert's Chinese bronzes) sets the stage for the Near and Far East inspiration

of Mainbocher's Collection. Opposite, a Russian dancer's tunic in flowered taffeta, the flared back balanced by an armful of flowers at the front of the bodice: Maison Arthur'.

French *Vogue*, March 1936, p.47:
'Contrastes, ce Printemps'
Caption reads: 'Du taffetas rigide couvert d'un décor floral estompé donne – cette tunique l'ampleur massée dans le dos, et s'évasant sur un fourreau en mousseline assortie. Du satin souple imprimé dans le tons de Chine ancien compose la longue tunique en biais atie fourreau plissé. Bijoux de Herz. Bronzes chinois – M. J. M. Sert'.

Plate 74
Louise Sheldon, dress by Mainbocher, 1936
Gelatin silver print
25.2 x 16.3 cm
Paris *Vogue* Archive

Photographed: 30 January 1936

Published:
Variant, American *Vogue*, 1 March 1936, p.55:
'Extremes Meet at Paris Spring Collections'
Caption reads: 'Now glancing Far Eastward, Mainbocher crystallizes an exquisite Chinese dream in this shining gown. Delicate, intricate Ming porcelain flowers, blue on red, shimmer on the satin, and the tunic ends below the knees in jagged beading over a slip of the finest possible pleats (Bonwit Teller; I. Magnin). The sleek bronze deer were loaned by José Maria Sert'.

British *Vogue*, 4 March 1936, p.59:
'Extremes Meet in Paris'
Caption reads: 'Mainbocher is no mere borrower of Eastern form and colour; his dresses are works of art executed with the delicate craftsmanship of the Orient. Here printed satin lustrous as Ming porcelain is fashioned into a narrow saw-edged tunic outlined with beads over a knife-pleated slip that falls to the ground.'

French *Vogue*, March 1936, p.46:
'Contrastes, ce Printemps'
Caption reads: 'Du taffetas rigide couvert d'un décor floral estompé donne – cette tunique l'ampleur massée dans le dos, et s'évassant sur un fourreau en mousseline assortie. Du satin souple imprimé dans les tous de Chine ancien compose la longue tunique en biais et le fourreau plissé. Bijoux de Herz. Bronzes chinois – M. J. M. Sert'.

Plate 75
Lyla Zelensky, dress by Molyneux, 1937
Gelatin silver print
24.1 x 18.1 cm
Horst Estate

Photographed: 26 January 1937

Published:
American *Vogue*, 1 March 1937, p.62:
'Fashion: Sparks from the Paris Openings'
Caption reads: 'Cleopatra's needle: Molyneux's hobbling sheath of gold and iridescent silk veiled with net (John Wanamaker, New York, Philadephia)'.

British *Vogue*, 3 March 1937, p.78: 'Sparks from Paris'
Caption reads: 'Harlequin gold-threaded stripes zig-zag round Molyneux's chrysalis gown, suspended on chains and veiled in green net'.

French *Vogue*, March 1937, p.26: 'Arlequines'
Caption reads: '[...] Dans le robe moulée ci-contre de Molyneux, ce sont des zig-zags multicolores traversés d'un fil d'or. Cape en tulle vert acide. Bijoux de Boucheron'.

Plate 76
Lisa Fonssagrives, coat by Molyneux, 1938
Gelatin silver print
27 x 16.4 cm
Paris *Vogue* Archive

Photographed: 8 August 1938

Plate 77
Lyla Zelensky, tunic by Alix, sandals by Bally, 1936
Gelatin silver print
25.4 x 20.3 cm
P. Garner

Photographed: 28 April 1936

Published:
American *Vogue*, 1 June 1936, p.52:
'First Impressions at the Paris Mid-Seasons'
Caption reads: 'Balinese: Alix threw high drama into her Mid-Season Collection with this Balinese dancer's jacket of stiff, stiff brocade in gold, blue, and orange. The circular peplum surges out below a taut bodice; and the dress underneath is a tube of navy-blue rayon jersey – cut fairly short as you see (Bergdorf Goodman)'.

British *Vogue*, 10 June 1936, p.78:
'Coated in Splendour'
Caption reads: 'Bold, swinging, flared, this Alix tunic-jacket, with the lilt of a Bali dancer's coat. It stands out gay and stiff in gold, blue and orange Chinese brocade. You can get it in London at Eve Valére'.

French *Vogue*, June 1936, p.29: 'La Demi-Saison'
Caption reads: 'Alix Jaquette-tunique en lamé chinois – godets trés prononcés. Robe en jersey de rayonne marine, Sandals Bally'.

Plate 78
Cora Van Millingen, dress by Lucien Lelong, jewellery by Mauboussin, 1937
Gelatin silver print
22.7 x 16.6 cm
Paris *Vogue* Archive

Photographed: 3 August 1937

Published:
American *Vogue*, 1 September 1937, p.84:
'Paris Collections Stress/Decorative evenings'
Caption reads: 'Sable-brown lace over white satin, as in this Lucien Lelong dress below ... Lelong's brown lace over white satin. Mauboussin jewels'.

Variant, British *Vogue*, 1 September 1937, p.50:
'Main Lines ... Out of Paris'
Caption reads: 'Lace in a formalised pattern, beautiful as Renaissance ironwork, is silhouetted over a white satin slip in the loveliest dress of Lelong's Collection. The white satin gets the upper hand in the deep corselette belt which bands you so firmly from breast to waist'.

French *Vogue*, September 1937, p.41:
'Tulle du Dentelle'
Caption reads: 'Lucien Lelong pose un voilage de dentelle très fine – clair sur une robe de satin blanc. Large ceinture corselet. Tous les bijoux Mauboussin'.

Plate 79
Helen Bennett and Lyla Zelensky, dresses by Maggy Rouff, jewellery by Mauboussin, 1938
Gelatin silver print
22.2 x 16 cm
Paris *Vogue* Archive

Photographed: 1 February 1938

Published:
British *Vogue*, 2 March 1938, p.56:
'Feminist Movements in Paris: Romantic Variations'
Caption reads: 'Tiny bodices and sweeping skirts. Pale blue and wine red. Maggy Rouff (London) takes a bolt of slipper satin and further stiffens it with hoops, scatters it with bows, and gathers it into a bodice of dark red chiffon shirrings. Next, Maggy Rouff takes white satin and impudently paraphrases upholstery by punctuating its smocked corners with satin-covered buttons. The corselette bodice of shirred chiffon, in a celestial blue, has white satin shoulder bows'.
French *Vogue*, April 1938, p.46:
'Le corselet, la jupe épanouie'
Caption reads: 'Une ample jupe de satin blanc coulissé contraste avec le petit corsage en mousseline bleu pâle, étroitement froncé. Derriére, une jupe largement épanouie en satin bleu et un corselet moulé bourgogne'.

Plate 80
Lud, dress by Jean Patou, jewellery by Mauboussin, 1938
Gelatin silver print
24 x 18 cm
Horst Estate

Photographed: 31 January 1938

Published:
American *Vogue*, 1 March 1938, p.67:
'Fashion: From the Paris Openings (Winterhalter flounces)'
Caption reads: 'Patou wakened nineteenth-century romanticism with a waltz dress delicate as a miniature, with its pleated net skirt, its taffeta basque bodice, its bouquet of four white roses. Imported by Milgrim. All jewels on these pages; Mauboussin'.

Variant, British *Vogue*, 2 March 1938, p.54:
'Feminist Movements in Paris: 19th Century Motif'
Caption reads: 'Wasp-waisted as a Winterhalter lady, she decks Patou's faille bodice, basqued and laced, with four cabbagy roses, [...]'.

Variant, French *Vogue*, March 1938, p.34
Caption reads: 'Toute la grâce fragile du xviii revue par le goût le plus actuel revit dans ces deux robes. Celle de Patou en faille-taffetas et tulle de Dognin. Celle de Molyneux tout en tulle noir finement plissé. Bijoux Mauboussin'.

Plate 81
Margaret Healey and Margot Taylor, dresses and veils by Mainbocher, jewellery by Boucheron, 1937
Gelatin silver print
24 x 18 cm
Horst Estate

Photographed: 10 August 1937

Published:
American *Vogue*, 15 September 1937, p.83:
'Fashion: Woman of the World: the Spirit of the Paris Openings'
Caption reads: 'Mainbocher's sequined black tulle dresses and veils with sequin eyebrows (opposite), the first dress flames with a peacock (John Wanamaker, New York, Philadelphia). The second has a red sequin hip-band (Henri Bendel). Jewels, Boucheron'.

Variant, British *Vogue*, 15 September 1937, p.33:
'*Vogue*'s Eye View of Collection Glitter'
Caption reads: 'Sex appeal is the prime motif of the Paris Collections and sequins its most spectacular manifestation. They have a Zeigfeld glitter that likes to be looked at – more, that insists on it. They flash like a glance from a bright eye and kill their man at ten yards. Here are a few of the millions that blaze over Paris. Top – Mainbocher's seductive eyebrows and lips on tulle veils. [...]'.

Variant, British *Vogue*, 15 September 1937, p.50:
'High Points from Paris'
Caption reads: 'Veiled, in Mainbocher's tulle sewn with sequin eyebrows; more multi-coloured sequins cascading, gaudy as a peacock's tail, down the side of his full-skirted tulle dress. This prodigal, audacious scattering of sequins is characteristic

of the Collections [...]'.

French *Vogue*, October 1937, p.67: 'Les Paillettes'
Caption reads: 'Mainbocher fait jouer le seintillement des paillettes – la matite du tulle, paillettes multicolores en queue de paon, ou rouge feu, tranchant sur la jupe noire. Des soureils et un grain de beauté en pailletés rose clair sont posés sur le grand voile, en tulle se Dognin. Bijoux de Boucheron'.

Plate 82
Madame Buchardt and Lisa Fonssagrives, dress and evening coat by Lucien Lelong, 1938
Gelatin silver print
27.4 x 16.1 cm
Paris *Vogue* Archive

Photographed: 29 July 1938

Published:
American *Vogue*, 1 September 1938, p.61: 'Fashion: Paris Openings First Impressions'
Caption reads: 'Designer: Lelong Evening coat: Strict black duvetine, with brocaded yoke and sleeves Dress: Gold lamé gauze (Both: Jay Thorpe)'.

British *Vogue*, 24 August 1938, p.22: 'Paris Collections Focus On: Material Magnificence'
Caption reads: 'Lelong's flashing, spun gold gown, slightly sobered by a black duvetyn coat with Oriental-potentate brocade sleeves'.

Variant, French *Vogue*, September 1938, p.38: 'Quant á la mode du soir ...'
Caption reads: 'Du voile Ariel, une gaze arachnéenne lamée or de Courdurier, est employé pour la robe de gauche. Le manteau est en Vellys noir de Rodier et brocart pour le buste'.

Plate 83
Cora Hemmet, hat by Reboux, jewellery by Boucheron, 1935
Gelatin silver print
26.1 x 16.7 cm
Paris *Vogue* Archive

Photographed: 4 September 1935

Published:
American *Vogue*, 15 October 1935, p.62: 'Fashion: Half a Hat'
Caption reads: 'Half a hat is smarter than a whole hat – says Reboux. Opposite – you see what a total success it is: bronze-green velours-felt cut like a petal over each eyebrow, rising high in a flange (notice the new height of this), then stopping dead on the crown of your head. Nothing at the back but curls and an anchoring band. The scarf is almost a gilet, in a delicate rose, bronze-green and palest blue'.

British *Vogue*, 13 November 1935, p.66: 'Half a Hat'
Caption reads: 'Half a hat is smarter than a whole hat, says Reboux. Opposite you see what a total success it is; bronze-green velours-felt cut like a petal over each eyebrow, rising high in a flange, then stopping dead on the crown of your head. Nothing at the back but curls and an anchoring band. Pissot and Pavy, Hanover Street, have this. The scarf is almost a gilet, in a delicate rose, bronze-green and palest blue'.

French *Vogue*, October 1935, p.56: 'La tête bouclée est dégagée derrière'
Caption reads: 'Reboux: En feutre-velours vert bronze, ce chapeau inspiré de la feuille du nénuphar s'applique de chaque côté du front et s'élève sur le sommet de la tête. Gilet-écharpe de trois tons. Bracelet Boucheron. Sur la page opposée: Haute toque d'astrakan noir, petite voilette. Grosse chaîne et bracelets en or'.

Plate 84
Agnetha Fischer, ensemble by Robert Piguet, hat by Louise Bourbon, 1936
Gelatin silver print
26.3 x 16.3 cm
Paris *Vogue* Archive

Photographed: 29 January 1936
Published:
'American *Vogue*, 15 March 1936, p.60: Fashion: "I Dress as I Please", from the Paris Collections'
Caption reads: 'Piguet's black wool cape, Piqué Revers (Bendel) – Louise Bourbon hat'.

Plate 85
Lisa Fonssagrives, jacket by Francevrament, hat by Maria Guy, 1938
Gelatin silver print
27.3 x 16.7 cm
Paris *Vogue* Archive

Photographed: 4 June 1938

Published:
British *Vogue*, 3 August 1938, p.30: 'Wider Brims, Higher Crowns'
Caption reads: 'Wider brims – they've taken Paris by storm, topping collarless coats. Maria Guy moulds her wine-coloured hat to your head without a single seam, rolls the wide brim up behind and holds it with a satin bow. Francevramant's boxy, collarless jacket, with the exaggerated shoulders is made entirely of mink tails, lined with soft wool'.

Plate 86
Helen Bennett, jacket and blouse by Molyneux, jewellery by Boucheron, 1938
Gelatin silver print
22.5 x 16.2 cm
Paris *Vogue* Archive

Photographed: 10 February 1938

Published:
Variant, British *Vogue*, 16 March 1938, p.59: 'Paris Puts it in Black and White'
Caption reads: 'White waves beat against black, in white shantung facing the full revers of this short black wool jacket curving over a shantung blouse. Lilies of the valley spray down the front of the plunging black grosgrain hat. All these Molyneux models are at his London salon'.

Variant, French *Vogue*, April 1938, p.71: 'Combinaison du noir et du blanc'
Caption reads: 'Le blanc et le noir s'opposent, se combinent, se rehaussent [...] Le second Molyneux comporte une blouse de shantung blanc; le même shantung double les revers de la jaquette noire. Chapeau garni de muguets. Bijoux de Boucheron'.

Plate 87
Lyla Zelensky, suit by Robert Piguet, hat by Suzanne Talbot, 1936
Gelatin silver print
24.1 x 18.1 cm
Horst Estate

Photographed: 24 January 1936

Published:
American *Vogue*, 1 March 1936, p.67: 'Extremes Meet at Paris Spring Collections'
Caption reads: 'Talbot peaks the crown of a felt hat (Macy's). Piguet wool suit'.

British *Vogue*, 4 March 1936, p.65: 'Highlight on White'
Caption reads: 'Piguet suit from Lilian Lawler. Talbot hat from Maison Ross. We told you at the start that there was a boom in individuality; here's more proof. High hat, high shouldered; flat hat, sloping shouldered [...] Piguet takes the opposite view, clamping half-white sleeves like canoe paddles on a black wool suit, the blades standing high above your shoulder blades. Shiny buttons fasten the high waisted jacket: Lilian Lawler. Talbot's hat (Maison Ross) continues the upward urge'.

British *Vogue*, 18 March 1936, p.77: '*Vogue*'s Eye View of the Mode', a sketch based on Horst's photograph
Caption reads: 'Piguet invented those banjo sleeves half white, half black, that stand inches above the shoulders'.

Variant, French *Vogue*, March 1936, p.54: 'Silhouettes Opposées'
Caption reads: 'Robert Piguet accentue d'autant plus le mouvement en hauteur de ses manches que toute leur surface extérieure est traitée en blanc, le costume étant en lainage noir. Talbot reste fidèle aux calottes hautes et aux plumes fusant en l'air'.

Plate 88
Loretta Young, New York, 1941

Published:
American *Vogue*, 15 June 1941, p.38: 'People and Ideas: Photogenic Loretta Young'
Caption reads: 'Primarily, of course, Loretta Young is photogenic because she's so beautiful. There are lots of specific clinical reasons, too, however. To wit: her small-featured, fine-boned face, with its unexpectedly dramatic-sized eyes and mouth. To wit: her long, graceful neck, set at a lovely angle to her clean-lined jaw and chin ... her pretty shoulders. To wit: her very fair, unusually fine-textured, flawless skin. Miss Young wears here a black silk crêpe dress, gilt buttoned. Falkenstein. Her huge picture hat is of yellow spun glass and black lace. Lilly Daché'.

British *Vogue*, April 1942, p.40: 'Loretta Young – The Philosophy of Being a Woman'
Caption reads: 'Photogenic, feminine – star of the new films "Bedtime Story" and "The Men in Her Life", and master of the philosophy of being a woman – she crowns her candid beauty with a huge hat of spun glass and lace'.

Plate 89
Susann Shaw, American *Vogue* cover, 15 May 1943

Published:
American *Vogue* cover, 15 May 1943
Caption reads: 'All seven faces are the same girl's. Natural, healthy, beautiful – helped by make-up. She is Susann Shaw. *Vogue*'s cover girl in Columbia's picture, "Cover Girl", with Rita Hayworth; Jerome Kern music. Horst photograph'.

Plate 90
Mistinguett, Paris, 1933
Gelatin silver print
24 x 18 cm
Horst Estate

Photographed: 21 December 1933

Published:
French *Vogue*, February 1934, p.33: 'Sur La Scène: Mistinguett aux Folies-Bergère'
Caption reads: 'La brillante revue des Folies-Bergere "Folies en Folie" est pour Mistinguett, incomparable vedette dont l'entrain fait merveille, un nouveau triomphe. Elle y porte cette très belle robe de Molyneux en crêpe-satin blanc, ornée d'aigrettes'.

Plate 91
Rita Hayworth, New York, 1947
Gelatin silver print
25.3 x 20.3 cm
Horst Estate

Plate 92
Jessica Tandy, New York, 1938
Published:
Variant American *Vogue*, 15 February 1939, p.65:

'In the News To-Day'
Caption reads: 'Jessica Tandy, English star, as the rebellious little Irish girl in "The White Seed"'.

Plate 93
Agnetha Fischer, Paris, 1931

Published:
French *Vogue*, November 1931, p.59
Caption reads: 'Le plus séduisant des cadeaux pour Noël / votre portrait signé du studio de *Vogue* qui, pour la première fois, offre – ses lectrices la possibilité de commander une photographie semblable – celle qu'elles admirent tous les mois dans ce magazine'.

Plate 94
Merle Oberon, London, 1934
Gelatin silver print
24.2 x 19.2 cm
Paris *Vogue* Archive

Photographed: 1 September 1934

Published:
British *Vogue*, 31 October 1934, p.82:
'Seen on the Stage'
Caption reads: 'Merle Oberon's mysterious beauty decked with seed pearls from Harvey & Gore'.

Plate 95
Natalie Paley, Paris, 1934
Gelatin silver print
23.9 x 17.9 cm
Horst Estate

Photographed: 15 October 1934

Published:
American *Vogue*, 1 December 1934, p.41:
'*Vogue*'s Eye View' (uncredited)
Caption reads: 'Especially in the last decade, dress designers have taken paradoxical delight in producing materials that look like other materials. Science has made playboys of the fabric people: they make silk that looks like tree-bark, Cellophane that looks like lamé, cloth that looks like glass. The fur people are no less pixy. At the right, the Reboux cape worn by Miss Nathalie [*sic*] Paley (all Paris wears furred capes and toques) is bordered, not with caracal, but with swan feathers [...]'.

British *Vogue*, 26 December 1934, p.9:
'*Vogue*'s Eye View of the Mode'
Caption reads: 'The fur people, like the fabric designers, take a paradoxical delight in producing materials that look like other materials. Right, the Reboux cape worn by Madame Natalie Paley is bordered not with caracal but with swan feathers'.

French *Vogue*, February 1935, p.31:
'Madame Natalie Paley'
Caption reads: 'Madame Natalie Paley, qui vient d'arriver à Hollywood, porte, sur la page opposée, une charmante robe du soir de Lucien Lelong en taffetas-faille noir, au corsage éclairé de boutons brillants, et ci-dessus une toque et une amusante cape garnie de plumes, de Reboux'.

Plate 96
Vivien Leigh, London, 1936
Gelatin silver print
23.5 x 18.4 cm
V&A: S.1038-2013

Photographed: 5 March 1936

Published:
British *Vogue*, 1 April 1936, p.64: 'London Lines'
Caption reads: 'Dilkusha (just opening at Lansdowne House) uses a double file of steel buttons to suggest a waistcoat on a black braid-edged town suit with hand-tucked organdie blouse. Miss Vivien Leigh posed'.

Plate 97
Tilly Losch, 1939

Published:
American *Vogue*, 1 August 1939, p.31:
'Fashion: Paris Brims over with Berets'
Caption reads: 'Descat's crimson velvet beret, tilted on Tilly Losch's head. (The sketch is Miss Losch's self portrait.) Vionnet's Persian lamb coat. Jewels from Mauboussin'.

Plate 98
Noël Coward, Paris, 1933

Photographed: 24 January 1934

Published:
Variant, British *Vogue*, 24 January 1934, p.46:
'Seen on the Stage'
Caption reads: 'Romney Brent, Noël Coward and Yvonne Printemps. Heads together over "Conversation Piece"'.

Variant, French *Vogue*, January 1934, p.32:
'Sur La Scène: Yvonne Printemps et Noël Coward'
Caption reads: 'On retrouvera dans cette photographie Yvonne Printemps et Noël Coward, qui ont été si applaudis au récent et brillant bal donné à l'Ambassade d'Angleterre. Yvonne Printemps, qui connaît à Londres le même succès qu'à Paris, va y créer tout prochainement à His Majesty's Theatre une oeuvre nouvelle de Noël Coward: "Conversation Piece". Sa charmante robe est de Jeanne Lanvin'.

Plate 99
Sybil Thorndike and Lewis Casson as Mrs Callifer and Dr Frederick Baston in *The Potting Shed*, New York, 1957

Published:
Variant, American *Vogue*, 15 February 1957, p.60:
'People Are Talking About: Sir Lewis Casson and his Wife, Dame Sybil Thorndike'
Caption reads: 'Sir Lewis Casson and his wife, Dame Sybil Thorndike, appearing on Broadway in Graham Greene's play, "The Potting Shed" [...] Sir Lewis and Dame Sybil have each played more than one thousand roles in their fifty-odd years on stage, spanning theatrical literature from Greek tragedy to drawing-room comedy. For forty-seven of those years they have been married, working in marvellous collaboration as actor-managers: she, as a commanding heroic star, he, as actor and director of their productions. Earlier on, their repertory company served as master school for glittering apprentices. Sir Laurence Olivier and Sir Carol Reed held Dame Sybil's queenly train in a 1935 *Henry VIII*. Later Olivier co-starred with her at the Old Vic, where she dominated as a leading tragedienne. Perhaps the Cassons' most dazzling play was *Saint Joan*, which Shaw wrote with Dame Sybil in mind. In 1924 Dame Sybil created Joan, directed by Sir Lewis, who played De Stogumber. Dame Sybil, a vibrant woman with lapis-lazuli blue eyes, and Sir Lewis, rockily British and erect, appear, off stage, a tea-cosy couple interested in their ten grandchildren. "On stage," said Dame Sybil, "we argue like hell"'.

Plate 100
Ethel Waters as Hagar in *Mamba's Daughters*, New York, 1939
Gelatin silver print
24.2 x 19.3 cm
Horst Estate

Published:
American *Vogue*, 15 February 1939, p.61:
'Ethel Waters in "Mamba's Daughters"'
Caption reads: 'Ethel Waters in "Mamba's Daughters" creates, with passion and great artistry, a character that is almost Greek in its capacity for tragedy. As Hagar, the daughter of Mamba, pursued by the twin Furies of bad luck and a wild temper, Miss Waters portrays a woman whose greatest crime is stupidity, whose love for her child runs like a crimson thread through the dark fabric of her life. Miss Waters' voice has long delighted Broadway, but in this, her first "straight" part, the wide scope of her acting ability is revealed. "Mamba's Daughters", written by DuBose Heyward and published as a novel in 1929, is dramatized by Mr. Heyward and his wife, Dorothy. Here, as in all their writing, they explore the gaiety and the despair of the American Negro. In the dusty country of the Deep South, this pitiful drama of a violent, uncomprehending creature, caught between her instincts and the law, marches to a classic end'.

Plate 101
Gary Cooper and his wife Rocky, New York, 1938
Gelatin silver print
25.3 x 20.3 cm
Horst Estate

Photographed: 29 March 1938

Plate 102
Louise Brooks, New York, 1979

Plate 103
Steve McQueen, San Francisco, 1967

Published:
Variant, American *Vogue*, 1 March 1967, p.135:
'Men in *Vogue*: Steve McQueen'
Caption reads: 'Steve McQueen comes on just the way you might hope – cool, hip, easy, very much his own man – a man of the sort that didn't exist before right now. McQueen himself feels he has "the California look": cigarette-slim suits from Cardin in Paris, Brioni in Rome, and DeVoss in Hollywood ... shoes from Cardin, or Lefcourt in New York ... plus Murray's space shoes "because I have bad knees from a motorcycle accident. The "California look" isn't standardized because everyone is finding his own bag now, that's the wonderful thing about clothes ... I always used to play it down, but now it's the time of the swinger, and you find what's best for you. One thing I don't like is the little boy look ... but the wide ties are great. ... Cardin is the tie man ... and the wide belt with a big buckle is really where it's at ... I love the way women like to play with your wide tie, and how they react to the big buckle on the belt. ... All my clothes are in earth colours, and fire colours ... I'm Aries, a fire sign ... and I like all the browns, rusts, olives. ... In California I get everything from DeVoss, it's really the boss store. ... I got a couple of suits in Hong Kong when we were filming *The Sand Pebbles* but they didn't work out. ... In California, I spend a lot of time at my production company, Solar ... we have offices over at Paramount ... but when I get up tight, I go out and drive my bike, it's a Triumph 650cc, around the dirt hills ... and I hit the gym a lot. ... My other big bag is cars ... I have a Ferrari and my wife Neile has an Excalibur. ... We work a lot on the house in Brentwood that we decorated ourselves with Spanish and Italian things ... it's a groovy place"'.

Plate 104
Marlene Dietrich, New York, 1942
Platinum-palladium print, printed later
35.6 x 27.9 cm
Horst Estate

Published:
American *Vogue*, 1 July 1942, p.35:
'People and Ideas: Marlene Dietrich'
Caption reads: 'On this page, you see her as she herself likes to look. As she looked when she came to New York recently. As she looked when she came to *Vogue*'s studio to be photographed. Her suit of black alpaca shrewdly understates her glamour, but has the force of an exclamation-point. Her hat – black. Her gloves – white. She carried an extra pair in her bag, she's that fussy about white-whiteness.

Always, she has her clothes made to order. She's a crank about the fit of her shoulders. Her skirts are sinuously narrow. She likes to look like a triangle on tiptoe. She'll spend hours at fittings ... but almost no time at the hair-dresser's. She washes her own un-permanented hair ... she washes it nearly every day. She rolls it in bobby-pins to dry as she dresses. Spectacularly tailored slacks are her passion in clothes. And because of her muchly vaunted and insured legs, she wears slacks better than most women do. Her legs (those beautiful gams) are part of the legendary Dietrich saga. But her hands give her away. They are the hands of a competent woman, a good cook, a cool, canny executive'.

Plate 105
Olivia de Havilland as Catherine Hilton in *Call It A Day*, New York, 1936
Gelatin silver print
25.3 x 20.3 cm
V&A: E.222-2014, Given by Gert Elfering

Published:
Variant, American *Vogue*, 1 January 1937, p.54: '*Vogue*'s Spotlight' (uncredited)
Caption reads: 'Olivia de Havilland, film star of "Call It A Day"'.

Plate 106
Noël Coward and Gertrude Lawrence on the set of *Tonight at 8:30*, Boston, 1936
Gelatin silver print
21.6 x 18.5 cm
Horst Estate

Plate 107
Marlene Dietrich, New York, 1942
Gelatin silver print
25.5 x 20.2 cm
Horst Estate

Published:
Variant, American *Vogue* 1 July 1942, p.34: 'People and Ideas: Marlene Dietrich'
Caption reads: 'Marlene Dietrich – Between movies she tours the Army camps, sings her smouldering songs for the U.S.O. Soldiers at more than one hundred camps have seen Marlene Dietrich on her recent U.S.O. tour, looking much as she does on the opposite page [...] A coiled siren in a slinky white skirt and a beige sequin tunic. A coiled siren singing her new song, "The Man's in the Army". This is how the soldiers like her. This is how the movie public likes her'.

Plate 108
Bette Davis, New York, 1939
Gelatin silver print
25.5 x 20.7 cm
Horst Estate

Published:
American *Vogue*, 1 January 1941, p.36: 'The World of Fashion: Cast and Forecast'
Caption reads: 'Bette Davis, now interpreting Somerset Maugham's "The Letter" as memorably as she did his "Of Human Bondage". Here, wearing a brown silk taffeta dress by Nettie Rosenstein. Bonwit Teller; I. Magnin, Jewels; Black, Starr and Gorham'.

Plate 109
Joan Crawford, New York, 1938
Gelatin silver print
34 x 25.5 cm
Horst Estate

Published:
American *Vogue*, 1 February 1938, p.103: 'Stars in their Courses'
Caption reads: 'Joan Crawford – who has never been on the stage [...] Joan Crawford, the hand-wrought, sometimes synthetic dignity of the movies, with its more startling effects [...]'.

British *Vogue*, 8 February 1939, p.46: 'Joan Crawford'
Caption reads: 'Joan Crawford, who has just finished work on "Ice Follies of 1939" with James Stewart and Lew Ayres, will soon be coming to Europe, and London, for a holiday – looking, if this photograph is any indication, more glamorous than ever'.

Plate 110
Gene Tierney, New York, 1940

Published:
American *Vogue* cover, 15 May 1940
Caption reads: 'Gene Tierney – who made a hit in "The Male Animal" is now in Hollywood – poses in a peppermint-striped play-suit with paradoxically-long sleeves, bare midriff. Best; Marshall Field. Du Barry's "Peppermint Pink" lipstick'.

British *Vogue* cover, July 1940 (uncredited)
Caption reads: 'Red and white cotton shirt and shorts: Fortnum & Mason. Elizabeth Arden's Chariot make-up, Honey suntan oil'.

Plate 111
Paulette Goddard, New York, 1940

Published:
American *Vogue*, 15 January 1941, p.63: 'People and Ideas: Paulette Goddard'
Caption reads: 'Actress-wife of Charles Chaplin. Co-starred with her husband, Charles Chaplin, in "The Great Dictator," she is now dancing with Fred Astaire in the new musical movie, "Second Chorus." Here she wears a "dinner-in-cabaña" costume designed by Hattie Carnegie for warm Florida nights. Shorts and coat of silk crêpe, sequin-embroidered. I. Magnin; Martha Weathered. Deep-sea note – real shell clip with diamonds; Verdura'.

Plate 112
Vogue cover, 1 September 1935

Published:
American *Vogue* cover, 1 September 1935
Caption reads: 'Aside from being pretty decorative – Princess Sherbatow's outfit chalks up at least five reasons for being in the photograph by Horst which makes the current cover. To wit: the soutache braid edging those drum-major tabs on the Creed suit; the Veronese-red of the velveteen jacket – a salute to the Italian spirit; those Schiaparelli strings of giant topazes; the Descat broadtail fur toque; and the Révillon's broadtail pillow-muff. Saks-Fifth Avenue has the suit and hat'.

British *Vogue* cover, 18 September 1935
Caption reads: 'Apart from being extremely decorative there are at least five sound reasons for Princess Sherbatow's outfit being photographed by Horst for the current cover. To wit: the soutache braid edging the drum-major tabs on the Creed jacket from Révillon, Regent Street; the rich Veronese-red and the use of velveteen – definite salutes to the Italian spirit; the Révillon broadtail pillow muff; and the Descat toque of the same fur'.

French *Vogue* cover, November 1935
Caption reads: 'Notre couverture représente un tailleur en velours de Creed porté avec une toque en breitschwanz de Rose Descat et manchon assorti de Révillon'.

Plate 113
Mrs Anthony Eden, 1934
Horst P. Horst/Vogue © The Condé Nast Publications Ltd.
Published:
British *Vogue*, 13 June 1934, p.68: 'Mrs Anthony Eden'
Caption reads: 'A tapestry background throws into relief the good looks of Mrs. Anthony Eden, a daughter of Sir Gervase Beckett. Her husband, the Lord Privy Seal, is a young statesman with a brilliant past and every prospect of a brilliant future. They have two boys, Simon and Nicholas, and a house in Lower Berkeley Street'.

Plate 114
Mrs Anthony Jenkinson, 1932
Horst P. Horst/Vogue © The Condé Nast Publications Ltd.

Published:
British *Vogue*, 30 March 1932, p.42: 'Wearing Worth's White Ottoman'
Caption reads: 'Mrs. Anthony Jenkinson, daughter of Sir James Dunn, wears a ravishing Worth dress of white ottoman silk in which to pose. Jet beads are twisted into a cord to outline the décolletage and fall over the shoulders'.

Plate 115
Lady Ursula Manners, Miss Charmian Fane, Lady Gloria Vaughan, Lady Elizabeth Paget, 'A Quartet of Débutantes', British *Vogue*, 2 May 1934
Horst P. Horst/Vogue © The Condé Nast Publications Ltd.

Published:
British *Vogue*, 2 May 1934, pp.84–5: 'A Quartet of Débutantes'
Caption reads: 'Lady Ursula Manners, whose photograph appears above, is the eldest of the Duke of Rutland's children. She has inherited the famous good looks of the Manners and the Tennants and is a "night beauty" with dark hair and dazzling white skin. Lady Ursula, who first came out at a hunt ball in the Midlands, completed her education in Florence, which is one of the smartest places to be "finished abroad" / A wavy mass of fine hair, enormous blue eyes, a witty tongue and a name like the heroine of an eighteenth-century romance are a few of the assets Miss Charmian Fane brings with her on her début. She is the daughter of the Hon. Mrs. Henry Fane. Like the other members of this débutante quartet she is to be a Maid of Honour at Queen Charlotte's Birthday Ball at Grosvenor House on May 24th / Caught in a pose which makes her look as if she has been painted by Greuze is Lady Gloria Vaughan, Lord Lisburne's eldest daughter. She is small and vivacious, with a dark Chilean beauty inherited from her mother, the former Mlle. Bittencourt, whose father was Attaché to the Chilean Legation. Present-day débutantes are full of accomplishments – Lady Gloria, for instance, has taken a course in millinery and dressmaking. / That intelligent and charming face at the right belongs to Lady Elizabeth Paget, the second of Lady Anglesey's daughters. Her elder sister, Lady Caroline, was presented two years ago and there are three younger girls to brighten the débutante ranks between now and 1940. Lady Elizabeth is musical and cultivated, and has lovely sensitive hands. She is a cousin of Lady Ursula Manners, who is seen opposite'.

Plate 116
Valentine Lawford, Dorset, 1948

Plate 117
Duke and Duchess of Windsor, 1963

Published:
American *Vogue*, 1 April 1964, p.176: 'Fashions in Living: The Duke and Duchess of Windsor in Paris'
Caption reads: 'H.R.H. The Duke of Windsor and the Duchess of Windsor'.

Plate 118
Duke of Windsor, 1963

Published:
American *Vogue*, 1 April 1964, p.186: 'Fashions in Living: The Duke and Duchess of Windsor in Paris'
Caption reads: 'The Duke's suit is of blue Scotch tweed with a big white check. (Although he has

his coats made in London, his suits – of English materials that he brings over – are done in New York, primarily because he believes that the trousers are cut better.)'.

Plate 119
Cecil Beaton (1904–80)
Horst and George Hoyningen-Huene, 1930
Gelatin silver print
16.3 x 15.7 cm
Collection of R. J. Horst
The Cecil Beaton Studio Archive at Sotheby's

Plate 120
Lord Eliot, Port Eliot, Cornwall, 1966

Published:
American *Vogue*, 1 August 1966, p.146:
'The Upswing Young'
Caption reads: 'In the Round Room, Lord Eliot sorting the enormous accumulation of family objects and treasures. Among his unexpected finds: a thirteenth-century, illuminated French missal and a manuscript by Charles I'.

Plate 121
Duke of Beaufort's hunt, Badminton Estate, Gloucestershire, 1983

Published:
American *House & Garden*, February 1983, pp.58–9:
'The Country Life'
Caption reads: 'Behind the great house built in 1680, with cupolas added later by William Kent, huntsman Brian Gupwell stands among the hounds bred for their special pale coats'.

Plate 122
Princess Michael of Kent, 1991
Horst P. Horst/Vogue © The Condé Nast Publications Ltd.

Published:
British *Vogue*, October 1991, p.36: 'Courtesans and Kings ... Princess Michael of Kent tells their tales'
Caption reads: 'Princess Michael of Kent, chronicler of royal love affairs, photographed by Horst P. Horst. Her tiara once belonged to Princess Marina'.

Plate 123
George Hoyningen-Huene
Cecil Beaton in his 'Circus Bedroom', 1930
© Estate of George Hoyningen-Huene:
Collection National Portrait Gallery, London

Plate 124
David Bailey (b.1938)
Horst, 1989
© David Bailey

Published:
British *Vogue*, August 1989, p.142:
'Horst on Horst'

Plate 125
Still life, the Silver Jubilee of King George V and Queen Mary, undated
Gelatin silver print
26.5 x 27.1 cm
Horst Estate

Plate 126
Still life, King George VI and the British royal family, undated
Gelatin silver print
27.4 x 27.5 cm
Horst Estate

Plate 127
Still life with fashion illustrations by Bérard, Dalí, de Chirico, Cocteau and Tchelitchew, undated
Gelatin silver print
27.5 x 27.5 cm
Horst Estate

Plate 128
Doris Hilditch, dress by Norman Hartnell, 1934
Gelatin silver print
24.2 x 19.5 cm
Paris *Vogue* Archive
Photographed: 1 September 1934

Published:
British *Vogue*, 17 October 1934, p.72:
'Shooting London Stars'
Caption reads: 'Black and silver striped lamé is the gleaming fabric of this Norman Hartnell afternoon dress, its jabot held by a huge mosaic clip. The hairy Cossack hat and cross fox scarf complete a superb outfit. Miss Doris Hilditch posed'.

Plate 129
Toto Koopman, dress by Victor Stiebel, jewellery by Chaumet, 1934

Published:
British *Vogue*, 4 April 1934, p.70:
'The London Collections Seen with a Parisian Eye'
Caption reads: 'Cool magnificence for grand evenings: Miss Koopman in Stiebel's silver-grey lamé with Chaumet jewels leans on Fryer's spinet'.

Plate 130
Gertrude Lawrence, dress by Schiaparelli, 1931
Gelatin silver print
27 x 20.9 cm
Collection of R. J. Horst

Published:
American *Vogue*, 1 July 1932, p.40:
'Fashion: Miss Lawrence In Widow's Crêpe'
Caption reads: 'Schiaparelli suddenly amazed the world by using a crinkly white mourning crêpe, and now Miss Gertrude Lawrence, Madame Agnès, Madame Schiaparelli herself, and all smart women are wearing it. This gown has a little train and a peau d'ange slip. Miss Lawrence adds a scarlet-and-white chiffon scarf'.

Plate 131
Ensemble by Victor Stiebel, 1934
Gelatin silver print
23.9 x 18.8 cm
Paris *Vogue* Archive

Photographed: 1 September 1934

Published:
British *Vogue*, 17 October 1934, p.5:
Victor Stiebel, advertisement

Plate 132
Elizabeth Jenns, cape by Enos, jewellery by Lacloche, décor by Syrie Maugham, 1934
Gelatin silver print
23.9 x 18.9 cm
Paris *Vogue* Archive

Photographed: 1 September 1934

Published:
British *Vogue*, 17 October 1934, p.65:
'Shooting London Stars'
Caption reads: 'Draped cape sleeves outlined with great bands of cross fox give a magnificent wide top to the slim column of geranium red velvet which is Enos's full-length evening wrap. Miss Elizabeth Jenns posed. Jewels from Lacloche'.

Plate 133
Princess Marina of Greece and Denmark, 1934
Horst P. Horst/Vogue © The Condé Nast Publications Ltd.

Published:
British *Vogue*, 28 November 1934, p.77: 'Classic Princess'
Caption reads: 'The moods of the Princess – these photographs tell how charming she is when serious, how singularly sweet her smile, how much of her expression is in her eyes, at one moment thoughtful and profound, at the next sparkling with gaiety; and how divinely tall she is – every inch a princess. Princess Marina posed specially in the Vogue Studio for M. Horst, who took all these lovely pictures'.

Plate 134
Yvonne Printemps as Mélanie in *Conversation Piece*, London, 1934
Horst P. Horst/Vogue © The Condé Nast Publications Ltd.

Published:
British *Vogue*, 4 April 1934, p.92:
'Conversation Piece'
Caption reads: 'The eyes of Yvonne Printemps, her lips, her curls, are not more ravishing than her conversation/Here are the principle ingredients of that pretty, witty, brew which is "Conversation Piece". Yvonne Printemps, a gay rogue in porcelain with her adorable head running over with curls and her expressive hands poking through a halo of ruffles. Noël Coward, author, composer, producer, actor – is there anything he doesn't do? Yes, he doesn't design the costumes or scenery but leaves them to Gladys Calthrop, who has done better than her best, and who is going to cap that unless she does it herself? Then Louis Hayward, a very personable young lover. Here they are in their delightful Regency clothes, and, not to be outdone, the creator of these clothes has decked herself out in earrings from finds at Ur. The elegant Regency chair in which Yvonne Printemps sits for her picture is from Sybil Colefax'.

Plate 135
Dress by Versace, jewellery by Chanel, shoes by Manolo Blahnik, 1986
Horst P. Horst/Vogue © The Condé Nast Publications Ltd.

Published:
British *Vogue*, November 1986, p.229:
'Pillars of Society'
Caption reads: 'Versace's frilled black velvet column, opposite, strapless bustier and skirt spun with silk taffeta and organza from waist to knees, £1,087, at Versace, 35 Brook St, W1; 92 Brompton Rd, SW1. Diamanté, pearl and gilt earrings, from £60, at Chanel. Black satin high heels, £145, at Manolo Blahnik, 49–51 Old Church St, SW3'.

Plate 136
Catherine Bailey, ensemble by Anouska Hempel, hat by Stephen Jones, 1989
Horst P. Horst/Vogue © The Condé Nast Publications Ltd.

Published:
British *Vogue*, August 1989, p.144: 'Horst on Horst'
Caption reads: 'British collections. Catherine Bailey photographed by Horst, wearing: Black velvet bodice with undulating peplum caught in a velvet and silk bow at the back. Ivory duchesse satin skirt. Both to order, at Anouska Hempel, 2 Pond Place, SW3. Black velvet trilby edged with violet fox fur, by Stephen Jones, £315, at Harrods. Fashion editor: Lucinda Chambers. Hair: Thomas McKiver. Make-up: Lucia Pieroni'.

Plate 137
Catherine Bailey, ensemble by Jasper Conran, shoes by Manolo Blahnik, 1989
Horst P. Horst/Vogue © The Condé Nast Publications Ltd.

Published:
British *Vogue*, August 1989, p.145: 'Horst on Horst'
Caption reads: 'British collections. Catherine Bailey photographed by Horst, wearing: Cream duchesse satin bolero, £278, over black botany wool body, £94, both at the Jasper Conran Shop, 303 Brompton Road, SW3. Satin court shoes at Manolo Blahnik, 49–51 Old Church Street, SW3. Fashion editor:

Lucinda Chambers. Hair: Thomas McKiver. Make-up: Lucia Pieroni'.

Plate 138
Ensemble by Chanel, 1986
Horst P. Horst / Vogue © The Condé Nast Publications Ltd.

Published:
British *Vogue*, November 1986, p.228: 'Pillars of Society'
Caption reads: 'Chanel's serpentine black silk jersey dress, *this page*: with pearl-embroidered snake, empire seaming and slanted pockets, bare back and fan-tailed train, about £3,000, at Chanel, 26 Old Bond St, W1; 31 Sloane St, SW1'.

Plate 139
Catherine Bailey, dress by Alistair Blair, shoes by Manolo Blahnik, 1989
Horst P. Horst / Vogue © The Condé Nast Publications Ltd.

Published:
British *Vogue*, August 1989, p.147: 'Horst on Horst'
Caption reads: 'Little black body-hugging velvet dress, with white silk gazar detachable cuffs, by Alistair Blair, £500, at Lucienne Phillips, 89 Knightsbridge, SW1; Harrods. Black satin courts, £170, at Manolo Blahnik. Black tights, £10.99, at branches of Marks & Spencer'.

Plate 140
Daniella, dress and wrap by Antony Price, vase by Alberto Giacometti for Jean-Michel Frank, 1991
Horst P. Horst / Vogue © The Condé Nast Publications Ltd.

Published:
British *Vogue*, June 1991, p.113: '*Vogue*'s Eye View: Great Dresses, Great Images'
Caption reads: 'Daniella strikes a pose in a "Sixties Surreal" moiré silk dress with wrap by Antony Price. Opaque velvet tights, by Christian Dior. Fashion editor: Liz Fremantle. Hair and make-up: Pierre Berube'.

Plate 141
Manolo Blahnik, 1990
Horst P. Horst / Vogue © The Condé Nast Publications Ltd.

Published:
British *Vogue*, September 1990, p.348: 'Footnotes from Manolo Blahnik'
Caption reads: 'Sporting a pale pink silk tie, which has been knotted with painstaking precision over a Savile Row cotton shirt and juxtaposed with peppermint-coloured Harris tweeds, he has all the refined, groomed looks of a dandified gentleman from a Henry James novel'.

Plate 142
Helen Bennett, American *Vogue* cover, 15 April 1939

Published:
American *Vogue* cover, 15 April 1939
Caption reads: 'Sharkskin slacks and button-less jersey shirt (both of Celanese), turban and Moroccan slippers; Lord and Taylor. Jewels; Olga Tritt. Tahiti make-up; Germaine Monteil'.

British *Vogue* cover, 17 May 1939
Caption reads: 'Sharkskin slacks and button-less jersey shirt (both Celanese) from Harrods. Twist a barbaric jewel-clasped turban round your head'.

Plate 143
The two-colour press room at the Condé Nast Press, Connecticut, late 1920s
Courtesy Condé Nast Archive, New York

Plate 144
'Chanel's Ode to Spring', American *Vogue*, 1 March 1935

Published:
American *Vogue*, 1 March 1935, p.56: 'Fashion: Chanel's Ode to Spring'
Caption reads: 'Green wool over printed silk (Jay-Thorpe) with white accessories'.

Plate 145
Shoes by Barnovi, Bentivegna, Paul Bernard, Georgette, Greco and R.R. Bunting; stockings by Gerard Fortier, La Manufacture du Bas de Soie and Selfix, 'Stockings Join the Colours', American *Vogue*, 1 May 1935

Published:
American *Vogue*, 1 May 1935, pp.70–1: 'Fashion: Stockings Join the Colours'
Caption reads: 'There are no heels at all on the evening slippers. Nor stockings on the legs. The satin Turkish slippers with their pointed toes are from Barnovi; the Arabian sandals of gold kid, strapped on, from Greco – both in Paris. Note those sheer blue stockings worn with the toeless and backless antelope sandals at the upper right. The stockings are from La Manufacture du Bas de Soie. The Paul Bernard shoes are imported by Bergdorf Goodman. The feet of new coloured stockings and shoes! They are, left to right: Selfix burgundy wool stockings; Bentivegna's antelope shoes imported by Bergdorf Goodman. Gerard Fortier's natural flax stockings gripped with Lastex; Greco kid shoes. Three pairs of Selfix ribbed stockings, gripped with Lastex, worn with Bentivegna, Georgette, and R. R. Bunting shoes'.

French *Vogue*, June 1935, pp.51–2: 'Pour le Sport, des Bas de Couleur'
Caption reads: 'Barnovi. Des pantoufles du soir en satin violet seront une très jolie note de couleur avec une robe blanche. Sans semelle, elles n'ont qu'une couture sous le milieu du pied. Gréco. Pour accompagner des robes grecques ou le sari des Indes, voici une sandale du soir sans talon, entièrement faite de fines lanières de chevreau d'or et portée sans bas. Paul Bernard. Des sandales en antilope marine découvrent les doigts de pied et se portent avec des bas marine très transparents, de la Manufacture du Bas de Soie. Bentivegna. Une nouveauté: des bas de couleur pour le sport. Ceux-ci sont en fine laine bourgogne, de Selfix. Avec un tailleur de flanelle grise et des souliers en antilope gris. Gréco. Des sandales en lin naturel et chevreau brun se portent avec des bas de lin s'arrêtant aux genoux, de la maison Gérard Fortier. Georgette. Parfait pour la plage, voici un mocassin de chevreau rose entièrement perforé et bordé de bleu pâle comme un soulier d'enfant, sans talon ni semelle épaisse. De chez Julienne, la seconde paire en toile bleu pâle monte haut sur le cou-de-pied et laisse libres les côtés et le dos. Talon, semelle et boutons sont en chevreau marine. Bentivegna. Encore des bas de couleur, ici bleu marine, pour accompagner des souliers de sport en box-calf blanc et marine. Bas Selfix serrés au genou par une bande de Lastex. Georgette. Ces bas de fine laine Selfix bourgogne maintenus par une bande de Lastex sont assortis au cuir acajou recouvrant la moitié des mocassins en peau d'antilope blanche perforée. R. R. Bunting. Ce soulier de box marron à bout carré s'accompagnera de bas vert de Selfix côtelés, en fil. Ensemble marron et sweater vert'.

Plate 146
Color Sells: Showing Examples of Color Photography, box cover, Condé Nast Publications, 1935 (first edition)
Courtesy Condé Nast Archive, New York

Note appended to inner box cover reads: 'The Dots on the Cover: The enlarged flower arrangement used on the cover of this box is a 16-time enlargement of the tiny color reproduction of the three anemones shown in the title. This illustrates the way in which the dot formations in the process plates serve to create the color combinations when run through the press. If the box cover is held off at a distance, it will be seen that the dot pattern disappears and the flowers retain their delicate gradations of color'.

Plate 147
'Color displays the product and the package', *Color Sells: Showing Examples of Color Photography*, Condé Nast Publications, 1935 (first edition)
Courtesy Condé Nast Archive, New York

Caption reads: 'Here is an outstanding achievement in detailed and accurate color-reporting, where color is the whole story at the point of sale. Exact shades of products in packages, and products in action on the face and hands, have been portrayed as they will appear to the purchaser and user. Packages themselves are not only immediately identifiable, but are made to look so attractive that no dressing table seems complete without them. To the expert who realizes the technical problems involved, this is a masterpiece of more than salesmanship, an assignment that could have been carried out only by means of perfect inks and exceptional quality in plate and press work. The difficulties lie in the multiplicity of colors, hues and shades involved, and that true, solid, beautiful black of the background, which is generally so hard to secure in process printing'.

Plate 148
Edward Steichen (1879–1973)
American *Vogue* cover, 1 July 1932
Edward Steichen / Vogue © Condé Nast

Published:
American *Vogue* cover, 1 July 1932
Caption reads: 'Cover Design – Colour photograph by Steichen'.

British *Vogue* cover, 20 July 1932 (uncredited)
Caption reads: 'No Cover Look in this issue'.

French *Vogue* cover, July 1932 (uncredited)
Caption reads: 'No Cover Look in this issue'.

Plate 149
John Rawlings,
Bette Davis, *Glamour* cover, January 1941
John Rawlings / *Glamour* © Condé Nast

Plate 150
American *Vogue* cover, 15 May 1941

Published:
American *Vogue* cover, 15 May 1941
Caption reads: 'Sun-bathed, but not sun-struck – the girl on the cover knows how to spend summer, how to be beautiful from head to toe. You summer-wise ones can follow suit – this issue shows how'.

Plate 151
Muriel Maxwell, American *Vogue* cover, 1 July 1939

Published:
American *Vogue* cover, 1 July 1939
Caption reads: 'For July – red, white, and blue. With shiny white sharkskin – a red-and-blue turban; Sally Victor. Striped bag; Paul Flato. Primrose House Carnival Make-Up. Revlon Amoa Red polish. Lugene glasses'.

British *Vogue* cover, 9 August 1939 (uncredited)
No Cover Look in this issue.

Plate 152
Lisa Fonssagrives, American *Vogue* cover, 1 June 1940

Published:
American *Vogue* cover, 1 June 1940
Caption reads: 'On the diver who folds herself into a V for *Vogue* – a little-boy suit of Crown-tested Rayon with "Lastex," by Brigance, with Joyce shoes

to match. The same suit in different colours spells out "*Vogue*". Lord and Taylor'.

British *Vogue* cover, August 1940 (uncredited)
Caption reads: 'No Cover Look in this issue'.

Plate 153
Dresses by Adele Simpson, mural painting by Salvador Dalí, 1943
Colour transparency
25.3 x 20.2 cm
Horst Estate

Published:
Variant, American *Vogue*, 1 March 1943, p.48: 'Fashion: In the Dalí Room'
Caption reads: 'In the famous Dalí room painted for Princess Gourielli. For the New York flat of Prince and Princess Gourielli (she is Helena Rubinstein), Dalí painted three murals. Gigantic miniatures, with light welling up from the background, a mocking perfection of detail, they show Dali's recurrent symbols – birds, insects, keys, sandaled feet – explained in his convoluted book, "The Secret Life of Salvador Dalí". In the Dalí room, short dinner-dresses, pink and turquoise-blue, etched with black. Adele Simpson designs of Enka rayon crepe; $10. Bonwit Teller: I. Magnin; L. S. Ayres'.

Variant, British *Vogue*, July 1943, p.38: 'Against a Dalí Background'
Caption reads: 'Against a Dalí background, these American beauties bloom in the new short evening dresses, low-necked, pastel-coloured, etched in black, each with a scarf snood drapery, romantic and practical. Horst photo'.

Plate 154
Mr Condé Nast, New York, 1942

Published:
American *Vogue*, 15 October 1942, p.26: 'People and Ideas: Condé Nast, 1874–1942'
Caption reads: 'On September 19th, 1942, Condé Nast, publisher of *Vogue* and founder of The Condé Nast Publications, died. We, who have worked with him for so many years and feel his loss so deeply, now receive, in his passing, the heritage of his principles and purposes. Ours is the responsibility to forward and maintain the distinguished traditions which he established. The qualities which we – his associates and friends – felt in him most strongly were his complete approachability and understanding. His door, like his heart, was always open'.

Plate 155
Still Life, 1949

Published:
American *Vogue* 15 October 1949, p.65: 'Fashion: New: A Flourish of Coral and Diamonds'
Caption reads: 'The gentle, half-forgotten beauty of coral, brought suddenly to life with the compelling brilliance of diamonds. Here, shown life-size, coral jewels designed in Paris by Mlle. Jeanne Toussaint of Cartier, for herself: a bouquet of coral buds, dewed with diamonds, on trembling-thin gold wires; a bracelet, clasped with a magnificent diamond dragon's head; a warm ivory rose, set in coral and diamond leaves; a ring, carved and curved, currently-large, currently-coral, banded by arcs of diamonds'.

Liberman, Alexander (ed.), documentation compiled by Jonathan Tichenor, introduction by Aline B. Louchheim, *The Art and Technique of Color Photography: A Treasury of Color Photography by The Staff Photographers of Vogue, House & Garden, and Glamour*, Simon & Schuster, New York, 1951, p.41: 'Coral and Marble'.
Caption reads: 'Photographed on the mantelpiece in my studio, with midday daylight through the windows. Camera, 8 x 10 Ansco View. Lens: 12" Zeiss Tessar, f/6.3. Film: Ektachrome Daylight Type sheet film. Light: Daylight at noon, through windows. Exposure: 4 seconds at f/22'.

Plate 156
Helen Bennett, ensemble by Bergdorf Goodman, jewellery by Olga Tritt, 1939

Published:
American *Vogue*, 1 December 1939, p.92: 'Features: Gala Green'
Caption reads: 'Zouave beach pyjamas of silk crêpe, two layers for the trousers; blue linen jacket, Bergdorf Goodman. Necklace; Olga Tritt. Lipstick; Chanel's deep "Garnet"'.

Plate 157
Dress by Jean Dessès, 1952

Published:
American *Vogue*, 1 April 1952, p.125: 'Fashions: Jewels from the Paris Collections'
Caption reads: 'One of the chiffon beauties for which Dessès is famous, in an important new Paris colour scheme: green, black, and biscuit. The whole point of the dress, a handsome, draped simplicity. Now in America, at Bergdorf Goodman and Marshall Field'.

Plate 158
Dress by Henri Bendel, jewellery by Harry Winston, 1948

Published:
American *Vogue*, 1 October 1948, p.137: 'Fashion: Made for You'
Caption reads: 'Lemon yellow, in this strength, for evening: sleeves, new, in this length for big evenings; above in a dress of stiff taffeta and heavy lace. Diamond jewellery by Harry Winston. In the background, red flock wallpaper, by Piazza Prints. [...] the dress made-to-order at Henri Bendel'.

Liberman, Alexander (ed.), *The Art and Technique of Color Photography,* 1951,
Caption reads: 'Camera: 8 x 10 Ansco View. Lens: 12" Ziess Tessar, f/6.3. Film: Kodachrome Type B sheet film. Light: 2000-watt spot overhead, 1500-watt flood. Exposure: ½ second at f/11.

Plate 159
Suit and headdress by Schiaparelli, 1947

Published:
American *Vogue*, 15 February 1947, p.151: 'Fashion: News from Schiaparelli'
Caption reads: 'Dinner suit of satin and crêpe – the suit Schiaparelli wore with great success on a recent trip to New York – is, in itself, a sort of summary of her designing tradition. First, because it is a dinner suit, an idea which Schiaparelli has always championed; and because the black has more than a flick of her famous shocking pink; because it's bustled and jet-embroidered, takes a long or short skirt, makes the headdress a part – not apart. Sequitur: Schiaparelli's fourth dimension in design – a sunburst of scent named, as the emblem was during Louis XIV's reign, "Le Roy Soleil"'.

Liberman, Alexander (ed.), *The Art and Technique of Color Photography*, 1951, G, p.38: 'Figure with color planes'
Caption reads: 'The entire background interest here is in pieces of vari-colored background paper, cut out and tacked on the walls. Camera: 8 x 10 Ansco View. Lens: 12" Zeiss Tessar, f/6.3. Film: Kodachrome Type B. Light: 5000-watt spot, 750-watt spot, 1500-watt flood, 3200° K lamps. Exposure: 1 second at f/11'.

Plate 160
Dress by Jo Copeland, mural paintings by Marcel Vertès, 1946

Published:
American *Vogue*, 1 April 1946, p.166: 'Vintage Year for Prints in America'
Caption reads: 'Black velvet makes a shadow of a waist on a Bianchini Fiberset rayon crêpe dress; Jo Copeland's gentle lines. $90; Saks Fifth. Antoine's new lipstick, '"Soleil"'.

Plate 161
Ensembles by Nettie Rosenstein, jewellery by Tiffany and Company, 1940

Published:
American *Vogue*, 15 November 1940, p.38: 'Fashion: Brilliant and Bejewelled'
Caption reads: 'Brilliant and bejewelled and covered up is this winter's way to go to dinner and the theatre. On the girl in red: diamond-and-ruby jewels, a cap to echo the embroidery of her silk crêpe dress. On the girl in blue: sapphire-and-moonstone clip, sapphire-and-diamond earrings and bracelet, a snood of sequins to echo those on her silk jersey dress. Nettie Rosenstein costumes from Bonwit Teller; I. Magnin. All the jewels are from Tiffany and Company'.

Plate 162
Ensemble by Bergdorf Goodman, jewellery by Cartier, 1939

Published:
American *Vogue* cover, 15 February 1939
Caption reads: 'Look for winged hats, bright hats, tweed hats like these. (Red jersey suit, white crêpe blouse.) All from Bergdorf Goodman. Cartier jewels. Elizabeth Arden's Redwood Make-Up'.

British *Vogue* cover, 8 March 1939
Caption reads: 'Look for winged hats, veiled hats, bright hats, and a bright new make-up – Elizabeth Arden's "Redwood"'.

Plate 163
Suit and coat by Handmacher, 1943

Published:
American *Vogue*, 15 August 1943, p.70: 'Fashion: Checked Suit, Greatcoat'
Caption reads: 'At Red Cross Headquarters. "How do I start a Red Cross Chapter on my campus?" Here an undergraduate visiting the New York Red Cross Fifth Avenue Production Workroom finds out how to establish a bandage-centre. The hound's-tooth check tweed suit, $35. The officer's black coat, $55. Both tailored by Handmacher. 10 to 18. Lord and Taylor; Marshall Field; Scruggs Vandervoort; Jordan Marsh'.

Plate 164
Susann Shaw, 1943

Published:
American *Vogue* cover, 15 May 1943
Caption reads: as for plate 89

Plate 165
Hats by Best, Lord and Taylor and Mme Pauline, gloves by Dawnelle, 1943

Published:
American *Vogue*, 15 February 1943, p.33: 'Fashion: Order of the Day'
Caption reads: 'Every hair in place. A vivid, glowing look (perhaps Lenthéric's new "Wonderful" make-up pictured here). Precisely tailored grey flannel suits with laundry-crisp blouses. Well-ordered accessories. Easy-to-wear hats such as these. Blue felt visored beret; Best. Red felt skull-cap (worn with a centre part); Lord and Taylor. White piqué beret; Mme Pauline. Dawnelle double-woven cotton gloves'.

Plate 166
Muriel Maxwell, hat by Lilly Daché, jewellery by Trabert and Hoeffer-Mauboussin, 1940

Published:
American *Vogue* cover, 1 August 1940

Caption reads: 'For your autumn reflection – this Lilly Daché felt pill-box, worn atop a red silk head-scarf the Peruvians call a chullo. It makes your face the focus. Ransohoffs. The jewels are from Trabert and Hoeffer-Mauboussin. The lipstick is Tangee's new "Red Red"'.

British *Vogue*, September 1940 (uncredited)
Caption reads: 'For your autumn reflection; this pill-box with a medieval head-scarf: Harrods. Matched by Lenthéric's No. 6 Lipstick'.

Plate 167
Dress by Hattie Carnegie, 1939

Published:
American *Vogue*, 15 June 1939, p.48:
'Fashion: Country Dinner: Skirts or Trousers?'
Caption reads: 'The page opposite speaks for the skirt side of the question. A simple, flounced dress of cool blue foulard, striped like a man's tie ... new soft use of a tailored fabric. Low and square, front and back. Choose it, to look impeccably cool on a very hot night. Wear blue beads, and red slippers to match the belt. Down your hair, shower lilies-of-the-valley'.

Plate 168
Muriel Maxwell, ensemble by Sally Victor, bag by Paul Flato, sunglasses by Lugene, 1939

Published:
American *Vogue* cover, 1 July 1939
Caption reads: 'For July – red, white, and blue. With shiny white sharkskin – a red-and-blue turban; Sally Victor. Striped bag; Paul Flato. Primrose House Carnival Make-Up. Revlon Amoa Red polish. Lugene glasses'.

British *Vogue* cover, 9 August 1939 (uncredited)
'No Cover Look in this issue'.

Plate 169
Dress by Mollie Parnis, background by Marcel Vertès, 1953

Published:
American *Vogue*, 1 May 1953, p.78:
'Fashion: Fashion analysis done here:
A Six-Page Production'
Caption reads: 'Fruit complex? An enviable thing (look at Envy grudging away backstage). Dress by Mollie Parnis, in grape-printed silk surah; $90. This, the Lennox bag, La Tausca pseudo-pearls, and McCallum stockings: all, Bergdorf Goodman. Shoes by Valley, at Best's. Dress, also at Hudson's; Younkers'.

Plate 170
Andrea Johnson, dress by Pierre Balmain, background by Marcel Vertès, 1953

Published:
American *Vogue*, 1 May 1953, p.80: 'Fashion: Fashion analysis done here: A Six-Page Production'
Captions read: 'To set the stage properly, *Vogue* enlisted the aid of the artist Marcel Vertès. A frequent contributor to our pages, winner of two Academy Awards for the décor and costumes that made *Moulin Rouge* a film of such extraordinary beauty, and author of that sharply drawn satire on the Freudians, *It's All Mental*, Vertès designed the six-page, tongue-in-cheek production about to unfold, all of it couched visually in psychiatric terms [...]'.

'A pretty picture of Infanta-ilism here – a dress of poppy cotton organdie puffing wide over a taffeta underskirt. Designed by Pierre Balmain-New York, at Saks Fifth; Montaldo's; Neiman-Marcus. (The setting: the studio of a mythical and most contrariwise painter – out of a surrealistic still-life, he creates a portrait of alive and classic beauty)'.

Plate 171
Madame Wellington Koo, New York, 1943

Published:
American *Vogue*, 1 January 1943, p.31:
'People and Ideas: Mme Wellington Koo'
Caption reads: 'Making friends for China is her talent, her lifework/Wife of an Ambassador, mother of two college-age sons, Mme. Koo is a Chinese citizen of the world, and international beauty. Here she wears her own version of China's dress, and her fabulous jade. On her inch-long nails – Chen Yu's "Temple Fire" lacquer' / 'Composed, complex ... the wife of the Chinese Ambassador to Great Britain'.

British *Vogue*, March 1943, p.38:
'Mme. Wellington Koo'
Caption reads: 'Making friends for China is her talent, her lifework'.

Plate 172
Coat by Connie Adams, 1946

Published:
American *Vogue*, 15 March 1946, p.160: '*Vogue*'s Junior Fashions: Ticking all Day'
Caption reads: 'Ticking for a Dandy – bright collar hooked up high. By Connie Adams; about $17. Bonwit Teller; Davison-Paxon; J.W. Robinson. Dorothy Gray's "Bright Touch" lipstick'.

Plate 173
Dorian Leigh, dress by Henri Bendel, 1946

Published:
American *Vogue* cover, 1 October 1946
Caption reads: 'Cover: the dress ... half blue, half black. Parma blue rayon satin from shoulder to waist in black; a huge Parma blue pouff bustle ties on over it when you want to add formality. The rest ... a stem of black rayon crêpe. Made-to-order; Henri Bendel. Scent to heighten evening elegance ... Henri Bendel's "10 West" perfume'.

British *Vogue* cover, November 1946
Caption reads: 'On the Cover: Evening news from New York: A sheath of black crêpe with Parma blue rayon satin from shoulder to waist. The bustle can be tied to add formality. Photographed by Horst'.

Plate 174
Jean Patchett, bathing suit by Brigance, 1951

Published:
American *Vogue*, 1 December 1951, p.151:
'Fashion: Brigance's Beach Ideas'
Caption reads: 'A bathing suit of pink Crompton velveteen (as dunkable as you are) cut with a high Empire waist and romper-pants. All of it banded – most strategically – with knitted, elasticized white. $25. The logical lipstick, "Pink Velvet" by Max Factor Hollywood. Bathing suit at Lord & Taylor; Hudson's; Woodward & Lothrop'.

Plate 175
Barbara 'Babe' Cushing Mortimer Paley, dress by Traina-Norell, 1946

Published:
American *Vogue*, 1 March 1946, p.74:
'Fashion: Mrs Stanley Grafton Mortimer, Junior'
Caption reads: 'The news of this blue is the sudden character it has, with black ... no longer candy-box pastel, but a colour that works like a flattering light. The dress, mat black rayon jersey; the pale yoke, simple as a sweater. Mrs. Mortimer adds a collar of pearls, a wonderful scramble of bracelets. The dress is a Traina-Norell design. At Bonwit Teller; I. Magnin; Marshall Field'.

Plate 176
Suit by Brigance for Frank Gallant, jewellery by Schreiner, 1951

Published:
American *Vogue*, 15 November 1951, p.136: 'Fashion: Italian Sky Blue Made For The American Resorts'
Caption reads: 'The silk suit in Italian sky blue: a resort Now, a spring Future. What we love about it: the keyhole collar; the degree of the short sleeves; the gored skirt; the fabric of the wild tussah and tame silk fibres. By Brigance, of Frank Gallant, of American Silk Mills suiting, $119; rhinestone jewellery, by Schreiner; Saks Fifth. Suit, also at Wanamaker's, Phila.; The Dayton Co. Her hair is sparked with Roux's "Dark Auburn" Color Shampoo; her lips and nails with Naylon's "Stop Light"'.

Unnumbered gatefold
Outer wrap, left:
American *Vogue* cover, 1 April 1939

Outer wrap, right:
American *Vogue* cover, 15 November 1954

Gatefold
Top row, left to right:
American *Vogue*, 15 February 1938
American *Vogue*, 15 April 1943
American *Vogue*, 15 February 1940

American *Vogue*, 15 September 1953
American *Vogue*, 15 May 1938
American *Vogue*, 1 August 1939

American *Vogue*, 15 May 1939
American *Vogue*, 1 October 1953
American *Vogue*, 15 October 1942

American *Vogue*, 1 June 1950
American *Vogue*, 1 August 1942
American *Vogue*, 1 April 1946

Centre row, left to right:
American *Vogue*, 15 November 1952
American *Vogue*, 1 November 1939
American *Vogue*, 15 November 1961

American *Vogue*, 1 April 1941
American *Vogue*, 1 September 1953
American *Vogue*, 15 September 1941

American *Vogue*, 15 February 1948
American *Vogue*, 15 September 1954
American *Vogue*, 1 January 1937

American *Vogue*, 15 June 1943
American *Vogue*, 15 November 1936
American *Vogue*, 1 May 1955

Bottom row, left to right:
American *Vogue*, 1 April 1948
American *Vogue*, 1 November 1941
American *Vogue*, 15 May 1950

American *Vogue*, 15 February 1946
American *Vogue*, 15 October 1941
American *Vogue*, 15 July 1936

American *Vogue*, 1 May 1940
American *Vogue*, 15 October 1953
American *Vogue*, 1 October 1952

American *Vogue*, 1 August 1938
American *Vogue*, 1 November 1946
American *Vogue*, 15 June 1942

Plate 177
Irving Penn (1917–2009)
Horst, New York, 1946
Gelatin silver print
25.4 x 20.7 cm
Collection of R. J. Horst
Inscription on reverse of print reads: 'Horst by I Penn NY 1946 for Horst's book "Patterns from Nature"'

Plate 178
Patterns from Nature, 1946
Horst, Horst P., *Patterns from Nature; Photographs by Horst* (J.J. Augustin, New York, 1946)
S. Brown

Plate 179
'*Vogue*'s eye view of summer beauty',
American *Vogue*, 1 May 1947

Published:
American *Vogue*, 1 May 1947, p.123:
'Fashion: Summer Beauty'
Caption reads: 'Part sun. Part shade. This is always the tempered pattern of summer days. And so the look of beauty and the look of fashion. There will be, as always, the standard summer look that is wholly a tribute to the sun: gilt-streaked hair, brown, sandaled feet, dresses which depend more on tanned skin than woven goods. But there will be – too new to be standard – another summer look: depending on pretty fabrics beautifully cut, on carefully calculated accessories, and on fragile, pale colours in face and dress. A tribute to leafy coolness. A dappling of summer beauty, of summer fashion'.

Plate 180
'Patterns in pictures by Horst', American *Vogue*, 15 October 1946

Published:
American *Vogue*, 15 October 1946, pp.192–3:
'People and Ideas: Patterns in pictures by Horst'
Caption reads: A leaf in a botanical garden/ Because a papaya leaf reminded him of a Gothic ceiling in Avignon, Horst, *Vogue*'s photographer, took a closer look at some everyday objects. Now, through the lens of his Rolleiflex, he metamorphizes the familiar into the extraordinary by taking close-ups of bark, shells, flowers, matting and vegetables. When printed – one negative straight, its twin in reverse – and placed in exact juxtaposition, the designs take on a new interest. These four, from Horst's new book of pictures, called *Patterns in Nature*, might be mistaken for eighteenth-century wallpaper stripped from a Loire château. Instead, two on the opposite page – the wickerwork and the cactus – actually are being used as abstract patterns for contemporary materials'.

Variant layout, British *Vogue*, December 1946, pp.66–7: 'Photo Patterns'
Caption reads: 'A papaya leaf reminded Horst, *Vogue*'s photographer, of a Gothic ceiling in Avignon ... Now he continues, through the lens of his Rolleiflex, to discover formalised design in Nature by taking close-ups of everyday objects and printing the negatives alternately straight and in reverse, to form repeat patterns. These four, for instance, might be mistaken for 18th-century wallpaper stripped from a Loire château. Actually, the wickerwork and the cactus patterns are being used for printed fabrics in America'.

Plate 181
Anthurium, 1946
Gelatin silver print
28.6 x 22.5 cm
Horst Estate

Published: *Patterns from Nature*, p.5
Caption reads: 'Rolleiflex, Medium Yellow Filter, Proxar #1, Hothouse, Botanical Gardens, Bronx'.

Plate 182
Paul Strand (1890–1976)
Iris, c.1928
Gelatin silver print
25.2 x 20.3 cm
V&A: PH.375-1982
© Aperture Foundation, Inc., Paul Strand Archive

Plate 183
Karl Blossfeldt (1865–1932)
Aristolochia spec. Birthwort, Shoots of Tendrils, undated
Long-term loan from Berlin University of the Arts – Karl Blossfeldt Collection at Die Photographische

Plate 184
Pyrite, Mineral and *Prunus Pennsylvania, Bark*, 1946
Published: *Patterns from Nature*, pp.42–3

Plate 185
Quartz and *Betula Lenta, Bark*, 1946
Published: *Patterns from Nature*, pp.44–5

Plate 186
Clay and *Boehmeria Argenta*, 1946
Published: *Patterns from Nature*, pp.32–3

Plate 187
Petrified Wood and *Brachet Fungus*, 1946
Published: *Patterns from Nature*, pp.50–1

Plate 188
Agave Rupicola and *Wing of Ornithoptera Cellularis, Butterfly*, 1946
Published: *Patterns from Nature*, pp.6–7

Plate 189
Rhipdogorin Flabellum, Coral and *Brassica Olerocea variety, Caulifower*, 1946
Published: *Patterns from Nature*, pp.58–9

Plate 190
Horst's sketchbook, 1940s
Pencil on paper
Hardcover sketchbook, red with black tape
(Closed) 22.2 x 18.3 x 1.2 cm
Collection of R.J. Horst

Plate 191
Kodak Negative Album, 1946
Album containing gelatin silver contact prints
(Closed) 8 x 10.3 x 3.5 cm
Horst Estate

Plate 192
Four contact prints from Kodak Negative Album, 1946
All:
Gelatin silver contact prints
6 x 6 cm, irregular
Horst Estate

Plate 193
Agave Attenuata, 1946
Gelatin silver print
28.7 x 22.8 cm
Horst Estate

Published: *Patterns from Nature*, p.8
Caption reads: 'Rolleiflex, Medium Yellow Filter, Proxar #1, Hothouse, Botanical Gardens, Bronx'.

Plate 194
Aednium Holochrysum, 1946
Gelatin silver print
28.6 x 23 cm
V&A: E.227-2014, Given by Gert Elfering

Published: *Patterns from Nature*, p.30
Caption reads: 'Rolleiflex, Medium Yellow Filter, Proxar #2, Hothouse, Botanical Gardens, Bronx'.

Plate 195
Wing of Ornithoptera Cellularis, Butterfly, 1946
Gelatin silver print
28.7 x 23.1 cm
Horst Estate

Published: *Patterns from Nature*, p.7
Caption reads: 'Graphic View Camera, 4 x 5, Outdoors, New York'.

Plate 196
Pyrite, Mineral, 1946
Gelatin silver print
28.6 x 23.7 cm
V&A: E.223-2014, Given by Gert Elfering

Published: *Patterns from Nature*, p.39
Caption reads: 'Graphic View Camera, 4 x 5 Outdoors, New York'.

Plate 197
Ligularia Kaempferi, 1946
Gelatin silver print
29.7 x 23 cm
V&A: E.226-2014, Given by Gert Elfering

Published: *Patterns from Nature*, p.77
Caption reads: 'Rolleiflex, Medium Yellow Filter, Hothouse, Botanical Gardens, Bronx'.

Plate 198
Trichocereus Candicans, 1946
Gelatin silver print
28.5 x 23 cm
V&A: E.225-2014, Given by Gert Elfering

Published: *Patterns from Nature*, p.29
Caption reads: 'Rolleiflex, Medium Yellow Filter, Proxar #2, Hothouse, Botanical Gardens, Bronx'.

Plate 199
Photographic pattern, made from *Peperomia Sandersii*, 1946
Gelatin silver print
31 x 26.8 cm
Horst Estate

Published: *Patterns from Nature*, p.100 (detail)
Caption reads: 'Graphic View Camera, 4 x 5, Outdoors, New York'.

Plate 200
Brachet Fungus, 1946
Gelatin silver print
28.6 x 22.7 cm
Horst Estate

Published: *Patterns from Nature*, p.51
Caption reads: 'Rolleiflex, Medium Yellow Filter, Proxar #1, Outdoors, Connecticut'.

Plate 201
Pinus Strobus, 1946
Gelatin silver print
28.4 x 22.8 cm
Horst Estate

Published: *Patterns from Nature*, p.65
Caption reads: 'Rolleiflex, Medium Yellow Filter, Outdoors, Botanical Gardens, Bronx'.

Plate 202
Nautilus Pompileus, Shell, 1946
Gelatin silver print
21.7 x 23.3 cm
Horst Estate

Published: *Patterns from Nature*, p.92
Caption reads: 'Graphic View Camera, 4 x 5, Outdoors, New York'.

Plate 203
Nautilus Pompileus, Shell, 1946
Gelatin silver print
28.7 x 23.1 cm
Horst Estate

Published: *Patterns from Nature*, p.87
Caption reads: 'Graphic View Camera, 4 x 5, Outdoors, New York'.

Plate 204
Photographic pattern, *Agave Rupicola*, 1946
Gelatin silver contact prints
23 x 20.4 cm
Horst Estate

Published: *Patterns from Nature*, p.101
Caption reads: 'Rolleiflex, Medium Yellow Filter, Proxar #1, Hothouse, Botanical Gardens, Bronx'.

Plate 205
Photographic pattern, *Coleus Blumei*, 1946
Gelatin silver contact prints
21.1 x 21.4 cm
Horst Estate

Published: *Patterns from Nature*, p.97
Caption reads: 'Rolleiflex, Medium Yellow Filter, Proxar #1, Hothouse, Botanical Gardens, Bronx'.

Plate 206
Photographic pattern, *Spathiphyllum Wallisi*, 1946
Gelatin silver contact prints
23.1 x 22.9 cm, irregular
Horst Estate

Published: *Patterns from Nature*, p.102
Caption reads: 'Rolleiflex, Medium Yellow Filter, Hothouse, Botanical Gardens, Bronx'.

Plate 207
Photographic pattern, 1946
Gelatin silver contact prints
22.9 x 22.2 cm
Horst Estate

Plate 208
Photographic pattern, *Peperomia Sandersii*, 1946
Gelatin silver contact prints
28.9 x 25.1 cm
Horst Estate

Published: *Patterns from Nature*, p.100
Caption reads: 'Graphic View Camera, 4 x 5, Outdoors, New York'.

Plate 209
Photographic pattern, 1946
Gelatin silver contact prints
16.5 x 20.9 cm, irregular
Horst Estate

Published: *Patterns from Nature*, p.104
Caption reads: 'Rolleiflex, Medium Yellow Filter, Hothouse, Botanical Gardens, Mexico'.

American *Vogue*, 15 October 1946, p.192: 'People and Ideas: Patterns in pictures by Horst'

British *Vogue*, December 1946, p.66: 'Photo Patterns'

Captions for American and British *Vogue*: see also Plate 180

Plate 210
Photographic pattern, *Echeveria Gibbiflora Crispa*, 1946
Gelatin silver contact prints
22.5 x 23.5 cm, irregular
Horst Estate

Pattern unpublished. For *Echeveria Gibbiflora Crispa*, see, *Patterns from Nature*, p.27

Plate 211
Photographic pattern, 1946
Gelatin silver contact prints
22.1 x 21.4 cm
Horst Estate

Plate 212
Photographic pattern, *Brachet Fungus*, 1946
Gelatin silver contact prints
22.4 x 22.4 cm
Horst Estate

Published: *Patterns from Nature*, p.96
Caption reads: 'Rolleiflex, Medium Yellow Filter, Proxar #1, Outdoors, Connecticut'.

Plate 213
Photographic pattern, *Calladium*, 1946
Gelatin silver contact prints
21.7 x 22.5 cm
Horst Estate
Published: *Patterns from Nature*, p.103
Caption reads: 'Graphic View Camera, 4 x 5, Outdoors, New York'.

Plate 214
Contact sheet, Persepolis, 1949
Gelatin silver contact print
25.4 x 20.3 cm
A. Cowan

Plate 215
Contact sheet, Qashqa'i tribe, c.1949
Gelatin silver contact print
25.4 x 20.7 cm
Horst Estate

Plate 216
Staircase wall, Persepolis, 1949
Gelatin silver print
19.9 x 19.4 cm
Horst Estate

Photographed: 6 September 1949

Plate 217
'People and Ideas: Persepolis', American *Vogue*, 15 November 1949

Published:
American *Vogue*, 15 November 1949, pp.132–5: 'People and Ideas: Persepolis'
Captions read: 'The capital of the Persian Empire under Darius and Xerxes: recent archaeological diggings reveal sculpture buried twenty-three centuries ago'.

'The great treasury building ruins; left by Alexander the Great who stripped and burned Persepolis, used ten thousand mules and five thousand camels to carry off the loot'.

'A lance-bearer and incense holder; two royal attendants: detail from a bas-relief'.

'Fragment of a double bull capital; a bull's head in ceremonial dress'.

'Fragment of the capital of the tripylon, the three-gated structure: an enormous human-headed bull, with the precisely curled hair and beard of the period'.

Plate 218
Persepolis Bull, 1949
Gelatin silver print
20 x 19.3 cm
V&A: E.233-2014, Given by Gert Elfering

Photographed: 1 September 1949

Published:
Variant American *Vogue*, 15 November 1949, p.134: 'People and Ideas: Persepolis'
Caption reads: 'Fragment of a double bull capital; a bull's head in ceremonial dress'.
Inscription on reverse of print: 'Among the ruins of the palace in the plain between Isfahan and Shiraz'.

Plate 219
Palace of Persepolis, 1949
Gelatin silver print
19.9 x 19.4 cm
Horst Estate

Photographed: 6 September 1949

Plate 220
Bas-relief from Palace of Xerxes, Persepolis, 1949
Gelatin silver print
26.9 x 27.5 cm
Horst Estate

Plate 221
Bas-relief from Palace of Xerxes, Persepolis, 1949
Gelatin silver print
26.8 x 22.8 cm
Horst Estate

Plate 222
Bas-relief from Palace of Xerxes, Persepolis, 1949
Gelatin silver print
27.4 x 20.8 cm
V&A E.232-2014, Given by Gert Elfering

Published:
American Vogue, 15 November 1949, p.133: 'People and Ideas: Persepolis'
Caption reads: 'A lance-bearer and incense holder; two royal attendants: detail from a bas-relief'.

Plate 223
Boy with eagle, c.1949
Gelatin silver print
19.5 x 19.6 cm
Horst Estate

Plate 224
Qashqa'i trumpeter, c.1949
Gelatin silver print
20.4 x 19.6 cm
Horst Estate

Plate 225
Colt and Qashqa'i tribesmen, c.1949
Gelatin silver print
20.8 x 19.3 cm
Horst Estate

Plate 226
Qashqa'i camp, 1950
Gelatin silver print
21.1 x 19.4 cm
Horst Estate

Photographed: 16 June 1950

Plate 227
Young girl with sheep, 1950
Gelatin silver print
20.6 x 19.3 cm
Horst Estate

Plate 228
A Qashqa'i shepherd and his son, 1950
Gelatin silver print
20 x 19.6 cm
Horst Estate

Inscription on reverse of print: 'Shepherds' camp, Qaradagh'

Plate 229
Camel, 1950
Gelatin silver print
20.2 x 19.3 cm
Horst Estate

Plate 230
Turkoman boy on steppe, c.1949
Gelatin silver print
20.4 x 19.4 cm
Horst Estate

Photographed: 14 June 1950
Inscription on reverse of print: 'Barefoot camel-herd on the Turkoman Steppe'

Plate 231
Male Nude, 1950

Plate 232
George Platt Lynes (1907–55)
New York Ballet production of *Orpheus*, 1950
Estate of George Platt Lynes

Plate 233
George Brassaï (1899–1984)
Young couple wearing a Two-In-One-Suit, Bal de la Montagne, Sainte-Genevieve, Paris, c.1931
© Estate Brassaï – RMN-Grand Palais

Plate 234
Luchino Visconti, Paris, 1936
Gelatin silver print
24.5 x 19.7 cm
Horst Estate

Plate 235
George Hoyningen-Huene
Horst in 1930 and 1932
Estate of George Hoyningen-Huene

Published:
Valentine Lawford, *Horst: His Work and His World*, (Alfred A. Knopf, New York, 1984), pp.36–7
Caption reads: 'Horst photographed by Huene on the roof of the *Vogue* studio in Paris, 1930, and in Huene's apartment, 1932. Horst: "Both George and I had this extraordinary feeling about Greece. The physical beauty of the men and women, the sun and the fresh air and the sea. The lighting here was brand new. We had tried to duplicate the lighting of the Acropolis at sunset"'.

Plate 236
Robert Mapplethorpe (1946–89)
Thomas, 1987
© The Robert Mapplethorpe Foundation.
Courtesy Art + Commerce

Plate 237
Minor White (1908–76)
Gino Cipolla, Portland, Oregon, 1940
The Minor White Archive, Princeton University Art Museum

Plate 238
Herbert List (1903–75)
Athens, 1938
Herbert List / Magnum Photos

Plate 239
George Hoyningen-Huene
Horst, 1931
Estate of George Hoyningen-Huene

Plate 240
Bruce Weber (b.1946)
Calvin Klein advertisement
Image courtesy of the Advertising Archives

Plate 241
Classical Torso, Paris, 1932
Gelatin silver print
A. Cowan

Plate 242
Male Nude, 1953
Platinum-palladium print
37 x 42 cm
The Elton John Photography Collection

Plate 243
Male Nude, 1952
Platinum-palladium print
57 x 45.5 cm
The Elton John Photography Collection

Plate 244
Male Nude, 1952

Plate 245
Male Nude, 1953
Platinum-palladium print
40 x 37 cm
The Elton John Photography Collection

Plate 246
Male Nude, 1952
Platinum-palladium print
46.5 x 55.3 cm
The Elton John Photography Collection

Plate 247
Male Nude, 1952

Plate 248
Male Nude, 1953
Platinum-palladium print
37.5 x 48.5 cm
The Elton John Photography Collection

Plate 249
Male Nude, 1952
Gelatin silver print
57.3 x 47.3 cm
The Elton John Photography Collection

Plate 250 and 251
Lord and Lady Eliot, Port Eliot, Cornwall, 1966

Published:
(Plate 250): American *Vogue*, 1 August 1966, pp.142–3: 'The Upswing Young'
Caption reads: 'The colour of Port Eliot: In the pearl-pale smaller drawing room called the Saloon, one of several family portraits by Sir Joshua Reynolds. This one: Jemima, Marchioness Cornwallis, with her son, Lord Broome. Below it, turquoise-bordered Minton plates. To the right, a Reynolds conversation piece. View from the long inner hall into the crimson Morning Room. Black portrait busts, one of William Pitt the Younger, flank the door. In the foreground, red poppies and blue lupins flare in the dim hall. Lord Eliot in the damask-walled Morning Room, in front of a rare, early Reynolds landscape view of Plymouth. To the right, a frame filled with family miniatures. Lady Eliot with the Labrador, Stick'.

(Plate 251) American *Vogue*, 1 August 1966, pp.144–5: 'The Upswing Young'
Caption reads: 'Treasures of Port Eliot: Lord and Lady Eliot, at the table in the dining room set with silver from the abundant family collection, which includes elaborate presentation pieces given to earlier Eliots, for instance, by the estate tenants as wedding presents. The century-old Irish linen cloth on the table was used by an Eliot who was Lord Lieutenant of Ireland. The great drawing-room, designed by Sir John Soane with, over the chimneypiece, left, a Hoppner of William Pitt the Younger. A parade of busts of Roman Emperors in the Orangery designed by Soane. A still life of family silver dominated by an early Victorian salver with the coat of arms of the Earls of St. Germans'.

Plate 252
Alexander Iolas, Athens, 1963

Published:
American *Vogue*, 1 December 1981, pp.290–1: 'Living: Where All That Glitters Is Gold'
Captions read: 'In Greece a marble "palace" houses the amazing, rich, sometimes zany world of the ultimate art collector – Alexander Iolas'.

'Alexander Iolas, with "Phryne," named for the fabled hetaera of ancient Greece, in front of the gold sheeted doors sculpted with warriors and centaurs by Pikionis, the architect of this extraordinary house. Holding up Iolas' private world, ancient stone pillars from Ravenna. Inside the front hall, a golden chair that does not invite you to sit down – a sculpture by Princess Michael (Marina) of Greece. Bannister: delicate wrought-iron tracery of flowers and leaves, created by Claude Lalanne'.

Plate 253
Samuel Reed and family, New York, 1966

Published:
American *Vogue*, 15 January 1966, p.114: 'The Reed Team'
Caption reads: 'Mr. and Mrs. Samuel Pryor Reed, their daughter Beatrice, in the drawing room of their New York flat – high-ceilinged, warmed by an Aubusson rug, and treasures gathered in their travels. The painted leather screen at the left is eighteenth-century Dutch, found in London. The portrait of a young woman was painted in Russia by an Italian, Rotari, and acquired in Austria. Mrs. Reed's black-and-silver caftan defines her evening-in clothes: long, lean, special, but never trousers'.

Plate 254
Cut flowers, Consuelo Vanderbilt Balsan's home, Southampton, New York, 1963

Published:
American *Vogue*, 1 February 1963, p.129: 'Consuelo Vanderbilt Balsan: Portrait of a Unique American'
Caption reads: 'Roses on a small table by a window of the Southampton dining room where Madame Balsan lunches almost as though al fresco'.

Plate 255
Consuelo Vanderbilt Balsan, Southampton, New York, 1963

Published:
American *Vogue*, 1 February 1963, p.124: 'Consuelo Vanderbilt Balsan: Portrait of a Unique American'
Caption reads: 'Madame Jacques Balsan in her Southampton drawing room where she can sit as though she were in a sunlit garden'.

Plate 256
Truman Capote at home, Long Island, 1965

Published:
American *Vogue*, 1 November 1965, pp.208–9: 'Truman Capote and the Country Studio He Designed for Work'
Captions read: 'Capote in the living room, partly double-storeyed. At his feet, an Andy Warhol portrait of Capote, painted ten years ago'.

'The spiral staircase to the gallery'.
'Capote in one of his collection of hats'.

Plate 257
Gloria Steinem's home, New York, 1970

Published:
British *Vogue*, January 1971, pp.104–5: 'A Writer's Study in Indian Colour and American comfort'
Caption reads: 'The couches at one end of the living-room are good ones, down-filled, second-hand, covered with the wall fabric. The Italian benches are remnants of another apartment, as is the Bermuda bed in my workroom. Its cotton flame-stich cover dictated the wall and curtains, but I liked Jane Holzer's idea of adding an under-curtain for depth. Posters and friendly faces disguise a cupboard. The cubicles are my favourite kind of bookcase, the country roulette was another wrecking company find, and that's actress Jeanne Moreau in the fireplace'.

Plate 258
'Baby Jane' Holzer, New York, 1969

Published:
American *Vogue*, 1 November 1969, pp.210–11: 'Jane Holzer the Lion-Hearted'
Caption reads: 'With a fling of pleasure, Mrs. Leonard Holzer has joined the most contemporary art with the eighteenth century. In her living room, in front of an enormous 1968 Larry Zox abstraction, she wears a Sant'Angelo gypsy dress, faces an eighteenth-century Chinese screen, thirteen feet high, covered in rare Chinese wallpaper, shimmering with birds and flowers. (Queen Victoria first ordered the two low stools, with their

white fabric, from India.) In the foreground, a sofa designed by Mrs. Holzer, with masses of pillows in suède thrown accurately in the most superb positions. At the right, a low table of polished petrified wood with a collection of shells'.

Plates 259 and 260
Jan Gardner Cowles at home, New York, 1971

Published:
(Plate 259) American *Vogue*, 1 October 1971, pp.180–1: 'A Reflection of Now'
Caption reads: 'Mrs. Gardner Cowles in her living room, its sense of space heightened by sleight-of-eye shutters. The rainbow reflections in the shutters, a 1969 painting by Frank Stella. The stacked stainless-steel sculpture is by Beverly Pepper. The entrance hall, now a showcase for Picasso's 1964 "Femme Couchée au Chat," paintings by Russell Cowles (Gardner's brother), and one by Rufino Tamayo. The Gaston Lachaise 1927 bronze in the distance is "The Elevation," hemmed by flowers'.

(Plate 260) American *Vogue*, 1 October 1971, pp.186–7:'A Reflection of Now'
Captions read: 'Bedroom of the Cowleses' daughter Virginia, arranged with tender austerity. Except for the Roy Lichtenstein print, "Brushstroke," sculptured furniture shapes – the mushroom seats, for instance – provide the decorative elements in this mostly golden and white space'.

'Jan Cowles in her not-so-secret garden – a flower-arranging corner especially tucked away just to the side of her kitchen, one of her private pleasures. Oranges and pinks are the preferred colors, "do most for the apartment," Mrs. Cowles said. She likes geraniums, daisies, arranges these and zinnias when in season in baskets or in glass bowls'.

'Jan Cowles's bedroom – a work of shining discipline, of waxed floors, clear colors, French blinds instead of curtains, a wooden Scandinavian sculpture, and a soft touch – a curvy sofa. The Marilyn Monroe portrait over the fireplace is Andy Warhol's as are the silkscreened flowers'.

'Mirrors cover Jan Cowles's bathroom wall – hundreds polka-dotted on a white ground – space-creating and reflecting Jim Dine's large lithograph, "Red Bathrobe," 1969, visible in the background through a transparent screen of mirror-dots-hung-on-string backing the bathtub sunken in an unmown rug'.

Plates 261 and 262
Cy Twombly and family at home, Rome, 1966

Published:
(Plate 261) American *Vogue*, 15 November 1966, pp.182–3: 'Roman Classic Surprise'
Captions read: 'In their serenely pale Roman palazzo, Mr. and Mrs. Cy Twombly, with, on the wall, a bust of the Emperor Hadrian, a Rauschenberg painting, and, above it, one of Cy Twombly's calligraphic paintings'.
'Under a green sunshade, a bust of the Emperor Septimius Severus'.

(Plate 262) American *Vogue*, 15 November 1966, pp.186–7: 'Roman Classic Surprise'
Captions read: 'Alessandro Twombly, aged six, in a Bersagliere hat (and sneakers), mounted on an eighteenth-century terra-cotta bust'.
'In front of his father's vast painting, "Triumph of Galatea," Alessandro, wearing a Knight of Malta's hat, with the Twomblys' silver-grey Neapolitan mastiff couchant on an Aubusson rug. The sum, a definition of Twombly magic'.

Plate 263
Baroness Pauline de Rothschild's bedroom, Paris, 1969

Published: American *Vogue*, 1 June 1969, p.150: 'Le Style Pauline'
Caption reads: 'Her bedroom, an exquisite jungle of eighteenth-century wallpaper with a steel-and-brass bed tented in taffeta, designed by Pauline de Rothschild. Over a Russian table of opaline, enamel, and metal hangs a seventeenth-century mirror-barometer. On the floor near a Louis XVI chair: a dressing-mirror of Tula metalwork'.

Plate 264
Table landscapes, Baron and Baroness Philippe de Rothschild's home, Château de Mouton, Pauillac, France, 1963

Published:
American *Vogue*, 1 December 1973, pp.198–9: 'Fashions in Living: Table Landscapes at Mouton'
Captions read: 'On a lunch table set for five – Pauline de Rothschild prefers an odd number of guests – branches of apple and pear, with growing fruit; white achillea, a wild plant; white candytuft. Pale apple-green tablecloth; early nineteenth-century Bordeaux plates with pale-green borders, black-and-white designs. In the background, a sixteenth-century Italian jointed figure used by artists'.

'Marie Gyselinck, Pauline de Rothschild's unflinching ally in planning and executing the Mouton "table landscapes," at work in her flower room. Plants and cuttings stand in water on the oilcloth-covered table until Marie can plant them in Japanese pots or low, moss-covered stands. This done, she carries them in baskets to the room where lunch or dinner will take place – which may be anywhere; at Mouton, all meals are movable feasts'.

'A cherry orchard on the lunch table – branches of wild cherry, with fruit, in blue-and-white or scarlet Japanese pots. White Porthault cloth embroidered with butterflies, flowers; white napkins and china. The seventeenth-century Italian wooden horse has a real horsehair tail'.

Plate 265
Louise Lawler (b.1947)
Pollock and Tureen, Arranged by Mr. and Mrs. Burton Tremaine, Connecticut, 1984
Courtesy of the artist and Metro Pictures, New York

Plate 266
Cindy Sherman (b.1954)
Untitled #474, 2008
Courtesy of the artist and Metro Pictures, New York

Plate 267 and 268
Emilio Pucci at home, Florence, 1964

Published:
(Plate 267) American *Vogue*, 15 March 1964, pp.157–8: 'Fashions in Living: Pucci the Magnificent'
Caption reads: 'Marchese Emilio Pucci di Barsento. The greatest colourist in the field of fashion design, a unique practical power in fashion, and a member of the Italian Parliament, Emilio Pucci was photographed here in one of his fantastic, frescoed workrooms in the Palazzo Pucci in Florence. In his sombre clothes, which are individual but never frivolous (his jacket may be of some discreet but unexpected pattern or weave), he moves like a dark flame among the glorious colours he thinks women everywhere should wear – the yachting pants, ski pants, dresses, jewellery, all designed with the Pucci perfection of cut. In fact, the only luxury Pucci recognizes is perfection'.

(Plate 268) American *Vogue*, 15 March 1964, pp.159–60: 'Fashions in Living: Pucci the Magnificent'

Caption reads: 'A romantic Pucci vision, photographed on the roof of his palazzo overlooking the great tiled dome of Florence's Duomo. On the opposite page, some of Pucci's early designs for scarfs which took their lunge of colour and geometry from Italian Renaissance Guild flags and the banners of the Palio horse race in Siena. On this page: The Pucci look as it runs today. An evening tunic, the print snowed under with sequins; an after-dinner skirt with a Balinese-prompted design; and, worn with white pants, one of Pucci's famous shirts which some women collect as if they were an armful of wildflowers. In the foreground: A scattering of present Pucci prints'.

Plate 269
Bombay Bathing Fashion, 1950
Platinum-palladium print, printed later
45.72 x 55.88 cm
Horst Estate

Plate 270
Interior of Horst's Oyster Bay house, Long Island, 1966

Published:
(Above) American *Vogue*, 1 June 1966, pp.134–5: 'Fashions in Living: The House that Horst Grew'
Caption reads: 'Horst's living room with Polynesian tapa screens given by Chanel, Persian rugs from the chieftain of me Qashqa'i tribe, a Roman statue, Braque lithographs. Apples and a Delft vase – a Horst play-off of textures, colours, the natural against the crafted'.

(Below) American *Vogue*, 1 June 1966, pp.138–9: 'Fashions in Living: The House that Horst Grew'
Captions read: 'In the library, strongly flowered print, a green-felt-lined door through a bookcase leading to the west wing, and a portrait of Horst by Christian Bérard'.

'In the woods, a stream, a bench, "a green shade"'.

'On a nineteenth-century British officer's travelling desk and drawers, Chinese porcelain, two Persian silver birds, and George III snuffboxes'.

'In Horst's rattan-coated bedroom, a Dali watercolour over the bed, a gouache by Bernard Lamotte next to a tall yellow Chinese vase. The small table is Japanese, polished from rosebush roots'.

'Horst's bathroom, carpeted in white sisal and papered with blue tiles, has a large Delft vase, small ancient bronzes, and mirrors repeating apple branches'.

'A Bérard sketch of Chanel on a table topped with leaves under glass'.

'In the west-wing bedroom, on an eighteenth-century English gesso table, a green Ming "mountain," and fourteenth-century Chinese gilt animals'.

Plate 271
Baron and Baroness Philippe de Rothschild's home, Château de Mouton, Pauillac, France, 1963

Published:
American *Vogue*, 1 July 1963, pp.96–7: 'Fashions in Living: Power of Dreams: What Imagination and Intelligence have created at Mouton – the Chateau of the Baron and Baroness Philippe de Rothschild'
Captions read: 'Baroness de Rothschild in the Second Empire fantasy drawing room; on the ornamented silk fire screen, a portrait of Queen Victoria and crown'.

'The Baron de Rothschild's tapestry evening slipper on a mid-nineteenth-century carpet (with an over-life-size figure of Napoleon III) commemorating a Franco-British Treaty of Commerce'.
'On the same carpet: Napoleon III's boots, a beadwork Victorian footstool, and another evening

slipper, this one of beadwork like the stool. This extraordinary room is dominated by a great portrait of Baron Philippe's mother. Painted about 1900 by Flameng, the portrait hung there throughout the war, and departing Germans and the Maquis in turn placed in front of it large vases of flowers'.

Plate 272
Baron and Baroness Philippe de Rothschild's home, Château de Mouton, Pauillac, France, 1963

Published:
American *Vogue*, 1 July 1963, pp.92–3: 'Fashions in Living: Power of Dreams: What Imagination and Intelligence have created at Mouton – the Chateau of the Baron and Baroness Philippe de Rothschild'
Captions read: 'Baron de Rothschild with his small granddaughter, Camille, and Gogo the golden retriever, outside the Château'.

'Still life of English and Dutch seventeenth-century silver brushes, against a background of an eighteenth-century Chinese paper panel in the new bedroom of the Baroness de Rothschild'.

'Table setting for luncheon: peach blossoms, jonquils, whitethorn, and sea sage on a moss foundation'.

'Butler's white-gloved hand pouring liqueurs: Framboise, Mirabelle, Kirsch'.

'For luncheon on outdoor terrace: white heather and blue-and-white Delft vases'.

'Balustrade – trompe-l'oeil red-ochre, white-grey marble; reverse stairway'.

'Doves and watchdogs at the entrance'.

'Marie, the flower-arranger, taught by the Baroness, gathering peach blossoms and pine for one of her masterpieces'.

'Still life in bathroom: vermeil boxes, wicker baskets, gilt handles like lemons'.

'Tortoiseshell still life: including a seventeenth-century Dutch miniature cabinet and candlestick, a tortoise snuffbox, all on a Chinese black lacquer table'.

'After luncheon: speckled tulips, brown Paisley-patterned cloth, with one of a vast collection of different coffee cups'.

'Lippold's "Cortège" in the living room'.

Plate 273
Karl Lagerfeld's apartment, Paris, 1974

Published:
American *Vogue*, 1 September 1974, pp.276–7: 'Fashions in Living: The Art Deco Life'
Captions read: 'Karl Lagerfeld is a young fashion designer whose special talent is to invoke the mood, the glamour of the 1920's and '30's – combining it with the ease and dash of the 1970's. The clothes he designs for Chloë, a top-flight Paris ready-to-wear house, are enormously pretty, feminine, alluring ... His passion for the 1920's doesn't stop at the drawing board. He loves, and collects, furniture, paintings, and objects of the Art Deco era, lives surrounded by them – in the Paris apartment shown on these four pages. All the rooms are in tones of white, cool or warm: one, a creamy white named for an Auvergne cheese – crême de cantal. Floors, black or dark brown: "They show off my Art Deco pieces like diamonds in a Cartier showcase"'.

' "Shell" sofa, armchairs, and pouf, in heavy ivory satin and gold lacquer – from a house decorated by Elsie de Wolfe, about 1930. Lacquered screen by Eileen Gray, about 1924. Painting, and two vases in silver bronze and black lacquer (1928), all by Jean Dunand'.

'Stainless-steel bed by Prinz, covered in rust-red satin specially woven in Lyons. Mirror designed by Grould, a brother-in-law of the couturier Paul Poiret. Standing lamp in bronze and Bakelite by Brandt and Dunand'.

Plate 274
J. Patrick Lannan's home, Palm Beach, 1973

Published: American *Vogue*, 1 May 1973, pp.186–7: 'Fashions in Living: Two Masterful Ways to Live with Art and Nature: For J. Patrick Lannan, Nature Serves Art'
Captions read: 'Art should be lived with, not just looked at, Patrick Lannan believes. Tall, white-haired, with shrewd blue eyes and a natural flamboyance, Mr. Lannan has turned "Four Winds," his house in Palm Beach, into a picture gallery and his grounds into a sculpture garden. The major aim of his collecting has always been to encourage young artists by buying and displaying their work. Patrick Lannan's early, and continuing, interest in electrical engineering and physics, coupled with an instinct for art, led him into the Buckminster Fuller group and on to kinetic art. He has built an outstanding kinetic-art collection. "He thinks big," said a friend. "The massiveness of sculpture is important to him"'.

'Lannan's strong sense that art should be a living environment is self-evident – especially in the outdoor gallery, where the lushness of Florida greenery is a superb backdrop for David von Schlegell's spacecraft-like aluminum sculpture "Marina," for Grace Knowlton's deceptively simple "Ceramic Spheres" arranged, with casual deliberation, beside the stark skyscrapers of "Red Realizations" by Mathias Goeritz. With emphasis on the new, the collection is eclectic – every culture, ancient and modern, represented: A rare Indian relief of gods looks down from the wall'.

'West African tribal masks frame the door and windows of the patio, and indoors, Japanese Tumuli-period figurines, pre-Columbian and Chinese terra-cottas, Han Dynasty jade share space with Egyptian sarcophagi'.

'Anyone interested in art can visit "Four Winds," by appointment – about ten thousand came last year. For the children who come with parents or teachers, works such as Bernard Kirschenbaum's "Walk Through," become, with Mr. Lannan's encouragement, natural playgrounds'.

Plate 275
Valentino's penthouse, Rome, 1970

Published:
American *Vogue*, 15 April 1970, pp.148–9: 'Fashions in Living: Valentino's Roman Roof-top'
Captions read: 'In a roof tent, Valentino has summer lunches and dinners. Against the roof's terra-cotta colours he played yellow sailcloth, a green splurge of potted plants and vines, the sharp whites of a classic sculpture and geometrically precise furniture, the chairs copied from Oriental ones'.

'In a turquerie tent, forming a glowing alcove off the coolly white and brown living room, the swathes of linen are printed with a design copied from a book of Persian art, the colours Valentino's choosing. Shining metal tables, square white planting boxes edged with chrome sharpen the opulence of pillows in linen and Indian silk, of leopard-skin rugs'.

Plate 276
Yves Saint Laurent's home, Marrakesh, 1980

Published:
American *Vogue*, 1 August 1980, pp.232–3: 'Living: A Quiet Splendor. YSL's Marrakesh House'
Captions read: 'The house with its rosy stucco and polished limestone walls, seen from water-lily pond'. and 'Yves Saint Laurent, in his Moroccan garden – as much an outdoor living room as a natural splendor – strewn with rugs, pillows from the bazaar – a peaceful place to drink mint tea offered by houseboys costumed in harem pants'.

Plate 277
Philip Johnson's sculpture gallery, New Canaan, Connecticut, 1971

Published:
American *Vogue*, 15 August 1971, pp.102–3: 'Fashions in Living: Art Under Glass. Philip Johnson's New Gallery'
Captions read: 'A sweep of the sculpture gallery, the sun pouring into the many-leveled room, with its works by American artists. From the left: a 1967-68 black felt sculpture by Robert Morris; hanging from the glass-and-pipe ceiling, Claes Oldenburg's "Soft Saw"; in one of the corner niches, a John Chamberlain sculpture made in the early 'sixties from junked automobiles; through the wall opening, metal plates – part of a 1969 Richard Serra; in front, Robert Morris's 1968 serial sculpture of nine fiber-glass forms; upper right in this photograph, Oldenburg's soft sculptures on two small shelves and hanging on the wall'.

'Outside the gallery, the soaring steel columns of a 1965 sculpture, 112 inches high, by Barnett Newman'.

Plate 278
Margaretta Fitler Murphy (Mrs Nelson A. Rockefeller) at home, Pocantico Hills, New York, 1975

Published:
American *Vogue*, 1 June 1975, pp.112–13: 'Features: Happy Rockefeller Now'
Caption reads: 'Mrs. Nelson A. Rockefeller: In the gallery her husband created in the cellar of the family house at Pocantico Hills, the real Happy Rockefeller with her acrylic, silkscreen portrait done in 1968 by Andy Warhol. Reconstructing basement corridors into a beautifully lighted, climate-controlled place for a daring collection of avant-garde art, Nelson Rockefeller created a vibrant, comfortable, modern hideaway in a 1908 house. Shown here, on the rear wall, one of a series of magnificent tapestries that extend down other corridors of the gallery, all made after Nelson Rockefeller's favorite paintings by Picasso with the artist's cooperation. "Picasso," Mrs. Rockefeller said, "chose the colors of the yarns himself." This one, woven in 1970 after Picasso's 1931 "Pitcher and Bowl of Fruit".

Plate 279
Mr and Mrs Joe D. Price's home, Oklahoma, 1972
Published:
American *Vogue*, 1 February 1972, pp.186–7: 'Fashions in Living: Masterwork: For Mr. and Mrs. Joe D. Price'
Caption reads: 'Sequins, glass, ghosts, and rock gardens. A sunray entrance to the guest bedroom is one of three remarkable doors designed by Bruce Goff for the Price house in a spangled spree of plate glass inlaid with colored glass, striped with metal, sequins, and tiles. Again, the triangle prevails in the chevron-shaped foot of the bed at the center. The scroll painting of a beautiful, eerie "ghost," page 187, by Goshun, is from the extraordinary collection of Japanese art in the museum, here, where Mr. and Mrs. Price sleep in Japanese fashion – on featherweight mattresses that, with the linens, are stored away by day'.

Plate 280
Roger Vivier's home, Château d'Aubeterre, Périgord, France, 1980

Published:
American *Vogue*, 1 April 1980, pp.284–5: 'Living:

Noble Alchemy: Roger Vivier's French medieval castle transformed to modern retreat, crammed with world art'
Caption reads: 'Stark fifteenth-century exterior of Château d'Aubeterre contrasts with luxurious sitting room, where African carvings, a seventeenth-century Chinese rug, Louis XVI fauteuils blend gloriously with paintings by Poliakoff and Antes, ancient Egyptian statues, Cycladic art collected by Vivier'.

Plate 281
Carmen Dell'Orefice, dress by Hattie Carnegie, 1947

Published:
American *Vogue*, 1 February 1947, p.165: 'People and Ideas: Compositions Around Four American Beauties: Miss Carmen Dell'Orefice'
Captions read: 'Already a finished contradiction in glamour and practicality, she cooks, sews, paints, spends long hours at a ballet bar. Here she wears Hattie Carnegie's timeless white lace, bead banded'.

'The subject. Horst said: "Little Carmen is the ideal painter's beauty; although only a sixteen-year-old school girl, she possesses an inherent gracefulness rarely found except among primitive races. Her almond-shaped eyes are those of a Renaissance beauty, a soft revelation when looking up – she tends to keep her well-defined eyelids cast down over them. The planes of her face are those of a Botticelli page, her long neck like that of Botticelli's figure of Spring. Her hands are long, aristocratic, and she always manages to keep her shoulders straight. Although she is extremely thin, she is not in the least angular, moves slowly, softly like an animal. She has two primary requisites of true elegance: the physical attributes of youth and the languor of the past. She is an American beauty of an antique other age"'.

Plate 282
Leonard McCombe (b.1923)
Carmen and Horst photographed for *LIFE* magazine, 1947
Time & Life Pictures / Getty Image

Plate 283
Carmen, Face Massage (unpublished variant), 1946
Gelatin silver print
25.3 x 20.4 cm
Horst Estate

Plate 284
Carmen, Face Massage, 1946
Gelatin silver print
25.2 x 20.3 cm
Horst Estate
V&A: E.215-2014, Given by Gert Elfering

Published:
Variant, British *Vogue*, June 1946, p.67: 'Facial Characteristics'

Caption reads: 'What good is a new hat without good facial characteristics – clear skin, clear tones, clear outlines?'

ACKNOWLEDGEMENTS

This publication, and the V&A exhibition it accompanies, would not have been possible without the energy and vision of Gert Elfering and Andrew Cowan. I am most appreciative of their connoisseurship and dedication to Horst's legacy. The 32 photographs donated to the V&A by Gert Elfering greatly enhance the Museum's holdings of Horst's work and will be accessible to future researchers in the Prints and Drawings Study Room.

The individuals who were closest to Horst during his life have enabled me to learn something of the photographer's character and enormous charm. I am indebted to Richard J. Horst, who also lent many works to the exhibition. A large proportion of Horst's photographs were commissioned by the Condé Nast organization and I was privileged to have been allowed access to the extensive Condé Nast Archives in New York, London and Paris. Staff there gave both their time and expertise. Particular thanks are due to Shawn Waldron and his colleagues in New York: Edward Klaris, Marianne Brown, Gretchen Fenston, Lindsay Foster, Pamela Griffiths and Gabriella Karefa-Johnson; Brett Croft, Adam Boon and Ben Evans in London; and Amélie Airault De Andreis and Vanessa Bernand in Paris. I am grateful to Anna Wintour OBE and Hamish Bowles of American *Vogue*, and the models Carol Alt, Lillian Macuson and Eva Malmstrom Shivdasani for sharing their memories of working with Horst. Carmen Dell'Orefice's personal recollections provide an insightful and fitting conclusion to this book.

For their flair, knowledge and generosity of spirit I am grateful to Vince Aletti, Ken Allen, Johan Andresen, Michael Bright, Christine Brown, Claire Brown, Paula Cowan, Ulla Elfering, Felix Elfering, Bill Ewing, Tim Jefferies and David Peckman of Hamiltons Gallery, Barry Joule, Herry Lawford, Johann D. Mayr, Kathleen Naundorf, Tim Peterson, Marissa Reibstein, Patty Sicular, Etheleen Staley and Takouhy Wise of Staley-Wise Gallery, Loic Tallon and James Watters. For their wonderful photographic skills and kindness, I thank Freddie Cowan and Francisco Soeiro. Numerous individuals have lent precious works from their collections; special thanks to Sir Elton John and the dedicated curators of his photography collection, Newell Harbin and Jane Jackson. For their assistance with archive research, I thank Kristin McDonough, Elizabeth Cronin and Ryan Haley of The New York Public Library, and David Brown for investigating the passenger lists of the great ocean liners of the 1930s.

Every V&A project is a creative collaboration and I am grateful to all the Museum colleagues I have worked with, especially Martin Barnes, Senior Curator of Photographs, with whom the initial selection of works for the exhibition was made, Marta Weiss, Bronwen Colquhoun and Erika Lederman of the Photographs Section, and my colleagues in the Word and Image Department and Research Department. Assistant Curator Anisa Hawes helped with many aspects of research and preparation, and diligently compiled the extensive Appendix; her calm and meticulous approach has been invaluable. Specialists in the Textiles and Fashion Department have shared their expertise, in particular Oriole Cullen, Cassie Davis-Strodder, Edwina Ehrman, Sonnet Stanfill and Claire Wilcox, and Conservators Sam Gatley and Sarah Glenn. Paper Conservator Simon Fleury prepared the works for exhibition and Paul Robins expertly photographed them for this publication. I would also like to acknowledge Linda Lloyd-Jones, Dana Andrew, Elodie Collin, Clare Everitt, Kerri Offord, Sarah Quantrill and Daniel Slater in the Exhibitions Department; Elinor Hughes and James Wainman at Cultureshock Media; and Katharina Weistroffer and Clara Sancho for their stunning exhibition design. For this beautifully produced book, I thank editor Anjali Bulley and copy-editor Denny Hemming for their patience and attention to detail; the talented Daniel Baer and Hannah Montague for such an elegant design; and colleagues Zara Anvari, Davina Cheung, Rachel Daley, Clare Davis, Mark Eastment, Liz Edmunds and Vicky Haverson.

Last but certainly not least, sincere thanks to the book contributors, the eloquent writers and scholars who have shed new light on Horst's œuvre.

Susanna Brown

Curator, Photographs
Victoria and Albert Museum

INDEX

Note: page references in italics refer to illustrations.

H

I

J

K

L

M

N

O

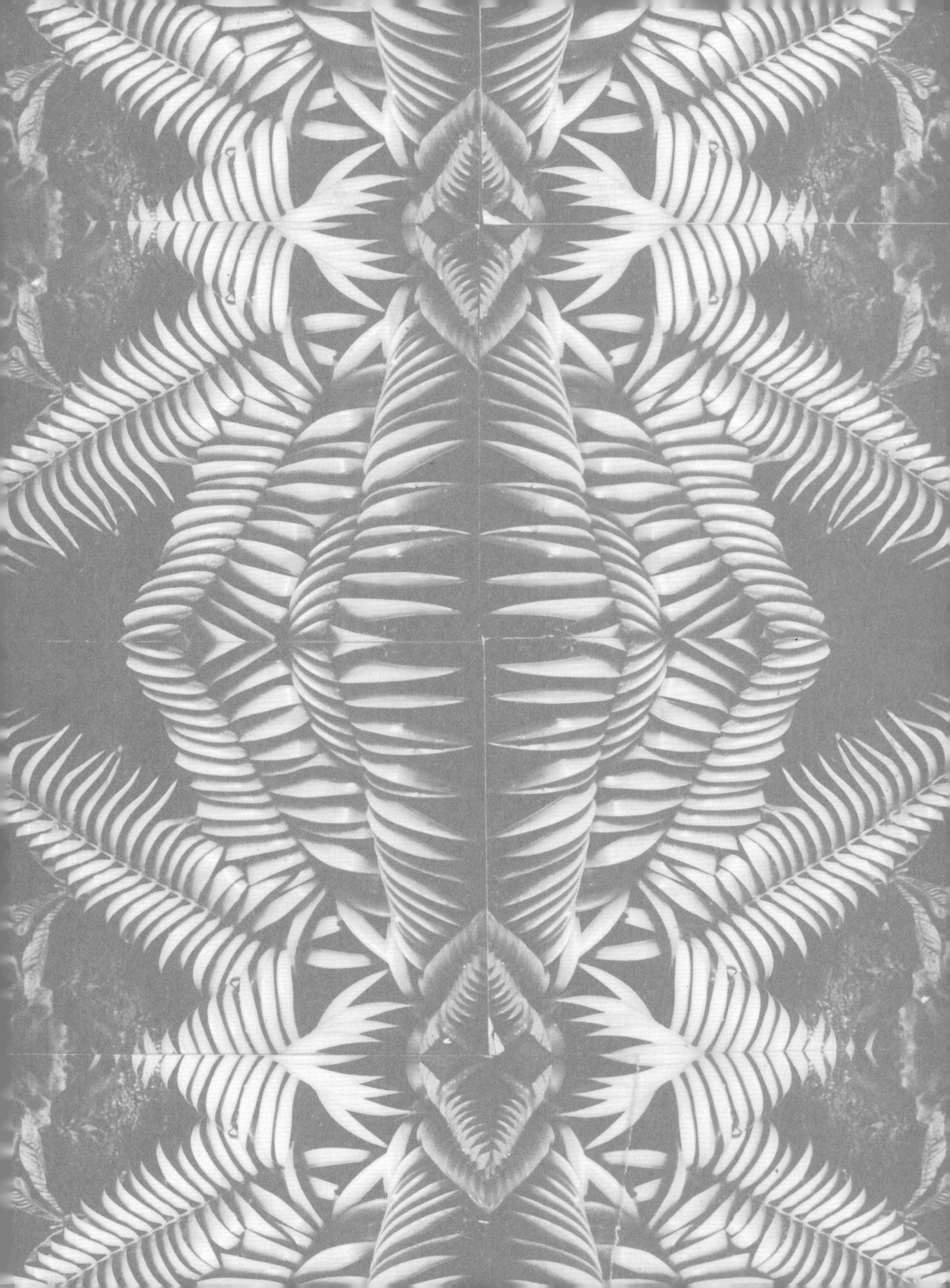

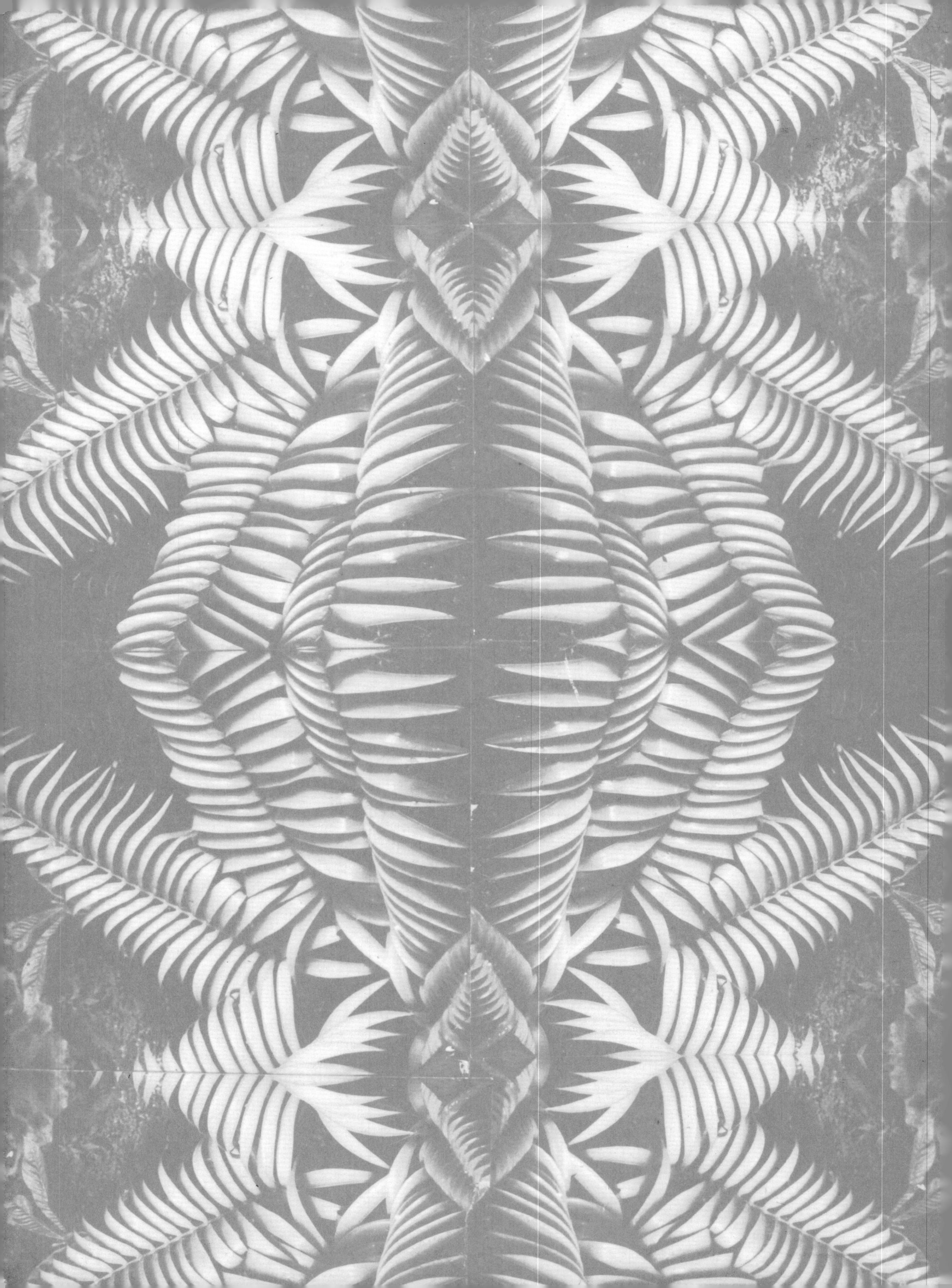